RESSOURCEMENT THOMISM

RESSOURCEMENT THOMISM

Sacred Doctrine, the Sacraments, and the Moral Life

ESSAYS IN HONOR OF ROMANUS CESSARIO, O.P.

Edited by Reinhard Hütter & Matthew Levering

The Catholic University of America Press
Washington, D.C.

Library of Congress Cataloging-in-Publication Data
Ressourcement Thomism : sacred doctrine, the Sacraments, and the
moral life : essays in honor of Romanus Cessario, O.P. / edited by
Reinhard Hütter and Matthew Levering.
p. cm.
"Publications of Romanus Cessario, O.P."—P.
Includes bibliographical references (p.   ) and index.
ISBN 978-0-8132-1785-7 (cloth : alk. paper)
1. Thomas, Aquinas, Saint, 1225?-1274.   2. Catholic Church—Doctrines.
I. Cessario, Romanus.   II. Hütter, Reinhard, 1958–
III. Levering, Matthew, 1971–   IV. Title.
B765.T54R465 2010
230'.2092—dc22
2010007561

Contents

Foreword

J. AUGUSTINE DINOIA, O.P.

It has been nearly twenty-five years now since Father Romanus Cessario and I sat in an empty classroom over the course of a week working through alternative models for a new curriculum at the Dominican House of Studies. We were striving for intelligibility, comprehensiveness, and integration—three elements of the Thomistic vision of theological education that was fundamental to the work of the faculty.

This vision of theology had been cultivated throughout years of shared fraternal and intellectual life in the Dominican Order. Our paths had for the most part coincided throughout our Dominican formation (just a year separated us)—from Providence College where we began, through philosophical studies at St. Stephen's Priory in Dover, Massachusetts, and theological studies in the pontifical faculty at the Dominican House of Studies. Over these years, we had the same Dominican teachers—Dominic Rover, Michael Stock, Raymond Smith, Thomas Heath, Alan Smith, and William Hill (names that I cannot fail to mention here, for they had a profound influence on our intellectual development). He had written theses on the metaphysics of the person and on the Blessed Trinity, I had written on Heidegger and Rahner. After ordination, we both returned to Providence College to teach for a few years before going off to pursue doctoral studies. Only at this point did our paths diverge— mine led to Yale, his to Fribourg.

By 1980, we were back together again. We had arrived at the Dominican House of Studies within months of each other—he to become the academic dean, and I to teach theology. Thus it happened that when we sat in that classroom to design a new curriculum, our ways of thinking about theology had been immeasurably enriched—his by O'Neill, Spicq, Nicholas, and Pinckaers, mine by Lindbeck, Frei, Kelsey, and Christian. He had greatly deepened his knowledge of Aquinas, writing a brilliant thesis on Christian satisfaction. I had rediscovered Aquinas, by way of Barth and Wittgenstein, and parted decisively with Rahner. Sharing the common patrimony of our Thomistic formation, we had come by different routes to similar convictions about the nature of theology. Thus it was that we had a clear idea of what the new curriculum should look like.

Working together during those years at the Dominican House of Studies—in the revision of the curriculum and in many other projects—we came increasingly to share a common vision of theology and of theological education. As far as Aquinas was concerned, Father Cessario was way ahead of me. His wide reading in Aquinas and in the commentators had shaped his own teaching and writing, and, through our many long and deep conversations, it also began to shape my own. This is a debt I cheerfully acknowledge in these prefatory paragraphs in his honor. Reading Barth had persuaded me of the dangers of the subjective turn in theology and philosophy. Listening to my good friend Romanus alerted me to the shortcomings of the linguistic and hermeneutical turns. Over the years, we understood that above all else we sought a robust theological realism in our writing and teaching. Theology is not just about discourse, or narratives, or texts, he used to say to me, but about the living God and the realities of his saving work.

Throughout twenty-five years of teaching at the Dominican House of Studies and at St. John's Seminary in Brighton, Father Cessario has touched the minds and hearts of many students and colleagues—something to which this volume bears eloquent testimony. The essays here range over most of the fields in which Father Cessario has worked and published: Christology, soteriology, sacramental theology, moral theology, and spirituality. Even those unfamiliar with his extensive output can recognize in this volume's table of contents the breadth of his theological interests and learning. It is a mark of the success of his teaching and writing that such an impressive array of scholars—young and not so young—should be united to honor him with this volume. It is a privilege for me to join my name to theirs in this brief but heartfelt foreword in homage to Father Romanus Cessario—my colleague, brother, counselor, and friend for more than forty years.

Preface

MARY ANN GLENDON

In the autumn of 1996, I received an invitation to join a most unusual reading group. For the next six years, a small band of professors gathered from time to time around an oval mahogany table in a seminar room at St. John's Seminary in Brighton, Massachusetts, to discuss just one book, one section at a time. The book was the *Summa theologiae* of Thomas Aquinas, and the discussions were led by such theological luminaries as Matthew Lamb, the late Ernest Fortin, Stephen Brown, Frederick G. Lawrence, and our host, Romanus Cessario. Among those of us who came to listen and learn were several young theologians, including Matthew Levering, a co-editor of this volume, and Law Professor Thomas Kohler. On occasion, we were joined by Bernard Cardinal Law, Bishop William Murphy, and my husband Edward Lev. Attendance varied over the years, but there was one constant. Father Cessario was always there to welcome us, radiating serenity in his white Dominican robes, ready to illuminate our path through the texts he loves so much and knows so well.

That seminar was my introduction to the range of gifts possessed by the new professor who was to become a cherished family friend. He had arrived in Boston in September 1995, the year before he celebrated the twenty-fifth anniversary of his ordination. His reputation as a leading moral theologian had preceded him, and I, as a member of the seminary's board of trustees, was well aware of our good fortune in securing the services of such an eminent scholar. In the context of the Aquinas Group, I soon had the opportunity to appreciate his pedagogical skills at first hand. With the Latin text in front of him, Father Cessario was as adept at elucidating an obscure point with a contemporary example as he was at correcting a faulty translation. His exchanges with his fellow theologians were inspiring for this law professor to behold—models of courtesy, collegiality, and openness.

The ministry of Romanus Cessario encompasses far more, however, than the teaching and scholarship deservedly celebrated by the contributors to this volume. Theology, as Bernard Lonergan has taught us, "mediates between a cultural matrix and the significance and role of a religion in that matrix."[1] When the cultural matrix is secular, skeptical, and materialistic, the theologian's lot is challenging indeed. Father Cessario squarely faces that challenge in his widely acclaimed *Introduction to Moral Theology*, where the state of the culture is a central preoccupation. Eschewing "high-minded moralizing" in favor of Thomistic "moral realism,"[2] he has made it his business to be an astute observer of contemporary social trends. Often, after a meeting of the Aquinas Group, the participants would adjourn to a nearby Korean restaurant where talk would turn to the events of the day. In that setting, we came to know our Dominican friend as a great conversationalist, extremely well informed about current affairs—local, national, international, and ecclesiastical, ever ready with penetrating questions, and never at a loss for insights from the tradition. That rare combination of eloquence, spirituality, learning, and worldly wisdom made him the perfect choice for the memorable Good Friday meditations that he delivered in St. Patrick's Cathedral in 2008.[3]

No armchair intellectual, Father Cessario has taken to heart the calls of Popes John Paul II and Benedict XVI to evangelize the culture. In 1997, he and a small group of associates in France and the United States launched an initiative that has reinvigorated the spiritual lives of many thousands of Catholics throughout the world. The idea was to create an attractive, pocket-sized monthly publication containing readings for each day's Mass, plus morning and evening prayers, interspersed with arresting stories from the lives of the saints, and with short meditations drawn from the best spiritual writers, ancient and modern. The supposition was that such a service would fill an unmet need. They were more right than they imagined. Even the founders of *Magnificat* must have been astonished to see how great that need was. Delighted subscribers spread the news rapidly by word of mouth. Today, *Magnificat*, with Romanus Cessario as senior editor, has 250,000 subscribers for editions in three languages, and it continues to grow.

1. Bernard Lonergan, S.J., *Method in Theology* (New York: Seabury Press, 1979), xi.

2. Romanus Cessario, O.P., *Introduction to Moral Theology* (Washington, D.C.: The Catholic University of America Press, 2001), xiv, xvii.

3. Romanus Cessario, O.P., *The Seven Last Words of Jesus* (Paris/New York: Magnificat, 2009).

In the wake of the Massachusetts Supreme Court decision mandating the issuance of marriage licenses to same-sex couples, Father Cessario joined the educational efforts of the Massachusetts Catholic Conference aimed at securing an amendment to the state constitution that would have permitted citizens of the state to vote on the issue. In the cold winter months of 2004, he was part of a hardy band of clergy and lay people who went from parish to parish night after night explaining why the preservation of marriage is important and what citizens can do to make their voices heard.

In these, and in countless other ways, Father Cessario has thrown himself into the new evangelization. To see him in action in different settings is to marvel at the way he is as much at home in a Brighton coffee shop as in a Roman academy. I am particularly struck, as I ponder his many "extra-curricular" activities on behalf of lay initiatives, by how effectively he has pioneered in giving real content to the concept of complementarity between clergy and laity. Having collaborated with him on a number of occasions, including the organization of a conference at the seminary on French and American visions of religious freedom and the preparation of a volume of the collected writings of Bernard Law,[4] I can personally attest to the boundless energy, intelligence, and good will that he brings to teamwork.

Truly it is fitting and just to honor this dedicated scholar whose presence has immensely strengthened St. John's Seminary, whose writing has done so much to reinvigorate the Catholic intellectual apostolate, whose work has been honored with membership in the Pontifical Academy of St. Thomas Aquinas, and who has poured himself out as a libation in the cause of advancing the civilization of life and love. It is a privilege to have been invited to preface these fine essays with a few notes about the Romanus Cessario I have come to know as a great priest, a wise teacher, a generous colleague, and a good friend.

4. Romanus Cessario and Mary Ann Glendon, eds., *Boston's Cardinal: Bernard Law, the Man and His Witness* (Lanham, Md.: Lexington Books, 2002).

The Cornerstone
Christian Faith and Modern Culture in Dialogue

GUY BEDOUELLE, O.P.

TRANSLATED BY MARTHA RITCHIE

The editorial adventure of *Pierre d'Angle*, a French annual review that has been published in Aix-en-Provence since 1995, began with a conversation in the train between Fr. Romanus and me about a book by Norman F. Cantor, which he had given me. Perhaps, we thought, there was a need for a review that could modestly contribute to filling the gap that had opened up during the past centuries between the Christian faith and all the various forms of contemporary culture, a gap that is made manifest by modern secularization. We had noticed that in each of our countries, the United States and France, there was a reciprocal ignorance between specialists in theology and in the spiritual domain (or the simple believer) and those who were dedicated to various arts. If the transcendentals—the Good, the True, and the Beautiful—are really convertible, how could the Christian be indifferent to the efforts of those who, according to the gifts they have received, give over their lives to find meaning in the enigma of existence?

Our ideas were not very clear about how this project for a new review would take shape, except that it ought to be truly beautiful in its presentation, its typography, and its illustrations. The title sprang immediately from a suggestion made by Fr. Romanus. It should be called *Pierre d'Angle,* and we never wavered on this point. A third editor, Fr. Daniel Bourgeois from the community of the Brothers of St. John of Malta in Aix-en-Provence, rallied to our cause, and his untiring curiosity and practical side have been ever so useful in assuring the realization of this *Cornerstone*.

As we said from the very first page of the first number: "Our modernity is the fruit of a prodigious meeting of many worlds and of great traditions . . . For the believer, the dynamic secret in this history, the cornerstone of this architecture, is the mystery of the living God Who never tires of enlightening and, in His truth and His beauty, creating human destiny. Christ, the Cornerstone, enables us to us to discover the past, the present, and the future of man, in light of this meeting of grace and freedom." The aim that this review pursues was more broadly presented in 1997 by the three sections of an issue, each of which was edited by one of the co-editors. Fr. Romanus's section urged theologians to take "another look, a free look" at the other sciences and at the arts.

Cautiously, the three editors of the review gave themselves five years to see if the challenge would be accepted. With a degree of self-assurance, we told ourselves that there had been short-lived reviews, the importance and quality of which had been recognized only after the fact! *Pierre d'Angle,* which has a limited print run, enters its fifteenth year with the 2009 issue. Producing a review such as ours is not done without discussion, but the differences that emerge are handled with mutual respect and friendship. The preparation of each number, which usually occurs in March, and in varying localities, gives us the opportunity to meet in order to share ideas and most particularly to hold on to the original intentions for the review.

In homage to Fr. Romanus I would like to emphasize the share he has had in contributing to the originality of our review. *Pierre d'Angle* is certainly not a theological review, but Fr. Romanus's varied contributions have always had a theological aspect, and that aspect has always been imbued with the thought of Thomas Aquinas. In addition, Fr. Romanus has persuaded such American scholars as John McIntyre, Carl A. Anderson, Mary Ann Glendon, George Weigel, Grace Goodell, and Peter John Cameron, among many others, to contribute articles to the review. In a sense, issue number 14 (2008), which collected the papers delivered at the colloquium organized by Fr. Romanus in Boston in October 2007 on the person and work of Fr. Ernest Fortin, is an example. The title is "God and Political Order: France and the United States." The number takes up the variations introduced by Tocqueville on the genius of two peoples and their institutions. Examining the different attitudes each country has toward religion, one can understand the source of some political and ideological misunderstandings that have arisen between France and the United States in spite of the friendship that has bonded them ever since the foundation of the American republic.

One should add here that Fr. Romanus has a great admiration, affection even, for such French saints as St. Louis-Marie Grignion de Montfort and St. Thérèse of the Child Jesus, the Little Flower. He knows pilgrimage sites like Ars, Lisieux, or Paray-le-Monial better than many a Frenchman does. He believes that the Catholic renewal through holiness will come from France, granting great things for our time.

Fr. Romanus has a keen interest in the Christian intellectuals, especially French, of the first half of the twentieth century, and particularly between the two world wars. His most recent contribution, to number 15 (2009), presents with elegance the strange character of Maurice Sachs, protégé of Jean Cocteau and of Jacques and Raïssa Maritain. Sachs belongs to the generation of Maritain's converts around 1926; he first thought he was called to the priesthood, but then he turned away to follow a less edifying life. In his article, Fr. Romanus shows how grace works within an exceptional being, the possibility of rejecting grace, and the pedagogical patience and caution practiced by the Maritains, and he also raises the question of the weight of homosexuality in a permissive society.

Our review gives Fr. Romanus the chance to wonder aloud about our society in crisis, to recall the teaching of the Church in reference to Thomas Aquinas as well as to recent encyclicals, and last but not least to put his thinking into the wider context of literature, the fine arts and occasionally international politics. The articles that Fr. Romanus has contributed to *Pierre d'Angle* ought one day to be published in their original language, for they are mostly rooted in a lucid vision of the American society.

Acknowledgments

On the occasion of his sixty-fifth birthday, this volume gratefully acknowledges the manifold contributions of Father Romanus Cessario, O.P. In addition to the merit of his own theological writings, he continues to contribute in countless other ways to the health of theology in the United States and abroad. Thomistic theologians owe him a special debt of gratitude. In this sense, we speak for the contributors and for many others in describing the entirety of the volume as an acknowledgment. In addition to these, some scholars and friends, not named elsewhere in this book, deserve our special thanks for enabling the book to come to fruition. As Father Cessario's birthday approached, two institutions hosted conferences where many of our contributors honed their thoughts: Ave Maria University (on the sacraments) and Providence College (on the common good). Among the organizers of these events, Michael Dauphinais, Paul Gondreau, and Russell Hittinger stand out. But for the fits and starts endemic to the festschrift genre, these distinguished scholars and friends would be among the contributors to the book—as indeed they are through their work on the symposia. Many thanks to them for their ongoing friendship and encouragement. Mercedes Cox's work at Ave Maria University on behalf of the 2007 conference was profoundly appreciated by Father Cessario and deserves grateful notice here. James Kruggel at the Catholic University of America Press took an immediate interest in this project and skillfully shepherded it through the process. Along with the director of the Catholic University of America Press, David McGonagle, James is a wonderful person to work with and an erudite theologian in his own right. During the production process, the generosity of Father Matthew Lamb enhanced the quality of the book, and we owe him an extra debt of gratitude. Gilles Emery, O.P., and Guy Mansini, O.S.B., both read the manuscript and offered helpful comments: their theological wisdom and friendship continue to prove simply invaluable. Copyediting of the manuscript prior to submitting the final version to the Press was kindly undertaken by Judith Heyhoe and Louise Mitchell: many thanks to them for their excellent work. In acknowledging these many gifts of time and talent, we thank God, our Creator and Redeemer, for the spiritual and intellectual fruitfulness of his son in Christ Jesus, Father Romanus Cessario.

January 28, 2009   *Reinhard Hütter*
Feast of St. Thomas Aquinas   *Matthew Levering*

RESSOURCEMENT THOMISM

Introduction

REINHARD HÜTTER AND

MATTHEW LEVERING

In a recent essay commenting upon the state of religious life in North America, Romanus Cessario observes, "The defining activity of all Dominicans is expressed in a phrase that St. Thomas Aquinas has penned: 'Contemplate and then share with others the fruit of contemplation.'"[1] From such contemplation and teaching, Cessario notes, "comes the impulse of friendship, which among intelligent creatures is the only way that they can realize the divine dynamic of being, namely, that goodness is diffusive of itself."[2] The present volume of essays honors Romanus Cessario by witnessing to the renewal of Thomistic theology that his friendships, rooted in his contemplation and teaching, have so greatly fostered.

The volume begins with a Foreword, a Preface, and a brief reflection by three of his dearest friends, all of whom have collaborated with him on many projects: Archbishop J. Augustine DiNoia, O.P., Secretary of the Congregation for Divine Worship and the Discipline of the Sacraments; Ambassador Mary Ann Glendon, Learned Hand Professor of Law at Harvard Law School and the United States's ambassador to the Vatican from 2008 to 2009; and Professor Guy Bedouelle, O.P., Rector of the Catholic University of the West in Angers, France. These testimonials to Father Cessario sketch, in succinct and eloquent fashion, the contours of his Dominican vocation. The body of the volume con-

---

1. Romanus Cessario, O.P., *"Tanquam spiritualis pulchritudinis amatores:* The Consecrated Vocation of Matthew Lamb," in *Wisdom and Holiness, Science and Scholarship: Essays in Honor of Matthew L. Lamb,* ed. Michael Dauphinais and Matthew Levering (Naples, Fla.: Sapientia Press, 2007), 41.

2. Ibid.

tains three sections. The first, "Sapientia Dei: Sacred Scripture and Sacred Doctrine," addresses an ever-present element in Cessario's writing and teaching, namely the nature and future of the theological task. Reinhard Hütter takes up this theme by way of dogmatic theology and the role of Magisterial teaching and metaphysical reflection; Matthew Levering focuses on how Aquinas's understanding of *sacra doctrina* flows from his discernment of God's ordering wisdom in Scripture; Thomas Joseph White, O.P., provides a programmatic exposition of the contemporary requirements of renewed Dominican theology.

The second section consists of four essays in sacramental theology, each of which presents the richness of insight made possible by the appropriation of St. Thomas Aquinas's teaching on the sacraments. Benoît-Dominique de La Soujeole, O.P., explores the implications of Aquinas's insistence that sacraments are signs. Bernhard Blankenhorn, O.P., examines the relationship of biblical revelation and metaphysical reflection in the doctrine of sacramental causality. Thomas Weinandy, O.F.M. Cap., underscores the activity of the risen Christ, who, far from ceasing to act in human history, acts through the sacraments. And Richard Schenk, O.P., reflects upon eucharistic sacrifice for the purpose of delineating what can and cannot be said about this extraordinary mystery. This section pays tribute to Father Cessario's decades of teaching sacramental theology and Christology.

The third section comprises seven essays that engage, from a wide variety of perspectives, aspects of moral philosophy and theology—the area of inquiry that has occupied most of Father Cessario's scholarly attention over the years. Lawrence Dewan, O.P., highlights the importance of Aquinas's teaching that the common good is the participation of all things in God's goodness; Stephen Brock takes up natural law and the common good; Joseph Koterski, S.J., surveys and evaluates recent writing on natural law; Steven Long probes difficulties within the contemporary debate regarding the moral object; Matthew Lamb provides a model of embodied interiority; Craig Steven Titus seeks to understand how moral development works in the context of the inherent connection of the virtues; and Graham McAleer addresses Catholic social teaching on economic markets. The volume ends with a short postscript by the eminent philosopher Alasdair MacIntyre, a longtime admirer of Father Cessario's work.

Those who know Father Cessario's many friends will both appreciate the contributors gathered here and wonder why many other good friends are not present. Given the large number and international range of his friendships, it is perhaps fortunate for the co-editors that our desire to bring out this volume in conjunction with his sixty-fifth birthday forced us to give potential contribu-

tors very short notice. Otherwise the book could easily have reached quite un-
publishable length! We hope that this volume, by God's grace, gives honor to
Father Cessario and testifies to the marvelous fecundity of his Dominican vocation. Realizing much sooner than many others that *ressourcement* does not
dispense with, but in fact requires, Thomism, he figures as one of the truly influential theologians of our time.

The Thought of Romanus Cessario, O.P.

This introduction would be incomplete if it did not include an effort to
distill the central themes of Father Cessario's theological research. Among
his many writings, we wish here to survey four of his books: *The Godly Image* (1990), *The Moral Virtues and Theological Ethics* (1991), *Christian Faith and
the Theological Life* (1996), and *Introduction to Moral Theology* (2001). A more
complete picture would require his *The Virtues, or the Examined Life,* where
he explores the three theological virtues and the four cardinal virtues, along
with their parts, their associated gifts of the Holy Spirit, and their opposed
vices.[3] Similarly, his *Perpetual Angelus: As the Saints Pray the Rosary* augments
his portrait of life in Christ and further demonstrates his familiarity with the
writings of the saints.[4]

The Godly Image

Cessario's *The Godly Image: Christ and Salvation in Catholic Thought from
Anselm to Aquinas* began as his doctoral dissertation, and the work demonstrates the speculative and historical mastery of Thomas Aquinas's texts that
a Fribourg-trained theologian acquires. Cessario opens his study with a brief
chapter on Aquinas's understanding of *sacra doctrina*. In chapter 7 of *On the
Reasons of Faith,* Aquinas states, "If a man will devoutly consider the suitabil-
ity of the passion and death of Christ, he will find there such an abyss of wisdom that more and greater things will continually reveal themselves to him."
Cessario comments: "[T]his stance characterizes Aquinas's whole theological
enterprise. The reasons ('rationes') which he gives for revealed truths of faith,
only accessible under the 'lumen fidei' of theological faith, come mainly from
prayerful meditation and reflection on the very mysteries themselves."[5]

3. Romanus Cessario, O.P., *The Virtues, or the Examined Life* (New York: Continuum,
2002). Matthew Levering reviewed this book in *The Thomist* 67 (2003): 143–47.

4. Romanus Cessario, O.P., *Perpetual Angelus: As the Saints Pray the Rosary* (New York:
Alba House, 1995).

5. Romanus Cessario, O.P., *The Godly Image: Christ and Salvation in Catholic Thought from*

Such "prayerful meditation and reflection" need not exclude philosophical reasoning that helps to clarify the mysteries of God, the human creature, and the gift of the grace of the Holy Spirit through the Paschal mystery of Christ Jesus. Divine revelation speaks of three kinds of realities, each of which has a certain kind of "necessity" that opens the mystery to philosophical clarification: the triune God, created natures with their intrinsic requirements, and the gift of salvation with its intrinsic requirements. Cessario observes of this threefold content: "These necessities—that of salvation history, that of natures as constituted by God, and that of the divine triune reality itself—are interlocking: the former two being grafted on to and deriving consistency and intelligibility from the divine 'necessity' that God be a Father uttering a Word with whom he breathes forth the force of loving recoil."[6] The goal of the *Summa theologiae* is thus to appreciate the "requirements" of God's free gifts, nature and grace, in light of the Trinitarian wisdom and will.

As *The Godly Image* proceeds, Cessario takes his readers through Aquinas's biblical commentaries (chapter 2), his *Commentary on the Sentences of Peter Lombard* (chapter 3), his *Summa contra Gentiles* and other writings (chapter 4), and his *Summa theologiae* (chapter 5). Each of these chapters explores satisfaction, whether the virtuous action of satisfaction, Christ's act of satisfaction on the Cross, or sacramental satisfaction (penance). As Aquinas's thought matures, he increasingly treats all three kinds of satisfaction under the rubric of charity. Cessario also points to the growing significance of the restoration and perfection of the *imago dei* for the theology of Christ's satisfaction. As Cessario works out these two aspects, restoration and perfection, we see the fruitfulness of his attention to natures from the perspective of a spiritual theology that recognizes deification as the goal of human existence. Cessario's sixth and final chapter, which explores our participation in Christ's charitable satisfaction, demonstrates the biblical and patristic character of Aquinas's conception of the Church's nature and mission. Rooted in "the recapitulation of the entire created order in Christ," the members of Christ's Body are manifold "expressions of divine charity in the world," whereby God reunites his "separated family" and "reveals himself as one who calls all men and women to a certain participation in his divine life."[7]

St. Anselm to Aquinas, Studies in Historical Theology VI (Petersham, Mass.: St. Bede's Publications, 1990), 7.

6. Ibid., 11. Cessario states, "The genius of a solution to this question of theological methodology is to find a course between theology as 'sacred history,' where the intelligible connection between the mysteries is simply narrative chronology as in Hugh of St. Victor's *De sacramentis,* and theology as necessitarian emanationism as in Plotinus's *Enneads*" (10).

7. Ibid., 193, 183, 201.

The Moral Virtues and Theological Ethics

The Moral Virtues and Theological Ethics draws from his years of teaching
moral theology to Dominican friars as a member of the Pontifical Faculty of
the Immaculate Conception at the Dominican House of Studies in Washington, D.C. Observing that "from the Renaissance until the middle of this century, moral legalism predominated in both Roman Catholic and reformed circles," Cessario credits the Second Vatican Council for the decline of casuistry
(although he points out that "revisionist moral theology still remains rule-
centered").[8] As Cessario recognizes, the full recovery of virtue-based ethics depends upon the renewal of Christian appreciation for the four moral or cardinal virtues, prudence, justice, fortitude, and temperance, because
"[t]hese cardinal virtues . . . provide the focal points for at least fifty other al-
lied and auxiliary virtues" that express human nature's requirements for flourishing.[9] Since "our lives find fulfillment only by following the rhythm which
Christ himself establishes," it follows that "Christian faith necessarily changes the way one considers virtue."[10] Above all, Christian faith reveals the ultimate flourishing to which God draws the human person, "beatific fellowship or union with the blessed Trinity."[11] To arrive at this flourishing requires
being configured to Christ Jesus and thereby to God's "eternal law" or plan for
the human attainment of beatitude.[12]

8. Romanus Cessario, O.P., *The Moral Virtues and Theological Ethics* (Notre Dame, Ind.:
University of Notre Dame Press, 1991), 3. He explains, "Today, efforts to revise moral theology
often employ ethical models based upon divine command or rule theories, usually moderated
by the principle of proportionate reason. Admittedly, the meanings and functions of 'proportion' differ according to the usage of the various authors. Still, in the final analysis, proportionalist authors identify the moral life with ethical obligations concretized in norms or precepts,
although, as is well known, they have relaxed the rigid moral legalism which the various systems
of moral casuistry had highly developed" (13).

9. Ibid., 4. Cessario credits Elizabeth Anscombe's "Modern Moral Philosophy" (*Philosophy*
33 [1958]; reprinted in *Ethics, Religion, and Politics* [Minneapolis: University of Minnesota Press,
1982]) for once more bringing "the concept of 'human flourishing' to the attention of moralists"
(17), and he notes also the contribution of Peter Geach (23).

10. Ibid., 2, 4. He goes on to observe, "If theology is to remain true to its character as a holy
teaching, a *sacra doctrina*, its practitioners should ensure that every element of the instruction
proceeds from and depends upon revealed wisdom" (12).

11. Ibid., 17. Cessario argues that "[p]hilosophical agnosticism about what constitutes human nature or its destiny need not undermine the task of elaborating a virtue-centered moral theology. In fact, some argue that we can only discover a comprehensive list of the created
goods which compose human flourishing under the guidance of Christian revelation" (18). As
he points out later, "the theologian must discover a means for establishing the concrete goals of
the Christian life. This requires agreement on the principal features of a Christian anthropology" (56).

12. Ibid., 21.

If this is so, what is the relationship between the transformation of human nature by grace and the paths of flourishing intrinsic to human nature? If the latter paths did not exist, then human nature would entirely disappear with the loss of grace. As Cessario puts it, "The perfecting of our human potential means, at least in part, that grace respects the built-in teleologies of human nature."[13] Yet how can this be so, if, as Cessario also states, "the New Testament authors make it remarkably clear that Christian existence constitutes an entirely new way of life for the one who accepts the Christian dispensation"?[14]

Chapter 1 of *The Moral Virtues and Theological Ethics* poses this question, and the remainder of the book works toward answering it. Chapter two explores the nature and development of *habitus*. Unlike mere "natural endowments," *habitus* possess an "openness to creative activity."[15] Because *habitus* develop through free and intelligent human choices, the interior action of the grace of the Holy Spirit can break vicious *habitus* and infuse virtuous *habitus*. Chapter three treats the nature of moral virtue in light of the human vocation to beatific communion with the Trinity. Cessario emphasizes that the development of virtuous *habitus* not only enables the person to act in accord with human nature, but indeed establishes a "new nature" by which the person can attain the ends befitting full human flourishing promptly, easily, and joyfully.[16] Grace accomplishes this transformation by infusing the moral virtues, which, unlike acquired moral virtues, receive their form from supernatural charity. The infused moral virtues show how profoundly the grace of the Holy Spirit takes hold of the human person, in whom virtues pertaining to natural flourishing now receive a "formal" ordering toward the goal of sharing in the Trinitarian life, aided by the gifts of the Holy Spirit.

But if the Holy Spirit infuses moral virtues in the believer, what further need is there to discuss moral virtues as acquired? Cessario replies that theological ethics must employ a philosophical understanding of human nature, and its corresponding virtues, in order to account analogously for the infused moral virtues that belong properly to the fulfillment of human nature in Trinitarian communion. This explains Aquinas's detailed exposition of the acquired moral virtues, which "constitute the primary analogates for their graced equivalents, the infused virtues."[17] As an example, Cessario offers the

---

13. Ibid., 23.   14. Ibid., 24.

15. Ibid., 36.

16. Ibid., 47; cf. 54. Cessario compares this position to that of Duns Scotus, who argues that (in Cessario's words) "one can only ethically evaluate the disposition to act in a certain manner by reference to some extrinsic principle or norm. So virtue for Scotus remains a matter of advised volition, but not actual transformation" (55).

17. Ibid., 57.

way that, in the life of grace, the supernatural virtue of hope interacts with the (infused and acquired) virtue of chastity, which belongs under the rubric of temperance. Similarly, he contends that the infused virtue of prudence no longer involves solely worldly judgments, but rather "embodies a real participation in the wisdom of Christ," and thus is linked with the moral virtue of humility.[18]

Chapter 4 begins with the goal of communion in the Trinitarian life, which occurs in the Holy Spirit through (sacramental) participation in the power of the Cross of Christ Jesus. As Cessario has shown, the grace of the Holy Spirit leaves no aspect of our human nature untouched: in restoring or healing the *imago dei*, for example, grace ensures that the married human person can accomplish the (natural) human goods associated with marriage from within the (graced) ordering of the married couple to communion with the Trinity. To see how this integration occurs in particular human actions, one must reflect upon the virtue of prudence, which consists in rightly understanding what is to be done. Appealing both to natural law and the Magisterium of the Church, Cessario comments that "prudence looks to introduce the *veritas vitae*, the truth about life, into the world."[19] By uniting intellectual virtue with moral virtue, prudence—and especially infused prudence—sheds light on the relationship between faith and the moral virtues of justice, courage, and temperance.[20]

In chapter 5, the way in which the indwelling of the Persons of the Trinity shapes the moral life of believers is again reflected upon, this time with the question of moral development in view. Cessario observes that even after the Fall and the gift of redemption, "[t]here does exist a sense in which the expression 'natural virtue' can be understood by the Christian theologian. This amounts to a distinguishable tendency within human nature to achieve its own perfection and to live in accord with right reason."[21] These virtuous *habitus* are the "acquired virtues," which Cessario discusses in the context of the infused virtues.[22] But since Christ Jesus reveals that human beings are ordered

18. Ibid., 60.
19. Ibid., 90. He adds, "Prudence extends divine providence so that it reaches even to the most particular of moral actions" (92).
20. See ibid., 115–16.
21. Ibid., 98.
22. Cessario points out that Scotus denies the need for the infused virtues, on the ground that charity suffices to elevate the acquired virtues (ibid., 103). Against this view, Cessario notes that "charity affects the direction, but not the substance of an action whereby the believer reaches out towards God. Charity, then, affects the doer's intention—in the strong sense of substantial purpose, not the weak sense of sporadic motive. Charity cannot account for why one act of abstinence embodies an intrinsic difference not found in another act of abstinence. Yet, since

to an end (Trinitarian communion) that natural capacities cannot attain, why should theologians attend to the tendencies "within human nature to achieve its own perfection and to live in accord with right reason"?

The answer, Cessario suggests, consists in the infused moral virtues. As an example, he points to the virtue of moderation in eating, which sustains health (and therefore is not negated by grace) but which also, during Lenten fasting, serves "to unite one more closely with Christ and the sufferings of his members."[23] As this example shows, the infused moral virtue does not make obsolete the acquired moral virtue: physical health remains a good end for the graced human person. Since the "matter" of the virtue remains the same, the acquired virtue and the infused virtue are not disjoined into separate realms of pure nature and pure grace. Instead, the matter of the natural virtue is taken up into the graced life of the person. This elevation does not negate the value of the (natural) acquired virtue, but it does somewhat relativize it through the freedom of the life of the spirit.[24]

On the other hand, what about persons who, as often happens in the case of adult baptism, receive the infused virtue despite lacking the acquired virtue? In such cases, the infused virtue provides a principle, namely cleaving to Christ, that offers the moral strength to overcome the vicious *habitus*.[25] Here Cessario adverts to St. Paul's complaint, "For I delight in the law of God, in my inmost self, but I see in my members another law at war with the law of

---

fasting in union with the Mystical Body counts as a distinctive feature of the Christian moral life, the *habitus* which makes the fasting possible should itself include an intrinsic reference to grace. Accordingly, only a distinct virtue, the infused virtue of abstinence, can fully account for the total reality caused in the believer by the working of the Holy Spirit" (107).

23. Ibid., 106. In this way "a totally new form has been given by faith to the virtuous deed" (109).

24. For instance, Cessario states that the acquired virtues of temperance and fortitude, far from being negated in the graced person, "remain ordered towards the indispensable human works of conserving and continuing both the individual person and the human species by facilitating resistance to threatening evils and promoting the pursuit of indispensable goods. The infused virtues of temperance and fortitude advance these same goals within the context of personal union with Christ in the Church of faith and sacraments" (ibid., 113). Since the "matter" of the virtues remains the same, "[t]he infused virtues impress the sign of the cross onto the human virtues" (113).

25. Cessario notes, "No empirical theory can explain how confidence in the power of the blood of Christ in our lives opens up the possibility for fulfilling the requirements of Christian virtue. Theologians who defend the compromise of certain virtues, especially chastity and purity, on the basis that specific individuals remain psychologically ill-disposed to live in accord with their moral requirements, unfortunately ignore a crucial element of Christian moral theology and life. As a result, those who follow the pattern of compromise not only settle for a kind of behavior which leaves the inclinations of human nature unfulfilled, they also miss the opportunity for realizing conformity with Christ. This results in a much larger compromise of Christian doctrine than that which occurs as the result of some immoral practice" (122).

my mind and making me captive to the law of sin which dwells in my members."[26] On this reading, St. Paul's "delight in the law of God" flows from his infused virtues, which oppose his ingrained vicious *habitus*. Insofar as St. Paul also possessed acquired virtues at the time of his conversion, those acquired virtues do not lose their value in the pattern of redemption.

The sixth and final chapter takes up the mean of virtue, the connection of the virtues, and the equality of the virtues. The mean of virtue, discerned by right reason, "avoids the extremes of excess and defect in moral matters."[27] Once right reason is enlightened by faith, would one need a new (graced) "rational mean" for the acquired virtues? Cessario shows that the rational mean of the acquired virtue is not negated by the graced enlightenment of the intellect. Consider the case of marriage: both acquired and infused prudence find that "the one who achieves sexual gratification outside the commitment which Christian marriage requires veers from the rational mean for venereal pleasures."[28] For its part, the connection of the virtues makes a common-sense point, namely, that a vicious *habitus* will hamstring one's ability to embody the other virtues. Even so, the connection or unity of the virtues does not mean that the virtuous person possesses, with regard to each virtue, "the kind of heroic virtue practiced by the saints."[29] Finally, the equality of the virtues does not mean that there is no hierarchy of virtues; rather it simply means that the virtues must develop together, or else the ensemble of virtues will be harmed. While this point holds for the acquired virtues, it holds even more clearly for the Christian life. As Cessario comments, "When moral theologians set forth characteristic qualities of the virtuous life, they attempt to explain coherently how a radical life of Gospel perfection, such as Jesus sets forth in the Sermon on the Mount, develops in the lives of those whom God calls to share in the image of his Son."[30] This development, Cessario emphasizes, occurs through the work of the Holy Spirit and cannot be accounted for when moral theology is reduced to casuistry.

Christian Faith and the Theological Life

In his introduction to *Christian Faith and the Theological Life,* Cessario presents the theology of the infused virtues and the theological virtues (faith, hope, and love) with special attention to their Trinitarian and Christological pattern. These virtues, which we receive through the imitation of Christ as members of his Body the Church, are no mere add-ons to natural human life,

26. Rom 7:22–3; cf. Gal 5:17.
27. Ibid., 130.
28. Ibid., 131.
29. Ibid., 143.
30. Ibid., 148–49.

but rather are "indispensable for every human creature."[31] He emphasizes that only God can give us these virtues, by which we are justified and come to "enjoy a loving conformity with each of the divine Persons,"[32] but he equally observes that these virtues require the "spiritual formation" and "instruction in the faith" that believers receive in the Church.[33] Thus he devotes his first chapter to exploring the instrumental causality of Christ's divine life in his members (the Church), the relationship of habitual grace to the human person's natural powers (insufficient in themselves for participating in the Trinitarian communion), and the relationship between the created image of God and the image of God as elevated by grace. In developing these themes, he shows how his work on faith arises from the insights of his earlier studies.[34] Along the way, he retrieves a wide swath of theological culture, as for instance in his account of the analogical meaning of "participation" in the Trinitarian life, in his richly nuanced analysis of "created grace," and in his amplification of his earlier reflection on the *imago dei*.[35]

If faith is infused by God, why is the Church's instruction necessary? To this question, Cessario devotes chapter 2, which explores faith as a "kind of knowing."[36] As always, his approach is both theocentric and ecclesial (rooted in the missions of the Son and Holy Spirit). In giving us faith, God enables us to know him with an intimacy far greater than what our natural power of knowing could achieve. God provides the spiritual light by which we know him as Truth; the assent to revealed Truth is a free act of faith in God revealing, rather than a logical or historical deduction.[37] But how do our minds, which obtain knowledge through discursive reasoning, apprehend the perfectly simple reality that is God? Following Aquinas, Cessario states that Christians know Truth through assenting to the creedal propositions of faith. Although the assent of faith, as a judgment of truth, terminates not in the propositions but in the reality of divine Truth, nonetheless, humans require diverse "articles of

---

31. Romanus Cessario, O.P., *Christian Faith and the Theological Life* (Washington, D.C.: The Catholic University of America Press, 1996), 7.

32. Ibid., 9.

33. Ibid., 10–11.

34. For instance, he comments that "grace radically changes us, but it does not accomplish this at the price of changing the kind of beings that we are, namely, human beings. In other words, although habitual grace represents a real, ontological endowment in the spiritual order, it does not turn human beings into pineapples, canaries, or angels" (ibid., 27).

35. Ibid., 32–38.

36. Ibid., 51.

37. On the light of faith, see ibid., 76–79. Cessario debates with Scotus's position, adopted by Molina and others, that "*fides acquisita* ('naturally acquired faith') remains a prerequisite for *fides infusa* ('supernaturally infused faith')" (59). On this topic see also 80–81.

faith" in order to be able to assent to divine Truth: "the human mind must 'articulate' divine truth into different elements or articles."[38] These articles of faith, revealed by God in his *sacra doctrina* (holy teaching), mediate the mind's direct contact with the reality or being of the triune God.[39] Cessario remarks that "Christ himself stands at the center of this entire process. For it is Christ who teaches both angels and men, and who alone fully communicates divine Truth to the world."[40] We receive Christ's "offer of truth and friendship" in his Body the Church, with its development of doctrine under the guidance of the Holy Spirit.[41]

Chapter 3 further probes the act of faith, particularly in light of the missions of the Son and Holy Spirit, which constitute the Church. It might seem that the revelation of the triune God in and through the Church limits human freedom, but Cessario shows that the contrary is true. As a free assent to God revealing, the act of faith receives its certitude from God. This fact locates faith within the believer's relationship with the Persons of the Trinity: faith contains not only cognitive but also affective dimensions. Faith inspires the quest for deeper knowledge of the God known in faith, and this quest goes hand-in-hand with a deeper love. As Cessario states, "theological faith sets us on the road to meeting God face to face."[42] The quest for deeper knowledge of the God known in faith also stimulates rational inquiry, including metaphysical questioning, investigation of the *praeambula fidei*, and theological contemplation. Despite their value, neither metaphysical knowledge nor arguments for the plausibility of faith (the *praeambula*) can substitute for the knowing that God gives us through the gift of faith, because it is in knowledge of the Trinity and the Incarnation that we attain to the mysteries of salvation.[43] For its part, theological contemplation belongs to the vocation to holiness: Cessario endorses "the classical perspective of the Eastern churches," according to which

---

38. Ibid., 65.   39. Ibid., 71–76.
40. Ibid., 69.   41. Ibid., 69–70. Cf. 109.
42. Ibid., 101.

43. Commenting on *ST* II-II, q. 2, a. 7, ad 3, Cessario praises the balance of Aquinas's solution regarding the content of faith's knowledge: "This assertion, that even those who have never heard revelation must have some expressed, explicit faith (at least in the reality of divine salvific providence) in order to be saved, goes against certain contemporary views that seem to overlook the necessity for some specific content in Christian faith. Aquinas helps the theologian avoid the relativism that easily surfaces in some contemporary Catholic speculation about the status of the unevangelized. At the same time, it is clear that Aquinas's position permits a wide latitude. Thus, the neo-scholastic commentator Reginald Garrigou-Lagrange concludes that 'if one considers those who enjoy supernatural faith, the majority [of these] have an explicit faith in Christ the Savior. In what *de facto* it consists, God alone knows!'" (Cessario, *Christian Faith*, 113).

"the title 'theologian' implies the actual living out of a holy life, and not simply a professorial rank."[44] Faith and charity are united in the public confession of faith.

Chapter 4 examines "the 'supernatural sense of faith' as it exists in the person who shares in Christ's kingly and prophetic offices."[45] In light of Hebrews 11:1, Cessario begins by exploring faith as a virtuous *habitus* that instills in the believer an interpersonal relationship with God (thus not solely cognitive, but also affective). Although formed faith requires charity, the movement of the will in the assent of faith is not the movement of charity, since "even the demons believe."[46] Nor is faith primarily our "response" rather than God's gift. Constituting "the beginning of eternal life," faith initiates the movement that leads to hope and charity, although the act of faith itself can be aided by moral virtues such as courage and humility.[47] In light of this examination of the *habitus* of faith, Cessario inquires into the relationship of faith to the preaching of the Gospel. In some detail, he describes a twofold graced movement in which the person hears the exterior preaching of the Gospel and receives the interior movement of divine grace that prompts the assent of faith. In the Church's proclamation of the Gospel, therefore, God is the cause of conversion, but "God instrumentally uses everything that is human in order to achieve a result that surpasses the abilities that any single person possesses."[48] Even faith formed by charity, however, needs further graced assistance. Cessario devotes the fifth and final chapter to explaining the service rendered to faith by the gifts of the Holy Spirit, in particular the gifts of understanding and knowledge that conform the believer ever more closely to the dynamics by which faith unites the believer to the divine realities.[49]

Introduction to Moral Theology

Cessario's *Introduction to Moral Theology* gives him an opportunity to explore, in a systematic fashion, how moral theology should be exposed. As elsewhere, he emphasizes that "[t]he great advantage that an authentically Christian moral theology affords the believer derives principally from the fact

---

44. Ibid., 116.

45. Ibid., 126.

46. Jas 2:19. Cessario observes that normally "the initial affect of credence leads straightaway to formed faith. The pattern of priority, then, is one of logic, not time" (*Christian Faith*, 156).

47. Ibid., 147.

48. Ibid., 152.

49. John of St. Thomas's view that the gifts provide "'mystical connaturality and union with divine truths'" (ibid., 175) guides Cessario's approach.

that moral teaching is located within a larger picture of saving doctrine."[50] In this vein, he devotes the first chapter to *sacra doctrina* as the context for moral theology. He highlights the Neoplatonic structure of *exitus-reditus*, which helps in the understanding of God's creative causality, the Incarnation of the Word as communicated across the generations by the Church, and the restoration and elevation of the human image of God accomplished by the Christian moral life. All three of these aspects, he suggests, require attention to the principle that "when the Church instructs about the good of human life, she enunciates truths that are not foreign and strange to human beings. The promise given us by the Church is that grace perfects nature."[51] On the other hand, neither will it do to place natural realities at the center of Christian moral reflection: following Aquinas, Cessario instead emphasizes "divine grace, the actions of infused charity, and the end of eternal life."[52]

Chapter 2 explores the wisdom expressed in the order of creation. Cessario points out that the Incarnation of the Word propels the search for a pattern of wisdom in the created order: "From the start of theological deliberation on the Incarnation of the eternal Logos, Christian apologists and theologians have sought to further the quest for the ultimate *logos* or intelligibility which undergirds and directs the created order."[53] Following St. Augustine, Cessario describes as the "eternal law" God's wisdom regarding the ordering of creatures to their ultimate end. God's "providence" indicates his active accomplishing of this ordering.[54] Natural law is human rational participation in God's wise ordering, his eternal law. Here Cessario adds the important specification that "natural law is not merely the *product* of practical reason but the *pre-condition* for its right exercise."[55] Because natural law is a received wisdom about God's ordering of human beings to our ultimate end, "Natural law is the normative theological and metaphysical order that undergirds, makes possible, and flows into our moral logic."[56] Far from being an autonomous ethic, natural law be-

---

50. Romanus Cessario, O.P., *Introduction to Moral Theology* (Washington, D.C.: The Catholic University of America Press, 2001), xiii.

51. Ibid., 12. Cessario argues that "because human nature exhibits a recognizable stability, universal statements about moral activity can be incorporated into a coherent body of knowledge" (19).

52. Ibid., 15.

53. Ibid., 56.

54. See also Cessario's "Brief Speculative Excursion into Freedom and Providence" (in *Introduction to Moral Theology*), 144–48.

55. Ibid., 64.

56. Ibid. Cf. Cessario's detailed discussion of natural law on 77–90, as well as his summary on 117: "Aquinas's action theory forms a central component of the *sacra doctrina,* and so adopts the dynamic features of the *imago Dei* anthropology: the human creature set between God as

longs within the Trinitarian and Christological patterns of our ordering to communion with the Trinity. Yet this ultimate end is not opposed to "the design and ends of human nature."[57]

Chapter 3 takes up human action as arising from human intelligence and freedom. Beginning with freedom, Cessario observes that it is not autonomous in a radical sense, because the human rational appetite, as created, possesses a "motion of natural desire."[58] As he puts it, "the will naturally desires happiness, and hence is free in respect to means but not to the end."[59] Thus the will does not possess a "transcendental" freedom: human freedom is not radically indeterminate, but rather is always ordered to the good. Freedom therefore cannot be set in opposition to nature, as if the former radically transcended what is meant by the latter. Having established the ordered character of human freedom, Cessario treats the ways in which violence, fear, ignorance, and lust restrict human freedom from attaining its full potential. He then provides a detailed synopsis—emphasizing the interaction of intellect and will—of the structure of the human act. Lastly, he returns to an analysis of freedom as ordered to the attainment of union with God and as guided by the Church's communication of Truth. As he shows in detail, virtuous action, guided by the theological and moral virtues (above all prudence), aims at attaining the good of union with God.[60]

---

principle and God as end. The eternal law, with its Trinitarian implications, provides the original pattern for the synergy of intellectual and appetitive powers which appears entitatively in natural law and operationally in the voluntary. God grants us an active rational share in our own government, but this activity presupposes our passive reception of being, nature, and the ordering of nature" (117).

57. Ibid., 69. Cessario points out, "Given the directions of modern moral philosophy, there exists the temptation to confuse the in-built structures of human nature with an inert physicalism, as if the Christian view of the body were that of a Cartesian machine. Although a sound natural law theory takes our physical being seriously, the basic grounds for natural law's claim to legitimacy rest on more than its ability to take full account of the biological and physical structures of the human person" (73).

58. Ibid., 104. In this regard Cessario remarks, "A thing's natural motion, like its natural being, is not self-generated. That which is positive within the volitional act—like being itself—is simultaneously most our own while yet being most a divine gift" (104).

59. Ibid.

60. Cessario states, "Prudence forms the theoretical nerve of a teleological conception on the moral life. It shapes human actions in accord with the dictates of right reason, so that human intelligence can easily discover the truth about human and divine perfection" (ibid., 130). He goes on to emphasize that conscience operates within the context of prudence. Thus, "[a] proper understanding of conscience does not introduce a covert system for bracketing general moral truths when it is judged that particular circumstances or personal convictions justify a conscientious exception to a general norm" (132). Appreciating the role of prudence allows one to avoid "accepting a fundamental tension between subjective conscience and objective law" (133).

Chapter 4 describes the "form" of good human action, that is, action configured to Christ Jesus. In this regard Cessario affirms that "Christians should
approach each of their specific actions as if it were a distinct sacramental expression of God's love."[61] Human action that is rightly ordered to the ultimate
end shares in the wisdom of God's eternal law, his ordering of all things to the
end of his goodness. Analyzing moral action, Cessario distinguishes three elements: object, end or intention, and circumstances. Regarding the moral object, which specifies the action, Cessario explains: "In order to show how different objects specify different specific kinds of activity, consider the generic
action of hitting any object, such as baseballs, nails, and your best friend's back.
Each one of these objects diversely specifies the generic action of hitting," and
thus the activities of "playing baseball, doing carpentry, and encouraging a
friend."[62] In other words, identifying the "object" enables one to describe what
concretely is happening in the action. Identifying the "end" (intention) of the
agent, and the circumstances in which the action takes place, then enables
one to evaluate the action more fully. Some objects—murder, adultery, and so
forth—cannot specify a good action no matter what the intention or circumstances.[63] As Cessario concludes, "Actions that embrace good moral objects re-

61. Ibid., 150. He adds, "Since Christ personally enacts the divine goodness in our human
history, that is, because he 'lived among us,' everything that the member of Christ does, insofar
as it flows from Christ, prolongs the original Incarnation of God's love throughout the course of
the ages. In a certain sense, Christian moral theology establishes the authentic forms in which
Christ himself appears again and again in the graced lives that believers originally receive in
Baptism, and in which they continue throughout a lifetime punctuated by reception of the other sacraments of initiation, forgiveness, and service to the communion" (151).

62. Ibid., 167, 168.

63. Against the accusation of physicalism, Cessario comments, "To explain sin by appeal to
objects does not mistake physical states for the moral order. The removal of a cancerous organ
specifies a different moral object from the removal of a healthy one. And although the physical
symptoms are identical, when a doctor anesthetizes a patient for surgery we identify a different
moral object than when a college student on a Saturday night drinks to excess" (ibid., 172). Similarly he points out that "there is an element of conscious willing which forms part of the constitution of the moral object itself. In this sense, how I choose to hit a baseball necessarily, viz., by
reason of the object, differs from how I choose to hit my friend on the back; or, to put it another
way, the moral object itself materially shapes a person's choosing. While this choosing already
expresses something of my personal willing or intention, it does not account for the full measure of my personal intentions, i.e., of what I am intending to accomplish by my action" (176). At
stake is the relationship of the formal and material aspects of the object; Cessario emphasizes
that "[t]he *finis operantis* receives its matter from the *finis operis*, and is limited thereby" (177).
Regarding the traditional distinction between "the *finis operis*, the end of the action, and the *finis operantis*, the end of the agent," Cessario notes that "it is still possible to employ the distinction in an overtly Platonic way, and to argue that an action receives the significant portion of its
moral meaning from the 'end' of the agent" (177). He also pauses to distinguish his view from
that of Peter Abelard, who argued that the morality of the action derives solely from the intention of the agent (175).

flect the providential order within which God heals and elevates human nature. Whatever is healthful and perfective for human persons respects their common human nature and orders them toward its uplifted fulfillment in grace."[64]

The fifth and final chapter treats the virtues, the gifts of the Holy Spirit, and the New Law of freedom. As elsewhere, Cessario has in view the person's transformation in Christ, a transformation that forms a communion of persons, the Church. After introducing his theme by means of St. Benedict's *Rule*, he surveys Aquinas's approach to the virtues, gifts, and New Law. After commenting on the distinction between theological, moral, and intellectual virtues, Cessario discusses the infused moral virtues in detail. In this context he observes the difference between Aquinas and Bonaventure with regard to infused fortitude and temperance: with Aquinas, Cessario holds that these virtues actually transform the sense passions, whereas Bonaventure argues that the sense passions are at best only restrained by the will.[65] Regarding the gifts of the Holy Spirit, he follows John of St. Thomas in distinguishing the virtues and the gifts by analogy with a boat that is moved both by oars and by wind. The gifts enhance the believer's freedom to respond to the prompting of the Holy Spirit. Lastly, Cessario argues that true freedom involves not autonomy but theonomy: the "New Law" of grace, which entails that "the human person is free only when he or she observes the commandments of God."[66] Concretely, observing the commandments of God means, for the believer, the celebration of the sacraments and the practice of the virtues within the context of conversion and trust in the divine mercy. The result, exemplified by the saints, is "the creation of a new people who, by their holy lives, offer a pleasing sacrifice to the Lord."[67] Marked by faith, hope, and charity, these new people embody nothing less than "restoration and perfection of the *imago Dei*."[68]

The Renewal of Thomistic Theology

In these four books, one sees the breadth of a master of *sacra doctrina* who apprehends Christ's centrality for the moral life without thereby losing touch with a theocentric perspective, and who consistently integrates the contributions of nature and grace toward our divinization. Before concluding, however, Cessario's unparalleled influence in spreading Thomistic theology within the English-speaking world merits attention.

Cessario's engagement in this task first manifests itself in an article pub-

64. Ibid., 191.   65. Ibid., 203.
66. Ibid., 217.   67. Ibid., 222.
68. Ibid., 226.

lished in the late 1980s, "Theology at Fribourg." This article quietly advances the claim that Fribourg Thomists—among them Jean-Hervé Nicolas, Servais Pinckaers, and Ceslas Spicq—offer a coherent alternative both to transcendental Thomisms, which in Cessario's view are "either beleaguered by concern for hermeneutical questions or pre-occupied with a self-consciousness about method,"[69] and to other *ressourcement* theologies that mistakenly renounce "the kind of philosophical infra-structure available in a theology employing realist metaphysics."[70] While Cessario recognizes that the dogmatic theologian Nicolas, the moral theologian Pinckaers, and the biblical scholar Spicq possess quite distinct perspectives, nonetheless he rightly observes that:

> their common efforts may be described as seeking to continue the program set for theology by Aquinas when he affirmed that theology "uses human reasoning, not indeed to prove the faith, for that would take away from the merit of believing, but to make manifest some implications of its message."[71]

In accord with the thesis of this seminal article, Cessario was among those most responsible for the publication in English, in the mid-1990s, of two of the most important fruits of Thomism in Fribourg, namely Servais Pinckaers's *The Sources of Christian Ethics* and Jean-Pierre Torrell's two-volume *Saint Thomas Aquinas, Volume 1: The Person and His Work,* and *Saint Thomas Aquinas, Volume 2: Spiritual Master.* His foreword to Pinckaers's book begins with what turned out to be a prescient understatement: "*The Sources of Christian Ethics* reaches its English-speaking readership at a particularly opportune moment."[72] Indeed, thanks in many ways to the growing influence of Cessario's own books and articles, the "moment" of which he spoke augured a renewal of Thomistic theology in the United States, which he also stimulated by editing, with his Dominican confrere J. A. DiNoia, a volume of essays on John Paul II's encyclical *Veritatis Splendor.*[73] During the same decade, Cessario brought back into print two works of sacramental theology by his dissertation director at Fribourg, the late Irish Dominican Colman O'Neill: *Meeting Christ in the Sacraments* and *Sacramental Realism.* In his introduction to his revised edition of *Meeting Christ in the Sacraments* (which originally appeared in 1964), he understands the current dire situation in sacramental theology as resulting

---

69. Cessario, "Theology at Fribourg," *The Thomist* 51 (1987): 329.
70. Ibid.   71. Ibid.
72. Cessario, foreword to Servais Pinckaers, *The Sources of Christian Ethics,* trans. Sr. Mary Thomas Noble, O.P. (Washington, D.C.: The Catholic University of America Press, 1995), ix.
73. J. A. DiNoia and Romanus Cessario, eds., *Veritatis Splendor and the Renewal of Moral Theology* (Princeton, N.J.: Scepter Publishers; Huntington, Ind.: Our Sunday Visitor; Chicago, Ill.: Midwest Theological Forum, 1999).

from "theologians who stopped their theological reflection short at the symbolic and anthropological aspects of the sacraments."[74]

Cessario also undertook two major retrievals of the history of Thomism. Together with Kevin White, he translated and published John Capreolus's treatise *On the Virtues.*[75] In retrieving the virtue ethics of the fifteenth-century "prince of Thomists," Cessario made the case that his own work must be read from within the Thomist commentatorial tradition. Second, he authored *A Short History of Thomism,* which first appeared in French.[76] This book briefly expounds the arc of Aquinas's career and Aquinas's understanding of theology, and then moves to a discussion of the various ways in which "Thomism" has been conceived. Against attempts to deconstruct the Thomist tradition, Cessario suggests that Thomism is in fact a unified and ongoing intellectual tradition. After having surveyed the debates about what being a "Thomist" involves (including ecclesial engagement with this issue) as well as the various efforts to distinguish historical periods within Thomism, Cessario proposes to "view Thomism as a continuum of intellectual achievement within the Western theological tradition."[77] In tracing the Thomists from Richard Knapwell and William of Macclesfeld onwards, he gives special attention to John Capreolus, Thomas de Vio (Cajetan), Dominic Báñez, and John of St. Thomas, but he also treats a wide array of lesser-known figures, all in the context of explaining the various theological and philosophical controversies that occupied Thomists in their efforts to "contribute to shaping the civilization of love whose foundation remains the one Truth that God has revealed in Jesus Christ."[78]

When the next history of Thomism is written, it will need to give a prominent place to Romanus Cessario, O.P. For this, and for his friendship, we are grateful to God. For Father Cessario we can wish nothing better than God's continued blessing: "May the God of peace himself sanctify you wholly; and may your spirit and soul and body be kept sound and blameless at the coming of our Lord Jesus Christ. He who calls you is faithful, and he will do it" (1 Thess 5:23–24).

74. Cessario, introduction to Colman E. O'Neill, O.P., *Meeting Christ in the Sacraments* (Staten Island, N.Y.: Alba House, 2002), xvi. He goes on to observe that "the fragmentation of sacramental theology, more than its construction, inauspiciously marks the immediate past of Roman Catholic theological culture" (xix), and he proposes that *Meeting Christ in the Sacraments* provides a good starting point for future constructive work.

75. John Capreolus, *On the Virtues,* trans. Kevin White and Romanus Cessario, O.P. (Washington, D.C.: The Catholic University of America Press, 2001).

76. Romanus Cessario, O.P., *A Short History of Thomism* (Washington, D.C.: The Catholic University of America Press, 2005).

77. Ibid., 34.

78. Ibid., 92.

PART 1

Sapientia Dei
Sacred Scripture and
Sacred Doctrine

Transubstantiation Revisited

Sacra Doctrina, Dogma, and Metaphysics

REINHARD HÜTTER

Ressourcement Reconsidered: Theology *ad Mentem S. Thomae*

It might not be too much of an exaggeration to claim that in many segments of contemporary North American, as well as European, Catholic theology, there is a twofold profound and interrelated sense of insecurity pertaining to the *intellectus fidei*. The *first* sense of insecurity relates to the nature and task of theology—to be precise, dogmatic or systematic theology—as well as its precise relationship to three distinct but interrelated points of reference and accountability: the canon of Scripture, tradition, and the living Magisterium. It seems indicative of this sense of insecurity and the ensuing lack of clarity that on May 24, 1990, the Congregation for the Doctrine of the Faith "deemed it opportune" to issue the statement *Donum Veritatis* ("Instruction on the Ecclesial Vocation of the Theologian") to help overcome this insecurity "by shed[ing] light on the mission of theology in the Church" (§ 1). The *second* sense of inse-

Earlier versions of this chapter were delivered as lectures or discussed as papers at the Symposium "Sacraments in Aquinas," at Ave Maria University, February 3, 2007; to the faculty of Duke University Divinity School, September 17, 2007; to the Pontifical faculty and the student body at the Dominican House of Studies, Washington, D.C., November 19, 2007; at the "Colloquium on Historical Theology" at Boston College, August 2, 2008; at the Theological Colloquium of the Lumen Christi Institute at the University of Chicago, May 15, 2008; and to the graduate student body in theology at Boston College, December 5, 2008. For valuable suggestions and criticisms I am indebted to many interlocutors present at these events.

curity plaguing the *intellectus fidei* pertains to the most central mystery of the faith, the sacrament of the Holy Eucharist and especially Christ's real presence or, more precisely, Christ's personal presence by way of his corporeal presence. In many quarters the impression has been fostered that the Second Vatican Council had given license to jettison the conceptual apparatus of the definition decreed by the Council of Trent. Numerous new interpretations have arisen, most of them trading on various transient post-metaphysical assumptions, and consequently without any lasting success. What is left is a widespread lingering, albeit mainly soft, agnosticism regarding the principal doctrinal tenets of this most central mystery—a situation most recently addressed by the late Pope John Paul II's last encyclical *Ecclesia de Eucharistia* (2003).

In this somewhat precarious theological situation, I regard it as salutary to move forward by first moving backward, "upstream, and *listening* to the sources."[1] The particular source overdue to be listened to again intently is Thomas Aquinas. Such renewed listening to the *doctor communis* serves a twofold *ressourcement:* first, regarding the nature and task of theology and, second, regarding the very core of the *mysterium fidei,* Christ's real, corporeal presence in the sacrament of the Holy Eucharist. For Thomas paradigmatically shows how the nature and task of theology bear immediately upon the mystery of Christ's Eucharistic presence, and it is in discursively contemplating the mystery of Christ's Eucharistic presence that the nature and task of theology come to a surpassing fruition.

But we have first to step back for a moment. For in the eyes of not a few, even among the most sympathetic observers over the centuries, too many barrels of ink have been spilled and too many library shelves filled with tomes by theologians affirming, denying, or qualifying Christ's real presence in the Eucharist. For example, all of the very precisely honed and defensively delineated theological definitions of Christ's sacramental presence (including the rejection of the doctrine of Eucharistic sacrifice, as well as of the doctrine of Eucharistic transubstantiation) became the settled identity markers of variant Protestant communities—Lutheran, Reformed, Puritan, (Ana)Baptist—and justified their separation from the Catholic Church. This situation did not leave Catholic theologians unaffected, for whom, especially after the Council of Trent, the doctrine of transubstantiation unsurprisingly became a central identity marker of Catholic orthodoxy under the condition of ongoing ecclesial division, polemic, and worst of all, protracted wars of religion in Ger-

---

1. I gratefully borrow this felicitous rendition from John Betz, who used it to describe an earlier instantiation of "going upstream" in his penetrating review essay of *Reason and the Reasons of Faith,* ed. Paul J. Griffiths and Reinhard Hütter, *Pro Ecclesia* 16 (2007): 222.

many, France, England, and Ireland. With the remarkable ecumenical progress among various Protestant communions in the first half of the last century,
and especially since the Second Vatican Council in its second half, the situation seems to have improved in unexpected ways. However, a complex set of
equally unexpected new problems has arisen. For the tangible ecumenical
progress achieved on many levels over the last four decades in Europe and in
North America, took place within the ever-intensifying onslaught of a disturb-
ingly post-metaphysical, as well as post-Christian, positivistic, relativistic, and
ultimately subject-driven consumer culture with increasing global outreach.
And the combined effects of the latter have caused in the minds and hearts of
many Christians the well-intentioned but premature and ill-informed judgment that the decisive symbolic step of immediate Eucharistic intercommunion is long overdue, a step that would indeed do nothing but acknowledge
and settle the status quo of reconciled difference, or better, reconciled indifference. Such impatient, enthusiastic ecumenism celebrates the indefinite post-
ponement of the question of truth as the welcome end of an already overly prolonged ecumenical effort. Not infrequently, and easily observable, in broad
segments of mainline Protestantism, and for that matter also in not a few Catholic circles, this ecumenical impatience is fueled by a remarkable indifference
regarding the most central truths of faith and doctrine. This agnosticism arises
to a large degree from the current widespread insecurity and unease regarding
the normative guidance that Scripture, dogma, the Fathers, and the Church's
Magisterium provide, as well as from a widespread departure from the expectation and hope that sustained intellectual contemplation, guided by faith,
will indeed illuminate the truth of the Christian mystery.[2] This situation is undoubtedly exacerbated by the present widespread disparagement of the science of sacred theology and its two integral components, positive and speculative theology. Contemporary theology in general and Catholic theology in
particular are distracted and confused by the currently popular dogmas of cultural constructivism and post-metaphysical relativism; of an increasingly ha-

---

2. The widely influential Reformed theologian Jürgen Moltmann can stand as a paradigmatic voice for those who like to regard themselves as the ecumenical avant-garde. Here the
axiom of the primacy and normativity of praxis, with theology as a subsequent after-the-fact
reflection, finds an all-too-clear application in the mandate of the instantly norming praxis of
intercommunion: "In eucharistic communion we actually do not arrive at a shared praxis on
the basis of a shared theory. Rather, on the contrary, we arrive at a shared theory on the basis of
a shared experience . . . First comes the communion with Christ and then, after the eating and
drinking, we may remain seated at his table and discuss our varying understandings of what has
happened to us there." Jürgen Moltmann, in Ökumene—wohin? Bischöfe und Theologen entwik-
keln Perspektiven, ed. B. J. Hilberath and J. Moltmann (Tübingen: Francke, 2000), 94 (my translation).

bituated hermeneutics of suspicion ceaselessly unmasking authority, tradition, and the "Truth" with a capital "T" as variegations of the "will to power"; of an uncritical accommodation to extraneous if not injurious criteria of academic excellence and productive research imposed by the late-modern, secular university; they are consequently encumbered by numerous and various self-doubts, as well as self-deceptions about the nature and task of sacred theology as a science.[3] In light of this theologically precarious situation, a conscious reconsideration of the way the *doctor communis* conceived of the task of *sacra doctrina* seems to me most salutary.

Sacra Doctrina: Positive as Well as Speculative Theology

What is at stake in such a *ressourcement* is nothing less than the contemporary recovery of what I regard as the two constitutive components of *sacra doctrina* according to Thomas. The first is the active reception of the Church's understanding of divine revelation as proposed in Scripture and as received by way of the Church's teaching, that is, by way of the Fathers, the councils, and the liturgy. This component of *sacra doctrina* was later called "positive theology," since its primary task was to establish *(ponere)* the truths of revelation. The second component of *sacra doctrina* is of a discursive metaphysical kind: first, to defend the revealed truths against objections; second, to draw out intelligible axioms entailed in, and possible further conclusions drawn from, the truths of revelation; and third, to contemplate the inner intelligibility of the revealed truths, that is, to participate discursively in the simplicity of *sapientia*. This component of *sacra doctrina* was later called "speculative theology." I will argue that Thomas's doctrine of Eucharistic conversion reflects the integral unity of the positive and the speculative components of *sacra doctrina*—a unity in urgent need of recovery in our contemporary intellectual context of theology.

Not a few contemporary dogmatic theologians—and especially liturgists —regard Thomas's doctrine of Eucharistic transubstantiation as inextricably entangled in an irretrievably lost medieval cosmological worldview. Upon closer inspection, however, it will become patent that it is precisely Thomas's surpassing reception and application of Aristotle's metaphysics and natural philosophy that saves the notion of *substance* from the fate of becoming a mere metaphor, a fate that would inevitably lead to the very loss of what the Church's dogma intends to maintain.

Upon closer inspection, it will become plain that Thomas's metaphysi-

---

3. See Alasdair MacIntyre, "The End of Education: The Fragmentation of the American University," *Commonweal*, October 20, 2006, 10–14.

cal contemplation of Eucharistic conversion—precisely *as* an integral component of *sacra doctrina*—provides surpassing intelligibility to the dogma of transubstantiation as defined and circumscribed by the Council of Trent and as continuously taught by the Church's Magisterium—a contemplation that gestures toward the blinding light of superintelligibility, experienced as the unique darkness that surrounds this most sublime of all mysteries of faith.

Intellectus Fidei

I submit and will substantiate the thesis that contemporary Catholic dogmatic theology reclaims, by way of a recovery of *sacra doctrina,* the positive as well as the speculative component of its task. It is nothing else than rejuvenating the comprehensive enactment of the *intellectus fidei* that seems to me at stake in the present precarious intellectual context for Catholic dogmatic theology.

In his 1998 encyclical *Fides et Ratio,* the late Pope John Paul II pointed quite clearly the direction such right enactment of the *intellectus fidei* should take:

> With regard to the *intellectus fidei,* a prime consideration must be that divine Truth "proposed to us in the Sacred Scriptures and rightly interpreted by the Church's teaching" [Aquinas, *ST* II-II, q. 5, a. 3, ad 2] enjoys an innate intelligibility, so logically consistent that it stands as an authentic body of knowledge. The *intellectus fidei* expounds this truth, not only in grasping the logical and conceptual structure of the propositions in which the Church's teaching is framed, but also, indeed primarily, in bringing to light the salvific meaning of these propositions for the individual and for humanity . . . For its part, *dogmatic theology* must be able to articulate the universal meaning of the mystery of the One and Triune God and of the economy of salvation, both as a narrative and, above all, in the form of argument. (§ 66)

Hence it is not vis-à-vis the primarily narrative approaches of the post–Vatican II dogmatic theologies, chiefly informed as well as structured by the economy of salvation (first and foremost the multivolume work *Mysterium salutis*),[4] but vis-à-vis the ensuing anti-metaphysical animus and the anti-Scholastic overreaction that a fresh consideration of *sacra doctrina,* of Thomas's unique integration of positive and speculative theology, offers a welcome relief. For Thomas, in a surpassing way, was able to integrate narrative and argument, or, in other words, positive and speculative theology, into one seamless enterprise of *sacra doctrina.*[5]

---

4. Johannes Feiner and Magnus Löhrer, eds., *Mysterium salutis: Grundriß heilsgeschichtlicher Dogmatik,* 5 vols. (Einsiedeln: Benziger, 1965–76).

5. On the central role of the economy of salvation and hence history and even narrative

Metaphysics

So far so good, many a post–Vatican II theologian might say. However, there is one other ingredient that is integral to Thomas's way of substantiating the discursive aspect of *sacra doctrina*—an ingredient that by broad late or postmodern theological and philosophical consensus is irretrievably passé, and that by some, especially Protestant theologians, is regarded as the subtle and specious Hellenistic attempt to destroy the pure and simple Hebrew essence of Christianity—in short, metaphysics.[6] Again, in his encyclical *Fides et Ratio*, Pope John Paul II challenges in a most salutary way this all too conventional wisdom of the day:

The word of God refers constantly to things which transcend human experience and even human thought; but this "mystery" could not be revealed, nor could theology render it in some way intelligible, were human knowledge limited strictly to the world of sense experience. Metaphysics thus plays an essential role of mediation in theological research.[7]

As we will see later, for Thomas, in regarding the truth of Eucharistic conversion, it is faith that preserves the human intellect from deception. This faith, however, does not operate *contra intellectum,* as an intellectually blind faith, commanded only by divine dictates to which the will submits in blind obedience—as notoriously conceived in a nominalist Scholastic and postnominalist Protestant theology. Rather this faith is one sustained, but not constituted, by the *intellectus fidei.* The *intellectus fidei*, however, relies on *received* reality—that

---

in the theological project of Thomas Aquinas, see Max Seckler, *Das Heil in der Geschichte: Geschichtstheologisches Denken bei Thomas von Aquin* (Munich: Kösel, 1964); and Thomas S. Hibbs, *Dialectic and Narrative in Aquinas: An Interpretation of the* Summa contra gentiles (Notre Dame, Ind.: University of Notre Dame Press, 1995).

6. For the classical argument promoting this lore, it is still instructive to read the *spiritus rector* of early twentieth-century, liberal Protestantism, Adolf von Harnack's *What Is Christianity?* trans. Thomas Bailey Saunders (London: Williams and Norgate; New York: Putnam, 1901), and especially his *Lehrbuch der Dogmengeschichte,* 3 vols. (Freiburg: Mohr, 1887–90). For the perpetuation of this prejudice into the Luther-renaissance of the early twentieth century, cf. Wilhelm Link, *Das Ringen Luthers um die Freiheit der Theologie von der Philosophie,* 2nd ed. (Munich: Kaiser, 1955). The most serious philosophical barrier in the twentieth century against returning to those profound Christian sources who freely drew upon metaphysics is Martin Heidegger's sprawling oeuvre. It is due to his influence (and to Karl Rahner's, who was very much Heidegger's disciple in this regard) that most post-conciliar theologians still take it as a simple given that "metaphysics" must be—what else could it be!—a closed system of thinking governed by the unthought that precisely determines this enclosure. Of course, thus conceived, metaphysics is nothing but a mental cage from which one must escape to be able to "think"— theologically. To put it mildly, Thomas would have been a tad surprised to learn about his captivity, as, I dare venture, would Aristotle.

7. John Paul II, *Fides et Ratio,* § 83.

is another way of saying *objective* reality—and this reliance is accounted for in our case, Eucharistic transubstantiation, by a most central *metaphysical* principle, a principle that antecedes and transcends culture as much as history, human subjectivity as much as the philosophy du jour, in short, the metaphysical principle of *substance*.

I do not wish to be misunderstood at the very outset. Let me therefore emphasize unequivocally that metaphysical analysis as employed by Thomas makes possible a profound understanding of the faith's most central *mystery*— precisely *as* mystery.[8] The subtle metaphysical analysis Thomas employed was not intended to resolve a conceptual or logical problem to everyone's satisfaction and then, after sufficient conceptual clarity had been achieved, to move on to the next problem.[9] For Thomas, Eucharistic transubstantiation is a mystery of faith in the strict sense. Hence, the *intellectus fidei* will explore the mystery by establishing and defending metaphysically its intrinsic, logical possibility, but instead of elevating the mystery from the level of the mere imagination to an allegedly higher plane of a truly conceptual comprehension, along the lines of Hegel's "Begriff,"[10] in its very metaphysical contemplation the *intellectus fidei* will preserve the utterly simple, literal sense of the received dominical word "τοῦτό ἐστιν τὸ σῶμά μου τὸ ὑπὲρ ὑμῶν διδόμενον" (Lk 22:19), more familiar to Thomas in its Vulgate rendition, "Hoc est corpus meum quod pro vobis datur."

8. As Thomas makes exceedingly clear in *Summa theologiae* I, q. 1, a. 8, in *sacra doctrina* such a metaphysical principle does not have any probative force. Rather, for the *intellectus fidei* metaphysical contemplation remains an extrinsically probable *"auxilium."* However, while in no way intrinsic to or even constitutive of *sacra doctrina,* metaphysical contemplation, as Thomas displays it throughout the whole *Summa theologiae,* remains indispensable in properly understanding the inner constitution of the reality on which the human intellect qua intellect (and hence also the *intellectus fidei*) relies in its very act of understanding.

9. I draw here upon a most helpful distinction employed by Gabriel Marcel, Jacques Maritain, and Thomas G. Weinandy: "Maritain states that where there is mystery 'the intellect has to penetrate more and more deeply the *same* object.' The mystery, by the necessity of its subject matter, remains . . . Many theologians today, having embraced the Enlightenment presupposition and the scientific method that it fostered, approach theological issues as if they were scientific problems to be solved rather than mysteries to be discerned and clarified. However, the true goal of theological inquiry is not the resolution of theological *problems,* but the discernment of what the *mystery* of faith is." Thomas G. Weinandy, O.F.M. Cap., *Does God Suffer?* (Notre Dame, Ind.: University of Notre Dame Press, 2000), 31–32, original emphasis.

10. It is "metaphysics" conceived along the lines of Hegel's rigorous explanatory conceptualism of "metaphysics as science in the strictest and most complete sense" that Wittgenstein abhorred in his *Blue Book* (*The Blue and Brown Books* [Oxford: Blackwell, 1958], 18) and over against which he claimed that "[p]hilosophy really is 'purely descriptive'" (*Wittgenstein and the Vienna Circle: Conversations Recorded by Friedrich Waismann,* ed. Brian McGuinness [Oxford: Blackwell, 1979], 117). I entertain strong and warrantable doubts that any but the most degenerate versions (and those tend to be of hearsay only) of Aristotelian natural philosophy and metaphysics could fall under Wittgenstein's verdict.

The *Mysterium Fidei* as Proposed in Scripture

A contemporary *ressourcement* in the *doctor communis* leads to a first, quite timely and sobering insight. Theology proper for Thomas is nothing else and nothing less than *sacra doctrina*. And the latter must strike contemporary sensibilities, imbued in historicity, perspectivity, and contextuality, as rather strange and hopelessly naïve, or worse. For *sacra doctrina*, according to Thomas, is indeed constituted by the simplicity of faith that rests on divine authority and embraces the truth as proposed in Scripture. After all, it is *sacra doctrina* that provides the truths necessary for salvation, as Thomas impresses upon the readers of the *Summa theologiae* in the very first article of the first question:

It was necessary for man's salvation that there should be a knowledge revealed by God, besides philosophical science built up by human reason.

Firstly, indeed, because man is directed to God, as to an end that surpasses the grasp of his reason . . . But the end must first be known by men who direct their thoughts and actions to the end. Hence it was necessary for the salvation of man that certain truths which exceed human reason should be made known to him by divine revelation.

Even as regards those truths about God which human reason could have discovered, it was necessary that man should be taught by a divine revelation; because the truth about God such as reason could discover, would only be known by a few, and that after a long time, and with the admixture of many errors. Whereas man's whole salvation, which is in God, depends upon the knowledge of this truth.[11]

Still true to this understanding of *sacra doctrina*, much later in the *Summa theologiae*, in its third part, in question 75, where Thomas treats sacramental

---

11. *ST* I, q. 1, a. 1: "[N]ecessarium fuit ad humanam salutem, esse doctrinam quandam secundum revelationem divinam, praeter philosophicas disciplinas, quae ratione humana investigantur. Primo quidem, quia homo ordinatur ad Deum sicut ad quendam finem qui comprehensionem rationis excedit . . . Finem autem oportet esse praecognitum hominibus, qui suas intentiones et actiones debent ordinare in finem. Unde necessarium fuit homini ad salutem, quod ei nota fierent quaedam per revelationem divinam, quae rationem humanam excedunt.

Ad ea etiam quae de Deo ratione humana investigari possunt, necessarium fuit hominem instrui revelatione divina. Quia veritas de Deo, per rationem investigata, a paucis, et per longum tempus, et cum admixtione multorum errorum, homini provenire: a cuius tamen veritatis cognitione dependet tota hominis salus, quae in Deo est. Ut igitur salus hominibus et convenientius et certius proveniat, necessarium fuit quod de divinis per divinam revelationem instruantur."

For consistency's sake, all citations from the *Summa theologiae* in English are taken from the translation of the Fathers of the English Dominican Province, St. Thomas Aquinas, *Summa Theologica* (New York: Benziger Brothers, 1948). The Latin original offered in the notes is taken from Sancti Thomae de Aquino, *Summa Theologiae*, 3rd ed. (Turin: Edizioni San Paolo, 1999), which offers an improved version of the Leonine edition.

conversion, he dedicates the whole first article solely to emphasizing the salvific significance of the real presence. When we compare Thomas's discussion
of this topic in the *Summa* with his early treatment of it in his commentary on
Lombard's *Sentences*,[12] we realize that Thomas intentionally inserted this article right at the beginning of the whole treatise on the Eucharist. It also becomes abundantly clear from this opening article of the treatise on the Eucharist that Thomas avows Eucharistic transubstantiation because the scriptural
affirmation of real presence requires it. According to Thomas, one cannot have
the one without the other. Truly making explicit the mystery of Christ's real
presence in the Eucharist requires developing an account of transubstantiation.

I shall now briefly turn to article 1 of question 75 in order, first, to review
Thomas's arguments for the salvific significance of the real presence and, second, to consider the striking way Thomas displays the nature of *sacra doctrina*.
The three reasons Thomas adduces in order to affirm "the presence of Christ's
true body and blood in this sacrament" are not probative but illuminative of
what is held "by faith alone, which rests upon Divine authority."[13] Each one of
these reasons adduced draws its strength from a particular perfection that is
ordered to salvation: first, in the order of salvation itself, second, in the order of
love, and third, in the order of faith.

First, the perfection in the order of salvation. Thomas points out the relationship between the figurative foreshadowing of the sacrifice of Christ's passion in Israel's sacrifices and its fulfillment in Christ's death on the Cross, of
which the Eucharist is the representation:

[T]herefore it was necessary that the sacrifice of the New Law instituted by Christ
should have something more, namely, that it should contain Christ Himself crucified, not merely in signification or figure, but also in very truth. And therefore this
sacrament which contains Christ Himself, as Dionysius says (*Eccl. Hier.* iii), is perfective of all the other sacraments, in which Christ's virtue is participated.[14]

---

12. See *In IV Sent.* d. 8, q. 1, a. 1.

13. *ST* III, q. 75, a. 1. In another way, this article can be read as a highly condensed reception of the early medieval and prescholastic Eucharistic doctrine. For a still greatly informative study of this rich period of prescholastic theological contemplation of the mystery, see Josef
Geiselmann, *Die Eucharistielehre der Vorscholastiker* (Paderborn: Schöningh, 1926).

14. *ST* III, q. 75, a. 1, c: "[I]deo oportuit ut aliquid plus haberet sacrificium novae legis a
Christo institutum: ut scilicet contineret ipsum passum non solum in significatione vel figura,
sed etiam in rei veritate. Et ideo hoc sacramentum, quod ipsum Christum realiter continet, ut
Dionysius dicit, 3 cap. *Eccles. Hierar.*, est *perfectivum omnium sacramentorum aliorum*, in quibus
virtus Christi participatur."

Second, the perfection in the order of love. It is because of his love for humanity and for the sake of humanity's salvation that "Christ assumed a true body of our nature." Drawing upon a famous insight from Aristotle—an insight that could as well have come from Augustine—namely that "it is the special feature of friendship to live together with friends," Thomas refers to Matthew 24:28 in order to point out that Christ promised to his disciples his everlasting bodily presence to them in the world to come. However, as a token of his surpassing friendship and love:

> in our pilgrimage He does not deprive us of His bodily presence; but unites us with Himself in this sacrament through the truth of His body and blood. Hence (John vi. 57) he says: "He that eateth My flesh, and drinketh My blood, abideth in Me, and I in him." Hence this sacrament is the sign of supreme charity, and the uplifter of our hope, from such familiar union of Christ with us.[15]

Third, the perfection in the order of faith. For faith, Thomas argues, pertains to Christ's humanity as much as to his divinity: "And since faith is of things unseen, as Christ shows us His Godhead invisibly, so also in this sacrament He shows us His flesh in an invisible manner."[16]

All three reasons adduced by Thomas are illuminative of the salvation in the service of which *sacra doctrina* stands. This becomes plain when we now, secondly, turn to consider the striking way Thomas displays, in the opening statement of the article, the nature of *sacra doctrina*:

> The presence of Christ's true body and blood in this sacrament cannot be detected by sense, nor understanding, but by faith alone [*sola fide*], which rests upon Divine authority. Hence, on Luke 22:19: "This is My body, which shall be delivered up for you," Cyril says: "Doubt not whether this be true; but take rather the Savior's words with faith; for since He is the Truth, He lieth not."[17]

It is deceptively simple but profoundly significant what Thomas is doing here: first, without quoting it at length, assuming that every reader would know it

---

15. *ST* III, q. 75, a. 1, c: "Interim tamen nec sua praesentia corporali in hac peregrinatione destituit, sed per veritatem corporis et sanguinis sui nos sibi coniungit in hoc sacramento. Unde ipse dicit, *Ioan. 6*, [57]: *Qui manducat meam carnem et bibit meum sanguinem, in me manet et ego in eo*. Unde hoc sacramentum est maximae caritatis signum, et nostrae spei sublevamentum, ex tam familiari coniunctione Christi ad nos."

16. *ST* III, q. 75, a. 1, c: "Et quia fides est invisibilium, sicut divinitatem suam nobis exhibet Christus invisibiliter, ita et in hoc sacramento carnem suam nobis exhibet invisibili modo."

17. *ST* III, q. 75, a. 1, c.: "[V]erum corpus Christi et sanguinem esse in hoc sacramento, non sensu deprehendi potest, sed sola fide, quae auctoritati divinae innititur. Unde super illud Luc. 22, [19], 'Hoc est corpus meum quod pro vobis tradetur,' dicit Cyrillus: 'Non dubites an hoc verum sit, sed potius suscipe verba Salvatoris in fide: cum enim sit veritas, non mentitur.'"

by heart, he alludes to Christ's words of consecration according to the Gospel of Luke, which is most crucial for the question at hand: "And he took bread, and when he had given thanks he broke it and gave it to them, saying, 'This is my body which is given for you. Do this in remembrance of me.' And likewise the cup after supper, saying, 'This cup which is poured out for you is the new covenant in my blood.'"[18] The dominical words themselves, taken in the *sensus literalis,* constitute the primordial point of departure for *sacra doctrina* among wayfarers, the mode of reception characteristic of positive theology, presupposing that the author of Scripture itself, the incarnate Word is speaking directly about himself.[19]

Second, again characteristic of the *modus procedendi* of positive theology, this presupposition is not simply made axiomatically, or aprioristically, to use a modern concept. On the contrary, this very presupposition is itself received, since it represents the Church's own understanding of the *sensus literalis.* To this purpose, Thomas cites St. Cyril of Alexandria, who enjoins the readers of his own commentary on the Gospel of Luke to take Christ simply at his word, because he is the truth: "Doubt not whether this be true; but take rather the Savior's words with faith; for since He is the Truth, He lieth not."[20] That is, Thomas lets the one authority among the Fathers who is most intimately associated with the dogma of Chalcedon make the fundamental point about Who is speaking about himself. Moreover, he prepares this reception of the *sensus literalis* through the Church's understanding by drawing, in the *sed contra,* upon two Western Fathers, St. Hilary, bishop of Poitiers, and St. Ambrose, bishop of Milan, both of whom antedate St. Cyril and hence represent even earlier voices of the Church's tradition.[21]

18. Luke 22:19–20 RSV.

19. Aquinas's point here is far from unreflectively naive in some allegedly "premodern" sense that we see ourselves regrettably forced to transcend toward some higher, modern, i.e., critical perspective. Rather, the Church's understanding, that is, *traditio* itself, reads this text as *Deus ipse loquitur.* Hence, when modern historical-critical exegetes are intent upon reconstructing the words of consecration as early post-Easter tradition instead of attributing the words to some construct of the "historical" Jesus, their work is to be gratefully received into a deeper theological understanding of the very apostolic *paradosis* whence arose the New Testament. For this is precisely what *traditio* is all about: the reception of God's Word in the Church that is Christ's body. In short, the post-Easter tradition *is* the apostolic *paradosis* that announces the truth that Jesus did indeed take bread and say, "This is my body."

20. PG 72, 92.

21. At this point it is appropriate to call to mind the status and role of the church doctors in Thomas's hierarchy of authorities. According to *ST* I, q. 1, a. 8, ad 2, the doctors cited have an authority intrinsic to *sacra doctrina,* albeit only a probable one. That is, church doctors and their writings do have a clearly lesser authority than statements of faith produced by church councils and ratified by the pope. Only the latter have an authority for *sacra doctrina* that is intrinsic as well as certain.

Third, we can observe here how Thomas displays what he calls the subal-
ternate character of *sacra doctrina* as *scientia* in *Summa theologiae* I, question 1,
article 2:

[S]acred doctrine is a science, because it proceeds from principles established by the
light of a higher science, namely, the science of God and the blessed [*scientia Dei et
beatorum*]. Hence, just as the musician accepts on authority [*tradita*] the principles
taught him by the mathematician, so sacred science is established on principles revealed by God.[22]

Consequently, in our instance, the first move of *sacra doctrina* as the sub-
alternate *scientia* of us wayfarers short of the beatific vision is, by way of the
Church's understanding *(traditio)*, the reception of a truth *(principium revelatum a Deo)*, that is, of a communication of the *scientia Dei et beatorum*, that
is not to be interpreted in light of some other more authoritative, profound,
or illuminating text of Scripture itself. Rather, *Christus ipse locutus est*. While
God, as Scripture's ultimate author,[23] surely speaks by way of and through all
of Scripture, the dominical words are exceptional, since they directly appeal to
the immediate assent of faith. Remember that Thomas understands that faith
adheres to the First Truth. In *Summa theologiae* II-II, question 5, article 3, ad 2,
he states: "[F]aith adheres to all the articles of faith by reason of one mean,
namely, on account of the First Truth proposed to us in the Scriptures, according to the teaching of the Church who has the right understanding of them."[24]
According to the Church's right understanding of the First Truth, that is, according to the *doctrina Ecclesiae*, in Luke 22:19, "the First Truth proposed to
us in the Scriptures" speaks himself, and thus constitutes immediately a *principium revelatum a Deo;* and St. Cyril's theological judgment (together with
St. Hilary's and St. Ambrose's teaching as adduced in the *sed contra*)[25] represents for Thomas paradigmatically "the teaching of the Church that has the right
understanding of [the Scriptures]."

22. *ST* I, q. 1, a. 2: "Et hoc modo sacra doctrina est scientia: quia procedit ex principiis notis
lumine superioris scientiae, quae scilicet est scientia Dei et beatorum. Unde sicut musica credit principia tradita sibi ab arithmetico, ita doctrina sacra credit principia revelata sibi a Deo."
23. *ST* I, q. 1, a. 10, c.: "[A]uctor sacrae Scripturae est Deus."
24. *ST* II-II, q. 5, a. 3, ad 2: "[O]mnibus articulis fidei inhaeret fides propter unum medium,
scilicet propter veritatem primam propositam nobis in Scripturis secundum doctrinam Ecclesiae intellectis sane."
25. *ST* III q. 75, a. 1, s.c.: "Hilary says (*De Trin.*, viii [PL 10, 247]): 'There is no room for doubt
regarding the truth of Christ's body and blood; for now by our Lord's own declaring and by our
faith His flesh is truly food, and His blood is truly drink.' And Ambrose says (*De Sacram.*, vi
[cap. 1; PL 16, 473]): 'As the Lord Jesus Christ is God's true Son, so is it Christ's true flesh which
we take, and His true blood which we drink.'"

Hence, what Thomas reminds us of in the opening article of the question on the conversion of bread and wine into the body and blood of Christ is that *sacra doctrina* is first and foremost the *act* of faith adhering to the First Truth in the concrete instance of its self-communication as apostolically mediated and interpreted by the *doctrina Ecclesiae*.[26] It is this doctrinally received and mediated *principium revelatum a Deo* that the *intellectus fidei* draws on in its subsequent metaphysical contemplation. Hence, the truth of faith is not established by the profound metaphysical exploration that follows; rather, having been established by the First Truth himself and subsequently taught by the *doctrina Ecclesiae*, the truth of faith is illuminated and defended by the discursive probings of the *intellectus fidei*. The truth does not depend on a successful metaphysical defense or even proof; rather, the revealed truth itself elicits the metaphysical contemplation that displays the truth's inherent intelligibility as a mystery of faith and contributes to a more comprehensive and penetrating intellectual reception of it. This is *intellectus fidei*. While the *intellectus fidei* is central to *sacra doctrina*, *sacra doctrina* among wayfarers arises from the First Truth, the author of Scripture, and hence, first and foremost, from the Incarnate Word himself. There is, however, no other access to this first datum than by way of Christ's body, the Church and her teaching.

Wittgenstein once rightly observed, "One is unable to notice something—because it is always before one's eyes."[27] Accordingly, it is often the novice who perceives with fresh eyes what has become all too obvious—and hence invisible—to all those already too accustomed to it, or even tired of it. I shall briefly turn to such a novice. Erik Peterson, a renowned theologian and historian of dogma, Lutheran in upbringing and theological training, was received into the Catholic Church on December 25, 1930. In the winter semester 1923–24, at the Protestant faculty of the University of Göttingen, Peterson offered a lecture course on Thomas Aquinas, an event quite extraordinary in that day and age, long before Vatican II and hence the cause of lively concern in many a quarter of Protestantism.[28] Subsequently, in 1925, in a small but intense treatise on the

---

26. For *doctrina* not as a "thing" but an act, see Frederick Christian Bauerschmidt, "That the Faithful Become the Temple of God," in *Reading John with St. Thomas Aquinas: Theological Exegesis and Speculative Theology*, ed. Michael Dauphinais and Matthew Levering (Washington, D.C.: The Catholic University of America Press, 2005), 293–311.

27. Ludwig Wittgenstein, "Philosophische Untersuchungen," § 129, in *Schriften* (Frankfurt am Main: Suhrkamp, 1960), 346: "Man kann es nicht bemerken,—weil man es immer vor Augen hat."

28. See Barbara Nichtweiß, *Erik Peterson: Neue Sicht auf Leben und Werk* (Freiburg: Herder, 1992), 384; and regarding the relationship between Peterson and Barth while both were lecturers at the University of Göttingen, ibid., 505–12; and on the dispute over the treatise "What Is

nature of theology, written in sharp opposition to the rising dialectical theology of Karl Barth, Erik Peterson had the following to say:

Just as there has been dogma and the church only since the ascension, so also has there been theology only from this particular point on. One cannot answer the question "what is theology" if one forgets that God's word became flesh and spoke about God. Nor can one answer the question "what is theology" if one forgets the other aspect as well, namely, that Christ ascended to heaven and that there is now dogma.[29]

Dogma, however, Peterson emphasizes "does not continue Christ's own discourse about God directly, but rather in such a way that there is now a teaching authority Christ has conferred upon the church in which dogma appears."[30]

Let me submit that Erik Peterson gleaned this fundamental insight about the nature of theology as *sacra doctrina*—its three necessary presuppositions being revelation, faith, and fidelity—from no one other than Thomas Aquinas. For, after all, it is Thomas who quite tersely states that "the formal object of faith is the First Truth, as manifested in Holy Writ and the teaching of the Church, [which proceeds from the First Truth]."[31] Peterson's rediscovery of theology as *sacra doctrina* is still relevant, possibly even more so in our day when theology has increasingly estranged itself by critical, hermeneutical hyper-sophistication under the rubrics of historical distance, epistemological difference, and cultural plurality. At a time when Protestant liberalism still reigned largely unchecked at most German Protestant university faculties, Erik Peterson learned from Thomas Aquinas that theology as *sacra doctrina* receives the First Truth, "proposed to us in the Sacred Scriptures and rightly interpreted by the Church's teaching,"[32] that is, by way of dogma as interpreted

---

Theology?" ibid., 512–17. According to Nichtweiß, Karl Barth regularly attended Peterson's lecture-course on Aquinas, which, in all likelihood, was Barth's first real encounter with the theology of Thomas Aquinas.

29. Erik Peterson, "Theologie als Wissenschaft," in *Theologie als Wissenschaft: Aufsätze und Thesen*, ed. Gerhard Sauter (Munich: Kaiser, 1971), 150. (The translation of the quotations is taken from the discussion of Peterson in my *Suffering Divine Things: Theology as Church Practice*, trans. Doug Stott [Grand Rapids: Eerdmans, 2000], 96–102.) More recently, Peterson's important essay has been made available in a new edition of his works: Erik Peterson, *Ausgewählte Schriften*, vol. 1, *Theologische Traktate*, with an introduction by Barbara Nichtweiß (Würzburg: Echter, 1994), 3–22.

30. Peterson, "Theologie als Wissenschaft," 149.

31. *ST* II-II, q. 5, a. 3, c.: "Formale autem obiectum fidei est veritas prima secundum quod manifestatur in Scripturis sacris et doctrinae Ecclesiae." The Editio Piana (Rome, 1570) contains the following addition, absent from the Editio Leonina (Rome, 1882ff.): "quae procedit ex veritate prima."

32. *Fides et Ratio*, § 66.

by the Church's Magisterium in the context of the Church's comprehensive sacramental reality: revelation, faith, fidelity.

Thomas gestures to this cardinal mode of receiving the First Truth in a hymn of his hand that became part of the new Office of the Blessed Sacrament he was asked to write for a new feast that originally arose locally from the Church's living faith.[33] On August 11, 1264, in his bull *Transiturus*, Pope Urban IV instituted this feast for the universal Church: it is, of course, the feast of Corpus Christi.[34] The sequence for Corpus Christi Mass, *Lauda Sion, Salvatorem*, opens its eleventh stanza with the line "Dogma datur Christianis," which has been translated as "[t]his truth to Christians is proclaimed," but after the Council of Trent's dogma on Eucharistic conversion and in light of Erik Peterson's profound understanding *ad mentem S. Thomae* of the First Truth speaking himself in the dominical words, it can as well be translated as "this dogma, this truth from and about the Word himself to Christians is given," namely by way of the *doctrina Ecclesiae*, "that bread passes over [*transit*] into flesh and wine passes over [*transit*] into blood":

> Dogma datur Christianis,
> Quod in carnem transit panis
> Et vinum in sanguinem.
> Quod non capis, quod non vides,
> Animosa firmat fides
> Praeter rerum ordinem.[35]

Dogma datur Christianis—By Way of the Magisterium's Continuing Affirmation of the Council of Trent's Teaching

The next step, consequently, of a continuing *ressourcement* in Thomas's procedure of *sacra doctrina* is to consider *doctrina Ecclesiae*, that is, "the teaching of the Church who has the right understanding of [the Scriptures]."

Since the Second Vatican Council, by its own explicit self-understanding a pastoral council, did not produce any new dogmatic definitions, and since the

---

33. It was through the initiative of St. Julienne of Mont-Cornillon that this feast began to be celebrated around 1240.

34. See Torrell, *The Person and His Work*, 129–36.

35. "This truth to Christians is proclaimed: / That to flesh, bread is transformed, / And transformed to blood is wine. / What you can neither grasp nor see, / A lively faith will yet affirm / Beyond this world's design." *The Aquinas Prayer Book: The Prayers and Hymns of St. Thomas Aquinas*, trans. and ed. Robert Anderson and Johann Moser (Manchester, N.H.: Sophia Institute Press, 2000), 102–4.

dogmatic definitions of the First Vatican Council have no immediate bearing upon our topic, the most recent relevant council is the Council of Trent. The more proximate normative context, however, is constituted by the teaching of the ordinary Magisterium in its ongoing affirmation of the dogma of Trent.[36] For this task, four encyclicals are pertinent: Pope Leo XIII's *Mirae Caritatis* from 1902, Pope Pius XII's *Mediator Dei* from 1947, Pope Paul VI's *Mysterium Fidei* from 1965, and Pope John Paul II's *Ecclesia de Eucharistia* from 2003. The first two encyclicals (I will only very briefly cite from them) treat the Eucharist in a comprehensive way and especially focus on the Eucharistic sacrifice. It is only with Pope Paul VI, in the immediate aftermath of the Second Vatican Council and in light of new theological interpretations (emerging especially in the Netherlands) of the mystery of Christ's real presence, that an explicit Magisterial averment of Eucharistic transubstantiation became necessary. Pope John Paul II, in *Ecclesia de Eucharistia,* as well as in the recent universal *Catechism of the Catholic Church* (1994; editio typica 1997), reaffirms the particular emphasis of the encyclical *Mysterium Fidei,* which on the specific topic of Eucharistic transubstantiation arguably remains the most important magisterial intervention in the twentieth century.

In both *Mirae Caritatis* and *Mediator Dei,* the primary emphasis lies on the inherent link between Christ's self-offering on the Cross and the Eucharistic sacrifice.[37] Christ's real presence in the Eucharistic sacrifice is affirmed pre-

---

36. To put it negatively, for theology, properly understood as *sacra doctrina,* the proximate normative context can never be the critically established pre-understanding of contemporary thought (the predominant intellectual climate, in German aptly called *Zeitgeist*), nor the deliverances of the sciences, nor the variant cultural contexts of the faithful. All of these concerns have their proper place in a subsequent hermeneutical and catechetical task of communicating the faith. Rather, theology, properly understood as *sacra doctrina,* first *receives, actively receives,* the Church's understanding—what Thomas formulated in the hymn in such a felicitous way as "dogma datur Christianis"—by way of the magisterial teaching of the twentieth and early twenty-first centuries.

37. Pope Leo XIII, in *Mirae Caritatis,* affirms that "the Eucharist, according to the testimony of the holy Fathers, should be regarded as in a manner a continuation and extension of the Incarnation. For in and by it the substance of the incarnate Word is united with individual men, and the supreme Sacrifice offered on Calvary is in a wondrous manner renewed . . . And this miracle, itself the very greatest of its kind, is accompanied by innumerable other miracles; for here all the laws of nature are suspended; the whole substance of the bread and wine are changed into the Body and the Blood; the species of bread and wine are sustained by the divine power without the support of any underlying substance; the Body of Christ is present in many places at the same time, that is to say, wherever the Sacrament is consecrated" (§ 7).

Pope Pius XII, in his extensive and rich encyclical *Mediator Dei,* reaffirms the teaching of Trent that "[t]he august sacrifice of the altar . . . is no mere empty commemoration of the passion and death of Jesus Christ, but a true and proper act of sacrifice, whereby the High Priest by an unbloody immolation offers Himself as a most acceptable victim to the Eternal Father, as He did upon the cross" (§ 68). "Likewise the victim is the same, namely, our divine Redeemer

cisely in the way the Council of Trent defined the matter. However, Eucharistic transubstantiation, while unequivocally affirmed, remains in the background of both encyclicals. This changes drastically with Pope Paul VI's encyclical *Mysterium Fidei*. Why? During the Second Vatican Council, the Dogmatic Constitution *Lumen Gentium*, § 11, had clearly, even if tersely, re-emphasized the teaching of Eucharistic sacrifice as laid down extensively in Pope Pius XII's encyclical *Mediator Dei*. But quite notably, *Lumen Gentium*, § 11, does not make mention at all of transubstantiation along the lines that the Council of Trent had explicitly defined it—quite possibly in light of the acutely felt modern conceptual difficulties, as well as equally acutely felt ecumenical sensibilities. Arguably, because of this silence and because of various new and not altogether unproblematic attempts at a new interpretation of the mystery of Christ's real presence in the Eucharist, *Mysterium Fidei* has the function of an explicit magisterial *addendum* on a most central aspect of Eucharistic doctrine, which was left unaddressed by Vatican II. Indeed, the opening paragraphs of *Mysterium Fidei* make it quite patent that this magisterial intervention is to be understood along these lines. Because *Mysterium Fidei* is affirmed by *Ecclesia de Eucharistia* and by the *Catechism of the Catholic Church*, it is advisable to attend more closely to this particular encyclical.

In *Mysterium Fidei*, Pope Paul VI addresses most directly the "dogma of transubstantiation" (§ 10) and declares unequivocally that it is impermissible

to discuss the mystery of transubstantiation without mentioning what the Council of Trent had to say about the marvelous conversion of the whole substance of the bread into the Body and the whole substance of the wine into the Blood of Christ, as if they involve nothing more than "transignification," or "transfinalization" as they call it; or . . . to propose and act upon the opinion that Christ Our Lord is no longer present in the consecrated Hosts that remain after the celebration of the sacrifice of the Mass has been completed.[38]

---

in His human nature with His true body and blood. The manner, however, in which Christ is offered is different. . . . For by the 'transubstantiation' of bread into the body of Christ and of wine into His blood, His body and blood are both really present; now the eucharistic species under which He is present symbolize the actual separation of His body and blood. Thus the commemorative representation of His death, which actually took place on Calvary, is repeated in every sacrifice of the altar, seeing that Jesus Christ is symbolically shown by separate symbols to be in a state of victimhood" (§ 70).

38. Paul VI, *Mysterium Fidei*, § 11. After having, by way of the words of St. Bonaventure, unequivocally affirmed Christ's real presence in the sacrament as indispensable for the integrity of the true Catholic faith, Pope Paul VI turns to what some contemporary theologians might want to call proper "word care": "Once the integrity of the faith has been safeguarded, then it is time to guard the proper way of expressing it, lest our careless use of words give rise, God forbid, to false opinions regarding faith in the most sublime things" (§ 23).

Because of their immediate relevance, we must recall some longer passages from §§ 24 and 25. For they describe in quite exact terms (a) the way *sacra doctrina* is to receive the Church's understanding by way of the definitions of dogma, and (b) the precise nature of the very concepts that the definitions of dogma employ:

> And so the rule of language which the Church has established through the long labor of centuries, with the help of the Holy Spirit, and which she has confirmed with the authority of the Councils, and which has more than once been the watchword and banner of orthodox faith, is to be religiously preserved, and no one may presume to change it at his own pleasure or under the pretext of new knowledge. Who would ever tolerate that the dogmatic formulas used by the ecumenical councils for the mysteries of the Holy Trinity and the Incarnation be judged as no longer appropriate for men of our times, and let others be rashly substituted for them? In the same way, it cannot be tolerated that any individual should, on his own authority, take something away from the formulas which were used by the Council of Trent to propose the Eucharistic Mystery for our belief. These formulas—like the others that the Church used to propose the dogmas of faith—express concepts that are not tied to a certain specific form of human culture, or to a certain level of scientific progress, or to one or another theological school. Instead they set forth what the human mind grasps of reality through necessary and universal experience and what it expresses in apt and exact words, whether it be in ordinary or more refined language. For this reason, these formulas are adapted to all men of all times and all places. (§ 24)

> They can, it is true, be made clearer and more obvious; and doing this is of great benefit. But it must always be done in such a way that they retain the meaning in which they have been used, so that with the advance of an understanding of the faith, the truth of the faith will remain unchanged. For it is the teaching of the First Vatican Council that "the meaning that Holy Mother the Church has once declared, is to be retained forever, and no pretext of deeper understanding ever justifies any deviation from that meaning." (§ 25)

After delineating these dogmatic guidelines for the ongoing work of *sacra doctrina,* let us turn to the way the encyclical applies them directly to Christ's real presence in the Eucharist:

> This presence is called "real" not to exclude the idea that the others are "real" too, but rather to indicate presence *par excellence,* because it is substantial and through it Christ becomes present whole and entire, God and man. And so it would be wrong for anyone to try to explain this manner of presence by dreaming up a so-called "pneumatic" nature of the glorious body of Christ that would be present everywhere; or for anyone to limit it to symbolism, as if this most sacred Sacrament were to consist in nothing more than an efficacious sign "of the spiritual presence of Christ and of His intimate union with the faithful, the members of His Mystical Body." (§ 39)

When we turn to Pope John Paul II's encyclical *Ecclesia de Eucharistia,* we can be very brief. For regarding Christ's real presence in the Eucharist and sacramental conversion, the encyclical cites *Mysterium Fidei* directly, and explicitly reaffirms the teaching of the Council of Trent.[39] Finally, also drawing upon Pope Paul VI's encyclical *Mysterium Fidei,* the *Catechism of the Catholic Church* unequivocally reaffirms, in one accord with the above encyclicals, the teaching of the Council of Trent that (a) Christ is substantially present in the sacrament and that (b) this substantial presence comes about through a change of the whole substance of the bread and wine into the substance of the body and blood of Christ.[40]

Let us step back now and gather some of the entailments of the Magisterium's teaching as they orient *sacra doctrina* in its active reception of the truth as proposed in Scripture. Several observations are in order.

The Church's Magisterium, in the course of the twentieth and the early twenty-first centuries (most explicitly in the encyclical *Mysterium Fidei*), makes it very hard, if not impossible, to deny that (a) the Council of Trent's teaching on Eucharistic sacrifice and Eucharistic transubstantiation indeed continues to obtain and, moreover, that (b) the Magisterium maintains a normative hermeneutic of these dogmatic definitions, in that these dogmatic definitions represent a priori, "quoad rem" true propositions, the "res" here refer-

---

39. "The sacramental re-presentation of Christ's sacrifice, crowned by the resurrection, in the Mass involves a most special presence which—in the words of Paul VI—'is called "real" not as a way of excluding all other types of presence as if they were "not real," but because it is a presence in the fullest sense: a substantial presence whereby Christ, the God-Man, is wholly and entirely present.' This sets forth once more the perennially valid teaching of the Council of Trent: 'the consecration of the bread and wine effects the change of the whole substance of the bread into the substance of the body of Christ our Lord, and of the whole substance of the wine into the substance of his blood. And the holy Catholic Church has fittingly and properly called this change transubstantiation.' Truly the Eucharist is a *mysterium fidei,* a mystery which surpasses our understanding and can only be received in faith, as is often brought out in the catechesis of the Church Fathers regarding this divine sacrament: 'Do not see—Saint Cyril of Jerusalem exhorts—in the bread and wine merely natural elements, because the Lord has expressly said that they are his body and his blood: faith assures you of this, though your senses suggest otherwise'" (§ 15).

40. *Catechism of the Catholic Church,* § 1374: "In the most blessed sacrament of the Eucharist 'the body and blood, together with the soul and divinity, of our Lord Jesus Christ and, therefore, the whole Christ is truly, really, and substantially contained'"; § 1376: "The Council of Trent summarizes the Catholic faith by declaring: 'Because Christ our Redeemer said that it was truly his body that he was offering under the species of bread, it has always been the conviction of the Church of God, and this holy Council now declares again, that by the consecration of the bread and wine there takes place a change of the whole substance of the bread into the substance of the body of Christ our Lord and of the whole substance of the wine into the substance of his blood. This change the holy Catholic Church has fittingly and properly called transubstantiation.'"

ring to principles that transcend historical change and cultural context. It is, furthermore, hard, if not impossible, to deny that (c) the Magisterium indeed assumes that the basic pre-philosophical apprehension of world and faith already entails metaphysical presuppositions pertaining to being and essence, presuppositions that classical metaphysics does not invent but systematically clarifies and analyzes with a lasting, fruitful pertinence, presuppositions on which the dogmatic tradition has drawn from early on. In addition, it is hard, if not impossible, to deny that (d) the Magisterium maintains that the dogma of Trent contains in and of itself theological accounts for truths of faith proposed in Scripture—theological accounts that are not again and again in need of further theological accounts. For these theological accounts entailed in the decree of Trent rely not on explanations that are historically relative, but on metaphysical principles that arise from reality itself. Finally, it seems hard, if not impossible, to deny that (e) the Magisterium assumes that these dogmatic propositions, as theological statements, intend God *as well as* the essence of things and hence presuppose certain abiding metaphysical principles.[41]

In our particular case, the Magisterium teaches unequivocally that the dogma of Trent clearly presupposes a pre-philosophical common knowledge of substance and hence draws on the abiding metaphysical principle of substance.[42] Furthermore, the Magisterium has unequivocally rejected the notion that "transubstantiation" might serve as a mere signifier in a quasi-nominalist sense, that is, as a notional placeholder for a range of interpretations that might only in the widest of senses fall under it. Hence, it seems extremely hard, if not simply impossible, for Catholic dogmatic theology, conceived as *sacra doctrina,* to give support to the widely held opinion that the dogmatic formulations decreed by the Council of Trent regarding Eucharistic conversion contain a doctrinal "intention" that can, and indeed must, be isolated from its conceptual "explanation," an explanation that expresses an essentially ineffable truth "quoad nos," whereby the explanation remains inherently contingent upon the historical situation from which it arises.[43]

41. Hence it seems quite obvious that while the Magisterium does not endorse the teaching of any one particular theological school, it is concerned to avoid the danger and problem of a late-medieval "double accounting," as then-Joseph Ratzinger, in his 1967 essay "Das Problem der Transsubstantiation," aptly called it. This "double accounting" means that while faith and dogma might say one thing—say, "transubstantiation"—philosophy, accountable to natural reason alone, will have to think quite another thing—say, "consubstantiation" or "transfinalization" or something else.

42. I draw here on and agree with Seidl, "Zum Substanzbegriff der katholischen Transsubstantiationslehre."

43. A rejection of such a specious hermeneutics of dogma, however, does not foreclose the possibility of some analogous hermeneutical approximation of what the dogma intends in

"Substance" and "Quantity": Their Indispensability for the Doctrine of Eucharistic Conversion

Clearly defined by magisterial teaching on transubstantiation, this situation calls for a fresh *ressourcement* of contemporary dogmatic theology in Thomas's positive as well as his speculative theology. Thomas's profound and compelling doctrine of Christ's Eucharistic presence offers itself anew because it grants surpassing intelligibility to the principles entailed in the doctrine of transubstantiation and especially to the abiding *metaphysical* notion of substance. For the *metaphysical* notion of substance employed by him and the whole Thomist school does not become passé with the crisis of the *physical* concept of material substance as it gained predominance in late medieval philosophy of nature and came into its own with Descartes's *res extensa* and the increasing divorce between natural philosophy and mathematical natural science at least since Newton, if not since Galileo. It is, I submit, the ongoing active reception of Thomas's doctrine of Eucharistic transubstantiation that saves the notion of substantial conversion from becoming a mere metaphor and in turn helps prevent Christ's substantial, corporeal presence in the Eucharist—and hence Christ's comprehensive personal presence as the crucified and risen Lord—from declining in the hearts and minds of not a few of the faithful into a mere symbol of the ecclesial communion of the Eucharistic assembly.

Let us first recall that the Council of Trent solemnly decreed that

by the consecration of the bread and wine, there takes place the conversion of the whole substance of the bread into the substance of the body of Christ our Lord, and of the whole substance of the wine into the substance of his blood. And the holy

---

contexts in which it is hard to communicate the depth of the principles involved. Then-Joseph Ratzinger provides an excellent example of such a hermeneutical approximation in his 1967 essay "Das Problem der Transsubstantiation." As Pope Benedict XVI, he continues such hermeneutical approximation in his post-synodal apostolic exhortation *Sacramentum Caritatis* (2007), where he seems to be at pains to use traditional terminology that at the same time does not commit him to one particular school of thought (e.g., "quorum sub specie" in § 8, and "substantialis transmutatio" in § 11): "The substantial conversion [*substantialis transmutatio*] of bread and wine into his body and blood introduces within creation the principle of a radical change [*principium extremae mutationis*], a sort of 'nuclear fission,' to use an image familiar to us today, which penetrates to the heart of all being, a change meant to set off a process which transforms reality, a process leading ultimately to the transfiguration of the entire world, to the point where God will be all in all (cf. 1 Cor 15:28)" (§ 11). Such a procedure, however, is categorically different from slicing dogma itself into two parts, so to speak, a transcendent "intention" that affirms the truth of faith on the one side and, on the other side, a time-conditioned, conceptual way of "expressing" said intention, this second part being in continuous need of contextual update by replacing outdated conceptual tools with contemporary ones.

catholic church has suitably and properly called this conversion transubstantiation.[44]

The encyclical *Fides et Ratio* reminds us by way of Thomas that indeed *sacra
doctrina* among wayfarers receives divine truth "proposed to us in the Sacred
Scriptures and rightly interpreted by the Church's teaching."[45] Hence the task
of the *intellectus fidei,* the task of understanding what conversion of a whole
substance into another substance entails, continues to be in front of *sacra doctrina,* and it is in this way that the ongoing reception of Thomas's profound and
profoundly satisfying doctrine remains in front of *sacra doctrina* as well.

But, first of all, what is "substance" as Thomas receives the notion by way of
Aristotle's philosophical analysis of reality and as he deploys it theologically?
Before we address this question, however, a succinct *caveat* is in order. For in
a contemporary intellectual context of such thoroughly nominalist character
that one is in constant amnesia about it (and "postmodernity" is nothing else
than nominalism in the state of amnesia), a context in which the "theories"
on which the "humanities" of the latter-day academy come and go at about
the frequency of the daily weather reports, it is imperative to recall a fundamental fact about Thomas's understanding of philosophy as an ordered set of
inquiries, lest we mistake his thought for another "theory" and its respective
jargon (that is, its technical language of set stipulations). Rather, ordered philosophical inquiry according to Thomas is fundamentally different. Referring
to Thomas's commentary on the Neoplatonic *Liber de causis,* Ralph McInerny
identifies three "disarming assumptions" that capture Thomas's understanding of philosophy in a nutshell. They are

1) that all philosophers are in principle engaged in the same enterprise; 2) that truths
he has learned from Aristotle are simply truths, not "Aristotelian tenets"; and 3) consequently that such truths as one finds in Neoplatonism or anywhere else must be
compatible with truths already known. This is the basis for saying that Thomism is
not a *kind* of philosophy.[46]

44. Council of Trent, thirteenth session (October 11, 1551), chap. 4, "De transsubstantiatione," in *Decrees of the Ecumenical Councils,* vol. 2, *Trent to Vatican II,* ed. Norman P. Tanner,
S.J. (London and Washington, D.C.: Sheed & Ward and Georgetown University Press, 1990),
695. Heinrich Denzinger, *Enchiridion symbolorum definitionum et declarationum de rebus fidei et
morum. Kompendium der Glaubensbekenntnisse und kirchlichen Lehrentscheidungen,* Lateinisch-
Deutsch, ed. Peter Hünermann, 40th ed. (Freiburg: Herder, 2005), § 1642: "[P]er consecrationem panis et vini conversionem fieri totius substantiae panis in substantiam corporis Christi
Domini nostri, et totius substantiae vini in substantiam sanguinis eius. Quae conversio convenienter et proprie a sancta catholica Ecclesia transsubstantiatio est appellata." All citations
from the Second Vatican Council and the Council of Trent are taken from Tanner.
45. John Paul II, *Fides et Ratio,* § 66.
46. McInerny, *Praeambula Fidei,* 175 n. 6.

Hence, it would be profoundly wrong, although not at all uncommon, to assume that Thomas submits a "theory" of the Eucharistic conversion. Rather, always proceeding conceptually from what is easier to what is more difficult to understand, Thomas analogically extends the "natural hearing," the inquiry into material being and subsequently into immaterial being as undertaken in Aristotle's *Physics* and extended in his *Metaphysics,* in order to guide the metaphysical contemplation into what remains irreducibly a mystery of faith, the *intellectus,* however, inevitably having to take departure, by analogical extension, from the world we know.[47]

Consequently, in the present intellectual context one can never recall often enough that—as John Wippel aptly put it—Thomas holds first and foremost in his theory of knowledge that "the order of thought is based upon the order of reality and reflects it. Because words in turn reflect thoughts, by attending to distinctive modes of predication we may ultimately discern different modes of being."[48] Differently put, "supreme and diverse modes of predication (as expressed in the predicaments) . . . follow from and depend upon supreme and diverse modes of being."[49] Hence, according to Thomas, we discover these supreme modes of being precisely by attending to the diverse modes of predication.[50]

The classical locus where Thomas exposits on this fundamental insight of Aristotle is in his commentary on Book III of Aristotle's *Physics,* in lecture 5 (# 322):

[Being] is divided according to the diverse modes of existing. But modes of existing are proportional to the modes of predicating. For when we predicate something of

47. In its document "On the Interpretation of Dogmas," the International Theological Commission reminds us unequivocally that this very procedure is indeed of an enduring importance for the interpretation of the mysteries of faith: "It was already the First Vatican Council which taught that a deeper insight into the mysteries of faith may be possible in considering them by way of analogy with natural knowledge and relating them to the ultimate goal of human beings (DS 3016)" (*Origins* 20, no. 1 [17 May 1990]: 13).

48. John Wippel, *The Metaphysical Thought of Thomas Aquinas: From Finite Being to Uncreated Being* (Washington, D.C.: The Catholic University of America Press, 2000), 216.

49. Ibid., 211.

50. "The mode or way in which words signify does not immediately follow upon the mode of being of such things, but only as mediated by the way in which such things are understood. To put this another way, words are likenesses or signs of thoughts, and thoughts themselves are likenesses of things, as Thomas recalls from Bk I of Aristotle's *De interpretatione*" (Wippel, *Metaphysical Thought,* 211). That is, "Thomas follows Aristotle in singling out being as it exists outside the mind and is divided into the ten predicaments . . . Therefore, in whatever ways being is predicated, in so many ways is *esse* signified, that is, in so many ways is something signified to be" (Wippel, *Metaphysical Thought,* 212). For an excellent analysis of this complex matter, see also John P. O'Callaghan, *Thomist Realism and the Linguistic Turn: Toward a More Perfect Form of Existence* (Notre Dame, Ind.: University of Notre Dame Press, 2003).

another, we say this is that. Hence the ten genera of being are called the ten predicaments. Now every predication is made in one of three ways. One way is when that which pertains to the essence is predicated of some subject, as when I say Socrates is a man, or man is animal. The predication of substance is taken in this way.[51]

The predicament "substance" connotes what subsists in itself. Differently put, of any existing thing, substance connotes nothing apart from the thing, but the thing itself. However, substance is not the same as the essence and the nature of the actually existing thing. While *substance, essence,* and *nature* express the same reality, *essence*—in distinction from substance—signifies that by virtue of which something is what it is, whereas *nature* signifies the substance as a principle of activity. Every finite substance has need of further perfections, called accidents, which are connoted by the remaining nine predicaments of Aristotle's list. That is, substance and accident must be treated in mutual relation, since accident is a principle that complements substance and together with it, through their common existence, constitutes the individually existing thing. In short, substance is not a separable thing by itself, but a metaphysical co-principle in composition with all its attributes. Hence, substance cannot be without at least *some* accidents.

If we were to consider substance in general, this would suffice. But in Eucharistic conversion we deal with the conversion of *material* substances. And because of this, we need to attend to the one accident necessarily proper to any material substance: *quantity.* Let us first return to Aquinas's fifth lecture on Book III of Aristotle's *Physics:*

Another mode is that in which that which is not of the essence of a thing, but which inheres in it, is predicated of a thing. This is found either on the part of the matter of the subject, and thus is the predicament of quantity (for quantity properly follows upon matter . . .), or else it follows upon the form, and thus is the predicament of quality.[52]

---

51. Thomas Aquinas, *Commentary on Aristotle's Physics,* trans. Richard J. Blackwell, Richard J. Spath, and W. Edmund Thirlkel; intro. by Vernon J. Burke; foreword by Ralph McInerny (Notre Dame, Ind.: Dumb Ox Books, 1999), 160 (#322). "Ad horum igitur evidentiam sciendum est quod ens dividitur in decem praedicamenta non univoce, sicut genus in species, sed secundum diversum modum essendi. Modi autem essendi proportionales sunt modis praedicandi. Praedicando enim aliquid de aliquo altero, dicimus hoc esse illud: unde et decem genera entis dicuntur decem praedicamenta. Tripliciter autem fit omnis praedicatio. Unus quidem modus est, quando de aliquo subiecto praedicatur id quod pertinet ad essentiam eius, ut cum dico *Socrates est homo,* vel *homo est animal;* et secundum hoc accipitur praedicamentum *substantiae*" (*In III Phys., lectio* 5 [#322]).

52. Aquinas, *Commentary on Aristotle's Physics,* 160 (§ 322). *In III Phys.,* l. 5 (§ 322): "Alius autem modus est quo praedicatur de aliquo id quod non est de essentia eius, tamen inhaeret ei. Quod quidem vel se habet ex parte materiae subiecti, et secundum hoc est praedicamentum

Significantly, in Thomas's listing of the predicaments, quantity is listed right after substance—here implicitly understood as the kind of substance immediately attainable, that is, the substance of a sensible, material thing.[53] Interestingly however, quantity itself cannot be properly defined, since it has no *genus proximum*. Thomas and the Thomist tradition, therefore, tended to circumscribe it by saying that it entails parts and divisibility into integral, quantitative parts.[54]

Quantity is a determination of being which gives extension to a material substance, hence "dimensive" quantity. Without quantity, a material substance would have no distinguishable parts, no parts outside of parts *("partes extra partes")*. Everything would, as Leo Elders puts it, "flow into each other" in the sense that there would be no spacial relationship anymore between the parts.[55] While quantity gives to material substance its dimensions, its intrinsic measure by way of the order of parts, the parts themselves are constituted and sustained by the substance itself.[56] The latter circumstance reminds us that, indeed, quantity modifies the being of substance by giving it the extension of space and hence relates *intrinsically* to the substance. Consequently, quantity is not something apposed into the closest proximity to substance. Rather, quantity is *of* the substance as the first of the other accidents that inhere by way of quantity in the substance.

However, in contrast with other Scholastic theologians, Thomas and the later Thomist tradition insist on the real distinction between substance and quantity. While quantity always gives spatial extension to something that subsists in itself, there is no identity between substance and quantity. The latter is

---

quantitatis (nam quantitas proprie consequitur materiam . . .); aut consequitur formam, et sic est praedicamentum *qualitatis.*"

53. For example, in the process of generation, matter antecedes form, since matter is what form reduces to a particular substance. Hence quantity antecedes quality. For while quantity inheres immediately in material substance, quality inheres only mediately in the material substance, by way of first inhering in quantity. For this very reason, quantity is the first accident of the substance of a sensible, material thing.

54. *In V Metaph.*, l. 15 (§ 977): "Quantum dicitur quod est divisibile in ea quae insunt." For a lucid exposition, see Leo J. Elders, S.V.D., *Die Naturphilosophie des Thomas von Aquin*, 70ff. For the precise differentiation between proper quantitative divisibility and other kinds of divisibilities, see John of St. Thomas, *Cursus philosophicus* I, Log., pt. II, q. XVI, a. 1; p. 463.

55. Leo J. Elders, *Die Naturphilosophie des Thomas von Aquin*, 75. He is drawing his image from John of St. Thomas, *Cursus Philosophicus* I, Log., pt. II, q. XVI, a. 1; p. 466: "In sententia S. Thomae propria et formalis ratio quantitatis est extensio partium in ordine ad totum, quod est reddere partes formaliter integrantes. Unde remota quantitate, substantia non habet partes integrales formaliter in ratione partis ordinatas et distinctas."

56. John of St. Thomas, *Cursus Philosophicus* I, Log., pt. II, q. XVI, a. 1; p. 464: "[Q]uantitas dicitur praebere partes integrales substantiae, non constituendo illas, sed ordinando inter se. Et haec ordinatio accidentalis est."

a real accident and, indeed, the first accident of material substances. Every substance composed of matter and form requires the first or immediately inherent accident of quantity. For in order to be itself, that is, *this* material substance, it requires dimensive quantity, the specific order of parts outside of parts. As Joseph Bobik puts it:

Dimensive quantity is quantity having within itself *partes extra partes*. It has within itself *distinguishable* parts outside other *distinguishable* parts . . . And the scholastic formula in turn brings out the unique vitality of dimensive quantity as a principle capable of contributing to individuation. By their very spread-out-ness or extendedness, the parts of dimensive quantity are situated or posited outside *(extra)* each other. Because of their very spread-out-ness, these parts cannot enter into each other so that they would coincide. By their very extendedness, these parts exclude each other, and are hence distinguishable from each other. By their very spread-out-ness within the whole, each requires a diverse situation or position in relation to the others within the whole.[57]

We can begin to see now the central role the predicamentals substance and quantity play in Thomas's metaphysical elucidation of the theological truth that indeed nothing less than the whole Christ is contained under this sacrament.

However, might not Thomas's concentration on the predicamentals substance and quantity in the elucidation of the Eucharistic mystery be ever so subtly reductive, in that such a concentration ultimately distracts from the fact that Christ's sacramental presence is a fundamentally personal presence? Might not the focus on "substance" and "quantity" give rise to a Eucharistic "essentialism" that obscures the fact that Christ's presence is irreducibly personal?

In order to address this question we must realize first of all that the terminus of the Eucharistic conversion is the substance of Christ's body in its respective present state. At the Last Supper, Christ was present to the twelve apostles in his natural mode as the incarnate Son of the Father instituting the Eucharist and thereby marking the very beginning of "his hour," his self-oblation to the Father on the Cross for the sake of "the many." His substantial, corporeal presence in the sacrament was that of his natural body in its concrete state at the beginning of his Passion. At each subsequent celebration of the Eucharist after Christ's Resurrection and Ascension, Christ's sacramental presence is that of his glorified bodily existence in heaven. Christ's body and blood are accompanied *(concomitari)* by all that is really associated with them

57. Bobik, "The Individuation of Bodily Substances," 62.

in his everlasting glorified state: in virtue of Christ's human nature, his human soul, and in virtue of the hypostatic union, the divinity of the Logos. Through real concomitance, because of the integral subsistence of the risen Christ in heaven, nothing less than the whole person of Christ is in the Blessed Sacrament. Because Thomas is absolutely unequivocal on this matter, it is worth citing him at length on this crucial point:

It is absolutely necessary to confess according to Catholic faith that the entire Christ is in this sacrament. Yet we must know that there is something of Christ in this sacrament in a twofold manner: first, as it were, by the power of the sacrament; secondly, from natural concomitance. By the power of the sacrament, there is under the species of this sacrament that into which the pre-existing substance of the bread and wine is changed, as expressed by the words of the form, which are effective in this as in the other sacraments; for instance, by the words—*This is My body,* or, *This is My blood.* But from natural concomitance there is also in this sacrament that which is really united with that thing wherein the aforesaid conversion is terminated. For if any two things be really united, then wherever the one is really, there must the other also be: since things really united together are only distinguished by an operation of the mind.[58]

Since body, blood, soul, and divinity of Christ are really united and distinguished from each other only by an operation of the human mind, it would be theologically misguided from the very outset to drive a wedge—and thus create a false dichotomy—between the *substantial* and the *personal* presence of Christ in the sacrament. The presence in the sacrament of the substance of Christ's body and the substance of Christ's blood entails by way of real concomitance the real substantial presence of Christ's undiminished humanity, body and soul; and the real presence of the undiminished substance of Christ's humanity, in virtue of its hypostatic union with the Divine Word, entails the personal presence of the Logos; and the latter, by way of a mediated concomitance also entails, because of the circumincession of Father, Son, and Spirit, the personal presence of the Father and the Spirit.[59] Hence, all that is in-

58. "[O]mnino necesse est confiteri secundum fidem Catholicam quod totus Christus sit in hoc sacramento. Sciendum tamen quod aliquid Christi est in hoc sacramento dupliciter: uno modo, quasi ex vi sacramenti; alio modo, ex naturali concomitantia. Ex vi quidem sacramenti, est sub speciebus huius sacramenti id in quod directe convertitur substantia panis et vini praeexistens, prout significatur per verba formae, quae sunt effectiva in hoc sacramento sicut et in ceteris: puta cum dicitur, Hoc est corpus meum. Hic est sanguis meus. Ex naturali autem concomitantia est in hoc sacramento illud quod realiter est coniunctum ei in quod praedicta conversio terminatur. Si enim aliqua duo sunt realiter coniuncta, ubicumque est unum realiter, oportet et aliud esse: sola enim operatione animae discernuntur quae realiter sunt coniuncta" (*ST* III, q. 76, a. 1c).

59. This latter extension of concomitance is held (I think rightly) by Reginald Garrigou-

trinsic to Christ's personhood in virtue of the Incarnation (his undiminished concrete humanity, body and soul) as well as all that is constitutive of his personhood in virtue of the divine Sonship (the subsistent trinitarian relations) is present in the sacrament.

On the basis of the principle of real concomitance, Thomas holds that the whole Christ is contained under each species of the sacrament, but differently in each case. Under the species of the wine, by the power of the sacrament, only the substance of Christ's blood is present, and in virtue of real concomitance, his body, soul, and divinity. Under the species of the bread, by the power of the sacrament, only the substance of his body is present, and in virtue of real concomitance his blood, soul, and divinity. Let us be mindful at this point that none of this is, of course, to be misunderstood, and hence all too quickly dismissed, as the allegedly typical way of the "scholastics" carrying matters to the extreme, but rather as a faithful and straightforwardly literal interpretation of Christ's words of consecration at the Last Supper.

The explanatory power of the predicamentals "substance" and "quantity" becomes surpassingly evident when, in the third article of question 76, Thomas discusses the way in which it is to be taken that the whole Christ is entirely under every part of the species of bread and wine.[60] Consider the second objection in order to feel the full force of the issue at stake. For this objection presses quite appropriately the entailments of what the real presence of the concrete physical nature of Christ's body does indeed involve:

[S]ince Christ's is an organic body, it has parts determinately distant; for a determinate distance of the individual parts from each other is of the very nature of an organic body, as that of eye from eye, and eye from ear. But this could not be so, if Christ were entire under every part of the species; for every part would have to be under every other part, and so where one part would be, there another part would be. It cannot be then that the entire Christ is under every part of the host or of the wine contained in the chalice.[61]

Lagrange in his *De Eucharistia accedunt De Paenitentia quaestiones dogmaticae Commentarius in Summam theologicam S. Thomae* (Rome: Marietti, 1943), 148; in principle we can find the position also in Matthias Joseph Scheeben, *The Mysteries of Christianity,* trans. Cyril Vollert, S.J. (St. Louis, Mo.: Herder, 1951), 479–82. The spiritual implications of this profound theological truth have been drawn out most beautifully in the small book by M. V. Bernadot, O.P., *From Holy Communion to the Blessed Trinity,* trans. Dom Francis Izard, O.S.B. (Westminster, Md.: Newman Press, 1952).

60. *ST* III, q. 76, a. 3.

61. "[C]orpus Christi, cum sit organicum, habet partes determinate distantes: est enim de ratione organici corporis determinata distantia singularum partium ad invicem, sicut oculi ab oculo, et oculi ab aure. Sed hoc non posset esse si sub qualibet parte specierum esset totus Christus: oporteret enim quod sub qualibet parte esset quaelibet pars; et ita, ubi esset una pars,

In his response, Thomas properly extends his use of the principle of real concomitance. By the power of the sacrament, the substance of Christ's body is in the sacrament; by the power of real concomitance, the dimensive quantity of Christ's body is also there—the latter, as we came to understand earlier, being indispensable for the proper constitution of a material substance. Consequently, Christ's body is in this sacrament "per modum substantiae," substantially, that is, "not after the manner of dimensions, which means, not in the way in which the dimensive quantity of a body is under the dimensive quantity of a place."[62] The explanatory power of the metaphysical principle of substance and its ontological precedence in relation to all the accidents, including dimensive quantity, carries far. Let us consider Thomas's response to the second objection:

The determinate distance of parts in an organic body is based upon its dimensive quantity; but the nature of substance precedes even dimensive quantity. And since the conversion of the substance of the bread is terminated at the substance of the body of Christ, and since according to the manner of substance the body of Christ is properly and directly in this sacrament; such distance of parts is indeed in Christ's true body, which, however, is not compared to this sacrament according to such distance, but according to the manner of its substance.[63]

In an additional step of deepening his argument, Thomas shows in which way we can understand that indeed the whole dimensive quantity of Christ's body is in the sacrament. We find the crucial axiom he applies already in the *sed contra* of article 4 of question 76:

The existence of the dimensive quantity of any body cannot be separated from the existence of its substance. But in this sacrament the entire substance of Christ's body is present . . . Therefore the entire dimensive quantity of Christ's body is in this sacrament.[64]

esset et alia. Non ergo potest esse quod totus Christus sit sub qualibet parte hostiae vel vini contenti in calice" (*ST* III, q. 76, a. 3, obj. 2).

62. "[C]orpus Christi est in hoc sacramento per modum substantiae, idest, per modum quo substantia est sub dimensionibus: non autem per modum dimensionum, idest, non per illum modum quo quantitas dimensiva alicuius corporis est sub quantitate dimensiva loci" (*ST* III, q. 76, a. 3c).

63. "[I]lla determinata distantia partium in corpore organico fundatur super quantitatem dimensivam ipsius: ipsa autem natura substantiae praecedit etiam quantitatem dimensivam. Et quia conversio substantiae panis directe terminatur ad substantiam corporis Christi, secundum cuius modum proprie et directe est in hoc sacramento corpus Christi, talis distantia partium est quidem in ipso corpore Christi vero, sed non secundum hanc distantiam comparatur ad hoc sacramentum, sed secundum modum suae substantiae" (*ST* III, q. 76, a. 3 ad 2).

64. "[Q]uantitas dimensiva corporis alicuius non separatur secundum esse a substantia eius. Sed in hoc sacramento est tota substantia corporis Christi . . . Ergo tota quantitas dimensiva corporis Christi est in hoc sacramento" (*ST* III, q. 76, a. 4 s.c.).

In his response, Thomas draws upon the by now familiar distinction between what is present by the power of the sacrament and what is present in virtue of real concomitance. "Vi sacramenti," the conversion is terminated at the substance of Christ's body and clearly not at the dimensions of the body for, after all, the dimensive quantity of the bread clearly remains after the consecration. Applying the axiom of the *sed contra* that the existence of the dimensive quantity of any body cannot be separated from its substance, he then adds the following: "Nevertheless, since the substance of Christ's body is not really deprived of its dimensive quantity and its other accidents, hence it comes that by reason of real concomitance the whole dimensive quantity of Christ's body and all its other accidents are in this sacrament."[65] In the response to the first objection he puts the decisive point even more succinctly:

Since, then, the substance of Christ's body is present on the altar by the power of this sacrament, while its dimensive quantity is there concomitantly and as it were accidentally, therefore the dimensive quantity of Christ's body is in this sacrament, not according to its proper manner (namely, that the whole is in the whole, and the individual parts in the individual parts), but after the manner of substance [*per modum substantiae*], whose nature is for the whole to be in the whole, and the whole in every part.[66]

The presence of the dimensive quantity of Christ's body "per modum substantiae" is possible because dimensive quantity relates intrinsically to substance. Hence, in order to obtain after the manner of substance, dimensive quantity does not require what is the manner of dimensive quantity, namely the relation to a place. In the body of the fifth article of question 76, Thomas gives a somewhat less condensed description of dimensive quantity realized according to its proper manner: "Every body occupying a place is in the place according to the manner of dimensive quantity, namely, inasmuch as it is commensurate with the place according to its dimensive quantity."[67] And it is quite obvious that according to the proper manner of dimensive quantity it is impossible for

65. "Quia tamen substantia corporis Christi realiter non denudatur a sua quantitate dimensiva et ab aliis accidentibus, inde est quod, ex vi realis concomitantiae, est in hoc sacramento tota quantitas dimensiva corporis Christi, et omnia alia accidentia eius" (*ST* III, q. 76, a. 4c).

66. "Quia igitur ex vi sacramenti huius est in altari substantia corporis Christi, quantitas autem dimensiva eius est ibi concomitanter et quasi per accidens, ideo quantitas dimensiva corporis Christi est in hoc sacramento, non secundum proprium modum, ut scilicet sit totum in toto et singulae partes in singulis partibus; sed per modum substantiae, cuius natura est tota in toto et tota in qualibet parte" (*ST* III, q. 76, a. 4, ad 1).

67. "Omne autem corpus locatum est in loco secundum modum quantitatis dimensivae, inquantum scilicet commensuratur loco secundum suam quantitatem dimensivam" (*ST* III, q. 76, a. 5c).

two dimensive quantities naturally to be in the same subject at the same time. But it is not impossible at all for the dimensive quantity of the bread after the consecration to remain commensurate with the place it occupies while the dimensive quantity of Christ's body is present "per modum substantiae."

Eventually the Thomist school had to unfold Thomas's teaching by developing a more explicit answer to the question how one can account metaphysically for the possibility for dimensive quantity to subsist solely "per modum substantiae."[68] Unfolding the tacit entailments of Thomas's teaching became necessary in light of different philosophical conceptualities giving rise to variant theological doctrines that emerged and spread in the centuries subsequent to Aquinas's death, conceptualities that in one or another way would identify substance itself with its property of quantitative extension and, in consequence, had strongly to compromise the genuine, whole presence of the dimensive quantity of Christ's body.

The late medieval school of the "via moderna"—largely indebted to the thought of William of Ockham and eventually identified by its opponents simply as the "nominalists" *(Nominales)*—came to regard material substance to be extended per se and not by way of being informed by the absolute accident of quantity. For Ockham there obtains no real distinction between substance and quantity. Quantity, rather, has a purely nominal status; that is, quantity is a connotative term that stands for substance in its aspect of extension.[69] Consequently, Ockham has to explain how after the consecration, the substance

68. This development occurred in part in response to an intense debate after Aquinas's death over the nature of quantity primarily among Francisan theologians, first and foremost Olivi, who challenged the view held by both Bonaventure and Aquinas, namely that (a) transubstantiation indeed was the only rationally satisfying metaphysical account for Christ's real, corporeal presence in the Eucharist and that (b) all remaining accidents are subjected to quantity. Olivi, Scotus, and Ockham form unfinished pieces of an alternative account of real presence that can be usefully studied in David Burr's informative essay "Quantity and Eucharistic Presence: The Debate from Olivi through Ockham" (*Collectanea Franciscana,* vol. 44, 5–44). (I am grateful to John Slotemaker for bringing this essay to my attention.) This debate is greatly instructive for the historical reconstruction of the highly complex discourse of late medieval scholasticism and, moreover, as a case study for the kinds of metaphysical objections that can be raised against the Thomist position—and the ensuing significant and, indeed grave metaphysical conundrums such an alternative metaphysical account subsequently has to face. From a properly theological perspective, however, this debate simply represents a path not taken by the Church's tradition. For the one crucial point Olivi, Scotus, and Ockham agree upon in this specific matter, namely, that substantial conversion is not what accounts for Christ's real presence, was a position eventually not accepted by the Church's tradition. On the contrary, without explicitly endorsing the Thomist metaphysical account of it, the Council of Trent essentially affirmed the position jointly held by Bonaventure and Aquinas, namely, that it is indeed substantial conversion that accounts for Christ's real, corporeal presence in the Eucharist.

69. See Gordon Leff, *William of Ockham: The Metamorphosis of Scholastic Discourse* (Manchester: Manchester University Press; Totowa, N.J.: Rowman and Littlefield, 1975), 207–13.

of Christ's body becomes present without being "quanta," without parts out-side of parts and the consequent natural order of parts *(ordo partium)*. This is his solution: Because "quantity" is a notion purely connotative to substance it can be removed without any real change in the underlying subject. And so, while the connotative notion of quantity is removed, Christ's body is never-theless definitively present under the host and each of its parts. Hence, the nat-ural parts of Christ's body have to interpenetrate each other and, consequent-ly, the natural order of parts *(ordo partium)* is dissolved. From the point of view of Thomas's teaching, the Ockhamist position fails to maintain the integrity of the dimensive quantity of Christ's body in the sacrament and consequently fails to make explicit the presence of the whole Christ in the sacrament.[70]

In order to consider the second major catalyst for a further specification of Thomas's teaching by the Thomist school, we need to advance from the four-teenth century to the seventeenth, from Ockham to Descartes. While sub-stance was a key notion in René Descartes' swiftly spreading philosophy, the notion underwent a profound transmutation in his doctrine. Inspired by the clarity and certainty of mathematics, Descartes searched for a new philosophy whose foremost criterion was the clarity and distinctness of ideas. Disregard-ing in a not all together unproblematic way the long tradition of metaphysical inquiry on this matter, he defined substance as a thing that exists in such a way that it needs no other thing for its existence. In light of this criterion, he identi-fied two kinds of substance: one intellectual, the other material. Thought con-stitutes the nature of the intellectual substance, and spatial extension (length, breadth, depth) the nature of corporeal substance.[71] The consequent identifi-cation in reality of substance and quantity does not come as a surprise: "There

70. For an extensive analysis of the excruciatingly detailed discussion Ockham provides on this matter in his philosophical and theological works, see Erwin Iserloh, *Gnade und Eucharis-tie in der philosophischen Theologie des Wilhelm von Ockham: Ihre Bedeutung für die Ursachen der Reformation* (Steiner: Wiesbaden, 1956), 174–283, esp. 186–202 for the discussion of the problem in Ockham's commentary on Lombard's *Sentences*, and 202–53 for a discussion of his position in his later *De sacramento altaris*. For a discussion of Ockham's doctrine more sympathetic than Iserloh's highly—and I think rightly—critical commentary, see Gabriel Buescher, O.F.M., *The Eucharistic Teaching of William Ockham* (St. Bonaventure, N.Y.: The Franciscan Institute, 1950), esp. 65–93.

71. René Descartes, *The Philosophical Writings of Descartes*, trans. John Cottingham, Rob-ert Stoothoff, and Dugald Murdoch (Cambridge: Cambridge University Press, 1985). Vol. 1: *Principles of Philosophy*, book 1, sections 48–53. Cf. esp. the following paradigmatic statements: "I recognize only two ultimate classes of things: first, intellectual or thinking things, i.e. those which pertain to mind or thinking substance; and secondly, material things, i.e. those which pertain to extended substance or body" (*The Philosophical Writings of Descartes*, vol. 1: *Princi-ples of Philosophy*, 208, section 48). "A substance may indeed be known through any attribute at all; but each substance has one principal property which constitutes its nature and essence, and to which all its other properties are referred. Thus extension in length, breadth and depth

is no real difference between quantity and the extended substance; the difference is merely a conceptual one, like that between number and the thing which is numbered."[72]

Cartesian theologians, especially in France and Italy, began to apply this deceptively simple but indeed radically changed notion of substance to the doctrine of Eucharistic conversion.[73] According to Descartes' new understanding of corporeal substance, Christ's substantial presence in the sacrament is conceived the following way: after the consecration, the dimensive quantity of the bread and the wine cannot remain (and with it none of the other accidents of bread and wine), for two corporeal substances cannot, of course, occupy the same space at the same time. According to the Cartesian theologians, what is present after the consecration is nothing but the glorious body of Christ per se. In order to veil the surpassing holiness of Christ's bodily presence and also in order not to deter the faithful from communion, God provides the sensible effects of bread and wine to the sensory organs. According to a different view defended by other Cartesian theologians, it is Christ's body that provides the sensible effects of bread and wine by taking on new surfaces similar to those of bread and wine. Furthermore, the Cartesian theologians hold that in virtue of being a corporeal substance, after the consecration Christ's body has to be locally extended. Consequently, by way of some mode

---

constitutes the nature of corporeal substance; and thought constitutes the nature of thinking substance" (210; section 53).

72. *The Philosophical Writings of Descartes*, vol. 1: *Principles of Philosophy*, 226; Part II, section 8. In this particular work of Descartes one can observe without difficulty the shift from a metaphysical consideration of the principles of reality as modes of being to the philosophical analysis of conceptions or ideas that take on the character of mental images. Such a transformation of metaphysical principles of being into univocal mental conceptions guided by the criterion of "ocular clarity" leads unavoidably to the loss of the metaphysical principle of substance itself in relationship to the accidents, and with it, to a profound lack of understanding of the nature and function of predicamentals, as well as of the real distinction between substance and quantity in a sensible thing. "When they make a distinction between substance and extension or quantity, either they do not understand anything by the term 'substance', or else they simply have a confused idea of the incorporeal substance, which they falsely attach to corporeal substance; and they relegate the true idea of corporeal substance to the category of extension, which, however, they term an accident. There is thus no correspondence between their verbal expression and what they grasp in their minds" (226f.; Part II, section 9).

73. For details of this intricate and theologically not at all unproblematic position, see Jean-Robert Armogathe, *Theologia cartesiana: L'explication physique de l'Eucharistie chez Descartes et dom Desgabets* (The Hague: Nijhoff, 1977), and his "Cartesian Physics and the Eucharist in the Documents of the Holy Office and the Roman Index (1671–6)," trans. Patrick Morgan, in *Receptions of Descartes: Cartesianism and Anti-Cartesianism in Early Modern Europe*, ed. Tad M. Schmaltz (London and New York: Routledge, 2005), 149–70; also Tad M. Schmaltz, *Radical Cartesianism: The French Reception of Descartes* (Cambridge: Cambridge University Press, 2002), esp. 34–74.

of contraction or condensation it must be reduced to the circumscriptive extension of what has the visual appearance of a host or wine in a chalice.

In light of these alternative positions, one might begin to appreciate in hindsight the profundity of Thomas's teaching that the dimensive quantity of Christ is in the sacrament by way of natural concomitance according to the mode of the substance. In view of the considerable metaphysical and theological problems entailed in the nominalist and the Cartesian positions, the Thomist school advanced its metaphysical investigation. Very much by way of extrapolating Thomas's metaphysical principles, Thomist theologians inquired how it is possible and what it means for dimensive quantity to be there by way of natural concomitance in the mode of the substance. The resulting development of Thomas's position comprises three central elements: (1) Because there obtains a real distinction between the principles of substance and quantity, material substance requires quantity as its absolute first accident. (2) Because local extension presupposes some distinction of parts from other parts, it is possible to distinguish between the essence of quantity, which is to have parts that are different from other parts, i.e., "outside of other parts," and the specific property of quantity, which is local extension. The Thomist commentators tended to identify the former as the *"ratio formalis,"* or the *primary formal effect of quantity* (*"ordo partium in toto"*), and the latter as the *secondary formal effect of quantity,* the *"ordo partium in loco"* or *"ubi et situs."* (3) Substance as such is indivisible and hence a substantial form or a separate substance (angel) has no capacity of local extension. Every material substance, however, has intrinsically—that is, in virtue of being a material substance—parts that are different from and hence outside of other parts, as well as a specific order among the parts, and consequently the capacity to be divided into parts and to be locally extended. While really distinct as a co-constitutive principle, in reality this essence of quantity is inseparable from a material substance. For quantity is the absolute accident of material substance. Hence, the essence of quantity obtains in virtue of its relation to substance alone, that is, it obtains always "per modum substantiae." In its normal, locally extended existence, the manner of dimensive quantity always already presupposes the essence of quantity to obtain "per modum substantiae," that is, the distinction of parts from other parts and the intrinsic (though not yet locally realized) order between them to obtain according to the manner of substance. And hence it is not intrinsically impossible for what is ontologically a distinct (though not independent) principle of the constitution of material substances in virtue of divine first causality to subsist solely "per modum substantiae."

In unfolding one aspect of Thomas's teaching in this particular way, the

Thomist school was able to continue to hold (against the nominalist position) that the *whole* Christ, including his undiminished dimensive quantity, is indeed in the sacrament, and (against the Cartesian position) that the Eucharistic species maintain their properly realized dimensive quantity in their local space, while Christ's body has its properly realized quantitative dimension in Christ's glorified state in heaven alone.

In summary: According to John of St. Thomas and other Thomist commentators, the primary formal effect of quantity, "ordo partium in toto," specifies the order of distinguishable parts as a whole. This order (in which consists the essence of quantity) gives rise to a really distinct determination, the secondary formal effect, the "ordo relationis" or "ordo partium." The order of parts denotes the position or situation of the parts under consideration relative to other parts in space ("ubi et situs").[74] Because the "ordo partium in toto" can be considered indeterminately, there obtains the logical separability and consequently the separability of modes of being between the primary formal effect of dimensive quantity and its secondary formal effect.

At this point, we can mark two vital results of this all too sketchy account of the predicamentals "substance" and "quantity" in the teaching of Thomas and the Thomist tradition. First, substance is not a mere conceptual name in the modern, nominalist sense—that is, a sheer linguistic pointer of the intellect's intentionality to some "Ding an sich." On the contrary, substances denote entities that subsist in their own existence—"unde solae substantiae proprie et vere dicuntur entia"[75]—entities that address the intellect and are formally received by it.

---

74. Gredt, *Logica / Philosophia Naturalis*, 145–46: "Definitio quantitatis . . . stricte autem sumpta pro quantitate *praedicamentali* definitur: ordo partium in toto. In qua definitione 'ordo' positionem significat partium extra partes, ita ut quantitas etiam definiri possit: accidens tribuens subiecto habere partes extra partes quoad se. Ordo, in quo consistit quantitatis essentia, non est relatio ordinis, sed fundamentum huius relationis; est ordo fundamentalis, i.e., fundamentum relationis secundum prius et posterius. Quantitas igitur duo continet: *multitudinem* partium, et huius multitudinis *ordinem* secundum positionem, quatenus partes ponuntur extra partes secundum prius et posterius . . . Quare quantitas praedicamentalis multitudini superaddit ordinem positionis secundum prius et posterius." Ibid., 252: "THESIS X: Effectus formalis primarius quantitatis seu eius ratio formalis est ordo partium in toto, effectus formalis secundarius est ubi et situs seu ordo partium in loco. Hic effectus secundarius distinctus est realiter et separabilis a primario." Ibid., 252, § 315: "*Effectus formalis primarius* seu ratio formalis est constitutivum metaphysicum quantitatis. Quantitas enim utpote accidens definitur per ordinem ad subiectum, ad substantiam. Quare indicando, quid *primo* faciat in substantia formaliter (per modum causae formalis), indicatur eius essentia metaphysica." Ibid., 254, § 318: "[O]rdo partium in toto potest considerari indeterminate, et tunc est *effectus formalis primarius* quantitatis." I am indebted to Romanus Cessario, O.P., for introducing me to the distinction between the primary formal effect of quantity and its secondary formal effect.

75. *ST* I, q. 90, a. 2: "Illud autem proprie dicitur esse, quod ipsum habet esse, quasi in suo

Second, Thomas's teaching on material substance allows for the real distinction between the primary formal effect of quantity (*ordo partium in toto*)
and its secondary formal effect (*ordo partium in loco*). That is, even under the
sacramental species of bread and wine, it is by way of the primary formal effect
of quantity that the substance of Christ's body and the substance of Christ's
blood are really present in their concrete particularity as *this* substance and as
that substance. This substantial presence, however, emphatically does *not* pertain to the *ordo partium in loco (ubi et situs)*.[76] While the substance of Christ's
body and blood are present without deficiency of substance (which includes
the primary formal effect of quantity, the *ordo partium in toto*), no further accidents need to be realized for the substantive, real presence of Christ's body
and blood to obtain. On the other hand, the Eucharistic species maintain their
dimensive quantity, that is, their specific *ordo partium in loco*, as sustained by
the primary formal effect of the quantity of bread and the quantity of wine.
And because quantity is not identical with substance, the logical separability of the two allows for the possibility that the primary (*ordo partium in toto*)
and the secondary (*ordo partium in loco*) formal effects of quantity are sustainable without the substance in which quantity inheres.[77] Since all the other accidents inhere in substance by way of dimensive quantity, their sustain-

---

esse subsistens: unde solae substantiae proprie et vere dicuntur entia. Accidens vero non habet
esse, sed eo aliquid est, et hac ratione ens dicitur; sicut albedo dicitur ens, quia ea aliquid est al-
bum. Et propter hoc dicitur in VII *Metaphys.*, quod accidens dicitur 'magis entis quam ens.' Et
eadem ratio est de omnibus aliis formis non subsistentibus."

76. Hence, it is crucial to remember that, when he distinguishes between substance and
quantity in *ST* III, q. 76, a. 1, ad 3, Thomas is concerned with the specific entailments of the *ordo
partium* in space, that is, the secondary formal effect of quantity, the *ordo partium in loco (ubi et
situs)*. Because of the increasing identification between substance and quantity in later Scholasticism, the Thomist tradition to an ever greater extent drew upon the distinction between the
primary formal effect of quantity (*ordo partium extra partes*) and the secondary formal effect of
quantity, dimensive quantity.

77. *ST* III, q. 75, a. 5, ad 1: "[S]icut dicitur in libro *De causis*, effectus plus dependet a causa
prima quam a causa secunda. Et ideo virtute Dei, qui est causa prima omnium, fieri potest ut
remaneant posteriora, sublatis prioribus." See John of St. Thomas, *Cursus philosophicus* I, Log.,
pt. II, q. XVI, a. 1; p. 463: "Caeterum oppositum hujus manifestavit nobis sacrosanctum Eucharistiae mysterium, in quo manet quantitas, quae antea erat panis, ut oculis videmus, et non
manet substantia panis, ut fides docet: distinguitur ergo et separatur quantitas a re quanta. Re-
spondent Nominales quantitatem substantiae non manere, cum ipsa enim evanuit; sed manere
quantitatem qualitatum caeterorumque accidentium extensorum. Sed contra est, quia ibi sunt
plura accidentia. Vel ergo unumquodque habet suam quantitatem distinctam, vel datur aliqua
communis omnibus. Si datur aliqua communis omnibus, illa distinguitur ab uno quoque acci-
dente, cum sit communis pluribus; et distinguitur etiam a substantia, quae ibi non est; ergo distinguitur quantitas a re quanta." For a discussion of this aspect of Thomas's doctrine and of the
sustainability of his teaching on the *accidentia sine subiecto remanentia*, see the essay by Sedlmayr, "Die Lehre des hl. Thomas von den *accidentia sine subjecto remanentia*—untersucht auf
ihren Einklang mit der aristotelischen Philosophie."

ability is consequent upon the separate sustainability of dimensive quantity.[78]

What difference does this distinction make? Consider the following argument advanced by Sylvester of Ferrara, the profound commentator of Thomas's *Summa contra gentiles (SCG)* on Thomas's discussion of how the body of Christ (as a proper material substance) can be in multiple places. Here is Thomas's text from *SCG* IV, 64, 5:

[T]he body of Christ in His own dimensions exists in one place only, but through the mediation of the dimensions of the bread passing into it its places are as many as there are places in which this sort of conversion is celebrated. For it is not divided into parts, but is entire in every single one; every consecrated bread is converted into the entire body of Christ.[79]

Sylvester of Ferrara, commenting on this text, advances a succinct version of the distinction between the two effects of quantity:

The effect of quantity is twofold. The one effect is completely intrinsic to that which has quantity [as it pertains to the *metaphysical order* of the constitution of a material substance], that is, quantification *(esse quantum)*, divisibility into parts, and the order of parts as a whole. The other effect is in some manner extrinsic [as it pertains to the *physical order* of material substances relating qua quantity to other material substances], namely insofar as quantity pertains to the thing in the outward order, that is, insofar as it corresponds to another distinguishable quantity, and the parts of the one correspond to the location of the parts of the other quantity. The first effect is necessarily and per se proper to quantity. The second effect, however, pertains to quantity only if it is ordered principally and per se to a place and toward extrinsic dimensions. Consequently, in the sacrament of the altar, the quantity of Christ's body, existing under the dimensions of the bread, has the first effect. For the body of Christ is in itself divisible and has an order of parts as a whole. It does not, however, have the second effect. For the parts of Christ's body do not correspond to the dimensive parts of the bread nor to the location of these parts, but the whole is under whatsoever part. Consequently it can be said that the body of Christ is under the dimensions of the bread in a divisible as well as an indivisible way, divisible insofar as it has in and of itself divisible parts; indivisible, however, because its parts do not correspond to the parts of those dimensions, but rather the whole corresponds to whatsoever part, similar to the way the soul as a whole is in each part [of the body].[80]

78. Cf. Thomas's nuanced discussion of this complex matter in *ST* III, q. 77, a. 2.

79. Translation from Saint Thomas Aquinas, *Summa Contra Gentiles. Book Four: Salvation*, trans., with introduction and notes by Charles J. O'Neil (Notre Dame, Ind. and London: University of Notre Dame Press, 1975), 262. ("Corpus enim Christi per suas proprias dimensiones in uno tantum loco existit: sed mediantibus dimensionibus panis in ipsum transeuntis in tot locis in quot huiusmodi conversio fuerit celebrata: non quidem divisum per partes, sed integrum in unoquoque; nam quilibet panis consecratus in integrum corpus Christi convertitur.")

80. My translation from *Sancti Thomae Aquinatis Doctoris Angelici Opera Omnia iussu edita*

Sylvester of Ferrara's commentary allows us to see with greater clarity what indeed is entailed in Thomas's own teaching. If Christ's words, "This is my body, this is my blood," are to be taken at face value and not as spiritual or metaphorical flights, the proper metaphysical avenue available to the *intellectus fidei* is material substance as inherently modified by quantity. Instead of diminishing or "reifying" the *mysterium fidei,* this kind of rigorous metaphysical contemplation lets the *mysterium* shine forth in its consummate glory.

At this point we must turn to two central sections of Pope Paul VI's encyclical *Mysterium Fidei:* first, its explicit reaffirmation of the decree of Trent, and second, its own extrapolation on it:

The Council of Trent, basing itself on this faith of the Church, "openly and sincerely professes that after the consecration of the bread and wine, Our Lord Jesus Christ, true God and man, is really, truly, and substantially contained in the Blessed Sacrament of the Holy Eucharist under the outward appearances of sensible things." And so Our Savior is present in His humanity not only in His natural manner of existence at the right hand of the Father, but also at the same time in the sacrament of the Eucharist "in a manner of existing that we can hardly express in words but that our minds, illumined by faith, can come to see as possible to God and that we must most firmly believe." . . .

To avoid any misunderstanding of this type of presence, which goes beyond the laws of nature and constitutes the greatest miracle of its kind, we have to listen with docility to the voice of the teaching and praying Church. Her voice, which constantly echoes the voice of Christ, assures us that the way in which Christ becomes present in this Sacrament is through the conversion of the whole substance of the bread into His body and of the whole substance of the wine into His blood, a unique and truly wonderful conversion that the Catholic Church fittingly and properly calls transubstantiation. As a result of transubstantiation, the species of bread and wine undoubtedly take

---

Leonis XIII P.M., vol. 15 (Rome: Leonine Commission, 1930), 208: "[D]uplex est quantitatis effectus. Unus est omnino intrinsecus subiecto quanto: scilicet esse quantum, et divisibilitas in partes, atque ordo partium in toto. Alius est aliquo modo extrinsecus, inquantum scilicet convenit subiecto in ordine ad extrinsecum: scilicet condividi alteri quantitati, et partes eius partibus loci correspondere. Primum convenit quantitati necessario et per se: secundum vero sibi non convenit nisi quando habet primo et per se ordinem ad locum et ad extrinsecas dimensiones. In sacramento ergo Altaris quantitas corporis Christi, sub dimensionibus panis existens, habet primum effectum, quia ipsum corpus Christi est in seipso divisibile, et habet ordinem partium in toto: non autem secundum effectum habet, quia partes corporis Christi non correspondent partibus dimensionis panis neque partibus loci, sed totum est sub qualibet parte. Ex quo sequitur potest dici corpus Christi esse sub dimensionibus panis et divisibiliter et indivisibiliter: divisibiliter quidem, quia in seipso divisibilitatem partium habet; indivisibiliter autem, quia partes eius non correspondent partibus illarum dimensionum, sed totum cuilibet parti, sicut anima est tota in qualibet parte." I am indebted to John F. Boyle for pointing me to this pertinent discussion of the matter in Sylvester of Ferrara's commentary, which is included in the Leonine edition of the *Summa contra gentiles.*

on a new signification and a new finality, for they are no longer ordinary bread and wine but instead a sign of something sacred and a sign of spiritual food; but they take on this new signification, this new finality, precisely because they contain a new "reality" which we can rightly call ontological. For what now lies beneath the aforementioned species is not what was there before, but something completely different; and not just in the estimation of Church belief but in reality, since once the substance or nature of the bread and wine has been changed into the body and blood of Christ, nothing remains of the bread and the wine except for the species—beneath which Christ is present whole and entire in His physical "reality," corporeally present, although not in the manner in which bodies are in a place. (§§ 45 and 46)

In order to receive this teaching according to the highest degree of its intelligibility, contemporary dogmatic theology, conceived as *sacra doctrina,* is well advised to continue to receive and reconsider Thomas's metaphysical analysis of (1) substance and quantity, (2) the non-identity of substance and quantity as modes of being, (3) dimensive quantity as the immediately inherent accident of material substance, and especially, (4) the real distinction and hence the possible separability of the primary formal effect of quantity, the *ordo partium in toto* from its secondary formal effect, the *ordo partium in loco (ubi et situs).* Furthermore, (5) it is Thomas—felicitously assisted by the Thomist commentators—who helps us understand why, in considering the conversion of one material substance into another material substance, it is impossible to disregard dimensive quantity.[81] It is indeed the latter—or more precisely and properly considered, its primary formal effect—that, under present intellectual conditions, can greatly assist in keeping substantial, corporeal presence from sliding into a mere metaphor of some atmospheric presence in general. "For," as John of St. Thomas avers in his succinct summary of Thomas's teaching, "once quantity is removed, substance lacks integral parts that are ordered formally by reason of the part and hence distinguishable."[82] Last but not least,

81. At this point I cannot delve into the arresting details of Thomas's demanding interpretation of the Eucharistic conversion as a *trans*-substantiation in the strict metaphysical sense. Stephen Brock, in his recent essay, "St. Thomas and the Eucharistic Conversion," has provided such an extraordinarily superb account of Thomas's argument that I happily and gratefully refer everyone to his work. Those students and connoisseurs of Thomas's philosophy of being who might have missed in my discussion so far any treatment of the *"actus essendi"* will find in Stephen Brock's essay what they might look for in vain here. For it is the metaphysical contemplation of substantial conversion that indeed makes a consideration of the *"actus essendi"* indispensible. Since, however, I focus in this chapter exclusively on the terminus of the conversion—Christ's real, corporeal presence—the metaphysical concepts of "substance" and "accident" (or "species") suffice. In short, not having mentioned the *"actus essendi"* explicitly, does not mean that I do not regard it as absolutely indispensible for a full metaphysical consideration of substantial conversion. To the contrary.
82. John of St. Thomas, *Cursus philosophicus* I, Log., pt. II, q. XVI, a. 1; p. 466: "In sententia

(6) because of real concomitance, Christ's surpassing personal presence in the
Eucharist has its indispensable anchor in the substantial presence of his body
and his blood under the Eucharistic species. For, according to Thomas, nothing less and nothing more than Christ's very humanity constitutes God's surpassingly efficacious instrument of the salvation of humanity.[83]

Most arresting in Pope Paul VI's encyclical *Mysterium Fidei,* with its very
precise and nuanced distinctions and demarcations, is undoubtedly the fact
that it advances sufficient conceptual specificity to encourage and invite further metaphysical contemplation of the *mysterium fidei* along the lines of
Thomas and also, if necessary under particular intellectual conditions, of the
classical Thomist tradition.[84] For the presence par excellence, the substantial
presence of Christ, as the result of the conversion of the whole substances of
bread and wine into the substances of Christ's body and blood, seems to require nothing less than the very presence of the specific *ordo partium in toto* of
Christ's precious body and blood, "contained in the Blessed Sacrament of the
Holy Eucharist under the outward appearances" of bread and wine.[85]

S. Thomae propria et formalis ratio quantitatis est extensio partium in ordine ad totum, quod
est reddere partes formaliter integrantes. Unde remota quantitate, substantia non habet partes
integrales formaliter in ratione partis ordinatas et distinctas."

83. For an extensive discussion of this crucial aspect of Thomas's Christology, see Theophil
Tschipke, *Die Menschheit Christi als Heilsorgan der Gottheit unter besonderer Berücksichtigung
der Lehre des heiligen Thomas von Aquin* (Freiburg: Herder, 1940). Cf. now the recent French
translation: *L'humanité du Christ comme instrument de salut de la divinité* (Fribourg: Academic
Press, 2003).

84. Lest I be misunderstood to claim that this developed Thomist position is necessarily
intended by or even entailed in the Church's teaching on Eucharistic conversion, allow me to
cite the words of one from whom such sobering warning and restraint in judgment might these
days be least expected. The following comment is made in response to the question "Is the distinction between two functions of quantity at all necessary?" ("Haec distinctio duarum func-
tionum quantitatis estne omnino necessaria?"): "Ad scientiam theologicam sufficit etiam terminologia S. Thomae in nostro articulo adhibita; scil. quantitas dimensiva corporis Christi est
in hoc sacramento, non secundum proprium modum ... *sed per modum substantiae* ... Haec
terminologia sufficit, et in his rebus difficillimis oportet sapere ad sobrietatem, nam velle nimis
explicare perducit ad falsam subtilitatem, ad acribologiam, ut dixit Aristoteles, quae elungat a
contemplatione mysteriorum ... S. Thomas qui generaliter sua manuscripta *abbreviando* non
evolvendo corrigebat, hanc sobrietatem egregie servavit, magis quam plures ejus commentato-
res, qui quandoque volunt ejus doctrinam nimis explicare per inferiora, non satis tendendo ad
contemplationem altiorum" (R. Garrigou-Lagrange, *De Eucharistia,* 146f.). Faced with an intellectual context shaped by Olivi, Scotus, Ockham, and eventually Descartes, Thomist commentators were led to go beyond what Garrigou-Lagrange, under different intellectual circumstances, rightly regards as the wisely restrained and indeed sufficient terminology of Thomas
Aquinas.

85. Paul VI, *Mysterium Fidei,* § 25.

"Hoc est corpus meum": *Intellectus per fidem a deceptione praeservatur*

Lest the Thomist deployment of substance becomes seriously lopsided, that is, be wrongly received along the lines of a crude, nonsacramental realism, I must hasten at this point to turn to the theological context into which Thomas squarely places his doctrine of Eucharistic conversion—the antecedent context of sacramental signification and causation—and even one step further in antecedence, the very root of sacramental signification as well as causation: Christ's passion on the Cross. For Thomas maintains that "the power of Christ's Passion is united to us by faith and the sacraments, but in different ways; because the link that comes from faith is produced by an act of the soul; whereas the link that comes from the sacraments, is produced by making use of exterior things."[86] The antecedent article in Thomas's discussion of the question offers the more substantive points. For, according to Thomas:

it is manifest . . . that Christ delivered us from our sins principally through His passion, not only by way of efficiency and merit, but also by way of satisfaction. Likewise by His Passion He inaugurated the Rites of the Christian Religion "by offering Himself—an oblation and a sacrifice to God" [Eph 5:2]. Wherefore it is manifest that the sacraments of the Church derive their power specially from Christ's Passion, the virtue of which is in a manner united to us by our receiving the sacraments. It was in sign of this that from the side of Christ hanging on the Cross there flowed water and blood, the former of which belongs to Baptism, the latter to the Eucharist, which are the principal sacraments.[87]

This use of exterior things as an instrumental extension of Christ's humanity, which is itself an instrument of his divinity, constitutes, in Abbot Vonier's apposite words, "the sacramental world." In his recently reissued *A Key to the Doctrine of the Eucharist*, a work of supreme clarity and profundity *ad mentem S. Thomae*, he aptly avers: "Sacraments are not substitutes for anything else,

---

86. *ST* III, q. 62, a. 6, c.: "Sicut enim ex praedictis patet, virtus passionis Christi copulatur nobis per fidem et sacramenta, differenter tamen: nam continuatio quae est per fidem, fit per actum animae; continuatio autem quae est per sacramenta, fit per usum exteriorum rerum."

87. *ST* III, q. 62, a. 5, c.: "Manifestum est autem ex his quae supra dicta sunt, quod Christus liberavit nos a peccatis nostris praecipue per suam passionem, non solum efficienter et meritorie, sed etiam satisfactorie. Similiter etiam per suam passionem initiavit ritum Christianae religionis, 'offerens seipsum oblationem et hostiam Deo,' ut dicitur Ephes. 5, [2]. Unde manifestum est quod sacramenta Ecclesiae specialiter habent virtutem ex passione Christi, cuius virtus quodammmodo nobis copulatur per susceptionem sacramentorum. In cuius signum, de latere Chrisi pendentis in cruce fluxerunt aqua et sanguis, quorum unum pertinet ad baptismum, aliud ad Eucharistiam, quae sunt potissima sacramenta."

they are their own end and justification. They produce their own grace, and in a way entirely different from all the other modes of participating in the divine life."[88] The sacraments signify the extension of Christ's humanity and thereby the *instrumental causality* of Christ's humanity.[89] Hence, the sacraments are essentially signs to which causality is joined. In other words, every sacrament is a sign, but "a sign of an efficaciousness."[90] Consequently, Vonier emphatically stresses that:

[a]t no time in the eucharistic mystery do we deal with Christ in His natural condition, *in propria specie* . . . He must be there *in specie aliena*—in a condition different from His natural one—in order to safeguard the character of the sacrament as a sign . . . His Presence in the sacrament must be truly such that at no time could it be seen otherwise than by the eye of faith.[91]

Abbot Vonier's point is absolutely essential, because it is by way of this theological insight of surpassing importance that Thomas provides the proper *sacramental* contextualization for the stark realism in which Cardinal Humbert of Silva Candida put the formula of submission that Berengarius of Tours had to sign at the synod of Rome, presided over by Pope Nicolas II in 1069. In this formula, one section maintains that after the consecration not only the sacrament but also the true body and blood of Christ are sensibly (not only in the sacrament, but also in truth) touched and broken by the priest and crushed by the teeth of the faithful.[92] It was Thomas's profound understanding of the *sui generis* sacramental order and its own proper efficacy by way of instrumental causality that significantly deepened and helpfully clarified the theological reception of the *mysterium fidei*.[93]

88. Vonier, *Key to the Doctrine of the Eucharist*, 25.

89. *ST* III, q. 62, a. 1, ad 1.

90. For an excellent treatment, to which I am greatly indebted in this section, see Chapter 4 in the present volume, by Benoît-Dominique de La Soujeole, O.P.

91. Vonier, *Key to the Doctrine of the Eucharist*, 21.

92. Denzinger (see note 44 above), § 690: "scilicet panem et vinum, quae in altari ponuntur, post consecrationem non solum sacramentum, sed etiam verum corpus et sanguinem Domini nostri Iesu Christi esse, et sensualiter, non solum sacramento, sed in veritate, manibus sacerdotum tractari et frangi et fidelium dentibus atteri." This section is interestingly not repeated in the later formulas of submission to Pope St. Gregory VII that Berengar had to sign in 1078 and 1079. It is this later formula that is cited in Paul VI, *Mysterium Fidei*, § 52.

93. Those who would like to understand Thomas's proper prioritization of sacramental signification as an ever so subtle acknowledgment of aspects of truth in Berengar's doctrine may want to recall Thomas's explicit and unambiguous reference to Berengar at the very end of the corpus of *ST* III, q. 75, a. 1: "Some men accordingly, not paying heed to these things, have contended that Christ's body and blood are not in this sacrament except as in a sign, a thing to be rejected as heretical, since it is contrary to Christ's words. Hence Berengarius, who had been the first deviser of this heresy, was afterwards forced to withdraw his error, and to

In unfolding the various aspects characteristic of this *sui generis* sacramental order, Thomas employs a set of traditional distinctions well established by his time that developed in a complex process of patristic and early medieval theological discourse: *sacramentum tantum*, the sign only; *res et sacramentum*, the thing and the sign; *res tantum*, the thing only. The first, the sign only, refers to what we know as the signification, that is, the species of bread and wine. The second, the thing and the sign, refers to the body and blood of Christ substantially present at the term of the Eucharistic conversion. Now, this is called *res et sacramentum* because not only is it the *res* which is signified by the *sacramentum tantum*; rather, what is signified, Christ's true body and blood, points beyond itself and signifies in turn the *res tantum*, the thing itself, that is, the spiritual effect of Eucharistic communion, which is the specific sacramental grace of further incorporation into the mystical body of Christ, the perfect union of charity between the head and the body. Hence, the pivotal middle term of the three sacramental terms, *res et sacramentum*, indicates the crucial double signification that occurs in the Eucharist: first, the reality of Christ's substantial, corporeal presence is signified by the *sacramentum tantum*, the species of bread and wine; and, secondly, the very reality of Christ's substantial, corporeal presence itself signifies (therefore *res et sacramentum*), namely the spiritual effects of Eucharistic communion. But this second signification occurs only by way of another, more proximate one. Because the whole order of sacramental grace derives from the power of Christ's Passion on the Cross, the *res et sacramentum*, as Abbot Vonier rightly stresses, "also signifies sacrifice, as being the immediate representation of Christ immolated on the Cross."[94] Christ's salvific presence in the Eucharist comes about by way of the *sacramental presentation* of his crucified humanity—the incarnate Son's utter self-giving to the Father in love, obedient to the point of death—his body and blood being sacramentally separated in the one sacrament. Is there a more abiding personal

---

acknowledge the truth of the faith." The one who explicitly adopted Berengar's doctrine was none other than John Wycliffe. (For Wycliffe's precise understanding of the doctrine of transubstantiation, of which he gives an accurate definition, see Gutwenger, "Substanz und Akzidenz," 269 n. 36.)

94. Vonier, *Key to the Doctrine of the Eucharist*, 49. The hurried reader of the *Summa theologiae* might easily miss where Thomas addresses this important matter in the context of accounting for the whole Christ being entirely present under the two distinct species of bread and wine: "For in the first place this serves to represent Christ's Passion, in which the blood was separated from the body; hence in the form for the consecration of the blood mention is made of its shedding" (*ST* III, q. 76, a. 2, ad 1). For Thomas, the Eucharistic sacrifice, in virtue of its sacramental representation, is identical with the sacrifice on the Cross. On this crucial matter see T. D. Humbrecht, O.P., "L'eucharistie, 'représentation' du sacrifice du Christ selon Saint Thomas," *Revue Thomiste* 98, no. 3 (1998): 355–86.

presence possible of Christ to the Church *in via* than in the sacramental form of his perfect, final oblation to the Father on the Cross (Eph 5:2; Heb 9:14)?

All of this is to say that in Thomas's doctrine of Eucharistic conversion, the substantial, corporeal presence of Christ in the Eucharist, does not at all occlude or thwart the abiding *sacramental* signification of the Eucharistic species. The *sacramentum tantum* with its proper instrumentality is in no way abolished by the Eucharistic conversion. On the contrary and contemporaneously put, the Eucharistic species remain signs "all the way down." They point beyond themselves, because faith, in assent to the dominical words, forbids the intellect to follow the path of the senses by way of the Eucharistic species to absent substances. For, as Thomas reminds us:

substance, as such, is not visible to the bodily eye, nor does it come under any one of the senses, nor under the imagination, but solely under the intellect, whose object is *what a thing is* . . . And therefore, properly speaking, Christ's body, according to the mode of being which it has in this sacrament, is perceptible neither by the sense nor by the imagination, but only by the intellect, which is called the spiritual eye.[95]

Accordingly, Thomas stresses that indeed "[Christ's body] can be seen by a wayfarer through faith alone [*sola fide*], like other supernatural things."[96]

Hence the character of the sacrament as a sign abides from beginning to end. It is by way of the instrumental causality inherent in sacramental signification that bread and wine constitute the irreplaceable and indispensable starting point for the sacramental conversion and that after the consecration, the remaining sacramental species continue to carry the *sacramental* signification of the Eucharistic conversion. Consequently, there is no deception at all taking place in this sacrament. "For," as Thomas argues, "the accidents which are discerned by the senses are truly present. But the intellect, whose proper object is substance . . . is preserved by faith from deception . . . because faith is not contrary to the senses, but concerns things which sense does not reach."[97]

---

95. *ST* III, q. 76, a. 7: "Substantia autem, inquantum huiusmodi, non est visibilis oculo corporali, neque subiacet alicui sensui, neque imaginationi, sed soli intellectui, cuius obiectum est 'quod quid est,' ut dicitur in III *De anima*. Et ideo, proprie loquendo, corpus Christi, secundum modum essendi quem habet in hoc sacramento: neque sensu neque imaginatione perceptibile est, sed solo intellectu, qui dicitur oculus spiritualis." "Consequently, the devils cannot by their intellect perceive Christ in this sacrament, except through faith, to which they do not pay willing assent; yet they are convinced from the evidence of signs, according to James 2:19: 'The devils believe, and tremble'" (Unde daemones non possunt videre per intellectum Christum in hoc sacramento, nisi per fidem: cui non voluntate assentiunt, sed ad eam signorum evidentia convincuntur, prout dicitur, Iac. 2, [19], quod 'daemones credunt et contremiscunt'). See also *In II De anima*, l. 14, § 420.
96. *ST* III, q. 76, a. 7.
97. *ST* III, q. 75, a. 5, ad 2 and 3: "[I]n hoc sacramento nulla est deceptio: sunt enim secun-

Remember Thomas's terse definition of faith as "the act of believing," that is "an act of the intellect assenting to the Divine truth at the command of the will moved by the grace of God."[98] This act of the believer, however, does not terminate in a proposition, but rather in a *res,* a "thing," a "reality." "For," Thomas avers, "as in science we do not form propositions, except in order to have knowledge about things through their means, so it is in faith."[99] And remember, *quid res est,* "what a thing is," that is, its "quiddity" or substance is the object of our intellect, our understanding. And it is only by way of our intellect beholding the substance of a *res* that we can say what it is. For we name things as we know them.[100]

The *res* of this particular truth of faith—*"hoc est corpus meum"*—is recognized by way of hearing alone, *solo auditu.* By way of beholding the pronoun "this" *(hoc)*[101] in its substantive sense, the "obscure knowledge" of faith does occur, and it is the will that "uses such knowledge well, to wit, by assenting to unseen things because God says that they are true."[102] By giving assent to the divine truth, received by way of the dominical words, faith's obscure knowledge preserves the intellect from deception. It is by way of the eye of faith

---

dum rei veritatem accidentia, quae sensibus diiudicantur. Intellectus autem, cuius est proprium obiectum substantia, ut dicitur in *III De anima,* per fidem a deceptione praeservatur."

98. *ST* II-II, q. 2, a. 9, c.: "Ipsum autem credere est actus intellectus assentientis veritati divinae ex imperio voluntatis a Deo motae per gratiam."

99. *ST* II-II, q. 1, a. 2, ad 2: "Actus autem credentis non terminatur ad enuntiabile, sed ad rem: non enim formamus enuntiabilia, nisi ut per ea de rebus cognitionem habeamus, sicut in scientia, ita et in fide." In an unjustly forgotten, but still highly important document, the International Theological Commission reminds us that this is not Thomas's personal opinion but indeed the Church's teaching: "All revelation ultimately is the self-revelation and self-communication by God the Father through the Son in the Holy Spirit, so that we may have communion with God *(Dei Verbum,* § 2). God is therefore the one and all-encompassing object of faith and theology (Thomas Aquinas). Therefore the following is true: 'The act of the believer comes to its term not in a formula but in a reality' *(ST* II-II, q. 1, a. 2, ad 2)" (International Theological Commission, "On the Interpretation of Dogmas," 9).

100. *ST* I, q. 13, a. 1: "Secundum igitur quod aliquid a nobis intellectu cognosci potest, sic a nobis potest nominari." In our particular case of faith's assent, though, the naming is received first, *solo auditu,* and subsequently, a knowing occurs, but an "obscure knowing," precisely because it is received *solo auditu.*

101. Brock, "St. Thomas and the Eucharistic Conversion," 556: "What the pronoun stands for is 'that which is contained under these species, in general,' or, more precisely, 'the substance contained under the accidents,' which previously was bread, and afterwards is the body of Christ."

102. *De malo,* q. 1, a. 3, ad 11: "[F]ides non est meritoria ex hoc quod est cognitio enigmatica, set ex hoc quod tali cognitione uoluntas bene utitur, assentiendo scilicet his que non uidet propter Deum." (Text and translation from *The De Malo of Thomas Aquinas,* ed. Brian Davies, trans. Richard Regan [Oxford: Oxford University Press, 2001], 90, 91.) In this particular response to an objection, Thomas accounts for the fact that a deficient vision (i.e., a "malum") can be the cause of merit. The key is that faith is meritorious insofar as the will uses the obscure knowledge by assenting to unseen things for God's sake.

(whose gaze is, so to speak, directed by the will's assenting to the truth of the proposition "This is my body, this is my blood") that the intellect beholds obscurely the substance of Christ's body and blood and hence indeed beholds the truth, the objective truth of the sacrament. What the intellect beholds nondiscursively by the eye of faith—which in this case is instructed *solo auditu*—can and indeed *must* be spelled out by the *intellectus fidei* in precise predicamental concepts.

To summarize: The intellect obscurely beholds Christ's substantial presence under the Eucharistic species, informed not by the senses, but by assenting to the divine truth *solo auditu* at the command of the will moved by the grace of God: "Dogma datur Christianis." By directing the intellect to the truth beyond the senses (a truth that in all its obscurity can indeed only be attained by the intellect), faith prevents the intellect from deception. As Thomas expressed it with unsurpassable clarity, simplicity, and beauty in his hymn *Adoro te devote:*

> Visus, tactus, gustus, in te fallitur;
> Sed auditu solo tuto creditur.
> Credo quidquid dixit Dei Filius.
> Nil hoc verbo veritatis verius.
>
> In cruce latebat sola Deitas;
> At hic latet simul et humanitas.
> Ambo tamen credens atque confitens
> Peto quod petivit latro poenitens.[103]

Quia dogma datur Christianis, intellectus per fidem a deceptione praeservatur. For Thomas there seems to obtain a rather subtle but nevertheless precise relationship between the doctrine of faith and the metaphysical notion of substance. The intellect is preserved from deception by faith because, at the will's command, the intellect assents to the doctrine of faith. Yet it is not a blind faith, *contra intellectum.* Rather, the intellect beholds the truth of the doctrine of faith by way of its own proper and primordial channel of beholding and understanding reality, that is, by way of the intellect's own proper object, substance. And the doctrine of faith as well as the truth that substance conveys transcends the vagaries of history, the contexts of culture and society, and

103. "Sight and touch and taste here fail; / Hearing only can be believed. / I trust what God's own Son has said. / Truth from truth is best received. / Divinity, on the Cross, was hid; / Humanity here comes not to thought. / Believing and confessing both, / I seek out what the Good Thief sought" (*The Aquinas Prayer Book*, 68–69). Regarding the authenticity of this hymn, see Torrell, *The Person and His Work*, 132–35.

the deliveries of the natural sciences. Hence, we dare not jettison the meta-physical contemplation of the *intellectus fidei* as it arises from the basic, pre-philosophical perception of the world, a metaphysical contemplation accessi-ble—if not de facto, so in principle—indeed to all human beings.[104] For as af-ter the consecration the intellect beholds *sola fide* indeed *quod quid est*, "what a thing is,"[105] that is, the very substance of Christ's body and blood under the Eucharistic species, the *intellectus fidei* properly understands what it indeed beholds by way of the predicament substance.

Consequently, in my view of things, the *first* formal act of *sacra doctrina* among wayfarers, that is, short of the beatific vision, is nothing but the ongo-ing active reception of the *principia revelata a Deo* as proposed in Scripture, ac-cording to the Church's understanding. This first formal act of *sacra doctrina* among wayfarers might properly be circumscribed with the Latin verb "pone-re" and hence by the name "positive theology."[106] The second formal act of *sa-cra doctrina* among wayfarers is the discursive activity of the *intellectus fidei*, lat-er called "speculative theology."[107] In this second formal act, the *intellectus fidei* draws upon created reality as it delivers itself to the human intellect, namely, precisely as "what things are," as substances.[108] But even more importantly, it is by this second formal act that *sacra doctrina* reaches beyond our state as way-farers. For, guided by the first formal act and, simultaneously, informed by the infused theological virtues of faith, hope, and charity, the second formal act is

---

104. While I remain uncertain whether the alternatives indeed are the right ones, if one ac-cepts the parameters set in the famous extended debate of the 1950s between F. Selvaggi and C. Colombo, I indeed tend toward the position of the latter. See Gutwenger, "Substanz und Ak-zidenz," 283–304, for an instructive exposition and summary of this debate.

105. *ST* III, q. 76, a. 7c.

106. Note that I make use of this notion only *gymnastikos* and do not suppose automatic identity with any particular claimant of this notion in the history of Catholic theology since the eighteenth century. In other words, I do not at all regard Denzinger (an indeed indispens-able tool) as anything even remotely close to an instantiation of "positive theology." Indeed, the first formal act of *sacra doctrina* should never be developed and worked out in isolation from or even in contrast to the second formal act. Consequently, genuine "positive theology" always gives rise to "speculative theology" and genuine "speculative theology" always remains rooted in "positive theology."

107. What I say in the previous footnote also pertains to this notion.

108. Hence, natural theology (in the precise sense of the *praeambula fidei* as understood by Vatican I) is the primordial as well as indispensable conceptual and ontological point of refer-ence for its discursive and argumentative operation. In the *ordo disciplinae*, i.e., in the specific order of learning of *sacra doctrina* as a *scientia*, Thomas rightly advises that the training in the sciences that culminate in metaphysics antecedes the training in theology proper. Would that, in the deeply confused state of philosophical and theological studies, only a glimpse of Thom-as's wisdom were to be caught and instantiated in an *ordo disciplinae* in which students would again move from A to B to C (an *ordo* that the natural sciences tellingly seem to have main-tained).

essentially ordered to its final end, the *scientia Dei et beatorum*, in which it already participates inchoately *sola fide*. Hence, the *intellectus fidei* is increasingly drawn—shall I say, elevated—by the Spirit to contemplate that *scientia*, the consummation of which will only be the beatific vision itself.[109]

Coda

Eucharistic transubstantiation, as defended doctrinally and interpreted discursively with surpassing profundity and simplicity by St. Thomas, is the hidden power that enables faith to preserve the intellect from deception and hence enables the intellect to "come along" and, by the eye of faith, in the very darkness of superintelligibility, to behold the hidden substance of Christ's body and blood and hence Christ's real presence in body, soul, and divinity. Such beholding, indeed, "belongs to the perfection of faith" for, after all, Thomas argues, "since faith is of things unseen, as Christ shows us His Godhead invisibly, so also in this sacrament He shows us His flesh in an invisible manner."[110]

In order to close the circle and return to the beginning of our consideration of *sacra doctrina*, it is opportune at this point briefly to revisit Thomas's opening article of question 75 of the third part of the *Summa theologiae*. For here, as already mentioned above, Thomas reminds his readers that in the Gospel of John, Christ, the incarnate Logos, makes the startling statement to his disciples: "You are my friends" (15:14). And, as Aristotle had rightly realized, "It is the special feature of friendship to live together with friends,"[111] to share each other's presence. So it is not really surprising that for Thomas, for

109. Thomas argues that the rectitude of judgment comes about in two ways, first by a perfect use of reason and, second, by a certain connaturality with that which the judgment of reason is about. In matters divine, such connaturality comes about by the gift of the Spirit that is charity and unites us with God. Consequently, this wisdom is caused, so to speak, by the will, that is charity, while it subsists essentially in the intellect: "Sic igitur circa res divinas ex rationis inquisitione rectum iudicium habere pertinet ad sapientiam quae est virtus intellectualis: sed rectum iudicium habere de eis secundum quandam connaturalitatem ad ipsa pertinet ad sapientiam secundum quod donum est Spiritus Sancti: sicut Dionysius dicit, in 2 cap. *De div. nom.*, quod Hierotheus est perfectus in divinis 'non solum discens, sed et patiens divina.' Huiusmodi autem compassio sive connaturalitas ad res divinas fit per caritatem, quae quidem unit nos Deo: secundum illud I ad Cor. 6, 17: 'Qui adhaeret Deo unus spiritus est.' Sic igitur sapientia quae est donum causam quidem habet in voluntate, scilicet caritatem: sed essentiam habet in intellectu, cuius actus est recte iudicare, ut supra habitum est" (*ST* II-II, q. 45, a. 2c).

110. *ST* III, q. 75, a. 1c.: "[H]oc competit perfectioni fidei, quae, sicut est de divinitate Christi, ita est de eius humanitate: secundum illud Ioan. 14, [1]: 'Creditis in Deum, et in me credite.' Et quia fides est invisibilium, sicut divinitatem suam nobis exhibet Christus invisibiliter, ita et in hoc sacramento carnem suam nobis exhibet invisibili modo."

111. *ST* III, q. 75, a. 1c. Thomas cites here from Aristotle's *Nicomachean Ethics*, 9, 12 (1171b32).

whom friendship with God is, after all, the path of deification, the Eucharist is Christ's central token of surpassing friendship, the "sign of supreme charity."[112] For "in our pilgrimage He does not deprive us of His bodily presence; but unites us with this sacrament through the truth of His body and blood" *(per veritatem corporis et sanguinis sui nos conjugit in hoc sacramento)*.[113] It is at this place that Thomas cites John 6:56: "He who eats my flesh and drinks my blood abides in me, and I in him" (RSV). It should therefore not come as a surprise that Thomas regards the ensuing sacramental union of Christ with the faithful in the Eucharist—a surpassing abiding in each other—as the reality of the sacrament, the *res sacramenti*: "The reality of the sacrament is the unity of the mystical body."[114] The unity of the mystical body ensues from the true personal, though sacramental, presence of Christ, the head, to whom each member is joined by faith and charity. And it is from the head that each member receives the Holy Spirit, who joins together all members who have Christ as their head. The Holy Spirit does this by infusing each member with the virtue of charity. Remember, it is charity alone that makes it possible in Eucharistic communion to receive the *res sacramenti*. Hence, in virtue of the charity infused by the Holy Spirit and sustained and increased by Eucharistic communion, the head abides in the members and the members in the head such that the Church is indeed the body of Christ.[115]

112. *ST* III, q. 75, a. 1c.

113. Ibid.

114. *ST* III, q. 73, a. 3: "Res sacramenti est unitas corporis mystici." The "thing" of the sacrament, or better, the sacramental grace, is the mystical body of Christ. This sacramental grace is not automatically received by everyone who receives the *sacramentum tantum* and with it the *res et sacramentum*, but is received only by the faithful whose faith is informed by charity, that is, who, enabled by grace, intellectually and volitionally embrace the substantial, personal presence of the one whose body and blood they receive sacramentally. Christ's mystical body comes about through Christ's sacramental body by way of the bond of charity that binds each member to the head. (On rightly distinguishing between Christ's mystical body and the visible Church without separating the one from the other, see *ST* III, q. 8, a. 3.) And when charity is lost, which is the case while one is in mortal sin, the sacrament cannot be received without lying to the sacrament, namely signifying that one is united with Christ in charity while one is actually in a state of alienation from God. "[W]hoever receives this sacrament, expresses thereby that he is made one with Christ, and incorporated in His members; and this is done by living faith [that is, faith informed by charity], which no one has who is in mortal sin. And therefore it is manifest that whoever receives this sacrament while in mortal sin, is guilty of lying to this sacrament, and consequently of sacrilege, because he profanes the sacrament: and therefore he sins mortally" (*ST* III, q. 80, a. 4c).

115. For inroads into Thomas's rich ecclesiology, hidden and diffused throughout his corpus and accessible to a large degree only by way of his Christology, pneumatology, and sacramentology, see Yves Congar, O.P., "The Idea of the Church in St. Thomas Aquinas," *The Thomist* 1, no. 3 (1939): 331–59; reprinted with revisions in his *The Mystery of the Church* (Baltimore: Helicon Press, 1960), 53–74. For a more recent insightful overview, see G. Sabra, *Thomas Aquinas' Vision*

Very much in contrast with the "decapitated body"[116] which seems to be the sad but inevitable outcome of a number of recent ecclesiologies "from be-low," it is nothing but the real, substantial presence of the head that—by way of a mutual Eucharistic abiding of Christ in the faithful and the faithful in Christ—causes and sustains the unity among the members. "It is a real pres-ence because it makes real."[117] In short, the Eucharist's "unifying function without the reality of the Presence could be only an illusion."[118] Hence it is indeed the case that "the Eucharist makes the Church,"[119] and it is Eucharis-tic transubstantiation that renders unmistakably explicit that the Eucharist makes the Church only because Christ makes the Eucharist.[120]

---

of the Church (Mainz: Grünewald, 1987), and the informative chapter by Thomas F. O'Meara, O.P., "Theology of the Church," in *The Theology of Thomas Aquinas*, ed. Rik van Nieuwenhove and Joseph Wawrykow (Notre Dame, Ind.: University of Notre Dame Press, 2005), 303–25.

116. For this expression I am indebted to Fr. Robert P. Imbelli from Boston College. Thom-as's ecclesiology, as well as his Eucharistic doctrine, remains a salutary safeguard against a pro-foundly problematic development that set in soon after Vatican II, a development prophetically sensed and anticipatorily denounced by Henri de Lubac in his important work, *Corpus Mysti-cum*. Referring to corporate aspirations that were a driving part of the liturgical movement of the 1930s and 1940s, Lubac fears the degeneration of those corporate aspirations into purely nat-uralist impulses: "Indeed there is always a risk of forgetting: it is not the human fact of gather-ing for the communal celebration of the mysteries, it is not the collective exaltation that an ap-propriate pedagogy succeeds in extracting from it that will ever in the very least bring about the unity of the members of Christ. This cannot come about without the remission of sins, the first fruit of the blood that was poured out. The memorial of the Passion, the offering to the heav-enly Father, the conversion of the heart: these, therefore, are the totally interior realities with-out which we will never have anything but a caricature of the community that we seek. But the Eucharist does not offer us some human dream: it is a *mystery of faith*" (Henri de Lubac, *Corpus Mysticum: The Eucharist and the Church in the Middle Ages*, trans. Gemma Simmonds, C.J., with Richard Price and Christopher Stephens, ed. Laurence Paul Hemming and Susan Frank Parks [Notre Dame, Ind.: University of Notre Dame Press, 2006], 261).

117. Ibid., 253. Now, it is indeed important to remember that also the reverse is true: "By vir-tue of the same internal logic . . . those in modern times who water down the traditional idea of the Church as the Body of Christ find themselves also watering down the reality of the Eucha-ristic presence" (Lubac, *Corpus Mysticum*, 252).

118. Henri de Lubac, *Catholicism: Christ and the Common Destiny of Man*, trans. Lancelot C. Sheppard and Sister Elizabeth Englund, O.C.D. (San Francisco: Ignatius, 1988), 319.

119. This famous phrase was coined by Henri de Lubac, S.J., in his 1944 study, *Corpus Mys-ticum*, 88. The phrase appears in the context of de Lubac's description how early medieval theo-logians understood the body of Christ to be enlivened by the Spirit, how the ecclesial body be-comes in reality the body of Christ: "Now, the Eucharist is the mystical principle, permanently at work at the heart of the Christian society, which gives concrete form to this miracle. It is the universal bond, it is the ever-springing source of life. Nourished by the body and blood of the Saviour, his faithful people thus all 'drink of the one Spirit', who truly makes them into one single body. *Literally speaking, the Eucharist makes the Church*. It makes of it an inner reality. By its hidden power, the members of the body come to unite themselves by becoming more fully members of Christ, and their unity with one another is part and parcel of their unity with the one single Head" (*Corpus Mysticum*, 88; my emphasis).

120. We find this relationship between cause and effect, between the Eucharist and the

In his unjustly forgotten but still greatly instructive and relevant res-sourcement in the Fathers and the medieval doctors, *The Mysteries of Christianity,*[121] Matthias Scheeben, the great and in many regards still unsurpassed Catholic theologian of the nineteenth century, grasped the intention of Thomas's Eucharistic doctrine with a remarkable profundity. Scheeben rightly emphasizes the active role of the Holy Spirit in the mutual abiding that builds up the mystical body of Christ. The infused virtue of charity that makes possible the genuine reception of the *res sacramenti,* the spiritual embrace of Christ, is the gift of the same Spirit, who because of a mediated concomitance caused by the circumincession of Father, Son, and Spirit, is also personally present in the sacrament:

It was not only to give some sensible indication of His presence that Christ has attached the real union of His body with us to the condition of our partaking of the consecrated bread, as we might suppose if the union itself were to be purely spiritual in form. He had a much higher purpose in mind: to effect a union that would be not simply the presence of His body in ours or a contact between the two bodies, but would be an organic connection between them. That our bodies may be assumed into His body and become one with it by being united to it, He takes that substance which naturally can and does become one body with us, and changes it into His body by conversion. To fuse our bodies with His body by the fire of the Holy Spirit, He melts down the food proper to our body by that same fire and changes it into His own body . . . That Christ might become a member and the head of our race, it was not enough for Him to assume a human nature like ours; He had to take His nature from the very midst of the race. Similarly, to perfect the organic bond which is to bind us to Him, He wills not merely to bring the substance of His body into contact with us, but to implant Himself in us, or rather us in Him; He wishes us to strike root in Him, just as He took root in our race at the Incarnation. This He

---

Church, explicitly affirmed by Henri de Lubac in the conclusion of his *Corpus Mysticum:* "Eucharistic realism and ecclesial realism: these two realisms support one another, each is the guarantee of the other. Ecclesial realism safeguards Eucharistic realism and the latter confirms the former . . . Today, it is above all our faith in the 'real presence', made explicit thanks to the centuries of controversy and analysis, that introduces us to faith in the ecclesial body: effectively signified by the mystery of the Altar, the mystery of the Church has to share the same nature and the same depth. Among the ancients, the perspective was often inverted. The accent was habitually placed on the effect rather than on the cause. But the ecclesial realism to which they universally offer us the most explicit testimony is at the same time, and when necessary, the guarantee of their Eucharistic realism. This is because the cause has to be proportionate to its effect" (251f.). It is noteworthy that Henri de Lubac, not at all unlike the presently all too confidently neglected and derided neo-Thomist theologians, does not hesitate to draw upon a metaphysical principle in support and illumination of a theological truth.

121. Matthias Joseph Scheeben, *The Mysteries of Christianity,* trans. Cyril Vollert, S.J. (St. Louis, Mo. and London: Herder, 1951).

does by changing into His body the food that nourishes our body; in this food and by means of it He inserts our body in Himself as a branch is engrafted on a vine.[122]

And whoever has ears to hear will indeed not fail to recognize the echo of Thomas's teaching, as well as that of Matthias Scheeben, resounding in *Ecclesia de Eucharistia,* § 22:

Incorporation into Christ, which is brought about by Baptism, is constantly renewed and consolidated by sharing in the Eucharistic Sacrifice, especially by that full sharing which takes place in sacramental communion. We can say not only that *each of us receives Christ,* but also that *Christ receives each of us.* He enters into friendship with us: "You are my friends" (Jn 15:14). Indeed, it is because of him that we have life: "He who eats me will live because of me" (Jn 6:57). Eucharistic communion brings about in a sublime way the mutual "abiding" of Christ and each of his followers: "Abide in me, and I in you" (Jn 15:4).[123]

Even before the most profound request for the ongoing presence of the friend was uttered, Christ had already instituted the surpassing gift of himself and thus responded to our deepest Christian longing: "Stay with us, for it is toward evening and the day is now far spent" (Luke 24:29). May our eyes of faith be opened each time when the priest, *in persona Christi,* speaks the words of consecration, the words of consummate divine friendship, "This is my body, this is my blood." What more can we ask for? And yet, we have received even more: Christ remains with us under the sacramental species in the Blessed Sacrament of the Holy Eucharist until the sacramental species disappear. He remains with us so that our faith may constantly grow and our hope increasingly rest assured in the abiding presence and everlasting nature of Christ's consummate friendship with those who love him. What more, indeed, can we ask for? Thanks be to God.

---

122. Scheeben, *The Mysteries of Christianity,* 500f.

123. Pope John Paul II, in *Ecclesia de Eucharistia,* seems to reemphasize and enlarge a theme present already in Pius XII's encyclical *Mediator Dei:* "It is on this doctrinal basis that the cult of adoring the Eucharist was founded and gradually developed as something distinct from the sacrifice of the Mass. The reservation of the sacred species for the sick and those in danger of death introduced the praiseworthy custom of adoring the blessed Sacrament which is reserved in our churches. This practice of adoration, in fact, is based on strong and solid reasons. For the Eucharist is at once a sacrifice and a sacrament; but it differs from the other sacraments in this that it not only produces grace, but contains in a permanent manner the Author of grace Himself. When, therefore, the Church bids us adore Christ hidden behind the eucharistic veils and pray to Him for spiritual and temporal favors, of which we ever stand in need, she manifests living faith in her divine Spouse who is present beneath these veils, she professes her gratitude to Him and she enjoys the intimacy of His friendship" (*Mediator Dei,* § 131).

APPENDIX 1

I would like to acknowledge my special indebtedness to the scholarship and expertise of John F. Boyle, Romanus Cessario, O.P., Guy Mansini, O.S.B., and Joseph Wawrykow. While I have consulted other authors, I have most profitably learned from and hence draw to varying degrees on the following studies: David Berger, *Thomas Aquinas and the Liturgy* (Naples, Fla.: Sapientia Press, 2004); Joseph Bobik, "Dimensions in the Individuation of Bodily Substances," *Philosophical Studies* 4 (1954): 60–79; Stephen L. Brock, "St. Thomas and the Eucharistic Conversion," *The Thomist* 65, no. 4 (2001): 529–65; Leo J. Elders, S.V.D., *Die Naturphilosophie des Thomas von Aquin: Allgemeine Naturphilosophie—Kosmologie—Philosophie der Lebewesen—Philosophische Anthropologie* (Weilheim-Bierbronnen: Gustav-Siewerth-Akademie, 2004); Reginald Garrigou-Lagrange, O.P., *De Eucharistia accedunt De Paenitentia quaestiones dogmaticae Commentarius in Summam theologicam S. Thomae* (Rome: Marietti, 1943); Joseph Gredt, O.S.B., *Elementa Philosophiae Aristotelico-Thomisticae,* vol. 1, *Logica / Philosophia Naturalis,* 11th ed. (Freiburg and Barcelona: Herder, 1956); Engelbert Gutwenger, S.J., "Substanz und Akzidenz in der Eucharistielehre," *Zeitschrift für katholische Theologie* 83 (1961): 257–306; John of St. Thomas, O.P., *Cursus Philosophicus Thomisticus,* vol. 1, *Logica* (Paris: Vivès, 1883); Charles Cardinal Journet, *The Mass: The Presence of the Sacrifice of the Cross,* trans. Victor Szczurek, O.Praem. (South Bend, Ind.: St. Augustine's Press, 2008); Matthew Levering, *Sacrifice and Community: Jewish Offering and Christian Eucharist* (Malden, Mass. and Oxford: Blackwell, 2005); Ralph McInerny, *Praeambula Fidei: Thomism and the God of the Philosophers* (Washington, D.C.: The Catholic University of America Press, 2006); Joseph Ratzinger, "Das Problem der Transsubstantiation und die Frage nach dem Sinn der Eucharistie," *Theologische Quartalschrift* 147 (1967): 129–58; Petrus Sedlmayr, O.S.B., "Die Lehre des hl. Thomas von den *accidentia sine subjecto remanentia*—untersucht auf ihren Einklang mit der aristotelischen Philosophie," *Divus Thomas* (F) 12 (1934): 315–26; Horst Seidl, "Zum Substanzbegriff der katholischen Transsubstantiationslehre: Erkenntnistheoretische und metaphysische Erörterungen," *Forum Katholische Theologie* 11 (1995): 1–16; Sylvester of Ferrara's commentary on Thomas's *Summa contra Gentiles,* esp. on bk. IV, in *Sancti Thomae Aquinatis Doctoris Angelici Opera Omnia iussu edita Leonis XIII P.M.,* vol. 15 (Rome: Leonine Commission, 1930); Jean-Pierre Torrell, O.P., *Saint Thomas Aquinas,* vol. 1, *The Person and His Work,* trans. Robert Royal (Washington, D.C.: The Catholic University of America Press, 1996); Anscar Vonier, O.S.B., *A Key to the Doctrine of the Eucharist* (Bethesda, Md.: Zacchaeus, 2003); John F. Wippel, *The Metaphysical Thought of Thomas Aquinas: From Finite Being to Uncreated Being* (Washington, D.C.: The Catholic University of America Press, 2000); and various chapters of the excellent introduction to the theology of Thomas Aquinas, *The Theology of Thomas Aquinas,* ed. Rik van Nieuwenhove and Joseph Wawrykow (Notre Dame, Ind.: University of Notre Dame Press, 2005), esp. Bruce D. Marshall, "*Quod Scit Una Uetula:* Aquinas on the Nature of Theology," in ibid., 1–35.

APPENDIX 2

One important indicator that indeed for Thomas Eucharistic real presence entails Eucharistic transubstantiation is to be found in his important doctrinal commentary on the decretal *Firmiter*, a profession of faith formulated at Lateran IV in 1215. The second decretal, *Damnamus*, of which Thomas offers a paraphrase, was also formulated at Lateran IV and deals with Joachim of Fiore's attack on the trinitarian doctrine of Peter Lombard. Thomas wrote this commentary during his Orviedo period (1261–65); its title is *Expositio super primam et secundam Decretalem ad Archidiaconum Tudertinum* (*Opuscula Theologica*, vol. 1 [Rome: Marietti, 1954], 415–31). As is well known, in its statement of faith, Lateran IV uses the participle for transubstantive change: "Transubstantiatis pane in corpus et vino in sanguinem potestate divina . . ." In his doctrinal commentary, Thomas understands the statement of faith to determine three distinct truths of the Eucharistic sacrifice, the first regarding the *"res"* contained under the sacrament, the second regarding the way Christ's body begins to be present under the sacrament, and the third regarding the valid ministry of the sacrament. In a strikingly seemless manner his interpretation of the second assertion, transubstantiation, flows directly from his interpretation of the first assertion, real presence:

> *Primo* quidem veritatem rei sub sacramento contentae, cum dicit: *Cuius corpus et sanguis in sacramento altaris sub speciebus panis et vini veraciter continentur.* Dicit autem *Veraciter*, ad excludendum errorem quorundam qui dixerunt quod in hoc sacramento non est corpus Christi secundum rei veritatem, sed solum secundum figuram, sive sicut in signo. Dicit autem: *Sub speciebus panis et vini*, ad excludendum errorem quorundam qui dixerunt quod in sacramento altaris simul continetur substantia panis, et substantia corporis Christi; quod est contra verbum Domini dicentis, Luc. xxii, 19: *Hoc est corpus meum.* Esset enim secundum hoc dicendum magis: Hic est corpus meum. Ut ergo ostendat quod in hoc sacramento non remanet substantia panis et vini, sed solum species, idest accidentia sine subiecto, dicit: *Sub speciebus panis et vini.*
>
> *Secundo* ostendit quomodo corpus Christi incipiat esse sub sacramento, scilicet per hoc quod substantia panis convertitur miraculose in substantiam corporis Christi, et substantia vini in substantiam sanguinis; et hoc est quod dicit: *Transubstantiatis pane in corpus et vino in sanguinem potestate divina, ad mysterium perficiendum unitatis,* idest ad celebrandum hoc sacramentum, quod est signum ecclesiasticae unitatis. *Accipimus* igitur *ipsi de suo quod ipse accepit de nostro.* In hoc enim sacramento accipimus de corpore et sanguine Christi, quae Filius Dei accepit de nostra natura." (*Opuscula Theologica*, vol. 1, 425)

So why does Thomas not simply cite in the opening question 75 of his Eucharistic treatise in *ST* III the statement of faith, *Firmiter*, of Lateran IV? In light of his understanding of *sacra doctrina*, is this not exactly what we should expect? In order to understand why Thomas did not simply refer to the *Firmiter*, it is crucial to grasp that in his own doctrinal commentary of it Thomas takes the council as doing nothing else but repeat what the words of institution, according to Luke 22:19, already entail—transubstantiation. For he understands any alternatives to transubstantiation to be excluded by the council's first affirmation, that of real presence. In short, according to Thomas, *Firmiter* does nothing but consistently affirm the witness of Scripture and gesture toward a direction to be taken in light of unacceptable alternatives. Eucharistic real presence is based on Scripture and transubstantiation is a necessary entailment, as the council affirms. And this is exactly the route Thomas takes in his Eucharistic treatise in *ST* III. To put it differently, the fact that Thomas does not cite *Firmiter* in the opening question 75 of his Eucharistic treatise is a strong indication that he is intending to make the case of *Firmiter* by way of an extended exposition based on the same fundamental assertion, namely that real presence and transubstantiation really are the two sides of the same coin. Making the case of *Firmiter* along the lines of *fides quaerens intellectum* makes it impossible to refer to the profession of faith as an authoritative source for the very case he wants to make, lest he create a vicious circle. In short, my suggestion is that the reader of Thomas's Eucharistic treatise who, because of the council's great influence upon the subsequent generations, will be aware of *Firmiter* or quite likely eventually to encounter it, might, in light of Thomas's treatise, turn to the council's profession of faith and say: "I see."

APPENDIX 3

In the first question of the *Summa theologiae,* Thomas unquestionably regards fidelity to God as the central requirement for those charged to expound *sacra doctrina.* We would, however, be profoundly mistaken if we were to infer from this that Thomas distinguishes between fidelity to God and obedience to the Church's Magisterium. Nevertheless, it is indeed the case that the fourteenth- and fifteenth-century conflicts between pope and councils eventually resulted in a form of papal primacy unknown to Thomas. (On this topic see the informative recent study by Ulrich Horst, O.P., *The Dominicans and the Pope: Papal Teaching Authority in the Medieval and Early Modern Thomist Tradition,* trans. James D. Mixson, foreword by Thomas Prügl [Notre Dame, Ind.: University of Notre Dame Press, 2006]). In light of these later developments, what Thomas does say about this matter is even more striking. For, arguably, he already held *in nuce* what is the result of overcoming conciliarism, namely a teaching Magisterium with the pope at its head. Yves Congar, O.P., brought together the most striking passages in Thomas's oeuvre that support and illustrate this claim:

> Thus a Christian cannot be excused from the vice of error if he assents to the opinion of any teacher that is contrary to the manifest testimony of Scripture or is contrary to what is publicly held on the basis of the Church's authority. (*Quodl.* III, 10)
>
> If we consider Divine Providence which directs his Church by the Holy Spirit, so that it may not err, just as Jesus promised in Jn. 16: 13 . . . it is certain that for the judgment of the universal Church to err in matters of faith is an impossibility. Hence, we must stand by the decision of the Pope rather than the opinion of other men, even though they be learned in the

Scriptures. For the Pope has the right and duty to determine concerning the faith, a determination he indicates by his judgment. (*Quodl.* IX, 16)

The custom of the Church has very great authority and ought always to be jealously observed in all things, since the very doctrine of Catholic doctors derives its authority from the Church. Thus, we ought to abide by the authority of the Church rather than that of Augustine or Jerome or of any other doctor. (*Summa Theol.,* II-II, q. 10, a. 12)

Thus some doctors seem to have disagreed either with reference to matters that have no bearing on faith, whether they should be explained thus or so, or they disagreed regarding certain matters of faith which were not then determined by the Church. But, after their determination by the authority of the universal Church, if anyone should pertinaciously call such a decision into question, he would be considered a heretic. This authority resides principally in the Sovereign Pontiff. For we read in the Decretals (dist. XXIV, qu. 1, can. 12, Friedberg 970): "Whenever a question of faith is in dispute . . ." (ibid., q. 11, a. 2, ad 3[um.])

—(Yves Congar, O.P., "Saint Thomas Aquinas and the Infallibility of the
    Papal Magisterium," *The Thomist* 38, no. 1 [1974], 81–105; 93f.)

The best commentary on the profound correlation between fidelity to God and obedience to the Church is to be found in Thomas's discussion of the object of faith in *ST* II-II, q. 1. Thomas moves from considering in the first article the contemplation of the First Truth to considering in its tenth article the question "Whether it belongs to the Sovereign Pointiff to draw up a symbol of faith?" We do not go wrong in assuming that Thomas suggests a profound interrelationship between the first and the tenth articles. In other words, fidelity to the First Truth takes on concrete form as obedience to the Church's teaching authority.

APPENDIX 4

Three essential points regarding Trent's decree need be made in due brevity. First, the decree emphasizes "the conversion of the *whole* substance of the bread into the substance of the body of Christ our Lord, and of the *whole* substance of the wine into the substance of his blood" (emphasis added). In the background of the decree's emphasis stands the argument with the position of Durandus of St. Pourçain, O.P., who understood the Eucharistic conversion as a kind of transformation with an underlying subject implying a common matter between the first and the second term of the conversion. As Stephen Brock ("St. Thomas and the Eucharistic Conversion," 535–36) rightly emphasizes, the Tridentine decree must be understood as a sound rejection of Eucharistic conversion as a mere substantial trans*formation* instead of a trans*substantiation*. The Tridentine emphasis on the conversion of the whole substance of bread and the whole substance of wine "would mean a substantial conversion that completely eliminates one substance, leaving a wholly distinct substance instead" (536). Second, in his important essay, Engelbert Gutwenger, S.J. ("Substanz und Akzidenz in der Eucharistielehre") has convincingly argued that the Council of Trent comprehensively endorsed the Eucharistic doctrine decreed at the Council of Constance (1414–18). Especially with regard to Eucharistic transubstantiation, the council fathers at Trent draw repeatedly and thoroughly on the definitions and the entailed theological suppositions of Constance. The council fathers at Constance, in turn, unreservedly endorsed the metaphysical notions of substance and accidents in relation to the Eucharist. Hence, it is very difficult, if not simply impossible, to deny that the council fathers at Trent not only acknowledged the definitions of Constance as normative, but also regarded the underlying theological account, including the entailed metaphysical principles, as the ineluctable implication of the definitions of Constance. The concrete issue at stake at Constance was the condemnation of John Wycliffe's rejection of Eucharistic transubstantiation (specifically his teaching that after the consecration the bread was still bread, "verus panis"), a rejection expressed in explicitly Scholastic conceptuality. Irrespective of how one might want to assess the finer historical points in Gutwenger's account, if what he claims indeed obtains in at least a proximate way, one point seems plain, namely that it is simply impossible to maintain what Herbert McCabe, O.P., states right at the beginning of an otherwise intriguing meditation on "Eucharistic change" (and what has taken the form of popular lore in many circles): "The Council of Trent did not decree that Catholics should believe in transubstantiation: it just calls it a most appropriate *(aptissime)* way of talking about the Eucharist, presumably leaving it open whether there might not be other, perhaps even more appropriate, ways of talking" (McCabe, *God Still Matters*, ed. Brian Davies, O.P. [London and New York: Continuum, 2002], 115). Third, and closely related to the second point, one frequently encounters the claim that the Council of Trent used the word "species," instead of "accident" in order to avoid any commitment to a "metaphysics of substance and accident." Gutwenger's extensive study makes the convincing case that all the council fathers, those favoring "species" as well as those favoring "accident," thought in broadly Aristotelian terms. Even Edward Schillebeeckx, O.P. (*The Eucharist* [New York: Sheed & Ward, 1968], 53–66), agrees on this point with Gutwenger, but he disagrees vehemently with Gutwenger's inference that the Council of Trent not only used—inescapably in its conceptual context, Schillebeeckx would say—but indeed *sanctioned* the descriptive use of the metaphysical predicamentals "substance" and "accident" as the ineluctable ontological entailment of the doctrine of faith on Eucharistic transubstantiation. Beware—such sanctioning is not the same as *imposing* these predicamentals (or as some like to put it, the Aristotelian "theory" of substance and accidents) as *de fide,* nor even as the exclusive way to unpack "transubstantiation" theologically. In this latter regard the matter clearly comes down to the very nature of dogma and, related, the nature of theology as an ecclesial discipline. If theology is understood as *sacra doctrina* in the sense developed here, Gutwenger's inference is perfectly appropriate. If, however, theology is primarily or even exclusively a contemporary hermeneutics of faith and doctrine in light of an ever antecedent, but ever newly to be construed, pre-understanding *(Vorverständnis)* of "modern man," or in the meanwhile "postmodern de-centered subject" and soon most likely post-postmodern "super-primate" (Daniel Dennett), Gutwenger's inference is illicit. But for that matter it also becomes dramatically unclear how any dogma is still to be received and defended theologically *as* dogma, and this pertains to Nicea and Calcedon as well. Only one generation after Schillebeeckx, these inferences have already been drawn; and as the present "signs of the times," the allegedly ineluctable contours of the "postmodern condition" have been invoked in order to understand the development of doctrine as the ongoing reconstruction of the faith itself.

APPENDIX 5

Let me at this point address a rather crude objection that most often occurs in the form of the question, Must I believe in Aristotelian "substance metaphysics" in order to be able to believe in transubstantiation? In short, is Aristotelian "substance metaphysics" itself "de fide"? (A slightly more sophisticated version of this question, but one displaying remarkable deficiencies of understanding of Aristotle's predicamentals, theory of language, and physics, can be found in Ian Robinson, "Thomas Cranmer on the Real Presence," *Faith and Worship* 43 [1997]: 2–10.) Three things need to be said in response to this question, which does not present a genuine objection but reflects rather a quite common misunderstanding. (1) Faith is guided by the dominical words of consecration as rightly interpreted by the Church's understanding, which from early on in unbroken continuity has understood them literally (and precisely this understanding was reaffirmed each time after it had been challenged by individual theologians such as Berengar, Wycliffe, and Zwingli). Hence, what is "de fide," that is, what indeed substantively and normatively constitutes that to which faith is the assent of the intellect commanded by the will due to grace is that faith receives the words "this is my body, this is my blood" in relationship to the bread and the wine as effectively signifying the complete conversion of what is constitutive of the bread and of the wine ("this" is bread, "this" is wine) into what is constitutive of Christ's body and Christ's blood ("this" is Christ's body, "this" is Christ's blood). What is "de fide" is not the precise metaphysical description employed, but the "that" of the reference of the words of consecration obtaining independently of the speaker and believer, a "that" that indeed has ineluctable ontological entailments. For that reference is beheld by divine faith alone, and divine faith entails the assent of the intellect, which—crucially—is ordered to receive and understand in its first act being (*ens*) by way of substance. It is in this way that the notion of "transubstantiation," which indeed is *de fide, aptissime* (Trent), expresses the mystery of Christ's real, bodily presence in the Eucharistic elements. (2) The *intellectus fidei*, accordingly, has to interpret and defend the proper assent of the intellect. In the course of this interpretation and defense, *sacra docrina* draws upon that science which investigates the constitutive principles of being. Acknowledging that indeed Aristotle has once and for all established this science of being, metaphysics—as Thomas does indeed acknowledge—does not entail any extrinsic antecedent belief in it besides that of the student at the beginning of a course of studies: *Oportet addiscentem credere.* This "credere" stands at the beginning of all learning, be it an art, a foreign language, or a science. (3) As it is very hard, if not impossible, for the *intellectus fidei* rightly to interpret and defend what is "de fide" about the Holy Trinity and Christ's divinity as well as humanity without continuously drawing upon the metaphysical notions and principles of essence, person, subsistence, nature, and relation, it is equally hard, if not impossible, to receive "de fide" the notion of "transubstantiation" as what "aptissime" expresses the mystery of faith of Christ's real presence in the Eucharistic elements without the *intellectus fidei* drawing upon the metaphysical notions and principles of being *(ens)*, form and matter, substance, and accident. It is in this subtle, indirect, but precise and irreversible sense that the Church's understanding by way of dogma continues to direct the ongoing labors of *sacra doctrina* in service of the *intellectus fidei* to metaphysics as the science of *ens inquantum ens* as the most proper handmaiden for *sacra doctrina*. It is a mode of inquiry that is neither passé (for its proper formal object can never be passé) nor falsified on empirical grounds or on grounds of mathematical natural sciences (for such a falsification could only occur by way of a superior science that does not exist, since metaphysics is by definition of its subject matter "first philosophy"). Accordingly, if one wants to be introduced into this inquiry, one has to adopt the proper natural faith of any student at the beginning of his or her course of studies. And that indeed entails that for all contemporary students of theology, the maxim obtains regarding *sacra doctrina,* as well as metaphysics: *Oportet addiscentem credere.*

[2]

Ordering Wisdom

Aquinas, the Old Testament, and *Sacra Doctrina*

MATTHEW LEVERING

Introduction

In 1912, among the writings of Thomas Aquinas's student Remigio dei Girolami, two previously lost works of Aquinas were discovered: two short treatises, preached by Aquinas as inaugural lectures, on the structure and content of the whole of Scripture.[1] Aquinas delivered these lectures as part of his formal installation as a *magister in sacra pagina* at the University of Paris.[2] In order to gain further insight into an oft-studied theme—Aquinas's understanding of *sacra doctrina*—the present essay investigates the view of the Old Testament that he presents in these inaugural lectures. I propose that Aquinas's explanation of the content and preaching of Old Testament may instruct contemporary theologians in the practice of *sacra doctrina*.

Before beginning, let me briefly summarize the two lectures. The first is ti-

1. See Ralph McInerny's note in Thomas Aquinas, *Selected Writings*, ed. and trans. Ralph McInerny (New York: Penguin, 1998), 5.

2. Jean-Pierre Torrell, O.P., holds that the second lecture I discuss, "On the Commendation of Sacred Scripture" (commonly known as "Rigans montes de superioribus suis"), "was given sometime between 3 March and 17 June 1256" as Aquinas's *principium* or inaugural lecture at the University of Paris. See Torrell, *Saint Thomas Aquinas*, vol. 1, *The Person and His Work*, trans. Robert Royal (Washington, D.C.: The Catholic University of America Press, 1996), 51. Torrell emphasizes the influence of Pseudo-Dionysius's theology of mediation upon the lecture. Torrell suggests that the first sermon-lecture that I discuss may have been delivered in September 1256: see *The Person and His Work*, 53.

tled "Commendation of and Division of Sacred Scripture." In it Aquinas presents the Old Testament as consisting first and foremost of laws, and secondarily of examples and stories that encourage obedience to the laws and that give instruction on how to apply them virtuously. He emphasizes the goodness and perseverance of God the Teacher, and the wisdom and usefulness of the laws that he gives Israel. The second sermon-lecture is titled "On the Commendation of Sacred Scripture." Aquinas argues that the revelation of divine wisdom far exceeds the understanding of even the most learned and holy preacher. In order to teach divine wisdom, preachers should first contemplate it through study, and then communicate it in language that the audience can understand. In short, the first lecture explores the structure of the Old Testament, whereas the second lecture engages the Old Testament as a resource for understanding how mere human beings dare to teach the Word of God.

"Commendation of and Division of Sacred Scripture": *Hic liber mandatorum Dei*

In Praise of Scripture's Wisdom and Order

In "Commendation of and Division of Sacred Scripture," Aquinas begins by praising Scripture by means of a quotation from Augustine, who states that "one skilled in speech should so speak as to teach, to delight, and to change; that is, to teach the ignorant, to delight the bored, and to change the lazy."[3] The "one skilled in speech" is most truly God himself.[4] For this reason, as Aquinas says, all Scripture teaches the ignorant, delights the bored, and changes the lazy. How so? To the ignorant, Scripture "firmly teaches with its eternal truth. Psalm 118 [119]:89: 'Thy word, O Lord, stands firm for ever as heaven.'" To the bored, Scripture "sweetly delights with its pleasantness. Psalm 118 [119]:103: 'How sweet are thy words to my mouth!'" To the lazy, Scripture "efficaciously changes with its authority. Jeremiah 23:29: 'Are not my words as a fire, saith the Lord?'"[5]

Aquinas then applies to the scriptural text upon which he is preaching,

---

3. Aquinas, "Commendation of and Division of Sacred Scripture," in Aquinas, *Selected Writings*, 5.

4. On Christ as Teacher according to Aquinas, see Michael Sherwin, O.P., "Christ the Teacher in St. Thomas's *Commentary on the Gospel of John*," in *Reading John with St. Thomas Aquinas*, ed. Michael Dauphinais and Matthew Levering (Washington, D.C.: The Catholic University of America Press, 2005), 173–93; Michael Dauphinais, *The Pedagogy of the Incarnation: Christ the Teacher according to St. Thomas Aquinas* (Ph.D. diss., Notre Dame, Ind.: University of Notre Dame, 2000).

5. Aquinas, "Commendation of and Division of Sacred Scripture," 5.

Baruch 4:1, this insight about how God the teacher instructs us, God's ignorant, bored, and lazy pupils. First, Baruch 4:1 bears witness to Scripture's life-
changing authority: "This is the book of the commandments of God." Second, Baruch affirms that Scripture consists of eternal truth: "the law that is
for ever." Third, Baruch explains the usefulness that Scripture's words possess:
"All that keep it shall come to life."[6]

I will not describe all the ways that Aquinas praises Scripture's authority,
truth, and usefulness. Instead, I wish to focus upon Aquinas's understanding
of how Scripture's "division" or arrangement conduces to the transformation
of God's ignorant, bored, and lazy pupils. If God is the most perfect Teacher,
then like human teachers and preachers, God will have arranged his scriptural teaching carefully so as to achieve his purposes. What kind of arrangement
or "division," then, does Scripture possess? Scripture's central "division," of
course, is that of the Old and New Testaments. Aquinas suggests that the Old
Testament instructs us by means of the commandments of justice, whereas the
New Testament, as primarily the grace of the Holy Spirit, helps us to attain
this justice. Turning to the structure of the Old Testament in particular, Aquinas argues that the Old Testament recalls sinful human beings to the knowledge of how to live justly by means of three steps. First, God teaches the law of
justice (the Torah). Second, God encourages obedience to this law (the prophets). Third, God offers prudential guidance for living out the law in daily life
(the hagiographers and apocrypha).

While this tripartite division of the Old Testament was standard in Aquinas's day,[7] Aquinas seeks to understand its divine rationale more deeply. He
distinguishes between three kinds of divine commandments: binding commandments that establish laws, binding commandments that encourage obedience to the laws, and "warning" commandments that offer prudential instruction about how to obey the laws.[8] Binding commandments of the first
kind come from God as king or ruler, and those commandments are found in
the Torah. Binding commandments of the second kind come from God in a
mediated fashion, through "his heralds and ambassadors,"[9] namely the prophets. Third, the "warning" commandments are contained in the hagiographers
and apocrypha.

---

6. Ibid., 5–6.
7. For a contemporary overview of the Old Testament that follows these three principal
parts, see Aidan Nichols, O.P., *Lovely, Like Jerusalem: The Fulfillment of the Old Testament in
Christ and the Church* (San Francisco: Ignatius Press, 2007), 13–74.
8. Aquinas, "Commendation of and Division of Sacred Scripture," 7.
9. Ibid., 7–8.

Following Aquinas, we can describe this tripartite structure in another way. First, God the Teacher gives his pupils laws of justice in the Torah. Second, lest the laws seem overly onerous, the divine Teacher encourages his pupils by setting before them (through the mediation of his teaching assistants, the prophets) his beneficence and the promised fulfillment. Third, recognizing the difficulty of applying laws to concrete situations, the divine Teacher gives fatherly advice in the hagiography and apocrypha regarding the prudential application of the laws.

However, what about the wide variety of content in the books that comprise the three parts of the Old Testament? When Aquinas inquires into this variety of content, does he need to change his portrait of the Old Testament's tripartite structure?

The Structure and Purpose of the Books of the Torah

The first book of the Torah, Genesis, contains "private law," which "is imposed for the observance of one person or one family."[10] The original justice of Adam and Eve is predicated on their obedience to God's commandment, "'But of the tree of the knowledge of good and evil, thou shalt not eat' ([Gen] 2:17)." When Adam and Eve sin by trying to become a law to themselves, God builds up a covenantal community through commandments to Noah and Abraham.

When Abraham's seed has grown into the people of Israel, God delivers to them "public law" through the mediator Moses, who represents the people before God. Exodus, Leviticus, and Numbers focus upon Moses receiving the law from God, while Deuteronomy focuses upon the people of Israel's receiving the law from Moses. Exodus, Leviticus, and Numbers are also distinguished from one another by the content of the laws that God teaches in each book. In Exodus, God teaches about "equity of judgment" through the Decalogue and the moral laws. Justice is twofold: toward God and toward fellow human beings. God devotes Leviticus to teaching about how to constitute a worship that does justice to the living God (ceremonial laws). Numbers teaches about how to constitute an "administration of the community" that does justice to fellow human beings (judicial laws).[11]

Thus the arrangement of God's teaching is wise and good in every way, from God's teaching of individuals in Genesis, to God's carefully ordered teaching of the people of God in Exodus, Leviticus, and Numbers—a teaching that proceeds through the mediation of Moses, as Deuteronomy emphasizes.

10. Ibid., 8.
11. Ibid., 9.

The Structure and Purpose of the Books of the Prophets

The second part of the Old Testament consists in the books of the prophets. Recall that Aquinas describes the prophets as God's "heralds and ambassadors." In preaching the Old Testament, what does Aquinas think we should learn from these "heralds and ambassadors"? Aquinas says that "a herald ought to do two things. He should manifest the beneficence of the king, so that men will be inclined to obey, and he should declare the edict of the law."[12] How do the prophets accomplish this task of supporting God's law?

We might first ask what Aquinas means by a prophet making manifest "the beneficence of the king." Aquinas has in mind what we call historical books, but which Jerome, following the rabbis, understood as "prophetic" books. Thus in different ways, the books of Joshua, Judges, Ruth, and Kings (including 1 and 2 Samuel) manifest the "beneficence" of God. Does God the Teacher arrange these books and their content in a particular way so as to manifest his beneficence most clearly? For Aquinas the question is whether these books show that God has been a good "king," a good father, to the family of Israel. As a good king and father, has God established a family worthy of note? Or is Israel dysfunctional, bearing witness not to a good king and father but to a negligent one who has brought his family to ruin? Does God's family in truth manifest God's royal and paternal "beneficence"?

The reader of Joshua, Judges, Ruth, and Samuel/Kings might be forgiven for answering in the negative. Joshua, while certainly not an unworthy heir to Moses, is nonetheless hardly on a par with Moses. Judges depicts the twelve tribes of Israel in a condition of profound, and at times horrific, spiritual and political disarray. The Moabite Ruth does not, it might seem, bring much distinction to David's ancestry. Lastly, Samuel/Kings attains its high point in David and Solomon—the former a murderous adulterer almost conquered by his son Absalom, the latter an idolater thanks in part to his large number of foreign wives. From this perspective, these books of Scripture show not God's "beneficence," but God's allowing his family to fall into almost complete ruin.

Without rejecting this negative reading, Aquinas offers an alternative perspective. First, God gives the people a noble lineage, as the book of Joshua shows. Second, the book of Judges shows that God repeatedly enables the people to unite and overcome their enemies, often against all odds. Third, by exalting the person of Ruth, God reveals his providential beneficence toward the people on an individual level. Fourth, God reveals his beneficence toward the entire people by exalting Israel during the prosperous reigns of David and

12. Ibid.

Solomon, during which time the Temple and much of Jerusalem were built. On this reading, what stands out is not so much the dysfunction of the people, which is often undeniable, but rather the fact that God gives so much to this people and cares for this people in so many beneficial ways.

In other words, even if the people have been unruly, God has established their lineage and their "house" in a condition of honor, not dishonor. It is a mark of honor to be an Israelite, a descendent of such noble leaders as Joshua and of such steadfast women as Ruth, a member of a people that has withstood enemies, and an inheritor of the high culture of the Davidic and Solomonic kingdoms. By exhibiting this "divine beneficence" enjoyed by Israel, these prophetic books thereby make it easier for God the Teacher's audience to desire to be spiritual Israelites by obeying the law of justice/holiness.[13]

In addition to manifesting "the beneficence of the king," the other task of the "herald" is to "declare the edict of the law" so that the people will observe its commands.[14] The "major prophets" did this by proclaiming the law to the whole people of Israel, whereas the "minor prophets" proclaimed the law to particular tribes within Israel. As a good father, God prompts his unruly children to obedience by a range of methods, including "cajoling by the promise of benefits, frightening with the threat of punishment, arguing by condemnation of sins."[15] God the Teacher ensures that each of these methods is present in each major prophet. Yet God also arranges that these methods are present in an ordered fashion, in accord with the degree of value that each method possesses.

Thus among the three major prophets, Aquinas notes, "Isaiah chiefly cajoles," Jeremiah primarily warns of punishment, and Ezekiel primarily argues with evildoers.[16] This threefold schema appears also in the three major prophets' declaration of the fulfillment of the law by Christ: "Isaiah chiefly foretells the mystery of the Incarnation, which is why he is read during the time of Advent by the Church, and Jeremiah the mystery of the Passion, hence he is read in Passiontide, and Ezekiel the mystery of the Resurrection, hence his book finishes with the raising of the bones and the repair of the temple."[17] Though all three prophets foretell each of the three mysteries, Isaiah's emphasis on the benefits to come fits with the Incarnation, Jeremiah's emphasis on the punishment of sins fits with the Passion, and Ezekiel's emphasis on confuting evildoers fits with the Resurrection. To these three prophets Aquinas adds Daniel, on the grounds that Daniel clearly possessed "a prophetic spirit" in foretelling "the divinity of Christ."[18]

13. Ibid.   14. Ibid.
15. Ibid.   16. Ibid., 9–10.
17. Ibid., 10.   18. Ibid.

The Structure and Purpose of the Hagiography and Apocrypha

The third part of the Old Testament that Aquinas marks out is the hagiography and apocrypha. Having set forth the law of justice in the Torah and encouraged its fulfillment in the prophets, God in the hagiography and apocrypha gives paternal advice about how to live out virtuously, in particular situations, the universal mandates of the law. Aquinas suggests that God the Teacher arranges the hagiography and apocrypha "according to the two ways fathers instruct their sons in virtue, namely, by word and deed, since in morals examples are no less important than words."[19] Aquinas finds that one book, Ecclesiasticus or Sirach, instructs by both word and deed, since it begins with wisdom sayings and ends by praising specific examples of virtuous deeds. The books that instruct by deed include Chronicles, Judith, Maccabees, Tobit, Ezra and Nehemiah (one book in the Vulgate), and Esther.

Certainly these books describe many deeds, but do these books, with their various historical tales, truly possess a unity that one can draw out for edification in preaching? Aquinas suggests that a helpful device for preaching these books is to recall the four cardinal virtues: prudence, justice, fortitude, and temperance. Each of the books emphasizes a particular virtue. Thus Chronicles teaches about justice in the ordering of communities toward the common good, even if Chronicles often does so by displaying the leaders' lack of justice. Ezra and Nehemiah teach prudence through their protagonists' exemplary efforts to rebuild the Temple and the walls of Jerusalem and to renew obedience to the Torah, in the face of daunting political challenges. The Book of Esther teaches prudence through Esther's exemplary handling of the violent threats of Haman. Tobit teaches fortitude under the aspect of perseverance through trials, while Maccabees teaches fortitude under the aspect of bold attack. Lastly, Judith teaches temperance, because Judith exemplifies how chastity strengthens a person's ability to serve the common good.

In addition to fostering obedience to the law by giving examples of virtuous actions, this third part of Scripture contains books in which wise persons seek to instruct others about how to live. Aquinas emphasizes, however, that these books are not solely didactic: rather, the purpose of the psalms is to ask "for the gift of wisdom," a petition that in fact constitutes the very heart of wisdom.[20] Joined to the psalms are the didactic wisdom books: Job, Wisdom, Proverbs, Ecclesiastes, and Song of Songs. Of these, Aquinas suggests that Job embodies one form of teaching wisdom, in that he uses disputation to refute

19. Ibid., 10.
20. Ibid., 11.

false teachers, even in the seemingly reasonable form of his three friends.[21] The other four books teach wisdom in a second way, namely, through positive precept rather than through disputation. Among these four books, Aquinas makes a further distinction: the book of Wisdom devotes itself to commending the pursuit of wisdom, whereas Proverbs, Ecclesiastes, and Song of Songs deliver "precepts of wisdom."[22]

One can understand why Aquinas describes Proverbs as setting forth precepts of wisdom, but Ecclesiastes and (still more) Song of Songs hardly seem to belong in this category. In this regard, however, just as with his use of the four cardinal virtues, Aquinas has recourse to a framework drawn from ancient philosophy: the three stages of human virtue, which according to Plotinus are the political, the purgative, and the perfect or contemplative. This template allows Aquinas to suggest how Proverbs, Ecclesiastes, and Song of Songs might fit together, on an ascending scale of wisdom, in their concern for the problem of how to live. Proverbs offers mundane wisdom regarding the political stage of virtue, "whereby a man moderately uses the things of this world and lives among men."[23] Ecclesiastes instills the "contempt of the world," whereby a person appreciates that this world is passing away and thus cannot provide a lasting source of happiness: this is the purgative stage of virtue.[24] Lastly Song of Songs, when read as celebrating the marriage of God and humankind, signals the desire for, and delight in, divine wisdom that belongs to the person who has fallen fully in love with God. The person who ascends to the third stage does not, in this world, lose the need of the first two stages, and thus all three find a place in God's teaching.

"On the Commendation of Sacred Scripture": ## *Rigans montes de superioribus suis*

Let us now turn to Aquinas's second lecture. He takes as his text Psalm 104:13, "Thou waterest the hills from thy upper rooms, the earth is sated with the fruit of thy works."[25] He suggests that Psalm 104:13 points to four realities: "the *height* of spiritual doctrine; the *dignity* of those who teach it; the *condition* of the listeners; and the *order* of communicating."[26]

For our purposes, the question is how Aquinas conceives of the Old Testa-

---

21. Ibid.   22. Ibid.
23. Ibid.   24. Ibid.
25. Aquinas, "On the Commendation of Sacred Scripture," in Aquinas, *Selected Writings*, 13. Scholars commonly name this university sermon by its Latin first line, *Rigans montes de superioribus suis*.
26. Ibid.

ment as he preaches about these four realities. I will survey his use of Old Testament texts and will leave to the side his use of New Testament texts.[27] He first explores Scripture as "the *height* of spiritual doctrine." Scripture is wisdom from God's "upper rooms" (Ps 104:13). It originates in God the Teacher: "The Word of God on high is the fountain of wisdom" (Sir 1:5, a verse not included in the RSV). God's wisdom is infinitely richer than our minds can conceive. As Wisdom personified puts it, "I dwelt in the highest places, and my throne is in a pillar of a cloud" (Sir 24:4). Yet God's wisdom has to do with realities that are not absolutely foreign to our minds. Aquinas quotes the Vulgate text of Job 36:25, "All men see him: every one beholdeth afar off," and he pairs this text with Romans 1:19. Although human reason can attain knowledge of God, the divine mysteries and most especially his Trinity remain obscure to our minds without revelation. Aquinas states that such mysteries "are so high that they completely transcend human reason, of which it is said in Job 28:21, 'It is hid from the eyes of all living,' and Psalm 17:12, 'He put on darkness as his covering.'"[28]

Second, Aquinas praises the dignity of "the doctors of the Church," who are "symbolized by mountains" because of their cleaving "to heavenly things above."[29] The doctors of the Church participate in the "height" of divine teaching by being "illumined by the first beams of divine wisdom," Christ himself.[30] In this respect Aquinas cites Isaiah 2:2, "And in the last days the mountain of the house of the Lord shall be prepared on the top of the mountain . . . and all nations shall flow unto it."[31] Because of their proximity to Christ, the doctors of the Church "participate in eternity" and "preach efficaciously."[32] They bear witness to Christ's coming: "Thou hast come, shining with light, powerful, from the everlasting hills. The foolish of heart have been despoiled" (Ps 76:4–5).[33] The doctors of the Church therefore remain authoritative teachers within the Church, because of their ability to "stand against errors."[34] With regard to the need for other teachers and preachers in the Church to rely upon the Church Fathers, Aquinas recalls Ezekiel 13:5, "You have not gone up to face the enemy, nor have you set up a wall for the house of Israel to stand in battle in the day of the Lord."[35] Thus preachers from every generation should learn from the Fathers and emulate their "highness of life," so that they too will "be

27. He quotes the Old Testament twenty-five times, compared to fifteen from the New Testament.

28. Ibid., 14.
30. Ibid.
32. Ibid., 15.
34. Ibid., 15.

29. Ibid.
31. Ibid.
33. Ibid., 14.
35. Ibid.

enlightened" and be able to "refute errors in disputation."[36] If their lives are not pure, their hearers will not believe their words, but if their lives are pure, then their words will carry weight, as Aquinas points out through Ecclesiastes 12:11.[37]

What about the congregation to which divine wisdom is preached? Aquinas suggests that their "condition" is expressed in Psalm 104:13's phrase, "the earth is sated with the fruit of thy works." He interprets this verse in light of three Old Testament texts: Proverbs 25:3, "The heaven above, and the earth beneath"; Ecclesiastes 1:4, "One generation passes away, and another generation cometh, but the earth standeth for ever"; and Genesis 1:11, "Let the earth bring forth the green herb, and such as may seed, and the fruit tree yielding fruit after its kind." Although the congregation lacks learning in sacred doctrine ("the earth beneath," Prov 25:3), nonetheless the congregation possesses a moral firmness ("standeth for ever," Eccles 1:4) and charitable fruitfulness ("yielding fruit after its kind," Gen 1:11). Regarding the virtues that the congregation must possess, Aquinas adds that we "should be low as the earth in humility. Proverbs 11:2: 'Where humility is, there also is wisdom.'"[38] If we possess humility and stand firm in virtue, God's teaching will "bear fruit" in us.

The practice of receiving God's teaching through the mediation of a preacher fosters the humility that enables the congregation to learn divine wisdom. Aquinas goes on to quote three further texts from the Old Testament wisdom literature: Sirach 6:34, "If thou wilt incline thy ear, thou shalt receive instruction: and if thou love to hear, thou shalt be wise"; Job 12:11, "Doth not the ear discern words?"; and Proverbs 9:9, "Give occasion to a wise man, and wisdom shall be added to him."[39] In short, humble listening to the word of God, when combined with moral rectitude, will bear fruit in a life of wisdom.

Let us pause and review the three steps that Aquinas has taken thus far. Using Old Testament texts, Aquinas first calls to mind that Scripture is divine wisdom. Second, Aquinas urges preachers to attend to the authoritative exegesis of the Fathers of the Church, because of their proximity to Christ in holiness. Third, again relying upon the Old Testament, Aquinas points out that the congregation must be humble and morally upright so as to receive fruitfully the scriptural wisdom.

Aquinas's fourth and final step, then, is to meditate upon the task of preaching, the "order" of communicating wisdom. Since the divine wisdom is infinite, "not everything that is contained in divine wisdom can be grasped by

36. Ibid. 37. Ibid.
38. Ibid. 39. Ibid., 16.

the minds of the teachers."[40] Aquinas finds it significant in this respect that Psalm 104:13 speaks of "upper rooms" rather than the *highest* rooms. Likewise, he quotes Job 26:14 as applicable here: "Lo, these things are said in part."[41] Just as God must adapt the infinite divine wisdom to the limits of the minds of human preachers, so also human preachers of the Old Testament must adapt their speech to their less learned audience. In thus adapting their speech, however, preachers should recall that they are fundamentally on the same level as the audience. Since the preacher's knowledge itself falls far short of exhausting the divine wisdom, the preacher in any case gives the audience a merely partial knowledge of the divine wisdom.

If the preacher's words fall so short of the divine wisdom, however, what use is the preacher? Calling to mind Job 12:13, "With him is wisdom and strength; he hath counsel and understanding," Aquinas contrasts God's natural possession of divine wisdom with human preachers' mere participation in divine wisdom. Thanks to God's generosity, however, this participation is not a stingy one. Aquinas states that "teachers share in wisdom abundantly. Hence they are said to be watered from on high. Ecclesiasticus 24:42: 'I said I will water my garden of plants, and I will water abundantly the fruits of my meadow.'"[42] The preacher of the Old Testament will receive abundant "water." Can such preachers share this "water" with the audience? They can indeed, but not by their own power. Aquinas emphasizes that in contrast to God the Teacher, who "communicates wisdom by his own power," the preacher is but a minister through whom God teaches.[43] To be a useful minister of God's teaching, the preacher must be innocent, wise, zealous, and obedient, as Aquinas preaches by means of Psalm 101:6, Proverbs 14:35, Psalm 104:4, and Psalm 103:21. Such a wise and holy preacher can lead others to the abundant participation in God's wisdom enjoyed by the preacher: "the satiety of the earth signifies this; Psalm 16 [17]:15: 'I shall be satisfied with the sight of thee.'"[44]

The first lecture that we examined offered an overview, a blueprint, of Aquinas's understanding of the Old Testament. In this second lecture, Aquinas is concerned with the communication of divine wisdom. Both lectures present the Old Testament as divine wisdom, God the Teacher's pedagogy, but the second one is more concerned to show whether and how divine wisdom can be efficaciously preached to those who do not devote their lives to seeking to understand divine wisdom.

40. Ibid.   41. Ibid.
42. Ibid.   43. Ibid., 17.
44. Ibid., 16.

Conclusion

Quoting the Second Vatican Council's Dogmatic Constitution on Divine Revelation, *Dei Verbum*, the *Catechism of the Catholic Church* observes: "[T]he books of the Old Testament bear witness to the whole divine pedagogy of God's saving love: these writings 'are a storehouse of sublime teaching on God and of sound wisdom on human life, as well as a wonderful treasury of prayers; in them, too, the mystery of our salvation is present in a hidden way.'"[45] The *Catechism* goes on to observe that "[e]arly Christian catechesis made constant use of the Old Testament," and that although Christians read the Old Testament "in the light of Christ crucified and risen," nonetheless "the Old Testament retains its own intrinsic value as Revelation reaffirmed by our Lord himself."[46] For Aquinas, too, Christ's fulfillment of the Torah reveals the "whole divine pedagogy of God's saving love." Since this fulfillment is not a negation, the Old Testament remains "a storehouse of sublime teaching on God and of sound wisdom on human life." The Decalogue, the prophets' teachings, and the hagiographers' and apocrypha's instruction in virtue continue to provide this "sound wisdom."

In Aquinas's lectures, the *Catechism*'s (and *Dei Verbum*'s) description of the Old Testament as "divine pedagogy," a "storehouse," and "sound wisdom" takes on further depth and richness. As we have seen, Aquinas does not envision the Old Testament as a jumbled storehouse. Instead, he recognizes in the Old Testament a wisdom—a well-ordered knowledge—that leads the human teacher and preacher to the divine Teacher. Guided by the divine Teacher, human teachers and preachers ponder the order of God's wisdom for human salvation in *sacra scriptura,* and seek to communicate this order to others. *Sacra doctrina* thus communicates an ordering that enlightens our minds and guides our loves. Although the teacher/preacher cannot hope to measure up to the divine wisdom that the Old Testament reveals, nonetheless the words of a holy and wise human teacher can communicate the divine wisdom that teaches, delights, and changes the hearer through the power of God. Read in this way, the Old Testament invites participation in the ordering wisdom of God. Aquinas thus finds the Old Testament to be "inspired by God and profitable for teaching, for reproof, for correction, and for training in righteousness, that the man of God may be complete, equipped for every good work" (2 Tim 3:16–17). Contemplating the Old Testament, "the man of God" discerns, and seeks to communicate to others, the ordering wisdom of God.

45. *Catechism of the Catholic Church,* § 122, citing *Dei Verbum,* § 15.
46. *Catechism of the Catholic Church,* § 129.

[3]

The Precarity of Wisdom
Modern Dominican Theology, Perspectivalism, and the Tasks of Reconstruction

THOMAS JOSEPH WHITE, O.P.

Theology is today passing through a serious crisis which has raised doubts concerning its very purpose. The fragmentation of the theological disciplines, which often more or less oppose one another, has led many theologians to speculate as to the validity of their efforts . . . To resolve this crisis, which has to do with the very notion of truth itself, there can be but one solution: to give back to theology an understanding of the Mystery of Christ, in the eschatological call to the beatific vision . . . There is no denying (to express the matter in patristic categories), that revelation has taken the form of an "economy," by which we mean a historical dispensation of salvation, made up of divine and human acts, and into which we gain access through our own time-conditioned acts, but this "economy" implies and necessarily calls for a "theology." By this we mean a revelation and a contemplation of the Mystery of God Himself, the supra-historical element without which sacred history would not be, and would never be truly known . . . It is thus history itself which, in the Mystery of Christ, calls for a perspective of Wisdom.[1]

This essay is an extended version of a talk delivered at the symposium "Albert the Great, Educator," November 27, 2007, at the Dominican School of Philosophy and Theology, Berkeley, California. A shorter version of the essay previously appeared in *Listening*, vol. 43, no. 3 (2008): 167–85. This particular issue of the journal was guest edited by Richard Schenk.

1. M. J. Le Guillou, *Christ and Church: A Theology of the Mystery*, trans. C. Schaldenbrand (New York: Desclee, 1966), 350–51.

I

The extremes touch, as the French like to say, and this is nowhere more evident in modern Dominican theology than in the symbolic internecine conflict surrounding Marie-Dominique Chenu's famous work *Le Saulchoir: Une école de théologie*, published in 1937, just as he had assumed the office of regent at the institution of that same title.[2] The book, as is well known, was placed on the Index by the Holy Office in 1942; and this led to the eventual purge of the Saulchoir in that same year, a reordering conducted under the theological and political direction of Reginald Garrigou-Lagrange, Michael Browne, and Thomas Philippe.[3] At stake in the interpretation of this work was nothing less than the central issue confronting modern Catholic theology in the twentieth century more generally: the relation between the historical character of human existence and human knowledge and the supposedly absolute, unchanging truth claims of Christian revelation. Chenu was a gifted medieval historian whose landmark treatment of Aquinas in his historical context demonstrated, among other things, the profound influence of Augustine and Dionysius upon Aquinas. His work contributed in important ways to the rise of modern historical Thomistic studies, especially in the Dominican Order.[4] Yet in *Une école de théologie* we find him applying historicizing theories not to the study of the context and composition of medieval works of theology, but to the doctrinal *content* of faith itself. Chenu claims therein that "Theological systems are only the expression of spiritualities" of a given historical epoch and setting. Therefore, "a theology worthy of the name is a spirituality, which finds the rational instruments adequate to its religious experience."[5] Religious experience is understood here in culturally situated terms, and somewhat individ-

2. Marie-Dominique Chenu, *Le Saulchoir: Une ecole de théologie* (Paris: Cerf, 1937).

3. See the recent discussion of these events by Fergus Kerr, *Twentieth-Century Catholic Theologians* (Oxford: Blackwell Publishing, 2007), 17–26. Of course the conflicts over *la nouvelle théologie* were more complex, and eventually developed into controversies between Roman Thomism and the Dominicans of Toulouse on the one hand, with multiple thinkers of (principally) the Society of Jesus and the Dominican Paris province on the other. See on this historical period, Etienne Fouilloux, "Dialogue théologique? (1946–1948)," in *Saint Thomas au XXe siècle: Actes du colloque centenaire de la "Revue Thomiste,"* ed. Serge-Thomas Bonino (Paris: Editions Saint-Paul, 1994), 153–98; and Aidan Nichols, "Thomism and the Nouvelle Théologie," *The Thomist* 64, no. 1 (2000): 1–19.

4. Along with the efforts of persons like his colleague Etienne Gilson. See Marie-Dominique Chenu, *Introduction à l'étude de S. Thomas d'Aquin* (Paris: Vrin, 1950), and the remarks of Kerr, *Twentieth-Century Catholic Theologians*, 27–29, 32–33. Kerr is no doubt correct in noting the contribution of this aspect of Chenu's example in the contemporary work of theologians such as Jean-Pierre Torrell and Gilles Emery.

5. Chenu, *Une ecole de théologie*, 148–49.

ualistically. The saints are those spiritual figures who "re-situate" the ongoing significance of Christianity in each historical age. The purposeful allusions to the themes of the modernist crisis in this form of thinking are, of course, evident. This seemingly historicizing interpretation of both faith and theological doctrine stands in some tension with the well-known condemnations of *Pascendi Dominici Gregis*, as Chenu was only too well aware.[6] That document, issued by Pope Pius X on September 8, 1907, specifically criticizes the idea that doctrines of the faith are elaborated primarily in and through recourse to individual historical experiences. In fact, as *Une école de théologie* and other writings of Chenu would suggest, not only are the *propositional forms of expression* of the faith considered here to be so many historically diverse ways of communicating a transcendent and timeless truth, but the *doctrinal content of faith itself* seems to be something intrinsically historical, subject to individual experience, historical unfolding, and individual apperception, in light of each person's "spirituality."

His brief statements in this text are admittedly ambiguous. But when one considers the possible trajectory of this path of thinking, it is not surprising that Chenu was asked by the Order in 1938 to sign statements in Rome asserting that he believed that "dogmatic formulas articulate absolute and immutable truths" and that "Sacred Theology . . . is true *science* . . . which has as its *principles* the articles of the faith" as expressed by the Creed.[7]

At the other extreme of this historical scenario we find Reginald Garrigou-Lagrange, the former teacher of Chenu at the Angelicum, and now his theological judge in 1938. In 1941, while Chenu's case was in process in Rome, Garrigou-Lagrange was composing a well-known, and in many ways helpful, theological book which many of us have read, titled *The Mother of the Saviour and Our Interior Life*.[8]

6. See Pius X, *Pascendi Dominici Gregis*, §§ 14–15. The "model" modernist whose work is often thought to be envisaged here is that of August Sabatier, the Protestant theorist and historian of St. Francis, whose theories of doctrine appeal to Schleiermacher's concepts of religious experience. An informative treatment of the modernist crisis in France is offered by Pierre Colin, *L'audace et le soupçon: la crise du modernisme dans le catholicisme français 1893–1914* (Paris: Desclée et Brouwer, 1997). Chenu was certainly well informed on this point; one may reasonably speculate that his language was meant to provoke.

7. "Formulae dogmaticae enunciant veritatem absolutam et immutabilem . . . Sacra Theologia non est quaedam spiritualitas quae invenit instrumenta suae experientiae religiosae adaequata; sed est vera scientia . . . cujus principia sunt articuli Fidei et etiam omnes veritates revelatae quibus theologus fide divina, saltem informi, adhaeret." For a list of the ten propositions Chenu was required to sign, see Kerr, *Twentieth-Century Catholic Theologians*, 19.

8. See Reginald Garrigou-Lagrange, *La Mère du Sauveur et notre vie intérieure* (Lyon: Edit. de l'Abeille, 1941), available in English as *The Mother of the Saviour and Our Interior Life*, trans. B. Kelly (St. Louis: Herder, 1948).

Consider for a moment some characteristics of this book of Mariology. Garrigou-Lagrange begins the discussion of the Blessed Virgin *in media res* with a discussion of the Baroque disputes between Thomists and Molinists concerning the theology of the merits of the Mother of God: *condigno* versus *congruo* merits, and among *congruo* merits those which are termed "proper" versus those which are "improper."[9] Herein the author makes an edifying theological point. "What Mary could merit by the first fullness of grace, which she received gratuitously in view of the foreseen merits of her Son, was an increase of charity and the higher degree of purity and holiness which was becoming in the Mother of God."[10] What this signifies is that grace is gratuitously given and yet permits a truly meritorious participation in the eternal designs of God. There is no opposition between the primary causality of God and the meritorious secondary causality of the creature, just as there is no opposition of grace and created freedom. Rather, there is an assimilation and augmentation of the latter by the former.[11]

This vision of theological anthropology is salutary, certainly. Yet consider what is missing from this presentation in the historical sphere. First, we are not offered any biblical examination of the mystery of the Blessed Virgin, nor any scriptural treatment of the subjects of grace and predestination. Second, there is virtually no acknowledgment, let alone examination, of the patristic development of Marian doctrine, with its inherent complexity and pluralism, and no acknowledgment of Augustine's impact upon Aquinas's mature doctrine of grace. (Rather, Augustine's doctrine is being "read back into" Scripture as a foregone conclusion.) Third, there is no acknowledgment that the author's presentation stems from the subsequent Thomistic commentary tradition (Cajetan, the *Cursus Salmanticensis*) rather than from Aquinas himself, and undoubtedly bears the imprint of a slightly "Franciscan" rereading of Aquinas. (According to this view, the Incarnation occurs only in view of the remedy of sin, yet simultaneously fulfills God's eternally desired plan for creation: the Incarnation of God.)[12] Last, there is no acknowledgment of the fact that *meritum*

9. Garrigou-Lagrange, *La Mère du Sauveur*, 20–25.

10. Ibid., 24.

11. Interestingly, this aspect of Aquinas's thought, duly highlighted in Garrigou's interpretation, has become important in contemporary ecumenical discussion between Catholics and Lutherans on the topic of merit. See Joseph Wawrykow, *God's Grace and Human Action: 'Merit' in the Theology of Thomas Aquinas* (Notre Dame, Ind.: Notre Dame Press, 1995); and Michael Root, "Aquinas, Merit, and Reformation Theology after the *Joint Declaration on the Doctrine of Justification*," *Modern Theology* 20, no. 1 (2004): 5–22.

12. See François Daguet's analysis of Aquinas and the Thomistic commentary tradition as regards Franciscan influences on this point in his *Théologie du dessein divin chez Thomas d'Aquin* (Paris: Vrin, 2003), 209–18.

is not a word ever used in the New Testament, but derives from the third century A.D. Latin speculation on the mystery of cooperation with God's grace.
For Garrigou-Lagrange, the medieval patrimony and the decrees of the Council of Trent on merit clearly suffice to justify the use of this apparently "timeless" notion, without explanation, applied retrospectively ("timelessly") to the
life of the Blessed Virgin (and in complete indifference to Protestant and post-
Enlightenment challenges to the doctrine). Might some theological explanation of all this historical complexity be in order, precisely to *defend* the perennial importance of the doctrines presented? Methodologically, here Scripture, patristic teaching, Aquinas, and post-Tridentine Baroque theology are
all fused into one indistinguishably. Ironically, in the absence of the acknowledgment of basic historical distinctions, this seemingly "timeless" portrayal of
the grace of Mary appears to be clearly indebted to a particular historical epoch in ways that are both idiosyncratic and methodologically arbitrary. Such a
way of proceeding would surely not have been so irregular one hundred years
beforehand, in an age before the advent of modern historical studies. But in
the age of Albert Schweitzer and Rudolf Bultmann, is it permissible for Catholic theology to disregard entirely the modernist claim that the doctrines of
the Virgin Mary are no more than the subjective fabrications of the collective
spiritual consciousness of medieval piety? How does one respond to such an
objection? Are these dogmas in fact the projections of the religious experience
of the Middle Ages? Can any viable modern treatment of Marian theology
afford to simply ignore such fundamental challenges?[13]

At base, the problems encountered in the Dominican theology of Chenu
and Garrigou-Lagrange respectively differ by extremes, which in turn share a
common problematic premise. To oversimplify, in one we find history without
sufficient recourse to dogma, while in the other we have dogma without sufficient recourse to history. Neither of these approaches aspires sufficiently to the
reconciliation of a trans-historical, sapiential dogmatic theology and a modern sensitivity to the historical context of all human thought and being. On the
one hand, with Garrigou-Lagrange, we encounter a formidable array of scholastic testimony, and an arsenal of argument *ex convenientia.* There is an "ontological" consideration of the "essential" trans-historical structure of Christian mysteries, and a corresponding confidence in the perennial truth of the
Catholic doctrine. This theology can rightly be considered sapiential insofar
as its entire structure is ordered toward the contemplation of the Triune God

---

13. Analogous things could be said, of course, about Garrigou-Lagrange's Christology, but
I have sought here to refer to a theological work from the very time of the examination of Chenu's case.

revealed in Jesus Christ and toward supernatural union with the Triune God by faith and hope, in charity.[14] Yet simultaneously, the same "essentialism" ignores some of the modern questions that challenge the deposit of faith most seriously. The historical dilemmas or nuances it does not permit us to confront are in many ways the most important for the modern sapiential articulation of the faith. In other words, this theology that is insufficiently sensitive to history renders the modern quest for a perennial and sapiential theology unstable and precarious. Ironically, the attempt to avoid doctrinal relativism can turn precariously toward an arbitrary perspectivalism of its own, an insufficient attempt to preserve a theological heritage supported too much by recourse to authority and not enough by argumentative engagement.[15]

With Chenu, however, we find the inverse tendency: the emergence of a refined interpretation of Aquinas leads to scientific understanding of the historical complexities of textual and doctrinal interpretation. At the same time, this study is bound to an interpretation of theological development within tradition that is insufficiently moored to the metaphysical and perennial aspects of faith and human thought. To this approach we can now turn to sketch out the emergence of a kind of doctrinal perspectivalism present in the thought of Chenu and his theological inheritors.

Chenu's theological monographs typically show a very delicate sensitivity to historical particularities and to the ways in which cultural and spaciotemporal influences conditioned the articulation of theology in any given age. Yet the work of the modern Dominican would also seem to suggest at frequent junctures that the process of discerning the deposit of faith is so radically characterized by its historical conditions that recourse to "trans-historical" ontological notions to express the content of the faith is at best naive and at worst an obscuring of the intrinsically "dynamic" and "historically individualistic" character of all human knowledge and divine grace. This facet of Chenu's thought has been analyzed helpfully by Henri Donneaud.[16] By examining a series of Chenu's writings on faith, Donneaud shows how the medievalist introduced a *trans-historical* modern concept of ongoing *dialectic* between dogma and experience into his evaluation of the history of doctrine, and that, ironically, this ahistorical philosophical presupposition stands in contrast to the

14. I will return to the notion of *sapientia*, or wisdom, below.

15. By this I mean not that Garrigou-Lagrange was in error to appeal to a notion of normative doctrinal absolutes, but that he did not always sufficiently distinguish such doctrines in themselves from particular theological interpretations, those derived from a particular theological school—such as Thomism, and a particular brand of Thomism.

16. See Henri Donneaud, "La constitution dialectique de la théologie et de son histoire selon M. D. Chenu," *Revue thomiste* 96, no. 1 (1996): 41–66.

characterization of faith by Aquinas, to whom Chenu appealed to justify his concept of faith.[17] Such "historicization" of the life of faith, while a constant theme throughout Chenu's life, was stated in a particularly transparent way in an essay written after the Second Vatican Council.[18] Here he writes directly against the conceptions of theology of (the now deceased) Garrigou-Lagrange himself:

The Word of God both creates history and is interpreted within history . . . Understanding of the unity of Word and event, in which the truth occurs, is a fundamental point of departure for theology . . . Biblical truth . . . in keeping with the Hebraic mentality, does not directly affront that which is, but that which happens, that which one experiences . . . Greek thought develops through a reflection on the substance of beings, and terminates in a philosophy of immutability and permanence. It ignores that which is proper to biblical thought: the dimension of time . . . One must not establish a division between the act of the divine Word and the formulas in which it takes shape and which give it its intellectual content. But one also must not cede to a facile concordism in which the historical and existential character of the truth of salvation dissolves, and where the Word of God is absorbed into and neutralized by a theological "science" . . . The truth is a radically Christological concept. It should not be treated as the manifestation of the eternal essence of things. [!][19]

Thus the very nature of faith itself is determined historically through an ongoing interaction between historical experience and propositional truth. Each age has to rearticulate the truth of the Gospel in terms that are adequate to its ongoing and contemporary experience.

In the immediate wake of the Council, it was this trajectory of thinking that was to become normative in much Dominican theology. However, the tendency was also progressively radicalized. Instructive in this respect is the work of Edward Schillebeeckx, which plunges us even more deeply (and somewhat uncritically) into the most acute problems of the post-Heideggerian her-

---

17. Of note in this respect are the perspectives elaborated in Chenu, "Raison psychologique du développement du dogme," Revue des Sciences Philosophiques et Théologiques 13 (1924): 44–51, where Chenu interprets Aquinas's theory of the Aristotelian agent intellect (knowledge by abstraction, in time, and by progressive synthetic judgments) as the anthropological basis for a historical "evolution of dogma." On p. 49 he suggests that a historically situated determination of the content of faith is "essential" to the faith as such.

18. Marie-Dominique Chenu, "Vérité évangélique et métaphysique wolfienne à Vatican II," Revue des Sciences Philosophiques et Théologiques 57 (1973): 632–40.

19. Ibid., 637–38. (All translations in this essay from the French are my own unless otherwise stated.) Yves Congar seems to admit in his Tradition et Traditions, vol. 1 (Paris: Fayard, 1960), 258–59, that there is an inadequate distinction in some of Chenu's work between the actual determination of the positive norms of faith in the present (whether by the Magisterium, great spiritual figures, or theologians) and the dogmatic Tradition, which such labor is meant to serve and in which it identifies the pre-existent, enduring doctrinal patrimony.

meneutical age. In his 1966 work *Openbaring en Theologie* (Revelation and Theology), Schillebeeckx offers reflections on the conceptual and ontological character of human knowledge in relation to doctrinal hermeneutics that are based upon an insightful study of Aquinas's theological epistemology. The essay offers helpful contributions for thinking out an appropriate response to the historical queries of the modernist crisis.[20] Yet by 1968, in an important essay on hermeneutics, Schillebeeckx has restructured his thinking in dialogue with Bultmann and Gadamer. The radical historicization of all concepts and doctrines calls forth a "praxis"-centered (experiential and practical) reevaluation, in every age, of classical theological enunciations. The latter are open to fundamental reevaluation and re-articulation based upon their potential contemporary political/intellectual significance:

The objective *perspective* of faith, which is not in itself thematic and cannot be conceptualized, is thus to some extent brought to light and expressed *in* reinterpretation as it were by a circuitous route (via the interpretative aspect of the act of faith), with the consequence that it becomes a power for action which is directed towards the future . . . There are no formulae of faith which are, as formulae, enduringly valid, capable of transmitting the living faith to men of all ages. Is this relativism? Not at all. It is what is meant by the identity of the faith with itself *in history*. For we do not possess the absolute which acts as an inner norm to our faith in an absolute way; we possess it only within our historical situation.[21]

Acute illustrations of this hermeneutical method are to be found in Schillebeeckx's works that followed, especially in *Jesus: An Experiment in Christology*. Here we are offered a quasi-Marxist, liberationist account of Jesus' ministry that (we are told) flowed from his own "*Abba* experience," and which implied metaphysically the radically kenotic historicization of God himself.[22] Jesus' own aims and teachings are presented as being in potential historical discontinuity with the subsequent reinterpretations of his person offered by New Testament "ontological" Christology. However, the tension is alleviated when we realize that the latter teachings merely decipher the meaning of Jesus for the early Christian movement in terms that were applicable to their historical epoch. The ontological Christology of the New Testament was in fact derived in

20. Edward Schillebeeckx, *Revelation and Theology*, vol. 2, trans. N. Smith (New York: Sheed and Ward, 1968).

21. This work is found in English in Edward Schillebeeckx, *God and the Future of Man*, trans. N. Smith (New York: Sheed and Ward, 1968), 1–50. The citation is taken from pp. 39–40. See the study by Leo Scheffczyk, "Christology in the Context of Experience," trans. R. Schenk, *The Thomist* 48, no. 3 (1984): 383–408, on this change in Schillebeeckx's theological method.

22. Schillebeeckx, *Jesus: An Experiment in Christology*, trans. H. Hoskins (New York: Crossroad, 1979), 140–271, 652–69.

large part through "experiences of forgiveness, grace, and liberation" that occurred *after* the crucifixion. The latter experiences are accessible to us even if
the ontological terminology in which they were originally articulated is problematic and no longer sustainable today.[23]

Such a viewpoint, of course, poses critical questions for theology. If doctrine is essentially constituted not only within a historical experience of transformation in Christ but also *by* that experience, is it then also "merely" the
expression of the human individual as a being in time, without recourse to a
trans-historical measure or corrective? But in that case, are theologies anything
more than the enunciation of the religious perspectives of various cultures,
bound by the limitations of their respective historical horizons? Are all dogmas
epistemically relative? Stated more critically, are they anything other than the
expression of the will to power of any particular theological sub-group, whether officially magisterial or not? Such a perspectivalist theological viewpoint is
certainly common today and would seem to suggest the inevitability of a kind
of doctrinal relativism. Consider in this respect the doctrinal perspectivalism of Chenu's Dominican disciple, Claude Geffré (also deeply influenced by
Schillebeeckx) in his 1987 *Le Christianisme au risque de l'interpretation:*

The earlier onto-theology which provided theology with its conceptual basis was
dismantled by the new ontology of Heidegger . . . The claim of theology to be a perfect and universal systemization of the Christian message has come into direct confrontation with the contemporary criticism of ideology and especially with the latter's vow of non-dialectical totalization, its rejection of all historical complexity, and
its stubborn resistance to what is real. All of us are, after all, marked by a Nietzschean suspicion of truth. Truth is not "perspectivalist," but we have to admit that it
can only be reached within a certain perspective. All discourse is therefore provisional and relative. There is no knowledge—only a language of interpretation that
is relative to the perspective of the one who speaks it . . . This sharpened consciousness does not necessarily lead to the destruction of a dogmatic faith in the Christian sense of the word, but it does make us view more cautiously a certain kind of
dogmatic theology that is offered to us as the only authentic way of interpreting the
Christian message . . . Autonomy of consciousness is an inescapable datum of modern life, and it goes together with a rejection of the claim, made in the name of the
authority of God or of the Church's Magisterium, that theological knowledge is infallible . . . "Authoritarian" theologies such as those of the Word of God in the Bar-
thian sense or Catholic theologies like those of the Roman school are no longer in
accordance with the contemporary order of the Spirit.[24]

23. See on these points, Schillebeeckx, *Jesus,* 390–97; *Christ: The Experience of Jesus as Lord,*
trans. J. Bowden (New York: Crossroad, 1981), 30–64.
24. Claude Geffré, *The Risk of Interpretation: On Being Faithful to the Christian Tradition in*

These conclusions are interesting due to their radicality. However, their radicality can be restated critically: On what grounds may one rule out a priori the epistemological *possibility* of infallible revelation? Whose perspective determines the identification of the "norms of the contemporary order" by which classical dogma is judged? What is the "Spirit" that the author identifies as governing the existing order of our world, what are its characteristics and how are they identified? And perhaps more fundamentally, if all discourse is provisional, are universal claims to the provisionality of discourse still philosophically advisable, or are they not inevitably subject to the accusation of a "hidden will to power"? In this case, should we not have recourse to the more logically consistent logical inconsistency and self-consciously self-contradicting perspectives of post-structuralists such as Jacques Derrida? In such a context, however, the project of a dogmatic theology would evidently be futile. In any event, it is clear that once we enter into the thick of a post-metaphysical, hermeneutical methodology, the claims of a perennial Christian truth seem deeply compromised, and the transcendent aspirations of a contemplative, sapiential theology, irrevocably undermined.

What might we conclude, then, from these reflections on perspectivalism? Tentatively, we could suggest the following two conclusions. First, without an explicit recognition of the human mind's orientation toward the transcendent wisdom of God, and a corresponding ontologically informed dogmatic approach to the mysteries of the Holy Trinity, Jesus Christ, the Church, and human beings, theology becomes a discourse disconnected from veridical necessities. It can then be accused (perhaps even rightly) of being primarily concerned with the uses and abuses of power, and the rhetorical discourse required to achieve cultural relevance for marginalized groups.[25] This vision of theology is as prevalent today as it is problematic. Clearly, then, the issues present in the debates of 1942 are still very much our own, and even more so.[26] Second, it is ironic to note that the perspectivalist tendency in modern theolo-

a Non-Christian Age, trans. D. Smith (New York: Paulist Press, 1987), 14–15. This is the English translation of *Le Christianisme au risque de l'interpretation.*

25. However, even this vision of theology—with both its post-modern proponents and its theoretically nihilist critics—relies implicitly upon an unsaid intellectual commitment to either a normative notion of the inclusive good or the normativity of the celebration of the will to power. Ironically, in either case, appeal to a certain form of metaphysical teleology becomes theoretically and existentially inevitable, even if such presuppositions are not explicitly acknowledged. Appeal to veridical necessities is not abolished, but only concealed.

26. On the question of perennial truth claims as related to the problem of hermeneutics, see the helpful statement by the International Theological Commission, "On the Interpretation of Dogmas," *Origins* 20 (1990): 1–14; Bernard Sesboüé, *Hors de l'église pas de salut* (Paris: Desclée de Brouwer, 2004), 323–74; George Cottier, "Thomisme et modernité," in Bonino, *Saint Thomas au XXe siècle,* 352–61.

gy briefly sketched above is hindered by the same methodological weakness as the theology of Garrigou-Lagrange previously considered, except in the form of a mirror image. Like two sides of the same coin, what these two approaches have in common is a failure to seek to resolve seriously the divide between,on the one hand, classical dogma and ontology, and, on the other, modern historical studies. Truth, however, like existence, embraces both being and time. In this sense, the relativism of a historicist account of theology—which is due precisely to the account's rejection of a classical ontology—also ignores the task of integration within the human subject just as much as (or even more than?) the forebear to which it reacts.

Is such perspectivalism theoretically remediable, however? There are some formidable reasons to think it is culturally insurmountable. For behind the intellectual problem of perspectivalism there stands the modern impact of the Kantian critique of metaphysics and its corresponding "Copernican revolution" in epistemology, compounded by the nineteenth-century, historical philosophy of Hegel and the twentieth-century, hermeneutical philosophies of Wilhelm Dilthey, Martin Heidegger, and Hans-Georg Gadamer. It goes without saying that this is not the place to attempt to present an argument on this vast topic of modern epistemology and hermeneutics. For the moment, let me make the suggestion that the Kantian and Heideggerian projects should be subject to critical scrutiny and are vulnerable to radical correction on a variety of fronts. They can and ought to be appropriately criticized and contextualized by sound considerations taken from classical ontology. I will refer briefly to these matters further below. First, however, I am going to return to some basic notions of theology as a sapiential discipline in Aquinas, as they are understood by some of his modern interpreters. In doing so I will simply allude to some Thomistic responses to the predicament delineated above, which I think are essential conditions of any possible response to the modern problem of this needed "reconciliation" between historical sensitivities and classical dogma. After this I will seek to illustrate three key areas of Catholic theology where the task of reconciliation between dogma and history is especially important and where I think future Catholic and Dominican theology will need to focus.

II

First then, the question of *sapientia*. Lest it seem profitless to turn from the quarrels of modern study back to the medieval vision of St. Albert and St. Thomas, let me begin by stating formally what I take to be the aspiration to theology as a form of wisdom in these thinkers, and especially in Aquinas's later thought. In doing so I would like to make clear in what way I understand their vision of theology to be extremely pertinent to the above-mentioned quarrels.

In the opening question of the *Summa theologiae* I, article 6, Aquinas asks in what sense is *sacra doctrina* a form of wisdom. And here he makes three key affirmations. Theological science that is based upon divine revelation aspires to be a wisdom, first because it allows us to consider our world in light of the most ultimate principles and causes of all things. This knowledge is itself already a graced participation in that ultimate knowledge which God has of himself and of the created order. To know the self-disclosing Triune God, then, is to know the source of all that is, *including all inferior and dependent causes*. Second, the knowledge transmitted by theology is inherently ethical in orientation. It unveils to us the final purpose of human existence: the union with God. It also provides understanding of the "natural law" inscribed in creation, itself stemming from and participating in the "eternal law" of the wisdom of God. Consequently, *sacra doctrina* as a form of "wisdom" should structure our prudence, teaching us how to live in this world in view of the beatitude which is realized by the grace of Christ.[27] Third, in response 2 of the same article, Aquinas insists that the highest wisdom may "judge" the adequacy of the conclusions of inferior disciplines for their truthfulness or falsity. However, it may not ever *substitute itself* for the adequate demonstrative processes of these sciences.[28] In other words, a theologian may rightly judge whether a conclusion of philosophy, natural science, history, or exegesis stands rightly in accord with the principles of faith and, therefore, determine, in certain cases, that such a conclusion is true or false. But he may not and cannot substitute this discernment of faith for the hard work of demonstration that is proper to the "secondary" or "subordinate" science in question. For to do this would require a competency of demonstrative knowledge in philosophy, natural science, exegesis, etc. Con-

---

27. *ST* I, q. 1, a. 6 (Leon. IV, 17): "Cum enim sapientis sit ordinare et iudicare, iudicium autem per altiorem causam de inferioribus habeatur; ille sapiens dicitur in unoquoque genere, qui considerat causam altissimam illius generis . . . Et rursus, in genere totius humanae vitae, prudens sapiens dicitur, inquantum ordinat humanos actus ad debitum finem . . . Ille dicitur qui considerat simpliciter altissimam causam totius universi, quae Deus est, maxime sapiens dicitur."

28. *ST* I, q. 1, a. 6, ad 2 (Leon. IV, 18): "Dicendum quod aliarum scientiarum principia [other than those of sacred doctrine] vel sunt per se nota, et probari non possunt vel per aliquam rationem naturalem probantur in aliqua alia scientia. Propria autem huius scientiae cognitio est, quae est per revelationem non autem quae est per naturalem rationem. *Et ideo non pertinet ad eam probare principia aliarum scientiarum,* sed solum iudicare de eis. Quidquid enim in aliis scientiis invenitur veritati huius scientiae repugnans, totum condemnatur ut falsum" (emphasis added).

sequently, as Aquinas states very explicitly in his *Commentary on Boethius's De Trinitate,* one aspect of the work of theology is the "integration" or assimilation of the valid reasoning of the lower sciences into the articulation of theological truths.[29] The theologian may make use of philosophy, for example, but to do so must also argue philosophically in a competent and integral way, employing philosophy in some real sense on its own terms. We could say similar things about the natural sciences, history, exegesis, and a host of other disciplines.

If we schematize succinctly these observations, we may note three chief characteristics of a sapiential theology, according to Aquinas. First of all, this theology concerns itself with ultimate perspectives. Theology is based upon some real knowledge of the ultimate truth about the source of reality. Insofar as it transcends the variegated perspectives of passing human civilizations, it finds its grounds not in mere conjecture or opinion, but in true knowledge concerning the transcendent mystery of God. Precisely because of this perspective, such "wisdom" also permits a *unification* of all lower forms of discourse and all inferior kinds of learning. Its subject matter offers "ultimate interpretive meaning" to all else that we can know through our natural cognitive acquisitions. Second, this wisdom offers us a certain answer to the ultimate question: "What may I hope for?" It is practically directive of our human acts because it spells out final purposes. Third, however, this form of knowledge must seek to make these two former truths (the first cause and final end of man) present or manifest in relation to the lower sciences, if it is to be sufficiently "incarnate" in the broader culture of human learning and activity. This requires competency in these "lower sciences" taken on their own terms. In other words, *sacra doctrina* gives ultimate perspective on the meaning of reality and human life, *but precisely in order to do so adequately*—in a comprehensive way—it must make itself manifest *in and through* the cultural matrix of philosophy, the natural sciences, history, and exegesis. In doing so it must also "relocate" these truths within the context of a more fundamental interpretation. Dogma and the spiritual life offer more determinate "explanations" of meaning than other forms of discourse. The partial viewpoints of the latter

---

29. See *Expos. de Trin.,* q. 2, a. 3. The case under consideration is that of philosophy. Aquinas notes here three uses of philosophy in theology (Leon. L, pp. 98–99): "primo ad demonstrandum ea que sunt praeambula fidei, que necesse est in fide scire, ut ea que naturalibus rationibus de Deo probantur, ut Deum esse, Deum esse unum, et alia huiusmodi uel de Deo uel de creaturis in philosophia probate, que fides supponit; secundo ad notificandum, per aliquas similitudines ea que sunt fidei, sicut Augustinus in libro *De Trinitate* utitur multis similitudinibus ex doctrinis philosophicis sumptis ad manifestandum trinitatem; tertio ad resistendum his que contra fidem dicitur, siue ostendendo ea esse falsa, siue ostendendo ea non esse necessaria."

take on their ultimate sense and signification only because of the unique perspective of the former.

The moral of the story is easy to discern: we cannot have dogma without historical learning. And here I am taking modern "historical learning" in the broader sense, so as to include the "histories" of modern cosmology, anthropology, biblical studies, and modern intellectual history. Yet conversely, this entire "explosion" of learning is ultimately unified and explicable, for Christian theology, only in light of the dogmatic, ontological, and contemplative perspectives of Christian theology.[30] These forms of discourse take on their ultimate meaning only in light of the revelation of the Triune God. And the ethical significance of modern scientific or historical discoveries needs to be interpreted always in light of the human being's most ultimate vocation to eternal beatitude, a gift that is possible only for a human being with a rational soul made in God's image, endowed with immaterial spiritual faculties of intellect and will. Anything less than this "dual integrity" of natural learning and supernatural, grace-induced perspective, would be wholly inadequate.

I will return shortly to this question of an integrated, assimilative perspective in dogmatic theology. First, however, I would like to note what I think are three required aspects of such a theology, corresponding presuppositions that would have to be present for any such theology to be possible today. This list is not meant to be exhaustive, but only suggestively relevant to our topic.

First, such a perspective presupposes that the human intellect is capable of a genuinely metaphysical range of knowledge.[31] This metaphysical dimension of human knowing is implicitly present in every basic act of cognition. In the words of Aquinas, "primo cadit in intellectu ens."[32] The first "thing" that enters

---

30. See the study related to this complex topic by Reinhard Hütter, "Aquinas: The Directedness of Reasoning and the Metaphysics of Creation," in *Reason and the Reasons of Faith*, ed. Paul J. Griffiths and Reinhard Hütter (New York and London: T & T Clark, 2005), 160–93.

31. Cf. Pope John Paul II, encyclical *Fides et Ratio*, § 83. The pope speaks about "the need for a philosophy of *genuinely metaphysical* range, capable, that is, of transcending empirical data in order to attain something absolute, ultimate, and foundational in its search for truth. This requirement is implicit in sapiential and analytical knowledge alike; and in particular it is a requirement for knowing the moral good, which has its ultimate foundation in the Supreme Good, God himself . . . [Here] I want only to state that reality and truth do transcend the factual and the empirical, and to vindicate the human being's capacity to know this transcendent and metaphysical dimension in a way that is true and certain, albeit imperfect and analogical. In this sense, metaphysics should not be seen as an alternative to anthropology, since it is metaphysics which makes it possible to ground the concept of personal dignity in virtue of their spiritual nature. In a special way, the person constitutes a privileged locus for the encounter with being, and hence with metaphysical enquiry."

32. *ST* I, q. 5, a. 2 (Leon. IV, p. 58): "Respondeo dicendum quod ens secundum rationem est prius quam bonum. Ratio enim significata per nomen, est id quod concipit intellectus de re, et

the mind is being. And of course with the intellectual apprehension of being, for Aquinas, one must simultaneously affirm the capacity to know truly (however imperfectly and progressively) essences *(essentia)* or natural kinds, as well as the capacity to make true judgments concerning existence *(esse)*. With the later there is also the implicit knowledge of truth, unity, and the goodness that is co-extensive with all that has being (in other words, the transcendentals).[33] This initial awareness can be formalized through the philosophical study of metaphysics, and it eventually offers us the possibility to contemplate indirectly and analogically the ultimate source of all beings, God. Consequently, I am claiming that a Catholic theology that is genuinely open to a contemplation of the transcendent mystery of God must also be a theology that acknowledges the natural capacity of the human mind for God. In order for ordinary human knowledge to be able to be oriented toward a higher and more ultimate perspective which illumines it *by revelation,* it must have an inbuilt orientation, as it were, toward the absolute, undisclosed truth about the source of all existence and toward the ultimate good for which the human heart strives. If the human person is not *naturally* capable of such trans-historical, metaphysical truth, the claim to a perennially valid "truth" and "goodness" of revelation is simply unintelligible. No architechtonic science of theology is possible, and revelation is either completely extrinsic to our nature and understanding (and situated toward us merely equivocally and dialectically) or intrinsically meaningless.[34]

---

significat illud per vocem, illud ergo est prius secundum rationem, quod prius cadit in conceptione intellectus. Primo autem in conceptione intellectus cadit ens, quia secundum hoc unumquodque cognoscibile est, inquantum est actu, ut dicitur in IX metaphys."

33. Consider, for example, *ST* I, q. 16, a. 4, ad 2 (Leon. IV, 211): "Ad secundum dicendum quod secundum hoc est aliquid prius ratione, quod prius cadit in intellectu. Intellectus autem per prius apprehendit ipsum ens; et secundario apprehendit se intelligere ens; et tertio apprehendit se appetere ens. Unde primo est ratio entis, secundo ratio veri, tertio ratio boni, licet bonum sit in rebus."

34. Today, the affirmation of such a claim immediately exposes one to the charge of "totalizing discourses," "onto-theology," and even ecclesio-political fascism. See, for example, Geffré, *The Risk of Interpretation,* 14–15. Here, however, some nuances are required. First, it is evident that some form of metaphysical universalism is the condition of possibility for a shared conception of truth and responsibility. If no "knowledge of natural kinds" is discernable, then the human mind is incapable even of the most basic narrative histories required for any realist hermeneutical project. In this case, even the goal of mutual comprehension and tolerance becomes impossible. Second, the Thomistic claim that we have an imperfect but real knowledge of being, essence, and the transcendentals is not to be confused with the claim that we have quidditative knowledge of the transcendent God. As Aquinas does not consider God to fall within the transcendentals or transcendental range of knowing as an "object" of knowledge, and since he rejects categorically the possibility of all but a mediated a posteriori knowledge of God from his effects, it is clear that the specific form of "onto-theology" delineated by Kant and Heidegger is not applicable to his form of thought in any kind of direct way. The contemporary literature on this is widespread. On onto-theology see the seminal work of Olivier Boulnois, *Être et représen-*

Second, all historical study presupposes ontology. Here there is no doubt a reckoning to be had with the legacy of Kant's philosophy. In the face of historicism, it is necessary to argue that a metaphysical capacity for deciphering natural forms is already implicitly active in our experience of things as they undergo change in and through time. This knowledge of essences or natural kinds is a *sine qua non* necessity for any narrative study of forms, because it allows us to chart alterations in distinct subjects of diverse kinds. Otherwise, we would be unable to identify the subjects of change and to chart their alterations intelligibly.[35] This is true not only in the modern sciences but even in the study of the history of ideas, which presupposes the possibility of identifying clearly an intelligible narrative of diversified forms of thought, for example, from the ideas of Wolff and Hume to those of Kant. Yet to be able to situate things within the context of their coming to be, their development, and their mutation or substantial alteration also presupposes that the mind has itself a level of reflection that transcends change and is superior to the temporal. In fact, in some real sense, thought is the condition of possibility for time, and not the inverse. Formally speaking, time is an intellectual measure of real change, and it can only occur within the mind. Yet it is possible as an intellectual construction only because the person who measures change has some reference or references beyond the changes in question, by which to regulate the measurements.[36] In "thinking time," then, the human mind is conditioned by the

tation (Paris: Presse Universitaires de France, 1999), esp. 457–554; and the recent work of Jean-François Courtine, *Inventio analogiae: Métaphysique et ontothéologie* (Paris: Vrin, 2005), esp. 243–90; and Thierry-Dominique Humbrecht, *Théologie négative et noms divins chez Saint Thomas d'Aquin* (Paris: Vrin, 2005), esp. 13–80. God, then, can in no way enter into a system of totalizing discourse, if approached in this way. Third, for Aquinas metaphysics allows us to grasp something of God analogically and indirectly. It thereby tends toward the knowledge of God as the origin of all human existence and as the universal good for all human beings. Such knowledge in turn facilitates the recognition of the ontological "space" in which other persons exist and act, as beings who participate in the goodness of God in different and complementary ways. Likewise, understanding of God in no way excludes a legitimate complementarity of diverse philosophical and theological discoveries. On the contrary, the simultaneous transcendence of God and possibility of true knowledge of God make place for a shared inquiry into truth, and they make possible the intellectual synthesis of legitimately concordant efforts.

35. See Jacques Maritain, *Œuvres Complètes*, vol. X, *Pour une philosophie de l'histoire* (Fribourg and Paris: Editions Universitaires and Editions St. Paul, 1985), 613–48. This idea is already present in Aristotle's *Physics*, II, 1–2, where he makes clear that the apperception of formal determinations within realities that undergo material change provides the condition of possibility for the intelligibility of becoming and, consequently, a "causal science" of becoming is possible. This can be affirmed without ignoring the modern scientific discovery that natural forms (both inorganic and organic) themselves have "cosmic histories" in which they have come to be and will eventually cease to be. Similar things can be said about teleology, a point I will return to below.

36. As Cottier points out in "Thomisme et Modernité," 355–57, perspectivalism derives

spacio-temporal, but its understanding extends to structures of reality that are more "fundamental" ontologically than the processes of change themselves. When we know that things *exist* and *what* things are *essentially,* we are in some sense situated on a level "beyond" that of mere flux and becoming; and it is this "transcendental range" of knowing that makes the scientific study of historical development possible at all.

On the other hand, however, this also means that historical study, whether that of the natural sciences or human culture, is a priori invested with an implicit higher significance. Change and the complexity of historical individuality are part and parcel of the nature of the real. And therefore not only are all the "positive" sciences implicitly dependent upon ontology: they also illustrate or manifest the ontological. The lesser causes in creation have the power to unveil the reality and presence of the superior source indirectly. Likewise, the historical has the power to unveil the true "shape" or the characteristics of the ontological. For this reason, the study of the historical character of reality is part and parcel of a higher sapiential study of the world. The lesser sciences are in no way "extrinsic" to theology, even if they are "distinct" from it. Rather they "participate" in its mission, each at its own level and with its degree of dignity.

Third, theological interpretation presupposes the existence of teleology and a teleologically oriented subject who construes meaning. Alasdair MacIntyre has demonstrated this point in compelling fashion on a philosophical level in his critique of Michel Foucault.[37] There really is not a possibility of a narrative of the self which does not presuppose a trans-narrative ontology. Even there where the deconstructionist formulates a speculative theory that negates the existence of the interpretive subject, his practical action of inter-

---

historically and logically from Kantian epistemological historicism, wherein the human intellect cannot transcend the spacio-temporal and in which ideas are always "situated" by such temporal context. By contrast, Aquinas affirms (see for example *ST* I-II, q. 53, a. 3, ad 3; I, q. 85, a. 5, ad 2) that the intellectual part of the soul is by both its nature and its object situated "above" temporal change. Aquinas distinguishes between the historical, sensible conditions of the intellect's exercise in time and the ontological character of its object. Metaphysically realistic knowing therefore takes place in time, but the objects of reason are not determined uniquely by the processes of temporal change. The intellect attains to "that which exists." He applies this distinction to the "object of faith," as well, as compared with the temporal expressions to which the faith gives rise, noting that the object of faith itself is not "diversified" by the plurality of expressions of the truth that stem from the historical *conditions* of human knowing. See *In Sent.* IV, d. 2, q. 2, a. 1 (ed. Moos, n. 95): "Fides, cum sit cognitio ideo quaedam, respicit rei veritatem; et quia diversitas temporum significatorum non diversificat veritatem, nec fides penes hoc diversificatur."

37. Alasdair Macintyre, *Three Rival Versions of Moral Inquiry* (Notre Dame, Ind.: Notre Dame University Press, 1990), 196–215.

pretation inevitably gives rise to a narrative through the habitual free action of the subject. In contrast to Nietzsche and his heirs, we should be prepared to argue that the articulation of voluntary desire presupposes an ontological unity of the personal subject in whom that desire inheres, and which this desire characterizes or manifests.[38] We are teleologically ordered beings. For Catholic theology, the interpretive project of understanding and explanation is itself teleological. It is rooted more fundamentally in the deeper human quest for meaning, and this quest is, in some sense, inevitable.

Furthermore, from a Christian point of view, this quest is only ever resolved in an ultimate way eschatologically, since the ultimate good of the human person is found in God alone. *Sapientia* implies finalization through union with God by grace. Correspondingly, the ways we unite ourselves to God by grace in this life—through practical action—are a proximate end or purpose for our theology. Quite concretely, then, all theology is moral, spiritual, liturgical, and sacramental in orientation, since in all these loci we are united with God in this life. Theology presupposes the vital influence of the gifts of the Holy Spirit conforming the activity of the soul to God in and through the sacramental and moral activity of the Church. And so all true theology aspires toward a deeper cooperation with these gifts.

Perhaps for some readers, this will all seem like a rather convoluted way of saying what is evident. For others it may seem like a nostalgic look toward the past. However, for these Garrigou-Lagrange– and Chenu-esque readers, I would like to suggest that there is much work to be done to make this distinctly Dominican and Thomistic vision of theology plausible today, *and* that there exists a very real possibility of making this kind of theology very plausible within the context of the cultural "structures of intelligibility" of our world today. In what remains of this article, I would like to present three arenas or domains in which I think the work of uniting the transcendent, dogmatic orientation of theology and an overt historical sensibility are both essential and readily possible, but also radically incomplete. Of course, what follows is merely a sketch, but I hope that it makes clear ways that the classical form of Dominican theology I have alluded to may be explored within the context of contemporary debate.

---

38. I am thinking here of Martin Heidegger's excellent analysis of Nietzsche's "will to power" as a depersonalized ontology of vital desire in his famous essay "The Word of Nietzsche: 'God is Dead,'" in *The Question Concerning Technology and Other Essays*, trans. William Lovitt (New York: Harper and Row, 1977), 53–114.

III

The first of these areas for exploration concerns the relationship between the modern scientific worldview and the classical metaphysics of creation. The factical life of the mind is ever expanding in our world due to the vast array of modern scientific discoveries, and this growth is accompanied by the crystal-lization of a modern cosmological narrative that develops from the Big Bang to the emergence of conditions favorable to organic life, and from the initial ap-pearance of living forms to the advent of homo sapiens. Now it is obvious that for all the talk about historical studies in twentieth-century theology, a seri-ous engagement with the modern scientific narrative of the universe and the origins of human life never really took place, or was exceedingly rare.[39] Argu-ably, even the work of Pierre Teilhard de Chardin is not an exception to this. The great Jesuit anthropologist fails to distinguish adequately the scientific and philosophical principles governing inanimate cosmic evolution on the one hand and the evolution of living species on the other.[40] He also seems to amal-gamate into one the laws of the animal world, the mental and artistic dynam-ics of human culture (the noosphere), and the life of grace.[41] Karl Rahner, who took inspiration from him, does not seem to acknowledge sufficiently in his "evolutionary" narrative of the world's becoming the irreducible role of the law of entropy. Everything, he tells us, is ordered toward an omega point in Christ, yet he fails to discuss the fact that the physical world is moving away from a point of highest maximal energy, and that this movement acts to undermine the world's qualitative arrangement.[42] What his viewpoint conceals, then, is

39. One might mention the exception of Wolfhart Pannenberg's work. See, for example, *Theology and the Philosophy of Science*, trans. F. McDonagh (Philadelphia: Westminster, 1976); and the collection of essays *Toward a Theology of Nature*, ed. T. Peters (Louisville: Westmin-ster, 1993).

40. Pierre Teilhard de Chardin, *The Phenomenon of Man* (New York: Harper and Row, 1975), 64–74.

41. Ibid., 174–84; 221–26; 257–59; 264–72.

42. See Karl Rahner, "Christology within an Evolutionary View of the World," in *Theologi-cal Investigations*, vol. V (London: Darton, Longman & Todd, 1966), 162–64, 168: "Only in re-lation to man is it possible to say what matter is—and not vice versa, what spirit is in relation to matter . . . Matter is the condition of what we experience directly as space and time . . . This temporal materiality understood as the pre-history of man considered as reflex freedom *must be understood as being orientated to* the history of the human spirit . . . This means, however, that if it is really to be taken seriously, 'becoming' *must be understood* as a real self-transcendence . . . If man is thus the self-transcendence of living matter, then the history of Nature and spirit forms an inner, graded unity in which natural history develops towards man, continues in him as *his* history, is conserved and surpassed in him, and hence reaches its proper goal with and in the history of the human spirit" (emphasis added). (I am grateful to Richard Schenk for point-ing out to me Rahner's silence on the law of entropy.) The view is foreshadowed by Teilhard's

that the study of the physical laws of the cosmos and its energy cannot of itself explain (nor even in a sense predictively foreshadow) the surprising production of a world favorable to organic life, the existence of that life itself, the emergence of human self-awareness, or the presence of divine grace in Christ. In fact, these must all transpire on differing ontological "levels," formally distinct from that of the more fundamental, non-animate evolutionary backdrop of the cosmos.[43] In amalgamating these "levels" of being, one might propagate a modern panentheistic mythology, but not philosophy nor theology.

The irony, however, is that, just as modern theologians seem to have neglected cosmological questions, the modern sciences have begun to transcend the artificial constraints of the positivistic ideologies which imprisoned them in the early twentieth century. We see the emergence of a new openness to transcendent meaning among modern scientists today, but often one mixed with great confusions. On the one hand, in contemporary scientific literature there is an increasing recognition of the seeming gratuity of existence, of degrees of perfection in nature, of the felicitousness of the emergence of life in our cosmos, the significance of order and teleology (teleonomy); and all this is connected to the mystery of human consciousness and its significance.[44] On the other hand, there is a widespread confusion, in this same literature,

---

affirmations (*The Phenomenon of Man*, 65–66) that "cosmic energy is constantly increasing" despite the fact that "[t]his would seem to be in direct contradiction with the law of conservation of energy." He goes on to explain (ibid., 66) that the increase of physical energy in the universe is distinguishable only in the "qualitative" instances of man and his social history. The inner perfections of the higher forms of life will, he claims, eventually attain a stasis of perfection that exhausts the universe's potential for physical transformation.

43. I am not seeking to weigh in here on the question of whether cellular life could have originated from inanimate matter without any kind of "special creation." My point is simply that biological life represents a substantially and qualitatively distinct *form* of being and that its "laws" of development cannot be derived merely from a consideration of the laws of non-living matter and energy.

44. On the gratuity of existence, see Paul Davies, *The Mind of God* (New York: Simon and Schuster, 1992), esp. 161–93; Stephen Hawking, *A Brief History of Time* (London and New York: Bantam, 1988), 174.

On the degrees of perfection in nature, see, for example, Stephen Weinberg, *Dreams of a Final Theory: The Scientist's Search for the Ultimate Laws of Nature* (New York: Pantheon, 1993), 39: "As we look at nature at levels of greater and greater complexity, we see phenomena emerging that have no counterpart at the simpler levels, least of all at the level of the elementary particles. For example, there is nothing like intelligence on the level of individual living cells, and nothing like life on the level of atoms and molecules . . . The emergence of new phenomena at high levels of complexity is most obvious in biology and the behavioral sciences, but it is important to recognize that such emergence does not represent something special about life or human affairs; it also happens within physics itself." See the helpful Thomistic reflections on this statement by Lawrence Dewan in his *Form and Being* (Washington, D.C.: The Catholic University of America Press, 2006), 101–5.

Regarding the emergence of life in the cosmos, I am alluding here in particular to John

of modern science with philosophical ontology and a confusion of ontology with natural theology per se or even Christian theology. There is something quite strange about Richard Dawkins or Ernst Mayr trying to tell us what the definition of chance or theological causality is based upon their studies of genetics.[45] Likewise, the effort of Michael Behe to determine what order is, or transcendent efficient causality, based upon the study of cell life, seems to me equally undiscerning.[46] Neither "side" in the erroneously conducted debate about "intelligent design" takes philosophical ontology sufficiently seriously as a discipline distinct from that of genetics. Yet it is a precondition for a study of the "meaning" of any possible history of evolution, however we want to narrate that history. Thus both the advocates and the detractors of "intelligent design" perpetuate confusion insofar as both tend to see the existence of order or teleology intrinsic to things as a topic that should be evaluated from within the methodologies of the modern sciences. They simultaneously tend to infer merely from the presence of such order that there is (or could be) a necessary theological meaning to creation. But surely there is a categorial difference between the scientific question of genetic development in organic forms and the philosophical question of the character of order and chance in the world per se, as there is a categorial difference between the identification of an intrinsic order in the world and the demonstration of a transcendent source of that order.[47] The affirmation of the existence of God does not follow automati-

---

Barrow and Frank Tipler, *The Anthropic Cosmological Principle* (Oxford: Oxford University Press, 1988).

On order and teleology, see, for example, Ernst Mayr's reflections on the problem of identifying natures or species in *Systematics and the Origins of Species from the Viewpoint of a Zoologist* (New York: Columbia University Press, 1942); and his reflections on "teleonomy" in *What Evolution Is* (New York: Basic Books, 2001). His views may be profitably compared and contrasted with those of Kenneth Miller, *Finding Darwin's God: A Scientist's Search for Common Ground Between God and Evolution* (New York: Harper Collins, 1999).

On human consciousness, see, for example, the perplexities concerning rational consciousness as discussed by Paul Davies in *God and the New Physics* (New York: Simon and Schuster, 1984), 72–87; 135–43; and Weinberg, *Dreams of a Final Theory*, 43–45, 58, 61.

45. Richard Dawkins, *The Blind Watchmaker: Why the Evidence of Evolution Reveals a Universe without Design* (New York: Norton, 1996), 21–41; Mayr, *What Evolution Is*, chap. 1.

46. See Michael Behe, *Darwin's Black Box: The Biochemical Challenge to Evolution* (New York: The Free Press, 1996), 230: "The discovery of design expands the number of factors that must be considered by science when trying to explain life . . . Unlike Darwinian evolution, the theory of intelligent design is new to modern science, so there are a host of questions that need to be answered and much work lies ahead. For those who work at the molecular level, the challenge will be to rigorously determine which systems were designed and which might have arisen by other mechanisms.[!]" See the critical remarks on this viewpoint by Dewan, *Form and Being*, 105–8. Form and finality seem to be presupposed here as something purely extrinsic to the object of the modern sciences and, therefore, in some sense, to material elements themselves.

47. In his *Commentary on the Metaphysics*, 1, sec. 11 [§ 177], Aquinas discusses the fact that

cally from the affirmation of an intrinsic natural order. Speaking in Thomistic terms, there is a fundamental difference between the primary cause of all that participates in being and goodness (God himself), and the "secondary" causes which operate according to their own intrinsic principles and essential autonomy—even while being in total dependence upon the primary cause. For a Thomist, the study of created being need not entail the study of God, but it can open us up to that study. However, conversely, any conflict envisaged between the world of creaturely activity and the transcendent government of God who sustains these very beings in existence (even in their chance encounters) is completely fatuous.[48]

Some years ago Herbert McCabe noted that, ironically enough, by refusing the question of the origin and meaning of the world as we have it, the modern positivist in one sense refuses to employ sufficiently the scientific method of causal question asking.[49] This is certainly true if we adopt a broad understanding of the "scientific method" in question: a search for the ultimate causal explanations of all that is. Yet on another level, this positing of the "ultimate" question of creation requires de facto the passage to a mode of understanding that is not open to confirmation or disqualification by quantitative measurement, and therefore to a mode of thinking that is distinctly ontological.[50]

---

the final cause was understood by Aristotle as an "intrinsic" principle of order within nature. He notes that this was an advance over pre-Socratic theories of nature, since Anaxagoras had previously considered teleology uniquely as an extrinsic principle of intellectual, efficient causality by mind (intended purpose) exerted *upon* the being and becoming of things. The distinction between these two "kinds" of final causality (intrinsic/natural versus extrinsic/intellectual) seems to be lacking in much of the modern discourse *pro et contra* concerning "intelligent design." I am indebted to Dewan, *Form and Being*, 106 n. 28, for the application of this text to the contemporary debate.

48. This point has been brought out with a marvelous clarity by the recent document of the International Theological Commission, *Communion and Stewardship: Human Persons Created in the Image of God*, esp, §§ 62–70. The document was issued July 23, 2004, and is available electronically at http://www.vatican.va/roman_curia/congregations/cfaith/cti_documents/ rc_con_cfaith_doc_20040723_communion-stewardship_en.html.

tters (London and New York: Continuum, 1987), 2–9; re- by Denys Turner, *Faith, Reason and the Existence of God* ʾess, 2004), 226–59.

ᴎ65–77, offers some suggestive remarks in this respect, re- ern scientific "theory of everything." Already, mathemat- s (while interrelated) are distinct theoretical fields. Yet atics can offer sufficient warrant for all of the principles ern sciences themselves have a certain heterogeneity due ᴉgical laws are in a sense radically different from those of order, beauty, and contingency of the universe (the "suf- ᴉnt to a genuinely "meta"-physical, theistic answer, rather

That theology must accept a sustained and serious conversation with the sciences is essential. My basic point, here, however, is that this conversation also has to be mediated by the contributions of philosophy. What Dominican theology may reasonably aspire to today is a more sustained integration of the modern scientific worldview with the distinctly metaphysical vision of Christianity. A conversation between science and revelation must concern itself with the reality in the natural world of order, causality, teleology, and essences (or natures), and with a corresponding metaphysics of creation, that respects the relative autonomy and history of creatures. Here a philosophical reflection on nature of the kind initiated by Thomists like Benedict Ashley and William Wallace is greatly needed.[51] The modern scientific worldview, in some sense, depends upon a "higher" philosophical order of thinking, even when it would refuse to acknowledge the metaphysical dimensions of that order and the source of that order, that source ultimately being God.[52] Consequently, an engagement with the sciences should also be concerned with the question of the primary transcendent cause of all being, yet as genuinely mediated by philosophy. In this way we can do justice to the truth of God's overarching governance of the secondary causes, which have their own remarkably complex and meaningful history, while simultaneously acknowledging God as the source of that intrinsically ordered historical sphere. If we do not wish to live with an epistemically schizophrenic worldview, the articulation of an integrated understanding of science, philosophy, ethics, and revelation is a necessity. Yet this project is (alas) very much under construction.

51. On science and philosophical realism, see the helpful reflections of Benedict Ashley, *Theologies of the Body: Humanist and Christian* (Braintree, Mass.: Pope John XXIII Center, 1985); idem, *The Way toward Wisdom: An Interdisciplinary and Intercultural Introduction to Metaphysics* (Notre Dame, Ind.: Notre Dame University Press, 2006); William Wallace, *The Modeling of Nature: Philosophy of Science and Philosophy of Nature in Synthesis* (Washington, D.C.: The Catholic University of America Press, 1996).

52. See the arguments to this effect by Jacques Maritain in *Science and Wisdom*, trans. B. Wall (London: The Centenary Press, 1940), 34–69. Aquinas argues in his *Commentary on the Metaphysics* VI, lect. 1, § 1150, that every particular science presumes the existence and "whatness" of its subject, such that no science reflects upon the being and essence of realities as being and essence per se, except metaphysics. In his *Commentary on the Physics* II, lect. 3 and 4, he argues that observational sciences such as astronomy or medicine rely implicitly upon principles proper to the philosophy of nature (form, matter, teleological actuality, potentiality) without being able to demonstrate (or deny) these principles. In continuity with such perspectives, it seems that post-modern thinkers are methodologically more insightful and consistent than positivists when they call into question the "objectivity" of scientific truth claims, given the incapacity of the mind to assure itself of trans-empirical, ontological notions. (Even while they are simultaneously more gravely mistaken concerning the nature of the real.) On the subject of the hierarchy of the sciences and the relation between philosophy of nature and metaphysics, see the important study of Lawrence Dewan, "St. Thomas, Physics and the Principle of Metaphysics," *The Thomist* 61, no. 4 (1997): 549–66.

A second domain concerns the question of the integration of history and dogma with respect to the incarnate life of God the Son made man. In a religiously pluralistic world, Christianity needs to be able to demonstrate the rational grounds for its truth claims, particularly in the historical realm. Any contemporary urban citizen of our world is bombarded by incompatible, competing meaning claims, and is presented with some scholarly material, as well as much sensationalistic popular literature (*The Da Vinci Code,* et alia) which would suggest that dogmatic truth claims concerning the historical Christ are arbitrary or erroneous. The person on the street may well believe that the claims of Christianity are as historically contestable as those of the Koran or as mythological as the Bhagavad-Gita.

Here I would like to make two points. First, there has been a healthy modern emergence of Christology conducted through rigorous historical inquiry, in which the identity of Christ is narrated by attempting to situate the aims, teachings, and events of his life, death, and resurrection within their original historical context. This so-called Christology from below is exemplified by thinkers such as Wolfhart Pannenberg, Walter Kasper, and N. T. Wright.[53] Thanks to their work, and that of others as well, we are now able to better situate Christianity within the matrix of a modern historiography and to understand the modern intelligibility of the claim that Christ was a truly historical personage and Christianity is a historically founded revelation. Of course, on one level there is the popularization of this work that still needs to be carried out. On a deeper level, however, there is also a more basic theological question that emerges concerning the relationship of "Christology from below" to the classical ontological Christology of the patristic and medieval heritage. My basic claim here, consistent with the arguments made above, is that the condition of possibility for any historically sensitive Christology from below is a capacity to recognize in Christ who he is and to think of him in ontological terms. In other words, just as any history presupposes an ontology, so any possible historical construal of Christ in time presupposes a theology of Christ's identity and being. If this is the case, then all historical studies of Christ have an ontological trajectory. Simultaneously, however, all "Christology from above" concerns the Incarnate Son, and therefore demands to be understood within time and history where the identity of God made man is manifested. To believe in the Incarnation is to believe that God had a public historical life among us, which is

---

53. See, in particular, Walter Kasper, *Jesus the Christ* (New York: Paulist Press, 1976); Wolfhart Pannenberg, *Systematic Theology,* vol. II (Grand Rapids: Eerdmans, 1994); N. T. Wright, *Jesus and the Victory of God* (Minneapolis: Fortress Press, 1996), and *The Resurrection of the Son of God* (Minneapolis: Fortress Press, 2003).

to some extent subject to "neutral" rational verification. These two approaches, "Christology from above" and "from below," are two different dimensions of the same science. The historical study of Christ is, I think, a sub-alternate discipline, in which one takes more profoundly into account how the Triune God has manifested his own identity to us in time and within history.[54] Evidently, if this is true, theology must seek a progressive unification of classical Christological "science" and modern historical study of Jesus. In this case, a number of Christological questions become acute: How is Jesus' human, historical consciousness related to the classical claim that he is the person of the Son existing in two natures, as God and man?[55] What is the relation between his eschatological message concerning the Kingdom of God and the revelation of his own identity as the Son of God?[56] How might the crucifixion and resurrection be understood as the historical revelation of the inner life of the Triune God?[57] And how did this revelation take place within the "categories" of the Second Temple Judaism of Jesus' time, such that it laid a groundwork for the later theology of Nicaea and Chalcedon?[58] The deepened consideration of these and similar questions must seek to integrate the historical and dogmatic/ontologi-

54. It follows from this that any hypothetical construal of the historical Jesus by a Christian theologian refers at least implicitly to the revealed principles provided by Scripture and Tradition, and therefore employs an "apologetic" methodology that seeks to defend the historical basis of the "high Christology" of the New Testament. This does not mean that the historical arguments contained therein have no intrinsic rational integrity or "natural" plausibility (on the contrary!), but it does mean that such argumentation is sub-alternated to a higher *scientia* concerning who Christ is, and that scientia is itself necessarily "ontological" in character. Because the Scriptures themselves in their historical claims contain such ontological affirmations ("Christ is Lord"), similar remarks can be made concerning the "agnostic" or anti-theological constructions of non-Christian historians of Christ. These too are "atheological" in their *implicitly* a priori (ahistorical, philosophical) refusal to entertain such ontological presuppositions, even hypothetically.

55. See the study by Bernard Lonergan, *Collected Works*, vol. 7, *The Ontological and Psychological Constitution of Christ* (Toronto: University of Toronto Press, 2002).

56. It seems to me that the work of N. T. Wright and Ben Meyer (who was influenced by Lonergan) are of great help on this point. I have recently attempted to employ arguments from Lonergan in order to consider theologically Christ's consciousness of his unity with the Father in announcing the Kingdom of God, as it relates to the classical theology of Christ's "two natures" and "two wills." See Thomas Joseph White, "Ditheletism and the Instrumental Human Consciousness of Jesus," *Pro Ecclesia* 17, no. 4 (2008): 394–422. Similarly, I have examined the traditional theology of the beatific vision of Christ in relation to some of N. T. Wright's analysis of the eschatological significance of the "cry of dereliction." See Thomas Joseph White, "Jesus' Cry on the Cross and His Beatific Vision," *Nova et Vetera* (English) 5, no. 3 (2007): 525–51.

57. See the Thomistic reflections on this point by the French Dominican theologian Emmanuel Durand, *La périchorèse des personnes divines: immanence mutuelle, réciprocité et communion* (Paris: Cerf, 2005).

58. On this last point, Larry Hurtado's work *Lord Jesus Christ* (Grand Rapids: Eerdmans, 2003) is of importance.

cal approaches to Christology if they are to form into one coherent narrative a modern sapiential understanding of the revelation of God given in Christ.

A second point that can be made on this front concerns the famous Rahnerian *Grundaxiom*, "the economic Trinity is the immanent Trinity, and the immanent Trinity is the economic Trinity." On one level, this famous axiom points us toward the classical truth that who God is in himself *(theologia)* is truly revealed in the manifestation of himself in history and time *(economia)*.[59] In response to an overly ahistorical theology, which was formulated in response to an overly ahistorical Enlightenment rationalism, this was a necessary reassertion. However, it is equally important to reaffirm today that theology does not terminate in the radical historicization of God and humanity. Rather the "economy" invites human beings to turn toward the transcendent "theology" of the inner life of God. As Gilles Emery and David Bentley Hart have recently argued convincingly, this requires a reaffirmation of an "analogical interval" between the immanent Trinity and temporal creation, such that the inner life of God is understood to transcend absolutely the historical sphere of creation.[60] In the soteriological realm, this leads to a corresponding sense of the eschatological orientation of all knowledge of God. While we have received true knowledge of the immanent life of God in Christ in time, the contemplation of God that begins in Christ's mission ultimately aspires to the vision of and union with God in himself in the life to come. The return toward the transcendent mystery of the inner life of the Holy Trinity is the deepest purpose of the human community, and therefore also of its theology.[61] In fact,

---

59. For a helpful analysis of the Rahnerian principle, see Emmanuel Durand, "L'autocommunication trinitaire: concept clé de la connexio mysteriorum rahnérienne," *Revue thomiste* 102, no. 4 (2002): 569–613, and "L'identité rahnérienne entre la Trinité économique et la Trinité immanente à l'épreuve de ses applications," *Revue thomiste* 103, no. 1 (2003): 75–92.

60. See the remarks of David Bentley Hart in *The Beauty of the Infinite* (Grand Rapids: Eerdmans, 2003), 165: "The God whose identity subsists in time and is achieved upon history's horizon—who is determined by his reaction to the pathos of history—may be a being, or indeed the totality of all beings gathered in the pure depths of ultimate consciousness, but he is not being as such, he is not life and truth and goodness and love and beauty. God belongs to the system of causes, even if he does so as its total rationality; he is an absolute *causa in fieri,* but not a transcendent *causa in esse* . . . Theology must, to remain faithful to what it knows of God's transcendence, reject any picture of God that so threatens to become at once both thoroughly mythological and thoroughly metaphysical, and insist upon the classical definitions of impassiblity, immutability, and nonsuccessive eternity." See also Hart's essay "No Shadow of Turning: On Divine Impassibility," *Pro Ecclesia* 11, no. 2 (2002): 184–206. Gilles Emery has offered parallel considerations in his essay "L'immutabilité du Dieu d'amour et les problèmes du discour sur la 'souffrance de Dieu,'" *Nova et vetera* (French) 74 (1999): 5–37.

61. I am indebted herein to the perspectives of Gilles Emery, "Theology as a Spiritual Exercise in Augustine and Aquinas," in *Trinity, Church and the Human Person* (Naples, Fla.: Sapientia Press, 2007), 33–72.

taking this seriously means affirming that the *De Deo Trino,* Aquinas's *prima pars,* so to speak, is the first starting point of theology and its heart as well, and not the *tertia pars,* or Christology. Despite the greatness of Karl Barth and Wolfhart Pannenberg, it is necessary to reassert over and against the trends of modern theology that Christomonism represents a distortion of theology. The purpose for the creation of humanity was the contemplation of the Triune God, not the Incarnation; and there is an order between these two mysteries. With all due respect to Immanuel Kant's dense arguments restricting the scope of the human mind to the historical sphere, our mind is not made merely for the historical sphere, and the classical contemplation of the immanent life of the Trinity developed by Sts. Gregory of Nazianzus, Augustine, Bernard, Bonaventure, Albert, and Aquinas remains an objective norm. Of course such theology does not in fact exclude a *theologia crucis,* a contemplation of the crucified God: nor does it exclude a consideration of the way in which the Trinitarian life of God is revealed to us in and through the mystery of the passion. But such reflection must ultimately stipulate that the "return toward God" by grace, toward the transcendent life of the Son as God, is the ultimate beatitude of the human intellect.[62]

This leads us to the last remaining point. How might we envisage today the Christian understanding of the teleological character of the human soul in confrontation with the modern sense of the radical historicity of the self? Nietzsche, Freud, and Foucault introduce us into a world in which the self is ultimately an epiphenomenon, undergirded by a vortex of quasi-anarchic, subconscious vital forces: the will to power, the id, the social constructions of others which have produced our own self-image and motivations. This modern "anthropology" calls forth an "archeology" of the subject, which would attempt to render us more lucid concerning the prevalence and power of these undergirding, pre-rational impulses and social forces that shape us. Contemporary "confessional" and psychoanalytic culture offers the modern person the incessant opportunity to scrutinize the historical layers of one's desires and frustrations and their linguistic and symbolic expression, so as to come to know better the subjacent psychological and cultural matrix that will determine the future, especially with regard to the structures of social power. Held up before the glare of these influences, the self as self evaporates.[63] Modernist novelists

62. This point was articulated poignantly by M. J. Le Guillou in *Christ and Church: A Theology of the Mystery,* trans. C. Schaldenbrand (New York: Desclee, 1966), 325–72, from which I have quoted at the heading of this essay.

63. See in this respect, in particular, Michel Foucault, *The Archeology of Knowledge and the Discourse of Language,* trans. A. M. Sheridan Smith (New York: Pantheon, 1972). "[My] essential

such as Proust, Joyce, Woolf, and Faulkner have illustrated more patently than any philosophy the plausibility of the anthropological theories of Nietzsche, Freud, and Foucault. Consider, for example, how a book like Faulkner's *Sanctuary* suggests so powerfully that what we call the self is in fact an entity motivated by unconscious vital forces, and structured externally by the manipulations of social conditions. The modernist desire either to construct a (seemingly arbitrary?) narrative interpretation of the self, or to deconstruct any such narrative, has become a constitutive feature of our culture, mediated by even the most banal of films or popular television shows.

Now it is true that Charles Taylor has argued convincingly that in many ways the modern narrative conception of the self is a product of Christian culture, from Augustine to the Puritans.[64] And one need look no further than to Dostoyevski, George Bernanos, or Sigrid Undset in order to find artists who have mastered the modernist narrative portrayal of the self in view of distinctly Christian ends.[65] Perhaps Christianity will even be necessary to maintain a sense of the narrative unity of human existence in a world in which the modern narratives of glib unbelief and deconstructing counter-narratives have left in shards any truly ontological conception of the person. Yet, one must also maintain the more fundamental theological affirmation that whatever the future of the modern liberal concept of the "subject," the fulfillment of the human spiritual soul does not occur uniquely within the horizon of spacio-temporal history. The fulfillment of the soul is meta-physical, and found ultimately in God alone, who transcends the world of the senses, even when he manifests his presence therein.

This fundamental truth is difficult to propose today, since the world of sensual, historical, and archeological scrutinizing of the self prohibits any delay in inner fulfillment or narrative resolution that would have to be put off until the eschaton.[66] On the other hand, however, the modern liberal and capital-

task was to *free the history of thought from its subjection to transcendence* . . . My aim was to analyse this history, in the *discontinuity that no teleology would reduce in advance;* to map it in a dispersion that no pre-established horizon would embrace; to allow it to be deployed in an anonymity on which *no transcendental constitution would impose the form of the subject;* to open it up to a temporality that would not promise the return of any dawn. My aim was to cleanse it of all transcendental narcissism . . . It had to be shown that the history of thought could not have this role of revealing the transcendental moment that rational mechanics has not possessed since Kant, mathematical idealities since Husserl, and the meanings of the perceived world since Merleau-Ponty—despite the efforts that had been made to find it there" (ibid., 203, emphasis added).

64. Charles Taylor, *The Sources of the Self* (Cambridge: Harvard University Press, 1989), esp. 127–42; 211–305.

65. See on this point, with particular reference to Dostoyevski, ibid., 447–55, 513–18.

66. Our culture surely cannot easily entertain the prospect of any asceticism in view of this

ist human being (perhaps naively) believes that he or she possesses a kind of natural right to happiness. Consequently, in a sense, classical Catholic theology has at its disposition in the larger culture the reflective acceptance of one of the most ancient principles of Christian ethics: the desire for happiness. It is not too difficult to argue even in the public square that the agonizing modernist search for meaning is in fact implicitly dependent metaphysically upon a fundamental, teleological orientation of the self, which is restless with the desire for happiness, and which can find final rest only in God. What the modern Thomistic tradition can do, then, is to offer the bewildered, materialistic, and modernist self the possibility of finding itself, yet only through the "project" of the life of the virtues ordered toward God. The virtues are in fact more architectural (or architectonic) than archeological. They offer a living form of progress to pursue currently, rather than the supposedly therapeutic inquiry into the historical self of the past. They invite the human person to look off into the encounter with God (now and in the future) as the condition of possibility for the deepest self-understanding of what has gone before. True self-discovery, then, while not excluding a needed narrative interpretation of one's personal history, occurs primarily in the recognition of the authentic goal of human existence and a practice in view of that end. It is this teleological orientation which "structures" the human person, and not archeology, however helpful the latter may be.

Following the work of people like Servais Pinckaers, Romanus Cessario, and Alasdair MacIntyre, this teleological form of self-discovery needs to be presented by modern theology in ways that are clear to the modern reader.[67] Yet we also need to develop a more practical, more spiritual theology which explains the teleological pursuit of the virtues to the modernist culture that is our own.[68] This study too, must be conducted in dialogue with the theories

---

end. Instead, the deeper and more disturbing asceticism of our time stems from the moratorium in the public square on deeper questions or convictions concerning the perennially true and the transcendent good. The liberal modern person is stifled by the ascetic embrace of a volitional immanentism.

67. See in particular, Servais Pinckaers, *The Sources of Christian Ethics*, trans. Sr. Mary Thomas Noble, O.P. (Washington, D.C.: The Catholic University of America Press, 1995); It seems to me that the work of Alasdair MacIntyre in his *Dependent Rational Animals: Why Human Beings Need the Virtues* (Peru, Ill.: Carus, 1999) offers suggestions for how a teleological vision of human fulfillment and community can in fact become the basis for a meaningful *evolutionary* interpretation of human beings, with regard to their pre-human historical state. The awareness of the enduring presence within us of this "archeology" of our evolutionary ancestry should condition (but not determine!) our understanding of the specifically *rational* character of human virtue.

68. Despite the absence in his work of an engagement with the modern genealogical traditions I am describing, I think an important example in this domain is provided by Reginald

of Nietzsche, Freud, and Foucault. The archaeologies of the self which these authors have developed can be used to effectively critique the naivety and hypocrisy of Enlightenment liberal culture. Their suspicions of the underlying factors behind publicly acceptable rationality can profitably be assumed by a Catholic theology of the fallen human condition which takes seriously the incurvature of the will, and its effects upon human motivation, particularly in academic, corporate, and governmental institutional structures. Yet the theoretical apparatus of a Nietzsche or a Freud is also deeply flawed due to its truncated, reductive anthropology. What is it to respond to the genealogical tradition critically, therefore, from within the Thomistic spiritual tradition? On the one hand, the introspective narrative biographies of St. Therèse of Lisieux or St. Edith Stein can serve as a resource for the articulation of a Thomistic anthropology, as they speak in the idiom of our age so effectively. To give examples: in a world in which the Freudian id has been so falsely absolutized, how would we explain, employing Aquinas and Therèse of Lisieux, what it is psychologically to try to live by the gifts of "fear" and understanding, the beatitudes of spiritual poverty and purity of heart? In response to Nietzsche, what does it mean to live like Edith Stein by the "gift of counsel" (the beatitude of the merciful) in the face of a culture dominated by the will to power as autonomy, a culture that fails to respect the dignity of human life as a result? Our presentation of the truths contained in Thomistic anthropology needs to be informed by the spiritual examples of the great figures of our modernist age.

In a more distinctly Dominican vein, however, it is worth asking in what ways the challenge of a teleological conception of human fulfillment invites us to rediscover (over and against the modern turn toward the subject) the distinctly "objective," theocentric perspective of our own mystical tradition, exemplified by figures such as Catherine of Sienna, Johannes Tauler, and Louis Chardon. In these theological writers, the self encounters its own deepest meaning only by turning away from self-scrutiny to worship, contemplate, and preach the objective mystery of God in all its splendor and transcendence. Instead of a theology of the gifts of the Holy Spirit in the lives of the saints, perhaps today we need to recover a theology of the gifts of the Holy Spirit acting in the humanity of Christ crucified. How does the Holy Spirit reveal to us in the dereliction and resurrection of Christ the goodness and beauty of God, so as to orient our subjective human existence toward its ultimate term? Or how do the missions of the Son and Holy Spirit in the divine economy (for ex-

Garrigou-Lagrange, *The Three Ages of the Interior Life, Prelude to Eternal Life,* 2 vols., trans. M. T. Doyle (St. Louis: Herder, 1947).

ample in the Incarnation or the Eucharist) allow us to understand the objective meaning of these same missions as experienced in the history of a given soul? All this can be done in ways that acknowledge the reality of our subjective comportment, our psychological desires, and the historical development of our self-understanding "within" a given historical-cultural setting. However, such reflection must also acknowledge the teleological accomplishment of our person in the encounter with the transcendent and ultimate truth about the Triune God. Otherwise the self at its deepest level remains indecipherable.

One might add to this a practical observation. In an age of ideology, actions inevitably offer at least as compelling a witness to an existential orientation as do words. Catholic Christians hope to communicate to others that we believe that the world is created by a transcendent wisdom, that the wisdom who created the world became a human being, and that this loving wisdom alone can fulfill in truth the desires of the human heart. This suggests that our liturgical life, where all three of these truths are proclaimed, should be the primary practical response to the crisis of the modern "historicist" self. It is in worship ultimately that we become what we are meant to be. The call to transcend the meanderings of our own historical narrative finds no more eloquent expression than that of the Eucharistic liturgy, where the biblical narrative is simultaneously proclaimed as our own deepest narrative and achieved existentially in the presence of Christ and the worship of the transcendent God. In the liturgy, all narratives are simultaneously achieved and surpassed by something greater. Perhaps today it is in the sensible vitality of liturgy and in the manifestation of a contemplative life that one can offer the most important witness to the reality of God.

Conclusion

By way of conclusion I would like to admit that these reflections may in fact seem quite unwieldy. We are used to a kind of cultural division between the lasting truths of our faith that we acknowledge in worship and the irreducibly pluralistic, perspectivalist culture in which we are immersed once we cross the threshold of our church doors. Perhaps these divisions seem inevitable and insurmountable. Yet we do also realize that on some level there is not so great a difference between the disoriented nonbeliever and ourselves. That person also is made to inquire into the ultimate meaning of his or her existence. He or she also is made for the grace of God and is offered redemption in Christ. And I and you are caught up in the questions and perplexities of the contemporary age. The trends, cultural instincts, and enigmas of moder-

nity are also very much my own. Therefore, the project of sapiential unification of modern "forms of knowing" within a larger "overarching" perspective
of revelation is a work that is salutary not only for one's world, but for one's self
as well. This work has to be conducted with realistic humility and not trium-
phalism, but it also should be conducted with joy and Christian hope. The Order of Preachers will continue to maintain a viable, meaningful charism in the
world today precisely to the extent that it is faithful to this heritage of seeking
ultimate wisdom within the plurality of discourses, by recourse to the unique
wisdom revealed in Christ. May it be said of Dominican theology what is said
of St. Dominic in the canon of the Mass: "Speaking either with you or about
you [O God], he disseminated wisdom and brought forth actions from the
plenitude of contemplation, spending all of himself for the building up of your
Church."[69]

69. *Proprium Ordinis Praedicatorum, Missale et Lectionarium* (Rome: Santa Sabina, 1985),
Augusti 8, p. 199: "Tecum vel de te iugiter loquens, sapientia profecit, et actionem de plenitudi-
ne contemplationis educens, aedificandae Ecclesiae tuae se totum impendit."

PART 2

Mysterium Fidei
Sacraments and
Metaphysics

[4]

The Importance of the Definition
of Sacraments as Signs

BENOÎT-DOMINIQUE DE LA SOUJEOLE, O.P.

What is a sacrament? All classical authors agree in holding that the concepts of sign and cause are fundamental in defining the sacraments. Yet there is an important speculative problem to be solved: the concept of sign and the concept of cause are formally distinct, and one cannot be the undetermined genus and the other the determining specific difference. They cannot be combined into an adequate definition: one or the other must be chosen. The one that is left out could nevertheless express an additional, essential property. The concept of cause is most prominent during the early Scholastic age: a sacrament is a cause of grace. This is the idea of the sacrament as medicine.

St. Thomas inherited this understanding of a sacrament from Peter Lombard. In the *Sentences*, a sacrament is a cause of grace which is fittingly signified to men. Going through a thinking process whose key moments are found in the *De veritate* and the *Summa contra gentiles*, St. Thomas finally defines the sacrament in the *Summa theologiae* as the sign of a sacred reality.

The expressions found in Aquinas's *Commentary on the Sentences* and in the *Summa* are almost identical:

Sacramentum autem debet intelligi signum rei sacrae ut est sacrans.[1]

Signum rei sacrae inquantum est sanctificans homines.[2]

---

1. *In IV Sent.* dist. 1, q. 1, a. 1, a. 1, sol. 1, ad 2 (Moos, § 27); St. Thomas insists likewise in the ad 3: "signum rei sacrae . . . inquantum sacrans est actu" (Moos, § 28).

2. *Summa theologiae* III, q. 60, a. 2, c.

127

These similar expressions, however, have different meanings. The most striking clue to their difference is found through an analysis of the Jewish sacraments. Whereas in the *Commentary on the Sentences,* St. Thomas claims that the sacraments of the Old Law are only sacraments *secundum quid*[3] because they only signify, in the *Summa* he argues that these same sacraments are "proprie sacramenta."[4]

What is the underlying reason for this change, and what are its main consequences?

The Underlying Reason for This Change

We can summarize thus St. Thomas's shift of emphasis: it is not necessary for a sacrament to be efficacious, and so the proper concept of sacrament does not include causality. However, it is necessary for *Christian* sacraments to be efficacious:[5] efficaciousness is an additional and specific Christian property.

Sacraments, therefore, are signs of a sacred reality. This sacred reality is none other than the holiness of God to which man is destined (that is, the final cause) and in which man can participate already here on Earth through faith (that is, the formal cause). Therefore, if efficient causality is not included in the sacrament as such, this is because the sacrament is a sign through which this holiness is expressed, regardless of the mode through which this holiness is given. As St. Thomas says in the *Summa*:

Sunt autem sacramenta quaedam signa protestantia fidem, qua homo justificatur.[6]

Thus all sacraments, whether they are found during the first period of the history of salvation before Abraham, the Jewish period, or during the Christian period, are signs of the saving faith; they are the cultic signification of a faith community.

What distinguishes Christian sacraments is not this aspect of sacraments as acts of the virtue of religion—which is found in sacraments through all periods of salvation—but an additional property: the efficient causality which imparts God's holiness to man. The manner in which this divine holiness is imparted gives its specificity to the properly Christian sacraments. How can this property be added?

3. *In IV Sent.* dist. 1, q. 1, a. 1, sol. 1 et ad 4 (Moos, §§ 24 and 30).
4. *ST* III, q. 60, a. 2, ad 2.
5. *ST* III, q. 62, a. 1, c.
6. *ST* III, q. 61, a. 4, c. See also *ST* III, q. 61, a. 3, c.: "Oportebat ante Christi adventum esse quaedam signa visibilia quibus homo fidem suam protestaretur de futuro Salvatoris adventu. Et hujusmodi signa sacramenta dicuntur."

We know how the Augustinian understanding distinguishes Jewish sacraments from Christian sacraments: the Jewish sacred signs designated the Savior who was to come—such was the faith of Abraham which saved Jews of upright heart—whereas the Christian sacred signs designate Christ, who has already come and who has achieved the Redemption of the world in the Paschal mystery. If the sign accomplished signifies Christ who is to come, there is no causality at work in the sacramental sign; if the sign accomplished designates Christ who has come (baptism, Eucharist, etc.), there is causality.

The Speculative Difficulty: How Can Sign and Cause Be Joined?

An intrinsic connection between sign and cause must be made manifest in the properly Christian sacraments. Yet we know that, however far we investigate the concept of sign, we shall not find the concept of efficient causality: a sign, as sign, can produce only signification.

This is where Thomas's mature development of sacramental causality, itself dependent on the evolution in his understanding of grace, has allowed things to be clarified in the *Summa*. Following from his developments in Christology, St. Thomas speaks of the instrumental causality of the sacrament.[7]

This signified causality belongs to Christ; it is he who acts in the Christian sacraments as he acted during his life on earth through miracles.[8] By reason of the personal mystery of Christ, true God and true man, there are two levels in this causality:

- As God, he is the principal cause: no one can cause grace but God alone.
- As man, he is the instrumental cause set in motion by God in order to cause grace.

The principal cause cannot be said to be a sign of its effect: fire (cause) is not a sign of smoke (effect). However, the instrumental cause, which is an interme-

---

7. See Theophil Tschipke, *L'humanité du Christ comme instrument de salut de la divinité* (Fribourg Br.: Academic Press, 2003) (German: *Die Menschheit Christi als Heilsorgan der Gottheit* [Freiburg: Herder, 1940]).

8. As is found in the Fathers of the Church, "Quod itaque Redemptoris nostri conspicuum fuit, in sacramenta transivit" (St. Leo the Great, *Sermo* 74, § 2 [PL 54, 398]). In other words, the miracles wrought by Christ during his public life are the "prototypes" of our sacraments. We will not dwell on the profound relation between the miracles of Christ and the sacraments of the Church, which is found throughout the patristic writings, and of which St. Thomas gives a good account; see on this topic, G. Berceville, "L'étonnante alliance: Evangile et miracles selon Saint Thomas," *Revue thomiste* 103, no. 1 (2003): 5–74 (particularly p. 55 and the long footnote 163).

diary cause, participates both in the cause and in the effect: a swinging ham-
mer may be a sign of nails being driven into wood.

At the natural level, the instrumental cause, because it is intermediary,
participates at once in the rationale of sign (of the principal cause) and in the
rationale of cause (of the effect toward which it contributes). The instrument
ut res, that is, accomplishing its proper, causal action (water washes) manifests
as a sign the efficient action of the principal cause (God who purifies the soul),
and also designates the final effect to which it participates *ut instrumentum* (filial adoption through the remission of sins).

Having reached this stage in our survey, we can see that the understanding
found in the *Commentary on the Sentences*—a sanctification (cause) appearing
in a visible figure (sign)—is not inexact. But the *Summa* starts from a different—I may add a higher—standpoint: God's will for salvation is constant since
original sin. It is made perfect and visible in the Incarnation (sign), in such a
way that the Incarnation is God's work of salvation made visible inseparably
from divine efficaciousness. Before the Incarnation, this same will for salvation
was made known by announcing (through words and events) the Incarnation
to come, and the sign that this saving will had been received and accepted by
man was the testimony of the faith of the chosen people. However, because the
active presence of Christ was lacking, this sign did not designate any causality
actually at work in and through the rite. Salvation is possible in the Old Testament, but it can be so only as a preview of the coming work of Christ. This is not
causality *actually* at work; causality is only announced and *morally* anticipat-
ed.[9] Therefore, we shall not say—as it was often said in baroque theology—that
the sacrament is an "efficacious sign," but that the sacrament is the *sign of an
efficaciousness* either announced and prepared (before Christ), or fully at work
through the sacrament itself (since Christ).

The Actual Fruitfulness of This Understanding

Through all the periods of salvation, man enjoyed the use of signs through
which he could profess a saving faith. Of course, before the revelation of the
mysteries of Christ, this faith was largely implicit, but precisely because it was

9. This is why Christ "descended into hell" in order to seek out the righteous ones of the
Old Testament and usher them into beatitude. This *moral* causality, which was signified only
through the prefigurations of pre–New Testament rites before the Incarnation, is based on the
fact that God, *foreseeing the merits of Christ,* bestowed sanctifying grace. The preeminent occur-
rence of this type of causality is found in the Immaculate Conception, wherein salvation was effected *through preservation* from original sin and personal sins, whereas all the other righteous
ones of the Old Testament were given salvation *through purification.*

a true theological faith, it was the faith without which no one can please God.

Christ having now come, is this mode of salvation over? The only pronouncement we possess from the Magisterium is found in *Gaudium et Spes*, § 22: "Since Christ died for all men, and since the ultimate vocation of man is in fact one, that is to say, divine, we ought to be certain that the Holy Spirit, in a manner known only to God, offers to every man the possibility of being associated with this paschal mystery."[10]

Hence there should not be any doubt that the pagans who are upright of heart can now receive the sanctifying grace that is both *Christic [origin] and Christo-conforming [finality]*. The council does not say how this sanctifying grace reaches pagans. It is an open question for us. St. Thomas's sacramentology in the *Summa theologiae* allows us to present a positive proposition, starting from the idea that the sacraments, because they are signs of God's will for salvation confessed by men, exist during each of the ages of salvation.

Based on the distinction of St. Thomas, developed by Charles Journet, between the *tempus* (the time of the economy) and the *status* (the state of the participant), we can clarify two ways to consider the history of salvation.[11] First of all, the conception of the Fathers of the Church and of St. Thomas is a chronological vision (see Figure 1).[12] The *tempus* is the objective historical time of the history of salvation, and the *status* is the subjective situation of persons. This chronological succession (that is, the different historical ages) has been achieved by Christ. There is today only one historical age for all people, that of Christ.

Christians, who come after Christ and benefit from the mediations instituted by the Savior (preaching of the Gospel, celebration of the sacraments, service of the ministers), enjoy a *status* which matches the *tempus* of the accomplishment of the economy of redemption. But what is the situation, now, of the people who have not yet heard the Gospel?

Those who—without any fault of their own—have not yet encountered the mediations instituted by Christ, although they are living during the *tempus* of the accomplishment, are still in the *status* antecedent to the coming of Christ. All men today are under only one *tempus* inaugurated by Christ, but according to different *status*. Consequently, the sacraments that existed before the com-

10. My translation.

11. Charles Journet, *L'Église du Verbe incarné*, vol. 3, *Sa structure interne et son unité catholique* (Paris: Desclée de Brouwer, 1969).

12. For the Fathers, see Auguste Luneau, *L'histoire du salut chez les Pères de l'Église: La doctrine des âges du monde* (Paris: Beauchesne, 1964). In St. Thomas, see in particular *ST* III, q. 61, a. 3; and Edward Schillebeeckx's rich commentary in *L'économie sacramentelle du salut*, trans. Yvon van der Have, O.S.B. (Fribourg: Academic Press, 2004), 113ff.

FIGURE 4-1

	Original Sin	Abraham	Moses	Christ	→	Church
Tempora						
	+	+	+		→	Eschatology
Status	First Covenant (Noah)	Promise	Old Law	Accomplishment	→	Communication to All
	Sacraments	Sacraments	Sacraments	Sacraments		Seven Christian Sacraments

ing of Christ remain for those who are today still in a *status* before Christ, but only as signs and not as causes of grace. However, the grace that is given today is always the grace of Christ.

This means, I propose, that these non-Christian persons can receive Christic grace within the mode of mediation that is theirs: their sacraments, insofar as they express a measure of truth (some more and some less), can offer them, by way of something which approaches instruction, the saving faith. Those sacraments also can be a response of faith which justifies them. However, we must affirm that the accomplishment remains solely Christian. For this, the following elements are necessary:

a. The first consequence of the historical coming of Christ is that the antecedent religions are now objectively accomplished. Whereas before Christ they were the ordinary way of salvation of their members, since Christ they are only an extraordinary way because they are meant for a full accomplishment which can only be Christian. The mission of evangelization of the Church is not cancelled by the salvation of the pagans made actually possible in, and in some measure *through,* their own religions. On the contrary, this mission presupposes the reality of God's ongoing work of salvation in non-Christian cultures and is founded on it (*Lumen Gentium,* § 17).

b. The second consequence relates to the grace offered since Christ. It is a *Christic* grace, since any grace of salvation can come only from the Savior, and it is *Christo-conforming,* since within any period of salvation, to be saved means to be configured to Christ. However, this sanctifying grace is not the *Christian sacramental* grace, which carries a unique intensity of quality: Christian sacramental grace unites the person, through the sacramental character, to the visible and invisible cult of the Church's mystery (baptismal character and character of confirmation). This perfection of the grace of Christ is not bestowed through the sanctifying grace given outside the mediations instituted by Christ.

c. All the non-Christian religions are mixed realities where truth and error are found together. There is an urgency for the Christian mission of evangelization, because, often, the errors are more numerous than the truths.

In another paper in a contribution concerning implicit faith, I have tried to show that St. Thomas, following St. Augustine, St. Gregory the Great, and many others, acknowledged God's intervention through certain heralds during each of the ages of salvation in order that the saving faith might come to birth.[13] The main goal of these divine interventions was to reveal the Savior to come and to provide the signs that could give support to the profession of faith.

A Broader Understanding Is Made Possible through the *Summa Theologiae*

The understanding that the whole of the economy of salvation is sacramental, according to the meaning defined above, enlightens the whole plan of divine redemption. The cultic signs of a faith community are not the only signs that deserve the name of sacrament and that actualize its essence. The concept of sacrament is perfectly actualized in Christianity, because the sign indicates a causality really at work. Yet the same sacramental reality is present in many

---

13. B.-D. de la Soujeole, "Foi implicite et religions non chrétiennes," *Revue thomiste* 106, no. 1–2 (2006): 315–34, esp. 328–29.: Commenting on the six jars of water in the miracle of Cana (Jn 2:6), St. Augustine affirms (*In Jo.* tr. IX, 6, *Bibliothèque augustinienn* 71, p. 519): "Sex ergo illae hydriae, sex aetates significant, quibus non defuit prophetia." The context clearly shows that this refers to Augustine's notion of the six ages of the world (from Adam to Christ). St. Thomas takes up this exegesis in his *Lectura sup. Jo.,* cap. II, lect. 1 (Marietti, 357). St. Gregory the Great says likewise, referring to the parable of the workmen sent into the vineyard at different hours of the day (Matt 20:1–16): the workmen are the preachers who are sent during the different ages of salvation, starting with Abel the Just: "Hic paterfamilias ad excolendam vineam suam mane, hora tertia, sexta, nona et undecima operarios conducit, qui a mundi huius initio usque ad finem ad erudiendam plebem fidelium praedicatores congregare non destitit. Mane etenim mundi fuit ab Adam usque ad Noe, hora vero tertia a Noe usque ad Abraham, sexta quoque ab Abraham usque ad Moysen, nona autem a Moyse usque ad adventum Domini, undecima vero ad adventu Domini usque ad finem mundi . . . Ad erudiendam ergo Dominus plebem suam, quasi ad excolendam vineam suam, *nullo tempore* destitit operarios mittere" (*In Evang. Homil.* XIX, 1 [PL 76], 1154 B). This homily on Matthew (XIX) is one of the three main sources (with Origen and St. John Chrysostom) that St. Thomas uses in the *Catena aurea* (in Mattheum XX, 1), where he quotes the sentence word for word: "Ad erudiendum . . . nullo tempore destitit (Dominus) operarios mittere" (Marietti, 292).

other realities which precede and give foundation to the sacramental acts of the divine cult. In the first place, and St. Thomas readily acknowledges it, this is true of the presence of prophecy during each of the periods of salvation.[14] Such prophecy is ordered toward the establishment of a mode of worship or cult through which the saving faith may be professed. This cult, fully accomplished in its Christian state, is—to utter a commonplace—the joint activity of the Bridegroom and the Bride. Thus, the acting is sacramental because the Actors who act are themselves sacramental beings. The Fathers considered the sacred humanity of Christ as the sacrament *par excellence,* and his Bride as homogeneous to him in some way. Therefore, if there is an analogy of the reality of the sacramental acts, then there is an analogy of the ecclesial sacramental being which allows us to acknowledge the presence of the ecclesial mystery within the non-Christian religions. We thus put into practice the patristic tradition of the *Ecclesia ab Abel justo,* while distinguishing today the *tempus* from the *status.*[15]

Conclusion

It seems to me that the coherence of the theological proposition I present here clarifies for us the economy of salvation by showing its profound unity. Moreover, such coherence can be also found in an inverted manner if we choose to remain with the definition of the sacrament given in the *Commentary on the Sentences.* If the Christian sacraments are the only true sacraments—it must be so if causality expresses the essence of the sacrament—then only in the Christian religion can there be a sacramental economy of salvation. On this basis, if some people were able to be saved before Christ, which is

14. Particularly in *ST* II-II, q. 2, a. 7, ad 3: "Dicendum quod multis gentilium facta fuit revelatio de Christo, ut patet per ea quae praedixerunt. Nam Job dicitur: 'Scio quod Redemptor meus vivit' (Job 19:25). Sybilla etiam praenuntiavit quaedam de Christo, ut Augustinus dixit . . . Si qui tamen salvati fuerunt quibus revelatio non fuit facta, non fuerunt salvati absque fide Mediatoris. Quia etsi non habuerunt fidem explicitam, habuerunt tamen fidem implicitam in divina providentia, credentes Deum esse liberatorem hominum secundum modos sibi placitos et secundum quod aliquibus veritatem cognoscentibus ipse revelasset." See Journet, *L'Église du Verbe incarné,* vol. 3, 387–88, for a good commentary. St. Thomas acknowledged that it was possible for a prophet of demons (St. Thomas's name for a prophet of a pre-Christian religion) to speak through genuine divine inspiration; see *ST* II-II, q. 172, a. 6, ad 1: "Prophetae daemonum non semper loquuntur ex daemonum revelatione, sed interdum *ex inspiratione divina* . . . quia Deus utitur etiam malis ad utilitatem bonorum." We see, therefore, that St. Thomas holds that all prophecy is ordained to the knowledge of God and to faith. See *De veritate,* q. 14, a. 8, ad 13.

15. For a discussion of this patristic theme, see Yves Congar, "Ecclesia ab Abel," in *Abhandlungen über Theologie und Kirche,* Festschrift für Karl Adam, ed. Marcel Reding (Düsseldorf: Patmos Verlag, 1952), 79–108.

certain, and if they can still be saved today without having explicitly encountered Christian revelation, which is equally certain, this could be explained
only through a different, non-sacramental economy of redemption. This non-
sacramental economy could include the incarnate Word and his Spouse the
Church at best only as a tendency, but not as an analogical participation. This
would be so, because such an economy would be either purely individual or
hidden—touching each man singularly—or communitarian but outside the
Church and, for certain theologians, without the Word Incarnate either. This
is certainly not St. Thomas's understanding. Let us recall the affirmations of
the declaration *Dominus Jesus* concerning, in particular, the necessity of the
Church for the salvation of all people.[16] It is why we must profess that there is
only one economy of salvation; and I add, that is a unique, sacramental economy, more or less present according to the *status* in which each person lives.

Let me be precise: I am not saying that all the non-Christian religions are
surely, certainly, today, in their present situation an analogical presence of
the mystery of Church. We must distinguish: a priori, the sacramental structure can be present in all non-Christian religions and can be the basis for their
positive contribution to the salvation of their members. To say that the entire
history of salvation, with the distinction between *tempus* and *status,* is sacramental expresses that. But, and this precision is important, we must verify *a
posteriori,* studying each religion in its concrete, historical state today, whether
its actual situation is good enough to be, in the concrete, an actual presence, by
participation, of the unique sacramental economy of salvation.

16. Congregation for the Doctrine of the Faith, Declaration *Dominus Iesus* (2000), §§ 20–21.

[5]

The Place of Romans 6 in Aquinas's Doctrine of Sacramental Causality

A Balance of History and Metaphysics

BERNHARD BLANKENHORN, O.P.

There is a rather widespread tendency to read St. Thomas Aquinas as taking an ultra-metaphysical approach to the question of sacramental efficacy, one that leaves little room for history. For example, the medievalist William J. Courtenay has pointed to the role of monetary theory in Aquinas's sacramental theology, arguing that a limited Aristotelian vision of money as needing to have inherent value (as in the case of gold coins) led Aquinas to reject covenant theology or *sine qua non* causality, which had been promoted as the best model for sacramental efficacy by, among others, St. Bonaventure and the Oxford Dominican Richard Fishacre.[1] Covenant theology proposes that God's grace is given simultaneously with the performance of a particular liturgical rite, but not through an intrinsic power that is somehow present in the performance of sacramental acts. Rather, God's gift of grace in the sacraments may be compared to a king who sets up an order or pact by which he guarantees that

1. Bonaventure, *Commentarii in quatuor Libros Sententiarum Petri Lombardi*, ed. P. Bernardini (Florence, Italy: Quaracchi, 1882–1902), IV, d. 1, part 1, a. 1, q. 4; cf. ibid., I, d. 14, a. 2, q. 2; III, d. 40, dubia 3; Richard of Fishacre, *In librum IV Sententiarum*, dist. 1, in *De sacramentorum efficacia apud theologos ordinis praedicatorum*, ed. H.-D. Simon and G. Meersseman (Rome: Pont. Institutum internationale Angelicum, 1936); A. Michel, "Sacrements," in *Dictionnaire Théologique Catholique*, vol. 14 (Paris: Librairie Letouzey et Ané, 1939), col. 579–80.

136

certain lead coins have a buying power of one hundred marks because he will redeem them at that value upon demand. The sacraments thus retain the status of effective signs by the exterior causality of a covenant or pact instead of by an intrinsic causality. For Courtenay, Thomas's rejection of this causal model is driven by a particular (and very limited) kind of metaphysics.

For Thomas, just as a lead coin that could be used in exchange for food far exceeding the intrinsic value of the coin's metal is not an adequate kind of currency, so a sacramental act that does not involve an intrinsic spiritual power in the ritual words and actions is not a real type of causality, but merely a sign.[2] Thus, for Thomas, the need for a strong apologetic defense of sacramental efficacy and a sacramental theology influenced by less sophisticated ideas of commercial contract and currency, especially as reinforced by his study of Aristotle, caused him to support first the theory of disposing causality and later on the theory of (perfecting) instrumental causality for the sacraments.[3] I will argue, by contrast, that salvation history and the biblical narrative have a significant place in Aquinas's mature doctrine of sacramental causality.

More recently, the French theologian Louis-Marie Chauvet has offered a postmodern, Heideggerian critique of Aquinas's mature teaching on sacra-

---

2. William J. Courtenay, "The King and the Leaden Coin: The Economic Background of 'Sine Qua Non' Causality," in *Covenant and Causality in Medieval Thought: Studies in Philosophy, Theology and Economic Practice* (London: Variorum Reprints, 1984), 187–88, 191–93, 200–208. Courtenay also argues that the covenant theology school has its roots in the teaching of St. Bernard of Clairvaux, and was thus in a sense the oldest medieval theological school of thought that addressed sacramental causality: "Sacrament, Symbol and Causality in Bernard of Clairvaux," in *Covenant and Causality in Medieval Thought*, 111–22.

3. Courtenay, "The King and the Leaden Coin," 209. For the development in Aquinas's thought mentioned by Courtenay, see my "The Instrumental Causality of the Sacraments: Thomas Aquinas and Louis-Marie Chauvet," *Nova et Vetera* (English) 4, no. 2 (2006): 255–93. The thirteenth-century debate over sacramental causality involved three main schools of thought. Starting in the 1220s, one group of theologians proposed that the sacraments dispose us for grace by imparting the sacramental character (in baptism, confirmation, and holy orders) and by effecting an "ornament of the soul," while God alone imparts sanctifying grace. Its adherents included William of Auxerre, Alexander of Hales, Roland of Cremona, William of Melitona, Albertus Magnus, the early Aquinas, and (with reservations) the early Bonaventure. Some theologians felt that this theory did not go far enough and proposed that the sacraments are direct or perfecting instrumental causes of sanctifying grace. This view was first proposed in the 1230s by Stephen Langton and Hugh of St. Cher and was developed somewhat extensively by the late Aquinas. Starting in the 1240s, covenant theology emerged as a reaction against both of these schools, first in Oxford with Richard of Fishacre, and then in Paris with William of Auvergne and Bonaventure (especially in his later works); these early proponents were later to be followed by Robert of Kilwardby and others. See Courtenay, "The King and the Lead Coin," 190–92; Hyacinthe Dondaine, O.P., "A propos d'Avicenne et de St. Thomas: de la causalité dispositive à la causalité instrumentale," *Revue thomiste* 51 (1951): 441–53; Berndt Hamm, *Promissio, Pactum Ordinatio: Freiheit und Selbstbindung Gottes in der scholastischen Gnadenlehre* (Tübingen: Mohr Siebeck, 1977), 479–89. See also the citations in n. 1 above.

mental causality. In his influential work *Symbol and Sacrament*, Chauvet laments the ahistorical nature of that doctrine, one that necessarily follows from the dominance of a metaphysics of causality, especially the metaphysics of the hypostatic union as the first cause of grace perpetuated in the sacraments. Thus, the historical acts of Christ matter little, since, beginning at his conception, the structure of Christ's being has already determined everything. The sacraments simply perpetuate the static power of the hypostatic union.[4] Chauvet's extensive critique of Aquinas has been widely received in sacramental theology.[5]

The challenge that Courtenay, Chauvet, and others present seems formidable, especially in light of Thomas's best-known passages on sacramental efficacy. Thomas's central text on this topic in his *Commentary on the Sentences* proceeds in a highly metaphysical fashion, eliminating various philosophical alternatives with the help of Aristotle while virtually ignoring Scripture.[6] The parallel article in the *Summa theologiae* (III, q. 62, a. 1) may be more accessible, yet Thomas's method hardly seems to have changed. *Sine qua non* causality is rather briskly rejected as inadequate, which leaves us with perfecting instrumental causality as the sole contender.[7]

It is my contention that, through the progressive appropriation of Romans 6:3–5 in several *Summa theologiae* articles on the life of Christ and in one early article on the sacraments, Thomas attains the core of his doctrine of sacramental instrumental causality before he ever arrives at question 62 of the *tertia pars*, where one finds the most formal, direct treatment of the topic. My study

4. Louis-Marie Chauvet, *Symbol and Sacrament: A Sacramental Reinterpretation of Christian Existence*, trans. Patrick Madigan, S.J., and Madeleine Beaumont (Collegeville, Minn.: Liturgical Press, 1995), 453–56. I have offered a response to Chauvet on this point and some of his other critiques of Aquinas in my "The Instrumental Causality of the Sacraments."

5. See David N. Power, *Sacrament: The Language of God's Giving* (New York: Herder and Herder, 1999). Power essentially ignores the themes of sacramental causality and grace. Kenan Osborne's extensive polemic against classical metaphysics and its place in sacramental theology adopts much of Chauvet's critique (*Christian Sacraments in a Postmodern World: A Theology for the Third Millennium* [New York: Paulist Press, 1999]). Two recent conferences at the University of Leuven also manifest Chauvet's widespread influence. Citing Chauvet, one participant notes in passing that "the causality-thinking of medieval theology—sacraments as instruments of grace—is surpassed in today's theological thinking and accomplished by the aspect of personal commitment: sacraments are by definition sacraments of faith!" (Laszlo Lukacs, "Communication—Symbols—Sacraments," in *The Presence of God in a Postmodern Context*, ed. Lieven Boeve and Lambert Leijssen [Leuven, Belgium: Peeters, 2001], 148). See also the following proceedings: *Contemporary Sacramental Contours of a God Incarnate: Sacramental Presence in a Postmodern Context*, ed. Lieven Boeve and L. Leijssen (Leuven: Leuven University Press, 2001).

6. Thomas Aquinas, *Scriptum super Libros Sententiis* (Paris: Sumptibus P. Lethielleux, 1933–47), IV, d. 1, q. 1, a. 4.

7. Thomas Aquinas, *Summa theologiae* (Rome: Editiones Paulinae, 1962), III, q. 62, a. 1.

of Thomas's appropriation of Romans 6 will begin with his treatment of Romans 4:25 and 6:3–5 in his *Commentary on Romans*, a work that is contemporaneous with the third part of the *Summa*. I will then move to a consideration of the ways in which he uses Romans 6:3–5 in the *tertia pars*. Having established the place and function of Romans 6 in Thomas's theology, we can then evaluate the place of the biblical narrative and salvation history in that theology.

Sacramental Causality in Thomas's *Commentary on Romans*

Thomas's sacramentology must always be read through his Christology. Before Thomas expounds on Paul's baptismal theology in Romans 6, he finds the occasion, in commenting on Romans 4:25, to summarize Paul's teaching on the power of Christ's humanity: "Jesus our Lord was put to death for our trespasses and raised for our justification." Aquinas notes:

It must be said that the death of Christ was salvific for us, not only by mode of merit, but also by mode of a certain efficiency. For since the humanity of Christ is in some way *an instrument of his divinity*, as Damascene says, all passions and actions of Christ's humanity were salvific for us, as proceeding from the power of his divinity. But because an effect has the similitude of the cause in some way, the death of Christ, by which mortal life was extinguished in him, is said to be the cause of the extinction of our sins. Now his resurrection, by which he returned to the new life of glory, is said to be the cause of our justification, through which we return to the newness of justice.[8] (Italics mine)

Thomas appropriates St. John Damascene's teaching that the operations of Christ's flesh have a salvific efficacy through his divine power. Aquinas explains this teaching with the Aristotelian category of efficient causality. Behind Damascene stands none other than St. Cyril of Alexandria. Yet we are hardly witnessing the reduction of Greek Christology to the categories of Aristotle. Thomas's intention is to affirm the real emanation of divinizing

---

8. Thomas Aquinas, *Ad Romanos*, in *Super Epistolas S. Pauli Lectura*, vol. 1 (Rome: Marietti, 1953), ch. 4, lectio 3, § 380: "Et ideo dicendum est quod mors Christi fuit nobis salutaris, non solum per modum meriti sed etiam per modum cuiusdam efficientiae. Cum enim humanitas Christi esset quodammodo instrumentum divinitatis eius, ut Damascenus dicit, omnes passiones et actiones humanitatis Christi fuerunt nobis salutiferae, utpote ex virtute divinitatis provenientes. Sed quia effectus habet aliqualiter similitudinem causae, mortem Christi, qua extincta est in eo mortalis vita, dicit esse causam extinctionis peccatorum nostrorum: resurrectionem autem eius qua redit ad novam vitam gloriae, dicit esse causam iustificationis nostrae, per quam redimus ad novitatem iustitiae." In this essay, all translations of quotations from the Romans commentary and from the *Summa theologiae* are my own.

power from the whole humanity of the suffering and resurrecting Christ, one that he can explain best with the Aristotelian concept of causal efficiency. Of course, Thomas is in some ways exploding Aristotle's understanding of causality, since the Stagirite hardly imagined the possibility of an infusion of a spiritual form through a physical instrument. Even when he sounds Aristotelian, Aquinas's metaphysics moves well beyond Aristotle's limits.

Thomas then explains Paul's attribution of the forgiveness of sins to Christ's death and of our justification to Christ's resurrection. The apostle's teaching is puzzling at first, in that it seems to separate a single event, that is, the forgiveness of sins and justification, while also distinguishing the two central events of the Paschal mystery that would seem to be a single cause of forgiveness and justification. Thomas implies that Paul does not attribute the effects of forgiveness and justification to distinct efficient causes. Rather, he thinks that Paul attributes these effects to distinct exemplary or formal causes. The formal causality or likeness of the Passion is especially present in the forgiveness of sin, the "negative" element of the coming of grace, while the inseparable "positive" element of that event, the arrival of new life, especially involves the formal causality or likeness of Christ's resurrection. The power of both mysteries imparts, as a united efficient cause, the one grace that wipes away sins and grants a share in the divine life, while the two effects of that single event in the believer are the fruit of distinct formalities.

The interplay of formal and efficient causality allows Thomas to explain Romans 4:25 while maintaining the real unity of the Paschal mystery and the coming of grace into the soul of the believer. The result is that the power of the Passion and the power of the Resurrection are not separated, while each mystery is still granted a unique role in the life of the believer. It becomes clear that the Christo-forming grace of forgiveness and justification is not the effect of a "static" hypostatic union, but rather the fruit of particular acts of the Word Incarnate. The fruitfulness has been made possible by the hypostatic union, yet the fruit is spiritually "shaped" or "molded" by the particular events of the life of Christ. Christ imparts a grace that has been marked by his acts of dying and resurrecting.[9]

Here we can see Aquinas undertaking a striking development of Aristote-

9. As Jean-Pierre Torrell has noted, this has nothing to do with a theory that would posit the perpetual nature of Christ's historical acts in order to make the saving efficacy of those events present. Rather, it is the power of the event that is made present in the sacramental event, a power that has been metaphysically marked by the event. Torrell cites Charles Cardinal Journet's metaphor of an invisible star whose light has been refracted to earth by a planet that no longer exists. See his "La causalité salvifique de la résurrection du Christ selon saint Thomas," *Revue thomiste* 96, no. 2 (1996): 201.

lian metaphysics in order to shed light on an obscure biblical passage in a way that goes beyond the Christology of St. Cyril of Alexandria and St. John Damascene. Cyril's Christology involves a certain balance between the power of Christ's divinizing humanity and the merits of his acts. From the beginning of the Incarnation, Christ's flesh is life-giving, yet his Passion and Resurrection truly merit our salvation, truly make a difference in the order of grace. This balance between Christ's being and the value of his deeds, between metaphysics and history, certainly does tip toward the metaphysical side in Cyril's thought. We most often find his emphasis placed on the constant divinizing power of Christ's humanity.[10] For Cyril, moreover, Christ's created nature tends to be a relatively passive instrument of the divine power. He seems to downplay the active role of Christ's humanity in the metaphysical giving of divine life, probably in order to highlight the activity of the Logos through the humanity of Christ, and to avoid any semblance of competition between his two natures. The active contribution of the Savior's humanity is usually found in the spheres of merit, sacrifice, and moral exemplarity.[11] Damascene adds relatively little to Cyril, as he remains faithful to his project of synthesizing the Greek Fathers. In the cited passage, Damascene focuses on Christ's divinizing humanity as he engages in anti-Monophysite and anti-Monenergistic polemics.[12]

Aquinas appropriates the theology of these two Greek Fathers and synthesizes it with the Aristotelian formal causality that is implied in his comments on Romans 4:25. An effect has a certain similitude of the cause precisely because the efficient cause is also the formal cause. Therefore, the death of Christ is the formal cause of the death of sin in us. The efficient power of the Passion causes this death in us because it has been marked by the formality of the Passion. Efficient causality "moves through" formal causality as through a metaphysical filter. Likewise, Christ's Resurrection is the cause of our new life in justice, for the efficient power of the Resurrection "moves through" Christ's

---

10. B. Fraigneau-Julien, P.S.S., "L'efficacité de l'humanité du Christ selon saint Cyrille d'Alexandrie," *Revue thomiste* 55 (1955): 615–28.

11. Bernard Meunier, *Le Christ de Cyrille d'Alexandrie: L'humanité, le salut et la question monophysite* (Paris: Beauchesne, 1997), 120–23, 128–37, 225, 242, 282–84; Daniel A. Keating, "Divinization in Cyril: The Appropriation of Divine Life," in *The Theology of St. Cyril of Alexandria: A Critical Appreciation*, ed. Thomas G. Weinandy, O.F.M. Cap., and Daniel A. Keating (New York: T & T Clark, 2003), 174–76; Jean-Miguel Garrigues, O.P., M.-J. Le Guillou, O.P., and A. Riou, O.P., "Le caractère sacerdotale dans la tradition des pères grecs," *Nouvelle Revue Théologique* 103 (1971): 811–12.

12. St. John Damascene, "The Orthodox Faith," in *The Fathers of the Church*, vol. 37, *Writings*, trans. Frederic H. Chase, Jr. (Washington, D.C.: The Catholic University of America Press, 1958), bk. III, ch. 19; Andrew Louth, *St. John Damascene: Tradition and Originality in Byzantine Theology* (New York: Oxford, 2002), 144, 154–55.

act of appropriating new life. Whereas Cyril's Christology can explain why all of Christ's actions and sufferings are life-giving, the Alexandrian theologian mostly employs categories such as merit or moral causality to explain the significance of particular historical events for salvation. By developing Cyril's metaphysical Christology through a synthesis with Aristotelian formal causality, Thomas can explain the significance of particular historical events on a metaphysical plane. Formal causality thus enables Thomas to synthesize history and metaphysics, to explain why the particular historical events of Christ's life have particular metaphysical significance. Because of formal causality, the metaphysics of grace is utterly marked by history, that is, the single grace of forgiveness and justification at once bears the spiritual marks or similitudes of Christ's Passion and Resurrection.[13] The concept of formal causality hardly exhausts or comprehends the nature of Christ's saving mysteries, since we are dealing with a divine power that has taken on flesh, yet it moves the mind toward a deeper and more harmonious insight into the meaning of a rather perplexing Pauline passage.[14]

We can now turn to Aquinas's treatment of Romans 6. In verse 3, Paul speaks of being "baptized into Christ." Thomas offers three meanings of the

---

13. Torrell summarizes the point well: "Il s'agit de la grande loi selon laquelle l'agent efficient ne peut produire que du semblable à lui en sorte qu'il y a dans tout agir une certaine assimilation de l'effet à sa cause . . . les mystères sont réalisateurs d'une assimilation à Jésus d'abord et, par lui, à Dieu lui-même . . . Notre grâce est une grâce de fils adoptifs, mais aussi de souffrance, de mort, de résurrection et d'ascension par lui, avec lui et en lui. Nous sommes ici au cœur de l'exemplarisme ontologique et du mystère de la grâce christoformante" (*Saint Thomas d'Aquin, maître spirituel, Initiation 2* [Paris: Cerf, 1996], 186).

14. For a study of Aquinas's doctrine of the instrumentality of Christ's humanity in light of its patristic background, see Theophil Tschipke, O.P., *Die Menschheit Christi als Heilsorgan der Gottheit: Unter besonderer Berücksichtigung der Lehre des Heiligen Thomas von Aquin* (Freiburg: Herder, 1940), 20–85. The text is also available in a recent French translation, *L'humanité du Christ comme instrument de salut de la divinité,* trans. Philibert Secrétan (Fribourg: Academic Press, 2003). For Thomas's doctrine of Christ's saving mysteries, see especially Jean-Pierre Torrell, O.P., *Les mystères: La vie et l'œuvre de Jésus selon saint Thomas d'Aquin,* vols. 1–2 (Paris: Desclée, 1999). See also Michael J. Dodds, O.P., "The Teaching of Thomas Aquinas on the Mysteries of the Life of Christ," in *Aquinas On Doctrine: A Critical Introduction,* ed. Thomas G. Weinandy, Daniel A. Keating, and John Yocum (New York: T & T Clark, 2004), 91–115; Philip L. Reynolds, "Philosophy as the Handmaid of Theology: Aquinas on Christ's Causality," in *Contemplating Aquinas: On the Varieties of Interpretation,* ed. Fergus Kerr, O.P. (London: SCM, 2003), 217–45; Richard Schenk, O.P., "*Omnis Christi Actio Nostra est Instructio:* The Deeds and Sayings of Jesus as Revelation in the View of Thomas Aquinas," in *Studi Tomistici,* vol. 37, ed. Leo Elders (Vatican City: Libreria Editrice Vaticana, 1990), 104–31; Leo Scheffczyk, "Die Stellung des Thomas von Aquin in der Entwicklung der Lehre von den Mysteria Vitae Christi," in *Renovatio et Reformatio: Wider das Bild vom "finsteren" Mittelalter,* ed. Manfred Gerwing and Godehard Ruppert (Münster: Aschendorff, 1985), 44–70. The recently translated doctoral dissertation of Edward Schillebeeckx remains very valuable as well: *L'économie sacramentelle du salut,* trans. Yvon van der Have, O.S.B. (Fribourg: Academic Press, 2004), 129–53.

phrase "into Christ," the last being our conformity to Christ as taught in Galatians 3:27. This conformity or configuration (the two terms seem to be synonymous for Thomas) is twofold. First, there is a moral similitude, the sacrificial life whereby Paul "bears the marks of Jesus in [his] body" (Gal 6:17). Second, being configured to Christ's death means conformity to Christ through the power of his death.[15] Here, Thomas evokes his teaching on the divinizing power of Christ's humanity as expounded in his comments on Romans 4:25. But for the moment, he offers a biblical explanation of the phrase "the power of Christ's death." He begins with Revelation 1:5: "He washed us from our sins." He assumes that his students need no help to remember the rest of the verse: "in his blood." The connection between Romans 6:3 and Revelation 1:5 is found in the purifying power of Christ's blood as it is shed, which is the purifying power of his death, of his voluntary suffering and sacrifice for sins. This purifying power was manifested at his death when blood and water flowed from his side in John 19:34.

Aquinas then proposes a "demonstration" of Paul's teaching that all are baptized into a conformity to Christ's death. His "proof" is nothing other than an explication of the liturgical practice of the Church, which manifests the deeper meaning of Scripture. The baptismal rite includes a symbolic conformity to Christ's death through the threefold baptismal immersion signifying Jesus' three days in the tomb. This is why baptism is celebrated on Holy Saturday, the day when Christ's corpse was in the grave. The same principle of signification is followed in the practice of baptizing on Pentecost, for the Holy Spirit's power imparts a purifying force to the baptismal waters.[16] The whole liturgical rite (and not just its matter and form) manifests the gift that is imparted, so that the symbolism of the believer's share in Christ's death points to the gift of a metaphysical participation in that death. He might have added that it is precisely the doctrine of the instrumental causality of Christ's humanity

15. *Ad Romanos*, ch. 6, lectio 1, § 473: "Sicut igitur eius morti configuramur, in similitudinem mortis eius, quasi ipsam mortem Christi in nobis repraesentantes. II Cor. ch. IV, 10: 'semper mortificationem Iesu Christi in corpore nostro circumferentes.' Gal. ult. [VI, 17]: 'stigmata Iesu in corpore meo porto.' Vel 'in morte ipsius,' id est, per virtutem mortis eius. Apoc. I, 5: 'lavit nos a peccatis nostris.' Unde de latere Christi pendentis in cruce post mortem fluxit sanguis et aqua, ut dicitur Io. XIX, 34. Sicut igitur eius morti configuramur, inquantum peccato morimur, sic ipse mortuus est vita mortali, in qua erat similitudo peccati, licet non esset ibi peccatum. Ergo omnes qui baptizati sumus, mortui sumus peccato."

16. We might be surprised to find an apparent reference in Aquinas to the contemporary practice of baptismal immersion. In fact, Augustine Thompson, O.P., has shown that this was the standard practice in northern Italian communes in the high Middle Ages. See his *Cities of God: The Religion of the Italian Communes, 1125–1325* (University Park: Pennsylvania State University Press, 2005), 309–35.

that explains why the Christo-forming grace symbolized by the whole rite is given in baptism.

The sign of Christ's death that takes place in the baptismal act causes a death in the baptized, for the sacraments of the new law effect what they signify. In Aquinas's view, Paul himself implies this scholastic axiom.[17] We have been buried with Christ in symbol, so that we might truly die to sin, and we rise from the water so that we might truly walk in a new life. The ritual act effects the mystical union with Christ that is symbolized by the ritual itself. Thus, concludes Aquinas, the sign of Christ's death that we receive in baptism obtains our death to sin. Conformity to Christ on the symbolic and ontological levels obtains death to sin.

It is noteworthy that the language of causality is virtually absent from the *lectio* on Romans 6:1–5. Only in this one instance does Aquinas refer to baptism as "causing" death to sin. The term never comes up elsewhere in his explication of the notions of configuration to, conformity with, and insertion into Christ. Instead, Aquinas prefers to use Pauline language (such as "insertion," "incorporation," and "putting on") or language close to that of St. Paul (such as "configuration" and "conformity") to interpret the Apostle to the Gentiles. For Aquinas, these Pauline terms have causal meaning.

Thomas approaches his reading of Romans 6 having connected his doctrine of Christological efficacy to Romans 4:25, and he now appeals to Romans 6:3–5 to argue that the baptismal rite itself is the means to metaphysical, mystical union with the suffering and resurrecting Christ. Aquinas's exegesis is far from naive or outdated. Joseph Fitzmyer's commentary on Romans 6:3–5 is strikingly similar on certain points. For Fitzmyer, Paul's teaching is that the Christian is not merely identified with the dying Christ but introduced into his very act of dying. The believer is not just symbolically "with Christ" but actually experiences union with him. Baptism unites us not just to a likeness of that death, but also to Christ himself and to his body. We are identified with our Lord's act of dying and with the glorified Christ, and we are thereby enabled to live with Christ's own life.[18] Fitzmyer shows that for Paul, the sacramental rite is not extrinsic to this spiritual union with Christ. The expression "in a likeness of his death" in Romans 6:5 confirms this interpretation: "The

---

17. *Ad Romanos*, ch. 6, lectio 1, § 475: "Est tamen considerandum, quod corporaliter aliquis prius moritur et postea sepelitur; sed spiritualiter sepultura baptismi causat mortem peccati, quia sacramentum novae legis efficit quod signat. Unde cum sepultura, quae fit per baptismum, sit signum mortis peccati, mortem efficit in baptizato. Et hoc est, quod dicit, quod *sumus sepulti in mortem*, ut per hoc ipsum, quod signum sepulturae Christi in nobis accipimus, consequimur mortem peccati."

18. Joseph A. Fitzmyer, *Romans* (New York: Doubleday, 1993), 433–35.

dative ['in a likeness of his death'] is better taken as a dative of instrument, referring to baptismal washing as the means of growing together."[19] Like Aquinas, Fitzmyer insists that Romans 6:3–5 teaches the realism and intensity of the believer's union with Christ through baptism.

Romans 6:3–5 in the *Tertia Pars*

We are now ready to trace Thomas's integration of his Romans exegesis into his *Summa* teaching on sacramental causality.

Fittingly, Thomas already begins to refer to his teaching on sacramental efficacy in the question on the effects of the Passion, that is, in the treatise on Christ (*ST* III, qq. 1–59) that precedes the treatise on the sacraments (*ST* III, qq. 60–90). In question 49, article 1, he asks whether Christ's Passion liberates us from sin. The fourth objection expresses doubt that Christ's Passion can be a sufficient cause of such liberation, since baptism and penance seem to be necessary for the remission of sins. Aquinas answers that Christ's Passion is a universal cause that needs to be applied to each individual.[20] An efficient cause and its effect must be present to each other in a certain way.[21] Only such a mutual presence enables a causal event, since efficient causality involves a certain transfer of actuality, a certain "causal influx." Thomas is employing a kind of universal metaphysical heritage, a causal logic proposed both by Aristotle and by the Platonists, in order to explain the biblical text and the faith of the Church.[22] Question 49, article 1, sets the stage for Thomas's appropriation of Paul later in the *quaestio*.

In question 49, article 3, Thomas interprets the language of "configuration" in Romans 6 as the biblical equivalent of the metaphysical language of the application of a universal cause to an individual recipient through a particular cause.[23] Thomas sees no distance between the Pauline language of union with

19. Ibid., 435.

20. *ST* III, q. 49, a. 1, ad 4: "Ad quartum dicendum quod, quia passio Christi praecessit ut causa quaedam universalis remissionis peccatorum, sicut dictum est, necesse est quod singulis adhibeatur ad deletionem propriorum peccatorum. Hoc autem fit per baptismum et poenitentiam et alia sacramenta, quae habent virtutem ex passione Christi, ut infra patebit."

21. Thomas Aquinas, *Summa contra Gentiles*, bk. III, ch. 68, § 2425.

22. See *ST* I, q. 76, a. 2, which cites Aristotle's *Physics*. See also idem, *In librum beati Dionysii de Divinis Nominibus exposito*, ch. 5, lectio 2, § 662, which seems to synthesize Aristotle and Dionysius; idem, *Super librum de causis exposito*, prop. 1.

23. *ST* III, q. 49, a. 3, ad 2: "Ad secundum dicendum quod, sicut dictum est, ad hoc quod consequamur effectum passionis Christi, oportet nos ei configurari. Configuramur autem ei in Baptismo sacramentaliter, secundum illud Rom. VI, 4, 'consepulti sumus ei per baptismum in mortem.' Unde baptizatis nulla poena satisfactoria imponitur." The meaning of the term "configuration" is explained through the reference to q. 49, a. 1, ad 4 and ad 5. The latter of these texts

Christ and the metaphysical language of universal and particular causality. Romans 6:4 speaks of sacramental configuration, and the metaphysics of the application of a universal cause by a particular agent leads to the doctrine that one must be configured to Christ's Passion to obtain its effects. For Aquinas, Paul's teaching on co-burial and union with Christ points to the principle that a particular cause is needed to account for unity between a recipient and a universal cause whose efficacy does not automatically reach all beings in potency to that causal power. For Aquinas, the notion of sacramental causality as the particular causality applying Christ's universal causality appears as a clear expression of a reality already implicitly taught in Scripture.

The key *Summa* passage that argues for the casual efficacy of the sacraments on the basis of Romans 6 is question 61, article 1, a text on the necessity of the sacraments for salvation. The answer to objection 3 states:

> The Passion of Christ is a sufficient cause of human salvation. Nor does it follow that the sacraments are not necessary for human salvation, because they operate in the power of the Passion of Christ, and the Passion of Christ is in some way applied to us through the sacraments, according to the Apostle (Rom 6:3): "Those of us who have been baptized into Christ have been baptized into his death."[24]

Aquinas now shifts the discussion he began in the *Commentary on Romans* in two ways. First, he is speaking of all of the sacraments, not just baptism, even though he refers to a biblical passage that mentions only baptism. The unity of the sacramental order is simply presumed.[25] Each of the sacra-

---

(ad 5) twice mentions that the Passion "is applied to us," though its focus is on faith as the way to receive the fruits of Christ's sufferings. Neither passage in q. 49, a. 1, uses the term "being configured to Christ" or its substantive "configuration."

24. *ST* III, q. 61, a. 1, ad 3: "Ad tertium dicendum quod passio Christi est causa sufficiens humanae salutis. Nec propter hoc sequitur quod sacramenta non sint necessaria ad humanam salutem, quia operantur in virtute passionis Christi, et passio Christi quodammodo applicatur hominibus per sacramenta, secundum illud apostoli, Rom. VI, 3, 'Quicumque baptizati sumus in Christo Iesu, in morte ipsius baptizati sumus.'"

25. It is not unusual for Aquinas to begin with a single sacrament and then to apply the conclusions of his argument to all of the sacraments. See *De veritate*, q. 27, a. 4c; *ST* III, q. 62, a. 1. I would suggest three reasons for this key assumption of the sacraments' unity. First, the Fathers' and scholastics' sacramental exegesis of John 19:34 identifies the blood and water as references to the sacraments of the Eucharist and baptism. Yet the two most powerful sacraments are symbols of all seven sacraments precisely because they are the most efficacious of the holy rites. Second, the stream of blood and water in John 19:34 also signifies the birth of the Church taken from the side of Christ, as Eve was taken from Adam (Aquinas, *Super Evangelium S. Ioannis Lectura*, ch. 19, lectio 5, § 2458; *ST* III, q. 64, a. 2, ad 3). But the Church is constituted and sustained by all of the sacraments. The Church is invisible and visible, spirit and body, sustained by the bodily communication of spiritual realties. The temple of the Holy Spirit is built up through the material elements of the sacraments in which the Holy Spirit is present in a unique way. A third reason for this automatic application of baptismal texts to all of the sacraments is

ments, not just baptism, configures us to Christ, especially to the suffering Christ. Second, the *Summa* article focuses on the activity of the sacraments themselves and their causal source, which is Christ's Passion. An expression like "the sacraments operate in the power of Christ's Passion" is not to be found in the *lectio* on Romans 6. Aquinas implies that if the power of the Passion is active in each of the sacraments, then this power has been marked by the historical event from which it proceeds. All sacramental grace is Christoforming and deeply historical. Yet the sacraments themselves have an active role in conforming us to the crucified Christ.

I would propose two foundations for this position. The first is Paul's baptismal realism that Aquinas has already identified: the baptismal rite itself effects union with Christ. The second is that Aquinas thinks of sacramental operation through the model of Christological operation.[26] For Aquinas, the hermeneutical key for Paul's teaching is an image that synthesizes mysticism with the realm of nature: the Incarnation of the Word and the real instrumentality of the body for the healing power of Christ's divinity (the *Logos-Sarx* analogy which Thomas appropriates from the Greek Fathers as an aid in explaining the real operative unity of Christ's two natures).[27] Given this Christological background to Thomas's Sacramentology, and given the legitimacy of a qualified extension of Paul's baptismal teaching to the whole sacramental order, Aquinas has found a sound biblical and metaphysical foundation for his doctrine of sacramental operation.[28] The sacraments themselves enjoy an active

---

phenomenological. Aquinas is naturally and perhaps even unconsciously applying some (though certainly not all) elements of biblical teaching on baptismal efficacy to all of the sacraments because the very practice of the Church manifests the profound unity of the sacramental order. The liturgical life of the Church, both in Aquinas's age and in ours, points to the profound unity of the same sacramental economy, and thus to its unity of efficacy. The common use, prayers, and external symbols, especially of the words manifesting the ritual's effect connected to each of the sacramental rites, point to a profound harmony in the sacramental life of the Church. The phenomenon of ritual practice guides Aquinas's doctrine of sacramental causality. Aquinas's teaching on the sacraments is constantly rooted in the Church's act of celebration. Edward Schillebeeckx insists that the ecclesial practice of the sacramental life was the founding principle that dominated all theological reflection in the patristic and medieval eras. See his *L'économie sacramentelle du salut,* 320.

26. Thomas moved from disposing to direct or perfecting instrumental causality in his sacramental theology as soon as he developed a Cyrillian Christology that moved him beyond disposing Christological causality. Both doctrinal developments occurred in book IV of the *Summa contra Gentiles.* I trace this development in my "The Instrumental Causality of the Sacraments," 276–79, 282–84.

27. See *SCG,* bk. IV, ch. 24, § 3609. For the patristic roots of this analogy, see Thomas G. Weinandy, O.F.M. Cap., *Does God Suffer?* (Notre Dame, Ind.: University of Notre Dame Press, 2000), 182–90; idem, "The Soul-Body Analogy and the Incarnation: Cyril of Alexandria," *Coptic Church Review* 17, no. 3 (1996): 59–66.

28. I would thus want to nuance the claim in my previous article on sacramental efficacy

spiritual power, a participation in the spiritual power of the Word Incarnate in his action and suffering. The sacraments are an active, effective means to union with Christ. They *can* effect such union because Christ himself imparts such power to them. Every effect bears a likeness of its cause. The sacraments themselves *do* effect such a union because this is what Scripture teaches *if* it is read through Thomas's Cyrillian Christology and the liturgical practice of the Church that reveals the profound unity of the sacramental order.[29]

Finally, we should note that an essential background for the notion of the Passion's application to us through the sacraments is a certain understanding of grace. For Aquinas and the Fathers, justification is not a strictly juridical event but a real participation in the spiritual gifts of the Savior. Grace is really intrinsic, not just extrinsic.[30] Grace is a deepening metaphysical participation in the life of the Trinity and in the life of the mediator of all grace, the life of Jesus in his humanity. The language of the application of Christ's Passion is thus one way to speak about grace with a focus on its Christo-centric, Christo-forming nature. Life in Christ and the life of grace are two sides of the same coin. Both are intrinsic metaphysical realities that truly change the soul of the believer.

Aquinas proposes that biblical passages such as Romans 6:3 teach the instrumental causality of the sacraments. Being baptized into Christ's death means being united to the grace that proceeds from the suffering Christ. Paul is essentially concerned about baptism as a means to life in Christ, the center of his entire spirituality, and Aquinas's sacramental doctrine manifests the same focus. Neither Paul nor Aquinas is interested in a generic kind of grace. For Paul and Aquinas, grace is never a product or a thing, but rather a participation in the life of the Savior and the life of the Trinity.

Conclusion

Courtenay's critique of Aquinas's theory of monetary value is essentially accurate. Thomas simply could not imagine how money might have value if a coin's metal did not have an inherent worth. Thus, the rejection of *sine qua non* causality as mere signification seems like a logical consequence. For Aquinas,

regarding the function of Titus 3:5 in Thomas's argument in *ST* III, q. 62, a. 1. Thomas's creative appropriation of Greek Christology is an essential preliminary step toward arriving at his interpretation of sacramental efficacy in St. Paul. Blankenhorn, "The Instrumental Causality of the Sacraments," 286–89.

29. See n. 25 above.

30. The doctrine of created, intrinsic grace is not at all restricted to Latin patristic and scholastic theology, for it can also be found among numerous Greek Fathers. See Jean-Miguel Garrigues, "La Doctrine de la Grâce Habituelle dans ses Sources," *Revue thomiste* 103, no. 2 (2003): 179–202.

the lead coin is not a cause but a sign in the realm of economics, and thus if the sacraments are simply ordered to grace in the way that a lead coin functioned in the emerging economic practices of the thirteenth century, then these holy rites are not causes either. Courtenay correctly points out that Aquinas misunderstood the new economic context from which the example of the lead coin emerged, a context within which it truly functioned as a kind of cause, and not just a sign. But Aquinas's best reasons to reject *sine qua non* causality are found in his Christological model for the sacraments and in his interpretation of St. Paul's sacramental realism. Even if Thomas had correctly understood the significance and power of the lead coin, his Christology and biblical exegesis would have led him to the same conclusion. Once the sacraments are understood through the model of Christological efficacy, any financial analogy becomes utterly inadequate. In its context, the lead coin exercised a true causality because of an extrinsic power that it possessed. But Christological efficacy is all about an intrinsic metaphysical power. Thomas's insistence on intrinsic sacramental power is ultimately rooted not in an Aristotelian theory of money, but rather in his Cyrillian Christology.

Indeed, Aquinas's doctrine of sacramental efficacy is the fruit of a meditation on St. Paul, guided by the Fathers, in light of the liturgical practice of the Church, with the help of Aristotelian, Platonic, and original metaphysical tools.[31] What we find in Aquinas's manner of approaching sacramental causality does not involve the simple insertion of the sacraments into a pre-determined metaphysical model of causality, but rather a subtle, complex dialectic between metaphysics and history, between philosophy, Scripture, and the Fathers. We cannot reduce Aquinas's sacramental theology to a simple historical or philosophical starting point that determines all that follows. Rather, Aquinas's discourse manifests a stream of theological reflection that is fed by various sources, which in turn mingle and penetrate one another. That complex process of theological reflection produces a notion of sacramental efficacy in which virtually every key aspect (the power of Christ's humanity, the intrinsic power of the sacraments, Christo-forming grace) is shaped by a dialectic of history and metaphysics, both in the process of intellectual recognition and in the very content of the doctrine. Aquinas's theology of sacramental causality is utterly immersed in salvation history, a history whose glory shines forth when we approach it with deeply metaphysical eyes. *Gratia perficit naturam . . . et historiam.*

---

31. One finds an original metaphysical development of instrumental causality in the *Summa contra Gentiles* that goes beyond Aristotle, Plato, and their respective disciples. This evolution enables Aquinas to lay the philosophical groundwork that helps him, in the middle of his life, to grasp the intelligibility and consequences of Cyril's Christology. See Blankenhorn, "The Instrumental Causality of the Sacraments," 275–76.

[6]

The Human Acts of Christ and the Acts That Are the Sacraments

THOMAS G. WEINANDY, O.F.M. CAP.

In their constitution on the sacred liturgy, *Sacrosanctum Concilium*, the fathers of the Second Vatican Council stated:

The liturgy, then, is rightly seen as an exercise of the priestly office of Jesus Christ. It involves the presentation of man's sanctification under the guise of signs perceptible by the senses and its accomplishment in ways appropriate to each of these signs. In it, full public worship is performed by the Mystical Body of Jesus Christ, that is, by the Head and his members.

From this it follows that every liturgical celebration, because it is an action of Christ the Priest and of his Body, which is the Church, is a sacred action surpassing all others. No other action of the Church can equal its efficacy by the same title and to the same degree.[1]

In this essay I will address, from within a Thomistic context, what is here professed by the Council fathers. As the Council emphasizes the primacy of the "sacred action" within the sacramental liturgy, so there is also a primacy of "act" that makes "action" possible within Aquinas's thought, which I believe extends to his understanding of the sacraments.[2] It is this conciliar and Thomistic focus on the sacraments as the personal "acts" of Christ and of his

---

1. *Sacrosanctum Concilium,* § 7. Translation from *Vatican Council II: The Conciliar and Post Conciliar Documents,* ed. Austin Flannery (Wilmington: Scholarly Resources, 1975).

2. We find this already within Aquinas's early work, *De ente et essentia,* where he detects this

Body that gives them their inherent dynamism and vitality, and thus their un-equalled efficacy.

In order to conceive rightly and to articulate adequately this primacy of act within Aquinas's sacramental theology, I want to demonstrate that the sacraments are founded upon Jesus' historic, priestly, human actions, which he now, as its risen Head, actively makes sacramentally present within his Body, through those ministers who act *in persona Christi*. I will also consider how all believers are empowered to participate actively in these dynamic sacramental acts and so actively lay hold of the salvific events that they make efficaciously present. While I will not always agree fully with Aquinas's presentation, my hope is that this essay will, in the end, not only further our appreciation of his understanding of the sacraments, but also enhance our contemporary appreciation of these marvelous acts that are the sacraments.[3]

---

primacy of act within the metaphysical composition of finite beings. Because there is nothing within the definition of any finite being—what it is *(essentia)*—that demands that it be, it must be given being, *esse,* in order to be and so be in act. Aquinas further concludes that, since finite beings do exist and cannot, by their own nature, account for their own existence, there must be a being whose very nature, *essentia,* is being itself, *ipsum esse,* and so *actus purus,* pure act, who is thus capable of bestowing being, *esse,* upon all other beings. This being is called God. In the act of creation, God, by the pure act that he is, bestows the act of existence upon finite reality, thus allowing it not only to exist, but also to act in accordance with the potential inherent within its essence. The Thomistic principle is that a being can act, perform actions, only insofar is it is in act, that is, only to the degree that it possess the perfection of "being."

Thus, for example, I have argued that the Persons of the Trinity, because they possess the fullness of being, are subsistent relations fully in act. While the terms "Father," "Son," and "Holy Spirit" are nouns, yet what they designate are the fully relational acts by which they are the one God. The term "Father" is that act by which he begets the Son and spirates the Holy Spirit and so is the Father eternally subsisting only in relation to them. The term "Son" is that act of being Son of the Father and co-spirator of the Holy Spirit, and so is the Son eternally subsisting only in relation to them. The term "Holy Spirit" is that act of conforming the Father to be the loving Father of the Son and conforming the Son to be the loving Son of the Father and so is the Holy Spirit eternally subsisting only in relation to them. See Thomas G. Weinandy, *The Father's Spirit of Sonship: Reconceiving the Trinity* (Edinburgh: T & T Clark, 1994), and *Does God Suffer?* (Notre Dame, Ind.: University of Notre Dame Press, 2000).

3. There are a number of excellent introductory studies and articles on Aquinas's understanding of the sacraments. For example, see Edward Schillebeeckx, *L'économie sacramentelle du salut* (Fribourg: Academic Press Fribourg, 2004), 107–53; Liam G. Walsh, "The Divine and the Human in St. Thomas's Theology of Sacraments," in *Ordo sapientiae et amoris: Image et message doctrinales,* ed. Carlos Josaphat Pinto de Oliveira and Jean-Pierre Torrell (Fribourg: Editions Universitaires Fribourg, 1993), 321–52; and his "Sacraments," in *The Theology of Thomas Aquinas,* ed. Rik Van Nieuwenhove and Joseph Wawrykow (Notre Dame, Ind.: University of Notre Dame Press, 2005), 326–64; and John Yocum, "Sacraments in Aquinas," in *Aquinas on Doctrine: A Critical Introduction,* ed. Thomas G. Weinandy, Daniel A. Keating, and John Yocum (London: T & T Clark, 2004), 159–81.

The Human Acts of the Son:
The Foundation of Sacramental Acts

To understand how the incarnate Son of God is the foundation of sacramental acts, it is necessary to grasp the metaphysics of the Incarnation and the
kind of acts that necessarily flow from it. Within his incarnate state it is always
the Son of God who is the principal actor, but the manner in which he acts is
always *as man*, for that is the manner in which he now exists. For Aquinas, the
assumed humanity is thus a personal instrument of the Son. "The humanity of
Christ is the instrument of the Godhead—not, indeed, an inanimate instrument, which nowise acts, but is merely acted upon; but an instrument animat-
ed by a rational soul, which is so acted upon as to act."[4] The Son of God does
not employ his humanity as an external or separate instrument, as a man employs a pen to write. Rather, the Son of God personally acts through his humanity as a man acts through his own arms and hands. The Son of God is acting and the manner in which he is acting is in accordance with his manner of
existing—as man.[5]

Most importantly for our study, the acts by which humankind is saved are,
for Aquinas, the human acts of the divine Son. While only God could achieve

4. *ST* III, q. 7, a. 2, ad 3. All translations will be taken from the Fathers of the English Dominican Province (New York: Benziger Brothers, 1947).

For an excellent study of this topic, see Theophil Tschipke, *L'humanité du Christ comme instrument de salut de la divinité,* trans. Philibert Secrétan (Fribourg: Academic Press Fribourg,
2003). See also Paul G. Crowley, "*Instrumentum Divinitatis* in Thomas Aquinas: Recovering the
Divinity of Christ," *Theological Studies* 52, no. 3 (1991): 451–75.

5. This becomes very clear when Aquinas speaks of the one operation within Christ. Although the Son of God exists as God and so possesses a divine operation, such as sustaining
the universe, yet he also possesses a human operation in that he exists as man. Miracles exemplify this unity of operation perfectly. Following upon Dionysius's understanding of a "theandric" act, Aquinas perceives such an "operation not by any confusion of the operations or powers of both natures, but inasmuch as his divine operation employs the human, and his human
operation shares in the power of the divine," and thus "he (the Son) wrought divine things hu-
manly, as when he healed the leper with a touch" (*ST* III, q. 19, a. 1, ad 1). Thus for Aquinas, "to
heal a leper is a proper work of the divine operation, but to touch him is the proper work of the
human operation. Now both these operations concur in one work, inasmuch as one nature acts
in union with the other" (*ST* III, q. 19, a. 1, ad 5). These operations concur in the one act of healing the leper because the divine Son of God performed the miracle through the instrumentality of his humanity. "If we speak of the soul of Christ as it is the instrument of the Word united
to him, it had an instrumental power to effect all the miraculous transmutations ordainable to
the end of the Incarnation, which is 'to re-establish all things that are in heaven and on earth'
(Eph 1:10)" (*ST* III, q. 13, a. 2). What should also be noted here is that, unlike within the Old
Testament, where the touching of a leper contaminates the person, the touch of Jesus does not
contaminate him but actually brings healing. The touching is thus essential to the healing. Because of their "matter," the sacraments will, literally, keep us in touch with Jesus so that we can
be healed and sanctified.

our salvation, yet such a work was accomplished by the Son of God through his human actions:

> The instrument is said to act through being moved by the principle agent; and yet, besides this, it can have its proper operation through its own form . . . And hence the action of the instrument as instrument is not distinct from the action of the principle agent; yet it may have another operation, inasmuch as it is a thing. Hence the operation of Christ's human nature, as an instrument of the Godhead, is not distinct from the operation of the Godhead; for the salvation wherewith the manhood of Christ saves us and that wherewith the Godhead saves us are not distinct.[6]

I now will argue that there is in place a dynamic, causal sequence, beginning with the Son's priestly, human, salvific acts, which find their efficacious end in being made present through the sacraments.[7] The dynamic, causal link is the risen High Priest Jesus Christ, who is now Head of his Body. As Head of his Body, he acts so as to make sacramentally present these saving mysteries within his Body. Thus the one who enacted these saving mysteries on Earth is the same one who makes these same saving mysteries sacramentally present now—the one Lord Jesus Christ. To this end, I will first examine the sacramental significance of Christ's priestly acts and only then consider the acts of the risen Christ as Head of the Church. In so doing I am purposely reversing the order of Aquinas's treatment. He first treats in question 8 of part three of *Summa theologiae* the grace of Christ's headship, which he possesses because of the incarnational union of the humanity to the divinity, and only treats of Christ's priesthood in question 22. I believe that because Aquinas founds, in question 8, the grace of headship upon the incarnational union, this will conflict with what he will say about Christ's priestly acts in question 22, and his acts as Head of his Body the Church. While Christ, throughout the entirety of his life, acts as priest and as Head of the Church, yet his priestly actions culminate in the offering of his own life to the Father on the cross; and it is only in his resurrection that he is fully empowered to be the Head of the Church. My concern throughout is to keep the dynamic bond between Christ's salvific acts and his sacramental acts.

---

6. *ST* III, q. 19, a. 1, ad 2.

7. Aquinas states: "Since, however, the death of Christ is, so to say, the universal cause of human salvation, and since a universal cause must be applied singly to each of its effects, it was necessary to show men some remedies through which the benefit of Christ's death could somehow be conjoined to them. It is of this sort, of course, that the sacraments of the Church are said to be" (*SCG* IV, 56, 1). The translation is taken from Charles O'Neil, *On the Truth of the Catholic Faith* (Garden City: Image Books, 1957).

The Human Acts of Christ as Priest
and as Head of the Church

For Aquinas, a priest is a mediator between God and man, and as such his office is twofold. A priest "bestows divine things on the people" and "offers up the people's prayers to God, and, in a manner, makes satisfaction for their sins."[8] Christ fulfilled this priestly function in a pre-eminent manner, for he made it possible for humankind to share in the divine nature by reconciling it to God. Christ accomplished such a great work because, as priest, the act that he performed was to offer his own sacred humanity as a loving sacrifice.

Aquinas developed this understanding further. Human beings are required to offer sacrifice to God for three reasons: first, for the remission of sins; second, for the preservation of grace; and third, for perfect union with God. Again, Aquinas stresses here the singular importance of Christ's human acts:

Now these effects were conferred on us by the humanity of Christ. For, in the first place our sins were blotted out . . . Secondly, through him we received the grace of salvation . . . Thirdly, through him we have acquired the perfection of glory . . . Therefore Christ himself, as man, was not only priest but also a perfect victim, being at the same time victim for sin, victim for peacemaking, and a holocaust.[9]

It is this threefold effect of his priestly, sacrificial act as man that Christ, as the risen empowered Head of the Church, will make present, in various ways, within the sacramental acts—the forgiveness of sin, the grace of salvation, and the perfecting of glory:

[G]race was in Christ not merely as in an individual, but also as in the Head of the whole Church, to whom all are united, as members of the head, who constitute one mystical person [*mystice una persona*]. And hence it is that Christ's merit extends to others inasmuch as they are his members; even as in a man the action of the head reaches in a manner to all of his members, since it perceives not merely for itself alone, but for all members.[10]

---

8. *ST* III, q. 22, a. 1.

9. *ST* III, q. 22, a. 2. A similar argument is found within the notion that Christ is the Mediator. Christ is mediator between God and man not insofar as he is God, but insofar as he is man. "It belongs to him as man, to unite men to God, by communicating to men both precepts and gifts, and by offering satisfaction and prayers to for men. And therefore he is most truly called Mediator, as man" (*ST* III, q. 26, a. 2). Again: "Although it belongs to Christ as God to take away sin authoritatively, yet it belongs to him, as man, to satisfy for the sin of the human race. And in this sense he is called the Mediator of God and man" (*ST* III, q. 26, a. 2, ad 3).

10. *ST* III, q. 19, a. 4.

As the Head of the Church, Christ's actions bear upon his Body, the Church, and thus the human actions by which he merited his own glory is the same merit that he now extends to his Body. Aquinas treats this notion more fully when he speaks of the grace of Christ as Head of the Church.

Since the whole Church forms "one mystic body" whose members perform "divers acts," so Christ, as the Head of the Body, performs specific acts that pertain to him as Head. These acts concern "order," "perfection," and "authority." First, as Head of the Church and being nearest to God, his "grace is the highest and first." Second, as Head, Christ "had perfection as regards the fullness of all graces" (this finds its supreme summit in the Beatific Vision).[11] Third, as Head, Christ "has the power of bestowing grace on all the members of the Church."[12] What is significant here is that there is a progression that leads to Christ's ability to act as Head of the Church. Because he possesses the highest order of grace and the full perfection of grace, he, as Head, has the power and authority to bestow that grace upon the members of the Church. Moreover, because Christ is the Head of the Church, he bestows this grace as man. "To give grace or the Holy Spirit belongs to Christ as he is God, authoritatively; but instrumentally it belongs also to him as man, inasmuch as his manhood is the instrument of his Godhead."[13] Aquinas further accentuates the ability of the Son of God to act as man in the bestowing of grace:

Since everything acts inasmuch as it is a being in act, it must be the same act whereby it is in act and whereby it acts, as it is the same heat whereby fire is hot and whereby it heats . . . Now . . . grace was received by the soul of Christ in the highest way; and therefore from this pre-eminence of grace which he received, it is from him that this grace is bestowed on others—and this belongs to the nature of head. Hence the personal grace, whereby the soul of Christ is justified, is essentially the same as his grace as he is the Head of the Church, and justifies others; but there is a distinction of reason between them.[14]

Because the Son's humanity possesses the fullness of grace, he, as man, is in act such that he is able to bestow grace upon the members of the Church. While Aquinas does clearly teach that, as Head, it is the Son of God as man who bestows grace upon the Church, it is precisely here that I believe he may not appreciate fully the dynamic causal relationship and sequence between Christ's priestly action and his ability to act as Head of the Church.

11. For Aquinas, the highest grace and the most perfect grace in Christ is the beatific vision, which is a necessary result of the incarnational union of the divinity and humanity. See *ST* III, q. 10, a. 4.

12. *ST* III, q. 8, a. 1.   13. *ST* III, q. 8, a. 1, ad 1.

14. *ST* III, q. 8, a. 5.

Although Aquinas does speak of Christ meriting the grace of salvation through his priestly acts, yet, when he actually treats of the headship of Christ, he does so exclusively within the context of the grace that flows into Christ's humanity because of its singular intimate union with his divinity. Thus the Son of God bestows the grace upon his Church that his humanity first received by the very nature of the incarnational union. As Aquinas later states concerning Christ being Head of the Church: "Now the interior influx of grace is from no one save Christ, whose manhood, through its union with the Godhead, has the power of justifying."[15] Christ's manhood does have the power to justify us, not simply because of its union with his divinity, but also because of the priestly acts Christ performs as Head of the Church. Aquinas himself will acknowledge this, as we will see shortly, but he fails to grasp that this conflicts with his other view that Christ possesses the fullest and highest grace solely because of the incarnational union of the humanity to the divinity.

The Priestly Acts of Christ the Head

The reason Aquinas gets himself into this tension is that he insists, as did all the Scholastics, that Christ, from the moment of his conception, when his humanity was united to his divinity, possessed the Beatific Vision and thus the fullest and highest grace. Thus, for Aquinas, Christ always possessed the grace of headship which he would bestow upon believers. It is this insistence on the Beatific Vision that is the cause of Aquinas's conflicted positions—between that of Christ possessing the fullness of grace at the moment of his incarnation or also through the merits of passion, death, and resurrection.

I would argue that, while Christ did possess the fullness of grace insofar as it pertains to his earthly existence, it was only through the entirety of his life, culminating with his sacrificial death on the cross, that he merited the glory of his resurrection and thus the complete perfection of his humanity with its perfect heavenly filial vision of his Father.[16] The fullest and highest grace accrued to Christ's humanity only when his humanity was glorified in the resur-

---

15. *ST* III, q. 8, a. 6. Aquinas also states that, because Christ's soul possesses the fullness of grace because of the nature of the incarnational union, "it is poured out from it to others" (*ST* III, q. 7, a. 9).

16. I have argued that the notion of the Beatific Vision is incompatible with Christ's earthly life and that it is the wrong category to employ with regard to the Son's incarnational state. See my "Jesus' Filial Vision of the Father," *Pro Ecclesia* 13, no. 2 (2004): 189–201. Thomas Joseph White has argued against my position. See his "The Voluntary Action of the Earthly Christ and the Necessity of the Beatific Vision," *The Thomist* 69, no. 4 (2005): 497–534. For my subsequent response see "The Beatific Vision and the Incarnate Son: Furthering the Discussion," *The Thomist* 70, no. 4 (2006): 605–15.

rection, and only then did he become the Head of the Church with full power and authority.[17] As the Letter to the Hebrews professes, Christ became perfect only through suffering (2:10, 5:9, and 7:28), for it was only through his sacrificial death that he merited for himself and his brethren the glory of the resurrection.[18] Aquinas rightly holds that a being is able to act only insofar as he is in act, but the Son of God as man is fully in act only as risen, and thus it is only as resurrected, possessing the perfection of grace concomitant with his heavenly life, that he establishes himself fully as Head of the Church and so is empowered to act fully as such, bestowing grace upon its members.

Moreover, if Christ's grace of headship is founded solely upon the incarnational union, the meaning and significance of the sacraments would be undermined, for the sacraments would then make present merely the grace of the Incarnation. However, as Aquinas himself acknowledges, the sacramental acts do not bestow graces that simply flow from the Incarnation, but they make present Christ's incarnate priestly graces merited through the Paschal Mysteries—his passion, death, and resurrection. As we will shortly see, Aquinas founds the instrumental, causal efficacy of the sacraments on the "passion of Christ." It is through these Paschal events/acts that Christ obtained for the Church the grace of forgiveness, justification, and the heavenly glory; and it is now the risen Christ, the heavenly High Priest, as Head of the Church, who makes present these saving actions of the sacraments.[19] The Church and sacra-

17. In *ST* III, q. 7, a. 12, ad 3, Aquinas does make the distinction between the habit of grace and effects of grace: "Anyone may increase in wisdom and grace in two ways. First inasmuch as the very habits of wisdom and grace increased; and in this way Christ did not increase. Secondly, as regards the effects, i.e. inasmuch as they do wiser and greater works; and in this way Christ increased in wisdom and grace even as in age, since in the course of time He did more perfect works, to prove Himself true man both in the things of God, and in the things of man." While Christ did do greater works such as die on the cross so as to obtain our salvation, I want to say that this not only manifested grace that he already processed, but actually contributed to his perfection, that is, his own resurrection, which fully established him in power as Head of his Body the Church.

18. In his *Commentary on the Epistle to the Hebrews*, Aquinas states that Christ was perfected after his suffering not with regard to the Beatific Vision, which he had from his conception as man, but only insofar as his passible humanity became impassible. Having obtained complete perfection, he was now able perfect others. See 5.9 (260). I would agree that after Christ's resurrection he was perfected and so was empowered to perfect others. However, I would also want to say that this perfection consisted in more than his human body taking on impassibility. The perfection pertained to the whole of his humanity—body and soul.

19. Aquinas may be addressing this issue when he makes a distinction between "personal and capital grace" and "the grace of union." "Personal and capital grace are ordained to an act; but the grace of union is not ordained to an act, but to the personal being." For Aquinas, while the grace of union pertains to the fact that the Son of God exists as man, the personal or capital grace pertains to his ability to act as Head of the Church in bestowing grace. However, Aquinas proceeds to say that "the grace of union, the capital, and the personal grace are one in essence,

ments were born not solely of the Incarnation but from the pierced side of the incarnate crucified High Priest (see Jn 19:34–35). As Aquinas himself states: "[T]he Church is said to be built up with the sacraments *which flowed from the side of Christ while hanging on the cross.*"[20] It is the risen Lamb who was slain who presides over the heavenly liturgy and who makes that heavenly liturgy present and active within the sacraments (see Rev 5:6).

I have labored over these issues because I want to ensure that the proper foundation for the sacraments is securely and correctly laid. In so doing, I have continuously emphasized the dynamic notion of "act." The sacraments are primarily acts founded upon the priestly human actions of the Son of God—his passion and death. Moreover, the glorious and risen High Priest makes present, as Head of his Body, these same saving mysteries through the acts that are the sacraments. We will now examine Aquinas's teaching on how Christ acts, as the Head of the Church, within the sacraments so that these sacramental actions allow believers to be incorporated into the saving mysteries and so obtain their eternal effect.

Sacraments: Efficacious Signs

Aquinas begins his treatment of sacraments by stating that, having considered "those things that concern the mystery of the Incarnate Word, we must consider the sacraments of the Church which derive their efficacy from the Word incarnate himself."[21] Here Aquinas is clearly acknowledging that the incarnate salvific acts of Christ are the source of the efficacy of the sacramental acts.

As is well documented, Aquinas's understanding of the efficacy of sacramental causality developed, its most mature expression being found within the *Summa theologiae*.[22] For Aquinas, a sacrament is not merely "a kind of

though there is a distinction of reason between them" (*ST* III, q. 8, a. 5, ad 3). I believe that there is more than a distinction of reason between them, since only upon his resurrection did Christ obtain fully the capital grace whereby he became the fully empowered Head of the Church. Only after, and not prior to, his resurrection did the grace of union and capital grace become one in the person of Christ, for only then was the glorified incarnate Son fully empowered to act as Head in the bestowal of grace. See Jean-Pierre Torrell, O.P., "La causalité salvifique de la resurrection du Christ selon saint Thomas," *Revue thomiste* 96 (1996): 180–208.

20. *ST* III, q. 64, a. 2, ad 3. See also III, q. 64, a. 3; and q. 66, a. 3, ad 3.

21. *ST* III, q. 60, prae.

22. For an excellent study on this development, see Bernhard Blankenhorn, O.P., "The Instrumental Causality of the Sacraments: Thomas Aquinas and Louis-Marie Chauvet," *Nova et Vetera* (English) 4, no. 2 (2006): 255–93. See also John F. Gallagher, *Significando Causant: A Study of Sacramental Causality* (Fribourg: Fribourg University, 1965); Nathan Lefler, "Sign, Cause, and Person in St. Thomas's Sacramental Theology: Further Considerations," *Nova et*

sign," but a specific kind of sign in that it is a "sign of a holy thing in so far as it makes men holy."[23] While a sacrament is a sign, it is not an inactive sign but an active sign, for the enacting of the sign is in itself what makes men holy. Thus, sacramental actions contain within themselves sanctifying causality that effects holiness. As Aquinas states: "Since a sacrament signifies that which sanctifies, it must needs signify the effect, which is implied in the sanctifying cause as such."[24] The efficacious causality of a sacrament is founded, for Aquinas, on "Christ's passion." This causality is the source of present "grace and the virtues," and it ultimately fosters the goal of "eternal life." "Consequently a sacrament is a sign that is both a reminder of the past, that is, the passion of Christ; and an indication of that which is effected in us by Christ's passion, that is, grace; and a prognostic, that is, a foretelling of future glory."[25]

Aquinas proceeds not only to define the nature of a sacrament, but also to put into place the nature of its causal activity. First, a sacrament by its very nature must be a sensible sign, for otherwise it would not be intelligible. "Now it is part of man's nature to acquire knowledge of the intelligible from the sensible . . . [I]t follows that the sacramental signs consist of sensible things." Second, the significance (literally, what is signified) of these sensible signs can be grasped only by the appropriate sacramental words that make evident the inherent meaning of the sign. "Therefore in order to insure the perfection of sacramental signification, it was necessary to determine the signification of the sensible things by means of certain words . . . When we say: I baptize you, it is clear that we use water in baptism in order to signify a spiritual cleansing."[26]

Third, and what is of the utmost importance here, the sensible sacramental sign and the sacramental words achieve their effect only when they together become the one act that is the sacrament. A sacrament is not merely the union of a sign and words, but the performing of the action that the sign and the words signify and embody.

Aquinas notes that some have thought (for example, Hugh of St. Victor) with regard to baptism, "that water itself is the sacrament":

But this is not true. For since the sacraments of the New Law effect certain sanctification, there the sacrament is completed where the sanctification is completed. Now, the sanctification is not completed in water; but a certain sanctifying instrumental virtue, not permanent but transient, passes from the water, in which it is, into man who is the subject of true sanctification. Consequently the sacrament is

Vetera (English) 4, no. 2 (2006): 381–404; and Philip McShane, "On the Causality of the Sacraments," Theological Studies 24, no. 3 (1963): 423–36.

23. ST III, q. 60, aa. 1 and 2.   24. ST III, q. 60, a. 3, ad 2.
25. ST III, q. 60, a. 3.   26. ST III, q. 60, a. 6.

not completed in the very water, but in applying the water to man, that is, in the washing.[27]

Thus, for Aquinas, sacraments are efficacious acts that are enacted by sensible signs and words. In baptism it is the combined action of the pouring of the water and the pronouncing of the words that effects what this one action symbolizes and speaks—the cleansing of sin and being incorporated into the life of the Trinity.[28] However, we have yet to speak of the nature of this sacramental, causal action that effects what it symbolizes and symbolizes what it effects. Aquinas addresses this issue when he treats of the instrumental causality of the sacraments.

The Sacraments as Instrumental Efficient Causes

Are the sacramental acts inherently instrumental efficient causes of grace? Aquinas answers this question by noting again that some "say that they (sacraments) are the cause of grace not by their own operation, but in so far as God causes grace in the soul when the sacraments are employed." Aquinas gives as an example a man who presents a leaden coin, and, on the king's command, is given a hundred pounds. The leaden coin itself did not effect the giving of the hundred pounds, but the "mere will of the king . . . For the leaden coin is nothing but a sign of the king's command that this man should receive the money."[29]

In contrast, for Aquinas, an efficient cause can be twofold, principal and instrumental. "The principal cause works by the power of its form, to which the effect is likened . . . In this way none but God can cause grace: since grace is nothing else than a participated likeness of the Divine Nature." The sacraments are instrumental efficient causes "for they are instituted by God to be employed for the purpose of conferring grace."[30] Thus, the sensible sacramental action is the cause of the interior effect of grace. "For example, the water of baptism, in respect to its proper power, cleanses the body, and thereby, inasmuch as it is the instrument of the Divine power, cleanses the soul: since from soul and body one thing is made."[31]

---

27. *ST* III, q. 66, a. 1.

28. Walsh rightly states: "The words 'inform' by saying what the action means, rather than simply what the water means. And since both words and actions require a person to make them happen, matter and form can never mean impersonal objects waiting around for someone to pick them up. There is matter and form, and therefore a sacrament, only when persons are doing and saying something significant" ("Sacraments," 340).

29. *ST* III, q. 62, a. 1.

30. Ibid. See also ad 1.

31. *ST* III, q. 62, a. 1, ad 2. See also q. 62, a. 3. Although Aquinas does not state this, instru-

For Aquinas, then, the sacraments contain within themselves the power to cause grace. Again, "those who hold that the sacraments do not cause grace save by a certain coincidence deny the sacraments any power that is itself productive of the sacramental effect." However, "if we hold that a sacrament is an instrumental cause of grace, we must needs allow that there is in the sacraments a certain instrumental power of bringing about the sacramental effects."[32] For Aquinas, the power residing within a sacrament as instrumental cause comes from being moved "by the principal agent." Thus, "a sacrament receives spiritual power from Christ's blessing and from the action of the minister in applying the sacramental use."[33] We are now at the heart of Aquinas's understanding of the efficient instrumental causality of the sacramental action.

Aquinas brings all the above to bear upon the question of "Whether the Sacraments of the New Law Derive Their Power from Christ's Passion?" He states, as said above, that "a sacrament in causing grace works after the manner of an instrument":

Now an instrument is twofold; the one separate, as a stick, for instance; the other, united, as a hand. Moreover, the separate instrument is moved by means of the united instrument, as a stick by the hand. Now the principal efficient cause of grace is God himself, in comparison with whom Christ's humanity is as a united instrument, whereas the sacrament is a separate instrument. Consequently, the saving power must needs be derived by the sacraments from Christ's Godhead through his humanity.[34]

For Aquinas then, since Christ freed us from sin through his passion and since it is through his passion that he perfected the soul "in things pertaining to Divine Worship in regard to the Christian Religion," "the sacraments of the Church derive their power specifically from Christ's Passion."[35] Here

---

mental sacramental efficient causality is similar to the theandric actions of the Incarnate Son. The Son of God performs a miracle by his divine power but he does so by the instrumentality of his humanity. So too the sacramental acts effect interior grace but they do so through the sensible outward signs.

32. *ST* III, q. 62, a. 4.

33. *ST* III, q. 62, a. 4, ad 3.

34. *ST* III, q. 62, a. 5. Because Blankenhorn is very insightful on this issue, I will quote him at some length. "[I]t is through the instrumentality of the sacraments that I attain a real participation in the efficacy of past historical events, a spiritual contact with the power of Christ's saving actions. Through the sacraments, I enter into communion with the Christ of history two thousand years ago. I am not simply connected to the power of his hypostatic union, but rather to the power emanating from his humanity, to the 'instrumental flux' that was active in the particular operations of the Jesus of history" ("The Instrumental Causality of the Sacraments," *Nova et Vetera* [English] 4, no. 2 [2006]: 288–89). Yocum states that "the sacraments and the humanity of Christ are connected in the line of instrumental causality" ("Sacraments in Aquinas," 170). See also Walsh, "Sacraments," 347.

35. *ST* III, q. 62, a. 5. See also III, q. 64, aa. 3 and 7. Blankenhorn states that "the sacraments

we perceive all of the logical causal connections that bear upon Aquinas's understanding of the causality of the sacramental acts. By the united instrumentality of his humanity, the Son, through his passion, obtains the forgiveness of sins whereby we are reconciled to God and thus also obtains for us the grace whereby we are enabled to worship God properly within the sacraments. The sacraments, through their separated instrumental causality, make present the meritorious effects of Christ's passion; and so Christians are able to worship God in righteousness and holiness.

In the above, Aquinas, it appears to me, rightly founds the sacramental actions, not simply upon the grace bestowed on Christ's humanity through its incarnational union with his divinity, but also upon the human salvific actions of the Son of God. The human acts that make up the entire Paschal Mystery are the human instrumental causes whereby the Son obtains our salvation and whereby, I have argued, he merited the perfection of his own glory and ours as Head of the Body, the Church. What I find unsatisfactory, and it pertains to my previous criticisms, is Aquinas's lack of a theological development concerning Christ's action within the sacraments as the risen priestly Head of his Body and, because of this lack, a somewhat misconceived understanding of the instrumental nature of sacramental causality.

While the incarnate salvific acts of the Son of God as High Priest do bring about humankind's salvation, and so become the source of the sacramental acts, it is as the glorified risen High Priest that he makes these earthly efficacious acts present within the sacraments. It is as the risen Lord, whose blood ever intercedes on our behalf (see Heb 12:24), that he is Head of the Body and as the Head acts so as to sanctify his Body through the sacraments. What Aquinas does not appreciate fully is that this action of Christ the Head within his Body demands a new conception and articulation of instrumental causality that is in keeping with this new reality.

As stated above, there are, for Aquinas, two types of instrumental efficient causality. The first is that the principal agent employs what is constitutive of who he is to bring about an effect, as a man employs his body to bring about an effect, or the Son of God acts as man through the instrumentality of his humanity. Aquinas refers to this as a "united instrument." The second type of instrumental efficient causality is that whereby one uses something other than oneself to bring about an effect, such as a man using a pen to write. Aquinas refers to this as a "separate instrument," and he sees the sacraments as possessing

effect a real ontological connection with Christ's saving activity. In other words, they cause grace" ("The Instrumental Causality of the Sacraments," 287).

this type of instrumental efficient causality. Christ employs the sacraments as separate from himself to bring about an efficacious salvific effect. However, I want to argue that from within the unity of Christ, the Head, with his Body, there is third type of instrumental efficient causality that is unique to the sacraments which allows Christ to act in the sacraments in a much more personally direct and immediate manner.

The Sacraments: Mystical Instrumental Efficient Causes

The Mystical Body, through the shared life of the Holy Spirit, is one living reality. It is composed of the risen Christ as its Head and the members of his Body, the Church. Within this one Mystical Body there is what I would call a mystical instrumental causality, by which Christ as Head acts so as to sanctify his Body. This mystical instrumental causality finds its fullest expression within the sacraments (the Eucharist being its definitive expression), for they are his own personal, instrumental efficient causes in which he himself acts as Head so as to sanctify his Body. The sacraments are constitutive of the living and life-giving reality of the Mystical Body, for they are the mystical instrumental actions of Christ within his Body and, as such, they are personal, instrumental causal acts of Christ himself.

Within his incarnate state, the Son of God acted as man because that was the manner in which he existed. Within his resurrected state, the Son of God now acts as a glorious man, and, as such, does so as the Head of his Body. Although the sacraments do not accrue to the Son of God's glorious humanity in the manner in which he now exists as a glorious man, since they are distinct from him and in this sense are "separate" from him, nonetheless, they do accrue to him as to the manner in which he now acts within his Body as its risen, human Head. The sacraments are then efficacious instrumental causes precisely because through them Christ himself is personally acting as Head within his Body.

Since Christ and his Church form the one Mystical Body, Christ's sacramental actions as Head are of a singular causal nature. What makes them unique is that they are "mystical," in that they take place within the one reality that is Christ and his Church, and they are "personal" in that they are the personal actions of Christ as Head by which he sanctifies the members of his own Body.

The Sacramental Character and the Sacramental Act

My argument concerning the unique instrumentality of the sacraments within the Mystical Body of Christ can be clarified and strengthened by examining the nature of the sacramental character. For Aquinas the sacramental character is a "seal" by which God "imprints his character on us."[36] This seal deputes Christians "to spiritual service pertaining to the worship of God."[37] Significantly, this character or seal empowers the Christian to act in a twofold manner:

Now the worship of God consists either in receiving Divine gifts, or in bestowing them on others. And for both these purposes some power is needed; for to bestow something on others, active power is necessary; and in order to receive, we need a passive power. Consequently, a character signifies a certain spiritual power ordained unto things pertaining to divine worship.[38]

For Aquinas, the sacramental character empowers a Christian to act either insofar as he is an active minister in the bestowing divine gifts, such as the priest who baptizes or presides over the Eucharist, or insofar as a he is an active recipient of the divine gifts, such as the baptized Christian who participates in the Eucharist.[39] The power of the active minister, since it is sacramental in nature, is, for Aquinas, instrumental. "But it must be observed that this spiritual power is instrumental . . . of the virtue which is in the sacraments. For to have a sacramental character belongs to God's ministers: and a minister is a kind of instrument."[40]

What must be noted here is that the minister, through his sacramental character, is empowered to be an instrument through which the sacraments are enacted. From where does this sacramental character derive its instrumental power, and in what manner does it exercise such power? Since, for Aquinas, this sacramental character pertains to divine worship either in the power of bestowing or in the power of receiving divine gifts, "the whole rite of the Christian religion is derived from Christ's priesthood":

Consequently, it is clear that the sacramental character is especially the character of Christ, to whose character the faithful are likened by reason of the sacramental

---

36. *ST* III, q. 63, a. 1, s.c.   37. *ST* III, q. 63, a. 1.
38. *ST* III, q. 63, a. 2.

39. With regard to this active and passive power, Aquinas states: "It is the sacrament of Orders that pertains to the sacramental agents: for it is by this sacrament that men are deputed to confer sacraments on others: while the sacrament of Baptism pertains to the recipients, since it confers on man the power to receive the other sacraments of the Church" (*ST* III, q. 63, a. 6).

40. *ST* III, q. 63, a. 2. See also III, q. 64, a. 5.

characters, which are nothing else than certain participations of Christ's priesthood, flowing from Christ himself.[41]

Through the sacramental characters, Christians are conformed into the likeness of Christ and so come to share in his priesthood.[42] Thus, through the sacramental characters, they are empowered to act in a priestly fashion, either in bestowing or in receiving divine gifts within Christian worship. Aquinas further specifies that the sacramental characters are ordained to priestly action.

Since the sacramental characters pertain to the bestowing or receiving of divine gifts within Christian worship, which consists "in certain actions: and the powers of the soul are properly ordained to actions, just as the essence is ordained to existence. Therefore a character is subjected not in the essence of the soul, but in its power."[43] For Aquinas, the act of existence empowers the essence to perform acts in keeping with that essence. Similarly, the sacramental character empowers the soul of the Christian to perform actions in a manner in keeping with its Christian nature, that is, to perform actions in conformity with Christ the priest:

In a sacramental character Christ's faithful have a share in his priesthood; in the sense that as Christ has the full power of a spiritual priesthood, so his faithful are likened to him by sharing a certain spiritual power with regard to the sacraments and to things pertaining to the divine worship.[44]

Again, for Aquinas, this spiritual power pertaining to the sacramental character, by sharing in Christ's priesthood, is "an instrumental power."[45]

I previously argued that the risen Christ personally exercised his priestly ministry within his Body, of which he is the Head, through the instrumental causality of the sacraments. Because the sacramental action resides within the one living reality of the Mystical Body, the sacramental actions are not instrumental actions separate from Christ, as a man employs a pen to write, as Aquinas holds, but his own personal and immediate actions within his Mystical Body. In the light of the nature of the sacramental character, we can see more clearly why this is the case. The sacramental character conforms the minister into the likeness of Christ the priest and so the minister, insofar as he is instru-

---

41. *ST* III, q. 63, a. 3.

42. This further supports my argument that the grace whereby Christ, as Head, sanctifies his Body is derived not merely from the incarnational union of his divinity and humanity, but primarily from his priestly acts.

43. *ST* III, q. 63, a. 4.   44. *ST* III, q. 63, a. 5.

45. *ST* III, q. 63, a. 5, ad 1.

mental in bestowing grace, is empowered to act in union with Christ, *in perso-na Christi*.[46] The sacraments are instrumental causes of grace, not as impersonal causes separate from Christ, but as personal instruments of Christ because they are personally enacted by the minister. By being a member of Christ's Body and through sharing in Christ's very own priesthood, by the power of the sacramental character, the ordained minister acts in the very person of Christ. The acts that are the sacraments are the personal acts of Christ, performed as Head of his Body, because they are enacted by the minister who personally makes present, as a living member of Christ's one Body and through sharing in Christ's one priestly power and activity, Christ's redemptive priestly acts.[47] Aquinas states in relationship to the Eucharist:

[S]uch is the dignity of this sacrament that it is performed only as in the person of Christ. Now whoever performs any act in another's stead must do so by the power bestowed by such a one. But as the power of receiving this sacrament is conceded by Christ to the baptized person, so likewise the power of consecrating this sacrament on Christ's behalf is bestowed upon the priest at his ordination.[48]

I have argued that the instrumental causality enacted within the sacraments is unique precisely because it is personally enacted by Christ as the priestly Head of his one living Body. The manner in which Christ exercises this sacramental instrumental causality is through the ordained minister, who, by sharing in Christ's priestly power, actually acts *in persona Christi*, and so the priestly sacramental actions that he enacts are the priestly sacramental actions that Christ himself enacts as Head of his Body.[49] In this understanding

46. For a study of Aquinas's understanding of the minister acting *in persona Christi*, see Bernard Marliangeas, *Clés pour une théologie du ministère: In persona Christi, In persona Ecclesiae* (Paris: Éditions Beauchesne, 1978). I am indebted to Professor Germain Grisez for providing me with this reference.

47. Aquinas states: "For, clearly, Christ himself perfects all of the sacraments of the Church: it is he who baptizes; it is he who forgives sins; it is he, the true priest, who offered himself on the altar of the cross, and by whose power his body is daily consecrated on the altar—nevertheless, because he was not going to be with all of the faithful in bodily presence, he chose ministers to dispense the things just mentioned to the faithful" (*SCG* IV, 76, 7).

48. *ST* III, q. 82, a. 1. See also III, q. 78, aa. 1 and 4.

49. While the ordained minister acts *in persona Christi*, it is not as if he is absorbed into the hypostatic union. This is probably one of the reasons that Aquinas speaks of the sacraments being "separate" instrumental causes. Christ and the ordained minister are two distinct individuals. It should also be noted that although the minister acts *in persona Christi* as an instrumental cause in what is necessary to enact the sacrament, to do so he must possess the proper intention precisely because he is a rational agent acting in union with Christ. Moreover, the preaching of the ordained minister and the manner in which he presides over the liturgy can be means of grace, but this very much depends upon the holiness, learning, and gifts of the minister and his cooperation with the grace of Christ. I am grateful to Dr. John Yocum for pointing out to me these various important nuances.

of the sacramental action, everyone is in act—Christ and the priest—and thus the sacramental actions make efficacious the mysteries that they symbolize.

Sacramental Acts: The Acts of the Participant

Before concluding, I want to examine briefly the nature of the acts by which the participants within the sacraments lay hold of their salvific effects.

Within the discussion of the nature of the sacramental character, we saw that Aquinas holds that divine worship consists of either bestowing or receiving divine gifts. For both, a specific power is required. "[T]o bestow something on others, active power is necessary; and in order to receive, we need a passive power."[50] It is through baptism that Christians are empowered, through the sacramental character, to participate in and so receive the benefits of the other sacraments. While it is a "passive power," in that it is a power to receive, yet the ability to participate and so receive the benefits of the sacraments is an activity, an act of participation and reception. There is not only a sacramental dynamism in the bestowal of God's gifts, but also an equal sacramental dynamism in the reception of God's gifts.[51] This notion is of the utmost importance, for it is inherent within a proper understanding of the sacraments as acts. The sacraments are both acts of bestowal and acts of reception.

While Aquinas emphasizes within his treatment of the sacraments the sacramental action of bestowal, he is not ignorant of the sacramental action of participation and reception. He notes, for example, that the priest within the Eucharistic Liturgy speaks not only on behalf of Christ but also on behalf of the Church.[52] It is through speaking on behalf of the Church that the priest, together with all those participating, offers prayers to the Father in union with Christ through the power of the Holy Spirit. It is through this act of liturgi-

---

50. *ST* III, q. 63, a. 2.

51. Walsh puts this very nicely: "In Christian worship receiving is every bit as active as giving, because it is the taking hold of grace. It is, indeed, the action that lasts forever" ("Sacraments," 353).

52. See *ST* III, q. 82, a. 7, ad 3. Aquinas stresses the active nature of the participation and reception when he speaks of the "virtue of religion." Religion, as all virtues, pertains to acts, which are "proper and immediate acts, which it elicits, and by which man is directed to God alone, for instance, sacrifice, adoration, and the like" (*ST* II-II, q. 81, a. 1, ad 1). For the active nature of the "virtue of religion" as well as the active nature of "devotion," see *ST* II-II, q. 81, aa. 2–7; and II-II, q. 82, aa. 1–3. As Walsh states: "He (Aquinas) has been criticized for placing an excessive emphasis on the sanctifying movement of sacraments, as God giving grace to humans, and not enough emphasis on their cultic movement, as worship given by humans to God. However, one must remember that the cult movement of all human action, its *ordo ad Deum,* has been established in his theology of religion, and sacraments have been expressly identified as acts of religion" ("Sacraments," 332).

cal prayer that the priest and people participate in the sacramental action and so reap its sacramental effect. Within the Eucharist, this finds its culmination in the active receiving of Holy Communion, where one receives the body and blood, soul and divinity of Christ, and so is united to him and to the body of believers. Such an active participation and reception is also seen within the sacrament of penance, where sinners not only actively confess their sins in repentance but also actively receive sacramental absolution through their response of "Amen" and the performing of the act of penance.

What we find then in the acts that are the sacraments is the meeting of a twofold act within each of the sacraments. The first is the action of the risen Christ made present through the sacramental action of the minister. The second is the sacramental act of the participant by which he or she grasps, in faith and worship, Christ's action. It is the meeting of these acts, the sacramental act of Christ and the sacramental act of the participant, that constitutes the completion and efficacy of all sacramental acts. Moreover, it is this sacramental union of act to act that anticipates the fullness of act in heaven. There, in an immediate and non-sacramental manner, the Son of God as man will act so as to bestow the fullness of his risen glory and life, and the saints will act so to lay hold of these in the fullness of love and worship. It is the everlasting union of these heavenly human acts between Christ and the members of his Body that will effect full participation within the life of the Trinity and so the fullness of the divine vision and life. Until that glorious consummation, we must satisfy our longing by participating in Christ's priestly acts that are the sacraments.

Verum sacrificium as the Fullness and Limit of Eucharistic Sacrifice in the Sacramental Theology of Thomas Aquinas

Historical Context and Current Significance

RICHARD SCHENK, O.P.

In the last of his many encyclical letters, Pope John Paul II reminded us that "the Church draws her life from the Eucharist." And since, as that text will help to show at the end of this essay, the Church does so largely by being drawn into his sacrifice, her vitality will rise and fall with the vitality of her mission of Eucharistic sacrifice. Yet we cannot approach this topic today "innocent" of the many challenges and misunderstandings that have enveloped the notion of Eucharistic sacrifice. The initial section of this paper will illustrate the *status quaestionis* with three contemporary configurations of the *prima facie* challenge to an affirmation of this Eucharistic dimension of the Church: Eberhard Jüngel and contemporary ecumenical dialogue; René Girard and comprehensive theories of sacrifice; and contemporary directions of theodicy following the decline in popularity of process theology. While not formulated primarily within Catholic theology, these challenges prevent Catholic theology today from an easy and in this sense "naive" revitalization of the theology of sacrifice.

In its final section, this essay will examine two of the most prominent Catholic attempts of late to reconfigure a Catholic answer to challenges of this sort: either by abstracting from sacrifice the negative undertones and limitations upon human self-affirmation that the language of sacrifice seems necessarily to impy, leaving only its affirmation of human merits (Karl Rahner's elimination of the language of sacrifice but not of its perceived meritoriousness); or by dramatically ascribing even the negative dimensions of sacrifice to the very nature of God (Hans Urs von Balthasar's retrieval of Christ's ongoing intercession, inclusive of a properly divine suffering).

The inability of these prominent Catholic attempts to successfully reconfigure what is at stake in the Catholic tradition of sacrifice will be more evident in contrast to prefigurations of the question in medieval theology, which will be considered in the middle section of this essay. In contrast to the same excesses of negative (Richard Fishacre) and positive (Robert Kilwardby) portrayals of sacrifice parallel to the recent Catholic refigurations of Rahner and Bathasar, Thomas Aquinas indicated in his own historical context the advantages of a studied ambivalence toward sacrifice. Illustrated by Thomas's treatment of pre-Christian sacrifices, the death of Christ as sacrifice, the Eucharistic sacrifice, and Christ as the principle subject of the Eucharistic sacrifice, the study of the prefiguration of the notion of Eucharistic sacrifice prior to the Reformation can aid us in the refiguration of the Catholic tradition, learning even from some of the most direct challenges facing it (*pace* Jüngel and Girard). Accordingly, this essay is articulated into three sections on the configuration, the prefiguration, and the refiguration of the question of sacrifice.

Contemporary Configurations of the Question

The Ecumenical Configuration

The interpretive situation in which we usually encounter the average pre-understanding of St. Thomas's reflections on the "verum sacrificium" is still dominated by the stubborn legacy of sixteenth-century Reformation controversies on sacramental theology and justification. This standard configuration of the sacrificial problematic of the Eucharist is shared even by those most convinced that a far-reaching consensus on justification is otherwise both a given and an advantageous state of affairs. The irenic study published in 1986 by the Ecumenical Working Circle (*Ökumenischer Arbeitskreis Evangelischer und Katholischer Theologen*), charged with exploring the possibility of intercommunion and intercelebration between Catholics and Protestants, underscored first of all the necessary link of justification, sacraments (especially the Eucharist/the Lord's Supper), and ministry. It then claimed that a sufficient, if still somewhat partial, consensus concerning the sacrificial sense of Eucharist was already and had always been a given; it would suffice to remove misunderstandings that had obscured the consensus that had always perdured in this regard.

After 1992, when the Pontifical Council for Promoting Christian Unity received the anonymous and highly harmonistic expertise it had commissioned to support the 1986 study, the suggestion was adopted to bracket out the topics of sacraments, Eucharist, and ministry from the Joint Declaration on the Doctrine of Justification, but that decision had little to do with the sacrificial interpretation of the Lord's Supper, which the expertise, along the lines suggested in 1986 and in strict accordance with the irenic principles of an exclusively convergent ecumenism, deemed to make but little difference (sec. 6). The questions of ministry were the primary issues that, according to the expertise, required greater consensus. But the tactic chosen in the wake of the expertise meant that those questions of justification that historically arose in the context of ministry and sacraments would also be left unanswered by the Joint Declaration. The following seemed to have been overlooked in many reports: if indeed justification is the chief criterion of what is genuinely Christian, then the fact of abiding differences on sacraments and ministry points to abiding differences on justification, differences that are obviously not yet in the reach of a consensus statement. These studies of 1986 and 1992 claimed that the "misunderstanding" of Eucharist as a meritorious work was at the heart of Lutheran objections to the sacrificial language of the Eucharist, though perhaps it was merely a misreading of the Catholic position indulged in by Catholics and Protestants alike. One is reminded of the implicit wordplay between *offerens* and *operans,* or between *Opfer* and *opus,* sacrifice and work, which Martin Luther seemed to suggest already in *De captivitate Babylonica ecclesiae praeludium.*[1] In any case, the rhetorical accident underlined the chief substantive issue. The chief debate about the sacrifice of the Mass was its appearance to supporters and detractors as a meritorious human work.

In the context of the concerns around justification, the debate about Eucharistic sacrifice as a work of the Church had arguably been and still remains more divisive than the question of real presence. Prominent, but less harmonizing, Protestant voices were quick to point out the abiding incompatibility of the Catholic notion of Eucharistic intercession and sacrifice with a genuinely Lutheran sense of justification. The official response in 1991 of the Protestant faculty in Göttingen, or in the end just its Lutheran members, to the 1986 study defended the "theological judgment of fact," though not the hard language, of the Reformed disqualification of the Catholic Mass as a "denial of the unique

---

1. Martin Luther, *De captivitate Babylonica ecclesiae praeludium,* 1520, e.g., 523 W: "Nihil enim de opere vel sacrificio in illis continetur."

sacrifice and suffering of Jesus Christ and as accursed idolatry *(vermaledeite Abgötterei)*."[2] Because of the sacrificial themes of the Catholic Eucharist (as the position paper stated it), a genuinely Lutheran position was indeed excluded by the Tridentine critique and today could neither sanction nor "respect" the Catholic liturgy and piety (94); Lutheran theology sees the abolition of the Roman Canon as a "necessity" of Christian faith (107).[3]

Eberhard Jüngel, one of the most prominent voices in the controversies around the Joint Declaration on the Doctrine of Justification, brought new precision to the traditional Lutheran critique of Catholic views of the Eucharist as sacrifice. In 1998, he published reflections on the original three themes of that Catholic-Lutheran dialogue which had followed the visit of Pope John Paul II to Germany in 1980: justification, sacraments, and ministry. In *Justification: The Heart of the Christian Faith. A Theological Study with an Ecumenical Purpose,* Jüngel argued for the connection between the passive, forensic sense of justification and the subsequent denial of any significant, qualitative difference between the common priesthood of the faithful and the ordained priesthood. In Jüngel's view, any significant difference between the two forms of ministry would tend to portray the ordained priest and so his community as active in a sense incompatible with the fundamental tenet of an abidingly extrinsic and thus thoroughly passive justification. Both justification and this denial of a special sacramental priesthood form one and the same "articulus stantis et cadentis ecclesiae."[4]

In a talk of the same year at the "Katholikentag" in Mainz, Jüngel added into this equation the denial of the sacrificial character of the Church's role

---

2. Cf. 20 n. 14, quoting the eightieth question of the Heidelberg Catechism, *Die Bekenntnisschriften der reformierten Kirche,* ed. E. F. Müller (1903; Zurich: Theologische Buchhandlung, 1987), 704. The position paper of the faculty at Göttingen enunciated a counterposition to the 1986 study that in the end was too gnesio-Lutheran for the Reformed colleagues to sign.

3. Cf. Richard Schenk, "Das jr ewre Leibe begebet zum Opffer: Zur Frage nach dem 'vernünftigen Gottesdienst,'" *Wort und Antwort* 39 (1998): 147–56, and "The Unsettled German Discussions of Justification: Abiding Differences and Ecumenical Blessings," *Dialog: A Journal of Theology* 44, no. 2 (2005): 153–64.

4. Eberhard Jüngel, *Das Evangelium von der Rechtfertigung des Gottlosen als Zentrum des christlichen Glaubens* (Tübingen: Mohr Siebeck, 1998), par. V, iv, 4, p. 213: "Man geht nicht zu weit, wenn man auch von dem Grundsatz des allgemeinen Priestertums aller Glaubenden behauptet, was vom Rechtfertigungsartikel als ganzem gilt: nämlich daß mit ihm die Kirche steht und fällt"; in English, *Justification: The Heart of the Christian Faith. A Theological Study with an Ecumenical Purpose,* trans. Jeffrey F. Cayzer (Edinburgh: T & T Clark, 2001). According to Erwin Iserloh, *Der Kampf um die Messe in den ersten Jahren der Auseinandersetzung mit Luther* (Münster: Aschendorff, 1952), 11, Luther, too, after devoting a good decade to the defense of the real presence against Zwingli et al., returned, especially in the Smalcald Articles of 1537–38, to his earlier concentration on the critique of the Catholic notion of the sacrifice of the Mass, which he saw as the most permanent hindrance to Church unity.

in the Eucharist. What is unacceptable from a Lutheran point of view has less to do with the misguided notion of a possible addition of sacrifices to Christ's own. Jüngel allows that Trent's denial of such a multiplication of sacrifices makes agreement on this aspect attainable in principle.[5] What does seem to Jüngel most resistant to future consensus, however, is that aspect of sacrificial imagery which gives to the Church an active role in intercession, even if together with Christ.

Of course it remains unfortunate that the Roman Catholic Church following Trent continues to speak widely of the sacrificial action of the priest or of the Church. On the contrary: the self-sacrifice of Christ calls precisely not for our sacrifice, it does not call for us to do anything, but rather it calls for us to receive (although from this receptivity Christian action does result—just as the work week results from the creative passivity of the Sabbath).[6]

Whenever we come together for the celebration of the Lord's Supper, what is at stake is our very being as being together with God; and nothing else. In the Lord's Supper no demand is heard that would require deeds of us. The law that issues commands falls silent here. Here there is no room for the demanding Imperative. Here rules alone that Indicative of the gospel from which grace flows. This is the Indicative which transforms us from actors to recipients, which takes human beings from whom much—and even too much—is demanded, and makes them again into beings who are glad that they are able to exist, glad that they are able to be together with Jesus Christ, and so also with one another. In the Lord's Supper there rules already now that gospel ("evangelische") Indicative of peace, which will determine the life in God's heavenly kingdom. Therefore: *Sursum corda*—lift up your hearts![7]

Jüngel thus calls upon the Catholic faithful (not excluding ordained priests) to join now in the concelebration of the Lord's Supper in this Lutheran sense

---

5. Jüngel, "Church Unity Is Already Happening: The Path Towards Eucharistic Community," trans. Richard Schenk, *Dialog: A Journal of Theology* 44, no. 1 (2005): 30–37: "On the basis of these statements (at the Tridentinum) about the character of the sacramental action as uniquely representing Jesus Christ, it must be possible to reach basic agreement between the Lutheran churches and the Roman Catholic Church that Jesus Christ makes himself present in the Lord's Supper and that he is the one who really acts in the sacramental action, making us to be recipients."

6. Ibid. On the contrast indicative/imperative, cf. also the essays by Jüngel, *Indikative der Gnade, Imperative der Freiheit* (Tübingen: Mohr Siebeck, 2000). The Roman Canon suggests something more like an optative: "We come to you, Father, with praise and thanksgiving, through Jesus Christ your Son. Through him we ask you to accept and bless these gifts we offer you in sacrifice. We offer them for your holy Catholic Church, watch over it, Lord, and guide it; grant it peace and unity throughout the world."

7. Jüngel, "Church Unity."

of the rite and its premises in the—characteristically Lutheran—doctrines of justification and ministry.

The question suggested by the present-day ecumenical situation is whether there are to be found in Thomas Aquinas's writings on sacrifice resources for developing a sense of sacrificial and intercessory activity on the part of the Church and her ministers that deepens, rather than weakens, the sense of the primacy of Christ's agency in the sacrament—an agency that is indeed reflected in his graced communication of intrinsic justification and an attendent participation in Christ's priestly office by the common priesthood of the faithful assisted by the ordained priesthood.

Configurations of Sacrifice in Contemporary Discussions of Theodicy and Mimetic Theory

Without confusing in principle the "is" of theological trends with the "ought" of where they could best be headed, it seems possible to identify two trends in recent theology that have a high degree of plausibility in themselves and can help shape well the anticipation of an appropriately "ambivalent" sense of Christ's death as the fullness and the limit of sacrifice. Both developments must be viewed in the context of deepened reflection upon the violence of the last hundred years.

The first of these trends can be observed in the discussion of theodicy. If patristic and scholastic theology, with a few well-known exceptions,[8] tended to stress the impassibility of God for God's sake, in the modern era it became increasingly common, though still far from predominant, to deny the impassibility of God for the sake of human hope. Recent reflections on theodicy seem today increasingly inclined to stress the impassibility of God for the sake of human hope, and this view is strengthened rather than weakened by God's maintaining his constant rejection of the *novissima inimica* (1 Cor 15:26). The divinization of suffering in God's own nature would undermine the belief that suffering is opposed to God's absolute and unconditioned will and of itself ought not to be.[9] The concomitant potential of the Chalcedonian formula for strengthening human hope by refusing to dismiss the destructiveness of suffering has become increasingly evident, but with that, too, the ambivalence of suffering as shared by God in an assumed humanity but renounced by him in

8. Cf. Thomas Rudolf Krenski, *Passio Caritatis: Trinitarische Passiologie im Werk Hans Urs von Balthasars* (Einsiedeln: Johannes Verlag, 1990), esp. 56–89.

9. Cf. Friedrich Hermanni and Peter Koslowski, eds., *Der leidende Gott: Eine philosophische und theologische Kritik* (Munich: Wilhelm Fink, 2001); and Armin Kreiner, *Gott im Leid: zur Stichhaltigkeit der Theodizee-Argumente* (Freiburg: Herder, 1997).

his divinity (both of these for the sake of human hope) has become more evident.

The second trend is to be found in the broad discussion of the provocative theses of René Girard. The concentration upon the scapegoat mechanism as *the* soul of the many diverse forms and dimensions of sacrifice and as *the* culturally significant moment in the social history of mimetic desire might well be exaggerated, but it has the advantage of identifying the abiding *negativum* in all forms of sacrifice. And yet an *aporeia* was implied already in the early works of Girard, that this dysfunctional, because repetitively violent, form of lessening for a time the potential for still greater violence might arguably be preferred to no restriction at all upon the spiral of violence (so the logic of *Caiphas propheta* in Jn 11:49f.). This counterpoint to the sheer negativity of sacrifice becomes even more pronounced as Girard's thought develops the necessity of the innocent victim in the process of unmasking and vitiating this otherwise unrecognized and unchallenged mechanism of violence.[10] The salvific necessity of genuine victimization for the elimination of sacrifice is something in which the disciples of the Christ will continue to share, but equally without eliminating from their suffering that abidingly negative dimension of sacrifice. As in the recent treatment of the theodicy problematic, this discourse on scapegoating sharpens rather than glosses over an ambivalent stance toward the notion of sacrifice. Taken together with the older ecumenical task addressed by the topic of sacrifice, these newer issues shape the question of whether there is an anticipation in the writings of Thomas Aquinas of a rightly ambivalent attitude toward the notion of sacrifice that can deepen our sense of the *mysterium fidei*.

Historical Prefigurations of the Question[11]

Looking back again at the texts in which our question first received its traditional formulation, two features stand out. The first is the lack of a unified, much less a comprehensive, theory of sacrifice comparable to what has arisen today in, say, the discussion of the work of René Girard. There is no overarching treatise *De sacrificio in generali*. Prior to the challenges by the churches of

10. Cf. René Girard, *Bouc émissaire;* in English, *The Scapegoat,* trans. Yvonne Freccero (Baltimore: Johns Hopkins University Press, 1986), esp. chap. 9, "The Key Words of the Gospel Passion"; and Jeremiah Alberg, "The Place of the Victim," in *Victims and Victimization in French and Francophone Literature,* ed. Buford Norman (New York: Rodopi, 2005), 111–18; as well as his *Reinterpreting Rousseau: A Religious System* (New York: Palgrave Macmillan, 2007).

11. For a more detailed analysis of medieval theories of sacrifice, cf. Richard Schenk, "Opfer und Opferkritik aus der Sicht römisch-katholischer Theologie," in *Zur Theorie des Opfers,* ed. Richard Schenk (Stuttgart–Bad Cannstatt: Frommann-Holzboog, 1995), 193–250.

the Reformation to the sacrifice of the Mass, the notion of sacrifice even in the
context of the Eucharist was thought too obvious and too close to the texts
of institution to deserve problematizing; the established controversies around
the interpretations of real and/or symbolic presence preoccupied the discussion. Scholastic treatises on the Eucharist either neglected the question of sacrifice almost entirely (as in Bonaventure's commentary on the *Sentences*) or
they treated it largely in passing in the context of other themes.[12] Thomas belongs to this second type. The dynamics of sacrifice appear only in more or less
fragmented segments of theology: in soteriology (the death of Christ as sacrifice), in sacramental theology (the Eucharist as sacrament *and* sacrifice), in
theories of Christian life (moral virtues, infused virtues, and mystical union)
and Christian death (especially martyrdom as sacrifice), as well as, notably, in
the Christian theology of non-Christian religions, from which much of the following material will be taken.[13]

The second salient feature of this prefiguration is that, on the scale of historical stances taken in pre-modern theology toward the notion of sacrifice,
from the most sacrifice-critical to the most sacrifice-friendly, neither Thomas nor the Council of Trent (which unfortunately lies outside the scope of the
reflections offered here) takes a maximum or unambiguous position. In comparison with his contemporaries, Thomas displays an awareness of the ambivalence of the positive and negative dimensions of the notion of sacrifice that
will be suggestive for the systematic refiguration of our question.

What medieval authors thought about the sacrifice of Christ's death, the
Mass, or an ideal Christian existence depended to a large degree on what they
thought of earlier, literal sacrifice in the sense of the religious offering of animals and plants. The more negative these literal sacrifices were thought to be,
the more metaphorical and selective would be the application of this motif to
Christian mysteries. Karl Rahner summed up well the underlying issue:

The dogmatic problem of the concept of sacrifice consists in this: to develop a notion of sacrifice that on the one hand can do justice to the (admittedly uneven) data
of the history of religions in general, while on the other hand being applicable to the
"sacrifice" of Christ on the Cross and to the celebration of the Mass as "sacrifice,"
without doing violence to these two New Testament sacrifices. While it is true that
in the end what "sacrifice" means for the Cross and the Mass can only be understood
from these realities themselves, the explanation that these two realities are sacrific-

---

12. Cf. Burkhard Neunheuser, *Eucharistie in Mittelalter und Neuzeit* (Freiburg: Herder,
1963), 24–51.

13. For a general overview of the other diverse facets of the question, cf. Guy Boissard, "Le
sens chrétien du sacrifice," *Nova et vetera* (French) 81 (2006): 35–50.

es would also be purely tautological, if we couldn't presuppose a concept of sacrifice independent of our knowledge of these realities that we are seeking to better understand. That does not deny that this presupposed concept of sacrifice cannot be applied to these two realities in a modified and analogous sense.[14]

Certainly from the twelfth century on, a growing rift could be observed between theories developing the more critical attitude toward pre-Christian religions evident in Peter Lombard († 1160) and the more positive interpretations that followed the lead of Hugh of St. Victor's († 1141) reflections on pre-Christian religions. While this divide did not always match the more publically debated and far better known divide begun a century later between "covenantal" and "causal" readings of sacramental symbolism, both debates received a new impetus from the Christian reception of Maimonides (1138–1204). At the conclusion of his labors on the *Sentences*, St. Bonaventure († 1274), in his poignant complaint about the acrimony even within the Franciscan community over the second debate, recalled that the much revered bishop of Paris, William of Auvergne († 1249), had been among the early champions of a programmatic interpretation that saw the graciousness of the sacraments not so much as mediated through the symbolic meanings of the sacraments but as granted on the basis of obedience to an explicit *pactum* or covenant with God.[15] William had drawn much of his thought from the covenantal explanation of the Old Testament rites by Moses Maimonides in the *Dux dubitantium aut perplexorum*.[16] While this line of interpretation necessarily played down the intrinsic

14. Karl Rahner, "Opfer. V. Dogmatisch," in *Lexikon für Theologie und Kirche*, 2nd ed., ed. Michael Buchberger, Josef Höfer, and Karl Rahner (Freiburg: Herder, 1957–68), VII Sp. 1174: "Das dogmatische Problem des Opferbegriffes besteht darin, einen solchen Opferbegriff zu entwickeln, daß er einerseits den (allerdings in sich selbst sehr schwankenden) Daten der allgemeinen Religionsgeschichte gerecht wird, anderseits sowohl auf das 'Opfer' Christi am Kreuz als auch auf die Meßfeier als 'Opfer' angewendet werden kann, ohne diesen beiden neutestamentlichen Opfern Gewalt anzutun. Denn so wahr es ist, daß letztlich bei Kreuz und Messe nur aus diesen Wirklichkeiten selbst heraus ... gewußt werden kann, was bei ihnen 'Opfer' bedeutet, so käme die Erklärung, diese beiden Wirklichkeiten seien Opfer, auf eine leere Tautologie hinaus, wenn nicht eben doch ein vom Wissen um diese Wirklichkeiten, die ja selbst verständlich gemacht werden sollen, unabhängiger Opferbegriff vorausgesetzt werden könnte, der auf diese Wirklichkeiten wenigstens analog und modifiziert angewendet werden kann." Cf. idem, *Die vielen Messen und das eine Opfer* (Freiburg: Herder, 1951), 10ff., meant as a critique of Michael Schmaus, *Katholische Dogmatik*, vol. 3, bk. 2 (Munich: M. Hueber, 1941), 210.

15. Cf. Bonaventure's impassioned appeal to William's authority in defense of Bonaventure's support for the covenantal theory against William of Militona and others of his confreres: *Scriptum in lib. III Sententiarum* (Quaracchi: Ad Claras Aquas, 1902), 895f.

16. For Maimonides' critique of sacrifice cf. *Dux dubitantium aut perplexorum*, esp. p. III, cap. 32, and to a lesser extent 46. Cf. also W. Orenstein, "The Maimonides Rationale for Sacrifice," *Hebrew Studies* 24 (1983): 33–39; Stephen D. Benin, "The 'Cunning of God' and Divine Accommodation," *Journal of the History of Ideas* 45, no. 2 (1984): 179–91; Ch. Leben,

importance of ritual elements and actions, it did not necessitate—much less provide the only need for—harsh judgments about pre-Christian sacrifice. Unbeknownst to Latin theologians, Maimonides himself had in his Mishna commentaries defended the hope for the Messianic restoration of the temple sacrifices.[17] In the *Dux perplexorum*, however, Maimonides had offered a far more influential view, that the sacrifices of the Old Testament were not initiated by God; but rather, taken over from pagan religions, they were merely tolerated by him for a time out of consideration for the initial weakness of the new people he was forming.[18]

Richard Fishacre and the Critique of Sacrifice

Maimonides' critique of sacrifice found followers among many who ignored his covenantal (as opposed to instrumentally causal) interpretation of the grace given by the cultic rituals of the Bible. William of Auxerre describes the sacrifices of the Old Testament as "quasi coacta"; Hugh of St. Cher claims they were "quasi extorta."[19] But in the first commentary on the *Sentences* to originate in magisterial lectures at Oxford, Richard Fishacre († 1248) draws heavily on Maimonides to promote both the covenantal interpretation of grace in the sacraments of the younger covenant *and* the critique of sacrifices practiced under the older one. Richard transforms the prophetic self-critique of Israel's cult in Hosea 2:4–5 into a praise of Christian rites in comparison to the alien ones that he now describes as "baser and less efficient decorations,"

"L'interprétation du culte sacrificiel chez Maimonide," *Pardès* 14 (1991): 129–45; and Amos Funkenstein, "Gesetz und Geschichte. Zur historisierenden Hermeneutik bei Moses Maimonides und Thomas von Aquin," *Viator* 1 (1970): 147–78.

17. Moses Maimonides, *Mischne Torah,* lib. XIV (Sefer Schofetim), cap. 11, § 1; cf. lib. IX (Sefer Korbanot).

18. Maimonides seems to have composed *Dux dubitantium aut perplexorum* in Arabic around 1190. The dates given for the completion of the entire Latin translation range from around 1220 (Smalley) to 1240 (Kluxen), but at least parts of the work were sufficiently known by 1225 to inaugurate their discussion and reception; cf. Beryl Smalley, "William of Auvergne, John of La Rochelle and St. Thomas Aquinas on the Old Law," in *St. Thomas Aquinas 1274–1974: Commemorative Studies*, vol. 2, ed. Armand A. Maurer et al. (Toronto: PIMS, 1974), 11–72; and Wolfgang Kluxen, "Literargeschichtliches zum lateinischen Moses Maimonides," *Recherches de Théologie ancienne et médiévale* 21 (1954): 23–50; idem, "Maimonides und die Hochscholastik," *Philosophisches Jahrbuch der Görres-Gesellschaft* 63 (1955): 151–65; as well as Adrian Schenker, "Die Rolle der Religion bei Maimonides und Thomas von Aquin," in *Ordo sapientiae et amoris: Hommage au Professeur J. P. Torrell*, ed. Carlos Josaphat Pinto de Oliveira (Fribourg: Éditions Universitaires, 1993), 169–93.

19. Guillelmus Altissiodorensis, *Summa aurea* (Grottaferrata: Editiones Collegii S. Bonaventurae ad Claras Aquas, 1985), lib. IV, 16f. Hugo de S. Caro, *Commentarius in IV librum Sententiarum*, ed. Fr. Stegmüller (Uppsala: Uppsala Universitets Arsskrift, 1953), dist. 1, p. 64.

"viliora et inefficaciora . . . ornamenta."[20] While Fishacre can appropriate the older self-critique to warn against a multiplication of liturgical or even superstitious practices among Christians,[21] he sees the negativity of the older sacrificial rites as founded in the pagan practices more proximate to the Old Testament:

Because ceremonial rites of this kind were not pleasing to God, but rather extorted, and because he merely tolerated that they be offered to him to prevent them from being offered to animals . . . Therefore, just as what happens merely by God's forbearance and by the extortion of him in the extreme is not meritorious, so, too, the observance of such rites is also not meritorious.[22]

Fishacre reveals something more of his attitude toward ritual in general by arguing that sanctifying grace would most likely have come to pre-Abrahamic religions not by sacrifices or oblations but by the only religious rite to be maintained in its literal form by Christianity, namely tithing.[23]

In a first example of how the flight from sacrifice can end in introducing new sacrifices, Fishacre's critique of Old Testament sacrifice shows its limitations where, under the pressure of biblical and patristic witnesses, he first admits for the sacrament of initiation into the older cult the same grace-filled effects as for the Christian sacrament of initiation.[24] Unlike contemporaries such as Robert Grosseteste or Richard Rufus, Fishacre had even drawn the conclusion from this acknowledgment of Old Covenant grace that the ability to observe the Decalogue would have been no weaker then than now. But then the question arose as to why this parallelism would end here and not apply to the cult as a whole, into which circumcision introduced its recipients.

20. Gonville and Caius, Ms. 329, f. 354ra. Joseph Goering's upcoming edition of Fishacre's commentaries on Book IV of the *Sentences* will allow for the first time a reliable assessment of what likely was a wide reception of Fishacre's sacramental theology, not just in England. I want to thank Prof. Goering for sharing some of his discoveries and transliterations during the early stages of his editorial work.

21. Ibid., f. 354vb. In his works *De legibus* und *De sacramentis in genere*, William of Auvergne had developed this application of prophetic critiques of sacrificial ritual to the pastoral admonition of Christians in ways still more programmatic than Fishacre.

22. Ibid., f. 357vb: "quia huiusmodi caerimonialia non sunt Deo placentia, sed quasi extorta, et concessit ea sibi Deus offeri, ne offerentur idolis . . . Igitur sicut quod per licentiam fit et maxime extortam non est meritorium, sic nec observatio talium caerimonialium."

23. Ibid., f. 360ra. Fishacre appeals here to Hugh of St. Victor, *De sacramentis*, lib. I, p. 6, cap. 3 (PL 176, 448 D): "Sub lege naturali primum data sunt sacramenta decimationes, sacrificia et oblationes, ut in decimatione peccatorum remissio, in sacrificiis carnis mortificatio, in oblatione boni operis exhibitio significaretur."

24. Ibid. (Gonville and Caius, Ms. 329), f. 361rb: "Igitur concedo in sacramento circumcisionis et vi sacramenti sicut vi signi conferri gratiam, id est et Deum facere suscipienti circumcisionem gratiam et excitare in eo caritatem, quae est substantia totius gratiae vel summa."

Fishacre answers with a reference to the limitation of all cultically accentuated religions:

> With the exception of the ritual ceremonies, there were the same commandments under both laws and so one and the same degree of difficulty in following them. But the higher part of reason is less eagerly inclined to fulfill those ceremonial laws than the other ones, namely the moral laws, since the former are not as consonant with reason but rather are, as it were, extorted. In this sense the old law was harder for the higher part of reason to follow than the new law.[25]

Fishacre's reserve toward ritual qualifies his sense of New Testament ritual as well. Thus he denies that the symbolism of bread has any greater weight than some other food that might have been agreed upon for the sacrament. In what will become a much-discussed image, the choice of bread for the Eucharist seems no more intrinsic to the sacrament than the choice of lead for the tokens used to organize the royal feeding of the poor.[26] Cult and sacrament are reduced to obedience and the fulfillment of contracts, the symbolic details of which play only an incidental role. The liberation from the burden of ancient sacrifices is paid for here by the loss of appreciation for the symbolic nature of human hope. What remains a sacrament in the new dispensation, does so by virtue of extreme heteronomy and arbitrary commands. The liberation from sacrifice demands here a new sacrifice of its own.

Robert Kilwardby and the Affirmation of Sacrifice

Transforming the first three distinctions of Peter Lombard's *Sentences* into a long, thematically unified treatise on non-Christian religions,[27] Robert Kilwardby († 1279) shared with his older confrere at Oxford the preference for a programmatic covenantal interpretation of the sacramental grace of the New Covenant.[28] These sacraments derive their meaning and their power more

---

25. Ibid., f. 358[va]: "exceptis caerimonialibus eadem sunt in utraque lege, et ita eadem difficultas et aequalis. Sed ad implendum illa caerimonialia superior pars rationis minus satis inclinatur quam ad implendum alia scilicet moralia, eo quod non sunt ita consona rationi sed quasi extorta, et ideo superiori parti rationis difficilior est lex vetus quam nova."

26. Cf. Richard Fishacre, *In librum IV Sententiarum*, 1, excerpted in H.-D. Simonin, and G. Meersseman, *De sacramentorum efficientia apud theologos Ordinis Praedicatorum. Fasc. I: 1229–1276* (Rome: Pont. Institutum Internationale Angelicum, 1936), 11–20; and William J. Courtenay, *Covenant and Causality in Medieval Thought: Studies in Philosophy, Theology and Economic Practice* (London: Variorum reprints, 1984); as well as Berndt Hamm, *Promissio, Pactum, Ordinatio: Freiheit und Selbstbindung Gottes in der scholastischen Gnadenlehre* (Tübingen: Mohr Siebeck, 1977).

27. Robert Kilwardby, *Quaestiones in librum quartum Sententiarum*, ed. Richard Schenk (Munich: Bavarian Academy of Sciences, 1993).

28. Richard Schenk, "Divina simulatio irae et dissimulatio pietatis: Divine Providence and

from their arbitrary choice by the Divine Initiator of the *pactum* than from what we today would call an analogous sense of sacrament, the symbolic expectations associated with the symbols and—precisely by symbolizing—with their instrumentalization as a secondary cause of grace.[29] Unlike Fishacre, indeed with an intentionality unparalleled in medieval theology, Kilwardby expands this model to serve as an argument for the grace-giving dimension of pre-Christian rites in general.[30] At times, Kilwardby will criticize Peter Lombard openly, but constantly he inscribes his own answers to Peter's questions into a triadic scheme of progressively salvific history even more favorable to religions than Hugh of St. Victor. Kilwardby is well aware of his innovation.[31] The pre-Abrahamic sacraments were not *revealed* and contracted in the details of their rites, but they were *inspired* by God, whose grace led humans under the natural law to invent rites by which they could respond to and embrace the hope that God had inspired within them. The silence of this still outstanding revelation feigned God's anger and masked his continued *pietas* and loyalty toward humanity, but even these pretenses of harshness were offset by the preverbal inspiration of hope in God; and it was this graced hope that found rites such as animal sacrifice to successfully strengthen trust in God.[32] With the *lex scripta* of the Old Covenant, the rites, including sacrifice, were offered explic-

---

Natural Religion in Robert Kilwardby's *Quaestiones in librum IV Sententiarum,*" in *Mensch und Natur im Mittelalter,* ed. Albert Zimmermann (Berlin and New York: De Gruyter, 1991), 431–55; idem, "Christ, Christianity, and Non-Christian Religions: Their Relationship in the Thought of Robert Kilwardby," in *Christ among the Medieval Dominicans: Representations of Christ in the Texts and Images of the Order of Preachers,* ed. Kent Emery Jr. and Joseph Wawrykow (Notre Dame, Ind.: University of Notre Dame, 1988), 344–63.

29. Contrast to Fishacre the point that Thomas will draw from Hugh of St. Victor, *Summa theologiae* III, q. 64, a. 2, ad 2: "Ad secundum dicendum quod res sensibiles aptitudinem quandam habent ad significandum spirituales effectus ex sui natura, sed ista aptitudo determinatur ad specialem significationem ex institutione divina. Et hoc est quod Hugo de Sancto Victore dicit, quod 'sacramentum ex institutione significat.' Praeelegit tamen Deus quasdam res aliis ad significationes sacramentales, non quia ad eas contrahatur eius affectus, sed ut sit convenientior significatio."

30. Cf. Richard Schenk, "Covenant Initiation: Thomas Aquinas and Robert Kilwardby on the Sacrament of Circumcision," in Pinto de Oliveira, *Ordo sapientiae et amoris,* 555–93.

31. Kilwardby, *Quaestiones in librum quartum Sententiarum,* q. 45, 238, 36–41; cf. 31, 121, 126–35, and 131, l. 436–43: "Sed, cum secunda opinio videatur probabilior, tamen istud non satis mihi liquet, quod dicunt sacramenta vetera non esse instituta ad iustificandum sicut nova, et ideo non habere efficacem ordinationem ad hoc. Videtur enim quod immo per hoc, quod, sicut Deus in evangelio dixit qui crediderit et baptizatus fuerit salvus erit, sic in Levitico dixit de oblationibus pro peccato et pro delicto quod oraret pro peccatore sacerdos et dimitteretur ei peccatum."

32. Ibid., q. 4, 19, l. 133–38: "Tamen interim, ne desperaret homo vel absorberetur nimia tristitia, occulta inspiratione praestitit ei paenitentiam de peccatis et modum colendi Deum et placandi in oblationibus, decimis et sacrificiis, in quibus conciperet fidem et spem salutis. Hoc enim dictat aeterna veritas humanae conscientiae, quod iustitia Dei non punit aeternaliter, cui sua misericordia praestitit paenitentiam de peccatis commissis."

itly by God as a covenantal means of grace. From their divine origin and explicit promises, Kilwardby argues that their observance must also have led to the promised state of sanctifying grace even more surely than in the previous epoch of the *ecclesia ab Abel.*

Given his chief stress upon the grace given by the older rites, Kilwardby is then at pains to explain why the *lex scripta* relaces the cult *de lege naturali* and why the *lex nova* replaces the *lex scripta.* The problem is especially evident in his theology of sacrifice. On the one hand, Kilwardby exalts the sacrifices. His contemporaries were at most willing to allow to the sacrament of circumcision the effects of sanctifying grace. Kilwardby stresses the gracious character of the entire cult. For newly born girls and for boys dying before the eighth day, sacrifices could accomplish what circumcision did for others.[33] Because of their divine ordination, the ancient sacrifices restored and increased grace. They did this more by their own immanent meaning as occasions for obedience and trust and by their immediate theocentric empowerment than by their transcendent reference to the Christ to come.[34]

Even prior to the reversal of strategies by which Kilwardby justifies the advent of each new era of salvation history by the—surprising—near failure of the previous one, Kilwardby finally lets something of the negative dimension of sacrifice be felt. There is something after all that is troubling about these purportedly divine institutions. Kilwardby notes that of the three forms of pre-Abrahamic sacrifice (plant and animal sacrifices, as well as tithes) only two forms are preserved in the New Covenant. He explains this observation by referring to the lack of "decentia" that sacrifices have for a spiritual covenant. They are all too crass, too carnal.[35] If Fishacre had shown the limits of

33. Cf. ibid., q. 15, 59, l. 164–71; q. 16, 62–65; and q. 18, 74f., 183–93.
34. Ibid., q. 31, 130, l. 389–98: "Ad primum dicendum, quod semper hic loquimur de legalibus sacrificiis ut sacramenta sunt; sed de sacramentis est loqui dupliciter: uno modo, ut nomine sacramenti non intelligatur nisi signum exterius tantum; alio modo, ut comprehendat simul signum et signatum. Et utroque modo verum est quod sacramenta illa iustificabant: Primo modo, secundum scilicet quod sacramentum dicitur solum signum, dici potest quod iustificabant, quia, licet illa opera praeter divinam institutionem non iustificassent, tamen, ut ex divina institutione facta sunt signa oboedientiae et caritatis internae, vim iustificativam habuerunt, quaedam ad conferendum illam, quaedam ad augendum"; ibid., q. 31, 127f., l. 327–34: "exposcebant oboedientiam, et sic meritoria et iustificatoria fuerunt; et hoc quaedam conferendo iustitiam et quaedam augendo collatam. Et aestimo, quod haec causa oboedientiae scilicet fuit praecipua causa institutionis in illis universaliter loquendo, ut per oboedientiam homo mereretur vitam. Alia vero causa scilicet significationis fuit, ut videtur, minus praecipua ad erudiendum de futuris, in quibus erat plena iustitia. Magis enim erat necessarium homini tunc iustificari ad praeparationem erga veram salutem futuram, quam per signa talia erudiri de futuris."
35. Ibid., q. 37, 168, l. 394–98: "Aliae sunt causae tres quae ponuntur, dist. 11, cap. 10, scilicet meritum fidei, cautela abominationis tollendae et cautela tollendae exprobrationis perfidorum.

the critique of sacrifice, Kilwardby demonstrated *nolens volens* the limits of a single-minded and programmatic affirmation of sacrifice.

Thomas Aquinas and Programmatic Ambivalence toward Sacrifice

Thomas and the Memory of Literal Sacrifice Thomas Aquinas († 1274) lacked the single-minded suspicion or affirmation toward sacrifice that characterized most of the work of his two confreres. While admitting the need for divine institution and ordination to raise human symbolism beyond its connatural effects, Thomas differed from these two contemporary Dominicans by also remaining committed to the interpretation of the newer sacraments as rites in which the symbolic action itself plays an intrinsic, if instrumental, role in gracing human lives. By the basic structure of their core argument that sacraments cause by signifying, theologies of instrumental causality tend to have a more vested interest in ritual signification than do covenantal ones, which need not be concerned with the reasons for the arrangements agreed upon in the *pactum*. Possibly with direct reference to our two previous authors, more surely with an eye toward Bonaventure, Thomas rejects in his own *Sentences* commentary, and from then on, a merely covenantal interpretation of the younger sacraments.[36] While a search for the immanent and immediate meaning *(significatio)* of rites new and old always paralleled the level of grace expected to be given there *(effectus)*, this sense of symbolic causality naturally increased the attention paid to the origin and meaning of the symbolic dimension of the sacrament. Once exclusively positive or negative views of earlier animal sacrifice are excluded, the question becomes: Which aspects of ritual sacrifice are and which aspects are not important to the sacrificial meaning of the Eucharist?[37]

For the most part, Thomas shared with Kilwardby the refusal to reject

Item. Decentia hoc iuvat, quia spiritualius est et honestius tractare panem et vinum quam carnem animalis et sanguinem"; cf. q. 49, 249, l. 26–29; q. 33, 144, l. 34–38; and q. 37, 157, l. 110–18.

36. Cf. Thomas Aquinas, *ST* III, q. 62, a. 1. For Thomas's development of the notion of instrumental causality, both intrinsic and extrinsic, cf. Bernhard Blankenhorn's essay "The Instrumental Causality of the Sacraments: Thomas Aquinas and Louis-Marie Chauvet," *Nova et Vetera* (English) 4, no. 2 (2006): 255–93. For the internal development of Thomas's theology specifically on the Eucharist, cf. also Pierre-Marie Gy, "Avancées du traité de l'eucharistie de S. Thomas dans la Somme par rapport aux Sentences," *Revue des sciences philosophiques et théologiques* 77 (1993): 219–28.

37. The articles on the details of the Old Testament rites are the longest in the *ST*. It is therefore no surprise that Thomas seeks a closer differentiation of the terms *sacramentum, sacrum,* and *sacrificium: ST* I-II, q. 101, a. 4. It becomes clear that even where the *sacra* are not themselves sacrificial victims, they are often ordered to cultic sacrifice, just as *sacramenta* tend to remain bound to sacrifice (ibid., ad 2). Thomas includes among the *sacramenta* the Passover feast, diverse rites of purification, including ones with sacrifices, sacrifices of satisfaction, and sin offerings with the entire feast of the Atonement (*ST* I-II, q. 102, a. 5).

historical sacrifice as thoroughly corrupt and despicable from the start. With that, the Eucharistic sacrifice, whatever its metaphorical dimensions, would not need to be interpreted *totaliter aliter* than the dynamics of pre- or Old-Covenant sacrifices: it could share or even intensify features that had been essential to them, such as the necessity of divine acceptance or their being most frequently "for others." Sounding at times rather like Kilwardby, Thomas, too, suggested the likelihood of divine inspiration and instigation ("instinctus" as distinct from legal institution) behind a good deal of pre-Abrahamic cult;[38] and he saw sacrifice as the core of such cult.[39] He was willing to admit that, where the divine provenance of the older rites is accepted, a hermeneutics of trust toward the rite is called for.[40] If, on the one hand, at least the core meaning of literal sacrifices was moral enough to allow the death of Christ to be designated as "potissimum sacrificium," "hoc unum singulare et praecipuum sacrificium," and "verum sacrificium," as the focal point and final reference of all Old Testament sacrifices, so too did every age need to find its ultimate meaning in reference to the Cross of Christ, including—*pace* Fishacre—the experience of hope in the midst of evil: "aliquod repraesentativum Dominicae passionis."[41] Thomas sees this need of an earlier era for "something representing the Lord's passion" as demanding, for example, something like the sacrificial rite of Passover. The older sacrifices and the Cross of Christ illuminate one another:

the chief sacrament of which [that is, of Christ's death on the Cross] in the Old Testament was the Paschal lamb. And thus St. Paul says in 1 Corinthians 5:7: "Christ, our Paschal lamb, has been sacrificed." Following upon this in the New Testament is the sacrament of the Eucharist, which is meant to recall the previous suffering [of Christ], just as that [older] rite had been meant to prefigure [his] future suffering.[42]

38. *ST* I-II, q. 103, a. 1 co.: "Sed quia etiam ante legem fuerunt quidam viri praecipui prophetico spiritu pollentes, credendum est quod ex instinctu divino, quasi ex quadam privata lege, inducerentur ad aliquem certum modum colendi Deum, qui et conveniens esset interiori cultui et etiam congrueret ad significandum Christi mysteria, quae figurabantur etiam per alia eorum gesta . . . Fuerunt igitur ante legem quaedam caerimoniae: non tamen caerimoniae legis, quia non erant per aliquam legislationem institutae."

39. *ST* I-II, q. 101, a. 4, co.: "Ipse autem cultus specialiter consistit in sacrificiis, quae in Dei reverentiam offeruntur." Cf. *ST* III, q. 63, a. 6, co.: "Per modum quidem ipsius actionis pertinet ad divinum cultum Eucharistia, in qua principaliter divinus cultus consistit, inquantum est Ecclesiae sacrificium."

40. Cf. *ST* III, q. 70, a. 3, co.

41. *ST* III, q. 73, a. 5, co.: "sine fide passionis Christi nunquam potuit esse salus secundum illud, Rom. 3:25: 'Quem proposuit Deus propitiatorem per fidem in sanguine ipsius.' Et ideo oportuit omni tempore apud homines esse aliquod repraesentativum Dominicae passionis"; cf. *In lib. IV Sent.*, dist. 8, q. 1, a. 2.

42. *ST* III, q. 73, a. 5, co.: "Cuius in veteri quidem Testamento praecipuum sacramentum

This does not exclude, but presupposes, what Thomas, not unlike Kilwardby, calls the *finis duplex* of the older rites: "For it was ordained both for the worship of God in its own time and for prefiguring Christ."[43] The literal meaning of Old Covenant rituals had mostly to do with the veneration of God and the reception of his graces at the time of their practice. The figurative meaning, including its explicitly or implicitly Christological hope, was distinct from these more direct areas of intention, even if the source of their enrichment. The respect for those who were saved in this often indirect anticipation calls for a respect for their rites as well: "Nevertheless, the fathers of the Old Testament were being justified through faith in the passion of Christ, just as we are. And the sacraments of the old law were certain protestations or confessions of that faith, inasmuch as they were signifying the passion of Christ and its effects."[44]

At the same time, Thomas shared with Fishacre a keen and arguably growing sense of the always inadequate, often destructive and ungodly dimension of sacrifice. Drawing on Maimonides, Thomas saw it as a strength of the Old Testament cult that it tended progressively to restrict and curtail sacrifice rather than extend it.[45] Thomas's critique of the older rites usually took the form of accentuating their inefficiency *ex opere operato*.[46] Over much of his lifetime, Thomas had reserved symbolic instrumental causality to the initiation rite of

erat agnus paschalis; unde et Apostolus dicit, 1 Cor. 5:7: 'Pascha nostrum immolatus est Christus.' Successit autem ei in novo Testamento Eucharistiae sacramentum, quod est rememorativum praeteritae passionis, sicut et illud fuit praefigurativum futurae."

43. *ST* I-II, q. 102, a. 2, co.: "ordinabatur enim ad cultum Dei pro tempore illo et ad figurandum Christum"; cf. in the text cited in n. 38 above: "*et* conveniens esset interiori cultui *et etiam* congrueret ad significandum Christi mysteria" (emphasis added).

44. *ST* III, q. 62, a. 6, co.: "Et tamen per fidem passionis Christi iustificabantur antiqui patres, sicut et nos. Sacramenta autem veteris legis erant quaedam illius fidei protestationes inquantum significabant passionem Christi et effectus eius"; cf. *ST* III, q. 70, a. 1, ad 2: "per haec fiebat aliqua professio fidei"; and *ST* III, q. 70, a. 2, co.: "Circumcisio erat praeparatoria ad baptismum inquantum erat quaedam professio Christi, quam et nos in baptismo profitemur"; as well as *ST* I-II, q. 103, a. 2: "Poterat autem mens fidelium tempore legis per fidem coniungi Christo incarnato et passo: et ita ex fide Christi iustificabantur. Cuius fidei quaedam protestatio erat huiusmodi caerimoniarum observatio, inquantum erant figura Christi. Et ideo pro peccatis offerebantur sacrificia quaedam in veteri lege, non quia ipsa sacrificia a peccato emundarent, sed quia erant quaedam protestationes fidei, quae a peccato mundabat. Et hoc etiam ipsa lex innuit ex modo loquendi: dicitur enim Levit. 4 et 5, quod in oblatione hostiarum pro peccato orabit pro eo sacerdos, et dimittetur ei; quasi peccatum dimittatur non ex vi sacrificiorum, sed ex fide et devotione offerentium."

45. Referencing *Dux dubitantium aut perplexorum*, p. III, cap. 32, Thomas wrote: "Vetus lex in multis diminuit corporalem cultum. Propter quod statuit quod non in omni loco sacrificia offerentur, neque a quibuslibet. Et multa huiusmodi statuit ad diminutionem exterioris cultus; sicut etiam Rabbi Moses Aegyptius dicit. Oportet tamen non ita attenuare corporalem cultum Dei, ut homines ad cultum daemonum declinarent" (*ST* I-II, q. 101, a. 3, ad 3).

46. Cf. Matthew Levering, *Christ's Fulfillment of Torah and Temple: Salvation According to Thomas Aquinas* (Notre Dame, Ind.: University of Notre Dame Press, 2002).

the *lex scripta;* toward the end of his life, he reduced even this exception to that status of causality *ex opere operantis* that he had assigned from the beginning to the rest of pre-Christian cult.

In accord with the awareness that the "efficacy" of any sacrifice depends upon its acceptance by God, an acceptance that the human action and its victim cannot itself guarantee, Thomas stresses divine acceptance as a constitutive part of sacrifice. The *verum sacrificium* is an accepted sacrifice; indeed, the self-offering of Christ was "maxime acceptum." "And therefore this work, namely that he voluntarily accepted the passion, was most accepted by God as proceeding from charity. And by this it is clear that the passion of Christ was a true sacrifice."[47]

The frequency with which Thomas mentions the criterion of divine acceptance in distinguishing true from false sacrifice is characteristic of Thomas's analysis of sacrifice. It is one of the features that Thomas most often alludes to in the Roman Canon, where the sacrifice of Christ on Golgotha and in the Eucharist is said to share with the best of pre-Christian sacrifice that it was accepted by the Father. As in Thomas's discussion of merit generally, his attention to the necessity of the divine acceptance of human activity and suffering underscores here the moment of divine liberty, but without portraying God's freedom as sheerly arbitrary. It seeks its reasons, by raising and regarding the quality of human agents and their actions.[48] As Thomas learned progressively from Augustine, God's crowning of human merit is the crowning of his own gifts.[49] By stressing the interior motivation of the one who brings sacrifice, Thomas can address a number of interrelated matters: the metaphorical description of all virtue as sacrifice,[50] the prophetic critique of merely ex-

47. *ST* III, q. 48, a. 3, co.: "Et hoc ipsum opus, quod voluntarie passionem sustinuit, fuit Deo maxime acceptum utpote ex caritate proveniens. Unde manifestum est quod passio Christi fuit verum sacrificium"; cf. ad 1: "ex eo, quod erat caro ipsius offerentis, erat Deo accepta propter caritatem suam carnem offerentis." The stress on divine acceptance as the criterion of the true sacrifice will return in the context of the sacrifice of the Mass; cf. *ST* III, q. 83, a. 4, co.: "Sic igitur populo praeparato et instructo, acceditur ad celebrationem mysterii. Quod quidem *et* offertur ut sacrificium, *et* consecratur et sumitur ut sacramentum, primo enim peragitur oblatio; secundo, consecratio materiae oblatae; tertio, perceptio eiusdem. Circa oblationem vero duo aguntur, scilicet laus populi, in cantu offertorii, per quod significatur laetitia offerentium; et oratio sacerdotis, qui petit ut oblatio populi sit Deo accepta."

48. Cf. Joseph Wawrykow, *God's Grace and Human Action: 'Merit' in the Theology of Thomas Aquinas* (Notre Dame, Ind.: University of Notre Dame Press, 1995).

49. Cf. Augustine, *Epist. 194*, 19 (PL 33, 880f.), now paraphrased in the Preface for Holy Men and Women.

50. *ST* II-II, q. 81 a. 7, ad 2: "Sed exhibentur Deo tanquam signa quaedam interiorum et spiritualium operum, quae per se Deus acceptat"; cf. *Scriptum in lib. III Sent.*, d. 9, q. 1, a. 1, qc. 2, ad 1. "Ad primum ergo dicendum, quod offerre sacrificia est tantum de illis quae pertinent ad

ternal or fruitless ritual, and the unique place of Christ's offering as uniquely motivating the acceptance of the Father. The person of the Son establishes in one sense a unique motivation for the Father's acceptance; in another sense, Christ reveals the measure of all sacrifice. Thomas's accentuation of divine acceptance and of its motivation in the human subject ("ex caritate proveniens") as realities close to the core of sacrifice becomes clear in the soteriological reflections on Christ's death and resurrection that Thomas developed as the basis for his interpretation of liturgy and sacrament.[51]

Thomas and the Interpretation of Christ's Death as Sacrifice The *data* belonging most directly to the theology of religions are thus reflected as well in Thomas's soteriological accounts of the sufferings of Christ and their interpretation as sacrifice. Not the suffering itself, but the charity of Christ in the midst of his suffering is salvific ("non satisfactio . . . nisi ex caritate"). In a sense not unique to his theology, Thomas therefore warns against attributing every suffering to Christ: failings that would prevent charity would also prevent salvation.[52] Indeed, Thomas can claim in the end that the human sacrifices of the pre-Abrahamic cult have more in common with the criminal violence against Christ than with his transformation of these sufferings into genuine sacrifice by his own love.[53]

In his question *De modo efficiendi passionis Christi,* Thomas lists five traditional modes or models, in which we can understand the salvific character of Christ's tortuous death: merit, satisfaction, sacrifice, redemption, and instrumental causality. The following question adds to the list liberation and reconciliation.[54] The prologue to the *tertia pars* had already singled out the category of salvation. The very plurality of these eight modes suggests that no one of them is exhaustive; they are all ways of unfolding what is contained in the "hyper," the "pro" *nobis,* of the earliest soteriological expressions. Each of these models is also addressing a situation of suffering, which, far from perfective, appears as something to be overcome, a *vitandum.* Each model sees some

---

latriam elicitive; unde hoc quod dicitur, 'omne opus quo Deo iungimur, esse sacrificium,' est metaphorice dictum; inquantum Deum placabilem reddit, ad quod sacrificium offertur."

51. *ST* III, q. 83, a. 4, co., speaking of the priest at Mass: "Quarto, petit hoc sacrificium peractum esse Deo acceptum, cum dicit, *Supra quae propitio,* etc. Quinto, petit huius sacrificii et sacramenti effectum, primo quidem, quantum ad ipsos sumentes, cum dicit, *Supplices te rogamus;* secundo, quantum ad mortuos, qui iam sumere non possunt, cum dicit, *Memento etiam, Domine,* etc. tertio, specialiter quantum ad ipsos sacerdotes offerentes, cum dicit, *Nobis quoque peccatoribus,* etc. Deinde agitur de perceptione sacramenti."

52. *ST* III, q. 14, a. 1, ad 1; and q. 46, a. 5f.   53. *ST* III, q. 22, a. 2, ad 2.
54. *ST* III, q. 48, a. 1–6; q. 49, aa. 1–4.

participation in that suffering quasi, as necessary (but not sufficient) to overcome it. Usually, this participation in sufferings is shown to be insufficient of
itself to overcome the negativity shared. Such weakness is one feature that distinguishes the Christ of the biblical tradition from the typical mythological
hero. Regarding the most formal of these eight soteriological modi, *efficientia,* Thomas refers first to the inability of humans to effect their perfection on
their own. In his mature theology, Thomas then refers to the instrumentality
of Christ's passion.[55] Finally, Thomas refers to *ipse Deus,* who as *causa principalis* overcomes both common human sufferings and the death of Christ.[56]
Thomas will underscore that Christ's resurrection was not effected by Christ's
humanity.[57] Each of the modi reflects something of this threefold structure:
the non-perfecting negativity of the expeience, the instrumentality of human
agency, and the decisive agency of God. In discussing the soteriological mode
of sacrifice, Thomas highlights the features characteristic of his notion of "true
sacrifice": the subordinate role of the violence done; the acceptance of the Father; and the charity and intercession of the Son. Taken together, these constitute the *verum sacrificium.*[58]

Prior to the treatise on sacraments, Thomas treats of the priesthood of
Christ, both in discontinuity with its literal practice[59] (for which reason it was
fitting for Jesus to be a layman in the society of his time and to be named a
priest only after the destruction of the temple) and in fulfillment of the positive dynamic of its sacrifices, though on intentionally different terms. Thomas's use of the Letter to the Hebrews shows his intention of deepening both
these lines of thought.[60] Reflecting the increased skepticism toward literal,

---

55. Cf. Blankenhorn, "The Instrumental Causality of the Sacraments."

56. *ST* III, q. 48, a. 6.

57. *ST* III, q. 50, a. 6, co., and ad 1: Whatever belonged to Christ in death, "fuit nobis salu-
tiferum virtute divinitatis unitae . . . Mors Christi est operata salutem nostram ex virtute divinitatis unitae et non ex sola ratione mortis."

58. *ST* III, q. 48, a. 3: "*Christus* autem, ut ibidem Eph. 5 subditur, *seipsum obtulit in passione pro nobis,* et hoc ipsum opus, quod voluntarie passionem sustinuit, fuit Deo maxime acceptum, utpote ex caritate proveniens. Unde manifestum est quod passio Christi fuit verum sacrificium"; and ad 3: "Ad tertium dicendum quod passio Christi ex parte occidentium ipsum fuit
maleficium, sed ex parte ipsius ex caritate patientis fuit sacrificium. Unde hoc sacrificium ipse
Christus obtulisse dicitur, non autem illi qui eum occiderunt."

59. Cf. *ST* III, q. 22, a. 1, ad 2.

60. *ST* III, q. 22, a. 2, co.: "Tertio, per ipsum perfectionem gloriae adepti sumus, secundum
illud Heb. X, 'Habemus fiduciam per sanguinem eius in introitum sanctorum,' scilicet in glo-
riam caelestem. Et ideo ipse Christus, inquantum homo, non solum fuit sacerdos, sed etiam
hostia perfecta, simul existens hostia pro peccato, et hostia pacificorum, et holocaustum." For a
largely "synchronic" and text-immanent reading of Thomas's commentary on the Letter to the
Hebrews, cf. Antoine Guggenheim, *Jésus Christ, grand prêtre de l'ancienne et de la nouvelle Alliance: Étude du Commentaire de saint Thomas d'Aquin sur l'Épître aux Hébreux* (Paris: Parole et

pre-Christian sacrifice characteristic of his late work, Thomas even claims at one point that the continuity between the pre-covenantal sacrifices and the cross of Christ was to be located more in the criminal violence toward Christ, not in that in which true sacrifice consisted: the free offering accepted by God for the salvation of humankind.[61] Here it becomes clear what Thomas has taken from the history of literal sacrifice to delineate what he sees as the truth of sacrifice, manifested in Christ's union and transformation of both victim and priest.

Thomas and the Sacrifice of the Mass　This same keen sense of freedom from the destructive passion of sacrifice is reflected in Thomas's short explanation of the Church's practice of not celebrating the Eucharist on Good Friday. The Eucharist is meant to recall not only the sufferings of the Crucified but his being heard and accepted "pro nobis." On Good Friday, the first moment is too strong to grasp the truth of the sacrifice, the benefits for us.[62] The vivid vision of Christ's execution obscures for a time the *verum sacrificium,* which consists primarily not in the suffering of violence but in liberation from it, in the communication of grace *pro vobis et pro multis.*[63] It is inimical to the true sacrifice that Christ's glory would not be shared by others.[64]

---

silence, 2004). Appended (ibid., 741–56) are some brief remarks on the problems posed by the longer (additions?) and the shorter (abbreviations?) redactions of the commentary, which presumably have added to the reasons for the delay of the critical edition. For the historical-critical difficulties in dating and ordering the uneven tradition of Thomas's writings on the entire *Corpus Paulinum,* cf. Jean-Pierre Torrell, *L'initiation à Saint Thomas d'Aquin: Sa personne et son oeuvre* (Paris: Cerf, 1993), in English, *Saint Thomas Aquinas,* vol. 1, *The Person and His Work,* trans. Robert Royal (Washington, D.C.: The Catholic University of America Press, 1996), 250–61.

61. *ST* III, q. 22, a. 2, ad 2: "Ad secundum dicendum quod Christi hominis occisio potest ad duplicem voluntatem comparari. Uno modo, ad voluntatem occidentium. Et sic non habuit rationem hostiae, non enim dicuntur occisores Christi hostiam Deo obtulisse, sed graviter deliquisse. Et huius peccati similitudinem gerebant impia gentilium sacrificia, quibus homines idolis immolabant. Alio modo potest considerari occisio Christi per comparationem ad voluntatem patientis, qui voluntarie se obtulit passioni. Et ex hac parte habet rationem hostiae. In quo non convenit cum sacrificiis gentilium."

62. *ST* III, q. 83, a. 2, ad 1: "In hoc sacramento recolitur passio Christi secundum quod eius effectus ad fideles derivatur. Sed tempore passionis recolitur passio Christi solum secundum quod in ipso capite nostro fuit perfecta. Quod quidem factum est semel; quotidie autem fructum Dominicae passionis fideles percipiunt. Et ideo sola commemoratio fit semel in anno; hoc autem quotidie et propter fructum et propter iugem memoriam."

63. *ST* III, q. 83, a. 2, ad 2: "Veniente veritate cessat figura. Hoc autem sacramentum est figura quaedam et exemplum passionis Dominicae . . . Et ideo in die, quo ipsa passio Domini recolitur prout realiter gesta est, non celebratur consecratio huius sacramenti. Ne tamen ecclesia eo etiam die sit sine fructu passionis per hoc sacramentum nobis exhibito, corpus Christi consecratum in die praecedenti reservatur sumendum in illa die."

64. On the significance of Eucharistic texts and practice for understanding sacrifice, cf. also Matthew Levering, "Aquinas on the Liturgy of the Eucharist," in *Aquinas on Doctrine: A*

From his writings on the *Sentences*[65] through the Eucharistic treatise in the *Summa theologiae*,[66] Thomas insisted on a dimension of sacrifice that is not a feature common to all the sacraments (*pace* Luther and Jüngel):

This sacrament is at once both a sacrifice and a sacrament: it has the character of sacrifice insofar as it is offered; and the character of a sacrament, insofar as it is taken. And thus it has the effect of a sacrament in the one who takes it, but the effect of a sacrifice in the one who offers it or in those for whom it is offered.[67]

This manner of identifying the chief structure of sacrifice is all the more striking, since Thomas repeatedly cited with approval Augustine's and Hugh's definitions of sacrifice as a kind of sacrament.[68] Presupposing the image made popular by Hugh of St. Victor,[69] namely that of the sacraments as vials (*vasa*) containing the medicine of spiritual grace to heal the sick who take it,[70] Thom-

---

Critical Introduction, ed. Thomas Weinandy, Daniel Keating, and John Yocum (London: T & T Clark, 2004), 183–98, esp. 190ff.

65. Cf. *Scriptum in lib. IV Sent.,* d. 8, q. 1, a. 1, qc. 3, ad 5; d. 12, q. 2, a. 2, qc. 2, ad 4. Included among those who do not receive the Eucharist as a sacrament but for whom it is offered as a sacrifice are those who are not actually members of the mystical body, with the intercession "ut sint membra."

66. Cf. *inter alia ST* III, q. 73, a. 4, ad 3; q. 82, a. 4, co.; q. 83, a. 4, co. and a. 6, ad 2; as well as q. 79, a. 7, ad 3: "Ad tertium dicendum quod sumptio pertinet ad rationem sacramenti, sed oblatio pertinet ad rationem sacrificii."

67. *ST* III, q. 79, a. 5, co.: "Respondeo dicendum quod hoc sacramentum simul est et sacrificium et sacramentum, sed rationem sacrificii habet inquantum offertur; rationem autem sacramenti inquantum sumitur. Et ideo effectum sacramenti habet in eo qui sumit, effectum autem sacrificii in eo qui offert, vel in his pro quibus offertur." Cf. ibid., a. 7, co.: "Respondeo dicendum quod, sicut prius dictum est, hoc sacramentum non solum est sacramentum, sed etiam est sacrificium. Inquantum enim in hoc sacramento repraesentatur passio Christi, qua 'Christus obtulit se hostiam Deo,' ut dicitur Ephes. V, habet rationem sacrificii, inquantum vero in hoc sacramento traditur invisibiliter gratia sub visibili specie, habet rationem sacramenti. Sic igitur hoc sacramentum sumentibus quidem prodest per modum sacramenti et per modum sacrificii, quia pro omnibus sumentibus offertur, dicitur enim in canone Missae, '. . . quotquot ex hac altaris participatione sacrosanctum corpus et sanguinem filii tui sumpserimus, omni benedictione caelesti et gratia repleamur.' Sed aliis, qui non sumunt, prodest per modum sacrificii, inquantum pro salute eorum offertur, unde et in canone Missae dicitur, 'Memento, Domine, famulorum famularumque tuarum, pro quibus tibi offerimus, vel qui tibi offerunt, hoc sacrificium laudis, pro se suisque omnibus, pro redemptione animarum suarum, pro spe salutis et incolumitatis suae.'"

68. Cf. a few examples among many, *ST* II-II, q. 81, a. 7, ad 2: "Unde Augustinus dicit, in X *De civ. Dei,* 'sacrificium visibile invisibilis sacrificii sacramentum'"; and III, q. 65, a. 1, obj. 7: "Praeterea, Hugo de sancto Victore dicit quod sacramenta veteris legis fuerunt *oblationes, decimae et sacrificia.*" Hugh's analysis is utilized by Thomas already in *Scriptum in lib. IV Sent.,* d. 1, q. 1, a. 2, qc. 3, co.; d. 2, q. 1, a. 2, ad 4. Thomas's awareness of the quote from *De civ. Dei* seems to begin much later.

69. Hugh of St. Victor, *De sacramentis Christianae fidei,* lib. I, p. 9, cap. 4 (PL 176, 323 B).

70. The degree to which the grace "contained" here is associated with the sacramental rather than the sacrificial dimension of the Eucharist can be seen in one of those rare passages where Thomas follows Peter Lombard's recommendation to privilege the "narrow" over the "broad"

as's chief characterization of sacrifice in contrast to sacramentality in general is that it is directed principally not toward the good of the recipient, but toward the worship of God or toward the good of created persons not receiving it.[71] The phrase "et sacramentum et sacrificium" is strictly parallel to the "pro vobis et pro multis": for you who are here taking ("sumentes") the sacrament and for those who are not, for whom—along with the recipients of the sacrament—the Eucharist is being offered as a sacrifice.[72] Jesus shows those present that his self-offering is "for you and not just for you."[73] Those who take com-

sense of sacrament: *ST* I-II, q. 101, a. 4, ad 2: "Ad secundum dicendum quod sacrificium novae legis, idest Eucharistia, continet ipsum Christum, qui est sanctificationis auctor. 'Sanctificavit enim per suum sanguinem populum,' ut dicitur Ad Heb. ult. Et ideo hoc sacrificium etiam est sacramentum. Sed sacrificia veteris legis non continebant Christum, sed ipsum figurabant, et ideo non dicuntur sacramenta." Thomas does not apply this restriction consistently, however, and it will not become common until after the Council of Trent and the *Catechismus Romanus* popularized it, so as to meet halfway the usage of the Reformers.

71. Cf. *ST* III, q. 82, a. 10, co.: "Quia unusquisque tenetur uti gratia sibi data cum fuerit opportunum, secundum illud I Cor. VI, 'Hortamur vos ne in vacuum gratiam Dei recipiatis.' Opportunitas autem sacrificium offerendi non solum attenditur per comparationem ad fideles Christi, quibus oportet sacramenta ministrari, sed principaliter per comparationem ad Deum, cui in consecratione huius sacramenti sacrificium offertur. Unde sacerdoti, etiam si non habeat curam animarum, non licet omnino a celebratione cessare, sed saltem videtur quod celebrare tenetur in praecipuis festis, et maxime in illis diebus in quibus fideles communicare consueverunt."

72. Cf. Thomas Aquinas, *Super I Cor.,* cap. 11, lect. 6: "Dicit autem signanter 'pro vobis et pro multis,' quia hoc sacramentum valet in remissionem peccatorum sumentibus per modum sacramenti, quod notatur signanter, cum dicitur 'pro vobis,' quibus dixerat 'Accipite.' Valet etiam per modum sacrificii multis non sumentibus, pro quibus offertur; quod significatur cum dicitur: 'et pro multis.' Secundo, virtus eius consideratur per comparationem ad vitam iustitiae, quam facit per fidem, secundum illud Rom. III, 24: 'Iustificati gratis per gratiam ipsius, per redemptionem quae est in Christo Iesu, quem proposuit propitiationem per fidem in sanguine ipsius.'" By way of contrast cf. Albertus Magnus, *De sacrificio missae, Opera Omnia 38,* ed. Augustus Borgnet (Paris: Vivès 1899), III, 13 n. 2 (p. 122): "'pro vobis,' discipulis, qui tamen estis perfectores sanctitatis: quia sicut diximus, Episcopus et sacerdos etiam indigent sanguine redemptionis, 'et pro multis': bonis scilicet efficaciter, pro omnibus tamen effusus est sufficienter."

73. Cf. *ST* III, q. 78, a. 3, co.: "'pro vobis et pro multis aliis effundetur in remissionem peccatorum.'" *In I Cor.,* cap. xi, lect. 6: "in consecratione corporis sufficit quod dicitur 'Hoc est corpus meum,' quia sanguis seorsum consecratus, specialiter repraesentat passionem Christi, per quam eius sanguis separatus est a corpore. Et ideo in consecratione sanguinis oportuit exprimere Christi passionis virtutem, quae attenditur, primo quidem, respectu nostrae culpae quam Christi passio abolet, secundum illud Apoc. I, 5: 'Lavit nos a peccatis nostris in sanguine suo,' et, quantum ad hoc, dicit 'qui pro vobis et pro multis effundetur in remissionem peccatorum.' Effusus est siquidem sanguis in remissionem peccatorum, non solum *pro multis,* sed etiam pro omnibus, secundum illud I Io. II, 2: 'Ipse est propitiatio pro peccatis nostris, non pro nostris autem tantum, sed etiam pro totius mundi.'" At the same time, Thomas takes care not to foster the always adventurous, sometimes reckless, hope of *apokatastasis,* as if this grace were likely to be accepted by all; rather, being for all who are even still potential members of his mystical body, its rejection weighs all the heavier: *Scriptum in lib. IV Sent.,* d. 8, q. 2, a. 2, qc. 3; *Reportatio in Mt.,* cap. 20, lect. 2. The effectiveness of the Church's Eucharistic intercession is conditioned by the devotion of the one for whom the Church prays in commemoration

munion can benefit from both the sacrament and the sacrifice; those who do not, are usually said to benefit from the sacrifice. The "pro-existence" of Christ in the Eucharist, as formulated in the words of institution, echoes the original soteriological *hyper*-formulae of Christ's death "for us" and reveals the Eucharistic sacrifice as part of Christ's ongoing intercession.[74] The other unique feature of the Eucharist, though usually thematized under the aspect of presence, underscores this aspect of sacrifice: namely that the *res et sacramentum* of this sacrament, in a way unlike the other sacraments, is Christ himself, worthy of our worship. As already given with the sacrament, Christ is already truly present *(res)*. But as *sacramentum,* he is also the source of further grace for all who in act or potency are part of his mystical body; it is his intercession that is the core of the sacrifice of the Eucharist even for those prayed for but not present to receive the sacrament. The one, historical sacrifice of the "Christus passus" is eternally brought before the Father by the *Christus vivus*—"pro vobis et pro multis." The acceptance by the Father of this loving intercession of the Son who gave his life for us makes the Eucharist not just a sacrifice, but a sharing in the one fully true and accepted sacrifice, which draws others into the Triune communion, a communion of interceding with Christ and being accepted by the Father. Thomas attributes the reverence with which the Eucharist is to be celebrated not only to the mystery of Christ's presence among those present, but also to the significance of the offering for those who are not present but who are being drawn into the Triune community and the mystical body of Christ.[75]

---

of her Lord: *Scriptum in lib. IV Sent.,* d. 12, q. 2, a. 2, qc. 2, ad 4: "Inquantum autem est sacramentum, habet effectum in omni vivente, in quo requirit vitam praeexistere. Sed inquantum est sacrificium, habet effectum etiam in aliis pro quibus offertur, in quibus non praeexigit vitam spiritualem in actu, sed in potentia tantum; et ideo, si eos dispositos inveniat, eis gratiam obtinet virtute illius veri sacrificii a quo omnis gratia in nòs influxit; et per consequens peccata mortalia in eis delet, non sicut causa proxima, sed inquantum gratiam contritionis eis impetrat. Et quod in contrarium dicitur, quod 'non offertur nisi pro membris Christi,' intelligendum est pro membris Christi offerri, quando offertur pro aliquibus ut sint membra."

74. Cf. *ST* III, q. 79, a. 7, co.: "Respondeo dicendum quod, sicut prius dictum est, hoc sacramentum non solum est sacramentum, sed etiam est sacrificium. Inquantum enim in hoc sacramento repraesentatur passio Christi, qua 'Christus obtulit se hostiam Deo,' ut dicitur Eph. V, habet rationem sacrificii, inquantum vero in hoc sacramento traditur invisibiliter gratia sub visibili specie, habet rationem sacramenti. Sic igitur hoc sacramentum sumentibus quidem prodest per modum sacramenti et per modum sacrificii . . . Sed aliis, qui non sumunt, prodest per modum sacrificii, inquantum pro salute eorum offertur, unde et in canone Missae dicitur, 'Memento, Domine, famulorum famularumque tuarum . . .' Et utrumque modum Dominus exprimit, dicens, Matth. XXVI, qui 'pro vobis,' scilicet sumentibus, 'et pro multis' aliis, effundetur in remissionem peccatorum"; and III, q. 78, a. 3, ad 8: "Et ideo signanter dicit, 'pro vobis' Iudaeis, 'et pro multis,' scilicet gentilibus, vel, 'pro vobis' manducantibus, 'et pro multis' pro quibus offertur."

75. *ST* III, q. 83, a. 4, ad 5: "Ad quintum dicendum quod in hoc sacramento maior devotio

Thomas on the True Priest of the Eucharist and His Concelebrants   The Eucharist would not be the offering of the true sacrifice, were it not the offering of *Christus passus,* the offering of what Christ fulfilled on the Cross, the offering accepted by the Father: "just as this celebration of this sacrament is an image representative of the passion of Christ, so, too, is the altar representative of his cross, on which Christ was immolated in his proper form."[76] The uniqueness of the true sacrifice also discloses the uniqueness of the true priest.[77]

The sacrifice that the Church offers daily in not different from the sacrifice that Christ himself offered, but rather its commemoration. Thus Augustine says in Book 10 of the *City of God* that "the priest is Christ who is offering, and he himself is also what is offered, and he willed that the daily sacrifice of the Church be the sacrament of its reality."[78]

---

requiritur quam in aliis sacramentis, propter hoc quod in hoc sacramento totus Christus continetur. Et etiam communior, quia in hoc sacramento requiritur devotio totius populi, pro quo sacrificium offertur, et non solum percipientium sacramentum, sicut in aliis sacramentis."

76. *ST* III, q. 83, a. 1, ad 2: "sicut celebratio huius sacramenti est imago repraesentativa passionis Christi, ita altare est repraesentativum crucis ipsius, in qua Christus in propria specie immolatus est"; cf. also Thierry-Dominique Humbrecht, "L'eucharistie, 'representation' du sacrifice du Christ, selon saint Thomas," *Revue thomiste* 98 (1998): 355–86. In contrast to some recent interpretations of the "Mysteriengegenwart," Thomas consistently names the one who is offered sacrificially "Christus passus," not "Christus patiens."

77. Thomas argues that the words used by the priest at the consecration and the words of original institution must be considered the same, "quia sacerdos, dum consecrat, non profert ista verba quasi ex persona sua, sed quasi ex persona Christi consecrantis" (*In I Cor* XI, lectio v). On Christ as the chief actor in the Eucharistic sacrifice, cf. also B. Valuet, "Le Christ, prêtre principal du sacrifice eucharistique et les prêtres ministériels agissant in persona Christi," in *Présence du Christ dans la liturgie. Actes du sixième colloque d'études historiques, théologiques et canoniques sur le rite romain,* ed. Centre International d'Études Liturgiques (Paris and Versailles: Centre International d'Études Liturgiques, 2001), 159–222; and the remarks on time and eternity by Robert Sokolowski, *Christian Faith and Human Understanding: Studies on the Eucharist, Trinity and the Human Person* (Washington, D.C.: The Catholic University of America Press, 2006), esp. chaps. 5 ("Phenomenology and the Eucharist," 69–85), and 6 ("Praying the Sacrifice of the Mass," 86–94). The latter author would only have strengthened his own arguments, e.g., on p. 84, if he had identified the "pro vobis et pro multis" as disclosive of the kind of sacrificial activity exercised by Christ in the Eucharist.

78. *ST* III, q. 22, a. 3, ad 2: "Sacrificium autem quod quotidie in Ecclesia offertur, non est aliud a sacrificio quod ipse Christus obtulit, sed eius commemoratio. Unde Augustinus dicit, in X *De civ. Dei,* 'sacerdos ipse Christus offerens, ipse et oblatio, cuius rei sacramentum quotidianum esse voluit Ecclesiae sacrificium'"; cf. *Super Decretales,* n. 1, co.: "Salus autem fidelium consummatur per Ecclesiae sacramenta, in quibus virtus passionis Christi operatur, et ideo consequenter exponit quid fides Catholica sentiat circa Ecclesiae sacramenta. Et primo circa Eucharistiam, cum dicit: 'In qua scilicet Ecclesia ipse idem Christus est sacerdos et sacrificium,' quia scilicet ipse obtulit semet ipsum in ara crucis oblationem et 'hostiam Deo in odorem suavitatis,' ut dicitur Ad Ephes. V, 2, in cuius sacrificii commemorationem cotidie in Ecclesia offertur sacrificium sub sacramento panis et vini."

Developing a somewhat different understanding of *oblatio* than Augustine's, Thomas can say that this—active, because graced—turning of the Church to the sacrifice of the Cross is repeated in the daily *oblatio* of the Church,[79] as the prayers and needs of our time are brought again and again before the Father in communion with the Son and in transparency to his one sacrifice of worship and intercession. The liturgical acts of such offering *in suam commemorationem* are many, though what they principally offer is one, and all that they offer is in this one sacrifice made by the one true priest.[80] It is the calling and graced privilege of the Church to intercede in this manner for a still suffering and historical world, for the still imperfect *corpus Christi mysticum*. The dialectic of participation includes here both the identification of the Church with Christ and her abiding difference from him.[81]

The intentional ambivalence that Thomas maintained regarding the pre-Christian sacrifices and the soteriological *interpretamentum* "sacrifice" finds its parallel in Thomas's description of the ministry and the self-experience of precisely the best ministers of the sacraments. Such are the ministers who most know themselves to be merely instrumental causes of grace, and indeed, to be merely *instrumenta separata* or (*pace* Jüngel) *instrumenta extrinseca*. Two liturgical practices of the day are cited here by Thomas. One was the prayer of consecration used at that time for the ordination of priests: "Receive the power of offering the *sacrificium* in the Church both for the living and for the dead."[82]

79. *ST* III, q. 83, a. 4, co., quoted above in n. 47.
80. Cf. *ST* III, q. 79, a. 7, ad 3: "In pluribus vero Missis multiplicatur sacrificii oblatio. Et ideo multiplicatur effectus sacrificii et sacramenti."
81. Thomas returns to this same dialectic of the mystical body's participation in Christ's salvific work again in the non-liturgical context of Col 1:24, which he admits can be easily misunderstood; *Super Col.* cap. 1, lectio 6: "Et etiam hoc fructu, 'ut adimpleam ea, quae desunt passionum Christi,' et cetera. Haec verba, secundum superficiem, malum possent habere intellectum, scilicet quod Christi passio non esset sufficiens ad redemptionem, sed additae sunt ad complendum passiones sanctorum. Sed hoc est haereticum, quia sanguis Christi est sufficiens ad redemptionem, etiam multorum mundorum. 1 Io. c. II, 2: 'Ipse est propitiatio pro peccatis nostris,' et cetera. Sed intelligendum est, quod Christus et Ecclesia est una persona mystica, cuius caput est Christus, corpus omnes iusti: quilibet autem iustus est quasi membrum huius capitis, 1 Cor. XII, 27: 'et membra de membro.' Deus autem ordinavit in sua praedestinatione quantum meritorum debet esse per totam Ecclesiam, tam in capite quam in membris, sicut et praedestinavit numerum electorum. Et inter haec merita praecipue sunt passiones sanctorum. Sed Christi, scilicet capitis, merita sunt infinita, quilibet vero sanctus exhibet aliqua merita secundum mensuram suam. Et ideo dicit 'Adimpleo ea quae desunt passionum Christi,' id est totius Ecclesiae, cuius caput est Christus. 'Adimpleo,' id est, addo mensuram meam. Et hoc 'in carne,' id est, ego ipse patiens." Cf. also Joseph de Sainte-Marie, "L'Eucharistie, sacrement et sacrifice du Christ et de l'Église : Développements des perspectives thomistes," *Divinitas* 18, no. 2 (1974): 234–86.
82. *De articulis fidei*, pars 2, co.: "Accipe potestatem offerendi sacrificium in Ecclesia tam pro vivis quam pro mortuis."

The examples from the rite of episcopal investiture that Thomas recalls here suggest that the crosier is given to the prelate to remind him that he is not the right hand of God but at best his tool;[83] this status as an extrinsic instrument characterizes all other participants in Christ's priesthood as well. While such a ministerial distance from the primary divine cause of grace and the conjoined instrument of Christ's humanity is unavoidable, insight into this distance is not; it is not enjoyed by all ministers equally, be they major or minor. The effectiveness of the ministering *sacerdos* will arguably be enhanced (and precisely not, as for Jüngel, reduced to passivity) in the measure in which he is aware of the abidingly external source and foundation of his activity. In the context of the general theory of sacraments and thus without discussing the heightened challenge that sacrifice will add to sacrament, Thomas revisited a question raised by Peter Lombard in the gloss on 1 Corinthians and in the third book of the *Sentences:* whether Christ has given every grace to his ministers that he possibly could have. Peter Lombard expresses this question with the notion of "potestas excellentiae." Great ministers, say Paul and Apollo, might have been given such a fullness of personal merit that humans could have been granted grace in their names, possibly even have been baptized in their names. Already in *De veritate,* Thomas had noted that Peter's views here had not been widely received, at least as regards his notion that creatures might be given the power to create or justify other creatures as well.[84] Thomas had noted early on that God should not, however, be called envious, even if he chooses to communicate less than the greatest possible grace and merit to his ministers. In the *Summa theologiae,* Thomas added as a reason: It is not because of envy that Christ does not communicate to his ministers the "potestas excellentiae," but rather for the advantage of the faithful, lest they put their hope in a mere human, leading to a fragmentation of Church unity.[85] The division in the Church

83. *ST* III, q. 62, a. 5, co.: "Respondeo dicendum quod, sicut dictum est, sacramentum operatur ad gratiam causandam per modum instrumenti. Est autem duplex instrumentum, unum quidem separatum, ut baculus; aliud autem coniunctum, ut manus. Per instrumentum autem coniunctum movetur instrumentum separatum, sicut baculus per manum. Principalis autem causa efficiens gratiae est ipse Deus, ad quem comparatur humanitas Christi sicut instrumentum coniunctum, sacramentum autem sicut instrumentum separatum."

84. *De veritate,* q. 27, a. 3, ad 17: "opinio Magistri non tenetur hic communiter, ut scilicet potestas creandi et iustificandi possit creaturae conferri."

85. *ST* III, q. 64, a. 4, ad 1: "Ad primum ergo dicendum quod Christus non ex invidia praetermisit potestatem excellentiae ministris communicare, sed propter fidelium utilitatem, ne in homine spem ponerent, et essent diversa sacramenta, ex quibus divisio in Ecclesia oriretur; sicut apud illos qui dicebant, 'Ego sum Pauli, ego autem Apollo, ego vero Cephae,' ut dicitur I Cor. I." Cf. ibid., ad 3: "Ad tertium dicendum quod ad hoc inconveniens evitandum, ne scilicet multa capita in Ecclesia essent, Christus noluit potestatem suae excellentiae ministris communicare. Si tamen communicasset, ipse esset caput principaliter, alii vero secundario."

that is thus avoided includes the division of the minister from Christ. Seeking
to be an instrument of grace, the extrinsic instrument must return to the conjoined one. In Thomas's view, sacrifice adds to sacrament that it is also for others, *pro vobis et pro multis,* both for those receiving the sacrament and for those
who are not, be they living or dead. Yet this prayer for others, which should
heighten the minister's sense of being separate and extrinsic, can be effectively
brought to the Father only by One who is immediate to those prayed for. Far
from obscuring Christ's unique agency in the Eucharist, the sacrifice of the
Mass is meant to underscore it. The Church's graced call to join her prayers to
the oblation of Calvary in communion with the living Christ is the only thing
that frees her from the temptation to seek salvation outside his true sacrifice by
doing violence to herself and others.[86]

Recent Catholic Refigurations of the Sacrificial Tradition

Even from the brief references provided above, the need for a revision of
the average pre-understanding of the Catholic interest in the theme of sacrifice seems obvious. Prior to Trent there was no universal, single-minded effort
to maximize the Catholic sense of sacrifice. The maxim seems plausible that
sacrifice, since it contains a destructive moment, rationally should be avoided
at least until the point is reached where the avoidance itself causes still greater
destruction. Past and present history is full of examples where the critique of
all sacrificing by others serves to disguise or justify the sacrificial intentions
of the critic. Identifying oneself with or as the victim need not, but easily can,
be a strategy for the victimization of others. Correspondingly, the maxim for
reflection on theories of sacrifice would urge us be slow to articulate positive
readings of sacrifice, until it is clear that the price of single-minded critique
would be too dear. That point has arguably been reached, when, in Jüngel's
words, "the sacrifice of Christ . . . does not call for us to do anything"; when the
Church, deeply aware of its own insufficiency, is no longer called by grace to
articulate within Christ's sacrifice its intercessions for those who are suffering;
when we drift into a Christianity that no longer has "aliquod repraesentativum
Dominicae passionis" in its charity, its prayer for itself and others, and its hope
for the Father's acceptance. A Church that could not intercede for others at the
Eucharist, a Church without the sacrifice of the Mass, would be a Church of a
different "type."[87] By way of contrast, the type of the Church with Eucharistic

86. Cf. again *ST* III, q. 79, a. 7, ad 3.
87. For the sense of "type" meant here, cf. John Henry Newman, *An Essay on the Develop-*

sacrifice was attested by Bishop Oscar Romero's final words: "May this Body, given up to the sacrificial fires, and may this Blood, sacrificed for humankind, so nourish us, that we too might give our body and blood over to suffering and pain, but as Christ did, not for ourselves, but to attain justice and peace for our people."[88] The Eucharist calls us to more than the "indicative" language allowed by Jüngel, but it is an "imperative" or at least an "optative" voice that can succeed only through the joining of our voices to Christ's (*pace* Jüngel) in a way that has not always been. It is far from "unfortunate that the Roman Catholic Church following Trent continues to speak widely of the sacrificial action of the priest or of the Church." That share in the action of Christ "pro multis" is one that the Catholic community would rightly be reluctant to disown or sacrifice by fleeing from sacrifice; but it is also a voice that will be heard and a sharing that will succeed only if the Catholic community sees its own work as secondary, founded in Christ's own voice and his sacrifice. What is formally a secondary or founded activity is not passivity; it is the highest activity in which the intercessory mission of the Church can be fulfilled.

Some of the most prominent voices in recent Roman Catholic theology have responded to the well-perceived need to retrieve what was most at stake in the theology of sacrifice, but in the pursuit of this goal they have sometimes sought a rehabilitation and affirmation of sacrifice that seems to pass all too quickly over that abiding *negativum* of sacrifice necessary for its "forced" recognition, the degree of "unwillingness," human and divine, that is a mark of genuine sacrifice. For God loves not too cheerful a giver (*pace* 2 Cor 9:7). The prefigurations of the theology of sacrifice discussed above have given us standards by which to measure the success of genuine "retrieval"; in particular, we must not lose sight of the abiding negativity presupposed by the *sacrificium verum*. Let us look briefly at two of the most prominent theologians to have interwoven affirmations and critiques of sacrifice, Karl Rahner and Hans Urs von Balthasar, before considering some general suggestions made by the late Pope John Paul II in the 2003 encyclical *Ecclesia de Eucharistia*.

Sacrifice-Critical Tendencies in Karl Rahner

Karl Rahner's critical reflections on sacrifice have managed to bring together in a remarkably unforced manner the three major concerns of soteriology, sacraments, and human existence. His most common critique of Anselm's

---

ment of Christian Doctrine, ed. Ian Ker (Notre Dame, Ind.: Notre Dame University Press, 1989), II, v. 4, p. 173.

88. Oscar Romero, *Voice of the Voiceless* (Maryknoll, N.Y.: Orbis, 1985), 193.

doctrine of satisfaction is that it misses that dimension of dying which—at God's initiative—is self-perfecting for us: a theme which had drawn his attention even prior to the controversial work on the Assumption in 1951. For Anselm, God seems to be capable of accepting any deed as satisfactory, for no deed could satisfy without his acceptance. Rahner seeks a motivation for God's acceptance of a freely embraced death that is even more distant from the arbitrary than was the motivation suggested by Thomas: quite in opposition to Thomas's theology, a properly embraced death was interpreted as self-perfective. Rahner's critique of the "sacrifice" of Jesus' death, as in his general theology of death, seems to minimize the diastasis of death and resurrection in favor of a claim to the self-perfecting dimension of an active embrace of hope in the face of mortality that should mark the whole of life.[89] Rahner

89. For his critique of the sacrifice, cf. Karl Rahner, *Grundkurs des Glaubens. Einführung in den Begriff des Christentums* (Freiburg: Herder 1976), 277: "Sagt man dagegen, dieses 'Opfer' sei als freie Gehorsamstat Jesu ... zu verstehen, Gott gebe durch seine eigene freie Initiative, durch die er diese Gehorsamstat ermöglicht, der Welt die Möglichkeit, der gerechten Heiligkeit Gottes genugzutun, und die um Christi willen gegebene Gnade sei ja gerade die Bedingung, sich selbst, das Heil Gottes frei ergreifend, zu erlösen, so hat man wohl Richtiges gesagt, aber die Vorstellung des Sühneopfers nicht nur erläutert, sondern auch kritisiert" ("If, on the other hand, one says that this sacrifice [i.e., Jesus' death] is to be understood as Jesus' free act of obedience; and that God gives to the world—through his own free initiative by which he makes this act of obedience possible—the possibility of doing satisfaction to the just holiness of God; and that the grace given for the sake of Christ is in fact the very condition of our self-salvation by our freely embracing the salvation of God: then one would surely have said something that is correct, but one would not only have explained the notion of propitiatory sacrifice, but one would have critiqued it as well"). Translations here and in the following are my own.

On Rahner's general theology of death, cf. Anselm Grün, *Erlösung durch das Kreuz. Karl Rahners Beitrag zu einem heutigen Erlösungsverständnis* (Münsterschwarzach: Vier-Türme-Verlag, 1975). Grün seems at times oblivious to the programmatic direction Rahner is taking; cf. the more critical assessment by Wolfhart Pannenberg, "Tod und Auferstehung in der Sicht christlicher Dogmatik," *Kerygma und Dogma* 20 (1974): 167–80.

On his minimizing the diastasis of death and resurrection, cf. Karl Rahner, "Dogmatische Fragen zur Osterfrömmigkeit," in his *Schriften zur Theologie*, vol. 4 (Einsiedeln: Benziger, 1967), 157–72. "Ist dem aber so ... dann ist die Auferstehung Christi nicht ein anderes Ereignis nach seinem Leiden und seinem Tod, sondern ... die Erscheinung dessen, was im Tode Christi geschehen ist: die getane und erlittene Übergabe der ganzen Wirklichkeit des einen leibhaften Menschen an das Geheimnis des erbarmend liebenden Gottes durch die gesammelte, über das ganze Leben und das ganze Dasein verfügende Freiheit Christi. Karfreitag und Ostern können dann als zwei wesentlich aufeinander bezogene Aspekte eines streng einheitlichen Ereignisses des Daseins Christi erscheinen" ("If this is the case, then the resurrection of Christ is not another event after his suffering and death, but rather ... the appearance of what happened in Christ's death: the active and passive, performed and suffered handing over of the entire reality of an embodied human being to the mystery of the mercifully loving God through the freedom of Christ, as this freedom collects and is in control of Christ's entire life and existence"; ibid., 165f.).

On hope in the face of mortality, cf. Rahner, *Grundkurs des Glaubens*, 260ff. and 414ff. Death is described as the maturation of eternity from out of time, as resurrection-in-death, as

argued that the negativity normally associated with the idea of sacrifice failed to do justice to the positive dynamic that he was reclaiming for a "good death," so that even to call Christ's death a sacrifice was either off the mark or in need of such a thorough-going critique of the notion of sacrifice as to be equivalent to its refutation.[90] His 1951 study of the sacrifice of the Mass acknowledges there is a sacrificial mentality but misses the sacrificial action of the Church required to call the Eucharist a sacrifice.[91] The "sacrificial" frame of mind, often prescribed as the ideal for Christian existence, is criticized by Rahner as a form of "jargon" too fixated on the *passio*-side of human existence rather than on its possibilities for active self-realization.[92] One can link the Eucharist to genuine Christian existence by referring to both as sacrifice, but one must then avoid "the appearance of misanthropy and vulgar hatred of life." "Talk of 'sacrificing the world' can be appropriate only in dialectical conjunction with a basic will to 'perfect the world.'"

In all these themes with their attempt to replace sacrificial models with largely evolutionary and existential ones, Rahner argues that the talk of sacrifice, since it does tend to bear negative undertones, should not blind us to the steadily progessive self-evolution of our existence and world, a world that for Rahner seems largely untroubled by the fear of atrophy or final loss. It is this predominance of inevitable self-evolution, a progression without the kind of interruption that calls for God's new gift or free acceptance from above vis-à-vis our de facto existence, that is arguably the least satisfying dimension in Rahner's impressive *opus*. His flight from sacrifice is bought at the price of understating our necessary solidarity with the painfully broken world of our day. It also helps us see where, despite all abidingly necessary defenses, a Catholic theology of sacrifice has much to gain by listening critically and selectively to the admittedly extreme critique of sacrifice in Jüngel. Some portion of Jüngel's insistence on the extrinsic nature of justification within, as well as outside, sacramental theology could be of use in the Roman Catholic critical self-examination of the place of Rahnerian thought in its recent history.[93] Christ is at once a source and goal of our graced acts and their counterpoint, the other

---

being born and giving birth, as liberating eternity from the prison (cf. Plato's "sema") of time, as the ultimate validation of history, and as at once self-salvation and salvation by another, etc.

90. Cf. the citation in n. 89 just above from Rahner, *Grundkurs des Glaubens*, 277.

91. Rahner, *Die vielen Messen und das eine Opfer.*

92. Karl Rahner, "Passion und Aszese," in *Schriften zur Theologie*, vol. 3, 73–109; idem, "Meßopfer und Jugendaszese," in *Sendung und Gnade*, 5th ed. (1959; Innsbruck: Tyrolia Verlag, 1988), 178, and esp. "Das 'jugendliche' Opfer," 177–80.

93. Cf. Eberhard Jüngel and Karl Rahner, *Was ist ein Sakrament? Vorstösse zur Verständigung* (Freiburg: Herder, 1971).

than ourselves. The ideal of a synergy of human acts with divine providence will be credible only if it can be set in the context of the limits of the immanent dynamics of human perfection, in a context of the experienced need for salvation from without, including the sense of what in the sacrifice of the Mass is *not* our own. The acknowledgment of Christ as the chief subject of the Eucharist, prior to and distinct from its being a celebration of the community, takes on here a special urgency. Just as the Eucharist is not for the individual communicant or even the communicating community alone, so it is not of the ordained or common priesthood of the Church alone. Because it is first and foremost the living Christ who intercedes *pro vobis et pro multis,* for those who could not intercede effectively for themselves, if left to themselves, it must be asked if there does not remain in Rahner's reflections too great an avoidance of the admittedly negative aspects of sacrifice to fulfill the task that he had set himself: namely, to draw closer to the world of our times, times marked by events that hardly support the optimism of unlimited and self-sustained evolution. In soteriology, sacramental theology, and a theology of the Eucharist, post-Rahnerian Catholic thought will need to give greater consideration to the ways in which the tradition of sacrifice can deepen our sense of alterity, our consciousness of our need to be saved by Another who for our sake does not allow us to identify apriori salvation-by-another with salvation-through-ourselves ("Fremderlösung" / "Selbsterlösung"). This seems to be in *nuce* the legitimate concern voiced first by Johannes Baptist Metz, whose sensitivity to the "apocalyptic" dimension of Christian hope arguably provides better conditions for the necessary "memoria passionis," one into which the Christian is drawn.[94] The anamnetic character of Christian existence and Eucharistic sacrifice "in meam commemorationem" could provide a basis for embracing that sense of Eucharistic community with Christ and the world that intercedes for those who do not see the dynamics of immanent self-perfecting as the hallmark of their histories.[95]

94. Cf. Johannes Baptist Metz, *Glaube in Geschichte und Gesellschaft* (Mainz: Grünewald, 1977) and *Memoria Passionis. Ein provozierendes Gedächtnis in pluralistischer Gesellschaft* (Freiburg: Herder, 2006). The references to transcendental and evolutionary systems of theology in the more recent work are as important as the direct discussion of Rahner in the older one.

95. For further reflections by the author on this aspect of today's problematic, cf. Schenk, "Opfer und Opferkritik"; "Ist die Rede vom leidenden Gott theologisch zu vermeiden? Reflexionen über den Streit von Karl Rahner und Hans Urs von Balthasar," in *Der leidende Gott: Eine philosophische und theologische Kritik,* ed. Friedrich Hermanni and Peter Koslowski (Munich: Wilhelm Fink, 2001), 225–39; and also "Tod und Theodizee. Ansätze zu einer Theologie der Trauer bei Thomas von Aquin," *Forum Katholische Theologie* 10 (1994): 161–78.

Sacrifice-Friendly Tendencies in Hans Urs von Balthasar

The dramatic theology of Hans Urs von Balthasar can be accused neither of understating the moment of suffering in his portrayal of sacrifice nor of downplaying the theological importance of sacrifice where this dimension of existence shows itself.[96] An often-polemical critic of Rahner's lack of a genuine "theologia crucis,"[97] Balthasar also expresses doubts about the all-too-negative qualification of sacrifice in Réne Girard's early work and its theological reception, notably by Raymund Schwager and his colleagues at Innsbruck, who were relating the dramatic methods of Girard and Balthasar.[98] It is telling, however, that Balthasar expresses as his chief concern the worry that the pejorative view of sacrifice in the Girardian tradition pays scant attention, not to properly human, but to Trinitarian action, most notably the handing over of the Son by the Father. Setting aside the classic location of suffering exclusively in the human nature of Christ, Balthasar seeks to interpret both the kenosis of the Incarnation and the passion of the cross as events of the immanent Trinity itself, involving God's own suffering. While Balthasar seeks to avoid both the classical forms of theopaschism and the violent, even "sadistic" (so the critique by Dorothee Sölle) portrayal of the Father by Jürgen Moltmann,[99] he programmatically insists on locating suffering and sacrifice within the Trinity. Throughout the final volume of his *Theodrama*, Balthasar presents his view of the suffering God in programmatic fashion, making his own the words of his colleague, the visionary, Dr. Adrienne von Speyr, whose visions he had helped to inspire and

96. Cf. especially Hans Urs von Balthasar, *Mysterium Paschale,* in *Mysterium Salutis,* vol. III, bk. 2, ed. J. Feiner and M. Löhrer (Einsiedeln: Benziger, 1969), 133–326, and *Theodramatik,* vol. 3, *Die Handlung* (Einsiedeln: Johannes Verlag, 1980), 295–395; cf. Thomas Rudolf Krenski, *Passio caritatis;* and Karl-Heinz Menke, *Stellvertretung. Schlüsselbegriff christlichen Lebens und theologische Grundkategorie* (Einsiedeln: Johannes, 1991), esp. 266–310.

97. Most famously in *Cordula oder der Ernstfall* (Einsiedeln: Johannes Verlag, 1966). Rahner's attempt to respond by simply referring the objector to Anselm Grün's dissertation amounts to something like an admission of Balthasar's critique.

98. Cf. Raymund Schwager, *Brauchen wir einen Sündenbock?* (Munich: Kaiser, 1978); idem, *Der wunderbare Tausch. Zur Geschichte und Deutung der Erlösungslehre* (Munich: Kaiser, 1986), 273–312; idem, *Jesus im Heilsdrama: Entwurf einer biblischen Erlösungslehre* (Innsbruck: Tyrolia, 1990); idem, "Christ's Death and the Prophetic Critique of Sacrifice," in *René Girard and Biblical Studies,* ed. Andrew J. McKenna (Decatur, Ga.: Scholars Press, 1985), 109–23; Hansjürgen Verweyen, "Offene Fragen im Sühnebegriff auf dem Hintergrund der Auseinandersetzung Raymund Schwagers mit Hans Urs von Balthasar," in *Dramatische Erlösungslehre,* ed. Józef Niewiadomski and Wolfgang Palaver (Innsbruck: Tyrolia, 1992), 137–46; and, by way of contrast, John P. Galvin, "Zur dramatischen Erlösungslehre Raymund Schwagers: Fragen aus der Sicht Karl Rahners," also in *Dramatische Erlösungslehre,* 157–64.

99. Cf. especially Jürgen Moltmann, *Der gekreuzigte Gott: Das Kreuz Christi als Grund und Kritik christlicher Theologie* (Munich: Kaiser, 1972).

edit, at once a concretization and a renewed impulse for Balthasar's own work as well.[100] The cross as the sacrifice of Christ is interpreted by these twin colleagues as the consequence of the Trinity's self-constitution: "From the very beginning, the Son had presented his sacrifice to the Father."[101] "Sacrifice, suffering, cross, and death, when considered in a Christian perspective, are merely the mirror of tremendous realities in the Father, in heaven, in eternal life."[102] They are "nothing other than the ways in which that which constitutes heaven becomes apparent: the love of God that extends into the ultimate."[103] It is not first the incarnate Son of God who brings sacrifice; rather, the Father himself, in a freely chosen giving up of himself, makes of himself a sacrifice, from which the Trinity first comes to be, so "that the Father, relinquishing his only-ness, begets the Son from out of his substance," "just as God will develop the salvific abandonment of the Son on the cross from out of the (pre-sacrifice) of the eternal begetting."[104] Whatever might have been abstracted even here from the realities of literal pre-Christian sacrifice, Balthasar was aware that he had left in his appropriation of sacrificial language more violence and suffering than had most of the Chalcedonian tradition, wherever it had attributed aspects of sacrifice to the Trinity.

More than twenty-five years ago, while reviewing the volumes of *Mysterium Salutis* that he had helped edit and now asking what would need to be amended in a future edition, Dietrich Wiederkehr remarked in reference to Balthasar's key work that there would be need for "a less passionistically legitimated and legitimating theology of the cross . . . where the theo-logical structure of Jesus' actions to create life and curtail suffering could be better reflected."[105] Despite his attempt to thematize a theology of suffering that could better address the situation of humanity than had the best-known forms of transcendental theology, despite his keen sense of the need for salvation from above, Balthasar's divinization of suffering and sacrifice threatens to make suffering normative and thereby obscures its character as a *vitandum*. What had

---

100. The index of persons at the end of *Theodramatik,* vol. 4, *Das Endspiel* (482) lists under "Speyer, Adrienne von" simply the reference: "1 passim"; cf. Hans Urs von Balthasar, *Unser Auftrag: Bericht und Entwurf* (Einsiedeln: Johannes Verlag, 1984); and Johann Roten, "The Two Halves of the Moon: Marian Anthropological Dimensions in the Common Mission of Adrienne von Speyr and Hans Urs von Balthasar," in *Hans Urs von Balthasar: His Life and Work,* ed. David L. Schindler (San Francisco: Ignatius Press, 1991).

101. Appropriated by von Balthasar, *Das Endspiel,* 466 (the translations here are my own); cf. ibid. the locations within von Speyr's work.

102. Ibid., 467.   103. Ibid.

104. Ibid.

105. Dietrich Wiederkehr, "Mysterium paschale und die Leidensgeschichte der Menschheit," in *Mysterium Salutis,* ed. Magnus Löhrer, Christian Schütz, and Dietrich Wiederkehr (Einsiedeln: Benziger, 1981), 243–46.

been thought to be God's antecedent, absolute, and unconditioned will for his and our complete happiness is replaced here by his fully originary desire for the beauty of suffering love, where the component of suffering is no longer merely tolerated and transformed but has been revealed as what constitutes the very Trinity itself. The sense that suffering ought not to be is obscured here. The anti-divine dimensions of literal sacrifice disappear behind the ultimate sanction. Future Catholic reflection would do well to learn, through a critical and selective reception of Girard's often overly reductionist theses, a greater sense of the earth-bound nature of literal sacrifice and of the need for metaphorical distance in the portrayal of "heavenly suffering." A more vigorous sense of the "Widergöttliche," the ungodly dimension, of unsubliminated sacrifice could further the otherwise laudable attempt among Balthasar's most gifted readers to take seriously the sufferings of humankind: an advantage in principle that they could claim over the accommodationist optimisms of the 1960s and '70s.

Inscribing Sacrifice in Communio: The Eucharistic Ecclesiology of Pope John Paul II

If both the medieval and the contemporary careers of the idea of sacrifice within Catholic theology suggest that neither too negative (Fishacre, Rahner) nor too positive (Kilwardby, Balthasar) a sense of sacrifice serves well the understanding of Christ's salvific work and its presence in the sacramental life of the Church, the question remains as to the shape of a theology that avoids these two extremes. The more ambivalent treatment of sacrifice in the writings of Thomas Aquinas provided one prefiguration of the possible renewal of sacrificial reflection. An ecumenically sensitive retrieval of a rich sense of the Eucharistic sacrifice was also at the heart of Pope John Paul II's last encyclical, the 2003 *Ecclesia de Eucharistia*.[106] Like Thomas, the encyclical neither excludes the image of sacrifice from the graced life of Christian existence (in contrast to Richard Fischacre and Karl Rahner) nor locates suffering in God's self-constitution and nature (unlike Balthasar) or in his antecedent and unconditional will for long epochs of human history (in distinction from Robert Kilwardby). Given the similar situation of Thomas and the encyclical within the options of their times, let us look in conclusion at the main lines of the encyclical's interest in the theme of sacrifice.

Ecclesia de Eucharistia situated the Eucharistic ecclesiology, explicated above

106. For the sacrificial thematic of the encyclical, cf. Romanus Cessario, "'Circa res . . . aliquid fit' (*Summa theologiae* II-II, q. 85, a. 3, ad 3): Aquinas on New Law Sacrifice," *Nova et Vetera* (English) 4, no. 2 (2006): 295–311.

all in the fourth chapter, in the context prepared for it by the initial chapters. "The Church lives from the Eucharist" also in the sense that she draws her life from her share *(communicatio)* in the mission of Christ (chap. 1). The letter presupposes but deals little with the affirmation and parsing of the real presence. Its focus is almost exclusively the mission carried out by Christ above all in the sacrifice of the Cross (chaps. 1 and 2). The encyclical brings together the Eucharistic themes of presence and offering by inscribing sacrifice into communion, that is, by showing how the Church's communion in and with Christ involves her in a communion in and with his ongoing intercession, which it takes as the irreducible core of the idea of sacrifice, one which therefore does not need to import suffering into the divine nature. The Church's ongoing share in the offering of the Eucharist is made possible by and deepens her share in the Trinitarian communion, at the same time developing ecclesial communion of the struggling Church, the *ecclesia militans,* where alone sacrifice continues to be marked by ongoing suffering.

The extent of the encyclical's emphasis on the work of Christ in the celebration of the Eucharist in the Church can be gauged by the frequency of the term sacrifice/sacrificial, used more than seventy times in the encyclical, not counting synonyms such as offering, paschal victim, or blood poured out. The entire encyclical is characterized by its emphasis on the Eucharist as containing the work of Christ, his sacrifice "for" humankind ("pro vobis et pro multis"). This includes the encyclical's emphasis on the ways in which the Church draws her life by benefiting from and sharing in this work of Eucharistic intercession. Without overlooking the gift of the real presence of Christ in the Eucharist, the encyclical was even more concerned with recalling the ways in which the real presence of Christ involves the Church ever anew in his unique and ultimate sacrifice, the source of all communion. The Eucharist is apostolic in the sense that here the Church, too, is for others; the further modes in which the Eucharist is apostolic (chap. 3, including "received through the apostles") are given to her to support her basic mission of Eucharistic "pro-existence." This communion in Christ's offering "pro vobis et pro multis" means that the Church is a communion which fosters the growth of that communion: with the Triune God and among all peoples. Neither the vertical nor the horizontal dimension of this communion, neither the invisible nor the visible notes of Eucharistic communion (§§ 35–38), could be lost without losing the Church herself. The communion of life, mission, sacrifice, and apostolate that the Church shares with her Lord is meant to increase humankind's communion in God's own life. Throughout the encyclical, the sacrifice of the Eucharist is inscribed into a theology of communion.

This theology includes an ecumenical dimension, drawing critically but substantially on the Eucharistic theologies of the Eastern churches. It is telling that the encyclical traces its ideas precisely on communion not to the Latin theologians of the thirteenth century, otherwise cited several times in the document, nor directly to patristic authors, but to the fourteenth-century Byzantine theologian, Nicolas Cabasilas. The work quoted in § 34 is not Nicolas's "Interpretation of the Sacred Liturgy," but his study "On Life in Christ." The fourth book of this work, dedicated to the Eucharist, has much to say about the unique, even foundational, character of the Eucharist vis-à-vis the other sacraments, especially about the communion with Christ that we attain in the Eucharist. While the Council of Trent had referred to Nicolas's erudition on the patristic sources for the theology of the sacrificial nature of the Eucharist, the encyclical's reference to his reflections on the unique status of the Eucharist seems to have the subsequent development of Orthodox theology in mind. It is the same ecumenical intent that is reflected in the several citations of Eastern-rite liturgies as a source of authentic teaching, a methodological innovation that had already been employed in the *Catechism of the Catholic Church,* expressing the fruit of ecumenical dialogue during the pontificate of Pope John Paul II between the Roman Catholic Church and the Eastern Orthodox churches. The frequency and weight of Eastern witnesses was a hallmark of that pontificate.

Beginning with the publications of Nicholas Afanasieff (1893–1966) in the 1930s, theologians of the Eastern Orthodox churches had been developing a "Eucharistic ecclesiology," a vision of the Church that takes its foundational idea from a vision of the Eucharist. Central to such Eucharistic ecclesiologies is the idea of communion. Included in the idea of Eucharistic communion are the taking of communion at the Eucharist, the communion with the Triune God, the communion of the local community immediately celebrating the liturgy, and finally the wider ecclesial communion—the communion with the bishop and the diocese, the communion in teaching, prayer, and charity among local, that is, diocesan churches, the communion in synods and councils. The initial intent of Afanasieff's programmatic essay of 1934 on "Two Ideas of the Universal Church" set the "Eucharistic ecclesiology" against the "universalistic ecclesiology" that he thought expressed the Roman Catholic theology of the Church. The interest in contrasting the two ecclesiologies led Afanasieff to stress initially the local liturgical community at the expense of those wider senses of ecclesial communion that were always implicit in his own thought and certainly of great importance to Orthodox theology as a whole. The subsequent development of this Eucharistic ecclesiology, involving

Orthodox theologians such as Aexander Schmemann, John Meyendorff, John Zizioulas, S. Charkianakis, and D. Papandreou, as well as Afanasieff himself, has shown a progressively keen sense of the wider implications of communion, moving from an almost exclusive emphasis on the particular community of worship to acknowledge more explicitly the communion of shared belief and of a shared episcopacy needed to frame, to proclaim, and to guarantee the belief and worship of a particular congregation. The fruit of this theological *ressourcement* has been a renewed insight into the manifold ways in which Eucharistic communion is embedded in and fosters a broader ecclesial communion.

The same Christ who is uniquely present in this unique sacrament is also the source of a further, unique grace. In the Eucharist, the really present Lord is both our ultimate good and the savior of the penultimate goods that reflect him; he is both "res et sacramentum." Most other sacraments are for the recipients themselves; for this reason, the prayers of petition added to the rite of baptism do not belong to that sacrament itself. But, in the Catholic understanding of the Eucharist (admittedly, not one shared by all ecclesial communities), praying for others belongs to the very heart of the Eucharist. Beyond the immediate gift offered to those receiving the sacrament, the Lord's sacrifice made present in the Eucharist is meant as an effective blessing for others: "pro vobis et pro multis." The encyclical shares with the work of St. Thomas this close association of the sacrifice of the Mass and the intercession brought there "pro multis" in the body of Christ, given up for me—but not only for me or the community presently gathered with me. When making the needs and wounds of the world transparent to the passion of Christ, when bringing them in the power of the Spirit before the Father, the Eucharistic Church is granted a share in the "pro-existence" of Christ's sacrifice on the Cross. It is a pro-existence that remembers its continuity with pre-Christian sacrifice: "In this gift Jesus Christ entrusted to his Church the perennial making present of the paschal mystery" (§ 5).

Theology often has something of a fugal character. Theologians of the Eucharist are asked to practice their counterpoint, avoiding the flight from and the flight into sacrifice, fathoming what sacrifice means by discerning the distinction of antecedent and consequent will in God.[107] The Eucharistic sacrifice is revealed as the compassion of God by the *discrimen* of Christ's *voluntas ut*

---

107. Cf. Brian Daley, "Apokatastasis and 'the Honorable Silence' in the Eschatology of Maximus Confessor," in *Maximus Confessor*, ed. C. Schönborn and F. Heinzer (Fribourg: Universitätsverlag, 1982), 318–27; and Thomas Joseph White, "Von Balthasar and Journet on the Universal Possibility of Salvation and the Twofold Will of God," *Nova et Vetera* (English) 4, no. 3 (2006): 633–66.

natura and his *voluntas ut ratio* in the face of death, as we pray with the Church the prayer the Lord taught her: that increasingly his will might be done on earth as it has always been done in heaven; affirming Christ as the Other of the Church and the Church as the vessel of his presence and work, affirming the one "verum sacrificium" and its daily offering by the Church, seeing there the fullness and yet also the limit of genuine sacrifice, looking in the Eucharist for the *corpus Christi verum* and the *corpus Christi mysticum*, the mysteries of presence and sacrifice, the *pro vobis et pro multis*. Especially when attentive to the beauty of this fugal revelation, the insight, dear also to the proponents of dramatic theology, would be strengthened: that the notion of *communio*, meant as a communion of persons, each *incommunicabilis*, provides a promising context for embracing this dialectic of Eucharistic participation. In letting Christ be "pro vobis," the Church is granted the gift of being actively with him in his Eucharistic presence "pro multis."

PART 3

Bonum—Lex—Virtus

Moral Theology

[8]

St. Thomas and the Divinity
of the Common Good

LAWRENCE DEWAN, O.P.

St. Paul, in the Epistle to the Romans 1:20, a text fundamental for the history of natural theology, writes: "For the invisible things of him [God] from the creation of the world are clearly seen, being understood by the things that are made. His eternal power also and divinity: so that they are inexcusable."[1] St. Thomas Aquinas, in commenting on this passage, explains (in part):

The third item known is "divinity," to which it pertains that they knew God as the ultimate end, unto which all tend; for by "the divine good" is meant the *common good which is participated in by all*; for this reason he said "divinity," which signifies participation, rather than "deity," which signifies the essence of God ([recall] Colossians 2:9: "and in him there dwells all the fullness of divinity"). Now, these three items relate to the three modes of knowing mentioned previously: for the *invisible* things of God are known by the way of *negation,* and his *eternal power* by the way of *causality,* but the *divinity* by the way of *excellence.*

Secondly, one must consider through what means they have been known, which is indicated when it is said: "through those things that have been made": for just as art is revealed through the works of the artist, so also the wisdom of God is revealed through creatures ([recall] Wisdom 13:5: for from the greatness of the beauty of the creature they could have seen well their creator).[2]

That is, St. Thomas understands "divinity" as a more participational word than "deity," which latter word is used to speak directly of the divine essence.[3] Divinity signifies God's goodness as a common good participated by all.

I take the point that God's divinity is known by the way of excellence to refer to the sort of thinking we see in Thomas's Fourth Way, with its levels of participation of perfections. The creatures' likenesses to God are by way of analogy, the more and the less.[4]

It is no wonder, then, that the "more divine" status of the common good is often signaled by St. Thomas. In the following I shall focus on the "more divine" status of the common good as a key for the metaphysical contemplation of the common good, which, as we shall see, is said in many ways, according to priority and posteriority.

Thomas, in the above text, also speaks of our knowing God as the wise artist at the origin of nature; and I will make that a theme in this meditation.

Thomas and the Greek Philosophical Heritage

One finds a focus on the divine in the moral discussions of Plato, Aristotle, and St. Thomas Aquinas. In the *Phaedo,* Plato presents the most appropriate life for human beings, the philosophical life, and contrasts the pursuit of the so-called virtues as found in non-philosophers with the philosophical cultivation of authentic virtue, precisely in the respect that the philosopher is seeking *communion with the divine.*[5] So also, Aristotle, at the end of the *Nicomachean Ethics,* sees the culmination of human striving in the attainment of the contemplation of truth, a life that makes one more like the gods and more lovable

---

Tertium cognitum est quod dicit *et divinitas,* ad quod pertinet quod cognoverunt deum sicut ultimum finem, in quem omnia tendunt. *Divinum enim bonum dicitur bonum commune quod ab omnibus participatur;* propter hoc potius dixit divinitatem, quae participationem significat, quam deitatem, quae significat essentiam dei. Col. II, 9: et in ipso habitat omnis plenitudo divinitatis. Haec autem tria referuntur ad tres modos cognoscendi supradictos. Nam invisibilia dei cognoscuntur per viam negationis; sempiterna virtus, per viam causalitatis; divinitas, per viam excellentiae.

Secundo, considerandum est per quod medium illa cognoverunt, quod designatur cum dicit per ea quae facta sunt. Sicut enim ars manifestatur per artificis opera, ita et dei sapientia manifestatur per creaturas. Sap. XIII, 5: a magnitudine enim speciei et creaturae cognoscibiliter poterit creator horum videri.

Thomas's immediate injection of the note of goodness into this interpretation seems to have to do with his relating the concept of divinity to participational likeness.

3. One can see this use of *"deitas"* by St. Thomas in such a text as *ST* I, q. 3, a. 3: whether God is his essence or nature (six occurrences in that one article).

4. Cf. *ST* I, q. 4, a. 3.

5. Plato, *Phaedo* 82b–84b; and cf. 69b–e.

to the gods. The divine life, to the extent that we can live it, is the most authentically human life.[6] And St. Thomas, as we recall, presents the subject of the moral part of *sacra doctrina* as the human being taken precisely as the image of God.[7]

Often in the writings of St. Thomas one finds the teaching, something of a commonplace, that the common good is more divine than the good of a particular person. For example:

> It is to be said that the providence of God, by which he governs things, as has been said, is similar to the providence by which the father of the family governs the household, or the king the city or kingdom: in which instances of governing this is common, that the common good is more eminent than the singular good: as the good of a people is more divine than the good of a city or family or person (as is found in the beginning of the *Ethics*). Hence, any provider attends more to what befits the community, if he governs wisely, than to what befits one only.[8]

This is referred to by Aristotle in *Nicomachean Ethics,* 1.2. We might begin the present meditation with a look at that latter text and Thomas's commentary on it.

Aristotle, in beginning the *Nicomachean Ethics,* focuses on the good as that which all pursue. He shows that there is *hierarchy* among such pursued goods, and that *such hierarchy cannot go to infinity.* Thus, he fixes our attention on an *ultimate* good worthy of human pursuit. Would not *knowledge* of the ultimate good in human affairs have a great effect on our action in its regard?[9]

Having associated these goods or ends with various productive sciences or arts, for example, health with the medical art or strategy with the military art, he proposes that we consider the end which pertains to the art or science of politics. The argument for introducing the consideration of politics is twofold. First, it is said that it belongs to the political art to determine who in the society shall study which arts, and generally what we are to do, how we are to act; thus, the end, that is, the good, of politics seems to be the end of the human being as such.

---

6. Aristotle, *Nicomachean Ethics,* 10, 8 (1179a22–33).

7. *ST* I-II, prologue.

8. Thomas, *De veritate,* q. 5, a. 3: "Responsio. Dicendum, quod providentia dei, qua res gubernat, ut dictum est, est similis providentiae qua paterfamilias gubernat domum, aut rex civitatem aut regnum: *in quibus gubernationibus hoc est commune, quod bonum commune est eminentius quam bonum singulare; sicut bonum gentis est divinius quam bonum civitatis vel familiae vel personae,* ut habetur, in principio ethicorum. Unde quilibet provisor plus attendit quid communitati conveniat, si sapienter gubernat, quam quid conveniat uni tantum."

9. Aristotle, *Nicomachean Ethics,* 1, 2 (1094a23–24).

Seemingly arguing further so as to bring on board as many hearers as possible, Aristotle acknowledges that while it might be the very same end or good
which would be for a single person and for the whole of a people or society, the
very attaining of such an end for the whole of a society would be a more "god-
like" action. To attain or to preserve that same end for an entire city would be
greater than so to do for one person. Aristotle thus concludes that "the end at
which our enquiry aims" is this end of the *political* art.[10]

Thomas Aquinas, in commenting on this work of Aristotle, at the very
point where there is the contrast between the single man and the society,
brings out the principles involved in the reasoning. Thus, we read:

Then when he says: "For if it is the same . . ." he shows that politics is *most primary*, from the very nature of its proper end. For it is evident that each sort of cause is
stronger to the extent that its effect reaches to more things; thus, the good, which
has the nature of final cause, is stronger precisely inasmuch as it extends itself to
more things. Hence, if the good is the same for one human being and for an entire
city, it seems much greater and more perfect to obtain, that is, to procure, and to
save, that is, to preserve, that which is the good of the whole city rather than that
which is the good of one human being.[11]

What I would underline here is the introduction of *the principle of causal superiority or hierarchy*. One thinks of Thomas's *Commentary on the Book of Causes*,
where he presents this conception as relating first of all to the efficient cause
spreading its influence to all other causality.[12] The doctrine has its background
in Aristotle's presentation of the modes of active potency at the beginning of
Metaphysics, 9.[13]

10. Ibid. (1094b10–11). Here I am using the Oxford (Ross) translation, but I revise it to
speak of one rather than many ends. I note that at line 11 the Latin (given in the Leonine edition
of *Sententia libri Ethicorum*) has "*hoc*," but with a variant as "*haec*," i.e., a plural "these." I will be
referring to Thomas Aquinas, *Sententia libri Ethicorum*, t. 47 of *Opera omnia* (Rome, 1969: Ad
sanctae Sabinae).
11. Thomas, *Sententia libri Ethicorum*, 1.2 (ll. 168–78): "Deinde cum dicit: 'Si enim et idem
est etc.,' ostendit quod *politica sit principalissima*, ex ipsa ratione *proprii finis*. Manifestum est
enim quod *unaquaeque causa tanto potior est quanto ad plura effectus eius se extendit*. Unde et
bonum, quod habet rationem causae finalis, tanto potius est quanto ad plura se extendit. Et ideo, si
idem est bonum uni homini et toti civitati: multo videtur maius et perfectius suscipere, id est
procurare, et salvare, id est conservare, illud quod est bonum totius civitatis, quam id quod est
bonum unius hominis."
12. Thomas Aquinas, *Super Librum de causis expositio*, prop. 1a (ed. Saffrey [Paris: Vrin,
2002], pp. 8.21–9.1). Recall *ST* I, q. 77, a. 3, ad 4: "A higher power relates essentially to a more
universal objectal note than does a lower power, because the higher the power, the more numerous the items to which it extends" (potentia superior per se respicit universaliorem rationem
obiecti, quam potentia inferior, quia quanto potentia est superior, tanto ad plura se extendit).
13. Cf. Thomas, *CM* 9.2 (1789); and cf. *ST* I, q. 19, a. 4 (134a34–46).

It might be noted that we are focusing here on the efficient cause, that is, the art or science of politics, and its production and maintenance of goodness. Still, the final cause, the good, is seen as proportionate to the power of that agent.[14] It is the common good itself, the final cause, which subsequently will be referred to as "more divine."[15]

Thomas adds an explanatory note on this whole consideration as including *both* the single person and the entire city. We read:

For it pertains to the *love* which ought to exist among human beings that a person seek and preserve the good even of one single person, but it is much better and more divine to show this [love and good] for a whole people and for cities.[16]

This is evidently a note on Aristotle's use of the word *"amabile:"* "Amabile quidem enim et uni soli, melius vero et divinius genti et civitatibus" (It is lovable for one alone, but better and more divine for a people and for cities).[17]

Next we get an alternative interpretation of what is being said: "Or [read] otherwise: it is lovable, indeed, that this be provided for even one city, but it is much more divine that it be provided for an entire people comprising many cities."[18] That is, Thomas sees the possibility that in the *"Amabile"* sentence, Aristotle has gone beyond the comparison of the good as obtained for one person and as obtained for a whole city, to a comparison of the good of one city and the good of a whole nation of cities.

Next, we have an explanation of the use of the word *"divinius."* We read: "But he says that this is more divine, in that it pertains more to likeness to God, who is the universal cause of all goods."[19] We then get, as regards Aristotle's words: "A method seeks this, therefore, that is, the civil,"[20] the following: "And this good, that is, that is common to one or several cities, is aimed at by a particular method, that is, an art, which is called 'the civil.' Hence to it most of

14. Cf. Thomas, *SCG* 1.72 (Pera § 625; Pegis § 9).

15. On the approach to the final cause through the efficient cause, cf. my paper: "St. Thomas and the Causality of God's Goodness," *Laval théologique et philosophique* 34, no. 3 (1978): 291–304.

16. Thomas, *Sententia libri Ethicorum*, 1.2 (ll. 178–82): *"Pertinet quidem enim ad amorem* qui debet esse inter homines quod homo quaerat et conservet bonum etiam uni soli homini, sed multo melius est et divinius quod hoc exhibeatur toti genti et civitatibus."

17. Aristotle, as in Thomas, *Sententia libri Ethicorum*, 1.2 (Leonine p. 7; 1094b9–10).

18. Thomas, *Sententia libri Ethicorum*, 1.2 (ll. 182–5): *"Vel aliter:* amabile quidem est quod hoc exhibeatur uni soli civitati, *sed multo divinius est, quod hoc exhibeatur toti genti, in qua multae civitates continentur."*

19. Ibid. (ll. 185–8): "Dicit autem hoc esse *divinius,* eo quod magis pertinet ad dei similitudinem, qui est universalis causa omnium bonorum."

20. Aristotle, as in Thomas, *Sententia libri Ethicorum*, 1.2 (Leonine p. 7; 1094b10–11): "Methodus quidem igitur hoc appetit, civilis quaedam existens."

all does it pertain, as to what is most primary, to consider the ultimate end of human life."[21] Thomas immediately adds a qualifier:

However, one must understand that he calls the political [art] most primary, not un-qualifiedly, but in the domain of active sciences, which bear upon human matters whose ultimate end politics considers; for the ultimate end of the entire universe is considered by divine science, which is most primary with respect to all. He says, still, that the ultimate end of human life pertains to politics, about which he determines in this book, because the doctrine of this book contains the first elements of political science.[22]

We see, thus, that the *Nicomachean Ethics* itself is expected to exhibit the very end at which human life aims, and that this is the end of city life.

Having passed in review the text of *Sententia libri Ethicorum,* 1.2, where the end of political science, the good for a whole society, is seen to be "more di-vine" than the same good as provided for only one person or only one city, let us look at further teachings in this line in the same work.

As we recall, the end aimed at is happiness, and the nature of this happi-ness is established by considering "the function of man." We read: "to say that happiness is the chief good seems a platitude, and a clearer account of what it is is still desired. This might perhaps be given, if we could first ascertain *the func-tion of man.*"[23] And Thomas Aquinas comments:

Then, when he says: "Whether, therefore, of a weaver, etc.," he proves that there is some operation proper to man . . . Firstly, through those things which are added to a man. For to a man it is added that he be a weaver or currier or grammarian or mu-sician or some other such thing. But there is none of these that lacks a proper opera-tion; otherwise, it would follow that these sorts of thing were added to a man use-lessly and vainly. How much more is it inappropriate that that which is by *nature, which is ordered by divine reason,* be useless and vain, as compared to that which is

21. Thomas, *Sententia libri Ethicorum,* 1.2 (ll. 188–92): "Hoc autem bonum, scilicet quod est commune uni vel civitatibus pluribus, intendit methodus quaedam, id est ars, quae vocatur ci-vilis. Unde ad ipsam maxime pertinet considerare *ultimum finem humanae vitae:* tamquam ad principalissimam."

22. Ibid. (ll. 193–202): "Sciendum est autem, quod politicam dicit esse principalissimam, non simpliciter, sed in genere *activarum* scientiarum, quae sunt circa res humanas, quarum ulti-mum finem politica considerat. *Nam ultimum finem totius universi considerat scientia divina, quae est respectu omnium principalissima.* Dicit autem ad politicam pertinere considerationem ultimi finis humanae vitae; de quo tamen in hoc libro determinat, quia *doctrina huius libri continet pri-ma elementa scientiae politicae.*" Thomas makes this last explanation, seemingly, because in his own prologue he has divided moral philosophy into three parts, the monostic ("monostica"), the economic, and the political, and has identified the *Nicomachean Ethics* with the monostic. Cf. Thomas, *Sententia libri Ethicorum,* 1.1 (Leonine, ll. 78–107).

23. Aristotle, *Nicomachean Ethics,* trans. David Ross, 1, 7 (1097b22–25), emphasis added; in Thomas, *Sententia libri Ethicorum,* 1.2 (Leonine p. 34).

through art, and thus ordered by human reason. Therefore, since man is something existing by nature, it is impossible that he be naturally idle, as [a thing] not having a proper operation. There is, therefore, some operation proper to man, just as there is of those [techniques] that are added to him. The cause of this is that each thing, whether natural or artificial, has being [*est*] through some form, which is the principle of some operation. Hence, just as each thing has its proper being [*proprium esse*] through its own form, so also it has its proper operation.²⁴

And it is in identifying reason as proper to man that we succeed in identifying happiness as an operation in accord with perfect virtue.²⁵

Aristotle had already argued that there must be one supreme final cause for the human being. In arguing for not going to infinity in final causes, he said that it is a natural desire, the desire for the end, and that a natural desire cannot be in vain (which it would be if the ends went on to infinity). And the reason for a natural desire not being possibly in vain? It is this:

But that it is impossible to proceed to infinity in ends he proves by a third reason which also leads to the impossible, in this way: If one proceeds to infinity in the desire for ends, such that one end is desired because of another, right to infinity, it will never come to this, that the man attain to the desired end. But it is pointless and in vain for someone to desire that which cannot be attained; therefore, the desire will be pointless and in vain. But this desire is natural: for it has been said above that the good is that which all naturally desire; therefore it will follow that a natural desire is inane and vacuous. *But this is impossible. Because a natural desire is nothing else but an inclination inhering in things resulting from the ordering by the primary source of events, which cannot be empty;* therefore it is impossible that in ends one proceed to infinity. And thus it is necessary that there be some ultimate end because of which all others are desired and it itself is not desired because of others. And thus it is necessary that there be one best end of human things.²⁶

24. Thomas, *Sententia libri Ethicorum*, 1.10 (Leonine ll. 46–66), commenting on Aristotle at 1097b28–30: "Deinde cum dicit: utrum igitur textoris etc., probat quod sit aliqua propria operatio hominis . . . Primo quidem per ea quae accidunt homini. Accidit enim homini, quod sit textor, vel coriarius, aut grammaticus, vel musicus sive aliquid aliud huiusmodi. Sed nihil istorum est, quod non habeat propriam operationem. Alioquin sequeretur quod huiusmodi otiose et frustra homini advenirent. Multo autem magis inconveniens quod sit otiosum et frustra id quod est secundum naturam, quod est ordinatum ratione divina, quam id quod est secundum artem, quod est ordinatum ratione humana. Cum igitur homo sit aliquid existens secundum naturam, impossibile est, quod sit naturaliter otiosus, quasi non habens propriam operationem. Est igitur aliqua operatio hominis propria, sicut eorum quae ei accidunt. Cuius causa est, quia unumquodque, vel naturale vel artificiale, est per aliquam formam, quae est alicuius operationis principium. Unde sicut unaquaeque res habet proprium esse per suam formam, ita etiam et propriam operationem."

25. Aristotle, *Nicomachean Ethics*, 1, 7 (1098a7–18).

26. Thomas, *In EN* 1.2.3 (Leonine ll. 32–52): "Quod autem sit impossibile in finibus procedere in infinitum, probat tertia ratione quae est etiam ducens ad impossibile, hoc modo. Si

It is Thomas who adds the interpretation as to why it is impossible that the natural desire be in vain. This really is a doctrine of the divine will as giving inclination to all things, as to their very natures.[27]

Aristotle eventually presents two levels of happiness as the goal of the human being.[28] The goal of politics, the achievement of virtue, constitutes a peace which in turn makes possible contemplation of the divine. Here I would recall the presentation by Thomas of Aristotle's point that ultimate happiness takes place in leisure. We read:

Happiness is found in a certain leisure; for someone is said to be at leisure when there remains nothing for him to do; which occurs when someone has already arrived at the goal. And so [Aristotle] adds that we are not at leisure in order to come to be at leisure, that is, we work laboriously, which is "not being at leisure," in order to come to repose in the goal, which is "to be at leisure." And he shows this with the example of those waging war, who wage war in order to arrive at participation in peace.[29]

Here Thomas sees a need for clarification:

---

procedatur in infinitum in desiderio finium, ut scilicet semper unus finis desideretur propter alium in infinitum, nunquam erit devenire ad hoc quod homo consequatur fines desideratos. Sed frustra et vane aliquis desiderat id quod non potest assequi; ergo desiderium finis esset frustra et vanum. *Sed hoc desiderium est naturale: dictum enim est supra quod bonum est quod naturaliter omnia desiderant;* ergo sequetur quod naturale desiderium sit inane et vacuum. Sed hoc est impossibile. Quia *naturale desiderium nihil aliud est quam inclinatio inhaerens rebus ex ordinatione primi moventis, quae non potest esse supervacua;* ergo impossibile est quod in finibus procedatur in infinitum. Et sic necesse est esse aliquem ultimum finem propter quem omnia alia desiderantur et ipse non desideratur propter alia. Et ita necesse est esse aliquem optimum finem rerum humanarum."

27. Cf., e.g., *ST* I, q. 59, a. 1.

28. Thomas teaches, at *ST* I-II, q. 3, a. 5 (ed. Ottawa, 731b18–24): "*Beatitudo autem imperfecta,* qualis hic haberi potest, primo quidem et principaliter consistit in *contemplatione, secundario* vero in operatione *practici intellectus ordinantis actiones et passiones humanas,* ut dicitur in X *Ethic*" (Imperfect happiness, such as can be had here [in this life], firstly and principally is to be found in contemplation, but secondarily in the operation of the practical intellect ordering human actions and passions, as is said in *Ethics* X). Here the Ottawa ed. sends us to 1177a12 and 1178a9. Note the second of these, at the beginning of Thomas's *Sententia libri Ethicorum,* 10.12. It opens with this: "Postquam Philosophus ostendit quod perfecta felicitas est et principalis secundum speculationem intellectus, hic inducit quamdam aliam secundariam felicitatem, quae consistit in operatione moralium virtutum" (After the Philosopher shows that perfect and principal happiness is in function of the contemplation by the intellect, here he introduces another, secondary happiness, which is found in the operation of the moral virtues).

29. Thomas, *Sententia libri Ethicorum,* 10.11, § 1: "*Felicitas enim consistit in quadam vacatione.* Vacare enim dicitur aliquis quando non restat ei aliquid agendum: quod contingit cum aliquis iam ad finem pervenerit. Et ideo subdit, quod non vacamus ut vacemus, idest laboramus operando, quod est non vacare, ut perveniamus ad quiescendum in fine, quod est vacare. Et hoc ostendit per exemplum bellantium, qui ad hoc bella gerunt quod ad pacem adoptatam perveniant."

Nevertheless one must consider that earlier the Philosopher said that repose is for the sake of operation. However, there he was speaking of the rest by which an operation is interrupted before achieving the goal, because of the impossibility of continuing; which rest is ordered toward the operation as toward a goal. Leisure, on the other hand, is rest in the goal toward which the operation is ordered; and thus, leisure befits happiness most of all, [happiness] which is the ultimate goal. [*This happiness] is not found in the operations of the practical virtues, which are especially those to be found in political affairs, maintaining the order of the common good which is most divine [divinissimum], or else in the affairs of war, by which the common good is defended against enemies, and nevertheless to these works leisure is not appropriate.*[30]

We note that "the common good which is divine" is here not the ultimate goal. Thomas goes on to review Aristotle's arguments that the ultimate good is not seen either in warfare or in political action. I will quote the latter point. We read:

it is also evident as regards political actions, that there is no leisure in them; rather, beyond the mere political dealings a man wants to acquire something else, say power and honors; or else, because in these there is not the ultimate goal, as was shown in book 1, it is more suitable that through political dealings someone wishes to acquire happiness for his own self and for the citizens, such that *the sort of happiness someone intends to acquire through the life of politics be other than political life itself;* for thus through political life we seek it as something other than that. For this is *contemplative happiness,* to which the whole of political life would seem to be aimed; thus, *through peace,* which is established and preserved through the ordering effected by political life, one gives to human beings the possibility of contemplating truth.[31]

Obviously, like "happiness," "the common good which is more divine" is said in many ways, according to priority and posteriority.

30. Ibid., § 2: "Est tamen considerandum, quod supra philosophus dicit, quod requies sit gratia operationis. Sed ibi locutus fuit de requie, qua intermittitur operatio ante consequutionem finis propter impossibilitatem continue operandi, quae quidem requies ordinatur ad operationem sicut ad finem. *Vacatio autem est requies in fine ad quem ordinatur operatio, et sic felicitati, quae est ultimus finis, maxime competit vacatio.* Quae quidem *non invenitur in operationibus virtutum practicarum, quarum praecipue sunt illae quae consistunt in rebus politicis, utpote ordinantes bonum commune, quod est divinissimum;* vel in rebus bellicis, quibus *ipsum bonum commune* defenditur contra hostes, et tamen *his operibus non competit vacatio.*"

31. Ibid., § 4: "*Secundo etiam hoc manifestum est in actionibus politicis,* quod non est in eis vacatio; sed *praeter ipsam conversationem civilem* vult homo acquirere aliquid aliud, puta potentatus et honores; vel, *quia in his non est ultimus finis ut in primo ostensum est,* magis est decens, quod *per civilem conversationem* aliquis velit acquirere felicitatem sibi ipsi et civibus, ita quod huiusmodi *felicitas,* quam intendit aliquis acquirere *per* politicam vitam, sit *altera ab ipsa politica vita;* sic enim per vitam politicam, quaerimus eam quasi alteram existentem ab ipsa. *Haec est enim felicitas speculativa, ad quam tota vita politica videtur ordinata; dum per pacem, quae per ordinationem vitae politicae statuitur et conservatur, datur hominibus facultas contemplandi veritatem.*"

Common Good, Divine Wisdom, and Nature

I have stressed the role of the natural in the argument in *Nicomachean Ethics* in order to take us toward some foundational considerations. I think of Gilson's point that it is the word "nature" that separates us from our contemporaries.[32]

To begin with, let us look at another prologue of Thomas's, by which he introduces his own *Commentary on Aristotle's Politics*. Interestingly it focuses on the teaching that art imitates nature. We read:

As the Philosopher teaches in *Physics* 2, art imitates nature.[33] The reason for this is that, as principles stand relative to each other, so also proportionately stand [their]

32. Cf. Étienne Gilson and Jacques Maritain, *Correspondance: 1923–1971*, ed. Géry Prouvost (Paris: Vrin, 1991), 250 (letter of Gilson, September 8, 1971). He is speaking of "la science moderne": "What separates us irreparably from [modern science] is the Aristotelian (and common sense) notion of Substantial Form . . . Descartes rid nature of it. They understand nothing anymore since they forgot Aristotle's great saying that 'there is no part of an animal that is purely material or purely immaterial.' *It is not the word 'philosophy,' it is the word 'nature' that separates us from our contemporaries.* Since I do not have any hope of convincing them of the truth (which yet is evident) of hylomorphism, I do not believe it is possible to propose our hypothesis to them as scientifically valid" (Ce qui nous en sépare irréparablement est la notion aristotélicienne (et de sens commun) de la Forme Substantielle . . . Descartes en a dépeuplé la nature. On ne comprend plus rien depuis qu'on a oublié la grande parole d'Aristote, qu'il n'y a "aucune partie d'un animal qui soit purement matérielle ou purement immatérielle." Ce n'est pas le mot philosophie, c'est le mot nature qui nous sépare de nos contemporains. Comme je n'espère pas les convaincre de la vérité [pourtant évidente] de l'hylémorphisme, je ne crois pas possible de leur proposer notre hypothèse comme scientifiquement valide). For the statement of Aristotle, cf. *Parts of Animals*, 1.3 (643a25).

Gilson argued that substantial form is the necessary foundation for natural teleology. Étienne Gilson, *D'Aristote à Darwin et retour: Essai sur quelques constantes de la biophilosophie* (Paris: Vrin, 1971), 33–34: "Aristotle found finality in nature so evident that he asked himself how his predecessors could have failed to see, and even worse, denied its presence there. Their error was explained, in his eyes, because they erred concerning the notions of essence and substance. [*Parts of Animals*, 1.1] The subsequent history of philosophy should confirm the accuracy of his diagnosis, because as long as the Aristotelian notion of substance as unity of a matter and a form survived, that of finality remained undisputed, but as soon as in the seventeenth century Bacon and Descartes [p. 34] denied the notion of substantial form (form that constitutes a substance by its union with a matter), that of final cause became inconceivable. Indeed, substance as defined by its form is the end of generation. What remained, once the form was excluded, was the extended matter, or rather extension itself, which is the object of geometry and is susceptible only to purely mechanical modifications. Descartes submitted to mechanism the entire domain of living beings, including the human body. The celebrated Cartesian theory of 'animal machines' which rightly astonished La Fontaine illustrates this point perfectly" (my trans.). (There does exist a published English translation, but I did not have it available to me: *From Aristotle to Darwin and Back Again: A Journey in Final Causality, Species, and Evolution*, trans. John Lyon [Notre Dame, Ind.: University of Notre Dame Press, 1984].)

33. This has never been truer: if one follows the scientific reports in the public press, one finds the likes of the following item rather often. Jonathan Abraham, "Eyeless Creature

operations and effects. Now, the principle of those things which are brought about by art is the human intellect, which in virtue of some measure of likeness is derived from the divine intellect, which is the principle of natural things. Hence it is necessary that the *operations* of art also imitate the *operations* of nature; and those *things* which are by virtue of art imitate those *things* which are in nature. For, if someone who is an instructor in some art were to bring about a work of the art, it would be necessary that the disciple who received the art from him look to that [teacher's] work so as himself to work in imitation of that. And therefore the human intellect, to which intelligible light is derived from the divine intellect, necessarily has it that in those things which it makes it be informed from inspection of those things which have been made naturally, so as to operate similarly.[34]

Thomas uses this approach to explain the development of human institutions. He eventually says:

Now nature proceeds in its operation *from simple items to composites,* in such fashion that in those things which are brought about by the operation of nature that which is maximally composite is perfect and a whole and the end of the other items, as is evident in all wholes with respect to their parts. Hence, also, the operative reason of man proceeds from simple things to composites, as from imperfect items to perfect ones.[35]

Turns Out to Be All Eyes," *The New York Times,* September 4, 2001: "The brittlestar, a relative of the starfish, seems to be able to flee from predators in the murky ocean depths without the aid of eyes. Now scientists have discovered its secret: its entire skeleton forms a big eye. A new study shows that a brittle star species called *Ophiocoma wendtii* has a skeleton with crystals that function as a visual system, apparently furnishing the information that lets the animal see its surroundings and escape harm. The brittlestar architecture is giving ideas to scientists who want to build tiny lenses for things like optical computing. 'This study shows how great materials can be formed by nature, far beyond current technology,' said Dr. Joanna Aizenberg, a material scientist at Lucent Technologies' Bell Laboratories and the lead author of the study. 'They form very interesting unique structures that have interesting mechanical and optical applications,' Dr. Aizenberg said. 'They form nearly perfect microlenses.' The study, published on August 23 in the journal *Nature,* was conducted by an international team that included material scientists, theoretical physicists, chemists and biologists."

34. Thomas, *Commentary on Aristotle's Politics,* prologue (in part): "Sicut philosophus docet in secundo *Physicorum,* ars imitatur naturam. Cuius ratio est, quia sicut se habent principia adinvicem, ita proportionabiliter se habent operationes et effectus. Principium autem eorum quae secundum artem fiunt est intellectus humanus, qui secundum similitudinem quamdam derivatur ab intellectu divino, qui est principium rerum naturalium. Unde necesse est, quod et operationes artis imitentur operationes naturae; et ea quae sunt secundum artem, imitentur ea quae sunt in natura. Si enim aliquis instructor alicuius artis opus artis efficeret; oporteret discipulum, qui ab eo artem suscepisset, ad opus illius attendere, ut ad eius similitudinem et ipse operaretur. Et ideo intellectus humanus ad quem intelligibile lumen ab intellectu divino derivatur, necesse habet in his quae facit informari ex inspectione eorum quae sunt naturaliter facta, ut similiter operetur."

35. Ibid., § 3: "Procedit autem natura in sua operatione ex simplicibus ad composita; ita quod in eis quae per operationem naturae fiunt, quod est maxime compositum est perfectum et

This is true even in the ordering of human beings amongst themselves:

> as *when it orders many men into some one community.* Of which *communities,* since there
> are *diverse grades and orders,* the *ultimate* is the *community of the city ordered to the es-*
> *sential completeness of human life.* Hence, among all human communities it [the city]
> is most perfect. And because those things which are used by man are ordered *to man*
> *as to an end,* which [man as end] is more primary relative to those things which are
> ordered toward the end, so it is necessary that *this whole which is the city* be more pri-
> mary relative to *all those wholes which can be known and constituted by human reason.*[36]

St. Thomas is here speaking from the viewpoint of achieved wisdom, and thus presents nature and human striving in the light of the divine influence. We should reflect on the philosophical pathway to that summit, and that means starting, not from God, but from those things which are more immediately known to us.

If we wish to make Thomas's own standpoint our own, we must realize the importance of the knowledge that nature is a cause which acts for an end. Without assurance of that, we have no basis for ethics, including the ethics of politics, at all.

As Thomas says in commenting on Aristotle's *Physics,* book 2, at the point where Aristotle defends the view that nature is a cause that acts for an end:

> And this is important for the inquiry concerning providence. For those things
> which do not know the end do not tend toward the end, except inasmuch as directed
> by some knower, like the arrow by the archer. Hence, if nature operates for the sake
> of an end, it is necessary that it be ordered [toward it] by some intelligence; and this
> is the work of providence.[37]

Lest we underestimate just how fundamental this view of nature is for our discussions, I will visit some texts basic for the existence of politics. Consider, first, Thomas's justification of obedience of one person by another:

> I answer that it is to be said that just as the actions of natural things proceed from
> natural powers, so also human operations proceed from the human will. Now, it was

---

totum et finis aliorum, sicut apparet in omnibus totis respectu suarum partium. Unde et ratio hominis operativa ex simplicibus ad composita procedit tamquam ex imperfectis ad perfecta."

36. Ibid., § 4, in part: "In ipsis autem hominibus, sicut cum multos homines ordinat in unam quamdam communitatem. Quarum quidem communitatum cum diversi sint gradus et ordines, ultima est communitas civitatis ordinata ad per se sufficientia vitae humanae. Unde inter omnes communitates humanas ipsa est perfectissima. Et quia ea quae in usum hominis veniunt ordinantur ad hominem sicut ad finem, qui est principalior his quae sunt ad finem, ideo necesse est quod hoc totum quod est civitas sit *principalius omnibus totis, quae ratione humana cognosci et constitui possunt.*"

37. CP 2.12 (ed. Maggiolo, 250 [1]).

necessary in natural things for the superiors to move the inferiors to their actions by virtue of the excellence of the divinely conferred natural power. Hence, so also, it is necessary in human affairs that the superiors move the inferiors by their [the superior's] will, by the power of the divinely ordered authority. Now, to move [that is, set in motion] by reason and will is to command [*praecipere*]. Therefore, just as on the basis of the divinely established natural order what are inferiors among natural things are necessarily subject to the motion of superiors, so also in human affairs inferiors are required to obey superiors on the basis of natural and divine fittingness [*iuris*].[38]

One can hardly overestimate the importance of the presence here of the argument from nature. Reason is seen to find its principles in an imitation of nature.

It is nature *seen as a manifestation of divine wisdom* that prompts our imitation of nature in our quest for what is right. This suggests that it is the line of thinking that we see in Thomas's Fifth Way that constitutes the basis for our morality. The operation of nature is a work of intelligence, and, ultimately, of something primary in the order of intelligence, a God.

Let us recall further how regular the appeal is to nature in justifying the doctrine of the primacy of the common good, particularly for the human being. The justification always takes the form of presenting the human being as a part of the society,[39] together with the argument that the part reveals its being for the sake of the whole, particularly by the sacrificing of itself for the well-being of the whole: the hand puts itself in the way of the spear-thrust aimed at the head.[40] Consider *Quodl.* 1.4.3:

38. *ST* II-II, q. 104, a. 1: "Respondeo dicendum quod sicut actiones rerum naturalium procedunt ex potentiis naturalibus, ita etiam operationes humanae procedunt ex humana voluntate. Oportuit autem in rebus naturalibus ut superiora moverent inferiora ad suas actiones, per excellentiam naturalis virtutis collatae divinitus. Unde etiam oportet in rebus humanis quod superiores moveant inferiores per suam voluntatem, ex vi auctoritatis divinitus ordinatae. Movere autem per rationem et voluntatem est praecipere. Et ideo, sicut ex ipso ordine naturali divinitus instituto inferiora in rebus naturalibus necesse habent subdi motioni superiorum, ita etiam in rebus humanis, ex ordine iuris naturalis et divini, tenentur inferiores suis superioribus obedire."

39. Society, of course, is a unity through order, not a substantial unity; cf. Thomas, *Sententia libri Ethicorum*, prologue, Leonine ll. 78–81.

40. I notice in the article of T. G. R. Bower, "The Object in the World of the Infant," *Scientific American* 225, no. 4 (1971): 30–38, that infants in their second week after birth "clearly showed a defensive response to an approaching object. They pulled their head back and *put their hands between their face and the object*. These responses were accompanied by distress and crying so intense that the experiment had to be terminated earlier than had been planned. We were nevertheless able to try a few variations. We found that the defensive behavior was specific to an approaching object; if an object moved away, it produced neither defensive behavior nor crying" (32, emphasis added). Bower's own interest was "that by the second week of life an infant

It is to be said, therefore, that to love God above all, [even] more than oneself, is natural, not merely for the angel or the human being, but also for every creature whatsoever, according as it is possible to love either sensibly or naturally. For natural inclinations can be known most of all in those things that naturally act without deliberation of reason: for in nature each thing so acts as it has a natural aptitude to act. Now, we see that each part by a natural inclination operates for the good of the whole, even accepting danger or detriment for its own self: as is evident when someone exposes the hand to the sword in order to defend the head on which depends the safety of the entire body. Hence, it is natural that every part whatsoever, on its own level, love more the whole than itself. Hence, in function of this natural inclination and in function of political virtue, the good citizen exposes himself to mortal danger for the common good. Now it is evident that *God is the common good of the entire universe and of all its parts.* Hence, any creature whatsoever, on its own level, naturally loves God more than its own self: things that lack sense [do so] naturally, brute animals sensitively, but the rational creature [does so] through intellective love, which [in Latin] is [sometimes] called *"dilectio."*[41]

This is the same doctrine as we have in *Summa theologiae* I, question 60, article 5. There I would note that, in the case of the virtue of the good citizen, it says that if the good citizen risking his life for the community were naturally a member of this particular community, his so acting would be an example of natural love. That is, where the *Quodlibetal* text carefully distinguishes between the natural inclination of the soldier and the political virtue of the soldier, the *Summa* text explains the same point by alluding to the fact that the *individual* political community is, after all, a work of "art" (to use the vocabulary of the prologue to the *Commentary on Aristotle's Politics*). We do not have the moral virtues naturally, but we have the active principles, the seeds, of those virtues naturally.[42]

---

expects a seen object to have tactile consequences" (ibid.) It seems impossible that the association of the tactile and the visual had been learned.

41. *Quodl.* 1.4.3 (Easter 1269, according to Weisheipl): "Dicendum est ergo, quod diligere deum super omnia plus quam seipsum, est naturale non solum Angelo et homini, sed etiam cuilibet creaturae, secundum quod potest amare aut sensibiliter aut naturaliter. Inclinationes enim naturales maxime cognosci possunt in his quae naturaliter aguntur absque rationis deliberatione; sic enim agit unumquodque in natura, sicut aptum natum est agi. Videmus autem quod unaquaeque pars naturali quadam inclinatione operatur ad bonum totius, etiam cum periculo aut detrimento proprio: ut patet cum aliquis manum exponit gladio ad defensionem capitis, ex quo dependet salus totius corporis. Unde naturale est ut quaelibet pars suo modo plus amet totum quam seipsam. Unde et secundum hanc naturalem inclinationem, et secundum politicam virtutem, bonus civis mortis periculo se exponit pro bono communi. Manifestum est autem quod deus est bonum commune totius universi et omnium partium eius. Unde quaelibet creatura suo modo naturaliter plus amat deum quam seipsam: insensibilia quidem naturaliter, bruta vero animalia sensitive, creatura vero rationalis per intellectivum amorem, quae dilectio dicitur."

42. *Sent.* 1.17.3: "Sicut autem videmus in formis naturalibus, quod per dispositiones acciden-

Art imitates nature, and *virtue* imitates nature. "Virtue and grace imitate nature," as Thomas says in explaining that we ought to benefit more those closer to us. We read:

> *grace and virtue imitate the order of nature,* which has been instituted by the divine wisdom. Now, the order of nature is such that each natural agent puts forth its action by priority to those things that are closer to it: thus, for example, a fire heats more the thing closer to it. And similarly God sends forth the gifts of his goodness by priority and more fully to those substances which are closer to him, as is clear from Dionysius in *On the Celestial Hierarchy* c. 4.
>
> Now, the conferring of benefits is an action of charity toward others. And therefore it is necessary that we benefit more those who are closer to us.
>
> However, *proximity of one human being to another can be considered in function of the diverse areas in which humans have things in common with each other: there is the* natural *community of blood relatives; there is the* political *community of fellow citizens; there is the* spiritual *community of the faithful; and so on.* And in keeping with the diverse links, diverse benefits are to be dispensed in diverse measures: for, to each one is more to be conferred the benefit pertaining to that thing in function of which the person is more conjoined to us, speaking generally. Still, this is subject to variation in keeping with diversity of places and times and undertakings: for, in some cases it is the stranger who is more to be aided, for example, if he is in dire necessity, than even [one's own] father who is not suffering so great a need.[43]

---

tales, sicut calorem et frigus et hujusmodi, materia efficitur magis vel minus disposita ad suscipiendum formam; ita etiam in perfectionibus animae ex ipsis operibus animae anima efficitur habilior vel minus habilis ad consequendum perfectionem suam. Sed tamen differenter se habent operationes animae ad perfectiones infusas vel acquisitas. *Acquisitae enim perfectiones sunt in natura ipsius animae, in potentia, non pure materiali sed etiam activa, qua aliquid est in causis seminalibus. Sicut patet quod omnis scientia acquisita est in cognitione primorum principiorum, quae naturaliter nota sunt, sicut in principiis activis ex quibus concludi potest. Et similiter virtutes morales* sunt in ipsa rectitudine rationis et ordine, sicut in quodam principio seminali. Unde Philosophus dicit esse quasdam virtutes naturales, quae sunt quasi semina virtutum moralium. Et ideo operationes animae se habent ad perfectiones acquisitas, non solum per modum dispositionis, sed sicut principia active" (Just as we see in natural forms, that through accidental dispositions, such as warmth and cold and the like, matter is rendered more or less disposed to receive a form, so also in the perfections of the soul, from the very operations of the soul the soul is rendered more able or less able to attain to its own perfection. However, the operations of the soul stand differently toward the infused perfections and the acquired perfections. For the acquired perfections are in the nature of the soul itself in potency, and not [in] a purely material potency, but indeed in an active [potency], the way something exists in seminal causes. Thus it is evident that every acquired science is within the knowledge of the first principles, which are naturally known, as in active principles from which they can be concluded. And similarly the moral virtues are in the very rightness and order of reason, as in a seminal principle. Hence the Philosopher says that there are some natural virtues which are in the role of seeds of the moral virtues. And so the operations of the soul stand related to the acquired perfections, not merely in the mode of a disposition, but as active principles).

43. *ST* II-II, q. 31, a. 3: "Respondeo dicendum quod gratia et virtus imitantur naturae

The objection we should consider here is as follows: "that benefit is maximal whereby a man helps someone in war. However, the soldier in a war ought to help his unrelated fellow-soldier rather than an enemy who is a blood-relative. Therefore, benefits are not rather to be conferred on those more closely united [to us]."[44] To which Thomas replies:

it is to be said that *the common good of many is more divine than the good of one.* Hence, for the common good of the republic (whether the spiritual or the temporal republic) it is virtuous for someone to expose *even his own life to danger.* And therefore, since cooperation in warfare is ordered to the preservation of the republic, in this [matter] the soldier giving help to his associated soldier does not give it to him as to a private person, but as aiding the republic as a whole. Thus, it is not surprising if in this matter he favors the unrelated person over someone related by blood.[45]

In this same line of imitation of nature, we might call attention to the argument in favor of the military being a distinct species of prudence. We read:

It is to be said that those things which are done in function of art and reason must be in conformity with those which are in function of nature, which have been instituted by the divine reason. Now, nature intends two things: firstly, regulating each thing in itself; but secondly, resisting external battlers and corruptors. And it is because of this that it gave to animals not only the concupiscible power, by which they are moved toward those things which are suitable for their well being, but also the irascible power, by which the animal resists opponents. *Hence, in the domain of rea-*

---

ordinem, qui est ex divina sapientia institutus. Est autem talis ordo naturae ut unumquodque agens naturale per prius magis diffundat suam actionem ad ea quae sunt sibi propinquiora, sicut ignis magis calefacit rem sibi magis propinquam. Et similiter deus in substantias sibi propinquiores per prius et copiosius dona suae bonitatis diffundit; ut patet per Dionysium, iv cap. *Cael. Hier.* Exhibitio autem beneficiorum est quaedam actio caritatis in alios. Et ideo oportet quod ad magis propinquos simus magis benefici. Sed propinquitas unius hominis ad alium potest attendi secundum diversa in quibus sibi ad invicem homines communicant, ut consanguinei naturali communicatione, concives in civili, fideles in spirituali, et sic de aliis. Et secundum diversas coniunctiones sunt diversimode diversa beneficia dispensanda, nam unicuique est magis exhibendum beneficium pertinens ad illam rem secundum quam est magis nobis coniunctus, simpliciter loquendo. Tamen hoc potest variari secundum diversitatem locorum et temporum et negotiorum, nam in aliquo casu est magis subveniendum extraneo, puta si sit in extrema necessitate, quam etiam patri non tantam necessitatem patienti."

44. Ibid., obj. 2: "Praeterea, maximum beneficium est quod homo aliquem in bello adiuvet. Sed miles in bello magis debet iuvare extraneum commilitonem quam consanguineum hostem. Ergo beneficia non sunt magis exhibenda magis coniunctis."

45. Ibid., ad 2: "Ad secundum dicendum quod bonum commune multorum divinius est quam bonum unius. Unde pro bono communi reipublicae vel spiritualis vel temporalis virtuosum est quod aliquis *etiam propriam vitam* exponat periculo. Et ideo, cum communicatio in bellicis ordinetur ad conservationem reipublicae, in hoc miles impendens commilitoni auxilium, non impendit ei tanquam privatae personae, sed sicut totam rempublicam iuvans. Et ideo non est mirum si in hoc praefertur extraneus coniuncto secundum carnem."

son it is necessary that there be, not only political prudence, through which those matters that pertain to *the common good* are suitably arranged, but also military [prudence], by which the attacks of enemies are repelled.[46]

The replies to objections in this article explain why the business of the military is not just one more undertaking in the community. Rather: "while other undertakings which are found in the city are ordered to some particular utilities, the military enterprise is ordered toward the protection of *the entire common good.*"[47]

I could continue this consideration of the role of nature in Thomas's judgment of what is appropriate in the domain of reason. We see it in his conception of the condition of the human being in paradise before the original sin. He teaches the rightness of man's dominance over the other animals, and a certain mastery over all of lower nature, in accordance with nature and the ways of providence.[48] Let us at least recall the situation as regards human government of humans in paradise. While he mentions various sources of inequality among humans in that state, most relevant to government was the fact that humans would have had free choice and some would have tried harder than others, and thus have been superior to others in knowledge and justice.[49]

Accordingly, on the question of government of some by others in paradise, the first thing Thomas does is distinguish two different modes of mastery or lordship [*dominium*]. One sort has one person as the servant of another, such that the subjected person is working strictly for the interests of the one commanding. This is punitive servitude and not admissible in paradise. However, the other sort includes any sort of "subjection," even such as befits the governing and directing of free persons. This latter was appropriate for the original state of things; and the reason? Thomas tells us:

---

46. *ST* II-II, q. 50, a. 4: "Respondeo dicendum quod ea quae secundum artem et rationem aguntur conformia esse oportet his quae sunt secundum naturam, quae a ratione divina sunt instituta. Natura autem ad duo intendit: primo quidem, ad regendum unamquamque rem in seipsa; secundo vero, ad resistendum extrinsecis impugnantibus et corruptivis. Et propter hoc non solum dedit animalibus vim concupiscibilem, per quam moveantur ad ea quae sunt saluti eorum accommoda; sed etiam vim irascibilem, per quam animal resistit impugnantibus. Unde et in his quae sunt secundum rationem non solum oportet esse prudentiam politicam, per quam convenienter disponantur ea quae pertinent ad bonum commune; sed etiam militarem, per quam hostium insultus repellantur."

47. Ibid., ad 2: "alia negotia quae sunt in civitate ordinantur ad aliquas particulares utilitates, sed militare negotium ordinatur ad tuitionem totius boni communis."

48. *ST* I, q. 96, a. 1 and 2; at a. 1, ad 3, it is interesting that while he conceived of man in that state as having no need of the animals for his clothing or for his nourishment or for his travel, he saw the need of them so as to obtain experimental knowledge of their natures.

49. *ST* I, q. 96, a. 3.

Someone rules over another as over a free person when he directs that person toward the proper good of the directed person or to the common good. And there was
such rule of the human being in the state of innocence, for two reasons.

Firstly, because man is *naturally* a social animal: hence, humans in the state of innocence lived socially. Now, the social life of many cannot exist unless someone presides, [someone] who focuses on the common good: for the many, just in themselves,
focus on the many, but one [focuses] on one. And so the Philosopher says, at the beginning of the *Politics,* that whenever many are ordered to one, there is always one to be
found in the role of principal person and director.

Secondly, if one man had superiority over another as to science and justice, it
would have been unsuitable had not this been exploited for the benefit of the others,
in accordance with the teaching of 1 Peter 4 [10]: "each one using the grace he has
received for the benefit of the other." Hence, Augustine says, in *On the City of God,* 19
[cap. 14], that "the just rule, not as coveting to dominate, but in the role of giving care;
this the natural order prescribes, for it is thus that God made man."[50]

God as the Common Good of the Universe

This teaching, God as common good of the entire universe, is asserted, as
we saw, in the passage quoted above from *Quodl.* 1. St. Thomas's treatment of
this doctrine is immense. Thus, for example, in the *Summa contra gentiles,* the
whole of book 3, comprising 163 chapters, bears "on the order of creatures toward God as toward an end." The last one hundred of these chapters are on
God's providence, in general and especially (111–63) as governing the rational
creature. Chapters 2–63 are on God as the end, that is, the good, of all things.

The view of God as common good of the universe means that it is natural to love God, by friendly love, more than oneself.[51] This love for God is a

---

50. *ST* I, q. 96, a. 4: "Tunc vero dominatur aliquis alteri ut libero, quando dirigit ipsum ad
proprium bonum eius qui dirigitur, vel ad bonum commune. Et tale dominium hominis, ad hominem in statu innocentiae fuisset, propter duo. Primo quidem, quia homo naturaliter est animal sociale, unde homines in statu innocentiae socialiter vixissent. Socialis autem vita multorum esse non posset, nisi aliquis praesideret, qui ad bonum commune intenderet, multi enim
per se intendunt ad multa, unus vero ad unum. Et ideo philosophus dicit, in principio politic.,
quod quandocumque multa ordinantur ad unum, semper invenitur unum ut principale et diri-
gens. Secundo quia, si unus homo habuisset super alium supereminentiam scientiae et iustitiae,
inconveniens fuisset nisi hoc exequeretur in utilitatem aliorum; secundum quod dicitur I Petr.
IV, unusquisque gratiam quam accepit, in alterutrum illam administrantes. Unde Augustinus
dicit, XIX *De civ. Dei,* quod iusti non dominandi cupiditate imperant, sed officio consulendi,
hoc naturalis ordo praescribit, ita deus hominem condidit."

51. For the distinction between friendly love *(amor amicitiae)* and concupiscible love, cf. *ST*
I, q. 60, a. 3; and especially I-II, q. 26, a. 4 (and already cf. I, q. 20, a. 1, ad 3); and for the application to the love of all creatures for God, cf. I, q. 60, a. 5.

primary precept of natural law.[52] This prompts me to talk about God as common good and our knowledge of natural law, including its having God as known promulgator.[53] I have already elsewhere proposed that one must incorporate into the conception of natural law the natural reasoning to the existence of God mentioned in the *In Psalm.* 8, and *Summa contra gentiles*, 3.38, and *Summa theologiae* II-II, question 85, article 1.[54] It now occurs to me that this is part of the identification of natural law, in its properly human mode, with *"ius gentium."*[55] Natural law in humans includes the human spontaneous reasoning concerning fundamental situations. One such fundamental situation is nature as acting for an end and its implications.[56] (The Fifth

52. Cf. *ST* I-II, q. 100, a. 3, ad 1.

53. Two essential features of law are that it be made by the one responsible for the common good for which it is law, and that it be promulgated to those subject to the law. I take this to mean that law appears *in its adequate reasonableness* only when it is *so promulgated as to reveal its proper origin.* This raises the question of natural law's adequate promulgation. So much is it an issue that in the article on the necessity for promulgation of law, in the question on the definition of law, an objection is based precisely on the case of natural law. One finds what is essential to law maximally in natural law, says the objector, and yet it stands in no need of promulgation. To this Thomas replies: "it is to be said that the promulgation of the law of nature [*legis naturae*] is from the very fact that God places it within the minds of human beings so as to be naturally known [*naturaliter cognoscendam*]" (*ST* I-II, q. 90, a. 4, ad 1). Now, for this reply to be sufficient, it seems to require that our knowledge of natural law include an appreciation of divine providence as its source. This is a point on which Suarez insisted in his presentation of natural law. On this, see especially Franciscus Suarez, S.J. (1548–1617), *Tractatus de legibus et legislatore Deo*, in *Opera Omnia*, ed. Carolus Berton (Paris, 1856): apud Vivès, t. V. Book II is *De lege aeterna, et naturali, ac jure gentium.* Cap. VI: *An lex naturalis sit lex divina praeceptiva* (104–12). Cf. my paper, "Natural Law and the First Act of Freedom: Maritain Revisited," *Études Maritainiennes— Maritain Studies* 12 (1996): 3–32, now available in my book: *Wisdom, Law, and Virtue: Essays in Thomistic Ethics* (New York: Fordham University Press, 2008), chap. 14; see especially 558 n. 13.

54. See my book review, "On Kevin Flannery's *Acts Amid Precepts: The Aristotelian Logical Structure of Thomas Aquinas's Moral Theory*," *Nova et Vetera* (English) 5, no. 2 (2007): 431–44.

55. I would use *ST* II-II, q. 57, a. 3, to present the "ius gentium" picture of natural law for human beings. It takes into consideration the human ability to size things up rationally and to see what is right. It seems to me that this is very much like natural law as presented in II-II, q. 85, a. 1 on the naturalness of offering sacrifice. I would say that we should conceive of natural law and its primary precepts in the light of these texts. See also my paper "St. Thomas, Rhonheimer, and the Object of the Human Act," *Nova et Vetera* (English) 6, no. 1 (2008): 71–72.

56. The first premise of the Fifth Way concerns the operation for the sake of a goal by things which lack knowledge, viz., natural corporeal substances. Is this a premise which itself needs proof, or is it per se known to all? In *Physics* 2.8, Aristotle *argues* in its favor. Is this the demonstration of a conclusion, or the dialectical defense of a principle? That this chapter of the *Physics* is the work of a metaphysician seems to me clear. The whole of bk. 2 concerns the nature and principles of physical science, and thus, e.g., contrasts physics with mathematics. This sort of comparison of the sciences requires the *universal* vantage-point proper to the primary philosophy. At the outset of bk. 2, Aristotle had said that it is absurd to attempt to prove the existence of *nature*, since knowledge of its existence is too primary an experience. By trying to prove its existence, one would merely reveal one's inability to distinguish the self-evident from the non-self-evident (Aristotle, *Phys.* 2.1 [193a2–6]). Then in 2.8 one of the claims Aristotle makes is that

Way line is alluded to in the spontaneous reasoning texts just mentioned.)[57]

One thing I have often pointed out,[58] and repeat here, is that in the much-studied *Summa theologiae* I-II, question 94, article 2, where three levels of natural inclination are presented, the first level presents the natural inclination *common to all substances*. This is almost always read as though having reference merely to the individual and its individual good. It surely should be read as relating to the inclination which all substances have, namely, as including their love for God more than for their own selves, each mode of substance in the mode of love appropriate to it.[59] We noted this doctrine of universal love above, as presented in *Quodl.* 1.

The natural love for God above all else is present in every creature, but in each according to its own mode or measure. In the rational creature, that is, angels and man, it is "in the mode of will." Such natural love presupposes natural intellectual knowledge of God.[60] In the angel such knowledge is a mediated

---

those who deny that nature operates for the sake of something actually *eliminate nature altogether* (Aristotle, *Physics* 2.8 [199b15–16]; *CP* 2.14 [267 (7)]). It appears to me, accordingly, that Aristotle teaches that nature's operation for an end is a per se *notum*. Indeed, it looks as if he considers it so known to *all*, or almost all. Aristotle does acknowledge the possibility of the state of mind in which a person might demand or attempt a proof of such a self-evident item, and compares such an arguer to a person blind from birth who engages in a discussion about colors (Aristotle, *Phys.* 2.1 [193a6–9]).

57. It is relevant that when preaching to the people in Naples in Lent of 1273, and using only one line of argument for the existence of a God, Thomas presents the atheist as one who views the universe as a result of chance, and the theist as convinced of a cosmic providence. *In Symbolum Apostolorum Expositio*, a. 1 (ed. Spiazzi, *Opuscula Theologica*, t. II [Rome and Turin: Marietti, 1954], § 869): "Among all those things which the faithful ought to believe, this is the first which they ought to believe, viz., that there is one God. Now, one must consider what this word 'God' signifies, which is nothing else but a governor and provider of all things. Therefore, that person believes that there is a God who believes that all the things of this world are governed and provided for by him. But someone who believes that all arise by chance does not believe that there is a God. But none is found to be so stupid as not to believe that natural things are governed, provided for, and disposed, since they proceed in a particular order and at certain times: for we see that the sun and the moon and the stars, and other natural things, all preserve a determinate course; which would not happen if they were by chance. Hence, if there were someone who did not believe there is a God, he would be stupid. *Psalms* 13.1 'The fool has said in his heart: "there is no God."'" Thomas goes on, however, to note those who admit such a governor for the natural world, but not for human affairs. He also finds it necessary to argue further that there is only one God.

For the date and occasion of this work, I am following James A. Weisheipl, O.P., *Friar Thomas d'Aquino* (Garden City, N.Y.: Doubleday, 1974), 401: Weisheipl uses the title "Collationes super Credo in Deum."

58. See my *Wisdom, Law and Virtue*, 237–39, and 564 nn. 59–62.

59. Cf. *ST* I, q. 60, a. 5, ad 3, where to an objector who thinks of the natural love as turning back toward the individual self, Thomas teaches that in the self there is a greater love for the specific self than for the individual self, and all the greater love for the divine good.

60. In *ST* I, q. 60, a. 1, it is seen that natural love is present in each creature according to its own mode, and that for angels and men, this is "secundum voluntatem." (Notice that the *sed*

intuition.[61] In the human being, it is a *natural conclusion*, the fruit of a spontaneous, universally inborn *discursive* operation. Our intellectuality is "rational,"
as possessed of a weaker light than the angelic.[62]

What I had not appreciated when I wrote my review of Fr. Kevin Flannery's
book is the relevance for this discussion of *Summa theologiae* II-II, question 57,
article 3, on "ius gentium." There, the human mode of "nature," including as it
does the rational power, is seen to make available to us objects of comparison,
such as are expressed in our allotment of property to this rather than that person. In the case of knowledge of the existence of God, there is a similar sizing
up of the situation in the real. It lacks the finesse of philosophical analysis, but
it belongs to the realm of those active starting points which should be developed by us into virtues, here the virtue of religion and the natural friendship
with God that charity is designed to perfect supernaturally. Let us listen to
Thomas once more:

> Therefore, because the universal good is God himself, and under this good is con-
> tained the angel and the human being and every creature, because every creature,
> in function of its very substance, belongs to God, it follows that by natural love both
> the angel and the human being naturally love God more, and more principally, than
> themselves. *Otherwise, if it naturally loved itself more than God, it would follow that
> natural love is perverse, and that it would not be perfected by charity, but rather de-
> stroyed.*[63]

Notice that it is inasmuch as God is known as the author of being, life, and
intelligence that he cannot be hated, but must be loved.[64] That we need a commandment concerning such love stems from the possibility (through habituation to sin) of our not living according to love of God in particular choices.[65]

My understanding is, then, that Thomas presents the existence of God as

___

contra argument in this I, q. 60, a. 1, sees the angelic natural love as following from its natural
knowledge.) In I, q. 59, a. 1, it was seen that will is the most perfect mode of inclination toward
the good, in that it follows upon the intellectual vision of goodness, considered universally. In I,
q. 60, a. 5, ad 1, it is seen that all naturally love God more than themselves, each in its own mode
(and notice that the *sed contra* there links this love to the natural law).

61. Cf. *ST* I, q. 56, a. 3.   62. Cf. *ST* I, q. 58, a. 3.
63. *ST* I, q. 60, a. 5.   64. Cf. *ST* II-II, q. 34, a. 1.

65. Cf. *ST* I-II, q. 99, a. 2, ad 2: "it is to be said that it was fitting for the divine law that it provide for man not only as to those matters which are beyond the capacity of reason, but also as to
those concerning which it does occur that human reason suffer impediment. Now, human reason concerning the moral precepts, as regards the most common precepts of the natural law,
could not err, taking them universally, but nevertheless, because of habituation in sinning, it
has been obscured regarding particular things to be done."

Cf. also *ST* I-II, q. 100, a. 5, ad 1, as to why the ten commandments speak of our duty to God
and to our neighbor, but not of our duty to ourselves: "the precepts of the decalogue are related to the precepts of love. But a precept had to be given to man concerning the love of God and

naturally known to all, even though naturally *reasoned to.* That someone professes ignorance of the existence of God stems from moral disorder (as the
Commentary on the Psalms as well as the *SCG* text asserts). I would say that this
natural knowledge would fill out the picture of the commandment of love as
known by virtue of itself to all. Given that one has knowledge of God as the author of being, one has knowledge of him as lovable by us, indeed as more lovable than ourselves.

Concluding Meditation

I want to conclude with the text in *Summa theologiae* I-II, question 19, on
the judge and the wife/child; this shows God as the highest common good, inasmuch as we learn it through art imitating nature (we use the judicial system
to present the higher order, just as Aristotle uses the army and its commander).

Thomas is asking whether the goodness of human willing depends on conformity to the divine willing, as regards the very thing willed [*in volito*]. As
usual, he begins with an appeal to our common experience:

as is clear from the foregoing, the will is borne unto its object according as it is proposed by reason. But it does happen that something is considered by reason in different ways, such that under one intelligible aspect it is good and under another intelligible aspect it is not good. And therefore if the will of someone wills that to be,
according as it has the aspect of the good, [the willing] is good; and the will of another, if it wills that same thing not to be, inasmuch as it has the aspect of the bad,
the willing will also be good. For example, the judge has good will, when he wills the
death of the criminal [*latronis*], because that is just; but the will of another, for example, the wife or the son [of the criminal], who wills that he not be killed, inasmuch as
death is something bad, as regards the nature, is also good.

Thomas pursues this difference of judgments, noting levels of the goodness involved:

But since the will follows the apprehension of reason or intellect, [therefore] according as the aspect of the good apprehended is more universal [*communior*], just in that
way the will is *directed to a more common good.* As is clear in the proposed example:
for the judge has care of *the common good* which is justice, and so he wills the death
of the criminal, which has the aspect of good relative to the common state [*statum*

---

neighbor because in that respect the natural law had been obscured because of sin; not as regards the love of himself, because in that respect the natural law was still in vigor."

Cf. also I-II, q. 109, a. 3, on our natural love for God above all else, and the effect of original sin.

communem]; but the wife of the criminal has to consider the *private good of the family*, and in accordance with that she wills that the criminal not be killed.

We then begin to apply the above to the question to be answered, concerning the divine will:

Now, *the good of the entire universe* is that which is apprehended by God, who is the maker and governor of the universe; hence, *whatever he wills, he wills under the aspect of the common good* which is his own goodness, which is the good of the entire universe. But the apprehension of the creature, in accordance with its own nature, is of *some particular good* proportionate to its nature.

And the result:

But it does occur that something is good according to some particular aspect, which is not good according to a universal aspect, or vice versa, as has been said. And so it happens that some will is good willing something considered according to the particular aspect, which nevertheless God does not will, according to the universal aspect, or vice versa. And thus, also, it is that diverse wills of diverse men concerning opposed things can be good, inasmuch as they will this to be or not to be, considered under diverse particular intelligible aspects.

And we come to a familiar consideration: "However, *the will of some man willing some particular good is not right, unless he refers that to the common good* as to an end, since even *the natural appetite of any part is ordered to the common good of the whole.*" And the ultimate conclusion:

Now, from the end is taken the formal intelligible aspect of the willing of that thing which is ordered toward the end. Hence, in order that someone by right willing will some particular good, it is necessary that that particular good be the willed thing [*volitum*] materially, but that *the universal divine good be that which is willed* [volitum] *formally*. Therefore, the human will is obliged [*tenetur*] to be conformed to the divine will as to the thing willed formally: for it is obliged to will *the divine and common good*; but not materially, for the reason already given.[66]

The entire moral life of the good person is viewed as organized under this union with the will of God: "doing the will of God" is the supreme name of every good act, in its kind (as regards moral species) or in its individual reality (as regards morally indifferent acts).

66. *ST* I-II, q. 19, a. 10 (830a17–b29).

9

The Primacy of the Common Good and the Foundations of Natural Law in St. Thomas

STEPHEN L. BROCK

According to Thomas Aquinas's famous definition of law, one of the essential features of any true law is order toward the common good.[1] Also according to Thomas, natural law is law in the proper sense of the term.[2] So we may assume that for him natural law does order toward the common good. However, his writings are not as direct or as explicit as one could perhaps wish about how it does so. In this essay I wish to propose that we should see order toward the common good as quite fundamental in the Thomistic conception of natural law.

For an initial sign of this, let us go at once to the passage where Thomas argues for the very existence of natural law: *Summa theologiae,* I-II, question 91, article 2. This is certainly a fundamental discussion, and in it we find two fairly clear references to the common good. The argument rests on the premises that all creatures are ruled by the eternal law of divine providence, insofar as their natural inclinations are from an impression of it, a kind of participation in it; and that "the rational creature is subject to providence in a special way, insofar as he himself becomes a sharer in providence, providing for himself and

1. *Summa theologiae,* I-II, q. 90, a. 2. Throughout this essay I conform to the usual practice of speaking of "the" common good when what is really meant is "a" common good, that is, some member of the class of common goods. The translations in the essay are mine.

2. *ST* I-II, q. 91, a. 2, ad 3.

others." Here we have at least an allusion to common good: "for himself and others."[3]

The article goes on to present natural law as the rational creature's distinctively intellectual and rational participation in the eternal law. Weaving a portion of the fourth Psalm into the account,[4] Thomas explains that reason's own natural light, "by which we discern what is good and what is bad" *(quid sit bonum, et quid malum),* is an "impression of the divine light." By this man has "a natural inclination toward the due *(debitum)* act and end"; he is shown "what are the works of justice." The mention of justice (and of the due, which is related to it)[5] can also be seen as a kind of reference to the common good. A little later we learn that the *ratio boni,* the intelligibility of the good, is that upon which is founded *(fundatur)* the very first precept of natural law: the good is to be done and sought, and the bad, avoided.[6]

At least for Thomists in North America, talk of the common good will bring to mind Charles de Koninck's potent little book, *On the Primacy of the Common Good.*[7] He showed, I think quite conclusively, that Thomas does uphold that principle, the primacy of the common good. In a sense, what interests me here is this principle's status as a precept of natural law in its own right; in particular, its having the kind of intelligibility enjoyed by such a precept. Each precept of natural law is what Thomas calls a first principle of practical reason. It is a practical truth that is naturally understood by all. One of its characteristic features is thus its mode of intelligibility—a very high-grade mode. It is so intelligible that it neither needs nor even admits of demonstration, properly speaking. Still, the understanding of it does have its sources and conditions. For instance, it presupposes the understanding of the principle's terms. I shall be especially concerned with how the principle of the primacy of the common good is rooted in the very term "good" and with the conditions of this term's

3. Another passage that connects natural law with order to the common good can be found in Thomas's treatment of the natural law precept to act virtuously—which is to say, according to reason. An objection to the existence of such a precept is that law is ordered to the common good, but some acts of virtue, especially acts of temperance, are ordered to someone's private good. The reply is that temperance concerns the natural urges for food and drink and sex, "which are ordered to the common good of nature, as other legal matters are ordered to the common moral good" (*ST* I-II, q. 94, a. 3, ad 1).

4. *Sacrificate sacrificium iustitiae . . . Multi dicunt, quis ostendit nobis bona? Signatum est super nos lumen vultus tui, domine;* Psalms 4:6–7. Thomas is not the first to apply this passage to the question of the existence of natural law; see Albertus Magnus, *Summa de bono,* tr. 5, q. 1, a. 2, obj. 8 and ad 8.

5. *ST* I, q. 21, a. 1, ad 3; see below, at n. 23.

6. *ST* I-II, q. 94, a. 2.

7. Charles de Koninck, *De la primauté du bien commun contre les personnalistes* (Quebec: Laval University Press, 1943).

own intelligibility; above all, the condition called "nature." Toward the end I shall try to say something about the relation between the primacy of the common good and the very first precept of natural law.

The Intelligibility of the Primacy of Common Good

The Primacy of the Common Good in Law and in Natural Law

A good place to begin, I believe, is back in *Summa theologiae*, I-II, question 90, article 2, where Thomas argues that an essential feature of all true law is order toward the common good. Here I think we find clear confirmation that the primacy of the common good belongs to natural law, as well as some important clarification of the very meaning of the expression "common good."

In the previous article Thomas had argued that law, being a rule and measure of human acts, must be a work of practical reason, since reason is the first principle of human acts. He now observes that in practical reason itself there is something that functions as principle to everything else in it; namely, the last end, happiness. Law then will regard above all the order toward happiness. Not, however, the happiness of a single individual; for "every part is ordered to its whole, as the imperfect to the perfect, and one man is only part of a complete community." Law properly regards the order toward the common happiness. In confirmation Thomas cites a passage from the discussion of legal justice in the *Nicomachean Ethics*.[8]

Thomas is not saying that precepts about particular matters cannot be laws. But he insists that these must at least share in the order to the common good. The precepts that frame this order are the primary laws. He cites a broad principle, illustrating it with a favorite example:

in any genus, that which is said [to be such] to the highest degree is principle of the others, and they are said according to their order toward it; as fire, which is hot to the highest degree, is cause of heat in mixed bodies, which are said to be hot to the degree that they partake in fire.[9]

Participant de igne. Thomas often speaks of participation in connection with this idea of stronger or weaker instances of some feature—most famously, I

---

8. *Nicomachean Ethics*, 5, 3 (1129b17). Thomas's argument here sheds light on the association between order toward the common good and the precept to act virtuously or according to reason (see above, n. 3). Since law is reason's chief rule and measure, to act according to reason will be chiefly to act according to law; and this will be chiefly to act according to the order toward the common good.

9. *ST* I-II, q. 90, a. 2.

suppose, when he applies it to being, as belonging to God and creatures.[10] The very notion of common good should also bring participation to mind. To be "common" *is* to be in some way participated in, shared by, many. In a moment we will see how Thomas thinks a common good is common and shared.

On the status of the primacy of the common good as a principle of natural law, the reply to the article's third objection is highly pertinent. It says: "just as nothing stands firmly according to speculative reason, except through resolution to first, indemonstrable principles, nothing stands firmly by practical reason except through ordination to the last end, which is the common good."[11] Thomas characterizes the precepts of natural law in just this way. They are the truths that stand in the same relation to practical reason as the very first indemonstrable principles stand to speculative reason.[12] It is also clear from this text that, just as the law that orders to the common good is that which is maximally law, so the common good itself is that which is maximally good, that is, maximally end. It is the very last end. The common happiness is higher than the individual happiness, by the very fact that it is common. A stronger assertion of its primacy, and of its primacy's being a matter of natural law, would be hard to imagine.

How the Common Good Is Common

It is in the article's second objection and reply that we are given some clarification of the meaning of "common good" itself. The objection says that since law directs man to action and human acts are in particulars, law is ordered to some *particular* goods. The reply grants this. But it maintains that even so, law is always ordered to a common good. "Operations are indeed in particulars. But those particulars can be referred to a common good, [which is common] not with the community of a species or a genus, but with the community of a final cause, according to which a common good is called a common end."[13] Thomas is observing that the word "common" is not entirely univocal. Sometimes it means what is predicated of many things, what has a shared *ratio* or definition, such as that of a species or a genus. But this is not what it means to be a "common good." Something's being ordered to a common good is not the same as its being an instance of a commonly predicated good. A common good is common, not as a *ratio*, but precisely as a good, that is, as an end.[14]

10. For instance in *ST* I, q. 44, a. 1. Here he cites fire and the fiery as an example.
11. *ST* I-II, q. 90, a. 2, ad 3.   12. *ST* I-II, q. 94, a. 2.
13. *ST* I-II, q. 90, a. 2, ad 2.
14. Clearly the word "particular" is similarly ambiguous. Although we speak of "the" common good, there are in fact many common goods, the common ends of many communities.

Think of a major league baseball team. Its ultimate common good, I suppose, is to win the World Series. (Which of course is not really a "world" series, only North American. But "World" makes it sound bigger, more universal and common, and therefore better, a higher end.) The players perform particular good acts, for example good hits, in order to reach and to win the series. Obviously it is not that each good hit is a winning of the series.

Of course a community's ultimate common good need not be its only one. Staying with our baseball team, what about the species of things that a good hit is an instance of: the species of *good hits*? This is not the team's ultimate end; but if we take *good hits* as a kind of whole, can it be regarded as some sort of common good for the team? I do not think so. This would mean that all good hits, as such, are somehow good for the team. But in fact the team tries to prevent good hits by its opponents, and it does so rightly and with no reluctance.

The Good of the Species as a Common Good

However, I do not mean to suggest that for Thomas the species to which a thing belongs can never be regarded, in itself, as a good, a common good, to which the thing is ordered. A good hit is merely an action, a kind of accident. I am inclined to say that it is ordered more to the good of the hitter, and to the common good that he is ordered to (his team's), than to the good of the species of good hits.[15] But if we consider substances, Thomas is really quite clear that a particular substance is ordered to the good of its own species, as to a common good.

For instance, he says that it is because an individual tends to the good of its species that it naturally tends to the good of others of the species. He uses a familiar example. "Each thing, inasmuch as it loves its species, loves with a natural love that which is one with it in species. And this even appears in things

---

"Common good" is predicated of each. So each of them is in a sense a "particular" common good, that is, a particular instance thereof. What is properly opposed to "common good" is not this sort of particularity, but the sort that Thomas sometimes designates with the word "private." A private good, as such, is a merely partial good. But some particular entities—singulars, not predicated of many—are quite public, and in that sense common. There is not always a relation of subordination among these; for instances, among sovereign nations. But there is sometimes subordination, with the lower common good being merely "particular" relative to the higher. This is reflected in Thomas's very conception of natural law. He calls it a participation in the eternal law. The eternal law orders to the good of all reality. In natural law this order is applied to the rational creature—a mere part of reality, though consisting of all mankind. That natural law is merely partial relative to the eternal law in itself comes out rather clearly in *ST* I-II, q. 91, a. 6.

15. On order toward the good, i.e. inclination, in accidents, see below, at n. 64.

lacking cognition; for fire has a natural inclination to communicate to another its own form, which is a good of the other."[16] This is from the *Prima pars*, in a question about love in angels. The article is on whether one angel naturally loves another as he loves himself. In the next article, which is on whether an angel naturally loves God more than himself, Thomas is very clear that the good of a thing's species has priority, for the thing, over that portion of the good of the species that is proper to it: "any singular naturally loves the good of its species more than its own singular good."[17]

Does this contradict the passage that says that the common good to which the particulars of an action can be ordered is not common with the community of a genus or a species? I do not think so. I think it is simply that a species can have two sorts of community. One is the community of predication, according to which the *ratio* or the definition of the species' nature is distributed to its members. Each member has the whole definition. But the species also has a community relative to which each member is only a part. In this sense the species is not predicable of its members. Socrates is a whole man, but he is only part of mankind. And even though he has the whole definition of man, he has only part of the perfection and the goodness found in mankind as a whole. This is what each singular is inclined to preserve: not the mere *ratio* of the species (which the species cannot lose in any case) but the being and the flourishing of the species. It is this that the individual loves more than the good proper to it. "The common good is always more lovable to each [individual] than is its proper good, as the good of the whole is more lovable for the part than is its own partial good."[18]

"Belonging" to the Common Good

The article on the angel's natural love of God contains a further clarification of the principle of the primacy of the common good:

The natural inclination in things lacking reason shows the natural inclination in the will of intellectual nature. But in natural things, if anything is by nature such that what it is is another's, it is inclined to what it belongs to more chiefly and more strongly than to itself . . . For we see that a part naturally exposes itself for the conservation of the whole, as a hand exposes itself to a blow, without deliberation, for the conservation of the body. And since reason imitates nature, we find this sort of inclination in political virtues; a virtuous citizen will expose himself to the risk of

16. *ST* I, q. 60, a. 4. I suppose that the form of the fire is "a good of the other" just insofar as the other is flammable, in potency to the form of fire.

17. *ST* I, q. 60, a. 5, ad 1.

18. *ST* II-II, q. 26, a. 4, ad 3.

death for the conservation of the whole republic. And if the man were a natural part of this city, this inclination would be natural to him.[19]

I find this helpful as a gloss on the primacy of the common good, because it indicates that the principle does not rest solely on the fact that a common good, as such, is more perfect, a "greater" good, than an individual good. That would suggest that one is bound to prefer the good of any community to one's own individual good—even if one does not belong to that community. If this is even true, it is surely not immediately evident, as a truth of natural law ought to be. But in this text the common good that has priority in an unquestionable way—"without deliberation"—is that of the community to which the individual belongs.[20]

What does "belong" mean here? The passage may sound as though it is the belonging of a part to a whole. The primacy of the common good would be as it were the practical companion of the speculative principle that whole is greater than part. However, although this fits the examples given in the passage, and although it is true that in some sense the individual good is always "partial" in comparison with the common good—always imperfect[21]—the belonging is not always strictly that of part to whole. This very article is arguing that all creatures "belong" to God and that he is the first, most universal common good, to which the proper goods of all creatures are duly subordinated. Creaturely good is very "partial" compared to God's, but creatures are not parts of God. Once again, I believe, we are meant to see the common good as "common" precisely as a good, an end. The "belonging" to it may or may not consist in being part of it. What it essentially consists in is being ordered to it or for the sake of it.[22]

Pertinent here is an earlier passage in the *Prima pars,* on divine justice.[23] There Thomas explains what it means to be "due" (*debitum*). What is due to one, he says, is what is one's "own" (*suum*); "as a slave is his master's, and not vice-versa, since the free is for his own sake [*sui causa*]." So it implies "a certain order of exaction [*exigentiae*] or necessity." To be due to some being, to belong to it, is to be *for* it, demanded by it, in a certain way bound to it.

---

19. *ST* I, q. 60, a. 5, c.

20. Of course there can also be the desire to join some community. Indeed it seems to be rather natural to desire to belong to something "bigger than oneself," even without yet having fixed on anything in particular.

21. Thus back in *ST* I-II, q. 90, a. 2: "every part is ordered to its whole as imperfect to perfect."

22. It is also important that the belonging may or may not be total; see *ST* I-II, q. 21, a. 4, ad 3.

23. *ST* I, q. 21, a. 1, ad 3.

This bond of belonging is not always the sheer bondage of slavery.[24] To be a slave means to be only for another's sake, not at all for one's own. If anything does belong to a slave (*qua* slave), it is not for his own sake but only for use in serving the master. But it is possible to be for one's own sake and also for another's (albeit not for a slave's). It is even possible to be more for the other's sake than for one's own, while still being truly for one's own. This is how Thomas understands the rational creature's order toward the common good of the universe and toward God.[25]

God is the end of all things, the first and most universal common good. He belongs only to himself, and all else belongs to him. His justice, his "rendering to each his due," therefore regards himself first of all. He gives himself his due by fulfilling the order of his wisdom, which directs all to the presentation of his goodness. Secondly, he works justice by giving to each creature "that which is due to it according to the proportion (*rationem*) of its nature and condition."[26] Thomas's examples of this creaturely "due" are also orders toward some kind of common good. He speaks of how the hand is ordered to the man, and more generally how parts are ordered to the whole. He also speaks of how accidents are ordered to substances. I think we can very well see a substance as the common end that all of its (per se) accidents are for.[27] Overall, it is clear that the priority of the common good is a basic principle of justice.

The Natural Presuppositions of the *ratio boni*

Practical Principles in Nature

In the second part of the essay, I mainly want to look at a text from even earlier in the *Prima pars:* from question 5, on "the good in general." It offers some rather precise information about the conditions of the very intelligibility of the good, the *ratio boni*. Seeing these will help us, I think, to relate the notion of the good to the primacy of the common good, and so to see the latter in relation to the very first precept of natural law. Before presenting the text, let me make a few remarks.

In the last passage that I quoted from the article on angelic love of God, Thomas cited the priority of the common good as a principle of political order. I suppose that this is what the expression "common good" first makes us think

---

24. See *ST* I, q. 96, a. 4.
25. *Summa contra gentiles*, III, ch. 112. See also *ST* I, q. 22, a. 2, ad 5; q. 103, a. 5, ad 2.
26. *ST* I, q. 21, a. 1, ad 3.
27. See *ST* I, q. 77, a. 6, c., and ad 2; also below, at n. 66.

of. Yet for Thomas the political order is in a way only secondary. The principle holds in politics because politics is a work of reason, and because reason imitates nature. He plainly means non-intellectual nature, physical nature.

Today some of Thomas's professed followers seem to find the doctrine of the "imitation of nature" a bit embarrassing. Apparently it smacks of "physicalism." But I do not see how to sweep it under the rug and still hold to a genuinely Thomistic account of practical reason. If space allowed, I would examine the beginning of the *proemium* to Thomas's commentary on Aristotle's *Politics*. What he says there sets up a strong connection between the "imitation of nature" and his fundamental conception of natural law as a participation in the eternal law.[28]

The imitation of nature is also very present in the moral part of the *Summa theologiae*. To cite just two examples: "human acts can be regulated according to the rule of human reason, which is gathered from the created things that man naturally knows."[29] And: "since the things that are by nature are ordered by divine reason, which human reason ought to imitate, whatever comes about from human reason that is against the order commonly found in natural things is vicious and sinful."[30] As this last passage indicates, the imitation of nature is not mere slavish mimicry of physical things. What imitation of nature really amounts to is a certain way of imitating the divine mind. Common principles of practical wisdom are first apprehended in physical activities. But they are grasped to be true in themselves, and to be applicable, in analogous ways, quite universally. I mean, applicable to everything, all beings: physical things, angels, and the works of our own reason. Their extension is quite metaphysical.

These remarks will, I hope, at least partly justify my turning to a passage from question 5 of the *Prima pars*. I do suspect that some readers may still be

---

28. Thomas Aquinas, *Sententia libri Politicorum*, proem., § 1: "As the Philosopher teaches in the second book of the *Physics*, art imitates nature. The reason for this is that as principles are related to each other, so in a proportional way are their works and effects. But the principle of the things that come about by art is the human intellect, which is derived according to a certain likeness from the divine intellect, which is the principle of natural things. And so it is necessary that the operations of art imitate those of nature, and that the effects of art imitate the things in nature. For if an instructor of some art makes a work of that art, the disciple who receives the art from him must attend to that work, so that he may work toward a likeness of it. And so the human intellect, to which intelligible light derives from the divine intellect, must be informed in the things that it does from the inspection of things done naturally, so as to work likewise." See also below, n. 40.

29. *ST* I-II, q. 74, a. 7. See also *SCG* III, ch. 81, § 1. We even find him teaching that a natural inclination in man derives from physical things: *ST* I-II, q. 87, a. 1. In *ST* II-II, q. 31, a. 3, he also says that *grace* imitates the order of nature (using fire again to illustrate the point).

30. *ST* II-II, q. 130, a. 1. See also *ST* II-II, q. 50, a. 4.

inclined to object that what the *Prima pars* can give us is only a speculative view of the good, not the practical sort of treatment that our topic calls for. I cannot go into the relation between speculative and practical reason here. Let me just mention a very simple point to which professor Jan Aertsen has called attention.[31] In *Summa theologiae* I-II, question 94, article 2, Thomas says that the first precept of natural law is founded on the *ratio boni*. The formula for this *ratio* that he gives there is the famous one from Aristotle's *Ethics:* "the good is what all desire."[32] The point is that it is this very same formula that begins and governs his account of the good in the *Prima pars*, question 5; and that both in question 5 and in his commentary on the passage in the *Ethics* itself, he stresses that the formula does not just mean what all rational beings, or even all beings with cognition, desire; it means what absolutely all beings desire.[33] I do not see why the first precept should not be part of the "rule of human reason that is gathered from the created things that man naturally knows."

Being, Goodness, and Perfection

In any case, the good is what all beings desire. Thomas's first conclusion, in *Summa theologiae* I, question 5, article 1, is that a good thing is good just insofar as it is a being. For what each thing desires is its perfection. The notion of good adds nothing to that of perfect except a relation to appetite, desirability. But a thing is perfect insofar as it is in act; and it is in act insofar as it is, or is a being.

Thomas is quick, however, to explain that what makes a thing good without qualification, a simply perfect and desirable thing, is not its sheer existence alone; for example, its merely being alive and not dead.[34] To be truly perfect is not just to have one's essential or substantial being. It is to be altogether "full"; not materially, of course, but with "fullness of being."[35] A thing is unqualifiedly perfect when it has all the being proportioned to its form or its nature.[36] This involves more than its substantial being, which is only its "being itself."

In article 1 Thomas does not say much about what this "more," this additional perfection, consists in. But the text that I want to look at more closely, article 4, makes it considerably more definite. The text goes to the very foundation of what we might call Thomas's ontology of the good.

31. Jan A. Aertsen, "Thomas Aquinas on the Good: The Relation between Metaphysics and Ethics," in *Aquinas's Moral Theory*, ed. Scott MacDonald and Eleonore Stump (Ithaca, N.Y.: Cornell University Press, 1999), 235–53.

32. *Nicomachean Ethics*, I, 1 (1094a3).   33. *In I Ethicorum*, lect. 1, §11.
34. *ST* I, q. 5, a. 1, ad 1.   35. See *ST* I-II, q. 18, a. 1.
36. See *ST* I-II, q. 5, a. 5.

The Presuppositions of the Good

The question raised in this article is whether the good has the *ratio* of end, of final cause. We have already seen Thomas stressing that a common good is common as an end. It is a "common cause." Here he offers a synopsis of the relations between the final cause and other causes. I will briefly comment on the body of the article, sentence by sentence.[37]

1. *Since the good is what all desire, and this has the* ratio *of end, it is clear that the good brings with it the* ratio *of end.*

Evidently for Thomas the connection between "desire" and "end" is quite immediate, with no need of reasoning. To desire something *is* to relate to it as to an end.

2. *Nevertheless, the* ratio *of good presupposes the* ratio *of efficient cause and the* ratio *of formal cause.*

As I think we can gather from the rest of the passage, Thomas has a twofold "presupposition" in mind here: first, in the natures of things themselves, in such a way that in order to *be* final causes, goods, they must already have formal and efficient causality; and second, in the natural order of understanding, such that we do not grasp the good until we have at least some grasp of these other causes. These are what I am calling the "natural presuppositions" of the *ratio boni.* I leave the word *ratio* untranslated because it can, and in this case I believe it does, have both an "objective" and a "subjective" sense: an intelligible feature in things, and an intelligible conception in the mind.

3. *For we see that what comes first in causing comes last in the caused.*

Thomas is treating the good as found in caused things. This I think fits with the fact that we are in a discussion of the "good in general." The next *quaestio* is on the "goodness of God." Obviously that is not the goodness of something

---

37. Here is the original, with the sentences numbered. (1) *Respondeo dicendum quod, cum bonum sit quod omnia appetunt, hoc autem habet rationem finis; manifestum est quod bonum rationem finis importat.* (2) *Sed tamen ratio boni praesupponit rationem causae efficientis et rationem causae formalis.* (3) *Videmus enim quod id quod est primum in causando, ultimum est in causato.* (4) *Ignis enim primo calefacit quam formam ignis inducat, cum tamen calor in igne consequatur formam substantialem.* (5) *In causando autem, primum invenitur bonum et finis, qui movet efficientem; secundo, actio efficientis, movens ad formam; tertio advenit forma.* (6) *Unde e converso esse oportet in causato, quod primum sit ipsa forma, per quam est ens.* (7) *Secundo consideratur in ea virtus effectiva, secundum quod est perfectum in esse; quia unumquodque tunc perfectum est, quando potest sibi simile facere, ut dicit Philosophus in IV Meteor.* (8) *Tertio consequitur ratio boni, per quam in ente perfectio fundatur.*

caused; and it is the primary goodness, indeed cause of the "good in general."[38] But the first goodness that we encounter is in caused things, created things.

4. Now, whereas fire heats before inducing the form of fire, the heat in the fire is the result of its substantial form.

Fire again. I suppose that few today would hold that there is such a thing as the substantial form of fire. Fire is not a substance after all. It is more like an activity. Still, even activities are beings, and they too have their formal principles. In any case the illustration is clear enough. The heat in a fire presupposes the fire, or results from it. But in order to ignite something else, the fire must first heat it.

5. Thus in causing, what comes first is the good and the end that moves the efficient cause; then comes the action of the efficient cause, moving to the form; and last comes the form.

This is the famous doctrine of the final cause as first cause, cause of the causality of the other causes.[39] The other causes cause for an end. This will be important when we get to the end of the passage. But what Thomas is in the midst of explaining is why, as it were, it is fitting to call the final cause not "first" but precisely "final" or "last"—the "end." Goodness or finality in the primary, unqualified sense is the last causality to take its seat in (caused) things or to be present in them. It is therefore also the last to present itself to us.[40] In a caused thing, the presence of goodness depends on, supposes, the presence of those other causes in it.

6. Hence in the caused thing the order is reversed. First there is the form itself, through which the thing is a being.

This is the formal cause: the form itself, in its role as the intrinsic principle through which a being has *esse*, that through which it is "a being" in the proper sense, something in act. The formal cause is the factor in a being that keeps it united in its own identity and determines it to its proper act of being. In a

---

38. As of *being* in general: see *ST* I-II, q. 66, a. 5, ad 4; II-II, q. 2, a. 3.

39. See *ST* I, q. 5, a. 2, ad 1; also Thomas Aquinas, *Sententia super Metaphysicam*, lib. V, lect. 2, § 775 (Marietti).

40. In the proemium to his commentary on the *Politics* (see above at n. 28), Thomas also presents reason as imitating nature in this respect, i.e., as bringing forth the end last. "Nature proceeds in its operation from simples to composites, in such a way that in those things that come about through the operation of nature, that which is maximally composite is perfect and whole and the end of the others, as is clear in all wholes with respect to their parts. Whence the operative reason of man also proceeds from simples to composites, as from imperfects to perfects"; *Sententia libri Politicorum*, proem., § 3.

substance, this is the substantial form; for instance, the soul, by which a living substance has its life, which is its act of being. In a way the act of being is "in" the form, not always in the sense that the form subsists or *is* "the being," but at least in the sense that the act of being follows on the form immediately and is proportioned to it.

7. Secondly there is considered in it effective power, whereby it is perfect in being; for a thing is perfect when it can make its like, as the Philosopher says in Meteorology IV.[41]

Here is where we are given a more definite notion of "unqualified perfection" and "fullness of being." A thing is judged perfect or complete when it can make its like. Organisms are mature when they can reproduce; scholars, when they can teach; rational creatures, perhaps, when they can "provide for themselves and others."[42] The perfection of a being, its "flourishing"—as the term suggests—is one with its fecundity. It is then that it is "full" of being: when it is robust and potent and impresses itself on others, when its being "overflows." Again, the fullness is not material. It is fullness of actuality, formal fullness.

Indeed the passage says that the effective power is "in it," in the form. Not only being but also action is in function of form. Thomas underscores this by identifying it as ability to make one's like. Just a little earlier he had said that likeness is "communication in form."[43] This is why, before grasping efficient causality, we must grasp formal causality. We cannot see one thing as the origin of another's existence—cannot see the efficient causality—unless we see them as existing according to a common form (with the cause existing according to it in some more perfect way).[44] At the same time, it seems clear that in grasping efficient causality, our understanding of the nature of form itself, and so of the nature of being, is also deepened. Now we appreciate the intrinsic "communicability" of form, its aptitude for affirming and promoting and diffusing itself.

8. Third comes the ratio of good, through which the perfection in the being is founded.

The corpus of the article finishes here, with this brief remark about the good. At first it may seem disappointing, perhaps not even very clear; but an equally brief remark in the reply to the first objection both clarifies it and, I think,

---

41. Aristotle, *Meteorologia*, IV, 3 (380a16).
42. *ST* I-II, q. 91, a. 2.
43. *ST* I, q. 4, a. 3.
44. "It is only through dependence on form that the thing has dependence on the efficient cause"; Lawrence Dewan, O.P., "Saint Thomas and the Principle of Causality," in *Jacques Maritain: Philosophe dans la Cité / A Philosopher in the World*, ed. Jean-Louis Allard (Ottawa: University of Ottawa Press, 1985), 64.

shows its significance. There, comparing the good and the beautiful, he says that these are the same in subject, because "they are founded"—*fundantur,* the same word as at the end of the corpus—"on the same thing, namely form."[45]

The article is arguing that goodness, or final causality, presupposes formal and efficient causality. Through these, a being is in act and is perfect in being. Both are "in the form."[46] And the thing's perfection is "founded" on the form. Not however merely by reason of its formal causality; that, he says, is how beauty is "founded" on form.[47] Nor merely by reason of its efficient causality. As we have seen, in a sense the efficient causality *is* the thing's ultimate perfection. But it is not what *founds* the thing's perfection. In order to be "founded" in the thing, the perfection must have the *ratio* of good. That is, it must be an object of desire or inclination. What inclination? Surely that of the formal and efficient causes themselves; in other words, the very inclination in the form.[48] A being has being through its form, and it acts by the power of its form, but only because its form inclines to its being and to its action. Without this inclination, the being's perfection, and its very being, would not be stable. It would

45. I am taking *fundatur* in the corpus of *ST* I, q. 5, a. 4, as the passive indicative of *fundo, -avi, -atum,* but it could also be taken as the passive subjunctive of *fundo, fudi, fusum,* with this result: "Third comes the *ratio* of good, through which the perfection in the being is poured forth." This is how it is taken by Lawrence Dewan, O.P., "St Thomas and the Causality of God's Goodness," *Laval Théologique et Philosophique* 34 (1978): 298 n. 34. (Dewan observes that Cajetan understands *fundo, -avi, -atum.*) This reading connects it directly with the principle that Thomas mentions in the second objection: *bonum est diffusivum sui esse.* The objection uses this to argue that the good is rather an efficient than a final cause. In reply Thomas says simply that here, *diffusivum* is to be understood in the sense in which an end is said to "move." Now, an end "moves" as the object that determines a movement of appetite (*ST* I-II, q. 9, a. 1). So really the two readings of *fundatur* come down to the same thing: the *ratio* of the good is that through which there is inclination toward the perfection in a being. I prefer *fundatur* both because of the presence of *fundantur* in ad 1, and because it seems to me that in line with I, q. 5, a. 1, we should be seeing the being's perfection first of all as object of the being's own appetite or inclination. On the *fundo, fudi, fusum* reading, especially with the *in ente* (ablative) rather than *in ens* (accusative), one is more apt to think of how the being's perfection attracts others.

46. See also *ST* I, q. 5, a. 5, c., and ad 3; I-II, q. 85, a. 2.

47. Beauty, he says, regards cognition, which is by "assimilation."

48. I think it is very much worth stressing that Thomas locates appetite or inclination in form itself. We have a certain tendency, I believe, to think of form only in its specificatory role, almost as though it only had to do with knowledge; we think of it as something abstract, mathematical—like a figure or a "configuration." (On the mathematicals and the good, see *ST* I, q. 5, a. 3, ad 4.) Certainly the forms of things have a specificatory role. They make their subjects determinate, definite. But for Thomas, they are also *determinations to* something, just in the sense in which a desire is. Notice the uses of *determinatio* in *ST* I, q. 80, a. 1, and in I-II, q. 1, a. 3. Thomas says that with respect to a thing's essential or substantial being, its substantial form *is* an appetite or a desire: *ST* I, q. 59, a. 2. Every form brings with it some inclination, some impulse or thrust: *ST* I, q. 80, a. 1. Ultimately this would be because all the forms and all the perfections of things proceed not only from the divine intellect but also from the divine will, and so they have a likeness of the divine will: *ST* I, q. 19, a. 2; I, q. 59, a. 1.

not have a solid foundation for its perfection.[49] The being would not be substantial.

Goodness as Founded on Nature

It is in just this sense, I take it, that the final cause is the first of the causes,
that on which the causalities of the other causes depend. These would not
cause if they were not inclined to their effects. Inclination is present in a being from the start, by nature, especially in its form. As inclination, it is determined or specified according to its object, which is the perfection of the being.
But the inclination in the form is also a being's first determination *to* its perfection. Without it the being would have no hold on its perfection, would not
truly *be* good.

Thus from the beginning the formal and the efficient causes are in function
of the final cause; and yet the thing cannot be said to be good—the final causality does not belong to what it actually is—except on the supposition of the
other causes. Nor is it known. Only by seeing the other causalities do we see
that the being is intrinsically inclining toward something and see what the object of its inclination is, what its good is.

In a sense its good is the form itself. Sometimes Thomas says the good of a
thing *is* its form. Evidently he means the form with its perfection in it. He also
presents the form as measure of a thing's good. "For each thing, that is good
which suits it according to its form; and evil, that which departs from the order
of its form."[50] This, I believe, is just the sort of order that he spoke of in the text
on divine justice: that by which a thing belongs to the principle of the order.

These considerations all lead me to suggest that we can sum up the argument in *Summa theologiae*, I, question 5, article 4, by saying that the *ratio* of
good or of final cause supposes the *ratio* of nature.[51] I mean, of course, nature

---

49. Thomas does not use the word *fundamentum* very often. An interesting and quite pertinent use of it is found in *ST* II-II, q. 23, a. 8, ad 2. He explains that charity is the "foundation" of
the other virtues insofar as it "sustains" them, makes them stable. Form certainly has the function of sustaining a thing's being, "holding" the thing in being: *ST* I, q. 59, a. 2. See also I-II,
q. 85, a. 6.

50. *ST* I-II, q. 18, a. 5. See also *ST* I, q. 5, a. 5; I, q. 49, a. 1; I-II, q. 71, a. 2.

51. This I would say is the most fundamental sense of the expression "the good is what all
desire," for Thomas: the good is first of all what things desire *by nature*. If each thing, insofar as
it is a being, is good, each is also, insofar as it is a being, desirous of its goodness; if goodness is
convertible with being, so is appetite. This is why we can say that the good is a cause of every being, insofar as it is a being. Every being has goodness, final causality; and its first final causality
is with respect to itself, the inclination of its nature, which is its essence. The will itself is "founded" (*fundatur*) on a certain nature: *ST* I-II, q. 10, a. 1, ad 1. Moreover, the good to which a thing is
inclined by nature is its true good: see *ST* I, q. 60, a. 1, ad 3. Other inclinations that a thing may
have are right only insofar as they are in harmony with its natural inclinations: *ST* I-II, q. 71,

in the sense of form, with form seen as principle of both being and operation. This is another reason why I speak of the "natural" presuppositions of the *ratio boni*.

But I am not now speaking of nature as confined to physical entities, to bodily or material things. It is noteworthy that this article in fact says nothing about the material cause. The discussion is about the good in general, the good that is co-extensive with being, as such. Not all beings have matter. The *ratio boni* does not strictly presuppose the material cause, and I am taking "nature" in a metaphysical sense. But we do gather it from physical things.

What Hume Presupposed

One offshoot of all of this, which I can mention here only briefly, regards David Hume's famous claim that the distinction between ought and ought not, or between good and bad, is not grasped by mere reason, and is not a matter of *truth*, at all.[52] Hume is saying, in effect, that there is no such thing as the *ratio boni*, no intrinsic "intelligibility" or "form" of the good whatsoever. There is only what we happen to feel impulses toward. In pure reason this could be absolutely anything, or a quite incoherent set of things, or nothing at all. The common good fares no better. "It is not contrary to reason to prefer the destruction of the whole world to the scratching of my finger."[53] I think that from Thomas's point of view it makes perfect sense that he, Hume, should hold this. For what Hume presupposes is that the presuppositions of the good do not exist.

Thomas is not saying that the notion of the good is contained in the notion of being, or of form, or of efficient cause, or of nature. The notion of the good adds a novelty, the relation to appetite. In some sense then he is in agreement with Hume that "ought" and "ought not" cannot simply be deduced from "is" and "is not." But Hume is maintaining that "ought" and "good" have no strictly intelligible content at all. And this, I say, is no surprise, given that prior to undertaking his critique of these notions, and notwithstanding the title of his book, Hume has entirely eliminated nature, in the sense just indicated. I am referring mainly to his famous critique of causality (which of course is just what *ST* I, q. 5, a. 4, is all about).

---

a. 2. Still, even appetites for false goods, bad appetites, insofar as they proceed "from within" their subject, must in some respect be "according to nature": *ST* I-II, q. 6, a. 4, ad 3.

52. David Hume, *A Treatise of Human Nature*, ed. L. A. Selby-Bigge (Oxford: Oxford University Press, 1888), bk. III, pt. I, sec. i ("Moral Distinctions Not Derived from Reason"), 469–70.

53. Ibid., bk. II, pt. III, sec. iii ("Of the Influencing Motives of the Will"), 416.

Causality itself, for Hume, has no intelligible "foundation" in things.[54] There is no active power. There is likewise no action, in Thomas's sense: no communicating one's actuality to others. There is neither act nor potency. There is no formal cause, nothing that holds a thing together and makes it stable over time. Hume calls the notion of substance an "unintelligible chimera."[55] As far as I can tell, when he examines the question of active power, he does not even take into consideration what is perhaps the decisive experience: that of things from which similar things emerge, not rarely but for the most part. For Thomas, as for Aristotle, reproduction is the "natural" event *par excellence*.[56] It is that in which the forms of things, their power and their inclination, are most fully set to work and most plainly set before us.

Without nature, the good is simply not intelligible.

The Primacy of the Common Good and the First Precept of Natural Law

The First Precept as Implicitly Ordering toward Common Good

My final considerations, which are somewhat tentative, concern the relation of the primacy of the common good to the first precept of natural law. Of course "the good is to be done and sought, and the bad, avoided," does not explicitly mention common good. I suppose that the notion of the common good must be somewhat posterior to that of the good simply, since it adds a note of comparison with a multitude. Still, the first precept must somehow be moving us in the direction of our common good.[57] Otherwise it could not it be a first precept of any law at all, let alone natural law, the law that first shows us "what are the works of justice."

The division of the good into common and particular is not a division of a genus into species, a division *ex aequo*. It is an analogical division, *per prius et*

54. For Hume causality is nothing but the regular succession of sensible phenomena. This induces us to associate the idea of the antecedent phenomenon with that of the subsequent one. The latter is called "effect," and the former, "cause." We do not grasp any *intrinsic* connection between the phenomena, nor any factor *in* the cause that makes it a cause.

55. On the formal cause, see *A Treatise of Human Nature*, bk. I, pt. III, sec. xiv ("Of the Idea of Necessary Connexion"), 155–72; bk. I, pt. IV, sec. vi ("Of Personal Identity"), 251–63.

On substance, see ibid., bk. I, pt. IV, sec. iii ("Of the Antient [sic] Philosophy"), 222.

56. See Aristotle, *De anima*, II, 4 (415a22–b2); *Metaphysics* V, 4 (1014b18–1015a19). In the *Treatise* Hume distinguishes several senses of "nature," but note of them refers to generation or reproduction: *A Treatise of Human Nature*, bk. III, pt. I, sec. ii ("Moral Distinctions Deriv'd from a Moral Sense"), 474–75.

57. It need not be what primarily frames the order toward the common good, since it is only a participation, in the eternal law. But it must participate in that order.

posterius, in which common good has the priority. The good of a part is truly good only insofar as it is ordered to the good of the whole. Now, the first precept of natural law is for Thomas a truth, a first, indemonstrable truth. It is true in a very absolute and unqualified way. I do not see how it can be true in this way unless the good and bad to which it refers are themselves unqualified good and bad, true good and true bad.[58] What is good only in a qualified way may well be something that is not to be done or sought, and what is bad only in a qualified way may be something that in truth is not to be avoided. Hence, as an ordination toward true good, the first precept seems to be in itself a disposition to "give the nod" to the common good.

It also seems to me that the account in I-II, q. 5, a. 4, of how the *ratio* of the good presents itself, suggests that the move to the notion of common good and to its priority does come quite naturally to us.[59] There Thomas focuses chiefly on good substances. This is where we first grasp the good. There are unqualified goods in the other categories too; but elsewhere he indicates that good and bad in other categories are to be understood in function of good and bad in substances.[60] An unqualifiedly good substance is a substance that has its full due perfection. It has this through its form and its active power, the power to make its like. Is this not almost as much as to say that an unqualifiedly good substance is one that is in some way a common good? It is one whose goodness other things—its effects—are ordered toward and share in. At least we can say that a substance is unqualifiedly good when it has both the being of its species, by its form, and something of the very self-diffusiveness or self-communicability of the form. This, I would submit, gives us the form as pertaining to the perfection of the species as such. To see a substance's unqualified goodness seems then to go hand in hand with seeing a true common good, namely the being of its species as a whole.

58. It is not to be overlooked that for Thomas the *ratio* of good also presupposes that of *true: ST* I, q. 16, a. 4.

59. I do not mean by this that it comes easy to us actually to give to the common good the priority that we naturally understand it to deserve. For the complete picture of Thomas's doctrine, it is essential to consider the effects that he assigns to original sin. Just one text: "In the state of integral nature, man referred the love of himself, and likewise the love of all things, to the love of God, as to its end. And so he loved God more than himself and above all. But in the state of corrupt nature, man fails in this as regards the appetite of the rational will, which on account of the corruption of nature seeks his private good, unless it is healed by the grace of God"; *ST* I-II, q. 109, a. 3. I take it that the expression "the appetite of the rational will" means deliberate appetite, choice. The natural inclination to love God above all remains even in the fallen state; one can see that doing so is right, and one can wish to do so. But without grace, some inordinate attachment or other to creatures inevitably prevails (*ST* I-II, q. 109, a. 8).

60. *ST* I-II, q. 18, a. 1.

The Analogical Universality of the Good

Now in *Summa theologiae* I-II, question 94, article 2, after presenting the very first precept of natural law, Thomas distinguishes three groups or levels of precepts that fall underneath the first one. The first level pertains to "an inclination that is according to the nature in which man communicates with all substances." By this "every substance desires the conservation of its existence according to its nature." For years now, Lawrence Dewan has been insisting, I believe quite rightly, that this refers not only to the individual's conservation, but also to that of its kind.[61] I think the very word "nature" suggests it, and in any case Thomas explicitly affirms such an inclination in many places. Back in the article on angelic love, he says: "nature is bent on itself not just as to what is singular for it, but much more as to what is common; for each is inclined to conserving not only its individual self, but also its species."[62] Much more as to what is common. Is it then among these precepts, those pertaining to the "nature of substance," that we should put the primacy of the common good? What I have just said about what makes a substance unqualifiedly good may suggest that it is.

I wonder, though, whether we should not put the primacy of the common good still higher, associate it even more closely with the very first precept. I am thinking of the first precept's greater universality, as founded on the good itself—the good that is a transcendental, convertible with being. Even substance is only one of the categories or genera of beings. The good is what all beings desire, in all genera. I see no reason why the first precept of natural law should be the only practical principle that is absolutely universal, a function of the nature of the good itself and of being itself, not of some particular genus of beings. Thomas compares it with the principle of non-contradiction, which is the first speculative principle. The principle of non-contradiction is certainly not the only speculative principle that extends to all genera.

It may sound strange to speak of desire belonging to accidents. Yet accidents are forms, and Thomas says without qualification that "some inclination follows on any form whatsoever."[63] In the same article, he makes it clear that he is not speaking only of substantial forms. "Each and every power of the soul is a certain form or nature, and has a natural inclination toward something."[64]

61. For example, in Lawrence Dewan, O.P., "St. Thomas, John Finnis, and the Political Good," *The Thomist* 64, no. 3 (2000): 366–67.

62. *ST* I, q. 60, a. 5, ad 3.

63. *ST* I, q. 80, a. 1; see above, n. 48.

64. *ST* I, q. 80, a. 1, ad 3; note the explicit mention of "nature." See also q. 78, a. 1, ad 3. On the powers of the soul as accidents, see *ST* I, q. 77, a. 1, ad 5.

The powers of the soul are not substantial forms but accidents, qualities. Each has appetite for its suitable object and its proper act—natural appetite (taken here as opposed to the appetite that follows cognition). More generally, I think we can also say that an accidental form is appetitive by the very fact that it brings a certain *esse*. It is a determination to that *esse*.

To be sure, what "has" the *esse* that the accident brings is not the accident itself but the substance in which it inheres. The status of accidents is utterly "slavish." The recipient, the "beneficiary," of the *esse* is strictly the substance. Properly speaking, what *is* a heater is not the quality of heat but the hot body.[65] Even an action, which is also an accident, is not what acts or what *is* acting; what *is* hitting is neither the power to hit nor the actual hit, but the hitter. This, however, only means that seeing the accidents of a substance as appetitive goes hand in hand with seeing them as ordered toward the substance—that is, with seeing the substance as their common end and good.[66]

So in a way we are merely back at the level of substance. Nevertheless, I think the precept of natural law must be kept "above" this level. For we should keep in mind that if the good extends to all the genera, it is not as still another, even broader genus. The good is not a genus any more than being is. It is too broad to be a genus. It applies directly not only to the species of things but also to their very differences. For instance, not only man, but also rationality, is a being and a good. As a result, what the good is differs for different species of things, even species in the same genus of substance. Even as confined to things of the same genus, the good is not univocal, as a genus is, but analogical. What the good is for plants is not what it is for animals.

The Analogical Universality of the Common Good

The same holds for the common good. This is clear even within Thomas's account of the precepts at the general level of substance. What each substance is naturally inclined to is the conservation in existence, not of the general nature of substance, but of its own nature, the nature of its proper kind. And obviously substances of different kinds have different ways of being ordered to the existence of their kind. In man's case, for example, conservation in existence requires the use of reason. For different kinds, what it is to be ordered to the common good differs. This again suggests that the principle of the priority of the common good belongs with the very first precept, "above" the three levels.

The principle's analogical character emerges even more clearly if we con-

65. See *ST* I, q. 75, a. 2.
66. See above, at n. 27.

sider the second and third levels. The second regards the nature that man shares with other animals, sensitive nature; the third regards the nature proper to man, reason. The goods that Thomas associates with these levels are even more explicitly common than the good that he associates with the first level. They pertain to communities found only at these levels and not at the first level: domestic or familial community, and properly rational community. And here, not only what these goods are, but also their very way of being common, is different from that of the first-level goods.

Thus, notice that at each of these levels, Thomas cites as objects of natural inclination not just one good, as at the first level, but two. At the general animal level, he cites the union of male and female, and the rearing of offspring. (Again, these will pertain to each kind of animal in its own specific mode.) Of course taken generally, the union of male and female is a common good for the whole animal species, since it is something to which all the members of the species are inclined and upon which the conservation of the species depends. But each particular union of male and female is also a common good, for the particular domestic or familial community—the community of this male and this female and their offspring. And it is a common good, not because all the members of the community are partners in it (the offspring are not partners in *this* union), but because the whole community originates with it and because it is the ruling principle of the community's other goods, such as the rearing of the offspring.[67]

At the properly human level, the two goods that Thomas cites are the knowledge of truth about God, and life in society. It is very significant that he says truth *about God*. Of course even truth in general could be cited as the object of a properly human natural inclination. But not all particular truths are such that all men need to know them. Even the rulers of society, who need to know much that the others may not, do not need to know all truths. They do, however, need to know the truth about God. It is a natural need. Knowledge of the truth about God is the core of what Thomas calls wisdom, and for him wisdom is both the highest perfection of the human mind and that which by nature ought to rule in human affairs. Earlier in the *Prima secundae* he had said that wisdom ought to rule even over prudence.[68] And here, just as he cites the

67. A community of this sort is possible only among beings that have cognition. Since they have diverse functions within the community, they must be able to relate differently to each other in accordance with their functions. They must also be able to distinguish between those of their kind that belong to this particular community and those that do not.

68. *ST* I-II, q. 66, a. 5, ad 1 & ad 2. It also belongs to wisdom to judge and defend the first indemonstrable principles, those which govern all the sciences: ibid., ad 4. See also Aquinas, *Sententia super Metaphysicam*, proem.

union of male and female before the rearing of offspring—the union being the ruling good—so he cites the knowledge of truth about God before life in society. On this truth depends the truth about justice itself. It is the truth about that to which men first belong and are first bound, the truth about the primary common good.[69]

Finally, we should keep in mind that all of these common goods are things to which man's reason naturally orders him. As rational, he is also ordered toward putting order among his inclinations, or toward giving each good its just priority. The primacy of the common good is a naturally understood principle of this ordering.

All in all, the principle of the primacy of the common good seems just too universal and polyvalent to be assigned to any of the levels beneath the first precept of natural law, even the level of the common nature of substance. Perhaps, however, it is in the inclination of a substance to the being of its kind that reason first discerns this universal law.

---

69. The ordination toward knowing the truth about God is proper to things having intellect, and it is distinct from the ordination toward the love of God, which somehow applies to absolutely everything (see *ST* I, q. 6, a. 1, ad 2; 44, a. 4, ad 3). I would suggest that the precept of the love of God also ranks with the first precept.

10

A Reading Guide for Natural Law Ethics

JOSEPH W. KOTERSKI, S.J.

By anyone's count, there has been an astonishing number of scholarly books and articles on natural law theory in recent decades. One might not have expected this trend, given the prevailing currents in academic philosophy and theology.

An Orphan from Theology

Despite attempts of various kinds since the Enlightenment to sever, or at least to ignore, the connection between the natural moral law and God as its ultimate source,[1] natural law theory is necessarily theological. This is not to say that one cannot come to know any number of moral precepts (for instance, that murder is wrong, or that promises should be kept, or that parents should be honored) without explicitly invoking God or having any particular theories about morality in mind.[2] To say that would be to ignore one of the most com-

---

1. There is an interesting account of this trend in Pauline C. Westerman, *The Disintegration of Natural Law: From Aquinas to Finnis* (Leiden: Brill, 1998). For a fine history of natural law theory, perhaps not as mindful of the perils of this trend but otherwise very reliable, see Alessandro Passerin d'Entrèves, *Natural Law: An Introduction to Legal Philosophy* (London: Hutchison University Library, 1970). For a somewhat dated but more detailed history, see the first half of a study that will be discussed later in this essay, Heinrich Rommen's *Natural Law: A Study in Legal and Social History and Philosophy*, trans. Thomas R. Hanley (Indianapolis: Liberty Fund, 1998), originally published in German as *Die ewige Wiederkehr des Naturrechts* (Leipzig: Verlag Jakob Hegner, 1936).

2. One of the recent authors who has done the most to bring out the undeniability of the

pelling features of natural law theory—that its most fundamental directives will be readily obvious to anyone of open mind and good will who reflects on human conduct, without any need to study natural law theory. But it is to say that when we are discussing not some particular precept of the natural moral law but natural law theory, considered precisely as a theory for explaining the nature of morality, natural law theory is ineluctably theological.

As a theologically grounded approach to morality, natural law theory has recurrently been an object of severe criticism by revisionist moral theologians, particularly since the publication of Pope Paul VI's 1968 encyclical *Humanae Vitae*. Disappointed in the re-affirmation of the Church's opposition to birth control, revisionist theologians have tended to treat that pope's appeal to the natural law within the larger argument of that encyclical as retrograde "physicalism."[3] The more general attack that some revisionist theologians have subsequently mounted against natural law reasoning objects to its view of nature as a classicist fossil from pre-historicist thinking that they feel needs to be retired in the name of progress and replaced by an approach that thinks of nature in terms of statistical normality, a notion that is conveniently without the hard edges of ever being able to discern the difference between what might be disadvantageous and what is intrinsically evil.[4] Even apart from such controversial issues, natural law theory has fared poorly in many professional theological circles, perhaps because of its distinctly philosophical character. Academic Scripture scholarship, for instance, has tended to regard its pedigree in Greek philosophy as a reason for suspecting natural law theory of being an

---

natural moral law in the normal experience of practical reasoning by even the most ordinary people who pass their daily lives without philosophical reflection is J. Budziszewski (*What We Can't Not Know: A Guide* [Dallas: Spence, 2004]). See also his *Written on the Heart: The Case for Natural Law* (Downers Grove, Ill.: InterVarsity Press, 1997) and *The Revenge of Conscience: Politics and the Fall of Man* (Dallas: Spence, 2000).

3. See Janet E. Smith, *Humanae Vitae: A Generation Later* (Washington, D.C.: The Catholic University of America Press, 1991).

4. One of the most significant targets of Pope John Paul II's *Veritatis splendor* is the tendency within consequentialist and proportionalist thinking to muddy the waters of the moral analysis of human acts in such a way that the category of intrinsically evil acts becomes unclear. Like Prof. Moriarty muddling the clue-pools of Sherlock Holmes, these revisionist thinkers have tried to recalibrate the normativity of nature with the metrics of relative normalcy over a range. In so doing they have rendered "nature" as a purely descriptive term rather than respected its appropriate normative use. In the third and fourth sections of *Veritatis splendor,* the pope offers an argument in the traditional natural law approach for the need to consider distinctly the intention (the *finis operantis* or motive of the agent), the circumstances (the factors in a situation that have moral bearing), and the end (the *finis operis* or intrinsic directedness of an action). By this strategy he makes a cogent case for retaining the notion of intrinsically evil actions as morally forbidden always and everywhere, regardless of any possible circumstances or any compensatory motivation that the subject who is considering a deliberate action might have.

alien influence upon the Bible rather than as intrinsic to the native soil of the biblical landscape.[5]

Natural law theory has done little better in the mainstream circles of professional philosophy. Twentieth-century philosophy has been dominated by analytic and continental approaches, and neither of them has offered much of a home for natural law theory when it is orphaned from its native theological domicile. The reception that the most prominent camps in mainstream philosophy have given natural law thinkers has rather been like that which Alice of Wonderland received when she arrived at the Mad Tea Party and found herself confronted by the uncivil riddles of the mad "March Hare" and the equally mad "Mad Hatter": "The table was a large one, but [they] were all crowded together at one corner of it. 'No room! No room!' they cried out when they saw Alice coming."[6] To the riddle they insisted that she answer (why is a raven like a writing desk?), they themselves had no answer. As Carroll's figure for common sense realism, Alice alone seems to have had eyes able to see the strangeness of their curiously endless banquet ever in search of clean plates.

For many analytic thinkers, an appeal to nature as a ground of ethics seemed to be impossible in principle, for they have been inclined to see the practitioners of natural law theory as invariably committing the "naturalistic fallacy" of trying to derive an "ought" from an "is" when aiming to argue for something morally prescriptive on the basis of descriptions of human nature.[7] Within the wide range of continental approaches to philosophy, some quarters have been suspicious of any talk of "nature," as if it necessarily reduces to some social construction and often involves the imposition of the values of one group upon another.[8] Others remain skeptical about the reality of any such thing as a "nature" (human nature, in particular) or about the possibility of ever knowing human nature well enough to employ it in ethics,[9] and most

5. For a fine review of this trend in scripture scholarship and a thoughtful critical response, see Matthew Levering, *Biblical Natural Law: A Theocentric and Teleological Approach* (Oxford: Oxford University Press, 2008).

6. Lewis Carroll, *Alice's Adventures in Wonderland,* I, chap. 7, in *The Complete Works of Lewis Carroll* (London: The Nonesuch Press, 1939), 68.

7. Thankfully, a small number of practitioners of analytic philosophy have given some indication of coming around to a viewpoint open to natural law reasoning on this question. See, for instance, Philippa Foot, *Natural Goodness* (Oxford: Clarendon Press, 2001). In addition to reporting the change in her own convictions on this subject, her book provides a sophisticated discussion of the history of the charge of the naturalistic fallacy in G. E. Moore's *Principia Ethica* (1903) and its roots in turn in David Hume, *A Treatise of Human Nature* (1739–1740).

8. For a thorough account of this trend, see Charles Taylor, *A Secular Age* (Cambridge, Mass.: Harvard University Press, 2007); Richard Rorty, *Philosophy and the Mirror of Nature* (Oxford: Blackwell, 1980).

9. Jean-Paul Sartre is typical of the Existentialist rejection of nature. As we will see below,

contemporary continental philosophers are dubious about linking theoretical reason and practical reason, especially in light of the Kantian tendency to focus ethics on reason and autonomy.

But the evidence of much fruitful work in the area of natural law theory suggests that we need to make a response like that of Galileo: *E pur si muove!* Quite contrary to what one might have suspected, natural law theory is not dead or dormant. It has continued to be the subject of countless scholarly and popular treatments. And quite unlike some parts of the modern academy, this area of thought has not just been the scene of a cottage industry that churns out scholastic commentaries for the sake of tenure files, but has been a lively area of inquiry with an important voice in the public square. The need always remains for a way to ground ethical positions on some basis that is universal, objective, and intelligible to anyone of open mind and good will.

Given the vast number of scholarly articles and books that have been produced—far more than could possibly be discussed here—this brief essay will not attempt the project of a comprehensive review,[10] but rather will offer a kind of reading guide, constructed by comment on some of the crucial issues that are in play and by the listing of some of the important materials (classical and contemporary) that deserve a careful reading for the understanding of these issues. It will prove helpful to focus on a select number of different questions that are important parts of the contemporary discussion on natural law ethics, both in the area of normative ethics philosophically considered and in certain areas where this approach to morality has proven particularly fruitful within jurisprudence and theology.

Although the ancient origins of natural law thinking are to be found in the area of law and statecraft, and even though some of the most fruitful applications of natural law theory have come in the realm of law, it would seem to be impossible to chalk up the current revival to trends within contemporary jurisprudence, which remains pervasively positivist. And yet even this point needs careful qualification, especially because of the complex nature of judi-

---

Sartre's *Existentialism Is a Humanism* (originally in French, 1946) took various Enlightenment philosophers to task for their inconsistency in wanting to retain the idea of nature as they departed from theism. In his view, the denial of God's relevance, let alone God's existence, required that one also give up on the notion of "nature" (or at very least, the idea of "human nature").

10. There have been a number of interesting review articles on recent natural law publications, each one featuring a different set of examples: Anthony J. Lisska, "On the Revival of Natural Law: Several Books from the Last Half-Decade," *American Catholic Philosophical Quarterly* 81, no. 4 (2007): 613–38; John Haldane, "Thomist Ethics in America," *Logos* 3 (2000): 150–68; J. Budziszewski, "Natural Born Lawyers," *The Weekly Standard*, May 14, 1999, 31–35; and Charles Covell, *The Defence of Natural Law* (New York: St. Martin's Press, 1992).

cial review. While traditional natural law jurisprudence has long recognized a category like equity by which judges could be justified in correcting the injustices that would result from a strict application of legislation and that could not have been foreseen by legislators, the unfortunate habits of the higher judiciary to use their powers of judicial review for the judicial legislation of policies that legislators have not seen fit to enact—often on the grounds of their personal vision of morality—gives reason for pause.

Out of concern with this issue, there is an important trend among traditional natural law theorists to insist that the judiciary ought to be entirely restricted to positivist considerations about what the law actually says and that judges should not consider themselves entitled to appeal to any principles of morality; it would be better to leave discussions about natural law ethics and the application of natural law principles to the realm of politics, legislation, and public opinion.[11] Given the emphasis recurrently found within the tradition of natural law to think of moral principles as a kind of higher law by which civil law can be judged, and in some cases to judge that a piece of legislation does not bind because it is not just, this emphasis on judicial restraint might seem a retreat from a stronger sense of natural law theory to a weaker one, but in the long run pruning the vine here may lead to a stronger stalk. The epistemic humility required for knowing where and how natural law theory can rightly be applied will mean fewer cases of overreaching.

The original force behind the natural law revival of the twentieth century, however, seems to me to reside in a theological question of an ecclesial nature, namely, the search for a suitable basis for Catholic social teaching. So, after offering a typology of the main objections to natural law reasoning and reviewing some of the classical sources for natural law thinking that are crucial for understanding the project, we will consider some of the trends that have led to a natural law revival.

The Typical Objections

A brief mention of certain common objections to natural law ethics today may aid in elucidating the philosophical challenges that have helped to stimulate the current renewal. It seems to me that there are four main groups.

1. For some, the very idea of a fixed common nature is unacceptable. This objection is typical of existentialism, skepticism, and post-modernism. Fur-

11. See, for instance, Robert P. George, *In Defense of Natural Law* (Oxford: Oxford University Press, 1999), esp. "Law, Democracy, and Moral Disagreement," 315–34. See also Mark C. Murphy, *Natural Law in Jurisprudence and Politics* (Oxford: Blackwell, 2007).

ther, there is often a strong sense today that human plasticity is sufficient for us to refashion ourselves almost indefinitely and that natural boundaries are all in principle able to be crossed, given enough time and energy.

2. A second objection arises from the denial of God's existence, and this objection is frequently found in connection with belief in some forms of evolutionary theory. These two positions are not necessarily connected, nor is one logically entailed by the other. Much depends on precisely how the term "evolution" is being understood (for example, whether a given theory denies or still affirms that the development of biological life on this planet has been guided by some intelligence).[12] In popular as well as in professional circles, a thing's "nature" tends to be used to designate the extent to which a given species has developed thus far. Seen in this light, there are numerous proponents of the view that morality is simply something that has evolved as a coping mechanism in the struggle for the survival of the fittest, rather than as something that could even possibly be normative for any higher reasons.[13] To try to develop an ethics on the basis of nature so understood tends to have a utilitarian cast, for the proponents of this approach reject the idea that nature contains divinely implanted obligations and insist instead that we should pragmatically consider how things presently are if we want to be successful in altering them in the ways that we prefer. At best we may be able to ascertain what is the most effective strategy for survival or flourishing, whether for individuals or for the group. But to assign any more weight than what is biologically pragmatic would seem unwarranted.

12. This is to take note of the fact that virtually all the currently viable theories of evolution under discussion today recognize the need to provide an explanation not only for natural selection but also for the differentiation of life forms prior to their being subjected to the natural selection process. In this context, when evolutionary theorists speak of "random variation" they do not mean variation that is "random" in the sense of being uncaused but only in the sense that the sequence of causal interactions are not systemically designed. What is at issue in this part of the debate is whether the physical causality operating at various levels (atomic, molecular, biochemical, etc.) is sufficient to account for the long chains of interactions that are needed to produce the biological structures and complex organisms that have sufficiently developed traits that are the means by which these organisms succeed in meeting the challenges of natural selection. For a discussion of this question, see, for example, the arguments about the need for an intelligent cause mounted by Michael Behe, *Edge of Evolution: The Search for the Limits of Darwinism* (New York: Simon and Schuster, 2007); and such critics of Behe as Kenneth Miller, *Finding Darwin's God: A Scientist's Search for Common Ground between God and Evolution* (New York: HarperCollins, 2007).

13. Among the raft of books on this subject, some make the argument in a more scholarly way, such as J. McKenzie Alexander, *The Structural Evolution of Morality* (Cambridge: Cambridge University Press, 2007); Richard Joyce, *The Evolution of Morality* (Cambridge, Mass.: MIT Press, 2006); and Franz B. Waal, *Primates and Philosophers: How Morality Evolved* (Princeton: Princeton University Press, 2006). There are also many popular books on the subject such as John Gray, *Straw Dogs: Thought on Humans and Other Animals* (London: Granta, 2002).

3. Third, the proponents of the hermeneutic of suspicion have voiced the notion that the theological aspects of natural law theory are really only the lurking evidence that natural law theory is another case of the imposition of the views of the powerful upon the powerless under the guise of something (nature) that is being claimed as objectively normative. The roots of this interpretive model can be traced back to such figures as Freud, Marx, and Nietzsche, who are often styled the great masters of this hermeneutic precisely by the manner in which they assert their charge against the natural law position. Instead of arguing a point in the traditional style of raising objections and setting forth arguments and counter positions within a framework of rational discussion, they frequently make their case by suggesting that some hidden motive lies behind the position of their adversary. The rhetorical result of this maneuver is that the adversary must spend so much energy clearing the air of the false charges that the positive presentation of the case is suspended; moreover, the poisoned atmosphere created by the charge makes anyone with a lingering resentment inclined to suspect that any serious effort to refute the charge is really an admission of guilt, on the assumption that where there is smoke there must be fire.[14]

4. Finally, there have been significant objections of a technical philosophical nature, as mentioned briefly above. Usually these objections have been associated with the charge of the "naturalistic fallacy," that is, the objection to the very possibility of defining "the good" that was formulated by G. E. Moore on the basis of David Hume's reflections on the difference between fact and value. The allegation here is that it is logically impossible to derive an "ought" from an "is." This is said to be the case because of the logical fallacy that is alleged to be invariably committed by any form of reasoning that tries to derive moral conclusions about obligation from descriptions of how human nature simply is.

All these objections to natural law ethics have a certain plausibility, and a reading program in natural law ethics needs to treat them seriously. They mainly arise in the areas where traditional natural law theory differs most

14. Interestingly, Pope Benedict XVI chose to focus on the thought and argument strategies of the Freudian, Marxist, and Nietzschean camps in his first encyclical, *Deus Caritas Est* (2005) and has thereby proven to be our German Shepherd guarding against certain German Wolves. In order to deal with the hermeneutics of suspicion that is their *modus operandi*, he wisely takes the course of citing examples of Christian sacrifice and charity for each area of consideration, in the expectation that these heroic examples can show that the suspicion is unwarranted and thereby return the discussion to the positive case that Christianity wants to make in the areas of sexual morality (contra Freud's theory of sexuality), truth (contra Nietzsche's reduction of truth to interpretation), and social charity (contra Marx's charges that religion neglects justice and oppresses the poor).

from modern thought. Without attempting a full philosophical response here, let us briefly consider each one in turn as a way to prepare the ground for further reading. The consideration of both classical sources and contemporary studies can be significantly enhanced by having in mind some of the debates that are in play.

1. In regard to whether "nature" is a legitimate philosophical concept and a possible source of moral knowledge, much depends on a correct understanding of the concept nature, and with it a proper appreciation for the multipronged problem of universals. The problem of universals has logical, metaphysical, and epistemological aspects but is irreducible to any one of these levels. The notion of nature that is needed for traditional natural law theory is not the sense of a Platonic Form (where the governing epistemic model is from the realm of mathematics rather than from living things); nor is it that of a timeless essence in the logical sense preferred by modern analytic philosophy. Rather, the focus is on the idea of nature that flows from the set of basic insights first formulated in the second book of Aristotle's *Physics* and in his *De anima*. The governing epistemic model here comes from the organic world, where questions about the sameness of an individual over time and about the identity of the many individuals within one species depend on a robust sense of potency and act as paired principles of being.

Conceived along these lines, "nature" refers to the dynamic principle of order that governs the unfolding of a being's inner structures and of the operations that are its typical activities. These principles can be discovered by the investigation of individual beings as they develop over the time from their generation to their destruction, beings that are living composite unities, beings that tend to grow and to operate according to patterns typical of their kind, beings whose initial stages may appear quite different from their mature and terminal states, and yet beings whose continuity over the course of time renders them able to be recognized as the same individual over the course of that lifetime and thus members of the same kind, whatever the differences in their appearance. The common features shared by a set of things allow us to recognize various individuals to be of the same kind as well as to understand why certain types of activity and nurture promote flourishing for members of this kind while the lack or distortion of those types of activity and nurture tends to harm them.

Considered in this sense, the notion of human nature that is operative in natural law theory is fundamentally continuous with what is used throughout the range of contemporary physical sciences, even though contemporary expressions of these sciences usually do not use the term "nature." The crucial aspect here is not the presence of terminology but the presence of the same mode of thinking. The ways in which every specialized science operates invariably involve the progressive accumulation of knowledge about the structural forms and the characteristic activities of the types of beings that are within the purview of that science. Whether the discipline is more given to understanding behavior or more interested in transforming the given situation, for example, by (bio)chemical processes, by medical therapies, or by behavioral training, there is invariably a use of discipline-specific terminology that is functionally equivalent to the philosophical notion of nature in regard to structures, activities, and the promotion or injury of individuals within the group. Whether or not a given discipline uses a term like "teleology" or "end-directedness" is less important than whether it does or does not in fact consider the phenomena of telic activity in the organisms that are the focus of its study. The claim that traditional natural law theory makes about these natures is not that natural structures, inclinations, or operations are themselves the ultimate ground for moral precepts, but that an appreciation of the teleological or end-directed nature of these structures, inclinations, and operations can help one to discover and articulate the appropriate moral precepts that govern beings with a nature of this type. Natural inclinations in particular have a special role in the discernment involved in natural law reasoning. A sound natural law theory does not take the inclinations themselves to deliver the content of moral precepts, but understands them as a kind of blinker: they point us to areas on which to reflect, so as to determine whether a given inclination is reliable in alerting us to something useful for the perfection of the organism, something obligatory or even something virtuous, or on the other hand, to something that is excessive, distorted, or somehow perverted that must be countered and resisted by the formation of a moral prohibition or discouragement.

2. A philosophical commitment to atheism would presumably preclude explicitly religious versions of natural law ethics; it might even make any discussion of nature illegitimate. One thinks, for instance, of Sartre's penetrating criticisms of thinkers from the Enlightenment who continued to talk about nature after banishing God from the picture. Consistency in the matter, he insisted, required that one not appeal to nature.[15] For this reason, he insisted that existence precedes essence and that there is no given nature; instead, one needs to construct one's essence. Now, that a human being has to make all sorts of choices that come to define the manner of one's existence is undeni-

---

15. Jean-Paul Sartre, "L'Existentialisme est un humanisme" (1946), in English, *Existentialism and Humanism*, trans. Philip Mairet (Brooklyn: Haskell House, 1977), 23–56.

able. But, of course, Sartre does not develop the point about the lack of a given nature for any other kind of being except for human beings. For all of his vigorous protests against the notion of a given human nature, one gets the impression that this is an arbitrarily delimited assertion that can be denied as easily as it is asserted, for human beings are no different in most respects from every other kind of being (for example, the fact that they have a common body structure, common ways of acting and feeling as member of the same biological structure, and so on). One cannot conduct a reasonable discussion about anything unless one adverts to the ways in which words designate this kind of being or that, and that is what one means by essence or nature—it is something found in things, not something constructed (except in the sense that we do have to find words and phrases adequate to represent in language what we discover to be the case in reality). But this applies to human beings according to their kind as well as to anything else, and so Sartre's point about the need for free choices (what he calls being condemned to be free) does not obviate the applicability of a concept such as nature but simply enhances the need for beings like us to choose well, given the type of nature that we have, namely, one with the power of free choice to determine, at least in part, our life-courses.

One could equally well ask if the cogency of natural law ethics in articulating certain moral precepts as objectively grounded might not actually require someone who professes to be atheistic or agnostic to reopen the discussion about the question of God's existence. Sartre's reasoning, one might say, can work in reverse: if, for good scientific reasons, one does need to retain the functional equivalent of "nature," one may also need to be more open to the notion of a designer of those natures than one might prefer.

3. The proponents of the hermeneutics of suspicion suggest that nature is really a term to disguise the impositions of power. To be sure, it is hard to do any philosophizing at all if one's conversation partner is ready to find a hidden meaning in anything that one says. If there is to be genuine philosophical conversation in this matter, the above remarks about the meaning of nature must be taken at face value, that is, as sincere efforts to discern structures that are given in the makeup of human beings that can be useful in determining the conduct appropriate for fulfillment rather than frustration of human life.

This is not to deny that natural law thinking has a checkered history because of the abuse of this theory.[16] But the ideological abuse of a legitimate

16. See Yves R. Simon, *The Tradition of Natural Law,* ed. Vukan Kuic (Bronx, N.Y.: Fordham University Press, 1992), for a wonderful discussion of the ideological uses of the term "natural law" by various individuals and schools of thought with pernicious agendas over the course of history.

term or a valid idea by those intent on some rhetorical or political gain does
not destroy the possible use of that concept in a philosophically respectable
way. Natural law ethics, when carried out responsibly, is the sort of moral theory that proposes intelligibility (that is, the ability of a natural structure to dis-
close reliable information to respectful inquirers about the being in question)
as a fundamental aspect of any moral criterion. The emphasis here is upon reason inquiring into the constitution of things prior to the use of practical reason
to determine a policy, practice, or action with regard to our use or alteration
of those things. Thus, by its self-understanding, natural law theory invites the
involvement of reasoning and discussion rather than authoritative pronounce-
ments or impositions of power.

4. Concerning the charge of the naturalistic fallacy, there has been much
recent fruitful discussion about whether there really is a logical fallacy here.[17]
In general, it is important to remember that traditional versions of natural law
ethics did not understand this approach as a matter of reading off a static or
complete set of dos and don'ts or of treating the idea of human nature as inflex-
ibly static or overly narrow in the ways that critics have sometimes charged.
Traditional versions have seen its dynamism as residing not in the evolutionary generation of one species from another but in the teleological drive to the
growth and maturation of an individual within a given species. What is permitted, forbidden, or obligatory does vary in relation to the individual's stage
of development, as well as the specific situation. But this relativity to such objective factors as the particular stage of maturation within the patterns that are
natural to a species or the obligations that one may bear by reason of one's situation (being a parent or a spouse, for instance) are not arbitrary; rather, they
gain specificity for an individual according to various circumstances and yet
are still related to the patterns typical for one's kind. The fact that achieving
knowledge about these patterns (for example, by parental rearing, by formal
education, by reflection on experience, and so on) is likely to be helpful does
not take away from the need to make use of one's freedom of choice; rather it
simply guides the chooser by providing information about which choices are
likely to be better and which worse.

In this regard, the contribution to one's moral knowledge by revelation,

17. Theorists of the "new natural law" camp generally accept the view that the naturalistic
fallacy is a genuine problem and have tried to revise the teleological views associated with such
medieval figures as Aquinas in order to avoid the problem. See, for instance, John Finnis, *Aquinas* (Oxford: Oxford University Press, 1998). Others have argued that a proper understanding
of teleology as a fact within human nature allows one to argue for the fact of certain obligations;
see, for instance, Anthony Lisska, *Aquinas's Theory of Natural Law: An Analytic Reconstruction*
(Oxford: Oxford University Press, 1996).

the Decalogue, or education in biblical wisdom is not something that curtails proper human autonomy. Instead, it can enhance freedom and liberate a person for making better choices.[18] Seen in this way, natural law involves a kind of moral reasoning that takes its lead from the natural inclinations. That moral reasoning is philosophically insightful about human nature through its careful consideration about which of these inclinations is likely to be helpful and which destructive, even while it remains appreciative of religious revelation about the designs of a providential creator, the weaknesses typical of a sinful humanity, and the resources of grace made possible through the divinely initiated process of human redemption.

In regard to the philosophical reasoning that is specifically at issue here for natural law's critics, the charge of the naturalistic fallacy has an initial plausibility, insofar as one presupposes that no descriptive statement about a thing's nature or about some state of affairs could ever contain a latent normative statement. At best, a description of a being will contain true statements about the being, whether timelessly true or true at a given time. But, ironically, this concentration on the analysis of temporal statements or of statements about timelessly true essences can be overly limiting if one fails to take account of the fact that things with organic natures necessarily have developmental aspects to them. To be adequate, these descriptions need to take into account the inherent dispositions toward realization that are the specific potencies and inclinations of a given nature. But potencies are not merely possibilities of a logical sort; they are already the actualizations of powers and inclinations. Thus these potencies and dispositions can be the grounds for statements of a normative character that are latent within an adequate description. Carefully articulated, they can provide the means by which traditional natural law theories can meet and overcome the charge of the naturalistic fallacy.

The central insight of Aristotelian natural philosophy that made natural law theory persuasive for so many medieval thinkers, as well as for contemporary philosophers with an openness to belief in God, was precisely the notion of teleology: the idea that beings of a given kind are not entirely manifest all at once but develop in the course of time according to certain patterns. Further, with regard to human nature, one of the crucial aspects is that human beings must contribute to their own flourishing by careful choices that can be consistent or inconsistent with the patterns of development that are intrinsic to them. That these patterns can be frustrated by the beings themselves and not

18. Pope John Paul II deals with the genuine and the deceptive senses of the concept of autonomy in the second section of the second chapter of *Veritatis splendor.* His own preferred term for the praiseworthy sense of autonomy is "participated theonomy."

Joseph W. Koterski, S.J.

just by external forces renders it crucial for the beings with powers of knowledge and choice to gain better and better knowledge of what these patterns are and what sorts of activities would fulfill or frustrate them in the attainment of their ends. When nature is thus seen in terms of teleology, potentiality, and intrinsic orientation toward an end, the descriptions of nature can be seen already to contain the data needed to elicit an ought statement through a careful combination of speculative and practical reasoning. In my judgment, there is more than adequate reason to think that natural law reasoning does not commit the naturalistic fallacy by pulling some normative language out of a purely descriptive hat. There are already in the hat descriptive statements of a teleological character that serve as the grounds for the normative statements that are included in the work of ethics.

Classical Resources for Natural Law Theory

The historical origins of natural law thinking can be traced back to classical antiquity. Anyone inclined to understand the perennial attractions of natural law theory will do well to make time for its classical loci, and yet it is good to bear in mind that the ancient sources that are truly seeds of natural law thinking are not yet its full flowering. Many fine modern accounts of the history of natural law rightly begin this history with the Greeks. In the plays of Sophocles, for instance, we find the appeal of Antigone to a law higher than the dictates of Creon that is her justification for undertaking the burial rites for her rebel brother that the king has forbidden. While the warrant for her action comes clearly from a divine source and concerns the "natural" relation of family kinship, there is, admittedly, no articulation of the theoretical connections between God, nature, and conduct.

Among classical sources, we can also rightly look to Aristotle's passing but undeveloped references to something called "natural law" in the *Rhetoric* and the *Politics*. As we have seen above, what Aristotle most contributes to the eventual articulation of natural law theory is his vibrant sense of teleology, plus the inclination to see nature as a ground for ethics. His theory of the virtues in the *Nicomachean Ethics* is thoroughly rooted in the application to human nature of his general philosophy of nature from the *Physics*.[19] But the essences of the be-

19. To account more generally for the variety of changes observable in terrestrial things (including the inorganic), he articulates in the *Physics* the notion of being as a unified entity ("substance") with various qualitative, quantitative, and relational features ("the accidents") and then accounts for changes in a being's substantial and accidental forms by a theory of the four types of causality, with "material cause" and "formal cause" referring to the constitutive

ings that constitute the universe as Aristotle knows it are apparently timeless essences, and the God of the Aristotelian universe is not envisioned as a creator who has designed the world but as a perfect sphere of thought endlessly engaged in contemplating its own perfection. While nature is a ground for ethics in Aristotle (since the moral virtues amount to a kind of "second nature" in us when we have developed from our natural potentialities the well-honed disposition for excellence in the choices that we make in the sphere of action and emotion), there is little sense of "natural law" as such in Aristotle. Law requires a legislator; an eternal universe like Aristotle's, with a deity whose perfection consists in self-contemplation rather than providential concern, has no particular place or need for a moral legislator. Yet Aristotle does envision a kind of normative role for nature, even though his thought takes the form of an ethics of the virtues rather than the form of a natural law theory, since the virtues all pertain to perfected dispositions of our natural abilities.

The ancient source for the idea of natural law as such is Stoicism, and medieval thinkers know this source largely through Cicero. Stoicism, however, tends to be fatalistic in ways that Christian authors found unacceptable. In this respect an indispensable element in the picture comes from certain non-negotiable religious commitments of Judaism and Christianity, such as belief in a providential creator who orders creatures toward ends of divine design even while stressing personal responsibility for one's deliberate actions.

The Aristotelian contribution to the medieval notions of natural law consists especially in adding a philosophically cogent notion like "nature" to the biblical notion of "creature." Patristic and early medieval reflection on the cosmos and the various kinds of beings to be found within the cosmos had tended to use the perspectives offered by Genesis and the biblical wisdom literature to handle the various sorts of creatures that God had made. The rediscovery of Aristotelian natural philosophy in the late twelfth and early thirteenth centuries made for a philosophically sophisticated understanding of the variety of creatures in terms intrinsic to their empirically observable structures and activities by considering them as instances of one or another distinct type of nature (including human nature), each one having its own deeply teleological patterns of development and activity.[20] In general, Aristotle saw a thing's

elements and structures of anything, "efficient cause" to the agents that induce changes, and "final cause" to the goals, purposes, and outcomes that are the result of the operation of structures and agents. Aristotle's most explicit argument for normativity in ethics is called the proper function argument and can be found at *Nicomachean Ethics*, I.7.

20. See Joseph W. Koterski, S.J., *Introduction to Medieval Philosophy: Basic Concepts* (Malden, Mass.: Wiley-Blackwell, 2009), chap. 6, "Cosmos and Nature."

nature as determined by the dominant ("substantial") form that is intrinsic to any natural object and that unfolds from within an entity according to the structures and patterns typical of the beings of that kind. By virtue of this orientation toward the goal of maturation within the species, there is a spontaneous inclination toward the full actualization of the potentialities within the being. As rational animals, human beings for Aristotle manifest the same basic goal-directed or teleological structure as other animals. But they differ in that the highest capabilities of this nature are rational. The rational control that humans have over their actions means that their inbuilt drives toward their ends need to be mediated by many deliberate choices. Among the points that Aristotle emphasizes in this regard is our capacity for speech and for life in community with others (domestic life, political life, social life). At the summit of the inclinations that characterize our existence are the desires for knowledge and for fulfillment (for what he called *eudaimonia* or happiness).

Although Aristotle's work on ethics is organized not around the idea of law but around that of virtue, he contributes at least as much as any other source to the medieval idea of natural or acquired virtue, and the vast bulk of the moral theory of a figure like Thomas Aquinas in the *secunda pars* of the *Summa theologiae* is actually about virtue, not natural law.[21] In the argument of *Nicomachean Ethics* I, 7, for instance, we find Aristotle's primary argument for the role of nature in ethics. This passage served as a springboard for medieval natural lawyers surpassing anything Aristotle himself seems to have managed. In that passage Aristotle argues that every species of animal has a "proper function," that is, a specific trait or ability that is its specific difference. Doing that function well constitutes virtue or excellence for beings of that nature. Reason is the function specifically characteristic of human beings, and reasoning well is the measure of virtue in general, as well as of justice for life in society. These remarks, and their development in his reflections on virtue in Book III of the *Ethics* and on specific virtues in subsequent books, thus have a basis in nature. In fact, Aristotle also argues for certain commonalities among the variety of political arrangements that human societies can devise. Yet he does not handle these matters primarily under the category of law. Why he does not do so is a matter for speculation, but it is possible that it is because in the very con-

---

21. So much of the work of Romanus Cessario, O.P., whom we honor in this volume, has been directed to elucidating the Thomistic understanding of moral virtue. It is a privilege to participate in this Festschrift as a way to acknowledge our common debt to his work and that of such confreres of his as Servais Pinckaers, O.P., to whose masterful *Sources of Christian Ethics*, trans. Sr. Mary Thomas Noble, O.P. (1983; Washington, D.C.: The Catholic University of America Press, 1995) Father Cessario contributed the preface and much guidance. We will consider this volume further below.

cept of law there is also an implication of will, that is, of someone's decision.[22]
Even though natures are intrinsic to physical objects, he understands these natures as eternal. They are not the result of any divine decision. With no divine author of natures in view, there is simply no reason to be thinking in terms of a divine legislator of morality. Indeed, morality for Aristotle has an entirely different ground, namely, the proper function of reason in practical matters of doing and making.

It is the Stoics who provided to the Middle Ages this crucial component of natural law ethics. Yet their view of natural law is very different from what medieval thinkers would produce. The basic Stoic notion is that all of the universe (all of nature) is permeated by a *logos* (reason) that gives the *nomos* (law) by which everything exists and acts. Rational beings (especially human beings and gods) have a special share in this *logos*, and human beings can become conscious of this *nomos* by right reasoning *(orthos logos)*. To live in accordance with this natural order is virtue. Not to do so is folly, for nature will invariably win out, and one will invariably suffer if one tries to go against nature. Thus, for the Stoics there is freedom of choice, but anything other than observing the natural law is ultimately futile. The Stoic picture thus includes a view of God as the mind of the universe, but it tends to be extremely fatalist. The range of free choice is curiously localized, for one has liberty only in regard to whether or not one will cooperate with the inexorable determinism of the forces of the universe. What sound practical reasoning can bring is a peace of mind that comes from indifference about whatever lies outside of one's control. Moral nobility comes from choosing to take a virtuous course by disciplined self-mastery over the centrifugal force of the baser passions.[23]

Christian authors found this Stoic fatalism unacceptable, both because it too severely restricts the scope of human freedom by not envisaging a way in which the decisions we make during our earthly lives have any bearing on our eternal destiny, and because it constricts the idea of God to the rationality within the universe and does not understand God as truly the one who intelligently designed a universe, brought that universe into being by a free choice, and providentially cares in a special way for the creatures made in his own image, whom he summons for eternal happiness with himself if they will use their intelligence and freedom for ordering their lives and conduct according to the plan that he has designed into their natures. Within the history of Christian thought

22. For this argumentation, see G. E. M. Anscombe, "Modern Moral Philosophy," *Philosophy* 33, no. 124 (1958): 1–19.

23. For a thoroughgoing account of Stoic ethics, see A. A. Long, *Stoic Studies* (New York: Cambridge University Press, 1996).

about God, the world, and morality there has from the very beginning been a readiness for a different approach to natural law thinking than what emerged in Stoicism. The new but indispensable element in the picture comes from certain non-negotiable religious commitments and, in particular, belief in a providential creator who orders creatures toward ends of divine design, as well as a tremendous emphasis on personal responsibility for one's deliberate actions.

Much of the technical terminology for subsequent formulations of natural law theory, however, comes from the Stoics through Cicero. Cicero is a skeptic rather than a Stoic, but he accurately transmitted to the Middle Ages some of the important contributions of the Stoics. There is a law of the universe, he tells us, a *lex aeterna et perpetua* (an eternal and perpetual law) that is the *summa ratio insita in natura* (highest reason built into nature). Human customs or decisions that contradict it may not legitimately claim the label "law" (a viewpoint that is the ultimate ground for the case that some natural lawyers offer when they are convinced of the need for civil resistance or even for the overthrow of a given political regime). What is more, every human being has the seed of the knowledge of this law (the *lumen naturae* or "light of nature"). As a result, there are insights of a moral character that we simply cannot fail to know. These things constitute *ius naturae* (what is "right by nature"), and thereby provide the source of knowledge about what it is right and just to do in the legal and political order. Cicero also provides the terms *ius gentium* ("law of the nations," later "international law") and *ius civile* ("civil law").

Another important stimulus for scholastic reflection on natural law ethics comes from the sphere of jurisprudence. The monk Gratian produced a massive work titled *Concordance of Discordant Canons*[24] in the 1140s in the effort to bring some coherence to the mass of church law that had accumulated by that time. Gratian's collection encouraged philosophical reflection both by its method of resolving difficulties and by some explicit and thematic consideration of questions about the nature of law and justice. Gratian's method involved the juxtaposition of conflicting legal positions, such as the canons issued by various ecclesiastical councils and various judicial opinions about the resolution of cases. He then attempted his own reconciliation of differences, often by the introduction of some decisive distinction. The influence of his method, not only on the legal education at Bologna but on philosophical and theological education at Paris and Oxford, is enormous. Richard Southern argues

24. *Decretum Gratiani emendatum et notationibus illustratum una cum glossis,* in English *Gratian: The Treatise on Laws (Decretum DD 1–20), with The Ordinary Gloss,* trans. Augustine Thompson and James Gordley (Washington, D.C.: The Catholic University of America Press, 1993).

that this highly formalized method is one important result of the pervasive medieval quest for a complete system of knowledge; it gives evidence of the reverent attitude to books and authorities typical of the entire period.[25] Scholastic explorations of natural law exhibit a similar pattern of analyzing such varied texts and authorities as the Bible, Church fathers, and Roman jurists.

As one particularly telling example, we might consider the reconciliation attempted between conflicting texts on the source of natural law from the tradition of Roman jurisprudence. As cited in the *Digests,* the jurist Ulpian held the view that natural law is what nature teaches all animals, including the human, in contrast to any form of human-made legislation. But other Roman jurists such as Gaius, apparently under Stoic influence,[26] treat natural law as virtually equivalent to the application of reason to human life. Aquinas suggests a resolution that affirms both positions by means of a careful distinction. There is, he argues, a natural law that is common to humanity and other animals. God, the author of all these natures, providentially directs each kind of creature to a useful course of conduct by implanting in every being an inclination toward what is good for beings of that kind. But human nature can be distinguished from every other form of animal nature precisely by the power of reason. Our human knowledge of the natural moral law, Aquinas insists, is a specifically human form of participation in the providence of God. Where other kinds of creature participate by instinctively responding to whatever appears to them as attractive or dangerous, human beings participate in it by subjecting whatever appears good or bad to the scrutiny of reason. Needless to say, the power of reason does not come fully formed in human children but needs to be trained. Thus our human participation in natural law is both like and unlike the way in which every other creature is governed by divine providence. Although the natural moral law governs all human beings, it is possible for a given human being to observe that law well or poorly, dependent not only on how well an individual is prepared to resolve questions requiring judgment and decision, but also on how well or poorly a culture prepares its members to do so.

The classic medieval source for the theory of natural law is the treatise on law within the *Summa theologiae* of Thomas Aquinas,[27] where Aquinas regards

25. Richard W. Southern, *Scholastic Humanism and the Unification of Europe,* esp. vol. 1, *Foundations* (Oxford: Blackwell, 1995), chs. 7–9, 235–318.

26. Marcia L. Colish, *The Stoic Tradition from Antiquity to the Early Middle Ages* (Leiden: E. J. Brill, 1985).

27. Aquinas's treatise on law is found in *Summa theologiae,* I-II, qq. 90–97, available in many good translations, including *St. Thomas Aquinas on Politics and Ethics,* ed. Paul Sigmund (New York: W. W. Norton, 1987), a volume that is replete with helpful introduction, commentary, and a plethora of appropriately chosen secondary literature.

natural law as our human participation by means of a providential use of human reason in God's providential care for the world in the form of eternal law. Aquinas argues at length for the general definition of law as an ordinance of reason, for the common good, promulgated by the one who has care of the community.[28] He then distinguishes eternal law (God's providential ordering of the whole universe) from natural law (our human participation in the eternal law by the right use of our reason in reflecting on our nature), from divine law (God's explicit declarations of law for the human community, such as the Decalogue or the Two Great Commandments of Christ) and from the various types of law established by human beings (including custom as well as constitutional law, administrative law, statute law, and jurisprudential precedent).

A careful reading of this treatise is absolutely fundamental for understanding the emergence of the natural law approach to ethics. Among the tasks facing a reader of this text, however, is the problem of understanding the place of Thomistic natural law theory within the larger context of Aquinas's moral theory. It is not a free-standing theory of ethics, nor complete in itself. Most immediately, one should note the connection of this general treatise on law with the sections that follow on the Old Law and the New Law. Ignoring these treatises in one's articulation of the Thomistic picture is an easy way for distortions of his views to creep in. But we should also caution against any inclination to treat even this larger set of Thomistic remarks on law as independent of the whole of the *secunda pars*. In point of fact, the account of natural law within the treatise on law is but one portion of an integrated account of ethics in terms of beatitude as the ultimate goal of human life, the human powers of reason and free choice, the appetites and passions, the virtues (both the natural virtues of intellect and will and the theological or supernatural virtues), the gifts of the Holy Spirit, and grace. It goes without saying, of course, that the *secunda pars* itself has a context within the whole of the *Summa*.

As possible ways of coming to understand this complex synthesis for the purposes of appreciating Thomistic natural law theory, let me mention three books that are especially useful. *The Sources of Christian Ethics* by the late Servais Pinckaers († 2008), as noted above, is simply a masterful account of the whole of the Thomistic approach to ethics; Pinckaers provides a balanced sense of the place of natural law theory in relation to happiness, the virtues, the gifts, and grace. He recounts at length the way in which Augustine came to an integrated understanding of the non-negotiable components of Christian morality through reflection on the Sermon on the Mount and the indispensable

28. *ST* I-II, q. 90, a. 4.

role of divine grace in making possible what would otherwise be beyond the reach of human capacities. From the basis of what Augustine established about the contours of morality, Pinckaers then examines the specifically Thomistic contribution to the understanding of morality, as well as points the way to such contemporary contributions to the field as *Veritatis Splendor* of Pope John Paul II.[29]

From the point of view of moral philosophy, one can rarely do better than to turn to one of the older treatises on natural law that has recently been reprinted, Heinrich A. Rommen's 1936 classic *The Natural Law*.[30] As the original German title directly suggests, this volume discusses at length the recurrence of the natural law idea again and again in the course of history. Rommen produced this volume as part of his own dedication to the cause of Catholic social action in Germany during the final years of the Weimar Republic. He served as director of the Department of Social Action of the Volks-Verein and held numerous offices in a variety of educational, social, and economic organizations of German Catholics. He worked closely with such figures as Oswald von Nell-Breuning, S.J., and G. Gundlach, S.J., who were deeply involved in the use of natural law theory for Catholic social teaching, to which we will turn in the next portion of this essay.

Arrested by the Nazis, Rommen spent a month in confinement and then lived under police surveillance after his release. It was during this period that he composed and published the original German edition of this text as a kind of protest against the abuse of the natural law idea. In 1938 he was given permission to leave the country and eventually became a professor of political science at what was then the College of St. Thomas in St. Paul, Minnesota. In 1945 he published an equally important volume, *The State in Catholic Thought*, but thus far it has not been republished.[31] In the first half of *Natural Law*, Rommen recounts the history of natural law reasoning, and it is particularly im-

29. Fr. Pinckaers's successor at Fribourg is Fr. Michael Sherwin, O.P., who has translated an abridgment of Pinckaers's masterpiece under the title *Morality: The Catholic View* (South Bend, Ind.: St. Augustine's Press, 2003), as well as authored a wonderful volume in his own name, *By Knowledge and by Love: Charity and Knowledge in the Moral Theology of St. Thomas Aquinas* (Washington, D.C.: The Catholic University Press of America, 2005).

30. Heinrich A. Rommen, *Die ewige Wiederkehr des Naturrechts* (Leipzig: Verlag Jakob Hegner, 1936); the translation by Thomas R. Hanley, O.S.B., as *The Natural Law: A Study in Legal and Social History and Philosophy* (St. Louis and London: B. Herder, 1947) is actually a revised and enlarged edition of the original, in which the author added many new sections; this is now available as *Natural Law: A Study in Legal and Social History and Philosophy* (Indianapolis: Liberty Fund, 1998).

31. Heinrich A. Rommen, *The State in Catholic Thought: A Treatise in Political Philosophy* (St. Louis: B. Herder, 1945).

portant to consider his argument that Hugo Grotius is a turning point in this history; with Grotius, the link between God and the natural law began to be detached, largely for pragmatic reasons. When Grotius argued that even if we were to grant that there is no God or that God is not concerned with human affairs (*etiamsi daremus . . . non esse Deum, aut non curari ab eo negotia humana*), he did so largely in the hope of retaining the objectivity and universality of moral obligation in confessionally divided Europe by his appeal to nature as a ground for ethics. As Rommen argues through his reading of the historical record, here began the philosophical movement toward regarding reason, and not nature, as the source of moral normativity that peaked in Kant.[32]

The second portion of Rommen's tome is invaluable for making the needed connections among ethics, anthropology, metaphysics, and revelation. One might put the point in a general way before making the specific application to natural law theory. Any philosophical approach to ethics will depend in significant ways on how one understands the nature of human existence, and this in turn depends on one's metaphysical commitments, which are in turn dependent on one's stance in regard to divinity. Just as a utilitarian approach to ethics depends on seeing human nature in terms of pleasure-seeking and pain-avoiding animals whose rationality is ultimately instrumental rather than contemplative, a part of an uncreated material universe, so too, by comparison, Kantian deontology is an ethics geared to protect and enhance the autonomy of beings whose most characteristic trait is reason, especially practical reason within a system of thought that is critical of what Kant called the pretensions of metaphysics to be knowledge and that regards faith in God as a postulate of practical reason. What Rommen does in these pages is to articulate the relations of traditional metaphysics and revelation, and progressively to show the implications of insights gained from these foundations for the vision of the human being as a hylomorphic composite unity of matter and form, of body and soul, and the necessity of an ethics along the lines of natural law and virtue if one is to provide due respect for the biological and psychic features of a creature that unites the material and spiritual orders as a creature brought into existence directly by God.

A similarly synthetic but briefer volume along these lines is Yves Simon's *The Tradition of Natural Law*.[33] Written with the freshness that marks all of Simon's books, the volume contains a brief history of natural law thinking (chap. 2) and a clear exposition of the Thomistic doctrine (chaps. 4–5); of spe-

32. See ibid., 71.
33. Yves R. Simon, *The Tradition of Natural Law*. See n. 16 above.

cial philosophical importance, though, are the sections that discuss the general problem of articulating a natural law theory (chap. 1) and certain theoretical questions about nature, universals, freedom, and obligation (chap. 3). Alert to Rommen's thesis on "the eternal return of the natural law idea," Simon focuses on the everlasting opposition to natural law that arises out of the contrast between the idea of actions that are right or wrong by nature and the divergence of moral opinions easily observable in the actual judgments that (presumably reasonable) people make, even on such fundamental issues as pre-natal human life. Simon argues for the inescapability of facing such questions as whether there is such a thing as a universal human nature, and the corresponding question of what we mean by "universal." He is also aware of the checkered history of the idea of natural law, which has been claimed by any number of individuals and causes, but which is sometimes better honored by those who do not claim the term yet respect its constituent ideas than by those who do claim the term and use it for racist or nationalist purposes.

Although this essay will forego a detailed discussion of what is generally called the New Natural Law tradition,[34] it is not for lack of respect for their contributions to ethics. It seems to me that there is a considerable difference between their generally intuitionist and deontological approach and the traditional natural law approach precisely on the question of the need for an explicit connection of ethical theory to metaphysics and anthropology.[35] While this school does claim the mantle of "natural law," its proponents generally tend

---

34. Among the many items that should also be included within a truly comprehensive list are the following: Germain Grisez, *Beyond the New Morality: The Responsibilities of Freedom* (Notre Dame, Ind.: University of Notre Dame, 1980); Germain Grisez, *The Way of the Lord Jesus*, 3 vols. (Chicago: Franciscan Herald Press, 1983); John M. Finnis, *Natural Law and Natural Rights*, rev. ed. (Oxford: Clarendon Press, 1982); John M. Finnis *Fundamentals of Ethics* (Oxford: Clarendon Press, 1983); A. Gomez-Lobo, *Morality and the Human Goods* (Washington, D.C.: Georgetown University Press, 2002); Robert P. George, ed., *Natural Law Theory: Contemporary Essays* (Oxford: Oxford University Press, 1992); Robert P. George, ed., *Natural Law and Moral Inquiry* (Washington, D.C.: Georgetown University Press, 1998); Robert P. George, *In Defense of Natural Law* (Oxford: Oxford University Press, 1999); H. Rhonheimer, *Natural Law and Practical Reason* (New York: Fordham, 2000); Mark C. Murphy, *Natural Law and Practical Rationality* (Cambridge: Cambridge University Press, 1991).

35. Among the critics of this position: Russell Hittinger, *A Critique of the New Natural Law Theory* (Notre Dame, Ind.: University of Notre Dame Press, 1987); Henry B. Veatch, *Swimming against the Current in Contemporary Philosophy: Occasional Essays and Papers* (Washington, D.C.: The Catholic University of America Press, 1990). Also valuable is Nigel Biggar and Rufus Black, eds., *The Revival of Natural Law: Philosophical, Theological, and Ethical Responses to the Finnis-Grisez School* (Aldershot: Ashgate, 2000), which offers a wide array of critics and responses. Of special importance within this volume is the essay by Ralph McInerny (pp. 53–72) on the liminal differences between Grisez and Aquinas in their respective understandings of the meaning of "good" and their accounts of the first principle of practical reason.

to argue that the necessary insights into the fundamental human goods and the basic modes of responsibility neither require nor allow us to enter into the discussions of metaphysics and anthropology that I have emphasized. A proper consideration of this issue would carry us beyond the bounds of this essay, but it is interesting to note that one of the most recent volumes by two of the standard-bearers of this school, *Body-Self Dualism in Contemporary Ethics and Politics* by Patrick Lee and Robert P. George, gives its entire first chapter to the presentation of the argument for the thesis that "human beings are animals" and its second to an argument that "human beings are persons" as preparation for its treatment in chapters three through six of the problems of hedonist drug taking, abortion, euthanasia, and sexuality. Unlike many of the publications in the New Natural Law tradition, this explicit recourse to anthropology and to metaphysics is a heartening sign of a possible return to a more traditional natural law approach.[36]

Before turning to the promised remarks on the ecclesial initiative that played such an important role in the modern revival of natural law thinking, I would like to mention two recent books of particular importance for the understanding of natural law theory in its traditional sense, *The First Grace* by Russell Hittinger and *Real Ethics* by John Rist.[37] In their own ways both make the case for the importance of connecting natural law reasoning with revelation, metaphysics, and anthropology. Before contending with a number of controversial issues from a natural law perspective, Hittinger explains and defends the irreducibly triple focus of natural law morality (theological, anthropological, and epistemological). One must attend not only to the role of *nature* (biological, psychological, and spiritual) and of natural inclination in the effort of *reason* to formulate moral precepts and to discern well-ordered from wayward inclinations, but also one must never forget the *theological* pole

---

36. Patrick Lee and Robert P. George, *Body-Self Dualism in Contemporary Ethics and Politics* (Cambridge: Cambridge University Press, 2008). See, for example, pp. 90–94 for an argument that the basic goods are not arbitrarily selected but are basic aspects of human well-being and fulfillment—not just what we happen to desire (different for different people), but really fulfilling or perfecting of us as human persons: "These fundamental goods are the actualization of our basic potentialities, the conditions to which we are naturally oriented and which objectively fulfill us, the various aspects of our fulfillment as human persons." The argument here is increasingly dependent on precisely those features that have been stressed in the traditional natural law argumentation: teleology, inclination, perfection of human potentiality, and so on. The New Natural Law tradition has usually tried to avoid consideration of these features as excessively metaphysical and anthropological in its efforts to generate a natural law ethics solely on the basis of intuitions about the basic goods as simply self-evident.

37. Russell Hittinger, *The First Grace: Rediscovering the Natural Law in a Post-Christian World* (Wilmington, Del.: ISI Books, 2003); John M. Rist, *Real Ethics: Reconsidering the Foundations of Morality* (New York: Cambridge University Press, 2002).

if one is to understand the source of moral *obligation.* Mindful of the recourse of recent popes to such scriptural texts as Genesis, the Gospels, and the letters of Paul when employing the argument patterns of natural law for purposes of making their case in the public forum, as well as instructing the faithful in their charge, Hittinger notes the distortions that are introduced into natural law reasoning when one tries to operate without all three of these sources together. Hittinger's account also includes some prudent cautions against the excessive use of natural law reasoning to try to resolve questions that are near or beyond its limits. He notes, for instance, the modern propensity to undermine the very idea of limited government by the variety of rights-claims and the tendency of contemporary jurisprudence to exalt a certain notion of privacy to sovereign status. His book's subtitle—*Rediscovering the Natural Law in a Post-Christian World*—issues a reminder about the need for understanding aright the relation of human nature and society to God if one is going to be able to make good sense of intramundane moral claims.

Rist's volume is not so much about natural law theory directly as about Platonic ethics, but it makes a related point about the need of any ethics worthy of the name for some sort of moral realism (like Platonism in a broad sense, Augustinianism, and Thomistic natural law theory), with the metaphysical commitments that this realism requires in order to have a transcendent ground. The rejection of moral realism, he shows, would require the embrace of deception in our moral and political life. By moral realism Rist means that there are at least some moral obligations that are not reducible to considerations of prudence or self-interest. In a masterful survey of a wide variety of ethical approaches, he shows that those ethical theories that do not claim such a grounding in the transcendent either tacitly have such a grounding or else dissolve upon analysis into incoherence. Without such an ultimate ground, there will be no defense against the skeptical attacks of such anti-realists as Thrasymachus, Macchiavelli, and Nietzsche. The argument of the book is a rich defense of the point that we have been making above about the indispensable connections among reason, nature, and God for a sound ethical theory.

Natural Law and Catholic Social Teaching

In Thomism we find one of the longstanding proponents of natural law theory. What is not often appreciated is the connection between the revival of Thomism at the end of the nineteenth century and the revival of natural law theory. The call for a Thomistic revival issued by Pope Leo XIII's 1879 encyclical *Aeterni Patris* precipitated a renewal of scholastic thought that was broad-ranging. The twentieth century witnessed the emergence not just of neo-Thomism but of other neo-Scholastic movements such as neo-Scotism and neo-Augustinianism, as well as the return to patristic sources in *nouvelle théologie* and the general renaissance of medieval studies in such disciplines as history and literature.

But, interestingly, it was a particular ecclesial project of Leo XIII, the articulation of certain Christian principles for the social order, that needed the Thomistic revival. Mindful of the secularization of the social order that came with the industrial revolution and the civil unrest that unseated the *ancien régime*, the loss of the papal states and the end of Christendom as a juridical order, the rise of socialism and communism, and the threats to religion and morality for the vast masses of country people who became disconnected from their roots as they flooded the cities, Leo looked for a suitable basis on which to set forth a vision of the social order that would respect religion and human dignity. The series of papal social encyclicals that began in 1891 with his *Rerum Novarum* has retained natural law as that basis. There has been supplementation of the argument by personalism, as well as a constant illumination of the situation from revelation in each of the documents within that tradition. But pope after pope has retained an appreciation for Leo's basic insight that in natural law theory was to be found the philosophical basis for a program of argumentation that could be offered in the public square as a non-sectarian platform for discussion and insight about the social order that was consonant with the fundamental insights of revelation, but that did not beg the question about the truth of those insights and thus alienate those parties to the discussion that do not share them.

What makes traditional natural law thinking especially suitable for its recurrent employment in Catholic social thought is its strongly philosophical character. This philosophical character enables its proponents to be perceived as being a reasonable voice in the public sphere when addressing issues of the social order, rights and duties, justice and the state, and so on. One can see the usefulness of this approach in the series of papal social encyclicals that have been issued since *Rerum Novarum*. Among the major documents in this tradition one might list the pair of social encyclicals by Pope Pius XI on marriage *(Casti Connubii)* and on the social order *(Quadragesimo Anno)*; the pair on peace *(Pacem in Terris)* and on social order *(Mater et Magistra)* of Pope John XXIII; the pair on human development *(Populorum Progressio)* and on social order *(Octogesima Adveniens)* of Pope Paul VI, as well as his heroic *Humanae Vitae*; and the trio of Pope John Paul II: *Laborem exercens* on the dignity of work, *Sollicitudo rei socialis* on human development, and *Centesimus annus* on the social order, which ought to be read in conjunction with his reflections on love, marriage, and sexuality in his *Theology of the Body* and his encyclicals on fundamental moral theology *(Veritatis splendor)*, the life questions *(Evangelium vitae)*, and the relations of faith and reason *(Fides et Ratio)*.

In *Pacem in Terris*, to take but one example of the profound use of natural law within this tradition, John XXIII sets the stage by arguing that world peace depends entirely on observing the order that God has set for the world (§§ 1–5). The various human rights that he lists are not asserted in the relatively abstract fashion of the natural rights tradition, where they tend to be taken as primitive and self-evident, but are in each case seen as flowing from the duties that human beings have to God and to family, and somewhat more remotely, to the juridical orders in which they find themselves (§§ 11ff.).

Even the sometimes maligned *Gaudium et Spes* from the Second Vatican Council employs a profoundly traditional natural law form of reasoning as its basis. The elaborate anthropological and sociological analysis found in the first part of the document provides something like what any good natural law theorist would ideally want to present as the vision of human life, human nature, and human personhood that is indispensable for ethics. The document recurrently refers both to a theological anthropology and to a philosophical one in its effort to address those people of good will and open mind who may not be of the household of the Faith and thus may not share the same religious suppositions, but who can be counted upon to join the Council in reading "the signs of the times." These signs of the times include the vast number of changes (both deep-seated changes and those that are more superficial) in the social order, in public morals, in culture and attitudes, in religious practice, in technology and economic life, in communications and the media, and so on.

The adversary that the conciliar text is repeatedly addressing here is the position that human nature itself changes and has changed, and that for this reason that there can be no unchanging or objective morality and certainly no absolute or exceptionless moral norms. Historicity, in short, seems to imply the relativity of moral truth, and it is for precisely this reason that the Council apparently felt the need to address the many ways in which the world has been changing, so as to affirm, against the view that human nature has essentially changed, that this is not the case. Not only does the Council bring to bear the theological and revealed notion that Christ, "the perfect man, reveals to human persons what human nature can and should be"[38] but also that there is an abiding human nature of a dynamic, teleological sort—the very claim

---

38. See *Gaudium et Spes*, §§ 22, 29, 41, 45; see also *Lumen Gentium*, §§ 13, 40.

that scholastic natural law theory perennially made. Whatever their own commitments, readers of this document are called upon to reflect on the permanent moral demands of the natural law for how human beings ought to choose
their actions and how they ought to form and reform their societies so as to ensure the protection of human persons, their marriages and families, their social associations, and their rights. For the Council, the vast amount of change
that can be catalogued testifies not to a change in human nature but to certain
changes in how we understand the abiding needs of human nature and especially to a deep awareness of the changing social challenges that need to be
met in order to respect human nature and human dignity.

There is considerable philosophical sophistication in the document's treatment of human nature. Not only does the document review and affirm the unity of matter and spirit, and body and soul, in each person, but it takes up the
gauntlet of inadequate anthropologies by criticizing materialist reductions of
the human person and the perversity of anthropological dualists (those who
would try to distinguish between human *being* and human *personhood*).[39] At
several points (for example, §§ 13, 16, 37–39) *Gaudium et Spes* also takes up the
disputed question of human freedom—the nature and proper description of
freedom, genuine and faulty notions of autonomy, and the legitimate and proper goals of free choice. In this respect it seems to anticipate some of the great
themes of the second chapter of John Paul II's *Veritatis Splendor*. In this section also we find the Council Fathers affirming the intrinsically social character of human nature, a point that is absolutely crucial to the tradition of Catholic social thought, for the human person "achieves integral fulfilment only in
the family, social life, and the political community."[40] And these insights in
turn justify the conclusion that society is not, as it tends to be for many political theorists, only a necessary evil or some artificial construct by virtue of a
social contract.[41] There are also important sections devoted to the differences
between male and female and their indispensable complementarity—points
that become crucial for the normative comments in the second part about the
morality of marriage, family, and society.

In a very direct appropriation of Thomistic natural law theory, the Council has an important section on conscience in general and on the need for human beings to follow certain fundamental moral principles of divine origin
that come to be known through conscience.[42] Not only does *Gaudium et Spes*

---

39. See *Gaudium et Spes*, § 25.   40. See ibid., § 29.
41. See ibid., § 25, and also § 75, which takes note of the fact that political community and
public authority are "founded on human nature."
42. See esp. ibid., § 16.

teach that "the more a correct conscience prevails, the more do persons and groups turn aside from blind choice and try to be guided by objective standards of moral conduct," but it also makes considerable use of this notion in its later discussion of sexual ethics and marriage in § 51, where it states that decisions about sexual activity and the regulation of the number and spacing of births depends not just on "a sincere intention and consideration of motives" but also on "objective criteria" that in turn need to be based on the "nature of the human person and his acts," as well as on the eternal life that each human person is called to share.[43]

Likewise, within the chapter on human community, the Council employs any number of other concepts and theses that are typical and distinctive of the natural law tradition, including the correlation of duties and rights, inviolable human dignity, shared humanity, and the demands of the common good.[44] Similarly, the third chapter of the second part on socioeconomic life is deeply in harmony with the previous tradition of Catholic social teaching, not only in its general claim that the inviolable dignity of the human person must be honored in the economic realm,[45] but also in its rather technical analyses of topics like productivity, labor, property ownership, and distributive justice. There is, for instance, a vigorous case made that theories that obstruct economic and social reform in the name of a false liberty and a view of *laissez faire* economics, as if moral principles were irrelevant, should be treated as erroneous, as should theories that subordinate the basic needs of individuals to the collective organization of production. There is a healthy respect for the economic laws of the market and for the technical intricacies of efficient decision-making processes in local, national, and world economies, but as is very typical of Catholic social teaching, the document repeatedly insists that there are moral norms that need to be respected and that may never be violated. On the topic of property and private ownership, for instance, there is considerable attention given (very much in the natural law tradition of moral argumentation) to the very purpose of private property (namely, to provide individuals with a kind of independence that enhances their ability to do their duties to their dependents and that extends their freedom). Correlated with the defense of private property is a sense of the social demands on private property that come from the common good and the communal purpose of all earthly goods.[46]

---

43. The Latin text of § 51 reads: "objectiva criteria ex personae eiusdemque actuum natura desumpta."

44. See ibid., §§ 24–31.   45. See ibid., § 63.

46. See ibid., §§ 70–71.

Overview

From this brief survey of publications in the area of natural law, offered in the spirit of a guide to assist those who would read in this area of thought on ethics, we can see a number of points that are of recurrent importance for this tradition and indispensable for its proper understanding. Let us summarize these points under three headings.

1. Traditional natural law thinking needs to be both theological and philosophical in character. Without sufficient attention to God, the project is sure to be distorted. It will lack attention to the ultimate *raison d'être* for human existence (union with God); it will lack a sufficient explanation for the order of things that have natures, as well as their intrinsic ordering by way of inclination; and it will lack the indispensable warrant for the obligations of natural law as law. Without sufficient attention to philosophical questions about human nature, the project is likely to be twisted beyond recognition into the creation of an ethics by human reason.

2. Rigorous thinking about natural law needs to have both an historical grounding and an appreciation of contemporary controversies. Without the proper formation in the history of philosophical and theological thought, one is likely to become lost or to go over ground that has already been charted. But considered more deeply, entering into the history of philosophy and theology in a reverent spirit of humility and docility is often the most profound way of engaging these disciplines. Truly to understand both Antigone and Creon as trying to do the right thing is to engage in the quest to grasp the relation of moral obligation and law. Truly to understand the Thomistic appropriation of Aristotelian natural philosophy and the unification of the category of nature with the category of creature is to engage in the pursuit of wisdom about the divine and the human poles of natural law theory. It goes without saying that these insights need to be brought to bear on current moral problems, and that those who wish to use the resources of ancient and medieval thought need to understand the nature of contemporary objections, questions, and insights in the ongoing effort to advance the field.

3. What is at issue in natural law theory is not the name but the thing. Some thinkers who never use the term are closer to the project than some who do. What a thorough-going program of reading in this area needs to have at hand is a resilient appreciation for the constituent parts of natural law ethics, in particular: a concept of nature adequately considered, an appreciation for teleology and for reason, a profound sense of law and the nature of moral obligation, and a sense of the relation of human conduct to God.

11

Natural Law, the Moral Object, and *Humanae Vitae*

STEVEN A. LONG

The purpose of this essay is threefold: first, to speak about St. Thomas's account of natural teleology and passive participation in relation to the natural moral law; second, to sum up Thomas's account of the teleological relation of the object and end of the moral act, and to address five strategic objections to this account; and third, to show how error regarding teleology can falsify our understanding of the object of the moral act and of the nature of the *malum* of contraception. This final point will advert to the recent controversy between Fr. Martin Rhonheimer and Janet Smith in the pages of the *National Catholic Bioethics Quarterly*.[1] I shall be making only the essential argument, leaving out a very great deal that is pertinent. Nonetheless, I hope that the exigency of the subject—enhanced by our recollection of the central affirmation of Thomas's

---

1. This entire essay was written prior to my exchange with Fr. Rhonheimer in the *National Catholic Bioethics Quarterly* (our letters crossing in the Colloquy section from Spring 2009 to Summer 2009), catalyzed by my essay published there in Winter 2008, "The False Theory Undergirding Condomitic Exceptionalism: A Response to William F. Murphy Jr. and Rev. Martin Rhonheimer." It was also written before it became fully clear to me that Fr. Rhonheimer no longer wishes to defend the argument that he initiated in *The Tablet* (U.K.), July 10, 2004, available online at http://www.thetablet.co.uk/articles/2284/. For that reason, and also because his argument in *The Tablet* does not adequately represent the breadth of his thought or his contributions to the appreciation of the thought of Aquinas, the argument I pose here with respect to his comments should be taken to regard the state solely of that argument as such, but not his entire account of the natural law. Of course, the exchange with Prof. Janet Smith occurs in the *National Catholic Bioethics Quarterly*, Autumn 2007, Colloquy, 403.

classical formulation of natural law doctrine in *Veritatis splendor,* and its eleven citations to the theological and philosophic elements of his teaching—as also the strategic character of the points articulated, may excuse the effort to tackle so weighty a subject in so brief a compass.

To this end this essay is divided into five sections: (1) concerning passive participation and teleology; (2) concerning the object of the moral act; (3) responding to five critical objections to the foregoing account of the object of the moral act (and here allow me to indicate that the response to the second objection, "B," is particularly of architectonic importance); (4) providing for the convenience of the reader a reprise of central points concerning the object of the moral act; and finally, (5) concerning contraception, *finis operis,* and Fr. Martin Rhonheimer.

I. Passive Participation and Teleology

In question 91, article 2 of the *prima secundae* of his *Summa theologiae,* St. Thomas Aquinas famously distinguishes the active and rational participation of the eternal law from merely passive participation, and insists that the first is properly law, while the second is merely law by participation and similitude. This has led some scholars to think that the passive participation of the eternal law is not genuinely important for his doctrine of natural law. Nothing could be further from the truth. The reason is that man's active, rational participation is necessarily founded upon the prior passive participation of the eternal law. Today, perhaps the most misunderstood aspect of the natural law is the truth that the rational and active participation of the eternal law which constitutes natural law, is nonetheless founded upon and presupposes passive participation and natural teleological order. This passive participation is now constantly scorned as merely physical and somehow contrary to the truly personal good. Yet the very existence of persons is itself a function of passive participation of eternal law, because persons do not create themselves.

What is passive participation? Passive participation is the sort of participation that every created being has simply by existing and by having a nature that is ordered toward certain ends. This sort of participation is not in and of itself natural law, but is only "law-like." The universe behaves as though it were subject to law, because there is written into it by God a certain order. Nonetheless, this order merely as it exists in subrational beings is not legal order because it is not received by a mind. For Aquinas, law in the strict sense is addressed to the mind of the recipient from the mind of the legislator, and anything less than this is not genuinely legal order, but only a similitude or likeness of legal order.

Yet it is of decisive importance that *all* legal order is founded upon the teleological structuring of our prior passive participation in the eternal law. We passively receive our being and nature—a nature that includes reason. Likewise passively received is the teleological ordering of human nature toward the ends that define it: for we define human nature in terms of its powers; we define these powers by their acts; and we define these acts by their objects and ends. Thus the ends of human living are definitory of human action. Human reason receives this ordering from without.

We do not make ourselves to be beings who need food and water to avoid death, or who need friends to avoid loneliness and alienation; we do not make ourselves to be beings who need knowledge and wisdom to avoid ignorance, confusion, and futility. We simply *are* such beings. This is all part of what Thomas identifies as passive participation of the eternal law. This ordering of our nature to ends is not chosen but is simply received by nature.

Yet because we possess reason as part of this passive participation, we are able to receive the entire ordering of human nature not merely passively—as do non-rational beings—but rationally and actively: as giving us divinely impressed reasons to do or not to do. These reasons to do or not to do flow from the teleology of human nature and are called *precepts*. It is this rational, preceptive participation in the eternal law—flowing from the passive participation, with its teleological structure—that is known as *natural law*. It is for this reason that St. Thomas always emphasizes, as for example in queston 91, article 2, that human reason is a "measured measure." In question 91, article 3, St. Thomas answers the following objection:

Further, a law bears the character of a measure, as stated above. But human reason is not a measure of things, but vice versa, as stated in Metaph. x, text. 5. Therefore no law can emanate from human reason.

His response to this objection is revealing. He writes:

Human reason is not, of itself, the rule of things: but the principles impressed on it by nature, are general rules and measures of all things relating to human conduct, whereof the natural reason is the rule and measure, although it is not the measure of things that are from nature.

In short: in order for reason to be the rule and measure of our action it must first be measured by "the principles impressed on it by nature" that "are general rules and measures of all things relating to human conduct." Although natural reason is "the rule and measure" of human conduct, "it is not the measure of things that are from nature" but rather is measured by natural realities. Only a reason that is measured by natural order is fit to be the measure for right action, because reason is perfected by truth, by the conformity to what is. The most significant datum for moral reason is its conformity to natural teleology and the essential hierarchy of ends.

Difficult moral questions implicate our knowledge of natural teleology. While we all share the same natural ordering that makes the evidence accessible, wisdom with respect to this evidence is not equally distributed. Knowing the right order of ends requires us to know the relation of subordinate ends to the final end, and this knowledge is only partially and incoherently achievable apart from knowledge of the existence and providence of God.

One cannot even define efficient causality—the kind of causality that produces or moves something—without referring to what the efficient cause is naturally ordered toward as an end. Thus, even when we try to define something as simple as "snow-shoveling" we must refer to the end, which is shoveling away the snow. No matter how complicated the efficient causality in play may be, it can neither be, nor be defined, without reference to finality: without reference to that for the sake of which it exists or acts.

As St. Thomas notes (SCG III, c. 2.), if there were no final cause, no *telos* or natural end, then efficient causing would be either uninitiable or unceasing. Either efficient causing could never begin, because there would be no reason for it; or else it would be naturally unending because lacking any point of natural termination and fulfillment. Yet both of these are contrary to fact. Actions are ordered toward ends which define these actions, and without which action would be impossible. Insofar as it is true that even the definition of efficient cause requires reference to teleology, it is likewise true that the affirmation of efficient causality implies the affirmation of teleology. But virtually everyone admits that efficient causes are operative in the world. Further, virtually everyone admits the reality of moral agency or efficiency. Logically speaking, the same persons ought to admit that natural teleology is likewise operative in the world, inclusive of the moral world. Of course, the end is not only essential to the being of agency, and to the knowledge of agency, but it represents the fulfillment and achievement of agency.

It is occasionally still argued that natural teleological order is irrelevant because one can't get "values" from "facts." However, the existence of "fact" as other than an abstraction from an already ordered nature is exactly what is at stake. It is either true or not true that nature is ordered to certain ends in relation to which the proper functioning of the nature is defined. Thus we say that an orchid is growing properly when such and such occurs; or that a child who cannot speak and who barks like a dog at the age of 15 is not developing properly;

or that one who needlessly alienates those with whom he lives is unreasonable; or that love of God and neighbor are ends of the moral law. Nature or "fact" is "value-laden" from the start. "Value" is an index of the relation of an act to the hierarchy of ends defining a good life, as likewise it is an index of our relation to the dispositions of character we require for a good life. In short, the only way to get something for consideration that isn't subject to teleology—something that isn't ordered toward an end defining it—is by abstracting from nature. A mere neutral "fact" that is ordered to no end is something that exists only in a mind, for in nature there is nothing remotely like it. After all, even quantity as it exists in the natural world is a function of beings and actions that are ordered toward ends. Subtract every being and relation to being, and every action and relation to action, and there is nothing even merely conceptual to be quantified.

One grants that an "ought" isn't merely any kind of "is" whatsoever. We cannot reasonably say that because cannibals like to eat visiting tourists for lunch that they *ought* to do so. The normative end of the good life isn't to be equated with merely anything that anyone may desire. As Aristotle taught more than two millennia ago in the *Nicomachean Ethics,* there is a distinction between the normative object and the factual object of *wish.* And the normative object of wish is a function of the teleological structuring of the human person.

St. Thomas teaches that "good" is *being* considered only with the addition of a conceptual relation to appetite. The objects of speculative and practical life interpenetrate, such that implicit within every practical ordering of the will is a prior *speculum,* a prior knowledge of reality which ignites inclinational motion. We do not seek the absence of being but the fullness of being. The "is" pertains to the "ought" because *good is being taken together with a conceptual relation of being to appetite as perfective of appetite.*

Thus the normative hierarchy of ends defines the good life as an ordered whole, a moral cosmos. For this reason, certain types of actions are simply incompatible with the structuring of a good life—they are *mala in se,* evils in themselves—and one can no more achieve a good life through such actions than one can melt water by freezing it or improve health by committing suicide.

II. The Object of the Moral Act

Here we come to the object of the moral act. It is precisely because certain acts cannot be ordered to the due end that they are generically evil, *mala in se.* No matter what the further purpose of an agent—the *finis operantis*—may be, the act chosen by the agent must be such as to be generically good in itself and its *per se* end (the *finis operis*). Acts that are generically incompatible with the normative teleology of the good life are not transubstantiated by the further purposes of the agent, for goodness is from integral causes. This, also, is why the integral nature of the act is always materially included within the object of the moral act. The unitary form or essence of the whole act, known as the object of the act, *never* excludes the external act and its natural teleology. This is why the object is the "moral essence," so to speak, of the act as a whole, and also why it is predicable of the external act—as it is predicable when we say what an act *is* objectively speaking. When the object of the moral act is likened to form,[2] it is being likened to the essential form of the whole and not merely to the form as a part (the essential nature gives species through the form, but it is more than the form).

The object of the moral act as such—the essential nature of the whole of the moral act—is, as Thomas puts it, *what the act is about relative to reason*.[3] There are two elements. There is the relation to reason, which signifies the ordering of the act known to reason that makes the act desirable to the agent in terms of what makes it a suitable means to the end sought.[4] This is the most formal element of the object. But just as the essence of a physical thing includes the common matter of the definition, so the object contains more than its most formal element: "what the act is about in relation to reason" cannot exclude the act itself and its teleology or *per se* effects. And if the act is not good of itself, it does not matter what the further intentions of the agent may be.

The act isn't reducible merely to what makes it an attractive object of choice to the agent; rather, it includes the *per se* order of the act chosen. One cannot, for example, justify killing in order to achieve the attractive aim of "ending the pain" of a suffering patient, because killing essentially not only ends pain but also by nature ends life, so that to choose it in such a case is necessarily to choose wrongful homicide. Essentially homicidal acts are only *per accidens* ordered to pain relief, but they are *per se* related to ending life.

2. *ST* I-II, q. 18, a. 2, ad 2: "The object is not the matter '*of which*' (a thing is made), but the matter '*about which*' (something is done); and stands in relation to the act as its form, as it were, through giving it its species." (Translations in this essay are those of the author or are taken from the English Dominican translation but generally tweaked in some way to reflect his preference.)

3. *ST* I-II, q. 18, a. 2, resp.: "And just as a natural thing has its species from its form, so an action has its species from its object, as movement from its term. And therefore just as the primary goodness of a natural thing is derived from its form, which gives it its species, so the primary goodness of a moral action is derived from its suitable object." See also *ST* I-II, q. 18, a. 10, resp.: "the species of moral actions are constituted by forms as conceived by the reason."

4. Cf. *ST* I-II, q. 18, a. 4, ad 2.

In the *Summa theologiae,* question 18, article 7, St. Thomas articulates a doctrine about *per se* and *per accidens* order between object and end of the moral act. This teaching is so important that I am now inclined to argue that not to understand it is to fail to understand his moral doctrine. To be clear about these terms "per se" and "per accidens" before exploring Thomas's teaching: when an object of itself naturally tends to an end, or when the end by its nature is such that it cannot be attained without a certain object, then the object is said to be *per se* or essentially ordered to the end.[5] But when the object does not essentially of itself tend toward the end, or alternately when the end is not of such a nature as always to require such an object, then the order between object and end is said to be *per accidens,* or accidental.

In question 18, article 7, St. Thomas teaches that when the object of the act is *per se* or essentially ordered to the end, the most containing, universal, and defining moral species is derived from the end.[6] For example, in opening the chest to do heart surgery, the end of repairing the heart is such as by nature to require the opening of the chest cavity, and so there is one unitary act whose moral species is medical, and not two acts, one of which is bodily mutilation

5. By "naturally" here, we advert not directly to the natural hierarchy of ends—which is natural in the strongest sense—but to the "natural" proportion of the action chosen by the agent to the end sought by the agent, even where that which the agent seeks is vicious. Thus, adultery involves certain actions that are *per se* proportioned to it. This is a teleology pertaining to the relation between objects and ends of actions, wherein the end either cannot be reached save through a certain object, or the object tends of itself toward the end. Thus, the adulterer who sets his sights on a good of pleasure apart from the rule of reason may pursue it remotely through first stealing to obtain money to aid in the pursuit of adultery, and here the relation is *per accidens.* But there are acts whose proximate end is adultery, and here the relation is "per se." Where there is *per se* order, the defining species is from the end; where it is *per accidens,* there is in truth a *distinct act* that is being accidentally further ordered by the agent. There is nothing about stealing that of its nature tends toward adultery, as there is nothing about the nature of adultery that requires theft, so the order of theft to adultery is *per accidens.* Without consulting this teleology of acts, we cannot place particular actions in their moral species.

6. *ST* I-II, q. 18, a. 7, ad 3. Speaking of the *per se* order of object to end, and of the respect in which the species derived from the end is like a genus containing the species derived from the object, Thomas makes it clear that in *this* case the sense of genus is "genus of formal cause": "Difference is compared to genus as form to matter, inasmuch as it actualizes the genus. On the other hand, the genus is considered as more formal than the species, inasmuch as it is something more absolute and less contracted. Wherefore also the parts of a definition are reduced to the genus of formal cause, as is stated in Phys. ii, 3. And in this sense the genus is the formal cause of the species; and so much the more formal, as it is more universal." (Text derived from the *Corpus Thomisticum, S. Thomae de Aquino opera omnia,* made available online by the University of Navarre www.unav.es/filosofia/alarcon/amicis/ctopera.html#OM: "Ad tertium dicendum quod differentia comparatur ad genus ut forma ad materiam, inquantum facit esse genus in actu. Sed etiam genus consideratur ut formalius specie, secundum quod est absolutius, et minus contractum. Unde et partes definitionis reducuntur ad genus causae formalis, ut dicitur in libro Physic. Et secundum hoc, genus est causa formalis speciei, et tanto erit formalius, quanto communius.")

and the other a medical act. Likewise, concentrated study tends of itself toward learning and so is an educational act. In these cases the most defining, containing, universal moral species is derived from the end.

However, when the object is not *per se* but only *per accidens* or accidentally ordained to the end, then the object is in reality a separate act with its own moral species. In this complex case we are viewing two acts not essentially ordered to one another as one act because the agent orders one to the other. While the one act is ordered by the agent to another, it nonetheless is not of itself essentially ordered to it. Thus one who steals in order to commit adultery is said to perform two evils, the first an act of theft, and the second an act of adultery. Theft is not of itself ordered to adultery, nor is adultery such that it can only be achieved through theft, and so any ordaining of theft to adultery is accidental. But because an agent may order one to the other, we can step back and view the two acts as parts of something that we can consider as a complex act. Since the theft is undertaken by the agent for the sake of adultery. Thomas argues that the agent is more adulterer than thief: but the agent is both. And notice that even if the remote end had been something good—say, to pay for a college education—the theft would remain a *malum*, an evil. In the complex act, one act is *per accidens* ordained by the agent to another act. By contrast are those acts in which the object is *per se* ordained to the end. All simple acts—theft, adultery, prayer, almsgiving, etc.—are acts in which the object of the external act is *per se* ordained to the end. All other acts, both in their being and their intelligibility, presuppose the most fundamental unit of the human action, the simple *per se* act, without the understanding of which we literally will not and cannot know *what we are doing*. What is most crucial here is perceiving that the simple, ordinary, and most universal instance of the human act is the case in which the object of the external act is *per se* ordained to the proximate end. Only a complex act *can* be such that the object is only accidentally ordered toward the end.

III. Three Objections

A. Objection based on misreading of the first example of question 18, article 7

Since in order to be an act, there must be an end, it is impossible for an external act to have only a remote end and no proximate end. This is important because St. Thomas, at the very beginning of I-II, question 18, article 7, offers two illustrations. The first is "fighting for victory," while the second is "theft for the sake of adultery." The first is clearly a simple and a *per se* ordering. The second is a complex act wherein one act is *per accidens* ordained to another. But some may wish to read the first example of St. Thomas as complex while yet also exhibiting a *per se* order between object and end. Although this is not of ultimate import for the pivotal truth that every simple act exhibits *per se* order betwixt object of the external act and end, and for the consequent truth that all other human acts depend in their being and their intelligibility upon this prior *per se* order of object and end, still it seems to be in disaccord with the text. For the text seems to wish to contrast the *per se* order of object and end in the simple case of action, with *per accidens* order. As Thomas puts it:

The object of the external act can stand in a twofold relation to the end of the will: first, as being of itself ordained thereto; thus to fight well is of itself ordained to victory; secondly, as being ordained thereto accidentally; thus to take what belongs to another is ordained accidentally to the giving of alms.[7]

Now, how can the object of the external act be "of itself ordained" merely to a remote end? It must first be ordained to a proximate end, or else we do not even have so much as a human act. Thus the very idea is nonsensical. In the case of complex, *per accidens* order, there is an act and object ordained to theft; and this whole act of theft is further ordained by the agent to adultery, to which it has no essential ordering but to which it is ordered *per accidens* by the agent. One act with its own object, end, and distinctive moral species is thus further ordained to another such act with its own object, end, and distinctive moral species. Because the latter is more sought by the agent than the former, we say that in this case the agent is more adulterer than thief: but he is both.

Whereas by contrast, in the first illustration of Thomas, he says that "to fight well is of itself ordained to victory." Victory is not an act, but an end.[8] If this is to be a complex act, we need two acts and not merely one. *Ergo*, it is not a complex act. Likewise, "fighting well" is, simply by itself, underdetermined as a moral act. Minus a proportion to a proximate end, it is a physical species,[9] and though this is included in the moral object materially, the moral object

7. *ST* I-II, q. 18, a. 7, resp.

8. Of course, one might mean, not "victory" but "triumphing," but then this is a distinct act to which a different object would also need to be appended, such as "going to Rome with prisoners for the sake of proceeding in the Roman triumph." It is fairly clear that this is not what St. Thomas has in mind.

9. It might indeed be the case that "fighting well" could serve as an *end* vis-à-vis some external act; for example, "the centurion trained daily for the sake of fighting well in the upcoming battle." But simply taken by itself, "fighting well" does not describe the external object of an act because it does not indicate any relation of reason to the end. Indeed, it is only when the proximate end is understood to be victory that "fighting well" is intelligible as a moral object.

is not reducible to physical species. An underdetermined physical description—"fighting well"—and an allegedly remote rather than properly proximate end—"victory"—do not constitute a human act. Only if fighting for victory is understood as one act whose proximate end is "victory" do we have a human act.

Remote ends *are* remote only in relation to the proximate end. What makes "fighting well" underdetermined is that no relation of reason with respect to the end sought is indicated in mere "fighting well." But if there is no proximate end, there is no act, and so no remote end, since the remote end is merely a further end, beyond the proximate end. It is like saying, "the agent performs a non-act, and then further orders this non-act to a remote end." Or, perhaps better, "the agent throws lint into an easterly wind for the sake of the remote end of world peace." "Throwing lint into an easterly wind" is a conduct, but it does not describe a human act until its proportion to some proximate end is designated, and so it is impossible for it to have *only* a remote end, because until it has some proximate end there is no act susceptible of being further ordered to a remote end.[10] Only *an act*, which thus has *an end*, can be further ordained to a remote end. Of course, it is manifest that fighting well is *per se* ordained to victory as proximate end, but the claim here criticized is that in St. Thomas's illustration "fighting well" is ordained exclusively to a remote end, and that the act is complex.

To call an act complex suggests it is not unified but plurified in species, whereas the proposal to view fighting for victory as complex does not even give us so much as one human act if "victory" is a remote end. Only if victory is a proximate end do we have an act susceptible of further ordering.

Thus in the first example, St. Thomas is treating fighting for victory in a way similar to the way we might view "running fast for the sake of winning the race," wherein there is a *per se* relation between the speed of the runner in the race and victory. Thomas is thinking of the close-in fighting (as distinct, for instance, from the relation of one skirmish to the end of triumph in a war) in which the one who fights better, wins: a simple act wherein the object is *per se* ordained to the end. But a mere physical act, minus any relation of reason with respect to the proportion of the act to the end, and then conjoined with a remote end, is a Frankensteinian conception.

To repeat: to have a *remote* end absolutely implies having already a *proximate* end. Whereas, treating Thomas's first example as a case of the *per se* or-

10. Of course, it is possible that someone is daffy enough to believe that throwing lint into an easterly wind is *per se* ordained to world peace, in which case the *proximate end* sought would be "world peace" and the agent would simply be deluded about the nature of things.

daining of object to end while also and simultaneously somehow a complex act will require us to posit an act with only a remote but no proximate end; and this is impossible. It will also require us to treat a physical act apart from all relation of reason to the end as though it were a human act; but with no relation of reason to the proximate end, there is no human act. For these reasons alone St. Thomas's example of fighting for victory cannot be considered a complex act with *per se* ordering of object to remote end. Rather, it is a simple act whose object is *per se* ordered to its proximate end. Even if a physical description with no relation of reason and putatively ordered only to a remote end could be— which it cannot be—one act, there would not be two acts, and so it would not be complex but simple. *But every simple act has a proximate end, and it is impossible for a simple act to have only a remote end.*

It follows that those who read the response to question 18, article 7 as giving us two instances of complex acts misprize the nature of the first illustration. Because the simple act wherein object is *per se* ordained to end is strategically and fundamentally presupposed for the reality and understanding of all other act structures, St. Thomas in this illustration is contrasting the simple act with complex act structures in which one act is *per accidens* ordered to another. The first example is that of a *simple* act whose object is *per se* ordained to the end—"fighting for victory"—by comparison with a *complex* act whose species is not unified because its object is actually an act to itself, with its own distinct moral species, and which is *per accidens* ordained by the agent to another act more desired for its own sake by the agent (e.g., taking what belongs to another to give alms; or theft for the sake of adultery).

And what is the lesson of question 18, article 7, resp. about simple acts whose objects are *per se* ordained to the end and complex acts whose objects are *per accidens* ordained to the end? In the former case, the most containing, universal, defining, and determining moral species or type is derived from the end. Whereas, in the latter case, one act with its own object, end, and distinct moral species is *per accidens* further ordained to another act with its own object, end, and distinct moral species: e.g., taking what belongs to another to give alms. For to take what belongs to another is not *per se* ordained to almsgiving, nor does almsgiving by its very nature require taking what belongs to another.

If we wish to determine the moral species of an action, it follows that we must know whether the object is, or is not, *per se* ordained to the end: for if and only if the object is *per se* ordained to the end will the most defining, containing, determining species derive from the end. We see in the complex, *per accidens* case that the agent's ordering of one act to another does not suffice to affirm that the one is *per se* ordained to the other. Rather, there is *per se* order of object to end when the object *of itself* tends to the end, or when the end *by its nature* is such as to require a certain type of act. St. Thomas says that, in the case wherein object is *per se* ordained to the end, the species derived from the end is like the genus of formal cause to which all the notes of the definition are reduced: i.e., it is most determining and formal.[11] This is the heart of the matter.

B. A second strategic objection considered

Nonetheless, are there not complex acts whose objects are per se ordained to the end? That what could otherwise be a *per se* simple act may also be a component part of a larger act, such that it is potentially "part" of one interconnected sequence of actions, is a far different thing from one act and end being merely accidentally ordained to the other. Yet such a *per se* order is never characterized by disjunct and non-unified moral species, but rather enjoys a unity of form derivative from the *per se* natural ordering of the act to the end. That there may indeed be acts that might stand alone, but that in the given case do not do so, but are rather all naturally required by the nature of a given end, unifies these potentially distinct acts into one. The likeness of this with the way in which higher forms possess the powers of lower forms *in virtute* is exact, because St. Thomas's understanding of the object of the moral act is *hylemorphic*: the unity of form derivative from *per se* order to the end embraces a material manifold that under other circumstances might have been, but in fact is not, freestanding. The question is one of relation to reason: does one choose the object because of its proximate end *simpliciter* in relation to happiness, or does one choose the object because its proximate end is essentially required for, and so part of, the achievement of some further end? If the latter, then the object of the act is such that its relation to reason includes the *per se* relation of proximate end to remote end. In this case, the proximate end is saturated with the species derived from the remote end. Thus while sequences of *per se* act structures (wherein object is *per se* ordained to the end) may be materially rich and manifold, they are not complex acts because they enjoy a unity of form and of moral species that is not the case in *per accidens,* complex acts.

Put yet differently: cases of *per accidens* ordering of object to end are always formally complex and disjunct, because they are always characterized by naturally disjunct species. In *per se* sequences of act, by contrast, there is always the simplicity consequent upon unity of form through the moral species deriva-

---

11. *ST* I-II, q. 18, a. 7, ad 3.

tive from the end. And just as the operational definition of hydrogen pertains to the human form, which by its nature possesses the powers of hydrogen, so the species of those acts that might have been freestanding *per se* acts (e.g., to administer anesthesia) are contained within the species derived from the end that naturally requires such acts (as, for example, by its nature heart surgery requires anesthesia, opening of the chest cavity, repair of the heart, closing of the chest cavity, etc.). Here we see in particular that the *per se* effects of the act performed are always included within the object of the moral act.

In my book *The Teleological Grammar of the Moral Act*, I argue that when an act is necessary to a particular end, that *vis à vis* that end, that act is contained within the species derived from the end.[12] Thus there are not two merely accidentally ordered acts, one of bodily mutilation (opening the chest cavity) and the other of medical surgery (operating on the heart); nor for that matter three (provision of anesthesia, bodily mutilation, and medical repair); but morally speaking rather there is one medical act of heart surgery with its essential component parts. These component parts are specified by proximate ends, but proximate ends saturated in the species of the further end that requires them and to which they are *per se* ordained: anesthetizing is not opening the rib cage which is not directly operating on the heart, and all are part of heart surgery. *Pari passu* with the realization of each simple component, the individual who thereby seeks the end whose nature requires these acts moves closer to it, and the species derived from that remote end saturates these acts essentially ordained to it. Hence, opening the rib cage is not an act of mutilation, but it does have a "close-in" end of opening up the rib cage *for the sake* of heart surgery.

Note that the relation of reason that connects opening the rib cage to the end of heart surgery—the datum that the end of heart surgery is of such a nature as essentially to require this—gives the object "opening the rib cage for the purpose of heart surgery" its moral character. Without this character it would not be a human act, because it would lack relation to reason—indeed, "opening the rib cage" might be sought for a number of reasons, not all of them good (torture; murder; medical surgery). The same logic whereby in the materially simplest case the object is per se ordained to the end and the object is most formally defined by the moral species derived from the end, extends to

12. Steven Long, *The Teleological Grammar of the Moral Act* (Naples, Fla.: Sapientia Press, 2007), 84, under point 4: "When acts of themselves tend toward an end, they are said to be naturally or *per se* ordered to it; likewise when attainment of an end *by the very nature of the end* requires a certain action, that action is also said to be naturally or *per se* ordered to the end." (Hereinafter cited as *TGMA*.)

the case wherein the rationes of what otherwise might have been several simple acts are necessitated by, and so contained within the species of, a further end. Thus if the individual who intends several simple acts for the sake of some further end that essentially requires these acts considers each material component act, each such component includes the relation/proportion of reason to the further end. Hence what is chosen is, for example, an act of delivering anesthesia for the sake of heart surgery, an act of opening the rib cage for heart surgery, an act of operating on the heart for the sake of surgical repair of the heart. Just as it is by reason of being human that this part of the body has the operational definition of iron, and not by its being iron, so it is by reason of being part of a heart surgery that what might otherwise have been a freestanding act of anesthesia with its proximate end exists.

Thus it is clear there may be sequences of acts each of whose constitutents could under other circumstances be pursued for different reasons, yet where in fact the end is such by its nature as to require one act, and that act is such by its nature as to require another, and so forth, like Chinese boxes each contained within the other, with the most containing moral species being derived from the end. Such sequences are not *per accidens* and disjunct. The understanding that an end of its nature requires a certain act presupposes the understanding of the nature of that act in relation to the end: one must know the purpose of heart surgery and the nature of anesthesia to judge that the end of heart surgery requires anesthetizing the patient. As St. Thomas teaches, the upshot is that where the end is such by its nature as to require the object, the moral species derived from the object is contained in and most formally defined by the moral species derived from the end. The sequence aspect resolves into the most containing species derived from the end, and what is materially manifold (sequence, acts) is in the case of *per se* order formally unitary. Not three distinct moral acts—anesthesia, opening the chest cavity, and repair of the heart—but one, heart surgery, whose moral species is that of medical surgery to repair the heart as defining a material manifold of acts that *might* but yet *do not* exist outside of the order to the end of heart surgery. For example, anesthesia, or opening the chest cavity, could be done to different purpose, but in the case of heart surgery this is not the case.

What renders the "simple" case to be simple is its *per se* order, which permits the greatest material diversification within formal unity. The simple case is simple not with the simplicity of the material atom, but rather with the simplicity of formal unity derivative from *per se* order in respect of the end. This is quite different from *per accidens* complex acts, wherein neither does the object essentially tend toward the end nor does the end essentially require the object;

similarly, theft does not tend toward adultery, nor does adultery require theft. Such acts are truly and formally complex because not unified in moral species.

So these are the alternatives: *simplicity of formal unity* derivative from *per se* order in respect of the end with its unifying and containing moral species; or *complexity of formal disjunction and disunity* derivative from lack of *per se* order in respect of the end with consequently distinct moral species.

From this vantage point, there is morally speaking one act of performing heart surgery, each of whose component acts is *per se* ordained to its particular proximate end, while itself being essentially part of the *per se* effect sought (e.g., in the medical illustration, if anesthesia does not suppress the pain and perhaps the consciousness of the patient; if opening the rib cage does not reveal the heart; and if surgical repair does not correct the disorder in the heart or palliate its effects, then there can be no achievement of the more global purpose). And the proximate end is conceived precisely along the lines of the powers of lower forms possessed *in virtute* by higher forms: that is, the higher unity of heart surgery possesses of its nature what the lower discrete act of anesthesia possesses, but possesses it in a distinct way as essentially part of heart surgery. The integral nature and *per se* order of the act is always retained, but under the *ratio* of the relation to reason, which is that whereby the act is appetible to the agent: in this case, because the end sought by the agent of its nature requires an act whose proximate end is anesthesia.

That is to say, just as the intention to play a piece of music on the piano involves playing all the notes essentially required for the piece, each of which is essentially ordained to the whole, so intending one act that essentially requires other acts involves moving toward component ends that are ordained to the further end. But just as in the human body iron is not "freestanding" but is defined by the formality of the human body, while retaining all that is requisite for the operational definition of "iron," so what might have been but is not a freestanding act of "giving the patient anesthesia" retains its character but as saturated by the moral species derived from the end which is repair of the heart.

A simple act that could be sought independently must be known in relation to its proximate end if one is to be able to judge and identify its further relation/proportion to a further end whose nature is such to require it. Yet when such an act that could be sought independently is sought because the very nature of a further end requires it, then that act and its proximate end are saturated in the most formal species derived from the further end (indeed: the component act would not exist save for the intention of the end). But the proximate end is required, just as the integral nature and *per se* natural ordering of one's action is always materially included within the object of the moral act.

The essential element constituting the intelligibility and simplicity of human action is *per se* order; that is to say, either the object is such by nature that it tends toward the end, or the end is such by nature that it requires the object. This order in *per se* sequences of acts is materially more complex but nonetheless formally simple—for even in the case of a sequence of acts that might have been freestanding, but which are only chosen as essentially required for some further end actively intended by the agent, this material sequence enjoys the simplicity of the unity of form. Such sequences, in moral terms, form components of one act with material parts, and the proximate ends of these parts exist within the given act only owing to the order to the further end which essentially requires them and whose moral species most formally contains and defines them: e.g., heart surgery. Formal simplicity in action derives from *per se* order of object to end, for in this case, the species derived from the end is most formal, definitive, and containing.

Yet it is surely true that both to be, and to be known, all other act structures presuppose prior acquaintance with the case of stand-alone actions wherein object is *per se* ordered to end with no further *per se* ordering: for example, anesthesia *simply* for the sake of pain relief with no reference to any further surgical act, as opposed to anesthesia performed solely owing to the intention of the end of heart surgery. For the performance both of *per accidens,* formally complex acts and of materially more extensive sequences of *per se* action (action that incorporates act components that might have been but in fact are not performed as stand-alone *per se* acts) presupposes prior awareness of simple "stand-alone" *per se* acts. The formally complex case is made up of two or more such acts (e.g., the famed illustration of theft for the sake of adultery); and the materially richer sequences of *per se* acts involve a prior judgment of proportion between the ends of the component acts and that end which by its nature requires them and whose species contains their species.

Hence both in order *to be* and in order *to be known,* all other act structures depend upon these "stand-alone" *per se* acts. If one likes, these "stand-alone" *per se* acts are accurately described as materially and epistemically the simplest of *per se* act structures. Yet all *per se* act structures nonetheless enjoy a certain unity and so simplicity of form owing to the *per se* order toward the end and the containing of all subordinate species in the species derived from the end. Not only these simplest of *per se* acts structures, but also materially rich sequences of *per se* action, enjoy the simplicity of unitary form, in which the species derived from the end contain all lesser species (the integral nature and *per se* ordering to the end/effects of action are always included in the object of the act). But the components of such rich sequences are understood as potentially freestanding—as stand-alone *per se* acts—prior to being included in such sequences. And so, while simplicity is a function of *perseity*, the clearest case of *perseity* is not the materially rich *per se* sequence, but the case of act *per se* ordained toward end as sufficing to define action (e.g., deliberately taking possession of what is not one's own as defining theft; administering pain relief for no intended purpose beyond relieving pain; and so on). Nonetheless, despite this material and epistemic greater simplicity of the stand-alone *per se* act structure, it is important to keep in mind that *perseity* always brings along with it the simplicity of formal unity derivative from the unitary containing species derived from the end.

Thus we may amend the earlier proposition, and speak of three alternatives:

1. a stand-alone *per se* act, e.g., theft (just for money) or administering anesthesia (just to relieve pain);

2. a sequence of what could have been such stand-alone *per se* act structures but in fact are not because these act components are willed into existence only owing to the nature of an intended end that (a) naturally requires the act components (e.g., anesthesia and opening the chest cavity for the sake of heart surgery) in question, and (b) whose species contains the species derived from these components;

3. a *per accidens* ordering of two *per se* act structures, whether neither of its nature requires or tends toward the other.

The first two cases both exhibit *per se* order to the end, and so the most defining, containing species is derived from the end, vouchsafing such acts a simplicity and unity of form (and retaining the *per se* ordering of the act components within that more defining and containing species: the integral nature and *per se* ordering of the act is always materially included in the object of the act). The first case is materially and epistemically simplest. Hence, provided that one realizes that all *per se* act structures enjoy the unity and simplicity of form, it is not unreasonable to refer to this as, *simpliciter,* the "case of the simple, *per se* act." The third case is formally complex and characterized by disjunct and non-unified species, as neither contains the other.

C. Objections based on the false identification of object with end

One final note about the misconstrual of the first illustration given us by St. Thomas in *prima secundae*, question 18, article 7 seems pertinent. Even if one were to cede the point that the first illustration is the oddity of a mere physical act lacking a proximate end and having only a remote end, and even if one were to call this a complex act—when so construed it is in fact no human act at all—it would still be necessary to distinguish the relation of object and end in simple (freestanding) acts as opposed to complex acts. This is because all simple acts exhibit *per se* order between object and end. Hence there is no getting around the fact that the most universal, foundational type of human act is the simple (freestanding) act wherein there is *per se* order between object and end (but again: it is *per se* order that is most central, and that can bestow upon rich material sequences the unity of species derived from the end that by nature requires them).

What is the relation of object to end in each of the simple acts constituting a complex act? For example, in adultery, what is the relation of object to end? The answer is obvious: in any simple act, the most determining and defining species derives from the end: this is the teaching of *ST* I-II, question 18, article 7, ad 3, wherein it is said that in the case of *per se* order between object and end, the species derived from the end is like a genus in the sense of the genus of formal cause to which all the notes of the definition reduce. Thus acts *per se* directed to the venereal arousal of another's spouse are adulterous acts, acts directed to taking what belongs to another are acts of thievery, and so forth.

At root, action is some means ordained to an end, and as the *per se* and simple must always be prior to the *per accidens* and complex, manifestly the most fundamental and universal act structure is that of simple acts exhibiting *per se* order between object and end; without such acts, no human acts whatsoever could be performed, and the genus of human action would be empty. Both in their being and in their intelligibility, *per accidens* act structures and *per se* act structures containing many component acts, presuppose *per se* simple (freestanding) acts.

Yet some may suppose that in stand-alone acts the object and end are identical. This supposition is contrary to the truth of the proposition that in all such cases the object is *per se* ordained to the end. Of course, it is possible for the object of the internal act of the will to be identical with the end to which the external act is *per se* ordered. But the object of the external act is *never* identical with the end. Thus, in simple acts, as intimate as the object and end of the external act are, they are not identical. The object is what the act bears upon and concerns in relation to reason, and the relation to reason is essentially the proportion of a given act to the *finis operantis*; it is that owing to which the act is appetible to the agent. Even where the end sought by the agent (*finis operantis*) is identical with the end to which the act is *per se* ordered (*finis operis*), the proportion of the act to the end is manifestly *not* the end: proportion to the end presupposes the end but it is not the end. Thus, even in simple acts (e.g., theft; adultery;

almsgiving; prayer) wherein the object is *per se* ordained to the end, there is a distinction between the object and the end, although the two are intimately related.

In simple acts the *finis operis* is *not* identical with "object of the external act" although the latter is essentially ordered to the former. While owing to their intimate relation it is a common error to conflate end and object in simple acts, this would void Thomas's proposition that the external act bears of itself a proportion to the end—for that which bears a "proportion to the end" is not identical with "end," and the object is formal with respect to the act and most articulates this proportion of the external act to the end:[13]

> And just as a natural thing has its species from its form, so an action has its species from its object, as movement from its term. And therefore just as the primary goodness of a natural thing is derived from its form, which gives it its species, so the primary goodness of a moral action is derived from its suitable object.[14]

Thus also St. Thomas writes: "Although the end is an extrinsic cause, nevertheless due proportion to the end, and relation to the end, are inherent to the action."[15] Due proportion to the end and relation to the end are not identical with the end. Once it is seen that in simple acts the object is not simply identical with the end, while yet the object receives its most defining and determining species from the end, it is clear that the structure of object as *per se* ordained to the end is the most fundamental unit of action, and that all other acts presuppose it as the *per accidens* presupposes the *per se,* and as the complex presupposes the simple.

D. Objection based on the denial that disordered actions exhibit proportion toward deprived/evil ends

Another significant objection to considering the teleology of acts is to the effect that this will require us to see that disordered appetites are ordered toward ends to which deprivation is annexed, such that we will be imputing "naturalness" to evil acts. After all, evil has no *per se* cause. But, to the contrary, to see that toward which an act tends, and to see that which a purpose essentially requires, is to discern the relation between object and end even in immoral actions. This teleology of action is not simply identical with the norma-

---

13. *ST* I-II, q. 18, a. 2, resp.
14. *ST* I-II, q. 18, a. 2, resp. See also I-II, q. 18, a. 4, resp., and ad 2. Note the body, wherein the goodness derived from the befitting object is contrasted with the goodness derived from the end which is, as it were, the cause of the act's goodness.
15. *ST* I-II, q. 18, a. 4, ad 2.

tive teleology of the unified hierarchy of ends, because it pertains to the way in which proportion to what is sought by the agent defines the act performed by the agent; and agents may seek ends to which deprivation is annexed.

Hence, for example, the end sought by Don Juan in touching a widow and the end sought by a physician in touching a widow are distinct, and Don Juan may be said to proportion his acts to a disordered good of pleasure that is morally wicked, whereas the physician proportions his acts to the medical curing of disease and promotion of health that is good. It is because there is such proportion that we can say that some acts are *per se mala*, wicked of themselves, because they are acts that are proportioned to purposes which reflect unrectified appetite, departing from the norm of reason. To say that certain actions are such as never to be reasonable, is to see that those actions are indeed proportioned in such a way as to be inconsistent with the normative hierarchy of ends defining the good life. That is, in moral terms they are proportioned to ends to which moral deprivations are essentially annexed.

The normative hierarchy of ends alone does not suffice to instruct us as to the relation between the act chosen by the agent and the end thereby sought, although it certainly will help us to judge what an agent seeks—for this will be either contributory to or detractive from the order of reason defining the good life. Nonetheless, we must have the teleology of acts, or else we lose touch with the virtue or vice of individual moral agents, and can neither place acts in their species nor even identify *per se mala* such as adultery, thievery, murder, and so on. The normative hierarchy of ends is essential for the right direction of action; but for knowing what we are doing we need to know whether what is at stake is a simple or complex act, and thus whether the "object" is in truth an act of its own with its own moral species (the *per accidens* case) or is *per se* ordained to the end such that the defining species is derived from the end. Thus, Don Juan's touches are said to be lascivious or salacious by reason of their *per se* ordering to disordered pleasure, whereas the touch of the conscientious doctor is said to be medical by reason of its *per se* ordering toward the cure of disease and the sustenance of health.

It is apparent, then, that in terms of the teleology of actions, "per se" does not designate "good" but only indicates the character of the order that obtains betwixt what the agent seeks and the agent's action. Nor does *per accidens* indicate "wicked," but only either that the action of the agent does not of itself tend to what the agent principally seeks, or that what the agent principally seeks is not such as by nature to require the action chosen—e.g., almsgiving does not by its nature require theft, nor does theft naturally tend of itself to almsgiving. We will not be able to place an act in its moral species if we do not know whether what the agent is doing is *per se* or *per accidens* ordained to what he seeks as an end,[16] or if we do not realize that all simple acts are *per se* ordained to ends from which their determining moral species are derived. It is these fundamental points that have been occluded by the reduction of the moral object merely into a "proposal" or logical entity, or into a function of the "transcendental self-constitution" of an agent's acts. *Sed contra:* without understanding that the object of the external act is either *per accidens* or *per se* ordained to the end sought, it will be impossible to place acts in their species. And whether the object is or is not *per se* ordained to the end sought, is a function *not* of the agent's preference or proposal, but of the natural teleological relation of object and end. The cuckolded husband who discovers Don Juan *in flagrante*, getting carried away with his wife, may or may not know that there is no *per se* cause of evil; but he does know that the acts performed by Don Juan are of their nature such as to incline to sinfully disordered pleasure, and so to fall under the species of adultery or fornication. This is a teleological consideration of acts that is needed to place acts in their species such that, in the light of the essential hierarchy of ends, their moral nature is clear.

E. The semantic objection

It may be objected that St. Thomas Aquinas did not use the terminology of "simple act." But he did suggest that sequences of acts are possible in which the relation of object and end is *per accidens*. By contrast, to be a simple act is (a) for there not to be two acts, and (b) for the object of the external act to be *per se* ordained to what the agent seeks. The requisite "complexity" of the complex act is formal complexity, the existence of disjunct and non-unified moral species derivative from the lack of *per se* order of object to end. By contrast, no matter how rich and internally differentiated is the material manifold and material sequence, *per se* order toward the end bestows formal unity whereby the species derived from the object(s) is essentially contained within the species derived from the end. No matter what one calls this latter case, and

---

16. And this is not a function of simply natural order, but of natural order as essentially related to the moral ordering of human actions; what is *per se* in moral order is what, morally speaking, an action tends to of itself or that which an end of its nature requires if it is to be achieved, even if the end be one to which deprivation is annexed. It is perhaps physically accidental to wax that fire melts it; but morally speaking, one who puts a message written in wax into the fire and keeps it there performs an act *per se* ordered to the destruction of the message written in the wax. That the melting of the wax is in a strict physical sense an accident is morally immaterial; what is morally material is that the melting is a type of necessary accident to which the heating of the wax is ordered by nature. Unless the person who places the wax in the fire is acting in ignorance of the effect of fire on wax, the person's action manifests a *per se* order toward destruction of the message in the wax.

whether one takes it at the simplest level—eating to stay alive, say—or at the most complex—giving the patient anesthesia for the sake of heart surgery—it is the central, most foundational, and universal type of human action. All other types of human acts presuppose this *per se* case of action, both for their being and for their intelligibility. That St. Thomas does not call such acts "simple acts" is no more pertinent than that he does not use the phrase "metaphysics of *esse*." What matters is that what the phrase designates is to be found in his teaching. Of course, as has been noted above, were there no *per se* natural ordering of object to end, no one could ever have a reason for doing anything, because everything would be equally likely and equally unlikely to achieve whatever the agent had in mind. The preeminent and obvious case of human action is: means essentially ordained to an end. The *per accidens* and complex case is the exception. That several acts which might have been but are not free-standing are integrated by being *per se* required owing to the nature of some end, such that they constitute one extended morally unified act, does not make these "complex"—for they are saturated in the species derivative from the end, formally unified thereby, and contained within the species derived from the end.

IV. Reprise of Central Points

Hence the critical points are these:

1. The integral nature of the act with its *per se* effects is always included materially in the object of the external act, which has a hylemorphic structure, similar to the *forma totius,* and is not to be reduced merely to that which renders the act appetible to the agent.

2. All stand-alone simple acts are acts wherein the object of the external act is *per se* ordained to the end.

3. Where the object of the external act is *per se* ordained to the end, the most saturating, containing, formal, and definitive species is derived from the end.

4. In *per accidens,* complex acts, one act with its object and end are further ordered *per accidens* by the agent to another act with its object and end, such that the first *is not* contained in the species derived from the second. The *per accidens* ordering is conspicuous only because the prior *per se* ordering of the simple constituent acts exists and is known.

5. Where the nature of an intended *end* is such as to *require* a certain object or objects, then in that case these objects are *per se* ordained to the end.

6. Nested sequences of *per se* acts in which either the end is such by nature as to require these acts, or in which all these acts by their natures tend toward that end, enjoy the simplicity of form consequent on the unified containing species derived from the end. Yet this simplicity of form obviously presupposes a prior acquaintanceship with the component objects that might have been but in fact are not stand-alone *per se* acts, and thus the simplicity of such prior stand-alone *per se* acts is presupposed for all other act structures either *to be* or *to be known*. This is because, most simply, action is *means per se ordained to the end,* and because owing to the discursive nature of human intelligence, we achieve more extensive *per se* unification of action on the basis of our understanding of potential components. To judge that anesthesia is required for heart surgery is to have some distinct apprehension of what anesthesia of itself tends toward, something that might have been desired for its own sake (but which here will be desired owing to its necessity for the end of heart surgery).

7. *In sequences of per se acts, the relation of the component acts to the unified moral species is precisely comparable to the presence of the powers of lower forms within higher forms in virtute.* That is, these are not acts that would be performed by the agent absent the *per se* order to the end naturally requiring them (although they could be so performed), and so while these structures are, as it were, present *in virtute,* they are not morally speaking separate acts (this is why their species are *contained* within the species derived from the end). Such sequences highlight the way in which various acts which might have been freestanding with their *per se* order to their respective proximate ends may be naturally required by the same further end, such that within that order of intention all the proximate ends that might have been freestanding are indeed saturated by the species derived from the further end and thereby form one moral act. If the surgeon doesn't know what is *per se* ordained to anesthetize for the sake of humanely blocking pain in heart surgery, the surgery is going downhill fast; yet, nonetheless, the complex material manifold of administering anesthesia, opening the chest cavity, repairing the heart, and closing the chest cavity are formally defined as constituting one moral act of heart surgery.

8. As has been argued above, the simple case is simple with the simplicity not of the material atom, but rather with the simplicity of formal unity derivative from *per se* order in respect of the end. This is quite different from *per accidens* complex acts, wherein the object does not essentially tend toward the end, nor does the end essentially require the object: as theft does not tend toward adultery, nor does adultery require theft. *Such acts are truly and formally complex because not unified in moral species.* So: simplicity of formal unity derivative from *per se* order in respect of the end with its unifying and contain-

ing moral species; or complexity of formal disjunction and disunity derivative from lack of *per se* order in respect of the end with consequently distinct moral species. The simplicity of formal species derivative from the end may be more or less materially comprehensive. But this does not alter either the priority of simple, stand-alone *per se* acts for the being and being known of all other act structures; nor does it alter the datum that *per se* order, even when materially more comprehensive (e.g., several objects all required by the nature of some intended end) always involves the simplicity of form owing to the unity of species derived from the end.

9. In conclusion: none of these distinctions can either be, or be known, without prior cognizance of the most universal, foundational, and central instance of human action, the case of the simple stand-alone action wherein the object is *per se* ordained to the end. But the simplicity in question is a formal simplicity derivative from *per se* order of object to end. The case where multiple objects are involved with respect to one end that by nature requires them, or where several objects by nature tend toward some end, presupposes the prior intelligibility of the potential act-components. Only the case of *per accidens* order is formally complex, because the species derived from the end does not essentially contain the species derived from the object (or objects). Thus, naturally speaking, it is *per se* order that is at the heart of human action. Indeed, if all order of object to end were naturally *per accidens*, there could be no reason for doing or not doing anything whatsoever, since nothing would of its nature be such as to bring about anything. The moral intelligibility of human action necessarily depends upon natural teleology.

V. Contraception, *Finis Operis,* and Martin Rhonheimer

The foregoing considerations enable one to see how the failure to advert properly to the teleological grammar of the moral act leads to an erroneous understanding of the morality of contraception. In a recent exchange with Janet Smith in the *National Catholic Bioethics Quarterly*, Fr. Martin Rhonheimer argues that the distinction between what the agent seeks as an end (the *finis operantis*) and the *per se* end of the act *(finis operis)* is a spurious distinction that is harmful to moral theology. He does so in the course of arguing that married couples may, when one is infected with AIDS, morally contracept to avoid the transmission of AIDS. As he argues in response to Smith:

she seems to follow an unfortunate revival of older theories based on treating acts in their natural or physical species, on the non-violation of natural ends, and on the casuist—not originally Thomistic—understanding of the distinction between *finis operis* (taken as the natural end) and *finis operantis* (the end of the agent). I have written elsewhere of how such approaches depart from Aquinas, contribute significantly to the postconciliar crisis in moral theology, and are alternatives to *Veritatis splendor's* recovery of the moral analysis of distinctively human actions as specified by Aquinas's idea of the moral object as *finis proximus,* which is also a kind of *finis operantis*. In my view, Smith's reversion to such approaches is a tragic mistake.[17]

Doubtless there are ways of making the distinction between the end sought by the agent and the *per se* end of the act performed that could confuse one's understanding of the moral act. But that there is such a pertinent distinction is nonetheless true, and it is demonstrably the teaching of St. Thomas. When Aquinas speaks of whether the object is *per se* ordained to the end, he quite clearly and undeniably means *the object of the external act.* He could not mean *the object of the internal act of the will* which is the end, because this would then be to ask whether the end is ordered to itself, which would be a remarkably silly and otiose question. It follows that the object can either be *per se* ordained to what the agent intends or not, and—since in either case the agent intends what the agent intends—whether the object is *per se* ordered to the end of the agent is not determined by the agent but by the objective nature of the act. If the act is not *per se* ordered but only *per accidens* ordained to the end of the agent, then the act has its own *per se* order to a distinct end, and for this reason it also has its own separate moral species. But clearly in this case of *per accidens* order, the end of that distinct act—the *finis operis*—and what the agent intends as end—*the finis operantis*—differ. To say that this is not originally Thomistic is like saying that the metaphysics of *esse,* or the distinction of act and potency— or, for that matter, the existence of the Dominican Order—was an invention of sixteenth-century commentators. That is to say, it is simply false.

Thus it is not enough for the couple to have a good intention with respect to the end they seek, for they must also select an act that is objectively choiceworthy. Now, the *per se* effect of choosing to perform a procreative act contraceptively is the obstructing of conception, and this is true by the very nature of the case. If the object of the act could be reduced merely to what makes it attractive to the agent, and did not always include the integral nature of the act itself with its *per se* ordering, then Fr. Rhonheimer's analysis could be correct. But on such an analysis, the teaching of St. Thomas Aquinas would necessarily be false, because Aquinas clearly insists that the object of the external act either *is* or *is not* essentially ordered to the end sought by the agent. And to re-

17. Martin Rhonheimer, "Colloquy," *National Catholic Bioethics Quarterly* 7, no. 3 (2007): 441–46, 443.

310 Steven A. Long

peat, clearly whether it is essentially ordered to the end sought by the agent is not merely a function of the agent's intention but also and critically of the *per se* order of the act itself. Procreation is not a medical act, and it is ordered to conception. To perform a procreative act while directly intervening to make its procreativity impossible of achievement is to contracept. That there are various reasons why someone might do this (e.g., in this case, to prevent transmission of AIDS, which of course involves also preventing transmission of the procreative matter), none of which is because contraception is itself independently sought as an end, is irrelevant. Someone might likewise seek to perform adultery with an employer, not because this is found independently attractive but as a means to guarantee secure employment, but this does not render the act less guilty of the malice of adultery. There are also various reasons why people lie, kill, cheat, steal, and so on *ad infinitum*, even when they find these acts distasteful. This does not render such acts less disordered, contrary to the radical intentionalism so widespread today that is found in Anglo-Saxon philosophic culture largely owing to analytic logicism, and that is found in continental philosophic culture largely owing to the transcendental turn. Each has forgotten *natura*.

Likewise, whether theft is essentially ordered to adultery is not merely a function of the agent's intention, but is a function of the nature of theft in relation to the nature of adultery. No matter how much the agent may principally intend adultery, the agent who steals for the sake of adultery nonetheless also commits an act of theft. Similarly, whether opening the rib cage is *per se* ordained to the further end of heart surgery is a function of the objective order between the proximate *per se* end of the object "opening the rib cage for the sake of heart repair" and the further end of "heart repair" which is such as essentially to require opening of the rib cage.

What I fear Fr. Rhonheimer has done in this case is inadvertently to reduce the moral and ontological density of the object of the moral act merely to that which is most formally judged choiceworthy by the agent. But just as the essence abstracted as a whole always includes the common matter of the definition—even though essence is formal with respect to the nature of the individual—so the object of the moral act always includes the integral nature and *per se* ordering of the act itself (even though the relation of the act to reason is formal with respect to the nature of the act). And whereas "opening the rib cage" is something that may be directed to torture or murder, but also may be directed to heart surgery which latter requires it, it is simply impossible to argue that the end of avoiding transmission of AIDS *requires* contraceptive sex. For one avoids transmission of AIDS by not performing the conjugal act, and the view that married couples *must* under all conditions perform the conjugal act is a belittling view of the dignity of marital love and commitment.

Of course, many cite *Veritatis splendor* § 78:

The object of the act of willing is in fact a freely chosen kind of behaviour. To the extent that it is in conformity with the order of reason, it is the cause of the goodness of the will; it perfects us morally, and disposes us to recognize our ultimate end in the perfect good, primordial love. By the object of a given moral act, then, one cannot mean a process or an event of the merely physical order, to be assessed on the basis of its ability to bring about a given state of affairs in the outside world.

This is true, but it does not mean that the generic nature of certain objects by virtue of natural teleology is "an event of the merely physical order." *That would be to view the moral act not in a hylemorphic but in a rationalist manner.* Of course, this is also why *Veritatis splendor* § 79 states:

One must therefore reject the thesis, characteristic of teleological and proportionalist theories, *which holds that it is impossible to qualify as morally evil according to its species—its "object"—the deliberate choice of certain kinds of behaviour or specific acts, apart from a consideration of the intention for which the choice is made or the totality of the foreseeable consequences of that act for all persons concerned.*

There remains much to be said about the various erroneous efforts to apply the principle of double effect to the moral permissibility of a married couple's use of condoms to prevent transmission of AIDS. I have tried to address this issue further myself in my *The Teleological Grammar of the Moral Act.*[18] But for now I will rest content with the proposition that in this dispute, Fr. Rhonheimer might indeed benefit from what I believe Janet Smith correctly sees as foundational: the role of natural teleology in St. Thomas's moral teaching.

18. See pp. 104–14.

[12]

Contemplata Tradere
Embodied Interiority in Cessario,
Pinckaers, and Lonergan

MATTHEW L. LAMB

The many publications of Fr. Romanus Cessario, as well as the many publishing ventures he has initiated or guided, testify to the fruitfulness of his Dominican vocation. I recall the first prolonged discussions I had with him. It was at a conference at the Dominican House of Studies in Washington, D.C. After the conference presentations he and Fr. J. Augustine DiNoia took me to the beautiful College Chapel where a great uncle of mine, who witnessed the marriage of my parents and taught me how to serve Mass, had been ordained a Dominican Priest in 1909. What struck me immediately was their very Dominican commitment to the wisdom of truth. The worship of the Holy Sacrifice of the Mass and Divine Office flowed for them into their research and scholarship, their teaching and preaching. This is the "Sitz im Leben," the formative context of life, out of which Cessario's and DiNoia's writing and teaching spring. I recall the joy and peace I experienced in that Chapel and in my conversations with Fathers Cessario and DiNoia. Here were fellow theologians for whom divine and Catholic faith enlightens minds and hearts to the living presence of our Risen Lord Jesus Christ, who is the way, the truth, and the life.

We discussed some of the implications of what Professor Alasdair MacIntyre was lecturing on at the time—later published as *Three Rival Versions of Moral Enquiry*. The absence of wisdom in contemporary cultures and universities was palpable. The challenges facing Catholic theology and Catholic higher education sprung from what MacIntyre identified as two dominant versions of inquiry in modern and postmodern cultures. One was a relativist pluralism and empiricist multiculturalism of the Encyclopedist position. Any overarching order in nature and history was dismissed in favor of fragmented investigations of the empirical sciences and historical scholarship. The fragments were then collected by the Encyclopedic tradition that could only list them alphabetically. The second version then came along in the Genealogists of power following Nietzsche. All "lists" and "orderings" of fragmented monadic things or people were no more than voluntarist impositions by the powerful. It seemed to me that these two versions or sets of positions were rooted in the nominalist pluralism (only individual entities exist) and concomitant voluntarist absolutizing of power *(potentia absoluta et voluntas ordinata),* both of which as MacIntyre showed influenced the Enlightenment and contemporary cultures decisively.[1]

The third version of inquiry MacIntyre termed tradition, giving it a rather cumbersome title of "Aristotelian Augustinian Thomist" tradition. It embraced the traditions of wisdom. Cessario told me about Fr. Pinckaers's *Les sources de la morale chrétienne,* that he was having translated, and that it provided a recovery of Aquinas's virtue orientation over against nominalist and voluntarist deformations. I told him about the work of Fr. Ernest Fortin and others who were researching and writing on the dialectic of the ancients and the moderns, indicating how many of the problems today had their source in the explicit rejection of the wisdom traditions of the ancients (Greek and Roman philosophers, the Greek and Latin Fathers, and the Medieval Schoolmen). The challenge of recovering wisdom traditions was enormous, requiring generations of dedicated scholars, philosophers, and theologians. A contemplative monk had once remarked that the centuries it took the moderns to dismantle the wisdom traditions would be needed to recover and advance them; then he wisely added: "So we do not have a day to lose."

When Cessario joined the faculty of St. John's Seminary in Boston, his courses soon attracted graduate students from other programs that, like the Seminary, were part of the Boston Theological Institute. Few theologians in the greater Boston area had Cessario's wonderful combination of Thomist theological scholarship and pastoral care. Fortunately, many students in the Boston area were able to take Cessario's courses and seminars, and they were especially important in aiding the students, whether seminarian or university,

---

1. See Romanus Cessario, *Introduction to Moral Theology* (Washington, D.C.: The Catholic University of America Press, 2001), 60–61; and Heiko Oberman, *The Harvest of Medieval Theology: Gabriel Biel and Late Medieval Nominalism* (Cambridge: Harvard University Press, 1963).

in overcoming the Cartesian and Kantian dualism so prevalent among those theologians seduced by either pluralist relativism or forms of power-analysis voluntarism.[2]

At that time, dissent from *Humanae Vitae* was widespread among academics, perhaps especially in theology faculties. Often the dissent was rationalized as a "personalist" approach to marriage rather than a "physicalist" one. Thus I would recommend graduate students in theology at Boston College to take Cessario's courses so that they could learn what I termed "Thomist personalism"—and by that I meant that he understood the fundamental importance, as Aquinas had, of Boethius's defining person relative to substance and nature. When personhood is defined as relational with no reference to nature, relations become free-floating. Person cut off from nature distorts both person and nature. This was a basic message of *Humanae Vitae*.[3] Contemporary calls for same-sex unions are entirely consequent with the divorce of nature and person first countenanced by those who rejected the encyclical.

When some of us decided we should set aside some time to discuss theology, given the declining state of Catholic intellectual life in the academy, we began an Aquinas Study group that met at St. John's Seminary on Saturday evenings once a month. Among the faculty participants besides Cessario, myself, and occasional visitors were Fr. Ernest Fortin, Professors Mary Ann Glendon and Thomas Kohler, and from Providence College, Professors Robert Barry, Matthew Cuddeback, Gary Culpepper, Paul Gondreau, and James F. Keating. Our good friend and distinguished lawyer Edward Lev also came when we were studying Aquinas's analysis of law in his *Summa Theologiae*. After several hours of *explication du texte,* we would adjourn for dinner at nearby Korean or Asian restaurants.

In honor of Cessario's sixty-fifth birthday, I will take up an issue both Ambassador Mary Ann Glendon and I would discuss with him. Dr. Glendon and I have found the work of Fr. Bernard Lonergan, S.J., a very helpful guide in understanding, among other things, how Aquinas can assist contemporary intellectuals in recovering metaphysical and theological wisdom so as to begin the task of integrating science and scholarship with wisdom and holiness. A key aspect of Cessario's own work,[4] following on his friend and mentor Fr. Servais Pinckaers, is his recognition of the attention to interiority in the

---

2. The importance of Cessario's teaching was evident given that fewer and fewer theologians had a proper formation in the wisdom traditions so important for Catholic intellectual life. See references in n. 21 below.

3. *Humanae Vitae* §§ 7–10, 8.

4. See the Introduction by Reinhard Hütter and Matthew Levering in this book.

work of Aquinas. I believe it would be instructive to review briefly Cessario's and Pinckaers's treatment of Thomist interiority. For the sake of comparison, I will then outline some aspects of Lonergan's notion of embodied interiority. In my great admiration and friendship with both Lonergan and Cessario, I have learnt from both of them the fundamental significance of a proper realist understanding of embodied interiority for the recovery and advance of wisdom traditions and the presentation of Catholic revealed truth.

Pinckaers and Cessario on Embodied Interiority

Cessario refers to interiority almost always relative to the theological virtues. So, for instance, "the Gospel and its new law of grace communicate an entirely unexpected kind of interiority, one that initiates a personal communion with God."[5] But this graced interiority perfects and elevates, never destroys, our natural knowing and loving. Every human being is created in the "imago Dei."[6] Following Pinckaers and Owens, Cessario emphasizes the importance of "realist cognitional theory." "There exists," Cessario writes, "an isomorphism between thinking and reality, a parallelism in structure."[7] In judgment we know things "inasmuch as *esse* is the radical actuality of the being-ness and actuality and intelligibility of a thing, it is the thing itself that is attained . . . This grasp at the truth of being, attained in the act of knowledge, stands at the heart of Aquinas's doctrine about theological faith."[8]

In defining Christian ethics, Pinckaers sees a definition that stresses duty rather than law as "connoting a greater interiority," but so formulated, it is "the tradition of Kant and his categorical imperative."[9] Pinckaers rejects any Kantian or Cartesian dualism. "Human acts have both an interior and an external dimension. We speak of interior acts such as knowing, willing, loving, choosing, praying, and of external acts such as vocal prayer, theft, restitution."[10] Pinckaers then contrasts ways of knowing in terms of interiority and exteriority. If one simply limits human knowing to the techniques and methods of the empirical sciences, there results a "one-dimensional world" that excludes human interiority.[11] He does not question the validity of such knowledge, only

5. See Cessario, *Christian Faith and the Theological Life* (Washington, D.C.: The Catholic University of America Press, 1996) 84; also 54–55, 90–91.

6. Cessario, *Introduction to Moral Theology*, 25–31.

7. *Christian Faith and the Theological Life*, 72.

8. Ibid., 73.

9. Servais Pinckaers, O.P., *The Sources of Christian Ethics*, trans. Mary Thomas Noble, O.P. (Washington, D.C.: The Catholic University of America Press, 1995), 5.

10. Ibid., 10.   11. Ibid., 77–82.

the "high-handedness" of those who claim it is the only form of valid knowing. In this contrast, Pinckaers was transposing what Augustine and Aquinas call two different orientations of human reason, "ratio inferior" and "ratio superior."[12] As Pinckaers indicates, nominalism fostered a reductionism that contracted knowledge and being to material objects and made ethics a matter of will imposing laws.[13]

Interiority in Aquinas is no introspective Cartesian "res cogitans" but an embodied interiority with, as Pinckaers writes, many levels. There is the spatial interiority of the human body with its organs; then there is biological interiority of the human person in "a continual exchange between exterior and interior that enables the person to act upon the world."[14] Then there is the "sensible interiority" that is human "openness to sense impressions from the outer world," converting them "into reactions and movements corresponding to needs and appetites." The deepest level is moral interiority that gives us "the radical ability to receive and experience within ourselves in a vital manner all truth and goodness, which render us fruitful and enable us to bring forth, in all the power of our free will, actions and works capable of transforming both ourselves and the world." It is at this deepest level that human interiority is open "to the action of the Holy Spirit through faith and love."[15] The unfathomable transcendence of the Triune God becomes immanently present, giving human interiority a graced participation in the very unfathomable depth of the Father, Son, and Holy Spirit. Cessario sees in the Church and her Christ mandated tasks of governing, teaching, and sanctifying the movement in history of the revealed and redeeming embodied interiority of the whole Christ, head and members.[16]

Pinckaers emphasizes that we must not imagine these levels as closed off from one another. The deeper the interiority, the more the other levels are affected. "We belittle human nature when we oppose the interior and exterior in a superficial way or downgrade the interior life in favor of personal or Christian commitment to the world."[17] Dynamic interiority has depth, height, solidity, and breath that requires cultivation of the virtues. To adequately un-

---

12. See Thomas Aquinas, *Summa theologiae* I, q. 79, aa. 8 and 9 and references to Augustine there. Also, Robert Mulligan, "Ratio Superior and Ratio Inferior: The Historical Background," *New Scholasticism* 29, no. 1 (1955): 1–32.

13. Pinckaers, *The Sources of Christian Ethics*, 240–53.

14. Ibid., 78.

15. Ibid., 78–79.

16. See Cessario's Introduction to Colman E. O'Neill, O.P., *Meeting Christ in the Sacraments* (Staten Island, N.Y.: Alba House, 2002) and the other works referenced by Reinhard Hütter and Matthew Levering in their Introduction to this book.

17. Pinckaers, *The Sources of Christian Ethics*, 79.

derstand and analyze human acts, Pinckaers warns against the false dualisms of modernity. "We need to understand clearly that the distinction between interior and exterior acts does not posit two completely different acts, but rather indicates the interior and exterior aspects of one concrete act."[18] "Therefore, the species of the human act is formally considered taken from the end [the object of the interior act of the will] and materially considered taken from the object of the exterior action."[19]

Cessario has shown the importance of this Thomist realist analysis of human action. Distinguishing the exterior and interior as material and formal can, he warns, be misunderstood in seventeenth-century, dichotomous ways utterly foreign to Aquinas:

The mention of a material-formal distinction prompts some moral theologians to interpret Aquinas as if he considered external actions—the material consideration—to hang like outer appendages on inner states, i.e., on the formal consideration of the will's activity . . . An act is integrally good only by the rightness of all its constituents, while it is flawed by any defect *(bonum ex integra causa, malum ex quocumque defectu)*. Hence the matter of an act may be such that it is not congenial to the form of an agent's purpose, just as clubbing with a baseball bat is not congenial to the form of the purpose of expressing friendly comradery.[20]

Now, the task of recovering the wisdom tradition of Aquinas is complicated, as Cessario and Long among others indicate, by the fact that we can read and study the texts of the past without realizing that we are not understanding the realities of which those texts are speaking. For one thing, it takes long years of study to allow biblical, patristic, and medieval theologians, and the Greek and Roman philosophers they studied, to challenge our contemporary preconceptions about the world and ourselves. Philosophy and theology graduate programs usually privilege modern and contemporary works, with nods or grimaces toward the ancients, who are generally consigned to historical sections as to quaint museums of the mind with little or no relevance today.[21] Also, we have trouble locating the interior realities Aquinas speaks of in the terms in-

18. Ibid., 183.

19. *Summa theologiae* I-II, q. 18, a. 6.

20. Cessario, *Introduction to Moral Theology*, 177. The fundamental importance of this proper understanding of the moral act is clearly and concisely analyzed in Steven A. Long's *The Teleological Grammar of the Moral Act* (Naples, Fla.: Sapientia Press, 2007).

21. See Matthew Lamb, "Will There Be Catholic Theology in the United States?" in *America* 162, May 26, 1990, 523–34. Also, "The Catholic Theological Society of America: Theologians Unbound," *Crisis: Politics, Culture, and the Church*, Dec. 1997, 36–37; "The Catholic Theological Society of America: A Preliminary Profile," *Fellowship of Catholic Scholars Quarterly* 21, no. 1 (1998): 8–10; also, the responses in *Crisis: Politics, Culture, and the Church* 16 (1998): 3, 14; and in *Fellowship of Catholic Scholars Quarterly* 21 (1998): 2–5. From 1968 to 1997, 75 percent of

herited from Augustine and Aristotle. It is to removing this last difficulty that
Lonergan devoted so much of his careful description, one might say phenomenology, of human knowing and loving.

Lonergan on Embodied Interiority

Fr. Bernard Lonergan complained to me often about a diminution of serious philosophical and theological study, often replaced in theologates and
seminaries with social activism. He would comment that well-formed theologians needed a context that facilitated three activities: study, prayer, and
exercise. He himself devoted many years almost exclusively to the study of
Aquinas. His writings in the 1940s and 50s were intent on recovering the metaphysics and cognitional theory of Aquinas in order, as he put it a 1955 article,
to elaborate the "isomorphism of Thomist and Scientific Thought."[22] His writings in the early period were marked by an engagement with Thomist philosophers and theologians in the task of the Leonine transposition: "vetera novis
augere et perficere."[23] By 1973, however, Lonergan could write of "the passing of Thomism" in the wake of Vatican II. He summarized the reflections of
a number of theologians on the passing of Thomism, in order to add his own
"further point that currently something like Thomism is very much to be desired."[24] At a minimum "something like Thomism" would require a serious
study of Aquinas. There is a note of urgency in the conclusion of the essay:

As yet, issues are unsettled. There is the danger that new notions in science, scholarship, philosophy can be exploited in the manner Karl Rahner would name substantial heresy. There is the opposite danger that the whole effort of renewal give rise to
a panic that now, as on earlier occasions, would close doors, and shut eyes, and stop
ears. But there exists the third possibility that the new can be analogous to the old,
that it can preserve all that is valid in the old, that it can achieve the higher synthesis

---

doctoral dissertations in theology written by members of the Catholic Theological Society of
America were on twentieth-century thinkers; 10 percent discussed nineteenth-century thinkers. Of the remaining 15 percent, most were in biblical studies. Research on specifically Catholic theological traditions—patristic, monastic, scholastic, counterreformation—was woefully
meager. See Walter Principe's plaintive presidential address and the responses in *The Proceedings of the Catholic Theological Society of America* (Atlanta, Ga.: Catholic Theological Society,
1991), 75–107.

22. Bernard J. F. Lonergan, *Collected Works of Bernard Lonergan*, vol. 4, ed. Frederick E.
Crowe and Robert M. Duran (Toronto: University of Toronto, 1988–2007), 133–44.

23. *Grace and Freedom: Operative Grace in the Thought of St. Thomas Aquinas*, vol. 1, *Collected Works; Verbum: Word and Idea in Aquinas*, vol. 2, *Collected Works*.

24. *Collected Works*, vol. 17, 282–298, quote on p. 292. In this essay and the previous one, Lonergan is attempting to make the best of what he sees as a crisis situation.

mentioned by Leo XIII in his bull *Aeterni Patris: vetera novis augere et perficere,* augmenting and perfecting the old by what is new. To that end we must labor and for it we must pray.[25]

Russell Hittinger recently described the situation that had led Lonergan to worry about the passing of Thomism in 1973. "As ecclesiastical discipline declined precipitously in the 1950s and 1960s, systematic Thomism underwent a kind of defenestration. No longer privileged in the curriculum of either seminaries or Catholic schools, Thomistic metaphysics became a scholar's specialty consigned to a chapter in the history of medieval philosophy."[26]

Cessario's concern is that Lonergan's work appears to be an instance of "transcendental Thomism" popular after Vatican II that conceded too much to modern (e.g., Kantian) philosophies and, in the words of Fr. Josef Kleutgen, S.J., "were not as well equipped to expound and defend the Catholic faith as the older Scholastic theology employed by the Church in pre-Enlightenment times."[27] As often happens among friends, Cessario's brief comments in print on Lonergan have led me to publish my understanding of Lonergan's work that could assist dedicated scholars like Cessario.

I recently published "Lonergan's Transpositions of Augustine and Aquinas"[28] in which I indicated the need for those who study Lonergan to study also what he studied, especially Augustine and Aquinas. The very extensive scholarly publications of Fr. Giovanni Sala, S.J., on Kant and Lonergan have established that Lonergan adopted Aquinas's cognitional theory in order to provide a thorough criticism of Kantian philosophy.[29] Thus it is not surprising that Fr. R. J. Henle, S.J., in his *American Thomistic Revival* would reject the notion that Lonergan was a transcendental Thomist.[30] To group Lonergan with

---

25. Ibid., 298.

26. Russell Hittinger, "Two Thomisms, Two Modernities," in *First Things,* June/July 2008, 38.

27. Cessario, *A Short History of Thomism* (Washington, D.C.: The Catholic University of America Press, 2005), 87–88.

28. John J. Liptay and David S. Liptay, eds., *The Importance of Insight: Essays in Honour of Michael Vertin* (Toronto: University of Toronto Press, 2007), 3–21.

29. Giovanni Sala, S.J., *Das Apriori in der menschlichen Erkenntnis: Eine Studie über Kants Kritik der reinen Vernunft und Lonergans Insight* (Meisenheim: Verlag Anton Hain, 1971); *Lonergan and Kant: Five Essays on Human Knowledge* (Toronto: University of Toronto Press, 1994); *Kant, Lonergan und der christliche Glaube* (Nordhausen: Bautz Verlag, 2005); *Kontroverse Theologie* (Bonn: Verlag Nova & Vetera, 2005); "What Use Is Kant for Theology?" in *Wisdom and Holiness, Science and Scholarship,* ed. Michael Dauphinais and Matthew Levering (Naples, Fla.: Sapientia Press, 2007), 293–314.

30. R. J. Henle's study of transcendental Thomism says Lonergan is not one; see his *The American Thomistic Revival* (St. Louis: St. Louis University Press, 1999), 348ff. Lonergan himself never, as far as I know, referred to himself as a transcendental Thomist. His use of transcen-

the transcendental Thomists influenced by Maréchal overlooks the fact that his studies concentrated on Plato, Aristotle, Augustine, and Aquinas—not the work of Maréchal. Lonergan recalled that when he came to hear of Maréchal's approach, he did not really study it so much as recognized Maréchal's treatment of judgment as confirming what he was more familiar with, namely, Augustine's key notion of *veritas* and Aquinas's notion of *esse*.[31]

In two of his essays in the 1970s, Lonergan articulated a dependence of his method on Aquinas. In his "Aquinas Today: Tradition and Innovation," of 1975 and four years later in "Horizons and Transpositions," Lonergan writes of the "emergence of method" in the thirteenth-century Schoolmen: the technique of the *quaestio* "resulted in a method, for it attracted a group of specialists following a common procedure in a determinate field of investigation."[32] Lonergan defines his own transposition of Aquinas's method of the question as "transcendental" in the Scholastic sense, where the transcendental is distinguished from the categorical as something not bound to one of Aristotle's predicaments. As Sala has shown, Lonergan's notion is a critical response to Kant by way of indicating that it is not some list of categories (cause, substance, etc.) that is prior to and imposed on the data of the senses, but the given nature of human intelligence itself, with the two sets of its operations analyzed by Aquinas and specified by the questions "Quid sit?" and "An sit?" that release for consciousness the intelligibility and truth of the real. Unfortunately, the subtleness of the method of the *quaestio* in the work of Aquinas gave way to

---

dental is indeed not in the Kantian but in the Thomist meaning of the term. I have also indicated the inadequacy of Fr. Gerald McCool's claim that Lonergan is a transcendental Thomist: cf. my "Divine Transcendence and Eternity" in *Continuity and Plurality in Catholic Theology: Essays in Honor of Gerald A. McCool, S.J.*, ed. Anthony J. Cernera (Fairfield, Conn.: Sacred Heart University Press, 1998), 75–106.

31. Lonergan, *A Second Collection: Papers* (Philadelphia: Westminister, 1974), 265: "I was sent to Rome for theology, and there I was subject to two important influences. One was from an Athenian, Stefanos Stefanu, who had entered the Jesuit Sicilian province and had been sent to Louvain to study philosophy at a time when Maréchal taught psychology to the Jesuit students and the other professors at the scholasticate taught Maréchal. Stefanu and I used to prepare our exams together. Our aim was clarity and rigor—an aim all the more easily obtained, the less the theses really meant. It was through Stefanu by some process of osmosis, rather than through struggling with the five great Cahiers, that I learnt to speak of human knowledge as not intuitive but discursive with the decisive component in judgment. This view was confirmed by my familiarity with Augustine's key notion, veritas, and the whole was rounded out by Bernard Leeming's course on the Incarnate Word, which convinced me that there could not be a hypostatic union without a real distinction between essence and existence. This, of course, was all the more acceptable, since Aquinas' esse corresponded to Augustine's veritas and both harmonized with Maréchal's view of judgment."

32. "Horizons and Transpositions" in *Collected Works*, vol. 17, 421. Also, *A Third Collection: Papers*, ed. Frederick E. Crowe (New York: Paulist Press, 1985), 35–54.

a conceptualist deductivism in nominalism and voluntarism that increasingly absorbed metaphysics into a conceptualist logicism. Lost was the embedded interiority of Aquinas's cognitional theory. Lonergan saw his work on Aquinas in *Verbum* as a retrieval of the contemplative-theoretical way of living. It is not an "epistemology"—that is a modern term from the seventeenth century resulting as a response to Cartesian and Kantian dualisms. Lonergan preferred the term "cognitional theory." He often would remark that cognitional theory answers the question "What do I do when I know?"; epistemology seeks to answer the question of "Why is doing that knowing?"; while metaphysics answers the question "What do I know when I do it?"

From Aquinas, Lonergan learned embodied interiority, for that is what comes to expression when one elaborates an answer to the question "What am I doing when I am knowing?" In a manner analogous to Pinckaers he distinguishes the external and internal dimensions of experience or "interiority" or "presence." "External experience is of sights and sounds, of odors and tastes, of the hot and cold, hard and soft, rough and smooth, wet and dry. Internal experience is of oneself and one's apprehensive and appetitive activities."[33] Like Pinckaers, Lonergan warns against a dichotomizing of internal and external. He also sees the importance not of only physical interiority or presence, but also of sensitive interiority in feelings and desires. The natural inclinations are fundamental indicators of the human desire for beatitude that are to be cultivated by what Lonergan terms ethical "rational self-consciousness" in acting virtuously. As Pinckaers analyzes the importance of natural inclinations for Aquinas, so Lonergan indicates the scales of preference in feelings as they respond to objects.[34] Where Pinckaers contrasts freedom of indifference and freedom for excellence, Lonergan speaks of man's natural essential freedom that becomes effective freedom through virtue.[35]

Lonergan realized that in the realm of intelligence, human beings are in potency for Aquinas; our senses are moved by sensible objects. The light of agent intellect bathes the human phantasm, raising the questions "Quid sit?" (What is it?) as the phantasm presents the data of our senses. Lonergan learned that abstraction for Aquinas is enriching, not impoverishing; it is the activity of intelligence grasping the intelligibility in the data of sense. The first two types of enriching abstraction are as follows: the first act of intelligence is the "objective abstraction" of the "species qua" of the illuminated phantasm; "ap-

33. Lonergan, "Cognitional Structure" in *Collection*, vol. 4, *Collected Works*, 209.
34. Lonergan, *Method in Theology*, 27–55.
35. Lonergan, *Insight*, 639–66.

prehensive abstraction" is intelligence in the second act grasping the "species quae," the universal in the particular, the "quidditas rei materialis." These two types of abstraction are fundamental because they emphasize objects moving the senses and, in the light of agent intellect, the mind. Lonergan called attention to how often Aquinas's embodied interiority would repeat "sensibile in actu est sensus in actu, et intelligibile in actu est intellectus in actu."

This twofold process of abstraction Lonergan later called "insight," for the universal is known in the particular; the whole post-nominalist opposition between universals and particulars is utterly foreign to Thomist interiority. From these, intelligence formulates *(dicere)* in "formative abstraction" the "species in qua," the universal common to many, the concept that proposes an answer to the question "Quid sit?"[36] Intelligence then raises the question "An sit?" (Is it so?) to determine if one has properly understood the object. In judging, reflective intelligence seeks out the relevant evidence in the sense data as it weighs the evidence for the truth or falsity of the concept relevant to the data. It is the cultivation of good judgment that fosters the acquisition of wisdom and can, in a theoretical way of living, make explict the realist metaphysics of being.[37]

Lonergan's reaching up to the mind of Aquinas changed him profoundly. He realized that to recover the wisdom of Aquinas, and bring the fruit of that recovery to the issues of our time, required making the intellectual, moral, and religious dimensions of Aquinas's embodied interiority explicit. This meant going back to a pre-modern, ancient and medieval cognitional theory wherein *Theoria* was a speculative-contemplative wisdom fostering the self-knowledge of the soul. In this task Augustine's narratives of his own intellectual, moral, and religious conversion proved a foundational guide. Augustine's intellectual conversion to the Truth, moral conversion to Goodness, and religious conversion to God revealed in Christ Jesus, together with the notion of doctrine arrived at by Athanasius and the other defenders of Nicea, grounded the shift toward theory in Thomas Aquinas.[38] The threefold conversion process of Augustine becomes in Aquinas the fundamental importance of the intellectual, moral, and theological virtues.[39] The notion of doctrine, on the other hand, in-

---

36. Lonergan, *Verbum*, 12–59.

37. *Verbum*, 60–105.

38. These three conversions are especially clear in St. Augustine's *Confessions*, Books V through IX; see also Ernest Fortin's several essays on Augustine in *The Birth of Philosophic Christianity*, ed. J. Brian Benestad (Lanham, Md.: Rowman and Littlefield, 1996), 1–120. On the movement toward theory, cf. Lonergan's "The Origins of Christian Realism," in *A Second Collection: Papers*, 239–61. For the foundational reality of intellectual, moral, and religious conversion, cf. Lonergan's *Method in Theology* (New York: Herder and Herder, 1972), 267–94.

39. Cf. *ST* I-II, qq. 55–67; II-II, qq. 1–170.

troduces into Christian consciousness the difference between how things are in relation to us and as grasped in the existential categories of the New Testament, and how things are in themselves, expressed in doctrine.

Theory is thus to be contrasted with common sense. In the realm of common sense meaning, we say how things concern us, are related to us and our desires and projects. Theory, however, is concerned with explanation, and of how things are related, not to us, but to one another. The shift from Greek drama to the dialogues of Plato is a shift from moral common sense to moral theory. The shift from the New Testament to Nicea is a shift from religiously informed revealed narratives to the beginnings of an *intellectus fidei*. To notice the difference between these two realms of meaning, moreover, is to enter another, third realm of meaning, that of interiority itself. Augustine and Aquinas both entered this realm; Lonergan has mapped it and named the streets. Furthermore, Lonergan's call for authenticity in the third stage of meaning repeats in its own order the ancient and medieval call to live by what is highest. For the philosophers this was reason as highest *quoad nos*—and indeed it is what Lonergan in *Insight* analyzes as the appropriation of rational self-consciousness.[40] For theologians what is highest *quoad se* is the Triune God revealed in Jesus Christ as the way, the truth, and the life. Lonergan analyzes this in how the supernatural solution to the problem of evil sublates the humanist quest for the good life into an absolutely supernatural fulfillment in eternal life.[41] The "law of the cross" in *De Verbo Incarnato* is a masterful transposition of the theologies of Augustine and Aquinas on how only the God who creates can redeem us by bringing life out of death and good out of evil—it shows how the only intellectually satisfying solution to the massive histories of evil and suffering is a Christ-centered theology of history rather than any philosophy of history.[42]

To recover the theoretical achievements of Aquinas, Lonergan realized that he had to attend to the acts and objects of human intentional consciousness. Recall the key elements in the self-knowledge of the human soul (see diagram).

Good habits perfect human powers such that we regularly perform acts that put us in possession of those objects which fulfill our natural inclinations to the true and the good. To know these terms and relations is to attend to inte-

40. *Insight*, 621–39.
41. *Insight*, 747ff.
42. See Bernard Lonergan, *De Verbo Incarnato* (Rome: Pontifical Gregorian University Press, 1964), 445–85; also my "Eternity and Time," in *Gladly to Learn, Gladly to Teach: Essays in Honor of Ernest Fortin* (New York: Lexington, 2002).

FIGURE 12-1

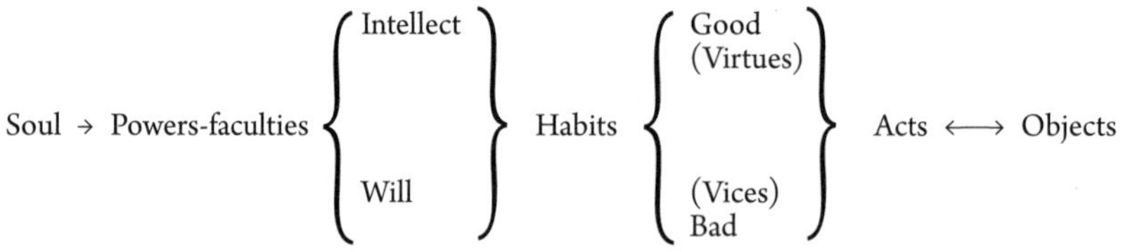

Soul → Powers-faculties { Intellect / Will } Habits { Good (Virtues) / (Vices) Bad } Acts ⟷ Objects

riority, embodied interiority. Such attention, however, is anything but Kantian or Cartesian. It is attentiveness to the aspects of the self-knowledge of the soul that fall within human conscious experience, namely, acts and objects.[43] This was the key in Lonergan's transposition of Aquinas. As he states in *Method in Theology*: "And if modern theologians were to transpose medieval theory into the categories derived from contemporary interiority and its real correlatives, they would be doing for our age what the greater Scholastics did for theirs."[44] This move is not the modern move to epistemology, but the cultivation of a heightened awareness of what we do when we know, as Lonergan sketched it out in the first two chapters of *Verbum*. This is clear by his phrase "and their real correlatives"—the object specifies the act as we saw above.

In our conscious living we are aware immediately of objects. The tree I see, the building I enter, the coffee I am drinking, etc. With a slight heightening of attention we are aware of the seeing, walking, drinking, that is, the acts. Most often, however, we do not advert to the acts or operations but to the objects we know or experience through those acts. Our self-presence or consciousness is in a world of objects. This is what Lonergan means by saying that our consciousness is intentional.

With this in mind, we can see how Lonergan's preliminary definition of method is really seeking to find a wise integration of the theological specialties by asking theologians to attend to their acts or operations. "A method is a normative pattern of recurrent and related operations yielding cumulative and progressive results."[45] This definition of method transposes Aquinas's teaching on skills and good habits into terms that contemporaries could grasp by attending to their operations and objects.

43. See the massive works of Giovanni Sala contrasting Lonergan and Kant. Kant excluded the "ratio superior" to which Lonergan calls our attention.
44. *Method*, 327–28.
45. *Method*, 4.

No human being can avoid forming habits, good or bad, for our faculties are naturally oriented to act, and actions or operations are either ordered (good) or disordered (bad). How do we know we have habits? We act in a certain way with ease. How do we know if the habit is bad? The easy acts are simply a repetitive constricting of our freedom, delivering us to the moral impotence of an habitual sinner, and tending to darken and weaken our minds and wills. How do we know they are good habits? The related and recurrent acts tend to enlarge our freedom and uplift our minds and hearts. So Lonergan's definition of method is a differentiated way of showing how method in theology means acquiring sets of intellectual and moral virtues, as well as skills. Nor can we exercise those virtues in theology without having received the theological virtues. Without a living faith, along with sets of acquired intellectual and moral virtues, Catholic theology ceases. Without the theological virtues, theology degenerates into inspections of dead texts in a very dead and deadening God-free, faith-free, privatized study of religion as purely exterior.

Lonergan's transcendental method with its functional specialties, then, is a set of skills and virtues. He attends to the related and recurrent acts or operations in each speciality. Note, for instance, that the speciality foundations is an explanatory theoretical analysis of intellectual, moral, and religious conversion, and it needs metaphysics since there is no one-to-one correlation between conscious acts and natural realities and revealed realities. Indeed, there could not be such a correspondence short of our enjoyment of the "lumen gloriae." For Lonergan, as for Aquinas, the science of theology will always be a science subaltern to Divine Knowledge and the knowledge of the Blessed in heaven.[46] Without acquiring metaphysical wisdom, theologians would be unable to understand fundamental aspects of their tasks as Lonergan outlines them in his *Method in Theology.*

This is especially the case with foundations, where Lonergan sees metaphysics as playing a role in articulating the explanatory nest of terms and relations in the "general theological categories."[47] These metaphysically articulated foundations provide the basis for doctrines, where the ongoing discovery of mind requires attention to the "fully metaphysical context," for an explanatory interiority ultimately leads to metaphysics as its completion, answering the question as to what it is we know when we are knowing it.[48] Finally, Lo-

---

46. See Lonergan, *De Deo Trino,* vol. 2 (Rome: Gregorian University, 1964), 249ff.; *De Verbo Incarnato,* 332ff.; Guy Mansini, O.S.B., "St. Thomas on Christ's Knowledge of God," *The Thomist* 59, no. 1 (1995): 91–124.

47. *Method in Theology,* 287.

48. Ibid., 308–9, 316.

nergan stresses how metaphysics has a twofold positive function in systematics: it provides both a heuristic structure and a criterion for proper distinctions between literal and metaphorical meaning, and between what is notional and what is real.[49]

The importance of metaphysics is also evident for moral theology and ethics in Lonergan's work. For example, his essay "Finality, Love, Marriage" carefully lays out the metaphysical aspects of finality central to Catholic teaching on human sexuality and marriage. It emphasizes these as the integration of nature and person, natural and interpersonal. It was published in a 1943 number of *Theological Studies*,[50] and the editor at the time, Fr. John Courtney Murray, added a note inviting comments and corrections, saying Lonergan would respond in a later issue. No one took up the invitation.[51] The essay sets out what Lonergan terms a preliminary speculative outline that will bring together nature, history, and graced personalist finalities.[52] Lonergan sets his study of marriage as "an ascent of love from the level of nature to the level of the beatific vision."[53] The hierarchy of ends of marriage is set up by attending to the three levels of human ends (life, the good life, and eternal life) and human activity (nature, reason ordered to virtue and friendship, graced theological virtues and the mystical body of Christ) in the wisdom traditions.[54] Taking what he terms "the dynamic Thomist position" Lonergan sees the excellence of the sacrament of marriage as calling spouses to the self-sacrificing love of Christ for his bride, the Church as the mystical Body of Christ destined to beatific vision. Life and the good life with the excellence of marriage and the Christian home wherein children are educated in the intellectual and moral virtues requires, in our fallen world, the graced and greater excellence of the theological virtues ordering all to "our eternal embrace with God in the beatific vision."[55]

What is key in Lonergan's analysis of the finality of human sexuality is the integration of what he terms the horizontal finality toward the procreation of

49. Ibid., 343.

50. "Finality, Love, Marriage," *Theological Studies* 4 (1943): 477–510.

51. "Finality, Love, Marriage," in *Collection*, vol. 4, *Collected Works*, 17–51: 52. On pp. 263–64, Frederick Crowe and Robert Doran give the note by the editor and speculate that a decree by the Holy Office in 1944 was instrumental in there being no response. I recall Lonergan telling me that he was told it was too difficult; he avered that John Ford, S.J., had not understood it properly (see Ford's "Notes on Moral Theology," *Theological Studies* 5, no. 4 [1944]: 530–31).

52. Ibid., 17–19: "For it is only in the cosmic breadth of a simultaneous context of nature, history, and grace, that appear at once the justice and assimilative capacity of the, on the whole, traditional view that the most essential end of marriage is the procreation and education of offspring but its most excellent end lies on the supernatural level of personalist development."

53. Ibid., 29.   54. Ibid., 27–48.

55. Ibid., 49–51.

children with the vertical finality of the unitive love. To remove the horizontal finality of the conjugal act is also to eliminate the vertical finality. This indicates the embodied interiority of marriage both naturally and supernaturally. As Fleischacker has written recently:

In the case of marriage, eliminate the horizontal finality of the procreative schemes of recurrence, and one destroys the unique rational and volitional relationship that emerges and develops between a man and woman. Thus, one does not have the "rational" relationship of a civic marriage without this conjugal relationship. And one does not have the sacred relationship of a sacramental marriage without this conjugal relationship. In initiating and then hindering these procreative schemes of recurrence and their developmental finality, one metaphysically destroys all of the vertical meanings that build upon these schemes. Attention and understanding of embodied interiority will make this manifest. Thus, Lonergan's position is not against the teaching of the Church on marriage and family. Quite the contrary. Some of Lonergan's most significant contributions to philosophy, especially to metaphysics, result in affirming the natural intelligibility of the procreative and unitive aspects of marriage, and the unity of these aspects with each other. The analogy of horizontal and vertical finality provides substantial grounds for making this claim.[56]

Fleischacker is, correctly in my judgment, criticizing those who take a private letter written in 1968 as evidence that Lonergan did not support Church teaching. He shows how the letter does not refer at all to Lonergan's writings on the finality of marriage. The statistical relation between insemination and conception in no way breaks the integrity of the procreative and unitive ends of marriage that Lonergan himself held.[57]

Lonergan's analysis of the human good and marriage, in conjunction with Pinckaers's criticisms of technical reductionism, does offer a clear differentiation of artifical birth control versus natural family planning. It is the difference

---

56. David Fleischacker, "Lonergan and the Surd and Sin of Contraception," forthcoming article. He shows how Lonergan maintains this embodied interiority throughout his later writings.

57. So Fleischacker writes: "The fact that a statistical relationship is part of the relationship between the conjugal act and conception may change the view of a natural causal relationship, but in turn, it is part of a larger relationship of finality that Lonergan over and over again affirms in his writings. In the end, contraception is just as much a surd as it was before. Why? Because initiating the procreative schemes and completing them in the conjugal act, and deliberately introducing something that blocks the schemes from completing is against the entire horizontal finality of these schemes and the conjugal act. One is actuating the finality for a child and yet standing against that same finality, and thus in the decision to introduce contraception, one is acting against the intelligibility, being, and goodness of the conjugal act and its meaning. Thus, objectively it is an evil, a privation of intelligibility, being, and goodness that should not take place. Thus, to avoid this evil, every conjugal act needs to be open to the finality that it intrinsically possesses."

between *technē* and *arēte,* between mere technique and the excellence of virtue. Using contraceptives requires no moral excellence or virtue. Instrumentalization and depersonalization of sex is all too widespread in what Lonergan
calls "the aberrations of reason in fallen human history."[58] But natural family
planning does require what in 1943 Lonergan praised as a "temporary absence
in marriage" that fosters the virtues, especially moderation and, with grace,
the self-sacrificing love central to sacramental union embodying the love of
Christ for his Church.[59]

Concluding Meditation

For Pinckaers and Cessario it is most important that one appreciate how
the embodied interiority of Aquinas provides alternatives to the subjectivism
and relativism of contemporary cultures. Cessario notes the criticism John
Finnis makes of Lonergan's notion of the good.[60] Finnis sees Lonergan as re-
ducing the good to the good as experienced. Like Aquinas, however, Lonergan seeks to develop what he terms "a cosmic or ontological account of the
good."[61] Indeed, it is the problems of living reasonably and responsibly that,
analogously with the Fathers and Schoolmen, leads Lonergan to insist upon
the importance of the absolutely supernatural revelation and redemption in
the Word Incarnate.[62]

Without the Missions of the Son and Spirit, without the Self-Communication of God in history and the higher viewpoint provided by faith as a knowledge born of the Love who is the Holy Spirit flooding our hearts (Romans 5:5),
sin and evil and death would overshadow all human history. We are not alone
like some cosmic orphans. We are called into the Interpersonal Community of
the Triune God, called to share with Christ in Infinite Understanding gener-
ating Infinite Truth spirating Infinite Love. Only God, no creature, can bring

---

58. "Finality, Love, Marriage," 51.

59. Ibid., 49–51; *Insight,* 251–67, 766–70; Pinckaers, *The Pinckaers Reader,* ed. John Berkman and Craig S. Titus (Washington, D.C.: The Catholic University of America Press, 2005),
236–70; see Giovanni Sala, *Gewissensentscheidung: Philosophisch-theologische Analyse von Gewissen und sittlichem Wissen* (Innsbruck: Tyrolia Verlag, 1993) for an analysis of conscience and natural law in Lonergan. See also Steven A. Long, "Natural Law, the Moral Object, and *Humanae
Vitae*" in this volume.

60. Cessario, *Introduction to Moral Theology,* 32, referring to John Finnis, *Fundamentals
of Ethics* (Washington, D.C.: Georgetown University Press, 1983), 44–45. Note that by "classi-
cism," Lonergan did not mean the great classics of philosophy and theology; see Benedict Ashley, O.P., *The Ashley Reader: Redeeming Reason* (Naples, Fla.: Sapientia Press, 2006), 13–26.

61. *Insight,* 618.

62. Ibid., 709ff. Also his *De Verbo Incarnato.*

life out of death, love out of hate, goodness out of evil. The leap of faith, as the analogy from our natural knowledge of God emphasizes, is not an irrational leap. It is a leap into a healed and supernaturally enlightened intelligence and reason. The light of faith does not blind our human intelligence, it heals and strengthens our understanding.

This account of the good brings together both metaphysics concerned with the proper understanding of the natural and Catholic theology concerned with the interiority of the mutual self-mediation of Divine and human persons knowing and loving each other. As Lonergan has written:

Once this is grasped, it follows that the divine persons, the blessed in heaven, and the justified here on earth are mutually present in each other as the known is present in the knower and as the beloved is present in the lover. Attention is to be given to this knowing and loving both with respect to its ultimate end, which is that good that is the good through its essence and with respect to its proximate end, which is a common good of order, the kingdom of God, the Body of Christ, the Church. Moreover, the consequent mutual indwelling differs in accord with the nature and state of each individual: for the divine persons are mutually present in each other on the basis of consubstantiality; the justified are present in God and in each other on the basis of intentional act of existence and on the basis of the kind of identification proper to love; we are in the Word as known to him and beloved by him both on the basis of his divine nature and on the basis of his human nature; the Word is in us in our knowledge and love for him as a sensible man as we are reaching toward a knowledge and love of God who dwells in inaccessible light (1 Tim. 6:16). And because the prior knowledge and love is easier for us in that it includes our sensitive memory of the past and our imagination of the future, we are led by it to that higher knowledge and love in which we now no longer know Christ in the flesh but our own inner word proper to the divine Word is spoken intelligibly in us on the basis of an emanation of truth and our own love proper to the divine Love is spirated on the basis of an emanation of sanctity. For the divine persons are sent on the basis of their eternal processions so that they may meet us and dwell in us on the basis of similar processions that are produced in us through grace. But those who proceed from and are sent by the Father do not come without the Father to whom all glory belongs through the Son and the Spirit.[63]

This certainly confirms Fr. Cessario's description of what happens in faith in his *Christian Faith and the Theological Life* as an "entirely unexpected kind of interiority, one that initiates a personal communion with God."

---

63. Lonergan, *De Deo Trino*, vol. 2, 255–56. My translation. This will appear in vol. 12 of the *Collected Works*.

[13]

Moral Development and Connecting the Virtues

Aquinas, Porter, and the Flawed Saint

CRAIG STEVEN TITUS

*The incontinent man is like a city which passes all the right decrees
and has good laws, but makes no use of them.* —Aristotle

The missing link between theory and practice in ethics is moral development.
Accounting for this link is the major challenge facing ethical theory today.
Some ethicists would grant moral development only a trivial place in relation
to issues of normativity, natural law, and the nature of rationality or in relation
to questions of the adequacy of utilitarian and consequentialist calculations.
Others would make it an issue for psychology or pedagogy alone, a minor concern. Neglecting moral development, however, risks the danger of construing
the moral agent as fragmented or determined. Aquinas and other virtue ethicists like Aristotle, by contrast, make it a principal element needed to understand the pursuit of a good moral life and true happiness (beatitude). A source
of confusion, however, in certain virtue approaches is found in the doctrine of

Earlier versions of this essay were delivered at the conference "Sujet moral et communauté" in Fribourg (CH) and published in French in a volume of the same name edited by Denis
Müller et al. (Fribourg: Academic Press, 2008). I am grateful for the constructive comments of
the conference participants.

The epigraph is taken from Aristotle, *Nicomachean Ethics*, trans. W. D. Ross (Princeton,
N.J.: Princeton University Press, 1984), 7, 10 [1152a20–22].

what has been called the unity of the virtues by some, the connection of the virtues by others.

St. Thomas Aquinas's mature works, the *Summa theologiae* and the *Disputed Questions on Virtue,*[1] on which I will focus, provide one of the primary reasons for a return to the virtues in ethics and in moral theology. His approach to virtue allows us a way to better integrate into ethics not only teleology and rational adjudication of the natural law, but moral development as well. The virtue revival, as is evidenced in the work of Josef Pieper, Elizabeth Anscombe, Alasdair MacIntyre, Servais Pinckaers, Stanley Hauerwas, and Jean Porter,[2] has made reference to a longstanding tradition of virtue-based philosophical anthropology and moral theology based on the Stoics, Aristotle, Scripture, Augustine, and Aquinas. Alongside this revival, caricatures have cropped up that reduce virtue ethics to moral psychology, at the expense of normativeness, or that view it as a meager agent-ethics. The present inquiry into Aquinas's doctrine of moral development gives us the opportunity to explore the promises and the ambiguities of virtue ethics.

The Virtues of the Flawed Saint?

In order to treat Aquinas's notion of the virtues and their connection, I would like to employ the counterexample of the flawed saint, that is, the troubling illustration of a person who simultaneously exhibits seemingly heroic virtues and patent vices. I raise this issue in order to apply virtue theory to the thorny issues of human struggles with imperfection, the uncertainty of moral development, and the gaps between normative theory and ethical practice. In particular, I will employ a counterexample presented by Jean Porter in her arti-

---

1. In this text, I cite the following translations: *The Summa Theologica of St. Thomas Aquinas* (Westminster, Md.: Christian Classics, 1981); and Thomas Aquinas, *Disputed Questions on Virtue,* trans. Ralph McInerny (South Bend, Ind.: St. Augustine's Press, 1999).

2. Josef Pieper, *The Four Cardinal Virtues: Prudence, Justice, Fortitude, Temperance,* trans. Richard Winston et al. (Notre Dame, Ind.: University of Notre Dame Press, 1966). G. E. M. Anscombe, "Modern Moral Philosophy," in *Collected Philosophical Papers,* vol. 3 (Oxford: Oxford University Press, 1981), 26–41. Alasdair MacIntyre, *After Virtue: A Study in Moral Theory* (Notre Dame, Ind.: University of Notre Dame Press, 1981); *Whose Justice? Which Rationality?* (London: Duckworth, 1988); *The Tasks of Philosophy* (New York: Cambridge University Press, 2006). Servais Pinckaers, *The Sources of Christian Ethics,* trans. Sr. Mary Thomas Noble, O.P. (Washington, D.C.: The Catholic University of America Press, 1995); *Morality: The Catholic View,* trans. Michael Sherwin, O.P. (South Bend, Ind.: St. Augustine Press, 2001); *The Pinckaers Reader,* ed. John Berkman and Craig Steven Titus (Washington, D.C.: The Catholic University of America Press, 2005). Stanley Hauerwas, *The Peaceable Kingdom: A Primer in Christian Ethics* (Notre Dame, Ind.: University of Notre Dame Press, 1983); *The Hauerwas Reader,* ed. John Berkman and Michael Cartwright (Durham, N.C.: Duke University Press, 2001). Jean Porter, *Moral Action and Christian Ethics* (New York: Cambridge University Press, 1995).

cle "Virtue and Sin: The Connection of the Virtues and the Case of the Flawed Saint."[3] In order to explain the case of the imperfect hero, Porter proposes reformulating Thomas Aquinas's conception of charity in order not to exclude persistent and grave sin. I will ask whether such a reformulation is necessary or adequate.

The Sins of a Flawed Saint

Porter engages salient aspects of the life of the Reverend Martin Luther King, Jr., the great civil rights advocate, popular leader, pastor, and Nobel laureate. He is widely known and rightly praised for his promotion of nonviolence, racial equality, and social justice. According to Porter, King is a martyr to the cause of equality; she affirms that he is a "genuine saint and martyr," who expressed "virtues in the fullest sense."[4] However, at the same time—and here is the foil—she calls him a "flawed saint." She reports that he also exhibited a pattern of vicious activity, namely, repeated marital infidelities. Some sources and supposed FBI recordings indicate that these marital infidelities are well documented; there are some, however, who believe that they are the fabrications of a defamation campaign against King. In any case—and our point is not to indict or acquit Rev. King—he demonstrated an intention to repent or, at least, to give himself a higher ideal in his public addresses, published writings, and private conversations. In his collection of sermons, *Strength to Love*, he describes the struggle in each person between the higher self (or ego) and the lower self, between good and evil, the last of which is expressed in "tragic lust and inordinate selfishness."[5] He often expressed, moreover, his desire to accomplish "the will of God" through his work of promoting social justice, while knowing that these efforts could cost him his life.[6]

3. "Virtue and Sin: The Connection of the Virtues and the Case of the Flawed Saint," *Journal of Religion* 75, no. 4 (1995): 521–39. Porter has repeatedly argued, against critiques, that Aquinas's theory of the connection of the virtues is neither patently false nor trivially true. See an earlier attempt at the issue, which she revised: Jean Porter, "The Unity of the Virtues and the Ambiguity of Goodness: A Reappraisal of Aquinas's Theory of the Virtues," *Journal of Religious Ethics* 21, no. 1 (1993): 137–63, and her book *Moral Action*, 159–66.

4. Porter, "Virtue and Sin," 528, 529.

5. Martin Luther King, Jr., *Strength to Love* (Cleveland, Ohio, 1963), 60, cited in Stephen B. Oates, *Let the Trumpet Sound: A Life of Martin Luther King, Jr.* (New York: HarperPerennial, 1982), 283–84.

6. Interview for the magazine *Time*; cited in Oates, *Let the Trumpet Sound*, 285. Moreover, according to his wife, Martin Luther King predicted his own assassination. Immediately after having heard of J. F. Kennedy's assassination in 1963, King said: "I don't think I'm going to live to reach forty . . . This is what is going to happen to me also." Conversation with his wife; cited in Oates, *Let the Trumpet Sound*, 270.

In the Catholic tradition, in which Porter speaks, the status of "saint" and "martyr" have great significance. To be considered a saint does not exclude mistakes, errors, imperfect acts, but it does demand evidence of repentance and conversion from known sins. St. Augustine was a "flawed saint" in the sense that he lived, according to his *Confessions,* a part of his life turned toward sin. After his conversion, though, he gave himself to God and took steps to contain his acquired weaknesses, which does not mean that he did not err or sin, but that he exhibited repentance and the intention to conform his person to Christ for the rest of his life. Furthermore, we call "martyr" a person who witnesses to Christ in righteousness at the price of his own life.[7] Nonetheless, we do not identify the saints and martyrs with their past sins or misdeeds, but recognize that the grace of charity permitted them to distance themselves from their sins and vices, even if traces of disordered tendencies remained. Thus we praise the saints for their greatness and heroic virtue (acts and qualities) without making norms of any past errors.

In contrast to this tradition, the manner in which her article renders Martin Luther King a flawed saint challenges what Porter believes to be a traditional understanding of virtue. She recognizes that his repeated unchaste behavior is paradoxical, especially inasmuch as she considers him a saint who expressed the fullness of the theological virtues of faith, hope, and charity, as well as all the infused virtues. It is in this context that Porter offers the example of Rev. King as a case for understanding—and revising—the thought of Aquinas on the connection of the virtues, and in particular the relation between the theological virtue of charity and serious "patterns of bad activities [and] vices,"[8] like marital infidelity. This case of the flawed saint will give us a chance to discuss its implications for Aquinas's theories of the possibility of moral development and the connection of the virtues.

I must make two caveats before employing this example, however. First, I am not judging the person of Martin Luther King (or someone such as John F. Kennedy, who might be put into the same category); discussions of a person's character flaws do not discredit God's offer of grace and salvation. Second, I can talk only about certain acts that people have observed or intentions that King has communicated; this information is limited and its interpretation problematic. Moreover, I do not intend to discredit the valiant work done by Martin Luther King and a great number of courageous people to overcome unjust laws and practices and to instill a reign of justice and compassion.

---

7. See Matt 5:10; also Aquinas, *ST* II, q. 124, aa. 1 and 5.
8. Porter, "Virtue and Sin," 529.

Aquinas on Virtue

Virtue involves good acts that make the person good.[9] Aquinas's thought on moral development is articulated around the virtues, which are understood through the concepts of *habitus* (quality or operational disposition) and connaturalization, which explain the possibility of continuity and creativity in moral agency. St. Thomas defines *habitus* as an acquired quality that we change only with difficulty. Even though it involves continuity and stability, a *habitus* is neither mechanical nor deterministic nor external. It should be distinguished from what is commonly referred to as a 'habit.' A *habitus*, as an operational disposition that involves rational, volitional, and emotional qualities, is unlike the habit of tying one's shoes without looking. It requires not only continued congruous acts in theoretical and practical matters (depending on the type of quality), but also creativity in novel situations. It involves the intelligence and creativity to bring the general notion of justice, for example, to adjudicate a dispute between neighbors about a broken window. *Habitus* is a quality that disposes one to act and that becomes a second nature *(connaturalis)*.[10] Virtue, as a good type of *habitus,* involves the internalization of the true good in our cognitive, affective, sensate, and intellectual faculties, at personal and social levels. It implies the normativeness of the true and the good acquired through reason (or natural law) seen as a human participation in Eternal Law. These normative and behavioral qualities are instilled in a person by natural disposition, discipline, rational adjudication, or as a gift of grace.[11] Vice, on the contrary, internalizes apparent goods or patent evil, in some way against human nature.

A current problem in virtue theory (and one that entraps Porter) is the equivocation that is discernable only when one has distinguished three related uses of "virtue" as: (1) a good quality that disposes one to act; (2) a good action itself; and (3) a norm, rule, or law that serves as the standard for an action or for a dispositional quality.[12] In the first sense, virtue is defined as a stable

9. See *De virtutibus in communi,* q. 1, a. 1.

10. See *Summa theologiae* I-II, qq. 49–54. The operational *habitus* cover three tightly related domains: (a) temperament or character traits, such as timidity or kindness; (b) acquired and stable dispositions to act, that is, the virtues and vices; and (c) individual acts.

11. See *De virtutibus cardinalibus,* a. 3; *ST* I-II, q. 66, a. 2; *ST* I-II, q. 106, a. 1, ad 2. Aquinas holds that natural dispositions and developments, while commensurate with human native capacities, depend also on the help of God *(auxilio Dei),* who is the first and efficacious cause of the goodness endemic to nature, cf. *ST* I-II q. 109, aa. 1 and 3; *ST* I-II, q. 61, a. 5.

12. Aquinas continually distinguishes operative dispositions from acts; see for example: *ST* I-II qq. 49–56; *ST* II-II q. 129, a. 3, ad 2. Something of this distinction is found in Halper, who identifies two definitions (and two notions) of the virtues in Aristotle: one is functional, based

quality or disposition to act morally, as a good operative disposition (*habitus operativus*).[13] Aquinas's most basic philosophical definition avers that "virtue denotes a determinate perfection of a power."[14] He also employs a definition that has been attributed to Augustine: "virtue is a good quality of the mind, by which we live righteously, of which no one can make bad use, which God works in us, without us";[15] the last clause refers specifically to infused virtue, which we will discuss in passing later. The perfection of any operative *habitus* involves the way in which the power inclines toward and correlates to its end or proper act that is judged virtuous inasmuch as it is in accord with reason, human and divine—that is, with natural and eternal law.[16] In addition to its normative characteristics (rectitude and being in accord with reason), a well-developed acquired virtue involves the tendency to express the psychological and behavioral characteristics of ease, promptness, and joy in action.[17] In the other two related senses, "virtue" is used to refer to the good acts themselves and to the norms, rules, or laws used to adjudicate goodness in practice. It is evident that virtue, when conceived as a good operative disposition, is closely related to concrete action and to a rational standard for judgment found in natural and divine law.[18]

Of these three senses, I would argue that, for Aquinas, virtue's prime analogue is a good operative disposition rather then a particular act or norm. However, operative dispositions are good only insofar as they tend toward normatively good action; moreover, they need to be distinguished according to the type of perfection to which they dispose. Thus the cardinal virtues as general conditions of all virtuous activity illustrate the draw toward greater moral coherence and normative unity. Rather than seeking simply to uphold an abstract norm willy nilly or an isolated good act, the goal of Aquinas's virtue ethics is to explain human dispositional goodness, and the correlation be-

---

on proper action that the virtue involves; the other is a psychic version of the virtue, concerning the psychological state constituted in the virtue. See Edward Halper, "The Unity of the Virtues in Aristotle," *Oxford Studies in Ancient Philosophy* 17 (1999): 115–43.

    13. *ST* I-II, q. 55, a. 4.

    14. *ST* I-II, q. 56, a. 1.

    15. Augustine, *De libero arbitrio*, II.19 (PL 32.1268), which Aquinas quotes in *ST* I-II, q. 55, a. 4; *De virtutibus in communi*, q. 1, a. 2; *ST* I-II, q. 65, a. 1. According to Odon Lottin (*Psychologie et morale aux XIIe et XIIIe siècles*, 8 vols. [Louvain: Abbaye Mont César, 1942–60]), although this definition is customarily attributed to St. Augustine, it is probably due to Peter of Poiters in his commentary on the *Sentences* (*ST* III, I [PL 211, 1041]).

    16. See *ST* I-II, q. 55, a. 4; *ST* I-II, q. 70, a. 4, ad 1.

    17. Cf. *De veritatis*, q. 20, a. 2; *Summa contra Gentiles*, bk 3, ch. 150, § 7; *De virtutibus cardinalibus*, a. 2, ad 2; *De virtutibus in communi*, q. 1, a. 1; cf. Romanus Cessario, *Introduction to Moral Theology* (Washington, D.C.: The Catholic University of America Press, 2001), 200–205.

    18. Cf. *ST* I-II, qq. 90–94.

tween the development of such a disposition and the norms and acts that either precede them or result from them.

Identifying the correlation of the dispositional, agentive, and normative aspects of virtue permits Aquinas to discern the developmental teleology that operates in virtue ethics and gives a different appreciation of the general cardinal virtues. For Aquinas's understanding of the general cardinal virtues involves within itself a conception of the unity of the person and the interrelationship of virtuous dispositions that seek to realize moral acts in fitting ways: with the good of reason (prudence); with firm will (justice); and with proper emotional states concerning attractive goods (temperance); and concerning difficulty in attaining good or resisting evil (fortitude).[19] These general cardinal virtues depict the dispositional centers around which coherent moral life and action turn.

What nuances can this threefold distinction bring to our discussion? If applied to a person, in statements such as: Martin Luther King was a "truly virtuous" person,[20] the first two senses carry different meanings. Certain discussions, though, including Porter's discussion of the flawed saint, seem to confuse the significance of dispositions and of acts in adjudicating a virtuous or vicious character. Noting the ambiguity in Porter's arguments will help to explain the riddle of Martin Luther King, or rather the problem of her interpretation of him. Porter identifies virtues or vices as "actions" in critical parts of her argument that concludes by disregarding Aquinas's thought on the connection of the cardinal virtues based on their being general conditions for all the virtues or as being a tendency in any truly virtuous act toward complete virtue. She says: "What [Aquinas's theory of general cardinal virtues] amounts to is a claim that no action can be said to be virtuous in an unqualified sense, unless it can fairly be said to exemplify all of the cardinal virtues in some way."[21] She concludes that the cardinal virtues, seen as general virtues, represent an uninteresting aspect of virtue.

Such differences in construing virtue, however lead to diverse interpretations of the flawed saint. The failures of such a person might seem to demonstrate that (1) at least his virtues are not infallible dispositions to produce objectively good acts or (2) at most his failures discredit him of any claim on virtue. The latter position is neither that of Porter nor that of Aquinas. However, it is in the significance of the first one—namely, the type of imperfection possible within the positive pull of the virtues toward further interconnection and completeness—that Porter and Aquinas differ, as we will see.

19. Cf. *ST* I-II, q. 65, a. 1.   20. Porter, "Virtue and Sin," 532.
21. Ibid., 524.

Moral Anthropology and Types of Virtues

In order to understand the flawed saint, our discussion needs to go beyond reflections on general dispositions. If the general cardinal virtues were to express the full extent of the connection of virtues—perhaps the weakest possible—we could rightly ask whether Aquinas's account is trivial or ethically meaningless, since isolated evil acts would disqualify a person from being considered a person with virtuous dispositions. But before drawing such a disqualificatory conclusion, let us look more carefully at moral development proper and the nature of failed acts and flawed characters.

Aquinas's conception of moral development is construed according to: the person as a whole in search of happiness (subjective aspect including intention); human faculties as ordered yet non-determined (as the seats or matters of the virtues); and the object of virtue and its acts as objectively discernable. Thus virtue (as a disposition) is not identified simply with human neurophysiological and psychological faculties per se, but with their interrelation with the finality, ends, and goods (personal and social, natural and divine goods) that fulfill the human person in partial, complete, and ultimate ways.[22] When considering the moral agent in terms of human potential, responsibility, and freedom, Aquinas's virtue approach takes into consideration four domains that he holds together: cognitive senses (internal and external sense powers); affective senses (emotion); intellectual cognition (intuitive and discursive reason); and intellectual affection (intuitive and discursive volition).

Aquinas's anthropological framework is crucial for understanding the possibility of the moral development that comprises the cardinal virtues as special virtues. This account of the virtues can help to explain moral growth in one domain but relative moral stagnation or disorder in another, for example, the moral shortfalls of the flawed saint. As I already mentioned, Aquinas considers that human moral powers are neither determined to one moral act (at the level of discursive reason and will) nor without a source of moral ordering (efficient, formal, and final causality). The potential for moral development is rooted in human nature, which is normative and which is expressed in the flourishing of the capacities to perceive reality, to manage emotions, to reason about ends and means, and to seek true goodness, which can all be summarized in terms of the quality and correlation of knowledge and love that are practically developed in comunities.[23]

Aquinas's conception of moral virtue as a good operative disposition fur-

22. See *ST* I-II, qq. 1–5.
23. See Alasdair MacIntyre, *After Virtue: A Study in Moral Theory* (London: Duckworth,

thermore is more modest in its pretensions than some thinkers have supposed. What have often been rejected in the past are static notions of virtues, conceptions that construe virtue as a type of fixed action, often only intelligible to a single cultural milieu. Porter herself refers to true and perfect virtues in ways that narrow Aquinas's thought. She even concludes that his doctrine of the connection of the virtues "cannot fully account for this kind of case."[24] However, Aquinas's typology of virtue permits us to understand the tendency toward the future (acts) and wholeness (a teleological end) and to account for the necessity for new and creative applications or for the possibility of actual error that brings us to the question of distinguishing true from false virtues.

Aquinas specifies that virtues are true when they have true and good ends, either at proximate or at ultimate levels.[25] On the one hand, at the level of proximate and particular goods, like being well disposed to pursue the goods of civil society, there are true but imperfect virtues. Thus we can have true patience and true courage that aim at proximate goods, but which could furthermore be directed to one's ultimate end (since they are not foreign to the final end, who is God).[26] These virtues, however, are not to be confused with the dispositions that pursue ends whose good is only apparent and that give counterfeit virtues (or semblances of virtue). In the latter case, people exhibit characteristics of one virtue, even seemingly in a heroic degree, but lack other cardinal virtues. A favorite example is the courage of those who use their bravery to do evil deeds: the bank robber, the assassin, and figures such as Thomas Cromwell (as cited by Porter).[27] In sum, the semblance of good leads a person away from his final good, while the true good (even when limited to human ends such as building houses and planting vineyards) is compatible with ultimate good.

On the other hand, Aquinas affirms that those virtues that aim directly at ultimate and universal goods and ends are true virtues, simply speaking (*virtus vera simpliciter*).[28] These virtues are based on the final end (God), who is obtained only through the gift of grace found in the virtue of charity. When

---

1985, second edition), and *Dependent Rational Animals: Why Human Beings Need the Virtues* (Chicago: Open Court Press, 1999).

24. Porter, "Virtue and Sin," 533.

25. See *ST* II-II, q. 23, a. 7; I-II, q. 65, aa. 1 and 2; II-II, q. 151, a. 7.

26. On the limits of this type of true virtue, see also: *De virtutibus in communis*, a. 7; *ST* II-II, q. 136, a. 3, ad 1, as well as the following discussion of perfect virtue.

27. On the problem of using a virtue for evil purposes, see: *ST* I-II, q. 66, a. 1; St. Augustine, *De lib. arb.* II. 19. As Josef Pieper specifies in his chapter on fortitude (in *The Four Cardinal Virtues*), true courage is not simply a matter of controlling one's fear, but it must be in the service of justice and right.

28. *ST* II-II, q. 23, a. 7.

treating true courage and true patience, Aquinas discusses whether true virtue can exist without grace and without charity.[29] In these questions, we see Aquinas's allegiance to Augustine, who considers virtue "true" only when it is simply perfect and theologically complete. Nonetheless, in so doing, Aquinas admits that there can be true but imperfect virtue at another level, as we will further discuss later on.[30]

The Possibility of Moral Development

Human Potential and Personal Differences

In addition to the considerations of true or counterfeit, right or wrong, good or evil, Aquinas's virtue theory demands consideration of personal potential and social differences which discount neither norms nor the effects of error and sin, but rather make them more evident. Aquinas ascribes the starting point for acquired virtues (both intellectual and moral) "to certain natural principles pre-existing in us."[31] Virtue (as second nature) is constructed (1) in accord with our specific human nature (essential nature) and (2) in function of a person's individual nature (temperament and character propensities). At the social level, family and peer influences, communal interactions, and culturally specific settings tend either to enhance or to restrict growth in virtue. The flawed saint, for his part, has embodied moral conflict, error, or weakness in three non-exclusive ways.

First, the natural inclinations are the cognitive and affective bases for moral goodness and drives for a virtuous life; they are, however, at first practically underspecified, for they must be put into practice and in this putting into practice the virtues are born. Negative practices and influences (including that of original sin) vie with the initial propensity to truth, goodness, self-integrity, or pro-social behavior.[32] For particular virtues to flourish, a person must actively nurture these principles, each one according to its specificity. If he does not, there will be immaturity at best, vice at worst.

Second, persons vary in temperamental, affective, and cognitive propensi-

---

29. See *ST* II-II, q. 123, a. 10, ad 3; II-II, q. 136, a. 3; and Craig Steven Titus, *Resilience and the Virtue of Fortitude: Aquinas in Dialogue with the Psychosocial Sciences* (Washington, D.C.: The Catholic University of America Press, 2006), 172, 326–33.

30. See *ST* I-II, q. 55, a. 4.

31. *ST* I-II, q. 63, a. 3; see also I-II, q. 51, a. 1; I-II, q. 63, a. 1; I-II, q. 63, a. 2. Aquinas's understanding of the interrelation of nature and nurture can be seen in his handling of *habitus* in *ST* I-II, q. 50, a. 1.

32. Cf. *ST* I-II, q. 94, a. 2; *ST* I-II, q. 63, a. 1. Cf. Matthew Levering, "Natural Law and Natural Inclinations: Rhonheimer, Pinckaers, McAleer," *The Thomist* 70, no. 2 (2006): 155–201.

ties. Some individuals are more fit and able for science, others for fortitude or temperance, and so on. A person's particular makeup of bodily sensory powers and emotions helps or hinders the exercise of rational powers.[33] While having natural strengths at this level, the flawed saint may also have other weaknesses. Often, as Aristotle said, an attitudinal strength that is not connected with the network of virtues may entail a tendency to an opposing weakness: for instance, a weakness in patience for the bold, in magnanimity for the timid, in courage for the fearful.[34]

Third, at the level of virtue and vice proper, since operative *habitus* are more or less mature and well-formed dispositions, the flawed saint will unremittingly need to bolster his integrity. He will have to persist to make progress in acquired virtue and in the interconnection of his virtues. If he has developed negative operative dispositions in the past, he will need to correct these by moving away from vice, through intermediate states, before being able to express fuller manifestations of virtue. Here we need to differentiate the personal disorders, relational weaknesses, inexperience, or errors—that are not in the realm of moral responsibility—from outright moral disorder as disposition or act (as vice or sin).

Aquinas's notion of perfection brings nuance also to the differences of personal capacity and state of life (for example, different commitments of the married, single, or consecrated persons) and it admits differences that are due to certain external situations (the lack of financial means to be magnificent, for example). Aquinas notes that the four cardinal virtues perfect a human being as regards his general state—in other words, these virtues are necessary and possible for everyone (withstanding cases of grave limitations at perceptual, psychological, or experiential level). Aquinas holds, nonetheless, that even without experience in eminent or particular virtues, the preparation of the general virtues does prepare a person for further developments, if experience so presents the possibility. Thus, he speaks of a "proximate potency" (*in potentia propinqua*) that a full range of basic (general) moral virtues provides,[35] but which without some experience and effort cannot become associated virtues. This also applies to different types of prudence that must be learned—family prudence, political prudence, military prudence, and, we might add, nonviolent prudence, in the case of Martin Luther King.

33. Cf. *ST* I-II, q. 63, a. 1.
34. Cf. *ST* I-II, q. 65, a. 1.
35. *ST* I-II, q. 65, a. 1, ad 1; *De virtutibus cardinalibus*, a. 2, ad 5.

Growth, Change, and Stability

Such considerations of the development of virtue are pertinent because neither does moral theory directly translate into moral action nor do natural inclinations directly become well-formed virtuous dispositions. The affective and cognitive capacities of the human person interact in the exercise of moral judgments and in more or less consequent moral action. Furthermore, just as one good action does not a virtuous disposition make,[36] so repetition and experience cut a path for constructing virtue or vice, conceived as stable acquired dispositions to act toward good or evil. But in the meantime, moral immaturity or neglect concerning these dispositions leads to inconsistencies and errors.

For Aquinas, the possibility of moral development means that we have to account for or at least presume that human beings are capable of intelligent, free, and responsible action.[37] Aquinas's approach is an anti-determinist position on the level of *habitus* and virtues (concerning discursive reason and will), for he seeks to provide an account of (1) change, contingency, and even inconsistency, as well as (2) stability, consistency, and even necessity, in a person's moral character. He construes the acquired virtues (good *habitus*), moreover, in a non-infallibilist way. The stability of a disposition to act does not eradicate the difficulty of translating the disposition into good actions, because of a number of circumstances: ignorance, novelty of the situation, technical incompetence, physical or psychosocial incapacitation (sickness, sleep, neuroses, psychoses), diversity of seemingly valid options, the pull of other dispositions, influences from peers or the culture, and so on.

Lastly, in the midst of these contingencies, Aquinas holds a nonrelativist position, in which the normative conception of goodness is grounded in the twofold rule of "human reason and Divine Law."[38] Human virtue, as a good operative *habitus,* demands the construction (perfection) of a natural human power according to the twofold rule: (1) directed by the order of human reason and the natural law (formal cause), and (2) guided by Divine Law of the New Law of grace (efficient cause).[39]

But the recognition of potential strength and weakness leads to further

---

36. Cf. *ST* I-II, q. 51, a. 3; I-II, q. 63, a. 1.

37. See Aquinas's preface to the *prima secunda,* which builds upon the Book of Genesis (1:27) and St. John Damascene (*De fide orthodoxa,* ii, 12).

38. *De virtutibus cardinalibus,* a. 2; *ST* I-II, q. 63, a. 2; q. 19, aa. 3 and 4.

39. Aquinas draws from both scriptural and Ciceronian authority in this regard. See *ST* II-II, q. 58, a. 3; *ST* II-II, q. 58, a. 12, s.c.; 3 *Sent.* d. 33, q. 1, a. 2, s.c. 2.

questions: Is the flawed saint an example of a person who has certain clearly developed virtuous strengths and, at the same time, certain clearly developed vicious weaknesses? Or is vice too much to admit? In order to respond to this question, we need to understand the possibility of partial developments and to distinguish between the types of perfection and completeness in the acquired virtues.

Does the Virtuous Mean Concern Acts or Dispositions?

Even though the human good must be appraised with respect to the two-fold rule of human reason and Divine Law, Aquinas exhibits practical modesty in recognizing that there is not always only one right practical answer. Moreover, contingencies increase as one moves from speculative theory to more concrete levels of practical theory and action. A person is not always rationally certain about the probity concerning practical details of his judgment. Furthermore, one may patently fail in a particular act (act of injustice, anger, or infidelity when drunk or ill) without losing the acquired disposition (in these cases, the acquired dispositions of justice, meekness, or chastity) because the use of a *habitus* is subject to our will and one act does not destroy such an acquired disposition.[40] Moreover, in Aquinas's construal, a large middle ground between diverse erroneous extremes constitutes pathways of virtue or moral development (and undevelopment). In reference to his notion of the virtuous mean, Porter overlooks crucial distinctions between general traits of virtues and what Aquinas calls true and perfect virtue.[41]

The doctrine of the mean of virtue helps one further understand the flawed saint in three ways. First, besides particular aspects of justice, the cardinal virtues do not involve an arithmetic mean or calculation. Rather, the other cardinal virtues exercise a rational mean regarding the matter of the virtue. In conformity to reason, as a maximum *(maxima bona* or *ultimum potentiae),* the moral virtues of courage and temperance seek a middle position between extremes of a particular passion in order to achieve the good: "where it is right; when it is right; and for an end that is right."[42]

Second, within the moral norm of being in conformity with reason, we can account for certain differences between two persons because different persons

40. Cf. *ST* I-II, q. 49, a. 3; and q. 63, a. 2, ad 2.

41. Porter states ("Virtue and Sin," 529) that Aquinas (*ST* I-II, q. 63, a. 2, ad 2) has not ruled out the possibility of perfect acquired virtue. In this particular text, though, Aquinas does not predicate "perfect" of the acquired virtues. Reference to perfect acquired virtue (as a disposition) needs to be made in the context of I-II, q. 65, aa. 1 and 2, which identify the limits of such perfection, as I shall outline presently.

42. *ST* I-II, q. 64, a. 1, ad 2.

(or the same person at different times) must consider different circumstances and have different resources on hand. This explains something of individual moral diversity within normative probity, for a virtuous disposition can be actualized (but also sidetracked) in various ways. Thus Aquinas says:

> In actions and passions the mean and the extremes depend on various circumstances: hence nothing hinders something from being extreme in a particular virtue as to one circumstance, while the same thing is a mean in respect of other circumstances, through being in conformity with reason.[43]

Thus, the practices of magnanimous or magnificent virtue will be rightly great and even "extreme" when requisite capacities or resources are on hand, according to Aristotle.[44] The mean in great gifts and acts involves having measured one's own capacities. They would be excessive for others. To strive for certain types of intellectual, political, and artistic excellences will overstep one person's capacities, but not another's. Nonetheless, according to Aquinas, there is also a proportionally great use of resources, even when they are slim; as in the case of the poor widow (Mk 12:43; Lk 21:3), whose mite is proportionally grand in relationship to her holdings and whose interior choice is magnificent.[45]

Third, according to Aristotle, not every virtuous person has all the virtuous dispositions in the same degree. The contemplative and the ruler have different measures of speculative and practical wisdom, although both fall into the mean of virtue, in each virtue and overall.[46] Aquinas is particularly nuanced concerning subjective differences between people and the changes of a developmental state over time. He states that one virtue, considered on the part of the subject, differs.

> Because one man is better disposed than another to attain to the mean of virtue which is defined by right reason; and this, on account of either greater habituation, or a better natural disposition, or a more discerning judgment of reason, or again a greater gift of grace, which is given to each one "according to the measure of the giving of Christ," as stated in Ephesians 4:9.[47]

Such variances in nature and grace explain something of the challenges that face the person who seeks to attain the rational mean of virtue.

---

43. Ibid.
44. See Aristotle, *Nicomachean Ethics*, 4, 3 (1123b13); and Eckart Schütrumpf, "Magnanimity, *megalopsychia*, and the System of Aristotle's *Nicomachean Ethics*," *Archiv für Geschichte des Philosophie* 71 (1989): 10–22.
45. Cf. *ST* II-II, q. 134, a. 3, ad 4; I, q. 95, a. 4; II-II, q. 32, a. 4, c. and ad 3.
46. Cf. Halper, "The Unity of the Virtues," 135–43.
47. *ST* I-II, q. 66, a. 1. Cf. 1 Cor 10:7–9; *ST* I-II, q. 66, a. 2.

The Connection of the Virtues

This discussion of moral development and the mean of virtue leaves two questions unanswered: Do the flawed saint's virtues admit of degrees? Do they call upon each other for fulfillment? Jean Porter, in employing Martin Luther King as an example of a flawed saint, wants to affirm that someone can express true virtue and persistent vice contemporaneously. The incommensurability of this portrayal with Aquinas's doctrine on virtue leads Porter to revise Aquinas's teaching on charity. However, Aquinas has other ways to solve the problem; one is his conception of the connection of the virtues.

A Unity or Connection of the Virtues?

Porter rightly confirms that Aquinas does not hold a Platonic or Stoic notion of the unity of the virtues.[48] Aquinas is clear: while agreeing with the Stoics that the nature of virtue in itself "consists in a maximum," he disagrees with them (through Simplicius's Commentary on Aristotle's *Categories*) regarding virtue construed as an acquired disposition. He says:

The nature of virtue does not require that man should reach the mean of right reason as though it were an indivisible point, as the Stoics thought; but it is enough that he should approach the mean, as stated in the *Nicomachean Ethics* (ii, 6 [1106b18–23]). Moreover, one same indivisible mark is reached more nearly and more readily by one than by another: as may be seen when several archers aim at a fixed target.[49]

Aquinas holds that the "essence of virtue" demands that one hit the target (and thus "approach the mean"). A Stoic interpretation demands hitting consistently an indivisible point (the bull's eye within a bull's eye). If, as such an interpretation has it, the doctrine of the unity of virtue seeks a monolithic or a static notion of perfection, then no one is just, temperate, courageous, or prudent if they miss any one of them in any part at any time. By contrast, Aquinas's no-

---

48. Plato construes the virtues in relation to the true Good. The virtue of wisdom gives a person the capacity to establish a just interrelation among the parts of the soul, among his virtues, and in his actions (cf. *Republic* IV; *Phaedo* 67c–70a; *Meno* 81a–e; *Laws* 643b–644c. See Thomas C. Brickhouse and Nicholas D. Smith, "Socrates and the Unity of the Virtues," *Journal of Ethics* 1, no. 4 (1997): 311–24. Plato speaks of a type of unity of the virtues, a unity that is founded on the interchangeability of the virtues with the good, which has been construed to reduce the virtues to a single point.

Stoic notions of virtue have a unity in the *logos*; however, they construe not so much a unity of the virtues but a mutual calling forth of the virtues. The essence of any virtue is found in the being in accord with reason or the natural law. See Simplicius's *Commentary on the Predicaments* [*Categories*], cited by Aquinas (*ST* I-II, q. 66, a. 1).

49. *ST* I-II, q. 66, a. 1; see also *De virtutibus cardinalibus*, a. 3.

tion of the connection of the virtues simply requires that one has a disposition to seek a virtuous mean in all these areas, which does not guarantee that the person will succeed every time in the actualization of a virtuous intention or plan; rather, it means that he will refine his acts in function of these goods in reasonable measure with the hope of greater ease, spontaneity, and joy in the doing over time. Thus, for Aquinas, there are degrees of attaining the essence of virtue.

Aquinas moreover construes two ways that virtues are interconnected, either by acquired prudence (the master skill of the cardinal virtues) or by charity (which pertains to the infused and theological virtues).[50] Prudence discerns, adjudicates, and puts into action the rational norm that has been discovered in the exercise of prudence.[51] In the work of prudence, preparedness of mind (*preparatione animi*) aids a person to be ready for virtuous acts even when they have no previous direct experience (magnificence for the poor and equanimity in bearing misfortunes for the prosperous person). Prudence does not function alone, however. Because of the significance of the four major areas of the cardinal virtues, it is hard to imagine a true and perfect virtue functioning without the assistance of the others. Can a person properly attend to a question of justice (with the whole repertoire of qualities), if he is subject to desires for domination or possessions, or if he is preoccupied by fear? He will at least be distracted, perhaps dulled, and find the task unpleasant. Nonetheless, he might also have a moment of clarity and concentration needed to do what is right and good, at the right time—however, without having a consistent disposition to do so. Aquinas holds that prudence needs the other dispositions, and vice versa: the other moral dispositions will not attain the norm of virtue without prudence, which is the means by which the rational norm is discerned and put into practice.

At this point, two further issues about the connection of the virtues arise. First, need everyone act identically in order to be considered virtuous? Concerning the virtue of seeking what is truly great (magnanimity or greatsouledness), Aquinas says: "The mutual connection of the virtues does not apply to their acts, as though everyone were competent to practice the acts of all the virtues. Wherefore the act of magnanimity is not becoming to every virtuous man, but only to great men."[52] Not everyone has the particular intellectual capacities needed (such as concentration and perspicacity). Two virtuous persons will not necessarily act exactly alike, because of other more mundane

50. Cf. *ST* I-II, q. 65, a. 1.   51. Cf. *ST* II-II, q. 47, a. 8.
52. *ST* II-II, q. 129, a. 3, ad 2.

skills, as well; for example, it would not be courageous for a non-swimmer to
jump into deep water to save a drowning child, when skilled swimmers are
willing and able.

A second issue concerns the connection of the virtues as a proximate disposition *(in propinqua dispositione),* that is, as a basis for virtues not yet explicitly developed.[53] The principles of all virtues support virtuous *habitus* because
of the unity of the person (the soul), either by way of actually possessing a *habitus* or by proximate disposition to one. When purposely performing virtuous
acts (like temperance, justice, patience, and so on), a person performs the acts
of the other virtues and is on the way to acquiring the related virtues as well.
However, if a person repeatedly performs divided acts (of which he is responsible for the immoral intention or object), he will develop imperfect virtue at
best, vice at worst, and these acts will lead to the corruption of prudence as
well.

Perfect and Imperfect Virtues

With the important discussion of true versus counterfeit virtues in mind,
Aquinas distinguishes the perfect (or complete) and imperfect (or incomplete) connections of the virtues. He thus seeks to account for the phenomenon of the inconsistency and partiality of acquired virtue. In a set of parallel
texts of his *Summa theologiae* (I-II, q. 65, aa. 1 and 2) and his *Disputed Questions
on Virtue (De virtutibus in cardinalibus,* a. 2), Aquinas identifies four types of
virtue by distinguishing perfect from imperfect virtues, based on whether or
not they are necessarily connected, and acquired from infused virtues, based
on their natural and supernatural supports.

A first grade of virtue involves inclinations that are poorly connected or
connected only by isolated dispositions and that tend toward disparate goods.
These inclinations, which can exist from an early age, are uneven and can be
used badly. They lack prudence, do not attain right reason, and do not fulfill
the definition of virtue. Such virtues are simply imperfect *(imperfecta quidem
moralis virtus* and *omnino imperfectae);* for example, we find people who by nature or habituation promptly exercise generosity, but not chastity.[54]

Second, there are acquired moral virtues that incline us to "do a good deed
well" and that are connected by the virtue of prudence. The connection of
such perfect moral virtues *(perfecta virtus moralis)* can be understood through
the concepts of general and specific cardinal virtues. Aquinas explains that
such acquired moral virtues are limited to works fitting to the natural good

53. See *ST* II-II, q. 129, a. 3, ad 2; *De virtutibus cardinalibus,* a. 2, ad 9.
54. *ST* I-II, q. 65, a. 1.

of man,[55] and to the use of right reason for the human good (*aliqualiter perfectae per comparationem ad bonum humanum*).[56] He adds that when these virtues "are acquired thus, they can be without charity, even as they were in many of the Gentiles (*gentilibus*)."[57] Aquinas holds that without grace, human beings can have an imperfect type of acquired virtue: "Wherefore, though man cannot avoid mortal sin without grace, so as never to sin mortally, yet he is not hindered from acquiring a habit of virtue, whereby he may abstain from evil in the majority of cases, and chiefly in matters most opposed to reason."[58] The perfection of acquired moral virtues is limited by their natural end and by the type of consistency that can be assured by acquired virtue. Aquinas explains not only that the perfection is limited, but also that these qualities are virtues only in a restricted sense (*secundum quid*), "for they direct man well in respect of the last end in some particular genus of action."[59] Inasmuch as they fall short of compatibility with the ultimate end (God through charity) such virtue does not attain the full notion of virtue.

Third, Aquinas considers the difference that grace makes for the life of virtue. It is only because of charity (which is grounded in faith and hope)[60] that the infused virtues can produce good acts according to a supernatural last end (*ultimum finem supernaturalem*); as such they are perfect and can be called virtues simply (*simpliciter perfectae*). Aquinas furthermore argues that being disposed well to one's ultimate end, namely God, is necessary for infused prudence to proceed aright. The work of infused prudence is more perfect than that of acquired prudence and, likewise, infused prudence perfects the other infused moral virtues in order not only to do what is good, but to do it well.[61] Infused moral virtues are in accordance with Divine Law, concern salvation, and make the human effort simply good.[62] Needless to say, infused moral virtues do not render a person necessarily competent in practical matters, such as adjudicating between the means of providing food and lodging for the needy. In this context, Aquinas affirms that infused prudence alone can draw reasons for action from this ultimate end, which is attained only through charity. This discussion of the connection of the virtues uses the perfect/imperfect distinction comparatively: a connected, acquired virtue is perfect in comparison with unconnected moral virtue, but imperfect in comparison with infused connected virtue.[63]

---

55. *ST* I-II, q. 65, a. 2.

56. *De virtutibus cardinalibus*, a. 2.

57. *ST* I-II, q. 65, a. 2.

58. *ST* I-II, q. 63, a. 2, ad 2.

59. *ST* I-II, q. 65, a. 2.

60. See *ST* I-II, q. 65, a. 5.

61. See *ST* I-II, q. 65, a. 4.

62. See *De virtutibus cardinalibus*, a. 2; *ST* I-II, q. 65, a. 1; *ST* II-II, q. 47, a. 14, ad 1.

63. For a discussion of prudence and the connection of the virtues, see the debate in *The Thomist* between Brian Shanley, "Aquinas on Pagan Virtue," *The Thomist* 63, no. 4 (1999):

Aquinas also identifies a fourth type of virtue, which Jean Porter does not discuss (to my knowledge). This is the infused virtue that is not connected with the others. Aquinas explains the possibility of possessing infused virtue in merely habitual or inchoate states *(habituales formae)*.[64] Although all the virtues are infused with charity, they are not necessarily exercised, as when there is an impediment (sleep, drunkenness, sickness, psychological disorders, the effects of lingering dispositions of past sins, or age-immaturity) or as when one exhibits perfect faith but imperfect charity.[65]

Imperfect infused virtue refers also to the process of connecting the virtues when the rational and affective capacities develop from childhood to maturity, as for example, after infant baptism has given infused grace, but before the infant's intelligent and affective capacities have matured. Even though all the virtues are infused with charity, each must be put into practice or else it will remain in an inchoate state. However, it should be noted that to wilfully neglect such theological development is neither innocent nor anything but a disordered state itself. Here we have numerous insights that are potentially useful to understand our flawed saint.

The Middle Ground between Virtue and Vice

One final aspect for adjudicating the counterexample of the flawed saint involves the developmental middle ground between virtue and vice. For Aquinas holds that virtuous acts can be produced in different ways, even in a type of developmental continuum that admits of gaps. This becomes apparent when we revisit Aquinas's account of the diverse states of temperance (and chastity). This issue is especially pertinent to our discussion because Porter's article, "Virtue and Sin," ignores the pertinent distinction between the virtues of temperance and continence, the state of incontinence, and the vice of intemperance.[66] Without these distinctions, some moral features in her account of Martin Luther King are impossible to account for.

553–77; Angela McKay, "Prudence and Acquired Moral Virtue," *The Thomist* 69, no. 4 (2005): 535–55; and Thomas Osborne, "Perfect and Imperfect Virtues in Aquinas," *The Thomist* 71, no. 1 (2007): 39–64.

64. *De virtutibus cardinalibus*, a. 2, c., ad 2 and 3; and *ST* I-II, q. 65, a. 3. ad 2.

65. For a discussion of impediments, see *ST* I-II, q. 65, a. 3, ad 2; *De virtutibus cardinalibus*, a. 2, ad 2 and 3; see also *De virtutibus cardinalibus*, a. 3, ad 12 and 13.

For a discussion of the need of faith for charity, see *ST* I-II, q. 65, a. 4. Moreover, by nature or a gift of grace even the saints are inclined to perform more promptly certain virtuous acts rather than others; cf. *De virtutibus cardinalibus*, a. 2, ad 1.

66. At the beginning of the treatise on temperance, Aquinas distinguishes the virtue (*ST* II-II, q. 141) from the vices opposed to it (II-II, q. 142). In the rest of the treatise, besides distinguishing continence (II-II, q. 155) from incontinence (II-II, q. 156), he discusses temperance's

For Aquinas, a virtue like chastity is not simply opposed to a contrary vice of lust or infidelity. Rather, Aquinas paints the full anthropological portrait of the virtue, at emotional, volitional, and cognitive levels. When the emotional or volitional elements are lacking a virtuous disposition, there are two different states that are not vice per se, but rather intermediate conditions on a developmental trajectory either toward vice or toward virtue.

First, in the condition of continence, there is external consistency but internal struggle. While having practical knowledge of what is good to do, a person may struggle with conflicts of desire, disordered fascinations with power, or compulsions to pleasure. These struggles may be due to certain acquired flaws, for example, in the capacity to manage emotions and to refocus imagination and memory. Such people pursue and ponder the attraction that they feel for men or women other than their spouse. They experience sadness, since they do not have new outlets for venereal pleasure and psychosexual attractions. They face difficulties in controlling their thoughts about genital arousal and interpersonal intimacies. These emotional and cognitive states do not bolster one's moral and spiritual goals. Nonetheless, thanks to a semi-virtue, namely continence, a person remains continent or faithful in act.[67] While he does not fall, he does not act with ease, spontaneity, and pleasure either. Such a person is a more or less flawed saint, holding on by sheer willpower.[68]

Another state is that of incontinence in which a person still understands what it means to be faithful to his or her spouse and longs to be so.[69] However, he fails because of weakness of will. This state is distinguished from that of vice, because he has not lost his practical judgment about what is good (precisely, that it is good to live conjugal fidelity). Thus, an incontinent disposition exhibits rational rectitude, but disorder at the level of emotions and, more specifically, failure at the level of the will. Some have considered it a temporary vice.[70] For Aquinas, one such act does not destroy an acquired virtuous dispo-

related virtues and vices, namely, shamefacedness, honesty, abstinence, fasting, sobriety, chastity, virginity, clemency and meekness, modesty, and humility, on the one hand, and gluttony, drunkenness, lust, anger, cruelty, and pride, on the other.

67. Cf. *ST* II-II, q. 155, a. 1; see also aa. 2–4.

68. For a more extensive treatment of weakness of will, see Tobias Hoffmann, "Aquinas on the Moral Progress of the Weak Willed," in *The Problem of Weakness of Will in Medieval Philosophy*, ed. Tobias Hoffmann, Jörn Müller, and Matthias Perkams (Leuven: Peters, 2006), 221–47.

69. Cf. *In Ethic.*, bk. VII, lect. 8, §§ 1430 and 1443; *ST* II-II, q. 156, aa. 1–4; *In Ethic.*, bk. VII, lect. 9, § 1454.

70. A "temporary vice" would involve a vicious act rather than a vicious disposition. Bonnie Kent says that Aquinas "stresses that intemperance is habitual, incontinence only temporary. Incontinence is like a transitory vice. The incontinent judges from passion, though not from habit, that bodily pleasures are good in themselves . . . In this the incontinent differs from the intemperate, who has a perverted conception of the good, but who chooses and acts in

sition, even though, if repeated, such acts erode a disposition and start to create another, the vice of intemperance. With grace or after the waning of the strong emotion, the incontinent person will repent, while the intemperate one will relish the act that has become second nature to him.[71]

Conclusion: Can We Value the "Flawed Saint"?

With these distinctions on hand, I return to Jean Porter's position on the paradox of the flawed saint. While recognizing, as did Aquinas,[72] that moral disorders skew the other domains of virtue, she claims that his view on the connection of the virtues

can indeed allow for the possibility that someone who is truly virtuous is nonetheless also morally flawed in some ways. However, I have since come to the conclusion that this solution is only plausible if the moral flaws in question are not *too* serious. Once we consider the case of someone like King, whose moral struggles apparently involved repeated extramarital affairs, it is less convincing. What makes this case so difficult is not the fact that many of King's struggles involved "sexual sins"; the difficulty lies in the fact that repeated infidelity seems to imply a kind of callousness, or at best a lack of appropriate regard, both toward one's spouse and also toward one's other partners.[73]

Porter goes on to adjudicate that a person can be a genuine saint, a subject of "perfect virtue," but also a subject of true and persistent vice, based on her conviction that King was a true saint and a serious sinner. Porter says, in sum: "My own view is that the example of King, and of other flawed saints, offers nearly conclusive evidence that Aquinas was wrong to say that the life of charity is inconsistent with serious sin."[74] It seems to me that if Porter had been more attentive to Aquinas's notions of intermediate states between virtue and vice, the imperfect-perfect distinction concerning the connections between the virtues, and the process of returning to grace and charity after grave sin, she could have accounted better for the type of flaw and the type of virtue exhibited by Martin Luther King. In particular, she would have recognized Aquinas's account of the possibility of an imperfect connection of charity and the other infused virtues, since one act of charity does not guarantee the next and since

accordance with it." (Bonnie Kent, "Transitory Vice: Thomas Aquinas on Incontinence," *Journal of the History of Philosophy* 27, no. 2 [1989]: 199–223, esp. 201 and 214).

71. Cf. *ST* II-II, q. 156, a. 3; *In Ethic.*, bk. VII, lect. 9, § 1454.
72. See *ST* I-II, q. 58, a. 5.
73. Porter, "Virtue and Sin," 532.
74. Ibid., 538.

the infused virtues are possessed in inchoate states *(habituales formae)*[75] before they are put into practice.

Moreover, at the level of acquired virtue, Aquinas's developmental perspective recognizes that there are two tendencies in acquired incontinence or continence: (1) as a movement away from vice and toward virtue—a growth in imperfect prudence; or (2) as a movement from a more virtuous tendency toward vice—a decrease in virtue. Aquinas's reflections on the connection of acquired moral virtue do not deny the possibility of error and sin in the so-called flawed saint. However, they affirm that every act counts, even though the odd act does not make or break an acquired disposition.

At another level, the infused virtues are gifts that depend not only on God's giving but also on a person's receiving them and persisting in their good use. Although they are not attained and possessed in the same way as acquired virtues—since they are gratuitously given—infused virtues must nonetheless be put into humble and obedient practice in cooperation with grace. True and perfect virtue requires persisting in progress, for Aquinas. A static point does not exist. At any moment, either a person advances toward a more coherent connection of these dispositions or he regresses,[76] even though fallow times do not demonstrate their necessity and fruitfulness until later. Thus for St. Thomas, charity (as a fledgling disposition) neither guarantees its own full development or the connection of the other infused virtues nor guarantees a coherent psychological structure of the acquired virtues (as dispositions).[77] Aquinas explains that in the exercise of infused moral virtues we can "experience difficulty in their works, by reason of certain ordinary dispositions remaining from previous acts. This difficulty does not occur in respect of acquired moral virtue: because the repeated acts by which they are acquired, remove also the contrary dispositions."[78] Nonetheless, a life of charity (with efforts to acquire natural dispositions through good and just practices) will aid one to come to maturity in theological virtue and to attain the psychological ease (or at least the lack of sadness) with which to exercise it. It also will overcome, in time, certain difficulties that have resulted from previous acts.

In conclusion, Aquinas's understanding of moral development and the connection of the virtues give us reason to better understand the example of

---

75. *De virtutibus cardinalibus,* a. 2, c., ad 2 and 3; and *ST* I-II, q. 65, a. 3, ad 2.

76. See *ST* II-II, q. 24, a. 6.

77. See his discussion of the three stages of charity in *ST* II-II, q. 24, a. 9. Moreover, Aquinas does say that the "acts of infused virtues do not cause *habitus,* but due to them pre-existing *habitus* are increased" (*De virtutibus in communi,* a. 10, ad 19).

78. *ST* I-II, q. 65, a. 3, ad 2. Cf. *De virtutibus cardinalibus,* a. 2, ad 2; *De virtutibus in communi,* a. 10, ad 14.

human inconsistency in our heroes and to appreciate the "flawed saint," but at a different level than that proposed by Jean Porter. Charity and prudence help us, in their proper ways, to make progress toward a more coherent moral and spiritual life, not only in good acts, but in virtuous dispositions as well. Charity explains the growth of coherence in the spiritual life, while its absence explains moral inconsistency and spiritual demise. For at the level of acts, charity does not cohabitate with certain deeds, that is, with serious sin. Therefore, Aquinas would praise King's heroic deeds of justice, while also recognizing that they are imperfectly connected with charity and other virtues, inasmuch as King was conjugally unfaithful or unjust. Aquinas's approach in this regard is nuanced and humble. It construes moral development as a process of habitualizing, connaturalizing, and connecting the virtues, while not losing hope for any "flawed saint," a term that Aquinas would not use. In particular, God can revive the person—after a grave sin—to repent, to seek forgiveness, and to repair (when possible) the damage done. The person thus returns to the pathway of development with renewed charity and infused virtue, which includes the possibility of further connecting the virtues, sanctifying desire, and even being disposed to martyrdom in a state of grace.

Vanity and Commerce

How *De malo* Supports Whig Thomism

GRAHAM J. MCALEER

Whig Thomism is a largely American school of Catholic reflection on economic, social, and political life. Perhaps it would be more accurate to say that Whig
Thomists tend to be Americans since this school, with some justice, points to
the Catholic social thought tradition, and most especially, *Centesimus Annus,*
for support. Whig Thomism's most famous thinkers are public intellectuals
rather than university professors: Fathers Richard John Neuhaus and Robert
Sirico, Michael Novak, and George Weigel. Romanus Cessario quite rightly warns us about the use of labels for complex intellectual positions.[1] Usefully then, Tracey Rowland, one of the critics of Whig Thomism, isolates the
core of the school: the conviction that there is, or ought to be, continuity between Catholic social thought and the Scottish Enlightenment.[2] Some Whig
Thomists might not accept this definition. In Neuhaus's work, the Scottish Enlightenment is a muted theme, so far as I can tell. His interest in the American
Founding is in some ways a surrogate for it, however.[3] This is another aspect of

1. Romanus Cessario, O.P., "Cardinal Cajetan and His Critics," *Nova et Vetera* (English) 3,
no. 1 (2005): 109–18.
2. Tracey Rowland, "Benedict XVI, Thomism, and Liberal Culture (Part 2)," *Zenit,* July
25, 2005. I cite the second part of this interesting interview available at http://www.zenit.org/
article-13666?l=english (last accessed on 11/5/09).
3. See my essay, "Business and Dignity: An Application of Edmund Burke's Analysis
of America," in *Festschrift for Fr. James Schall* (South Bend, Ind.: St. Augustine's Press, forthcoming). For an interesting account as to why there might be a deeper connection between

the school, and one that rankles many: these American Catholics think that the principles of the American Founding ought to be something of a gold standard for the development of Catholic social thought. Though some might dispute the accuracy of Rowland's definition, I like it: I think the proposition is a powerful intellectual formula for Christian engagement with culture.[4] Rowland thinks that the American liberal economic and political order is "really toxic" to faith. To a degree, I concur with Rowland,[5] though much hangs on what "liberal" means, as Whig Thomists constantly emphasize. I hope to return to Rowland's criticism of Whig Thomism in the future. Here, I want to argue that Catholic social thought can safely adopt the Scottish school's theory of commercial motivation—vanity.

The point is crucial. Eighteenth-century Scottish thinkers argued that vanity is basic to business motivation. This suggests that beauty and aesthetics, rather than the good and ethics, structure commercial societies like those of the West and now much of the world.[6] Can any self-respecting Thomist accept this? The idea that beauty underwrites ethics is certainly a respectable intellectual position with many supporting arguments. Great thinkers like C. S. Pierce hold this position, some interpreters of Aristotle,[7] and it may be implicit in Scheler's ethics. The disgust reaction, which Kolnai regards as a central moral phenomenon, is aesthetic in character.[8] If beauty is basic to moral order,[9] vanity may well be as crucial as the Scots think. Thomists, however, must be wary.

Montesquieu cites evidence of a link between vanity and abortion.[10] Does vanity serve the culture of death? Abortion is an abandonment of the living. Scheler identifies such abandonment as a structural feature of vanity. He was much taken with Sombart's thesis that capitalism is, most essentially, a system

Catholicism and American popular culture, see Steve Sherwood, "American Pop Frankenstein? Andy Warhol, Iconic Experience and the Advent of the Pop Society" (pro manuscripto).

4. The Scottish Enlightenment was a British phenomenon in some way. Smith and Hume were English in sensibility to a significant degree and Hutcheson, Smith's teacher, was Northern Irish. Burke must also be included, and he was Anglo-Irish. Smith, Hume, and Burke were all pro-American.

5. See my Ecstatic Morality and Sexual Politics (New York: Fordham University Press, 2005), chap. 9.

6. See my discussion in "Business Ethics and Catholic Social Thought," Nova et Vetera (English) 4, no. 1 (2006): 17–27.

7. See the extremely interesting essay by Frank Knight, "The Ethics of Competition," Quarterly Journal of Economics 37, no. 4 (1923): 579–624.

8. Aurel Kolnai, Disgust (Chicago: Open Court, 2004).

9. Aurel Kolnai, "Aesthetic and Moral Experience," in Ethics, Value and Reality: Selected Papers of Aurel Kolnai (New Brunswick, N.J.: Transaction, 2008), 187–210.

10. See my Ecstatic Morality and Sexual Politics, 166 n. 48.

of business organization in service of luxury. In fact, Sombart argues that capitalism is an erotics: luxury is the expression of men's fascination with feminine style and sensibility. Hume also notes the centrality of gallantry in commercial society.[11] Vanity might bring people together but, argues Scheler, vanity trips the abandonment of the self. Ever sensitive to how he is received by others, the vain man lives out a social self, leaving his personal, individual self untended. There is a reversal of value here, one that defines the modern world, according to Scheler. The high value of personal discrimination is forsaken for lower generic values of assimilation.[12] This reversal is the hallmark of a *ressentiment* civilization.[13] According to Sombart, up until the eighteenth century, luxury was tied to the court and aristocrats set styles;[14] since then, adds Scheler, commercial society had slipped into a utility-driven ethos. Initially a supporter of World War I, Scheler, soon disillusioned, came to the view that it was a capitalist war: life was destroyed unrelentingly but government made no demands on people's property. It was a war to protect property and markets, he concluded: low values, therefore, forced the sacrifice of high values.[15] According to Scheler's lights, the West, victim to *ressentiment,* is a declining civilization under capitalism.[16]

Does vanity entail this abandonment and reversal? Elsewhere, I argue that Smith defends the ethos of commercial society on account of aesthetic, not utilitarian, values.[17] The present essay argues that Aquinas's treatment of vanity shows that abandonment and reversal are not strict implications of vanity. I do not dispute the basic thrust of Scheler's ethics—inversion of value is destructive of environments and persons—but the Church can work for the reform of commercial society rather than criticize the very form of a trading civilization. Aquinas provides the framework for this reform and shows that modernity need not be "toxic" to the faith.

It is easy enough to glean from the foregoing why vanity is enumerated as one of the deadly sins. In Thomas's presentation of these sins, vanity ranks im-

---

11. David Hume, *Essays Moral, Political and Literary* (Indianapolis: Liberty Fund, 1987), 131–33.

12. Max Scheler, *The Nature of Sympathy* (New Brunswick, N.J.: Transaction, 2007), 39–44.

13. For my use of Scheler's *ressentiment* argument in relationship to gay marriage, see "Two Case Studies in Schelerian Moral Theology: The Vatican's 2005 'Instruction' and Gay Marriage," *Nova et Vetera* (English) 6, no. 1 (2008): 205–17.

14. Werner Sombart, *Luxury and Capitalism* (Ann Arbor: University of Michigan Press, 1967), 86, 113.

15. Max Scheler, *Ressentiment* (Milwaukee, Wis.: Marquette University Press, 2003), 144 n. 25.

16. Max Scheler, *The Nature of Sympathy,* 103–7.

17. See my essay "Business Ethics and Catholic Social Thought."

mediately below pride and is the first enumerated sin: pride, of course, being the source of all sin and not, strictly speaking, one of the seven enumerated, but at the root of all of them. Yet what are we to make of Nemo's recent thesis about the West? Building on the seminal work of law historian Harold Berman, Nemo argues that the Gregorian Reform established the basic framework of law and property that endures today. Commercial society operates within this framework. In Nemo's telling, Gregory sought to Christianize the world in a thoroughly concrete manner, and his chosen instrument was Roman law. The task was to infuse the law with the spirit of the Gospel and to bring both to bear on the matter-of-fact realities of ordinary domestic, commercial and civic, life.[18] Assuming Nemo is correct, does not Benedict XVI's Regensburg Address—wherein the pope argues that there is something essentially Greek, Western, about Christianity—favor the claim that the liberal tradition is an integral part of the Christian understanding of the world?

Critics of Whig Thomism are skeptical of, among other things, the role of markets. These criticisms invariably boil down to the question of the nature of property and especially whether corporations have a moral obligation beyond what they owe their individual investors. The Corporate Social Responsibility movement assumes that private property is, at heart, as Rawls puts it, a "common asset."[19] The Enlightenment idea is quite different. Vanity and luxury, says Daniel Defoe, "feed trade and consequently the poor."[20] Volume sales is the hallmark of capitalism—the idea makes both moguls (Bill Gates and Sam Walton, say) and the (near) worldwide increase in calorie consumption possible and such sales occur on the back of demand for luxury and refinement: "these volume sales take place by the grace of luxury."[21] The most recent work on poverty and development does seem to confirm the Enlightenment idea of the likes of Hume and Smith.[22] Paul Collier has argued recently that the one billion people living in rich countries are thriving economically and that real, sustained growth is found among the four billion in the high growth developing world spurred on by globalization.[23] There is, however, a bottom billion cut out of economic growth almost entirely. Collier offers a number of reasons for

18. Philippe Nemo, *What Is the West?* (Pittsburgh, Pa.: Duquesne University Press, 2006), chap. 4.

19. See the discussion of John Rawls in John Kekes, *The Illusions of Egalitarianism* (Ithaca, N.Y.: Cornell University Press, 2003), chap. 4.

20. Defoe, as quoted by Sombart, *Luxury and Capitalism*, 115.

21. Sombart, *Luxury and Capitalism*, 147.

22. See the famous discussion of the Invisible Hand as akin to an operation of grace in Adam Smith, *The Theory of Moral Sentiments* (Indianapolis: Liberty Fund, 1982), 183–84.

23. Amongst an enormous literature, see Paul Beckett, Krishna Pokharel, and Eric Bellman, "India's Surging Economy Lifts Hopes and Ambitions," *Wall Street Journal*, November 28,

this development failure and they all have to do with structural issues: endemic civil war, land-locked countries with poor natural resources, and so on.[24] Collier offers strategies for how the West can help, but the main point is: this failure of development is not a market creation. Neither markets nor Corporate Social Responsibility can be the solution either, at least not directly. Drastic action is required, and Collier flirts with the idea of temporary colonial administrations, among other strategies.

Market institutions and private property serve the peoples of the world well. Liberal economy is one of the meanings of the West and, if Berman and Nemo are right, a meaning consequent to the Gregorian Reform and, at a deeper remove still, the Greek rationality that Benedict encouraged at Regensburg. Could it be that the dispute with Whig Thomism is also a dispute with the Gregorian Reform? This might seem an odd formulation: surely that boat sailed long ago?[25] To the contrary, Nemo shows that significant bodies of Christian opinion have, down through the centuries, contested the Reform.[26]

The Scottish school correctly identifies the centrality of vanity in commercial motivation and, I argue, support of the Reform requires Christians to acknowledge this (ultimately phenomenological) fact. But Thomas rightly asserts the good over beauty, moral norms over vanity. To my mind, Whig Thomism is, at root, a theoretical position on the relationship between beauty and good: both are acknowledged as legitimate values of enormous scope, but an emphasis is placed on the good as controlling. Vanity has a relative autonomy, one might say, but is it (only) a conditional good? That is, is vanity only a consequence of sin? I do not think Aquinas thought so.

My thesis—that Catholic social thought should adopt vanity as a licit motivator of business practice—has strong and weak versions. The argument for Whig Thomism still works even if vanity is a conditional good; it is a failing able to be used for good purposes. A leading critic of Whig Thomism is Bob Kraynak. In a marvelous book, *Christian Faith and Modern Democracy*, he argues that Catholic social thought must stop being so doctrinaire. It is time to

2007; and Justin Lahart, Patrick Barta, and Andrew Batson, "New Limits to Growth Revive Malthusian Fears," *Wall Street Journal,* March 24, 2008.

24. See the book review by Fr. Raymond de Souza, "Paul Collier: The Bottom Billion: Why the Poorest Countries Are Failing and What Can Be Done about It," *Religion and Liberty* 17, no. 3 (2007): 4–5.

25. It would be an interesting thesis for a Church historian to pursue: Is the history of the later Church a series of contests about the worthiness of the Reform? For example, I think Robert Kilwardby was a dissenter. Please see my "Individuation and Incarnation: The Role of Metaphysics in the Theology of Robert Kilwardby," in *Companion to Robert Kilwardby,* ed. Paul Thom (E. J. Brill, forthcoming).

26. Nemo, *What Is the West?,* chap. 4.

realize, he insists, that absolutism about human rights and other political veri-
ties of the modern age are contrary to the deepest political traditions of the
Church: that is, *any* economic, social, or political form is, for the Church, always only a conditional good; conditional upon how well, given that we are
sinners and given the times and situation, a social form curtails what is worst
in us and sustains spiritual Christian brotherhood.[27] The Church must stop
insisting that only democratic forms of government are congruent with the
Gospel and accept that monarchical or even authoritarian regimes can serve
the wayfarer and the Church equally well. *At times,* my concerns intersect
with Kraynak's.[28] Given the success of markets, as sketched in the paragraph
above discussing Collier's research, a Whig Thomist could happily acknowledge the role of vanity in commercial society as a conditional good. A Whig
Thomist might confidently argue that vanity does happen to serve the goals of
the Church well in the midst of a fallen world.

A stronger version of the thesis can hold that vanity is either a permanent
condition of the wayfarer or, stronger still, an ontological condition of human
nature as such. The (lesser) strong version stems from *De malo:* Thomas believes that we are comparative creatures—compared to God in the first place,
ontologically, and to other persons, socially. He grants that pride—and vanity
is a functional pride—is a structure of the human spirit. Not all pride is good
(obviously!) but there is some that is good: it prompts humans to seek excellence amidst the goods of the world. If my interpretation of Thomas on this
point is correct below, an upshot is that vanity is not a conditional but a structural good. That is, humans seek excellence in the regard of one another and attain the good in imitation of each other. In both these versions of the thesis—
the weak and the (lesser) strong—the liberal order, consequent to the Reform,
is likely as not a providential aid to broken humanity. I leave to a marginal discussion the stronger of the strong versions.[29]

27. Robert P. Kraynak, *Christian Faith and Modern Democracy* (Notre Dame, Ind.: University of Notre Dame Press, 2001).

28. See my *Ecstatic Morality and Sexual Politics,* especially chap. 9.

29. There are some tricky issues here and the topic really warrants a book. Catholic social thought, at least as developed by John Paul II, regards work as an essential structure of being human. It is a little unclear, but an implication appears to be that even if the Fall had never happened, work, in some of its dimensions at least, would have played a role in Eden. Some
might wonder about this and it is perhaps too difficult to arrive at a clear pronouncement. But
would vanity have existed even if work did? As shown below, Thomas approves of vanity when
it encourages virtue. In an Edenic state, to what degree is there need, if any, of encouragement? Hume treats vanity ontologically, but he had little time for a *Christian* sense of history. If
Christology is emphasized, however, perhaps an ontological treatment of vanity is possible. If
Christ's glory is an exemplary cause (John Paul II), and if, even in Eden, humans would mediate

There are a number of books with titles something like "How the Scots In-vented the Modern World." Scots the world over no doubt think this is true, and, with a pinch of salt, there is truth to the claim. We live in a commercial culture rather than an aristocratic or military or priestly culture, and Scot-tish thinkers were the first to reflect on this fact; indeed, they helped make it a fact. The Scottish Enlightenment picks out a group of intellectuals, some of the very first rank, who flourished in eighteenth-century Scotland. Lesser-known thinkers like Lord Kames and Francis Hutcheson set a framework of inquiry that flowered in the towering minds of Adam Smith, David Hume, and Thom-as Reid. Volumes abound on these thinkers, but what I take as defining of this school is its moral realism. In contemporary ethics, it is Catholic moral phi-losophy that is most rigorously realist. I think this is why Catholic thinkers find the Scots fellow-travelers. Exactly why Catholic thinkers do not find the English, French, and German Enlightenment thinkers so appealing could fill many books, and nuances would abound. Perhaps crucial is the fact that this school emerged from the law books of Lord Kames: Catholic ethics being, in part, and ultimately, a law-based ethics. Amongst the Scots, nuance is warrant-ed: Reid might be more appealing and Hume less. These emphases cannot be pursued here. Needful now is justification of the claim that vanity—and I rely on Hume's treatment—can play a useful role in Catholic social thought.

Neanderthal or Consumer? This is, with a little bit of finessing, a basic question for the Church today. Ours strikes some as a narcissistic culture.[30] Hume would deny this but grant it is a culture of vanity. Hume argues that vanity is a part of human nature.[31] Archeological digs of Neanderthal dwell-ings show no convincing evidence of jewelry or adornment. The earliest hu-man settlements have an abundance of such evidence. Certainly, Hume takes adornment as basic to humans.[32] Manufacturers generate what is "necessary and ornamental to human life,"[33] and fostering opulence in the private domain builds the greatness of the state.[34] The state contributes security to trade and trade contributes labor to the state; that is, trade educes from a population in-novation and technological prowess and these qualities become a resource for the state in times of need.[35] Trade also elicits work and refinement from the people because luxury, adornment, and opulence provoke vanity. People

---

this glory to one another modeling Christ, then (given the definitions below in Thomas's treat-ment) vanity might have ontological standing.

30. Ralph D. Ellis, *Eros in a Narcissistic Culture* (Dordrecht: Kluwer, 1996).
31. David Hume, *Essays Moral, Political and Literary*, 259.
32. Ibid.   33. Ibid., 256.
34. Ibid., 255.   35. Ibid., 262.

covet beauty. Cities flourish and novelty ranks high as people come together "to show their wit or their breeding; their taste in conversation or living, in clothes or furniture."[36] Underwriting industry, knowledge, and benevolence is vanity and the quest for luxury, and commerce is the result.

A consequence of vanity, and one of real significance, is property. About property, Hume, in full Whig character, says: property draws "authority and consideration to that middling rank of men, who are the best and firmest basis of public liberty."[37] Hume's is a minimal political order, limited primarily to rule of law,[38] since social order is maintained through the socially observed conventions of vanity. Refinement provokes ingenuity, security, and law, says Hume, and thus beauty is a basic motivator. Consumerism, though much-maligned,[39] is central to government, and even more central to limited government, and liberty therefore. Hume convincingly shows, I think, how commerce secures the link between the liberal economic and political orders.

Does moral theology give a positive account of vanity? Thomas's *De malo* offers the classic analysis of the topic. It is indisputable that Thomas provides there a positive analysis of vanity, as well as cautioning about its dangers. This is just as well. As far as I can see, this is an aspect of Catholic social thought that is seriously underdeveloped: the problem of commercial motivation. Seminal texts in the Catholic social thought tradition, texts like John Paul II's *Laborem exercens* and *Centesimus annus,* are superb engagements with the world of business and commercial life. In these texts, work is identified as "the key to the social question"[40] and for the same reasons that Whigs like Hume and Burke championed property: work builds dignity.[41] Work "confirms" man's dominion of the world when, and such is the onus of ethical business practice, work engages the intellect, requires self-management, and tends to human flourishing. That is, work builds dignity when it addresses man's basic powers: intellect, will, and the appetites more broadly.[42] And so of work, John Paul II writes: "And this mark [work] decides its [the human person's] interior characteristics; in a sense it constitutes its very nature."[43] But what provokes work?

There are hints that John Paul II recognizes the role of vanity as there are intriguing passages where the question of vanity surfaces in *Centesimus An-*

---

36. Ibid., 271.   37. Ibid., 277.

38. Ibid., 272.

39. "Shopping and Philosophy: Post-Modernism Is the New Black," *The Economist,* December 23, 2006, 106–7.

40. *Laborem exercens,* § 3.

41. *Centesimus annus,* § 43; *Laborem exercens,* § 9.

42. See my "Business Ethics and Catholic Social Thought," 22.

43. *Laborem exercens,* greeting; cf. *Centesimus annus,* § 6.

nus. Making Collier's point—that some Third World countries suffer because they cannot gain access to global markets[44]—John Paul II adds that populations within thriving, globalized, countries struggle for opportunity to actualize the resources they have. The condition of the marginalized in this sense is hard indeed: they are goaded into cities, abandoning their traditional ways, "allured by the dazzle of an opulence which is beyond their reach."[45] The vocabulary is Hume's and his underlying philosophy is not dismissed. What is regretted is not the role of vanity, opulence, and refinement, but the suffering of people unable to actualize resources to adequately meet the rigors of a market-driven economy. Refusing to make an idol of the market, John Paul II nonetheless praises its mechanisms: "above all they give central place to the person's desires and preferences, which, in a contract, meet the desires and preferences of another person."[46] There is a legitimate place for self-interest and the person is, by virtue of fundamental inclinations and powers, entrepreneurial.[47] Consumerism can be a profound problem but only when a culture has (echoes of Scheler) reversed the objective hierarchy of value.[48]

Thomas's *De malo* is divided in two: the first part concerns the structure of action,[49] the second, the question of motivation. My argument has support in what Thomas says about pride. In *De malo*, question 8, article 2, Aquinas writes:

And one of the things that human beings naturally desire is excellence. For it is natural for both human beings and everything to seek in desired goods the perfection that consists of a certain excellence. Therefore, the will will indeed be morally right and belong to loftiness of spirit if it seeks excellence in accord with the rule of reason informed by God.

Pride, understood as "loftiness of spirit," is natural as humans seek excellence. Excellence is specified by reason and ultimately God. In the paragraph preceding, Thomas tells us that "every good naturally desired is a likeness of God's goodness." God's goodness is ecstatic: for the good, as Thomas frequently notes in the words of Pseudo-Dionysius, *diffusivum sui est*. This generosity is always ennobling, aiming, as Scheler would put it, at enhancement of the value of the beloved. These themes are present in Thomas's discussion of vanity. In the objections, Thomas cites various Roman authors who, unsurprisingly, dwell

---

44. *Centesimus annus*, § 28.
45. Ibid., § 33.
46. Ibid., § 40.
47. Ibid., §§ 25, 32.
48. Ibid., §§ 36, 28, 41, 47.

49. For the importance of Thomas's action theory to issues in business ethics, see the first chapter of my *To Kill Another: Homicide and Natural Law* (New Brunswick, N.J.: Transaction, 2010).

on the naturalness of vanity. He also cites the argument that since humans want to know the truth, they also want the truth about themselves known.[50] Thomas promptly dispatches this argument: to know the truth is to perfect the intellect and humans naturally desire to perfect their appetites: "But to desire that others know one's goodness is not a desire for one's own perfection." Here, Thomas appears to set his face against vanity as the Scots understood it: a regard for how one is viewed in the eyes of the spectator. Moreover, telling us that the glory sought in vanity is a clarity, Thomas leaves us in no doubt that he rejects the priority of aesthetics later affirmed the Scots: "And clarity implies some evidence that makes something apparent and manifest in its splendor, and so glory implies a manifestation of someone's goodness."[51]

It is the rest of Thomas's argument which intrigues though. A sign of *rapprochement* with the Scots is Thomas's use of Ambrose as an authority: glory, says Ambrose, is "clear recognition accompanied by praise."[52] Thomas argues that vanity, underwritten by the right norms, is good. These norms are: truth, the common good, and care of the self. To desire that one be known by others to be good can be a laudable desire: if manifesting one's goodness redounds to the glory of God, if it works for the good of one's neighbor, and if one is strengthened in virtue and encouraged to persevere. Indeed, preempting the language of the Scots, and even more so Burke, Thomas argues that manifesting glory helps neighbors, "who, perceiving one's goodness, are drawn to imitate it."[53]

Thomas and Hume agree that vanity is not accidental to human nature. For Thomas, vanity is an aid in the human pursuit of excellence which, at its deepest level, is an imitation of God's generosity. It is not a conditional good, in the sense Kraynak means. That is, the comparative nature of being human is, for Thomas, permanent. Kraynak wants Catholic social thought to acknowledge that a multiplicity of regimes—democratic, monarchical, authoritarian—might promote social order, leaving the Church free to tend to the spiritual. What Thomas suggests is that irrespective of regime, as it were, vanity will build community and encourage virtue. Vanity is a dependent good, however. John Paul II makes the point: "It is therefore necessary to create lifestyles in which the quest for truth, beauty, goodness and communion with others for the sake of common growth are the factors which determine consumer choices, savings and investments."[54] A corollary to vanity is the Scottish Enlightenment interest in what the Scots called "the spectator," moral consensus. Whig

---

50. *De malo*, q. 9, a. 1, obj. 3. 51. Ibid., q. 9, a. 1.
52. Ibid. 53. Ibid.
54. *Centesimus annus*, § 36.

Thomists are right to see that in the Scottish Enlightenment not just any version of self-development is tolerable. Hume and Smith are quickly misunderstood if their interest in vanity is read as a promotion of self-interest. Vanity
is a social phenomenon governed by the spectator's ideas of luxury or beauty, which entails, as Smith's portrait of the ambitious young man makes clear,
great sacrifice for the sake of commonly affirmed values.[55]

Much hinges, though, on the right relationship between beauty and the
good. This is an intrinsically difficult question, one compounded by recent developments within Catholic theology. Nuptial theology—the claim that conjugal love is normative for human action, a love, in turn, rooted in the meaning of Christ as the Bridegroom—clearly relies on certain aesthetic ideals of
comeliness, what is becoming and lovely about the beloved. Yet, this theology
is also likely a fertile approach to globalized culture if Sombart's theory about
the relationship between commerce, luxury, and erotic life is correct. The theory is by no means uncontested—not least by his colleague, Weber—yet some
confirmation of Sombart's research is found in Hume: Hume links refinement
and gallantry and argues that love relations in commercial society take on a
distinctive, positive hue. Scheler argued that the ethos guiding contemporary
economic life could be corrected only by a truer assessment of sexuality. This
claim is tied into his overall ethical theory and need not delay us here. But a
not dissimilar idea is found in *Deus Caritas Est,* where Benedict lays out the
elements of what might be called a social erotics.[56] This text makes one wonder whether Catholic social thought might develop a nuptial commerce as an
interpretive model for adjudicating trends with commercial culture. Understanding vanity is a small, but crucial, beginning to elucidating the idea of a
nuptial commerce and the role it might play in Catholic social thought.

55. Adam Smith, *The Theory of Moral Sentiments,* 181–82.
56. On the erotics of this text, see my "Pleasure: A Reflection on *Deus Caritas Est,*" *Nova et
Vetera* (English) 5, no. 2 (2007): 315–24.

Postscript: "There Is Only One Sadness . . . Not to Be Saints"

An Expression of Gratitude to Father Romanus Cessario, O.P.

ALASDAIR MacINTYRE

Christian saints are a strange and oddly varied lot. Assemble in one place, say, Columcille, Catherine of Siena, Thomas More, Theresa of Avila, John of the Cross, Philip Neri, Robert Bellarmine, Thérèse of Lisieux, Maria Goretti, and Teresa Benedicta of the Cross, and two things are at once evident about this congregation of the unexpected. The first is that, although they have some notable qualities in common—energy, conviction, and a prayerful care for the needy—they are extraordinarily different from one another. And I do not think that this is just because the list that I have assembled is one of names drawn from different times, places, and cultures. The second is that none of them is a model of human goodness, as understood by the great moral philosophers.

This may not seem in the least problematic, if the moral philosophers that we have in mind are Mill or Kant or Hume. Obviously the saints would not win prizes as utility-maximizers or performers of duty for duty's sake or examples of the virtues as understood by Hume. But when we take note of the fact that they equally certainly seem not to be models of the Aristotelian virtues either—and not only because so many of them are women—we need to pause and take stock, especially if we are Thomistic Aristotelians. None of the saints resemble Aristotle's magnanimous man. Yet perhaps too often we have taken it for granted that the exercise of the theological virtues supplements and perfects the exercise of the natural virtues, understood as Aristotle understood them, in such a way that the goodness that we owe to grace is simply a heightened version of the goodness that we are capable of by nature, understood as Aristotle understood it. But that is not how saints are. So what has gone wrong in our thinking about natural goodness and about holiness?

I have reason to be grateful to Father Romanus Cessario for a number of things, but most of all perhaps for the help that his writings have given me in thinking about this problem—my problem, I hasten to add, not his. But, like many others, I am of course grateful for more than this, above all that he, together with a small number of others—notable among them Father Servais Pinckaers, O.P., and Stanley Hauerwas—gave moral theology a new life. What we are peculiarly in debt to Cessario for is not primarily that his answers differ from those of that unfortunate generation of Catholic moral theologians who prospered in the wake of the Second Vatican Council, but that he asked different questions. They asked questions about rules. He asked questions about virtues. And, just because he focused upon virtues, he was able to understand rules better than they did.

Enquiry into the theological virtues is of the first importance for at least two reasons. First, their exercise is one of the ways in which grace enters the world and changes the world. And, secondly, without their exercise we are deficient even in the natural virtues. For, as Aquinas puts it, to perform the acts of the natural virtues as we are required to perform them, that is, with charity, is impossible without grace, and this would have been so even if we had not been corrupted by sin.[1] It follows that the forms taken by prudence, justice, courage, and temperateness in the lives of saints may be unpredictably different from those which they take in the lives of those lacking grace. So we have the beginning of a solution to my problem, although no more than a beginning. To go further we need to consider the difference between the types of conflict that arise in the course of the development and exercise of the natural virtues and those that arise in those whose actions are informed by the theological virtues. In both cases the needed background for the enquiry has been provided by Cessario's discussions.

In *The Moral Virtues and Theological Ethics* Cessario has an illuminating discussion of prudence, contrasting Duns Scotus's account with his own Thomistic view. On Scotus's account prudence is an intellectual, but not a moral, virtue, instructing us as to what is to be done, but itself in no way an expression of our desires or our emotions. Aquinas by contrast said of prudence

1. *ST* I-II, q. 109, a. 4.

that it "requires that a human being be rightly disposed with regard to ends; and this depends on rightness of appetite."[2] And Cessario commented that prudence can therefore "only reach completion in the concrete affairs of life when the moral virtues, which steady the movement of the appetites, supply prudence with the right ends-in-intention,"[3] noting in a footnote that Aquinas's conception of prudence presupposes his account of the relationships between intellect and will, another matter on which he is at odds with Scotus.

Prudence therefore may always be misled in particular situations by even momentarily disordered appetites. And the attempted exercise of prudence may lead to quandaries when an agent seeks to avoid both the sins of excess and those of defect, both, for example, precipitous rashness in the face of some danger and excess of caution. "In the case of a reasoned mean," Cessario has argued,

prudence weighs two factors indispensable for the correct development of virtue in the sense appetites. The first is a material factor, the biological stuff, if you will, out of which the virtue emerges . . . Next . . . the actual circumstances of a virtuous act also figure in assessing the reasoned mean. This second factor can include as many different people, events, and things as one might encounter in the course of a lifetime.[4]

At once it is clear that there are large possibilities for conflict even within those who have developed their capacity for exercising both the moral virtues and prudence to a significant degree. For each of us has to reckon both with her or his own natural propensities, rooted in her or his own peculiar neurophysiological and biochemical makeup, and with the complexity and the unfamiliarity of the circumstances of some of the situations in which we have to choose and to act. And it therefore is a central task of prudence to acknowledge the reality of inner conflicts that are engendered, both in the course of striking a mean between the type of excess and the type of defect that may arise from one's biological makeup and in the course of trying to give due weight to this or that type of circumstance. It is during the deliberations by which an agent thinks her or his way through these competing and conflicting considerations toward decision and action that she or he may be most dangerously vulnerable to prudential misjudgments arising from disordered appetites.

There is of course no general solution to this problem, no set of maxims— other than those enjoining the perfecting of prudence—that will guide us

2. *ST* I-II, q. 57, a. 4.
3. Romanus Cessario, O.P., *The Moral Virtues and Theological Ethics* (Notre Dame, Ind.: University of Notre Dame Press, 1991), 91.
4. Ibid., 131.

through such conflicts and lessen our vulnerability. Each individual has to find her or his own way, guided, if possible, by the deliberative advice of more seasoned others, so that she or he comes to know how to avoid both the faults of excess and those of defect and how to give due weight to what sometimes appear incommensurable considerations. Both of these are a matter of knowing how, not of knowing that, of practical, not theoretical, intelligence. But, just because of this, those whose exercise of the virtues owes nothing to grace will also be liable to fail morally for yet another reason.

In our practical decision making, we all of us presuppose a double rank ordering of the ends toward which we direct ourselves, a rank ordering, on the one hand, of types of end and a rank ordering, on the other, of those particular ends that we choose to pursue or not to pursue on particular occasions. So the achievement of a good education may be a type of end that a student rightly ranks higher than the end of amusing her or himself, but at particular times and places that student may rightly judge that for the next hour at least a little amusement is in place rather than preparing for an examination. Now consider one way in which both types of rank ordering may go wrong, namely, by misconceiving our ultimate end. It is our ultimate end that provides the measure according to which we rank-order all lesser ends, both types of end and particular ends. It is our ultimate good that provides the standard by which we judge what place all other goods should have in our lives.

I do not mean to suggest in saying this that we are generally aware of making use of this measure. In the cultures of modernity most people are not aware that there is such a measure, let alone that they themselves employ it. But it is nonetheless presupposed. And, insofar as we are virtuous, we will be rightly directed toward our ultimate end, and will give to each good its due place in our life. If we lack grace, the happiness at which we aim will be no more than that imperfect happiness of which Aquinas speaks. The difficulty is that it is only from the standpoint of the life of grace that we are able to recognize that imperfection and the standard by which it is to be judged imperfect. And, given our sinfulness, we will be apt to fall into error.

A comparison between Aristotle's discussion of courage and Aquinas's is instructive. Aristotle took it that the paradigmatic expression of courage is a willingness to confront danger nobly and, if need be, to die in battle the kind of death that is honored in political communities.[5] And it is not difficult to understand why, since elsewhere Aristotle argues that it is only in and through our participation in our political community that we are able to enjoy a shared,

---

5. *Nicomachean Ethics*, III (1115a29–32).

adequately human life governed by law and justice.[6] So it is better to die than to lose everything that makes life worthwhile.

Aquinas agrees with Aristotle that willingness to confront such dangers in battle is the mark of a courageous human being, but this willingness is perfectly exemplified by Christian martyrs, who have confronted the dangers of a battle, a contest with their persecutors.[7] And Aquinas goes on to argue that to die willingly as a martyr is an act of the greatest perfection, since "of all virtuous acts martyrdom is the greatest proof of the perfection of charity."[8] But this of course is something that can be understood only from the standpoint of grace. Someone who lacked nothing in respect of the natural virtues, but who had not been given grace, could not, when risking her or his life as a patriot in the just defense of her or his country, have the thought that "This is not the best possible way to offer one's life for the sake of a greater good."

Aquinas, however, goes even further, when he says that "something judged excessive by the one standard [that of nature] could actually become virtuous by the other standard [that of grace]"[9] in a passage that Cessario quotes in the course of distinguishing the infused from the acquired virtues.[10] So what is, on Aquinas's view, "proportionate to the good of society" may not be "a proportion ordered toward the good of eternal life," and Cessario concludes that "the particular shape or 'form' which the infused virtues give to one who lives by faith amounts to more than just a new motive." What accords with the mean from the standpoint of a life directed toward the good of eternal life may, perhaps must, appear excessive from the standpoint of a life directed toward the imperfect happiness of this world. The saint is, from the standpoint of the prudent Aristotelian, liable to seem an unbalanced extremist.

We are thus one stage closer to the solution of the problem that I posed at the outset. But we still need to take one further step. Consider once again the possibilities of conflict that arise for us both on account of our biological makeup and on account of the variety and complexity of the circumstances in which we sometimes have to act. Someone who is on the way to acquiring the virtue of courage will often have to recognize that some of his fears are inordinate and unreasonable and therefore will have to discipline himself, with the aim not only of acting other than as his fears bid, but also of lessening those fears. But he may well in consequence make the mistake of supposing that, as he becomes fully courageous, he should expect his fear to cease to have *any* motivating power, perhaps to disappear altogether, so that in battle the fear of

---

6. *Politics*, I (1253a1–39).
7. *ST* II-II, q. 124, a. 2.
8. *ST* II-II, q. 124, a. 3.
9. *In III Sententiarum*, d. 33, q. 1, a. 2.
10. Cessario, *The Moral Virtues and Theological Ethics*, 111.

death would no longer weigh with him at all in his deliberations. And, if he did indeed achieve this condition, in which fear was no longer any kind of motive, he might of course often do what a courageous human being would do, but he would not in fact be courageous. He would instead have become insensible to danger, a far from desirable condition. To have the acquired virtue of courage is to be willing to risk death for a just and appropriate cause, in spite of one's continuing reasonable and ordinate fear of death.[11] So both in the case of courage and in the cases of the other natural virtues, we continue to have, in a variety of ways and degrees, competing desires and passions—the desire to act courageously *and* the fear of death—and we therefore remain liable to disordered desires and passions, and to the possibility of their dictating our actions, even when we are well advanced in the exercise of the natural virtues.

With those whose actions are, by grace, informed by infused virtues it is quite otherwise. "For infused virtue effects that one in no way obey the concupiscence of sin; and, while this virtue remains, it does this infallibly. Acquired virtue falls short in this respect."[12] It was on the basis of this distinction between the acquired and the infused virtues that Cessario constructed his own contemporary account of the dynamic of infused virtues.[13] And by his so doing, Aquinas and he cooperate in providing the final piece needed for the puzzle from which I began. For the saints, just because of their infused virtues, the promptings of disordered passions and desires have no motivating force at all. They have not been freed from temptation, but their ability to resist such promptings gives them a distinctive kind of intransigent single-mindedness, one that differentiates them sharply from many good people.

I have chosen to express my gratitude to Father Cessario by focusing on a single problem, one in which he helped me to arrive at a conclusion, both by directing my attention to the relevant texts of Aquinas and by his commentary on and development of a theology out of those texts. Yet in arriving at this conclusion, I have drawn only on one of his books. And I therefore need to stress how much else he has given us and how central to the enterprise of moral theology his further thoughts on the infused virtues, especially as developed in *Christian Faith and the Theological Life* and, we may hope, in its successor volumes, have been and will be. But I want also to return once more to my problem, with two additional observations about the relationship between holiness and natural goodness.

11. On the importance of the distinction between inordinate fear and reasonable fear, see *Summa theologiae* II-II, q. 125, a. 1.

12. *De virtutibus in communi*, 10, ad 14.

13. Cessario, *The Moral Virtues and Theological Ethics*, 117–25.

The first of these I owe to John of the Cross, who contrasts the anxiety that is generated by attachment to earthly things with the clarity of understanding that becomes possible through detachment from them. Since such detachment is a work of grace, we might well suppose that in the movement from nature to grace we leave behind any pleasure that we previously took in those earthly things. Not so, according to John of the Cross. Detachment issues in a new and different enjoyment of just those same earthly things: "this man, then, has joy in all things, since his joy is dependent on none of them—just as though he possessed them all."[14] So grace through detachment returns us to nature and enables us to enjoy nature more fully, so that even the imperfect happiness that is the goal of the good human being without grace is itself better achieved through grace. Holiness is after all an enhancement of goodness.

A second observation has provided me with my title, translated from the last sentence of Léon Bloy's novel *La Femme Pauvre,* too often misquoted and even misascribed. Bloy's characters, like Bloy himself, have a vein of real craziness, as well as an aspect of holiness. And it is important to distinguish the two and not to suppose that what I have called the unbalanced extremism of the saints is a form of madness. But what Bloy had grasped and gives voice to through his characters is his understanding that, once we know what holiness is and how it stands to natural goodness, we have only one thing left to be sad about: the inadequacy of our charity, of ourselves as we now are. And it is one of Father Cessario's achievements that he has provided just the account of the virtues that we need in order to understand why this is so.

14. St. John of the Cross, *The Ascent of Mount Carmel,* III, XX, 2, 3, in *The Voice of the Spirit: The Spirituality of St. John of the Cross,* ed. and trans. Elizabeth Hamilton (Huntington, Ind.: Our Sunday Visitor, 1976), 70–71.

Publications of
Romanus Cessario, O.P.

BOOKS

Christian Satisfaction in Aquinas. Washington, D.C.: University Press of America, 1982.

The Godly Image: Christ and Salvation in Catholic Thought from Anselm to Aquinas. Petersham, Mass.: St. Bede's Publications, 1990.

Meeting Christ in the Sacraments by Colman E. O'Neill, O.P., and revised by Romanus Cessario, O.P. New York: Alba House, 1991.

The Moral Virtues and Theological Ethics. Notre Dame and London: University of Notre Dame Press, 1991.

Le Virtù. Volume 19 of Manuali di Teologia Cattolica (AMATECA), Sezione sesta: *La persona umana.* Milan: Editoriale Jaca Book, 1994. (Spanish edition: *Las virtudes.* Valencia: Edicep, 1998. English edition: *Virtues, or the Examined Life.* New York: Continuum, 2002. Croatian edition: *Kreposti.* Zagreb: Kršćanska sadašnjost, 2007.)

Perpetual Angelus: As the Saints Pray the Rosary. New York: Alba House, 1995.

Christian Faith and the Theological Life. Washington, D.C.: The Catholic University of America Press, 1996.

The Love That Never Ends: A Key to the Catechism of the Catholic Church. With J. A. DiNoia, B. G. O'Donnell, and P. J. Cameron. Huntington, Ind.: Our Sunday Visitor Press, 1996.

Jean Capreolus en son temps (1380–1444). Mémoire Dominicaine, numéro spécial, 1. Edited with Guy Bedouelle and Kevin White. Paris: Les Éditions du Cerf, 1997.

Veritatis Splendor and the Renewal of Moral Theology: Studies by Ten Outstanding Scholars. Edited with J. A. DiNoia, O.P. Chicago: Midwest Theological Forum, 1999.

Le thomisme et les thomistes. Paris: Les Éditions du Cerf, 1999.

John Capreolus (1380–1444). On the Virtues. Trans. Kevin White and Romanus Cessario, O.P. Washington, D.C.: The Catholic University of America Press, 2001.

Introduction to Moral Theology. Washington, D.C.: The Catholic University of America Press, 2001.

Boston's Cardinal: Bernard Law, the Man and His Witness. Edited with Mary Ann Glendon, and including a "Biographical Essay." Lanham, Md.: Lexington Books, 2002.

The Virtues, or the Examined Life. New York: Continuum, 2002.

A Short History of Thomism. Washington, D.C.: The Catholic University of America Press, 2005.

The Moral Virtues and Theological Ethics. 2nd ed. Notre Dame, Ind.: University of Notre Dame Press, 2008.

The Seven Last Words of Jesus. Paris and New York: Magnificat, 2009. Chinese edition: Taiwan: Catholic Window Press, 2010.

ARTICLES

"Theology at Fribourg." *The Thomist* 51, no. 2 (1987): 325–66.

"The Meaning of Virtue in Catholic Moral Life: Its Significance for Human Life Issues." *The Thomist* 53, no. 2 (1989): 173–96.

"Christian Satisfaction and Sacramental Reconciliation." *Communio* 16, no. 2 (1989): 186–96.

"Casuistry and Revisionism: Structural Similarities in Method and Content." In *"Humanae Vitae": 20 Anni Dopo. Atti del II Congresso Internazionale di Theologia Morale,* 385–409. Vol. III. Milan: Edizioni Ares, 1990.

"Aquinas on Nature and Grace." In *Catholicism and Secularization in America,* edited by David L. Schindler, 207–10. Notre Dame, Ind.: Communio Books, 1990.

"La tradition thomiste et l'oeuvre de l'Esprit: les dons d'intelligence et de science." *Nova et vetera* (French) 65 (1990): 259–67.

"Christ and Reconciliation." *Faith & Reason* 17 (1991): 15–50.

"Lacordaire et les États-Unis." In *Lacordaire, son pays, ses amis et la liberté des ordres religieux en France,* edited by Guy Bedouelle, 333–47. Paris: Les Éditions du Cerf, 1991.

"A Thomist Interpretation of Faith: The Gifts of Understanding and Knowledge." In *Novitas et Veritas Vitae : Aux Sources du Renouveau de la Morale Chrétienne. Mélanges offerts au Professeur Servais Pinckaers à l'occasion de son 65e anniversaire.* Edited by Carlos-Josaphat Pinto de Oliveira, 67–102. Fribourg: Editions Universitaires, 1991.

"Incarnate Wisdom and the Immediacy of Christ's Salvific Knowledge." In *Problemi teologici alla luce dell'Aquinate (Atti del IX Congresso Tomistico Internazionale). Studi Tomistici* 44, 334–40. Vatican City: Libreria Editrice Vaticana, 1991.

"St. Thomas Aquinas on Satisfaction, Indulgences, and Crusades." *Medieval Philosophy & Theology* 2 (1992): 74–96.

"Virtue Theory and the Present Evolution of Thomism." In *The Future of Thomism,* edited by Deal W. Hudson and Dennis William Moran, 291–99. Notre Dame, Ind.: American Maritain Association, 1992.

"An Observation on Robert Lauder's Review of G. A. McCool, S.J." *The Thomist* 56, no. 4 (1992): 701–10.

"Lacordaire and the United States." *Catholic Historical Review* 78, no. 2 (1992): 197–206.

"Boethius, Christ, and the New Order." *Carmina Philosophiae* 1 (1992): 53–64. (Reprinted in *New Directions in Boethian Studies* [Studies in Medieval Culture], edited by Noel Harold Kaylor, Jr., and Philip Edward Philips, 157–68. Kalamazoo, Mich.: Medieval Institute Publications, 2007.)

"Is Aquinas's *Summa* Only About Grace?" In *Ordo Sapientiae et Amoris: Hommage au Professeur Jean-Pierre Torrell OP à l'occasion de son 65e anniversaire,* edited by Carlos-Josaphat Pinto de Oliveira, 197–209. Fribourg: Editions Universitaires, 1993.

"Moral sexual christiana dentro de una estructura más amplia." *Anámnesis* 3 (1993): 5–25.

"Le Père Garrigou-Lagrange (1877–1964)." *Sources* 20 (1994): 206–8.

"Early Dominican Confessional Practice." *New Blackfriars* 75, no. 885 (1994): 425–28. (French translation: "Les Premiers Dominicains et la confession." *Mémoire Dominicaine* 5 [1994]: 283–86.)

"The Church, Higher Education, and Global Concerns." *Josephinum Journal of Theology* 2, no. 1 (1995): 25–33.

"Moral Absolutes in the Civilization of Love." In *The Splendor of Truth and Health Care. Proceedings of the Fourteenth Workshop for Bishops, Dallas, Texas,* edited by Russell E. Smith, 43–57. Braintree, Mass.: The Pope John XXIII Medical-Moral Research and Education Center, 1995. (Reprinted in *Crisis* 13 [May, 1995]: 18–23.)

"Boèce, le Christ et la civilisation européenne." *Pierre d'angle* 1 (1995): 51–60.

"Toward Understanding Aquinas' Theological Method: The Early Twelfth-Century Experience." In *Studies in Thomistic Theology,* edited by Paul Lockey, 17–89. Notre Dame, Ind.: Center for Thomistic Studies, 1995.

"*Epieikeia* and the Accomplishment of the Just." In *Aquinas and Empowerment: Classical Ethics for Ordinary Lives,* edited by G. Simon Harak, 170–205. Washington, D.C.: Georgetown University Press, 1996.

"The Spirituality of St. Thomas Aquinas." *Crisis* 14 (July/August 1996): 14–16.

"Evangelization and Our Present Circumstances: In Praise of Virtue." In *The Church's Mission of Evangelization,* edited by William E. May, 129–52. Steubenville, Ohio: Franciscan University Press, 1996.

"Éloge des vertus chrétiennes pour un temps de crise." *Pierre d'angle* 2 (1996): 53–71.

"Saint Thomas, Durand de Saint-Pourçain et Capreolus: Le Débat sur la foi." In *Jean Capreolus en son temps (1380–1444),* edited by Guy Bedouelle, Romanus Cessario, and Kevin White, 159–64. Paris: Les Éditions du Cerf, 1997.

"Christian Virtue and Public Morality." *Rivista Teologica di Lugano* 2 (1997): 27–42.

"À nos lecteurs: sur le paradoxe de l'existence chrétienne entre foi et modernité. La foi comme Dieu l'a révélée." *Pierre d'angle* 3 (1997): 18–26.

"On Bad Actions, Good Intentions, and Loving God: Three Much-Misunderstood Issues about the Happy Life That St. Thomas Clarifies for Us." *Logos* 1, no. 2 (1997): 100–124.

"Assent and Dissent," "Atheism," "Bishop," "Celibacy, Priestly," "Deacon," "Holy Orders," "Ministry," "Modernism," "Priest," and "Priesthood of Christ." In *Encyclopedia of Catholic Doctrine,* edited by Russell Shaw. Huntington, Ind.: Our Sunday Visitor Publishing Division, 1997.

"Theological Literacy and Theological Science." In *Boston Theological Institute Newsletter* 27, no. 24 (18 Mar 1998): 1–2.

"More Good News." *Catholic Dossier* 4, no. 2 (March–April 1998): 54–55.

"The Holy Spirit, Spirit of Truth, Person of Love." *Catholic International* 9 (May 1998): 220–24.

"Tommaso D'Aquino (santo)" and "Garrigou-Lagrange, Reginald." In *Dizionario di Mistica,* edited by L. Borriello et al. Vatican City: Libreria Editrice Vaticana, 1998.

"The D.E.S. Motto and the Benedictine Tradition: A Thomistic Connection." *Delta Epsilon Sigma Journal* 43 (1998): 88–90.

"St. Therese, Seminarians, and the Future." *Catholic Dossier* 4, no. 6 (November–December 1998): 14–16.

"John Poinsot: On The Gift of Counsel." In *The Common Things: Essays on Thomism and*

Education, edited by Daniel McInerny, 163–78. Mishawaka, Ind.: American Maritain Association, 1999.

"The Reason for Reason: *Fides et Ratio.*" *Crisis* 17, no. 1 (January 1999): 16–19.

"Thomas Aquinas: A Doctor for the Ages." *First Things* (March 1999): 27–32. (Reprinted in *The Second One Thousand Years: Ten People Who Defined the Millennium,* edited by Richard John Neuhaus, 28–39. Grand Rapids: Eerdmans, 2001.)

"Reply to Professor Gilbert Morris." *First Things* (June/July 1999): 7.

"Fides et Ratio: Un appel à la vérité et à la reconciliation." *Pierre d'angle* 5 (1999): 32–38.

"What the Angels See at Twilight." *Communio* 26 (Fall 1999): 583–94. (French translation: "Ce que les anges voient au crepuscule." *Communio* 25 [nov.–déc. 2000]: 41–51.)

"Custodia Condicional de la Vida Humana: Un principio moral de Juan Pablo II." In *El Dios y Padre de Nuestro Señor Jesucristo,* edited by José Luis Illanes et al., 427–32. Pamplona: Servicio de Publicaciones de la Universidad de Navarra, 2000.

"Infallible Teaching and the Gift of Divine Truth." *Catholic Dossier* 6, no. 3 (May–June 2000): 5–8.

"Un 'salut civil'? Vie et famille dans la doctrine catholique." *Pierre d'angle* 6 (2000): 185–97.

"Sacramental Confession and Addictions." In *Addiction and Compulsive Behaviors. Proceedings of the Seventeenth Workshop for Bishops, Dallas, Texas,* edited by Edward J. Furton, 125–39. Boston, Mass.: The National Catholic Bioethics Center, 2000.

"Schönborn, Christoph." In *New Catholic Encyclopedia, Jubilee Volume: The Wojtyla Years,* edited by Berard L. Marthaler, Richard E. McCarron, and Gregory F. LaNave, 406–7. Detroit: Gale in association with The Catholic University of America Press, 2001.

"Towards an Adequate Method for Catholic Bioethics." *National Catholic Bioethics Quarterly* 1, no. 1 (2001): 51–62.

"Gilson, Étienne (1884–1978)." In *The Dictionary of Historical Theology,* edited by Trevor A. Hart, 227–29. Grand Rapids: Eerdmans, 2001.

"En partant d'une chanson de Gershwin . . ." *Pierre d'angle* 7 (2001): 41–47.

"Duplex ordo cognitionis." *Doctor Communis* II, n.s., Atti della II Sessione Plenaria, 22–24 Giugno 2001, 102–9; 141–42. Vatican City: Pontificia Academia Sancti Thomae Aquinatis, 2002.

"The Theological Virtue of Hope (IIa IIae qq. 17–22)." In *The Ethics of Aquinas,* edited by Stephen J. Pope, 232–43. Washington, D.C.: Georgetown University Press, 2002.

"The Sacramental Mediation of Divine Friendship and Communion." *Faith & Reason* 27 (2002): 7–41.

"Consequentialism." In *New Catholic Encyclopedia.* 2nd ed., Vol. 4: 159–60. Detroit: Gale; Washington, D.C.: The Catholic University of America, 2002.

"Casuistry." With E. Hamel in *New Catholic Encyclopedia.* 2nd ed., Vol. 3: 219–221. Detroit: Gale; Washington, D.C.: The Catholic University of America, 2002.

"Mary in the Dominican Tradition." *Nova et Vetera* (English) 1, no. 1 (2003): 27–42.

"Entendre les Mystères : Musique liturgique et foi théologale." With Jonathan Gaspar. *Pierre d'angle* 9 (2003): 135–50.

"Cooperation, *Veritatis splendor,* and the Luminous Mysteries." In *Walk as Children of Light: The Challenge of Cooperation in a Pluralistic Society. Proceedings of the Nineteenth Workshop for Bishops, Dallas, Texas,* edited by Edward J. Furton, 47–67. Boston: The National Catholic Bioethics Center, 2003.

"Life and Family as Themes in Catholic Social Thought." In *Indubitanter ad Veritatem. Studies Offered to Leo J. Elders, S.V.D. in Honor of the Golden Jubilee of His Ordination to the Priesthood,* edited by Jörgen Vijgen, 69–79. Budel, Netherlands: Damon, 2003.

"Aquinas on Christian Salvation." In *Aquinas on Doctrine: A Critical Introduction,* edited by Thomas Weinandy, Daniel Keating, and John Yocum, 117–37. London: T & T Clark International, 2004.

"Response." In "Book Symposium," *Nova et Vetera* (English) 2, no. 1 (2004): 208–10.

"Mel Gibson and Thomas Aquinas: How the Passion Works." ZENIT, 9 April 2004. Available from http://www.zenit.org/ (German translation: "Wie die Passion Christi die Erlösung bewirkt—Mel Gibson und Thomas von Aquin." *Una Voce—Korrespondenz* 34 [2004]: 131–38.)

"Conditional Stewardship of Life: A Moral Principle of John Paul II." In *Moral Issues in Catholic Health Care,* edited by Kevin T. McMahon, 120–38. Overbrook, Pa.: Saint Charles Borromeo Seminary, 2004.

"Sex, Lies, and Freud." *Logos* 7, no. 3 (2004): 47–59.

"Mel Gibson et saint Thomas d'Aquin: Un regard théologique sur *La Passion du Christ.*" *Pierre d'angle* 10 (2004): 185–94.

"Why Aquinas Locates Natural Law within the *Sacra Doctrina.*" In *St. Thomas Aquinas and the Natural Law Tradition: Contemporary Perspectives,* edited by John Goyette, Mark S. Latkovic, and Richard S. Myers, 79–93. Washington, D.C.: The Catholic University of America Press, 2004.

"The Light of Tabor: Christian Personalism and Adoptive Friendship." *Nova et Vetera* (English) 2, no. 2 (2004): 237–47. (Reprinted in *L'Antropologia della Teologia Morale Secondo L'Enciclica "Veritatis Splendor." Atti del Simposio promosso dalla Congregazione per la Dottrina della Fede, Roma, settembre 2003,* 92–101. Vatican City: Libreria Editrice Vaticana, 2006.)

"Mel Gibson's Movie & Thomas Aquinas's Modes: How the Passion of the Christ Works." *Saint Austin Review* 4 (2004): 27–32. (Dutch translation: "Mel Gibson en Thomas van Aquino over de Passie van Christus." In *Doctor Humanitatis.* Vol. 1, *De actualiteit van Sint Thomas van Aquino,* edited by Jörgen Vijgen. Hoofddorp: Uitgeverij Boekenplan, 2005.)

"Mel Gibson's 'Passion' & Aquinas's Five Modes: How the Passion of Christ Works." The Premier International Fan Website: Mel Gibson's "The Passion of the Christ." Available from http://www.passion-movie.com/promote/cessario.html.

"Walk According to the Light: An Illustration from North America." In *Camminare nella Luce: Prospettive della teologia morale a partire da 'Veritatis splendor,'* edited by Livio Melina and José Noriega, 401–7. Rome: Lateran University Press, 2004.

"Capreolus on Faith and the 'Theologal' Life." In *Essays in Medieval Philosophy and Theology in Memory of Walter H. Principe, CSB: Fortresses and Launching Pads,* edited by James R. Ginther and Carl N. Still, 135–41. Aldershot, England; Burlington, Vt.: Ashgate Publishing, 2005.

"*Duplex Ordo Cognitionis.*" In *Reason and the Reasons of Faith,* edited by Paul J. Griffiths and Reinhard Hütter, 327–38. New York: T & T Clark, 2005.

"'Worthy of the Temple': Liturgical Music and Theologal Faith." With Jonathan Gaspar. *Nova et Vetera* (English) 3, no. 4 (2005): 673–88.

"Catholic Hospitals in the New Evangelization." *National Catholic Bioethics Quarterly* 5, no. 4 (2005): 675–686.

"Person and Being: Theological and Psychological Considerations." *Doctor Communis,* Atti della IV Sessione Plenaria, 25–27 Giugno 2004, 75–84. Vatican City: Pontificia Academia Sancti Thomae Aquinatis, 2006.

"'Circa res . . . aliquid fit' (*Summa theologiae* II-II, q. 85, a. 3, ad 3): Aquinas on New Law Sacrifice." *Nova et Vetera* (English) 4, no. 2 (2006): 295–312.

"The Sacred, Religion, and Morality." *Doctor Communis* VII, n.s., Atti della V Sessione Plenaria, 24–26 Giugno 2005, 173–86. Vatican City: Pontificia Academia Sancti Thomae Aquinatis, 2006.

"Johannes Capreolus." In *Thomistenlexikon,* edited by David Berger and Jörgen Vijgen, 302–11. Bonn: Nova & Vetera Verlag, 2006.

"The Sacred, Religion, and Morality." *Logos* 9, no. 4 (2006): 16–32.

"Catholic Considerations on Palliative Care." *National Catholic Bioethics Quarterly* 6, no. 4 (2006): 639–50.

"Moral Theology on Earth: Learning from Two Thomases." *Studies in Christian Ethics* 19, no. 3 (2006): 305–22.

"Hommage au Père Servais-Théodore Pinckaers, O.P.: The Significance of His Work." *Nova et Vetera* (English) 5, no. 1 (2007): 1–16.

"The Theological Heritage of Pope Benedict XVI." *Nova et Vetera* (English) 5, no. 2 (2007): 267–70.

"Moral Realism and Christian Values." In *The Person and the Polis: Faith and Values within the Secular State,* edited by Craig Steven Titus, 153–73. Arlington, Va.: The Institute for the Psychological Sciences Press, 2007.

"*Tanquam spiritualis pulchritudinis amatores:* The Consecrated Vocation of Matthew Lamb." In *Wisdom and Holiness, Science and Scholarship: Essays in Honor of Matthew L. Lamb,* edited by Michael Dauphinais and Matthew Levering, 17–45. Naples, Fla.: Sapientia Press, 2007.

"Saint Thomas and the Enculturation of the Natural Law: Doing Moral Theology on Earth." *Doctor Communis,* Atti della VI Sessione Plenaria, 23–25 Giugno 2006, 41–53. Vatican City: Pontificia Academia Sancti Thomae Aquinatis, 2007.

"Reply to Edward T. Oakes, S.J." *First Things* (October 2007): 8–9.

"Thomas d'Aquin, apôtre du sens commun." *Pierre d'angle* 13 (2007): 49–56.

"Sonship, Sacrifice, and Satisfaction: The Divine Friendship in Aquinas and the Renewal of Christian Anthropology." *Letter & Spirit* 3 (2007): 71–93.

"In Honor of Avery Cardinal Dulles, S.J.: Priest, Scholar, and Living Memory." *Nova et Vetera* (English) 6, no. 2 (2008): 245–46.

"The Sacraments of the Church." In *Vatican II: Renewal within Tradition,* edited by Matthew L. Lamb and Matthew Levering, 129–46. Oxford: Oxford University Press, 2008.

"On Moral Theology." In *Love Alone Is Credible: Hans Urs von Balthasar as Interpreter of the Catholic Tradition,* edited by David L. Schindler, 297–302. Vol. 1. Grand Rapids: Eerdmans, 2008.

"Scholarship and Sanctity." *Second Spring* 10 (2008): 13–20.

"Love, Friendship, and Beauty: On the Twenty-fifth Anniversary of a Magisterial Document about Religious Life and the Apostolate." *Logos* 11, no. 4 (2008): 147–63.

"The Quarry Workers." *Nova et Vetera* (English) 6, no. 3 (2008): 669–74.

"*Humanae Vitae,* the Maritains, and Maurice Sachs." *Nova et Vetera* (English) 6, no. 4 (2008): 711–30.

"O que os anjos vêem: natureza e grace." *Lumen Veritatis* 2, no. 5 (2008): 121–25.

"Freedom and Satisfaction." In *The Human Person and a Culture of Freedom,* edited by Peter A. Pagan and Terese Auer, O.P., 207–25. Washington, D.C.: American Maritain Association, 2009.

"On the Place of Servais Pinckaers († 7 April 2008) in the Renewal of Catholic Theology." *The Thomist* 73 (2009): 1–27.

"Hommage au Père Servais Pinckaers, O.P. : L'importance de son œuvre." In *Renouveler toutes choses en Christ : Vers un renouveau thomiste de la théologie morale,* edited by Michael S. Sherwin and Craig Steven Titus, 6–19. *Etudes d'éthique chrétienne,* NS 5. Fribourg: Academic Press, 2009.

"Saint Thomas Aquinas : 'The Apostle of Common Sense.'" *Nova et Vetera* (English) 7, no. 3 (2009) : 563–68.

"Consequentialism." *New Catholic Encyclopedia Supplement 2009,* 2 vols., edited by Robert L. Fastiggi, Vol. 1: 191–93. Detroit: Gale/Cengage Learning, 2010.

Works Cited

Aertsen, Jan A. "Thomas Aquinas on the Good: The Relation between Metaphysics and Ethics." In *Aquinas's Moral Theory*, edited by Scott MacDonald and Eleonore Stump, 235–53. Ithaca, N.Y.: Cornell University Press, 1999.

Alberg, Jeremiah. "The Place of the Victim." In *Victims and Victimization in French and Francophone Literature*, edited by Buford Norman, 111–18. New York: Rodopi, 2005.

———. *Reinterpreting Rousseau: A Religious System*. New York: Palgrave Macmillan, 2007.

Albertus Magnus. *De sacrificio missae. Opera Omnia 38*. Edited by Augustus Borgnet. Paris: Vivès, 1899.

Alexander, J. McKenzie. *The Structural Evolution of Morality*. Cambridge: Cambridge University Press, 2007.

Anscombe, G. E. M. "Modern Moral Philosophy." *Philosophy* 33, no. 124 (1958): 1–19.

Aristotle. *Nichomachean Ethics*. Translated by W. D. Ross. New York: Random House, 1941.

Armogathe, Jean-Robert. *Theologia cartesiana: L'explication physique de l'Eucharistie chez Descartes et dom Desgabets*. The Hague: Nijhoff, 1977.

———. "Cartesian Physics and the Eucharist in the Documents of the Holy Office and the Roman Index (1671–6)." In *Receptions of Descartes: Cartesianism and Anti-Cartesianism in Early Modern Europe*, edited by Tad M. Schmaltz, 149–70. London and New York: Routledge, 2005.

Ashley, Benedict, O.P. *Theologies of the Body: Humanist and Christian*. Braintree, Mass.: Pope John XXIII Center, 1985.

———. *The Ashley Reader: Redeeming Reason*. Naples, Fla.: Sapientia Press, 2006.

———. *The Way toward Wisdom: An Interdisciplinary and Intercultural Introduction to Metaphysics*. Notre Dame, Ind.: Notre Dame University Press, 2006.

Balthasar, Hans Urs von. *Cordula oder der Ernstfall*. Einsiedeln: Johannes Verlag, 1966.

———. *Mysterium Paschale*. In *Mysterium Salutis*. Vol. 3, bk. 2. Edited by J. Feiner and M. Löhrer, 133–326. Einsiedeln: Benziger, 1969.

———. *Theodramatik*. Vol. 3, *Die Handlung*. Einsiedeln: Johannes Verlag, 1980.

———. *Unser Auftrag. Bericht und Entwurf*. Einsiedeln: Johannes Verlag, 1984.

Barrow, John, and Frank Tipler. *The Anthropic Cosmological Principle*. Oxford: Oxford University Press, 1988.

Bauerschmidt, Frederick Christian. "That the Faithful Become the Temple of God." In *Reading John with St. Thomas Aquinas: Theological Exegesis and Speculative Theology*, edited by Michael Dauphinais and Matthew Levering, 293–311. Notre Dame, Ind.: University of Notre Dame Press, 2005.

Beckett, Paul, Krishna Pokharel, and Eric Bellman. "India's Surging Economy Lifts Hopes and Ambitions." *Wall Street Journal,* November 28, 2007.

Behe, Michael. *Darwin's Black Box: The Biochemical Challenge to Evolution.* New York: The Free Press, 1996.

———. *Edge of Evolution: The Search for the Limits of Darwinism.* New York: Simon and Schuster, 2007.

Benin, Stephen D. "The 'Cunning of God' and Divine Accommodation." *Journal of the History of Ideas* 45, no. 2 (1984): 179–91.

Berceville, G. "L'étonnante alliance: Evangile et miracles selon Saint Thomas." *Revue thomiste* 103, no. 1 (2003): 5–74.

Berger, David. *Thomas Aquinas and the Liturgy.* Naples, Fla.: Sapientia Press, 2004.

Bernadot, M. V., O.P. *From Holy Communion to the Blessed Trinity.* Translated by Dom Francis Izard, O.S.B. Westminster, Md.: Newman Press, 1952.

Biggar, Nigel, and Rufus Black, eds. *The Revival of Natural Law: Philosophical, Theological, and Ethical Responses to the Finnis-Grisez School.* Aldershot: Ashgate, 2000.

Blankenhorn, Bernhard, O.P. "The Instrumental Causality of the Sacraments: Thomas Aquinas and Louis-Marie Chauvet." *Nova et Vetera* (English) 4, no. 2 (2006): 255–93.

Bobik, Joseph. "Dimensions in the Individuation of Bodily Substances." *Philosophical Studies* 4 (1954): 60–79.

Boeve, Lieven, and L. Leijssen, eds. *Sacramental Presence in a Postmodern Context:* Bibliotheca Ephemeridum Theologicarum Lovaniensium, vol. 160. Leuven: Leuven University Press, 2001.

Boissard, Guy. *Die vielen Messen und das eine Opfer.* Freiburg: Herder, 1951.

———. "Le sens chrétien du sacrifice." *Nova et vetera* (French) 81 (2006): 35–50.

Bonaventure. *Commentarii in quatuor Libros Sententiarum Petri Lombardi.* Edited by P. Bernardini. Florence, Italy: Quaracchi, 1882–1902.

Boulnois, Olivier. *Être et représentation.* Paris: Presse Universitaires de France, 1999.

Brickhouse, Thomas C., and Nicholas D. Smith. "Socrates and the Unity of the Virtues." *Journal of Ethics* 1, no. 4 (1997): 311–24.

Brock, Stephen L. "St. Thomas and the Eucharistic Conversion." *The Thomist* 65, no. 4 (2001): 529–65.

Budziszewski, J. *Written on the Heart: The Case for Natural Law.* Downers Grove, Ill.: InterVarsity Press, 1997.

———. "Natural Born Lawyers." *The Weekly Standard,* May 14, 1999, 31–35.

———. *The Revenge of Conscience: Politics and the Fall of Man.* Dallas: Spence, 2000.

———. *What We Can't Not Know: A Guide.* Dallas: Spence, 2004.

Buescher, Gabriel, O.F.M. *The Eucharistic Teaching of William Ockham.* St. Bonaventure, N.Y.: The Franciscan Institute, 1950.

Burr, David. "Quantity and Eucharistic Presence: The Debate from Olivi through Ockham." *Collectanea Franciscana* 44 (1974): 5–44.

Capreolus, John. *On the Virtues.* Translated by Romanus Cessario, O.P. and Kevin White. Washington, D.C.: The Catholic University of America Press, 2001.

Carroll, Lewis. *Alices's Adventures in Wonderland.* Vol. I, *The Complete Works of Lewis Carroll.* London: The Nonesuch Press, 1939.

Chauvet, Louis-Marie. *Symbol and Sacrament: A Sacramental Reinterpretation of Christian*

Existence. Translated by Patrick Madigan, S.J., and Madeleine Beaumont. Collegeville, Minn.: Liturgical Press, 1995.

Chenu, Marie-Dominique. "Raison psychologique du développement du dogme." *Revue
   des Sciences Philosophiques et Théologiques* 13 (1924): 44–51.

———. *Le Saulchoir: Une ecole de théologie.* Paris: Cerf, 1937.

———. *Introduction à l'étude de S. Thomas d'Aquin.* Paris: Vrin, 1950.

———. "Vérité évangélique et métaphysique wolfienne à Vatican II." *Revue des Sciences
   Philosophiques et Théologiques* 57 (1973): 632–40.

Colin, Pierre. *L'audace et le soupçon: la crise du modernisme dans le catholicisme français
   1893–1914.* Paris: Desclée et Brouwer, 1997.

Colish, Marcia L. *The Stoic Tradition from Antiquity to the Early Middle Ages.* Leiden:
   E. J. Brill, 1985.

Congar, Yves, O.P. "Ecclesia ab Abel." In *Abhandlungen über Theologie und Kirche*, edited
   by Marcel Reding. Düsseldorf: Patmos-Verlag, 1952.

———. "The Idea of the Church in St. Thomas Aquinas." *The Thomist* 1, no. 3 (1939):
   331–59; reprinted with revisions in Yves Congar, O.P., *The Mystery of the Church*,
   53–74. Baltimore: Helicon Press, 1960.

———. *Tradition et Traditions.* Paris: Fayard, 1960.

———. "Saint Thomas Aquinas and the Infallibility of the Papal Magisterium." *The
   Thomist* 38, no. 1 (1974): 81–105.

Cottier, George. "Thomisme et modernité." In *Saint Thomas au XXe siècle: Actes du
   colloque centenaire de la "Revue Thomiste,"* edited by Serge-Thomas Bonino, 352–61.
   Paris: Editions Saint-Paul, 1994.

Courtenay, William J. *Covenant and Causality in Medieval Thought: Studies in Philosophy,
   Theology and Economic Practice.* London: Variorum Reprints, 1984.

Courtine, Jean-François. *Inventio analogiae: Métaphysique et ontothéologie.* Paris: Vrin,
   2005.

Covell, Charles. *The Defence of Natural Law.* New York: St. Martin's Press, 1992.

Crowley, Paul G. "*Instrumentum Divinitatis* in Thomas Aquinas: Recovering the Divinity
   of Christ." *Theological Studies* 52, no. 3 (1991): 451–75.

Daguet, François. *Théologie du dessein divin chez Thomas d'Aquin.* Paris: Vrin, 2003.

Daley, Brian. "Apokatastasis and 'the Honorable Silence' in the Eschatology of Maximus
   Confessor." In *Maximus Confessor,* edited by C. Schönborn and F. Heinzer, 318–27.
   Fribourg: Universitätsverlag, 1982.

Damascene, St. John. "The Orthodox Faith." In The Fathers of the Church. Vol. 37, *Writings.* Translated by Frederic H. Chase Jr. Washington, D.C.: The Catholic University
   of America Press, 1958.

Dauphinais, Michael. *The Pedagogy of the Incarnation: Christ the Teacher according to
   St. Thomas Aquinas.* Ph.D. diss., University of Notre Dame, 2000.

Davies, Paul. *God and the New Physics.* New York: Simon and Schuster, 1984.

———. *The Mind of God.* New York: Simon and Schuster, 1992.

Dawkins, Richard. *The Blind Watchmaker: Why the Evidence of Evolution Reveals a Universe without Design.* New York: Norton, 1996.

de Souza, Raymond. "Paul Collier: The Bottom Billion: Why the Poorest Countries Are
   Failing and What Can Be Done about It." *Religion and Liberty* 17, no. 3 (2007): 4–5.

Denzinger, Heinrich. *Enchiridion symbolorum definitionum et declarationum de rebus fidei
   et morum: Kompendium der Glaubensbekenntnisse und kirchlichen Lehrentscheidungen,*

Lateinisch-Deutsch. Edited by Peter Hünermann. 40th ed. Freiburg: Herder, 2005.

Descartes, René. *The Philosophical Writings of Descartes.* Vol. 1, *Principles of Philosophy.* Translated by John Cottingham, Robert Stoothoff, and Dugald Murdoch. Cambridge: Cambridge University Press, 1985.

"De transsubstantiatione." In *Decrees of the Ecumenical Councils.* Vol. 2, *Trent to Vatican II.* Edited by Norman P. Tanner, S.J., 695. London: Sheed & Ward; Washington, D.C.: Georgetown University Press, 1990.

Dewan, Lawrence, O.P. "St. Thomas and the Causality of God's Goodness." *Laval théologique et philosophique* 34, no. 3 (1978): 291–304.

———. "Saint Thomas and the Principle of Causality." In *Jacques Maritain: Philosophe dans la Cité / A Philosopher in the World,* edited by Jean-Louis Allard, 153–71. Ottawa: University of Ottawa Press, 1985.

———. "Natural Law and the First Act of Freedom: Maritain Revisited." *Études Maritainiennes—Maritain Studies* 12, no. 4 (1996): 3–32.

———. "St. Thomas, Physics and the Principle of Metaphysics." *The Thomist* 61 (1997): 549–66.

———. "St. Thomas, John Finnis, and the Political Good." *The Thomist* 64, no. 3 (2000): 366–67.

———. *Form and Being.* Washington, D.C.: The Catholic University of America Press, 2006.

———. "On Kevin Flannery's *Acts Amid Precepts: The Aristotelian Logical Structure of Thomas Aquinas's Moral Theory.*" *Nova et Vetera* (English) 5, no. 2 (2007): 431–44.

———. "St. Thomas, Rhonheimer, and the Object of the Human Act." *Nova et Vetera* (English) 6, no. 1 (2008): 71–72.

———. *Wisdom, Law, and Virtue: Essays in Thomistic Ethics.* New York: Fordham University Press, 2008.

DiNoia, J. A., O.P., and Romanus Cessario, O.P., eds. *Veritatis Splendor and the Renewal of Moral Theology.* Princeton: Scepter Publishers; Huntington, Ind.: Our Sunday Visitor; Chicago, Ill.: Midwest Theological Forum, 1999.

Dodds, Michael J., O.P. "The Teaching of Thomas Aquinas on the Mysteries of the Life of Christ." In *Aquinas On Doctrine: A Critical Introduction,* edited by Thomas Weinandy, Daniel Keating, and John Yocum. New York: T & T Clark, 2004.

Dondaine, Hyacinthe, O.P. "A propos d'Avicenne et de St. Thomas: de la causalité dispositive à la causalité instrumentale." *Revue thomiste* 51 (1951): 441–53.

Donneaud, Henri, O.P. "La constitution dialectique de la théologie et de son histoire selon M. D. Chenu." *Revue thomiste* 96, no. 1 (1996): 41–66.

Durand, Emmanuel, O.P. "L'autocommunication trinitaire: concept clé de la connexio mysteriorum rahnérienne." *Revue thomiste* 102, no. 4 (2002): 569–613.

———. "L'identité rahnérienne entre la Trinité économique et la Trinité immanente à l'épreuve de ses applications." *Revue thomiste* 103, no. 1 (2003): 75–92.

———. *La périchorèse des personnes divines: immanence mutuelle, réciprocité et communion.* Paris: Cerf, 2005.

Elders, Leo J., S.V.D. *Die Naturphilosophie des Thomas von Aquin: Allgemeine Naturphilosophie, Kosmologie, Philosophie der Lebewesen, Philosophische Anthropologie.* Weilheim-Bierbronnen: Gustav-Siewerth-Akademie, 2004.

Ellis, Ralph D. *Eros in a Narcissistic Culture.* Dordrecht: Kluwer, 1996.

Emery, Gilles, O.P. "L'immutabilité du Dieu d'amour et les problèmes du discour sur la 'souffrance de Dieu.'" *Nova et vetera* (French) 74 (1999): 5–37.

———. "Theology as a Spiritual Exercise in Augustine and Aquinas." In his *Trinity, Church and the Human Person*, 33–72. Naples, Fla.: Sapientia Press, 2007.

Feiner, Johannes, and Magnus Löhrer, eds. *Mysterium salutis: Grundriß heilsgeschichtlicher Dogmatik*. 5 vols. Einsiedeln: Benziger, 1965–76.

Finnis, John M. *Natural Law and Natural Rights*. Rev. ed. Oxford: Clarendon Press, 1982.

———. *Fundamentals of Ethics*. Oxford: Clarendon Press, 1983.

———. *Aquinas*. Oxford: Oxford University Press, 1998.

Fishacre, Richard, O.P. *In librum IV Sententiarum*. In *De sacramentorum efficientia apud theologos Ordinis Praedicatorum. Fasc. 1: 1229–1276*. Edited by H.-D. Simonin and G. Meersseman. Rome: Pontificum Institutum Internationale Angelicum, 1936.

Fitzmyer, Joseph A. *Romans*. New York: Doubleday, 1993.

Fleischacker, David. "Lonergan and the Surd and Sin of Contraception." Forthcoming article.

Foot, Philippa. *Natural Goodness*. Oxford: Clarendon Press, 2001.

Ford, John, S.J. "Notes on Moral Theology." *Theological Studies* 5, no. 4 (1944): 530–31.

Fortin, Ernest. *The Birth of Philosophic Christianity: Studies in Early Christian and Medieval Thought*. Edited by J. Brian Benestad. Lanham, Md.: Rowman and Littlefield, 1996.

Foucault, Michel. *The Archeology of Knowledge and the Discourse of Language*. Translated by A. M. Sheridan Smith. New York: Pantheon, 1972.

Fouilloux, Etienne. "Dialogue théologique? (1946–1948)." In *Saint Thomas au XXe siècle: Actes du colloque centenaire de la "Revue Thomiste,"* edited by Serge-Thomas Bonino, 153–98. Paris: Editions Saint-Paul, 1994.

Fraigneau-Julien, B., P.S.S. "L'Efficacité de l'humanité du Christ selon saint Cyrille d'Alexandrie." *Revue thomiste* 55 (1955): 615–28.

Funkenstein, Amos. "Gesetz und Geschichte: Zur historisierenden Hermeneutik bei Moses Maimonides und Thomas von Aquin." *Viator* 1 (1970): 147–78.

Gallagher, John F. *Significando Causant: A Study of Sacramental Causality*. Fribourg: Fribourg University, 1965.

Galvin, John P. "Zur dramatischen Erlösungslehre Raymund Schwagers: Fragen aus der Sicht Karl Rahners." In *Dramatische Erlösungslehre,* edited by Józef Niewiadomski and Wolfgang Palaver, 157–64. Innsbruck: Tyrolia, 1992.

Garrigou-Lagrange, Reginald, O.P. *La Mère du Sauveur et notre vie intérieure*. Lyon: Edition de l'Abeille, 1941.

———. *De Eucharistia accedunt De Paenitentia quaestiones dogmaticae Commentarius in Summam theologicam S. Thomae*. Rome: Marietti, 1943.

———. *The Three Ages of the Interior Life, Prelude to Eternal Life*. 2 vols. Translated by M. T. Doyle. St. Louis: Herder, 1947.

———. *The Mother of the Saviour and Our Interior Life*. Translated by B. Kelly. St. Louis: Herder, 1948.

Garrigues, Jean-Miguel, O.P., M.-J. Le Guillou, O.P., and A. Riou, O.P. "Le caractère sacerdotale dans la tradition des pères grecs." *Nouvelle Revue Théologique* 103 (1971): 801–20.

———. "La Doctrine de la Grâce Habituelle dans ses Sources." *Revue thomiste* 103, no. 2 (2003): 179–202.

Geffré, Claude. *The Risk of Interpretation: On Being Faithful to the Christian Tradition in a Non-Christian Age*. Translated by D. Smith. New York: Paulist Press, 1987.

Geiselmann, Josef. *Die Eucharistielehre der Vorscholastiker.* Paderborn: Schöningh, 1926.

George, Robert P., ed. *Natural Law Theory: Contemporary Essays.* Oxford: Oxford University Press, 1992.

———, ed. *Natural Law and Moral Inquiry.* Washington, D.C.: Georgetown University Press, 1998.

———. *In Defense of Natural Law.* Oxford: Clarendon Press, 1999.

Gilson, Étienne. *D'Aristote à Darwin et retour: Essai sur quelques constantes de la biophilosophie.* Paris: Vrin, 1971.

———. *From Aristotle to Darwin and Back Again: A Journey in Final Causality, Species, and Evolution.* Translated by John Lyon. Notre Dame, Ind.: University of Notre Dame Press, 1984.

Gilson, Étienne, and Jacques Maritain. *Correspondance: 1923–1971.* Edited by Géry Prouvost. Paris: Vrin, 1991.

Girard, René. *The Scapegoat.* Translated by Yvonne Freccero. Baltimore: Johns Hopkins University Press, 1986.

Gomez-Lobo, A. *Morality and the Human Goods.* Washington, D.C.: Georgetown University Press, 2002.

Gratian. *Gratian: The Treatise on Laws (Decretum DD 1–20), with The Ordinary Gloss.* Translated by Augustine Thompson and James Gordley. Washington, D.C.: The Catholic University of America Press, 1993.

Gray, John. *Straw Dogs: Thought on Humans and Other Animals.* London: Granta, 2002.

Gredt, Josephus, O.S.B. *Elementa Philosophiae Aristotelico-Thomisticae.* Vol. 1, *Logica / Philosophia Naturalis.* 11th ed. Freiburg and Barcelona: Herder, 1956.

Grisez, Germain. *Beyond the New Morality: The Responsibilities of Freedom.* Notre Dame, Ind.: University of Notre Dame, 1980.

———. *The Way of the Lord Jesus.* 3 vols. Chicago: Franciscan Herald Press, 1983.

Grün, Anselm. *Erlösung durch das Kreuz: Karl Rahners Beitrag zu einem heutigen Erlösungsverständnis.* Münsterschwarzach: Vier-Türme-Verlag, 1975.

Guggenheim, Antoine. *Jésus Christ, grand prêtre de l'ancienne et de la nouvelle Alliance: Étude du Commentaire de saint Thomas d'Aquin sur l'Épître aux Hébreux.* Paris: Parole et silence, 2004.

Guillelmus Altissiodorensis. *Summa aurea.* Grottaferrata: Editiones Collegii S. Bonaventurae ad Claras Aquas, 1985.

Gutwenger, Engelbert, S.J. "Substanz und Akzidenz in der Eucharistielehre." *Zeitschrift für katholische Theologie* 83 (1961): 257–306.

Gy, Pierre-Marie. "Avancées du traité de l'eucharistie de S. Thomas dans la Somme par rapport aux Sentences." *Revue des sciences philosophiques et theologiques* 77 (1993): 219–28.

Haldane, John. "Thomist Ethics in America." *Logos* 3 (2000): 150–68.

Halper, Edward. "The Unity of the Virtues in Aristotle." *Oxford Studies in Ancient Philosophy* 17 (1999): 115–43.

Hamm, Berndt. *Promissio, Pactum Ordinatio: Freiheit und Selbstbindung Gottes in der scholastischen Gnadenlehre.* Tübingen: Mohr Siebeck, 1977.

Harnack, Adolf von. *Lehrbuch der Dogmengeschichte.* 3 vols. Freiburg: Mohr, 1887–1890.

———. *What Is Christianity?* Translated by Thomas Bailey Saunders. London: Williams and Norgate; New York: Putnam, 1901.

Hart, David Bentley. "No Shadow of Turning: On Divine Impassibility." *Pro Ecclesia* 11, no. 2 (2002): 184–206.

———. *The Beauty of the Infinite*. Grand Rapids: Eerdmans, 2003.

Hauerwas, Stanley. *The Peaceable Kingdom: A Primer in Christian Ethics*. Notre Dame, Ind.: University of Notre Dame Press, 1983.

———. *The Hauerwas Reader*. Edited by John Berkman and Michael Cartwright. Durham, N.C.: Duke University Press, 2001.

Hawking, Stephen. *A Brief History of Time*. London and New York: Bantam, 1988.

Heidegger, Martin. "The Word of Nietzsche: 'God is Dead.'" In *The Question Concerning Technology and Other Essays*, translated by William Lovitt, 53–114. New York: Harper and Row, 1977.

Heidelberger Katechismus: Die Bekenntnisschriften der reformierten Kirche. Edited by E. F. Müller. 1903. Reprint, Zurich: Theologische Buchhandlung, 1987.

Henle, R. J. *The American Thomistic Revival*. St. Louis: St. Louis University Press, 1999.

Hermanni, Friedrich, and Peter Koslowski, eds. *Der leidende Gott. Eine philosophische und theologische Kritik*. Munich: Wilhelm Fink, 2001.

Hibbs, Thomas S. *Dialectic and Narrative in Aquinas: An Interpretation of the* Summa contra gentiles. Notre Dame, Ind.: University of Notre Dame Press, 1995.

Hittinger, Russell. *A Critique of the New Natural Law Theory*. Notre Dame, Ind.: University of Notre Dame Press, 1987.

———. *The First Grace: Rediscovering the Natural Law in a Post-Christian World*. Wilmington, Del.: ISI Books, 2003.

———. "Two Thomisms, Two Modernities." *First Things*, June–July 2008.

Hoffmann, Tobias. "Aquinas on the Moral Progress of the Weak Willed." In *The Problem of Weakness of Will in Medieval Philosophy*, edited by Tobias Hoffmann, Jörn Müller, and Matthias Perkams, 221–47. Leuven: Peters, 2006.

Horst, Ulrich, O.P. *The Dominicans and the Pope: Papal Teaching Authority in the Medieval and Early Modern Thomist Tradition*. Translated by James D. Mixson. Foreword by Thomas Prügl. Notre Dame, Ind.: University of Notre Dame Press, 2006.

Hugo de S. Caro. *Commentarius in IV librum Sententiarum*. Edited by F. Stegmüller. Uppsala: Uppsala Universitets Arsskrift, 1953.

Humbrecht, Thierry-Dominique, O.P. "L'eucharistie, 'représentation' du sacrifice du Christ selon Saint Thomas." *Revue thomiste* 98, no. 3 (1998): 355–86.

———. *Théologie négative et noms divins chez Saint Thomas d'Aquin*. Paris: Vrin, 2005.

Hume, David. *A Treatise of Human Nature*. Edited by L. A. Selby-Bigge. Oxford: Oxford University Press, 1888.

———. *Essays Moral, Political and Literary*. Indianapolis: Liberty Fund, 1987.

Hurtado, Larry. *Lord Jesus Christ*. Grand Rapids: Eerdmans, 2003.

Hütter, Reinhard. *Suffering Divine Things: Theology as Church Practice*. Translated by Doug Stott. Grand Rapids: Eerdmans, 2000.

———. "Aquinas: The Directedness of Reasoning and the Metaphysics of Creation." In *Reason and the Reasons of Faith*, edited by Paul J. Griffiths and Reinhard Hütter, 160–93. New York and London: T & T Clark, 2005.

International Theological Commission. "On the Interpretation of Dogmas." *Origins* 20, no. 1 (1990): 1–14.

International Theological Commission. *Communion and Stewardship: Human Persons Created in the Image of God*. July 23, 2004. http://www.vatican.va/roman_curia/congregations/cfaith/cti_documents/rc_con_cfaith_doc_20040723_communion-stewardship_en.html.

Iserloh, Erwin. *Der Kampf um die Messe in den ersten Jahren der Auseinandersetzung mit Luther.* Münster: Aschendorff, 1952.

―――. *Gnade und Eucharistie in der philosophischen Theologie des Wilhelm von Ockham: Ihre Bedeutung für die Ursachen der Reformation.* Steiner: Wiesbaden, 1956.

John of St. Thomas, O.P. *Cursus Philosophicus Thomisticus.* Vol. 1, *Logica.* Paris: Vivès, 1883.

John of the Cross. *The Ascent of Mount Carmel.* In *The Voice of the Spirit: The Spirituality of St. John of the Cross.* Edited and translated by Elizabeth Hamilton. Huntington, Ind.: Our Sunday Visitor, 1976.

Journet, Charles. *L'Église du Verbe incarné.* Vol. 3, *Sa structure interne et son unité catholique.* Paris: Desclée de Brouwer, 1969.

―――. *The Mass: The Presence of the Sacrifice of the Cross.* Translated by Victor Szczurek, O.Praem. South Bend, Ind.: St. Augustine's Press, 2008.

Joyce, Richard. *The Evolution of Morality.* Cambridge: MIT Press, 2006.

Jüngel, Eberhard. *Das Evangelium von der Rechtfertigung des Gottlosen als Zentrum des christlichen Glaubens.* Tübingen: Mohr Siebeck, 1998.

―――. *Indikative der Gnade, Imperative der Freiheit.* Tübingen: Mohr Siebeck, 2000.

―――. *Justification: The Heart of the Christian Faith. A Theological Study with an Ecumenical Purpose.* Translated by Jeffrey F. Cayzer. Edinburgh: T & T Clark, 2001.

―――. "Church Unity Is Already Happening: The Path Towards Eucharistic Community." Translated by R. Schenk. *Dialog: A Journal of Theology* 44, no. 1 (2005): 30–37.

Jüngel, Eberhard, and Karl Rahner. *Was ist ein Sakrament? Vorstösse zur Verständigung.* Freiburg: Herder, 1971.

Kasper, Walter. *Jesus the Christ.* New York: Paulist Press, 1976.

Keating, Daniel A. "Divinization in Cyril: The Appropriation of Divine Life." In *The Theology of St. Cyril of Alexandria: A Critical Appreciation,* edited by Thomas G. Weinandy, O.F.M. Cap., and Daniel A. Keating. New York: T & T Clark, 2003.

Kekes, John. *The Illusions of Egalitarianism.* Ithaca, N.Y.: Cornell University Press, 2003.

Kent, Bonnie. "Transitory Vice: Thomas Aquinas on Incontinence." *Journal of the History of Philosophy* 27, no. 2 (1989): 199–223.

Kerr, Fergus, O.P. *Twentieth-Century Catholic Theologians.* Oxford: Blackwell Publishing, 2007.

Kilwardby, Robert, O.P. *Quaestiones in librum quartum Sententiarum.* Edited by Richard Schenk. Munich: Bavarian Academy of Sciences, 1993.

King, Martin Luther, Jr. *Strength to Love.* Cleveland, Ohio, 1963.

Kluxen, Wolfgang. "Literargeschichtliches zum lateinischen Moses Maimonides." *Recherches de Théologie ancienne et médiévale* 21 (1954): 23–50.

―――. "Maimonides und die Hochscholastik." *Philosophisches Jahrbuch der Görres-Gesellschaft* 63 (1955): 151–65.

Knight, Frank. "The Ethics of Competition." *Quarterly Journal of Economics* 37, no. 4 (1923): 579–624.

Kolnai, Aurel. *Disgust.* Chicago: Open Court, 2004.

―――. "Aesthetic and Moral Experience." *Ethics, Value and Reality: Selected Papers of Aurel Kolnai,* 187–210. New Brunswick, N.J.: Transaction, 2008.

Koninck, Charles de. *De la primauté du bien commun contre les personnalistes.* Québec: Laval University Press, 1943.

Koterski, Joseph W., S.J. *An Introduction to Medieval Philosophy: Basic Concepts.* Malden, Mass.: Wiley-Blackwell, 2009.

Kraynak, Robert P. *Christian Faith and Modern Democracy.* Notre Dame, Ind.: University of Notre Dame Press, 2001.

Kreiner, Armin. *Gott im Leid: zur Stichhaltigkeit der Theodizee-Argumente.* Freiburg: Herder, 1997.

Krenski, Thomas Rudolf. *Passio Caritatis: Trinitarische Passiologie im Werk Hans Urs von Balthasars.* Einsiedeln: Johannes Verlag, 1990.

La Soujeole, Benoît-Dominique de, O.P. "Foi implicite et religions non chrétiennes." *Revue thomiste* 106, no. 1–2 (2006): 315–34.

Lahart, Justin, Patrick Barta, and Andrew Batson. "New Limits to Growth Revive Malthusian Fears." *Wall Street Journal,* March 24, 2008.

Lamb, Matthew. "Will There Be Catholic Theology in the United States?" *America,* May 26, 1990.

———. "The Catholic Theological Society of America: Theologians Unbound." *Crisis: Politics, Culture, and the Church* (Dec. 1997): 36–37.

———. "Divine Transcendence and Eternity." In *Continuity and Plurality in Catholic Theology: Essays in Honor of Gerald A. McCool, S.J.,* edited by Anthony J. Cernera, 75–106. Fairfield, Conn.: Sacred Heart University Press, 1998.

———. "The Catholic Theological Society of America: A Preliminary Profile." *Fellowship of Catholic Scholars Quarterly* 21, no. 1 (1998): 8–10.

———. "Eternity and Time." In *Gladly to Learn, Gladly to Teach: Essays in Honor of Ernest Fortin.* New York: Lexington, 2002.

Le Guillou, M.-J., O.P. *Christ and Church: A Theology of the Mystery.* Translated by C. Schaldenbrand. New York: Desclee, 1966.

Leben, Ch. "L'interprétation du culte sacrificiel chez Maimonide." *Pardès* 14 (1991): 129–45.

Lee, Patrick, and Robert P. George. *Body-Self Dualism in Contemporary Ethics and Politics.* Cambridge: Cambridge University Press, 2008.

Leff, Gordon. *William of Ockham: The Metamorphosis of Scholastic Discourse.* Manchester: Manchester University Press; Totowa, N.J.: Rowman and Littlefield, 1975.

Lefler, Nathan. "Sign, Cause, and Person in St. Thomas's Sacramental Theology: Further Considerations." *Nova et Vetera* (English) 4, no. 2 (2006): 381–404.

Levering, Matthew. *Christ's Fulfillment of Torah and Temple: Salvation According to Thomas Aquinas.* Notre Dame, Ind.: University of Notre Dame Press, 2002.

———. "Aquinas on the Liturgy of the Eucharist." In *Aquinas on Doctrine: A Critical Introduction,* edited by Thomas G. Weinandy, Daniel A. Keating, and John Yocum, 183–98. London: T & T Clark, 2004.

———. *Sacrifice and Community: Jewish Offering and Christian Eucharist.* Malden, Mass. and Oxford: Blackwell, 2005.

———. "Natural Law and Natural Inclinations: Rhonheimer, Pinckaers, McAleer." *The Thomist* 70, no. 2 (2006): 155–201.

———. *Biblical Natural Law: A Theocentric and Teleological Approach.* Oxford: Oxford University Press, 2008.

Link, Wilhelm. *Das Ringen Luthers um die Freiheit der Theologie von der Philosophie.* 2nd ed. Munich: Kaiser, 1955.

Liptay, John J., and David S. Liptay, eds. *The Importance of Insight: Essays in Honour of Michael Vertin.* Toronto: University of Toronto Press, 2007.

Lisska, Anthony. *Aquinas's Theory of Natural Law: An Analytic Reconstruction.* Oxford: Oxford University Press, 1996.

———. "On the Revival of Natural Law: Several Books from the Last Half-Decade." *American Catholic Philosophical Quarterly* 81, no. 4 (2007): 613–38.

Lonergan, Bernard, S.J. *De Deo Trino.* Vol. 2. Rome: Gregorian University, 1964.

———. *De Verbo Incarnato.* Rome: Pontifical Gregorian University Press, 1964.

———. *Method in Theology.* New York: Herder and Herder, 1972.

———. "The Origins of Christian Realism." In *A Second Collection: Papers.* Edited by William F. J. Ryan and Bernard J. Tyrrell. Philadelphia: Westminster, 1974.

———. *A Second Collection: Papers.* Edited by William F. J. Ryan and Bernard J. Tyrrell. Philadelphia: Westminster, 1974.

———. *A Third Collection: Papers.* Edited by Frederick E. Crowe. New York: Paulist Press, 1985.

———. "Cognitional Structure." In *Collection: Papers by Bernard J. F. Lonergan.* Vol. 4, *Collected Works.* Edited by Frederick E. Crowe and Robert M. Duran. Toronto: University of Toronto Press, 1993.

———. *Verbum: Word and Idea in Aquinas.* Vol. 2. *Collected Works.* Edited by Frederick E. Crowe and Robert M. Duran. Toronto: University of Toronto Press, 1997.

———. *Grace and Freedom: Operative Grace in the Thought of St. Thomas Aquinas.* Vol. 1, *Collected Works.* Edited by Frederick E. Crowe and Robert M. Duran. Toronto: University of Toronto Press, 2000.

———. *The Ontological and Psychological Constitution of Christ.* Vol. 7, *Collected Works.* Edited by Frederick E. Crowe and Robert M. Duran. Translated by Michael G. Shields. Toronto: University of Toronto Press, 2002.

———. "Horizons and Transpositions." In *Philosophical and Theological Papers, 1958–1964.* Vol. 17, *Collected Works.* Edited by Robert C. Croken and Robert M. Duran. Toronto: University of Toronto Press, 2004.

———. *Collected Works of Bernard Lonergan.* Edited by Frederick E. Crowe and Robert M. Duran. Toronto: University of Toronto Press, 1988–2007.

Long, A. A. *Stoic Studies.* New York: Cambridge University Press, 1996.

Long, Steven A. *The Teleological Grammar of the Moral Act.* Naples, Fla.: Sapientia Press, 2007.

Lottin, Odon. *Psychologie et morale aux XIIe et XIIIe siècles.* 8 vols. Louvain: Abbaye Mont César, 1942–60.

Louth, Andrew. *St. John Damascene: Tradition and Originality in Byzantine Theology.* New York: Oxford, 2002.

Lubac, Henri de, S.J. *Catholicism: Christ and the Common Destiny of Man.* Translated by Lancelot C. Sheppard and Elizabeth Englund, O.C.D. San Francisco: Ignatius, 1988.

———. *Corpus Mysticum: The Eucharist and the Church in the Middle Ages.* Translated by Gemma Simmonds, C.J., with Richard Price and Christopher Stephens. Edited by Laurence Paul Hemming and Susan Frank Parks. Notre Dame, Ind.: University of Notre Dame Press, 2006.

Lukacs, Laszlo. "Communication—Symbols—Sacraments." In *The Presence of God in a Postmodern Context,* edited by Lieven Boeve and Lambert Leijssen. Leuven, Belgium: Peeters, 2001.

Luneau, Auguste. *L'histoire du salut chez les Pères de l'Église: La doctrine des âges du monde.* Paris: Beauchesne, 1964.

MacIntyre, Alasdair. *After Virtue: A Study in Moral Theory.* Notre Dame, Ind.: University of Notre Dame Press, 1981.

————. *Whose Justice? Which Rationality?* Notre Dame, Ind.: Notre Dame University Press, 1988.

————. *Three Rival Versions of Moral Inquiry.* Notre Dame, Ind.: Notre Dame University Press, 1990.

————. *Dependent Rational Animals: Why Human Beings Need the Virtues.* Peru, Ill.: Carus, 1999.

————. "The End of Education: The Fragmentation of the American University." *Commonweal,* October 20, 2006, 10–14.

————. *The Tasks of Philosophy.* New York: Cambridge University Press, 2006.

Mansini, Guy, O.S.B. "St. Thomas on Christ's Knowledge of God." *The Thomist* 59, no. 1 (1995): 91–124.

Maritain, Jacques. *Science and Wisdom.* Translated by B. Wall. London: The Centenary Press, 1940.

————. *Pour une philosophie de l'histoire.* Vol. X, *Œuvres Complètes.* Fribourg and Paris: Editions Universitaires and Editions St. Paul, 1985.

Marliangeas, Bernard. *Clés pour une théologie du ministère: In persona Christi, In persona Ecclesiae.* Paris: Éditions Beauchesne, 1978.

Mayr, Ernst. *Systematics and the Origins of Species from the Viewpoint of a Zoologist.* New York: Columbia University Press, 1942.

————. *What Evolution Is.* New York: Basic Books, 2001.

McAleer, Graham J. *Ecstatic Morality and Sexual Politics.* New York: Fordham University Press, 2005.

————. "Business and Dignity: An Application of Edmund Burke's Analysis of America." In the forthcoming Festschrift for Fr. James Schall, to be published by St. Augustine's Press.

————. "Business Ethics and Catholic Social Thought." *Nova et Vetera* (English) 4, no. 1 (2006): 17–27.

————. "Individuation and Incarnation: The Role of Metaphysics in the Theology of Robert Kilwardby." In *Companion to Robert Kilwardby.* Leiden: E. J. Brill, forthcoming.

————. "Pleasure: A Reflection on *Deus Caritas Est.*" *Nova et Vetera* (English) 5, no. 2 (2007): 315–24.

————. "Two Case Studies in Schelerian Moral Theology: The Vatican's 2005 'Instruction' and Gay Marriage." *Nova et Vetera* (English) 6, no. 1 (2008): 205–17.

————. *To Kill Another: Homicide and Natural Law.* New Brunswick, N.J.: Transaction, 2010.

McCabe, Herbert. *God Matters.* London and New York: Continuum, 1987.

————. *God Still Matters.* Edited by Brian Davies, O.P. London and New York: Continuum, 2002.

McInerny, Ralph. *Praeambula Fidei: Thomism and the God of the Philosophers.* Washington, D.C.: The Catholic University of America Press, 2006.

McKay, Angela. "Prudence and Acquired Moral Virtue." *The Thomist* 69, no. 4 (2005): 535–55.

McShane, Philip. "On the Causality of the Sacraments." *Theological Studies* 24, no. 3 (1963): 423–36.

Menke, Karl-Heinz. *Stellvertretung: Schlüsselbegriff christlichen Lebens und theologische Grundkategorie.* Einsiedeln: Johannes, 1991.

Metz, Johannes Baptist. *Faith in History and Society: Toward a Practical Fundamental Theology*. New York: Seabury, 1980.

———. *Memoria Passionis: Ein provozierendes Gedächtnis in pluralistischer Gesellschaft*. Freiburg: Herder, 2006.

Meunier, Bernard. *Le Christ de Cyrille d'Alexandrie: l'humanité, le salut et la question monophysite*. Paris: Beauchesne, 1997.

Michel, A. "Sacrements." In *Dictionnaire Théologique Catholique*. Vol. 14. Paris: Librairie Letouzey et Ané, 1939.

Miller, Kenneth. *Finding Darwin's God: A Scientist's Search for Common Ground between God and Evolution*. New York: Harper Collins, 1999.

Moltmann, Jürgen. *Der gekreuzigte Gott: Das Kreuz Christi als Grund und Kritik christlicher Theologie*. Munich: Kaiser, 1972.

———. *Ökumene-wohin? Bischöfe und Theologen entwickeln Perspektiven*. Edited by B. J. Hilberath and J. Moltmann. Tübingen: Francke, 2000.

Mulligan, Robert. "Ratio Superior and Ratio Inferior: The Historical Background." *New Scholasticism* 29, no. 1 (1955): 1–32.

Murphy, Mark C. *Natural Law and Practical Rationality*. Cambridge: Cambridge University Press, 1991.

Murphy, Mark C. *Natural Law in Jurisprudence and Politics*. Oxford: Blackwell, 2007.

Nemo, Philippe. *What Is the West?* Pittsburgh, Pa.: Duquesne University Press, 2006.

Neunheuser, Burkhard. *Eucharistie in Mittelalter und Neuzeit*. Freiburg: Herder, 1963.

Newman, John Henry. *An Essay on the Development of Christian Doctrine*. Edited by Ian Ker. Notre Dame, Ind.: Notre Dame University Press, 1989.

Nichols, Aidan, O.P. "Thomism and the Nouvelle Théologie." *The Thomist* 64, no. 1 (2000): 1–19.

———. *Lovely, Like Jerusalem: The Fulfillment of the Old Testament in Christ and the Church*. San Francisco: Ignatius Press, 2007.

Nichtweiß, Barbara. *Erik Peterson: Neue Sicht auf Leben und Werk*. Freiburg: Herder, 1992.

O'Callaghan, John P. *Thomist Realism and the Linguistic Turn: Toward a More Perfect Form of Existence*. Notre Dame, Ind.: University of Notre Dame Press, 2003.

O'Meara, Thomas F., O.P. "Theology of the Church." In *The Theology of Thomas Aquinas*, edited by Rik van Nieuwenhove and Joseph Wawrykow, 303–25. Notre Dame, Ind.: University of Notre Dame Press, 2005.

O'Neill, Colman E., O.P. *Sacramental Realism: A General Theory of the Sacraments*. Princeton, N.J.: Scepter, 1998.

———. *Meeting Christ in the Sacraments*. New York: Alba House, 2002.

Oates, Stephen B. *Let the Trumpet Sound: A Life of Martin Luther King, Jr.* New York: HarperPerennial, 1982.

Oberman, Heiko. *The Harvest of Medieval Theology: Gabriel Biel and Late Medieval Nominalism*. Cambridge: Harvard University Press, 1963.

Orenstein, W. "The Maimonides Rationale for Sacrifice." *Hebrew Studies* 24 (1983): 33–39.

Osborne, Kenan B., O.F.M. *Christian Sacraments in a Postmodern World: A Theology for the Third Millennium*. New York: Paulist Press, 1999.

Osborne, Thomas. "Perfect and Imperfect Virtues in Aquinas." *The Thomist* 71, no. 1 (2007): 39–64.

Pannenberg, Wolfhart. "Tod und Auferstehung in der Sicht christlicher Dogmatik." *Kerygma und Dogma* 20 (1974): 167–80.

———. *Theology and the Philosophy of Science.* Translated by F. McDonagh. Philadelphia: Westminster, 1976.

———. *Toward a Theology of Nature.* Edited by T. Peters. Louisville, Ky.: Westminster, 1993.

———. *Systematic Theology.* Vol. 2. Grand Rapids: Eerdmans, 1994.

Passerin d'Entrèves, Alessandro. *Natural Law: An Introduction to Legal Philosophy.* London: Hutchison University Library, 1970.

Peterson, Erik. "Theologie als Wissenschaft." In *Theologie als Wissenschaft: Aufsätze und Thesen,* edited by Gerhard Sauter. Munich: Kaiser, 1971.

———. *Ausgewählte Schriften.* Vol. 1, *Theologische Traktate.* Würzburg: Echter, 1994.

Pieper, Josef. *The Four Cardinal Virtues.* Translated by Richard Winston, Clara Winston, Lawrence E. Lynch, and Daniel F. Coogan. Notre Dame, Ind.: University of Notre Dame Press, 1966.

Pinckaers, Servais, O.P. *The Sources of Christian Ethics.* Translated by Mary Thomas Noble, O.P. Washington, D.C.: The Catholic University of America Press, 1995.

———. *Morality: The Catholic View.* Translated by Michael Sherwin, O.P. South Bend, Ind.: St. Augustine's Press, 2003.

———. *The Pinckaers Reader.* Edited by John Berkman and Craig Steven Titus. Washington, D.C.: The Catholic University of America Press, 2005.

Porter, Jean. "The Unity of the Virtues and the Ambiguity of Goodness: A Reappraisal of Aquinas's Theory of the Virtues." *Journal of Religious Ethics* 21, no. 1 (1993): 137–63.

———. *Moral Action and Christian Ethics.* New York: Cambridge University Press, 1995.

———. "Virtue and Sin: The Connection of the Virtues and the Case of the Flawed Saint." *Journal of Religion* 75, no. 4 (1995): 521–39.

Power, David. *Sacrament: The Language of God's Giving.* New York: Herder and Herder, 1999.

Principe, Walter. "Presidential Address." In *The Proceedings of the Catholic Theological Society of America.* Atlanta: Catholic Theological Society, 1991.

Proprium Ordinis Praedicatorum, Missale et Lectionarium. Rome: Santa Sabina, 1985.

Pseudo-Dionysius, the Areopagite. *La hiérarchie céleste.* Paris: Éditions du Cerf, 1958.

Rahner, Karl, S.J. *Die vielen Messen und das eine Opfer.* Freiburg: Herder, 1951.

———. "Opfer. V. Dogmatisch." In *Lexikon für Theologie und Kirche.* 2nd ed. Edited by Michael Buchberger, Josef Höfer, and Karl Rahner. Freiburg: Herder, 1957–68.

———. "Christology within an Evolutionary View of the World." In *Theological Investigations.* Vol. V. London: Darton, Longman & Todd, 1966.

———. "Dogmatische Fragen zur Osterfrömmigkeit." In *Schriften zur Theologie,* 157–72. Vol. 4. Einsiedeln: Benziger, 1967.

———. "Passion und Aszese." In *Schriften zur Theologie,* 73–109. Vol. 3. Einsiedeln: Benziger, 1967.

———. *Grundkurs des Glaubens: Einführung in den Begriff des Christentums.* Freiburg: Herder, 1976.

———. "Das 'jugendliche' Opfer." In *Sendung und Gnade.* 5th ed. Innsbruck: Tyrolia Verlag, 1988.

———. "Meßopfer und Jugendaszese." In *Sendung und Gnade.* 5th ed. Innsbruck: Tyrolia Verlag, 1988.

Ratzinger, Joseph. "Das Problem der Transsubstantiation und die Frage nach dem Sinn der Eucharistie." *Theologische Quartalschrift* 147 (1967): 129–58.

Reynolds, Philip L. "Philosophy as the Handmaid of Theology: Aquinas on Christ's Causality." In *Contemplating Aquinas: On the Varieties of Interpretation,* edited by Fergus Kerr, O.P. London: SCM, 2003.

Rhonheimer, H. *Natural Law and Practical Reason.* New York: Fordham, 2000.

Rhonheimer, Martin. "Colloquy." *National Catholic Bioethics Quarterly* 7, no. 3 (2007): 441–46.

Rist, John M. *Real Ethics: Reconsidering the Foundations of Morality.* New York: Cambridge University Press, 2002.

Robinson, Ian. "Thomas Cranmer on the Real Presence." *Faith and Worship* 43 (1997): 2–10.

Romero, Oscar. *Voice of the Voiceless.* Maryknoll, N.Y.: Orbis, 1985.

Rommen, Heinrich A. *Die ewige Wiederkehr des Naturrechts.* Leipzig: Verlag Jakob Hegner, 1936.

———. *The State in Catholic Thought: A Treatise in Political Philosophy.* St. Louis: B. Herder, 1945.

———. *The Natural Law: A Study in Legal and Social History and Philosophy.* Translated by Thomas R. Hanley, O.S.B. St. Louis and London: B. Herder, 1947.

Root, Michael. "Aquinas, Merit, and Reformation Theology after the *Joint Declaration on the Doctrine of Justification.*" *Modern Theology* 20, no. 1 (2004): 5–22.

Rorty, Richard. *Philosophy and the Mirror of Nature.* Oxford: Blackwell, 1980.

Roten, Johann. "The Two Halves of the Moon: Marian Anthropological Dimensions in the Common Mission of Adrienne von Speyr and Hans Urs von Balthasar." In *Hans Urs von Balthasar: His Life and Work,* edited by David L. Schindler. San Francisco: Ignatius Press, 1991.

Rowland, Tracey. "Benedict XVI, Thomism, and Liberal Culture (Part 2)." *Zenit,* July 25, 2005. http://www.zenit.org/article-13666?l=english.

Sabra, G. *Thomas Aquinas' Vision of the Church.* Mainz: Grünewald, 1987.

Sainte-Marie, Joseph de. "L'Eucharistie, sacrement et sacrifice du Christ et de l'Église. Développements des perspectives thomistes." *Divinitas* 18, no. 2 (1974): 234–86.

Sala, Giovanni, S.J. *Das Apriori in der menschlichen Erkenntnis: Eine Studie über Kants Kritik der reinen Vernunft und Lonergans Insight.* Meisenheim: Verlag Anton Hain, 1971.

———. *Gewissensentscheidung: Philosophisch-theologische Analyse von Gewissen und sittlichem Wissen.* Innsbruck: Tyrolia Verlag, 1993.

———. *Lonergan and Kant: Five Essays on Human Knowledge.* Toronto: University of Toronto Press, 1994.

———. *Kant, Lonergan und der christliche Glaube.* Nordhausen: Bautz Verlag, 2005.

———. *Kontroverse Theologie.* Bonn: Verlag Nova and Vetera, 2005.

———. "What Use is Kant for Theology?" In *Wisdom and Holiness, Science and Scholarship,* edited by Michael Dauphinais and Matthew Levering, 293–314. Naples, Fla.: Sapientia Press, 2007.

Sartre, Jean-Paul. *Existentialism and Humanism.* Translated by Philip Mairet. Brooklyn: Haskell House, 1977.

Scheeben, Matthias Joseph. *The Mysteries of Christianity.* Translated by Cyril Vollert, S.J. St. Louis, Mo. and London: Herder, 1951.

Scheffczyk, Leo. "Christology in the Context of Experience." Translated by R. Schenk. *The Thomist* 48, no. 3 (1984): 383–408.

————. "Die Stellung des Thomas von Aquin in der Entwicklung der Lehre von den Mysteria Vitae Christi." In *Renovatio et Reformatio: Wider das Bild vom "finsteren" Mittelalter,* edited by Manfred Gerwing and Godehard Ruppert. Münster: Aschendorff, 1985.

Scheler, Max. *Ressentiment.* Milwaukee: Marquette University Press, 2003.

————. *The Nature of Sympathy.* New Brunswick, N.J.: Transaction, 2007.

Schenk, Richard, O.P. "Christ, Christianity, and Non-Christian Religions: Their Relationship in the Thought of Robert Kilwardby." In *Christ among the Medieval Dominicans: Representations of Christ in the Texts and Images of the Order of Preachers,* edited by Kent Emery, Jr., and Joseph Wawrykow, 344–63. Notre Dame, Ind.: University of Notre Dame, 1988.

————. "*Omnis Christi Actio Nostra est Instructio:* The Deeds and Sayings of Jesus as Revelation in the View of Thomas Aquinas." In *Studi Tomistici,* vol. 37, edited by Leo Elders. Vatican City: Libreria Editrice Vaticana, 1990.

————. "Divina simulatio irae et dissimulatio pietatis: Divine Providence and Natural Religion in Robert Kilwardby's *Quaestiones in librum IV Sententiarum.*" In *Mensch und Natur im Mittelalter,* edited by Albert Zimmermann, 431–55. Berlin and New York: De Gruyter, 1991.

————. "Covenant Initiation: Thomas Aquinas and Robert Kilwardby on the Sacrament of Circumcision." In *Ordo sapientiae et amoris: Image et message de Saint Thomas d'Aquin à travers les récentes études historiques, herméneutiques et doctrinales,* edited by Carlos-Josaphat Pinto de Oliveira and Jean-Pierre Torrell, 555–93. Fribourg: Éditions Universitaires, 1993.

————. "Tod und Theodizee: Ansätze zu einer Theologie der Trauer bei Thomas von Aquin." *Forum Katholische Theologie* 10 (1994): 161–78.

————. "Opfer und Opferkritik aus der Sicht römisch-katholischer Theologie." In *Zur Theorie des Opfers,* edited by Richard Schenk, 193–250. Stuttgart–Bad Cannstatt: Frommann-Holzboog, 1995.

————. "Das jr ewre Leibe begebet zum Opffer: Zur Frage nach dem 'vernünftigen Gottesdienst.'" *Wort und Antwort* 39 (1998): 147–56.

————. "Ist die Rede vom leidenden Gott theologisch zu vermeiden? Reflexionen über den Streit von Karl Rahner und Hans Urs von Balthasar." In *Der leidende Gott: Eine philosophische und theologische Kritik,* edited by Friedrich Hermanni and Peter Koslowski, 225–39. Munich: Wilhelm Fink, 2001.

————. "The Unsettled German Discussions of Justification: Abiding Differences and Ecumenical Blessings." *Dialog: A Journal of Theology* 44, no. 2 (2005): 153–64.

Schenker, Adrian. "Die Rolle der Religion bei Maimonides und Thomas von Aquin." In *Ordo sapientiae et amoris: Image et message de Saint Thomas d'Aquin à travers les récentes études historiques, herméneutiques et doctrinales,* edited by Carlos-Josaphat Pinto de Oliveira and Jean-Pierre Torrell, 169–93. Fribourg: Éditions Universitaires, 1993.

Schillebeeckx, Edward, O.P. *The Eucharist.* New York: Sheed & Ward, 1968.

————. *God and the Future of Man.* Translated by N. Smith. New York: Sheed and Ward, 1968.

————. *Revelation and Theology.* Vol. 2. Translated by N. Smith. New York: Sheed and Ward, 1968.

————. *Jesus: An Experiment in Christology.* Translated by H. Hoskins. New York: Crossroad, 1979.

————. *Christ: The Experience of Jesus as Lord.* Translated by J. Bowden. New York: Crossroad, 1981.

————. *L'économie sacramentelle du salut.* Translated by Yvon van der Have, O.S.B. Fribourg: Academic Press, 2004.

Schmaltz, Tad M. *Radical Cartesianism: The French Reception of Descartes.* Cambridge:
Cambridge University Press, 2002.

Schmaus, Michael. *Katholische Dogmatik.* Vol. 3, bk. 2. Munich: M. Hueber, 1941.

Schütrumpf, Eckart. "Magnanimity, *megalopsychia,* and the System of Aristotle's Nicomachean Ethics." *Archiv für Geschichte des Philosophie* 71 (1989): 10–22.

Schwager, Raymund. *Brauchen wir einen Sündenbock?* Munich: Kaiser, 1978.

————. "Christ's Death and the Prophetic Critique of Sacrifice." In *René Girard and
Biblical Studies,* edited by Andrew J. McKenna, 109–23. Decatur, Ga.: Scholars Press,
1985.

————. *Der wunderbare Tausch: Zur Geschichte und Deutung der Erlösungslehre.* Munich:
Kaiser, 1986.

————. *Jesus im Heilsdrama: Entwurf einer biblischen Erlösungslehre.* Innsbruck: Tyrolia,
1990.

Seckler, Max. *Das Heil in der Geschichte: Geschichtstheologisches Denken bei Thomas von
Aquin.* Munich: Kösel, 1964.

Sedlmayr, Petrus, O.S.B. "Die Lehre des hl. Thomas von den *accidentia sine subjecto remanentia*—untersucht auf ihren Einklang mit der aristotelischen Philosophie." *Divus
Thomas* (F) 12 (1934): 315–26.

Seidl, Horst. "Zum Substanzbegriff der katholischen Transsubstantiationslehre: Erkenntnistheoretische und metaphysische Erörterungen." *Forum Katholische Theologie* 11
(1995): 1–16.

Sesboüé, Bernard. *Hors de l'église pas de salut.* Paris: Desclée de Brouwer, 2004.

Shanley, Brian, O.P. "Aquinas on Pagan Virtue." *The Thomist* 63, no. 4 (1999): 553–77.

Sherwin, Michael, O.P. *By Knowledge and by Love: Charity and Knowledge in the Moral
Theology of St. Thomas Aquinas.* Washington, D.C.: The Catholic University Press of
America, 2005.

————. "Christ the Teacher in St. Thomas's *Commentary on the Gospel of John.*" In *Reading
John with St. Thomas Aquinas,* edited by Michael Dauphinais and Matthew Levering,
173–93. Washington, D.C.: The Catholic University of America Press, 2005.

Sherwood, Steve. "American Pop Frankenstein? Andy Warhol, Iconic Experience and the
Advent of the Pop Society." *Pro manuscripto.*

Simon, Yves R. *The Tradition of Natural Law.* Edited by Vukan Kuic. Bronx, N.Y.: Fordham University Press, 1992.

Smalley, Beryl. "William of Auvergne, John of La Rochelle and St. Thomas Aquinas on the
Old Law." In *St. Thomas Aquinas 1274–1974: Commemorative Studies.* Vol. 2. Edited by
Armand A. Maurer et al., 11–72. Toronto: PIMS, 1974.

Smith, Adam. *The Theory of Moral Sentiments.* Indianapolis: Liberty Fund, 1982.

Smith, Janet E. *Humanae Vitae: A Generation Later.* Washington, D.C.: The Catholic
University of America Press, 1991.

Sokolowski, Robert. *Christian Faith and Human Understanding: Studies on the Eucharist,
Trinity, and the Human Person.* Washington, D.C.: The Catholic University of America
Press, 2006.

Sombart, Werner. *Luxury and Capitalism.* Ann Arbor: University of Michigan Press, 1967.

Southern, Richard W. *Scholastic Humanism and the Unification of Europe.* Vol. 1, *Foundations.* Oxford: Blackwell, 1995.

Suarez, Franciscus, S.J. *Tractatus de legibus et legislatore Deo.* In *Opera Omnia.* Edited by Carolus Berton. Paris, 1856.

Sylvester of Ferrara. Commentary on Thomas's *Summa contra Gentiles.* In *Sancti Thomae Aquinatis Doctoris Angelici Opera Omnia iussu edita Leonis XIII P.M.* Vol. 15. Rome: Leonine Commission, 1930.

Taylor, Charles. *The Sources of the Self.* Cambridge: Harvard University Press, 1989.

———. *A Secular Age.* Cambridge: Harvard University Press, 2007.

Teilhard de Chardin, Pierre, S.J. *The Phenomenon of Man.* New York: Harper and Row, 1975.

Thomas Aquinas. *Ad Romanos. In Super Epistolas S. Pauli Lectura.* Vol. 1. Rome: Marietti, 1953.

———. *Commentary on Aristotle's Physics.* Translated by Richard J. Blackwell, Richard J. Spath, and W. Edmund Thirlkel. Notre Dame, Ind.: Dumb Ox Books, 1999.

———. *Corpus Thomisticum, S. Thomae de Aquino opera omnia.* University of Navarre. www.unav.es/filosofia/alarcon/amicis/ctopera.html#OM.

———. *Disputed Questions on Virtue.* Translated by Ralph McInerny. South Bend, Ind.: St. Augustine's Press, 1999.

———. *Expositio super primam et secundam Decretalem ad Archidiaconum Tudertinum. Opuscula Theologica.* Vol. 1. Rome: Marietti, 1954.

———. *In Symbolum Apostolorum Expositio. Opuscula Theologica.* Rome and Turin: Marietti, 1954.

———. "On the Commendation of Sacred Scripture." In *Selected Writings.* Edited and translated by Ralph McInerny. New York: Penguin, 1998.

———. *Sancti Thomae Aquinatis Doctoris Angelici Opera Omnia iussu edita Leonis XIII P.M.* Vol. 15. Rome: Leonine Commission, 1930.

———. *Sententia libri Ethicorum.* In *Opera omnia.* Vol. 47. Rome: Ad sanctae Sabinae, 1969.

———. *Scriptum super Libros Sententiis.* Paris: Sumptibus P. Lethielleux, 1933–47.

———. *St. Thomas Aquinas on Politics and Ethics.* Edited by Paul Sigmund. New York: W. W. Norton, 1987.

———. *Summa Contra Gentiles.* Translated by Charles J. O'Neil. Notre Dame, Ind. and London: University of Notre Dame Press, 1975.

———. *Summa Theologiae.* 3rd ed. Turin: Edizioni San Paolo, 1999.

———. *Summa Theologica.* Translated by the Fathers of the English Dominican Province. New York: Benziger Brothers, 1947–48.

———. *Super Librum de causis expositio.* Edited by Henri Dominique Saffrey. Paris: Vrin, 2002.

———. *The Aquinas Prayer Book: The Prayers and Hymns of St. Thomas Aquinas.* Edited and translated by Robert Anderson and Johann Moser. Manchester, N.H.: Sophia Institute Press, 2000.

———. *The De Malo of Thomas Aquinas.* Edited by Brian Davies. Translated by Richard Regan. Oxford: Oxford University Press, 2001.

Thompson, Augustine, O.P. *Cities of God: The Religion of the Italian Communes, 1125–1325.* University Park: Pennsylvania State University Press, 2005.

Titus, Craig Steven. *Resilience and the Virtue of Fortitude: Aquinas in Dialogue with the Psychosocial Sciences.* Washington, D.C.: The Catholic University of America Press, 2006.

Torrell, Jean-Pierre, O.P. *L'initiation à Saint Thomas d'Aquin: Sa personne et son oeuvre.* Paris: Cerf, 1993.

———. "La causalité salvifique de la résurrection du Christ selon Saint Thomas." *Revue thomiste* 96, no. 2 (1996): 179–208.

———. *Saint Thomas Aquinas, Volume 1: The Person and His Work.* Translated by Robert Royal. Washington, D.C.: The Catholic University of America Press, 1996.

———. *Saint Thomas d'Aquin, maître spirituel, Initiation 2.* Paris: Cerf, 1996.

———. *Les mystères: La vie et l'œuvre de Jésus selon saint Thomas d'Aquin.* Vols. 1–2. Paris: Desclée, 1999.

———. *Saint Thomas Aquinas, Volume 2: Spiritual Master.* Washington, D.C.: The Catholic University of America Press, 2003.

Tschipke, Theophil, O.P. *Die Menschheit Christi als Heilsorgan der Gottheit unter besonderer Berücksichtigung der Lehre des heiligen Thomas von Aquin.* Freiburg: Herder, 1940.

———. *L'humanité du Christ comme instrument de salut de la divinité.* Translated by Philibert Secrétan. Fribourg: Academic Press, 2003.

Turner, Denys. *Faith, Reason and the Existence of God.* Cambridge: Cambridge University Press, 2004.

Valuet, B. "Le Christ, prêtre principal du sacrifice eucharistique et les prêtres ministériels agissant in persona Christi." In *Présence du Christ dans la liturgie. Actes du sixième colloque d'études historiques, théologiques et canoniques sur le rite romain,* edited by Centre International d'Études Liturgiques, 159–222. Paris and Versailles: Centre International d'Études Liturgiques, 2001.

Van Nieuwenhove, Rik, and Joseph Wawrykow, eds. *The Theology of Thomas Aquinas.* Notre Dame, Ind.: University of Notre Dame Press, 2005.

Veatch, Henry B. *Swimming against the Current in Contemporary Philosophy: Occasional Essays and Papers.* Washington, D.C.: The Catholic University of America Press, 1990.

Verweyen, Hansjürgen. "Offene Fragen im Sühnebegriff auf dem Hintergrund der Auseinandersetzung Raymund Schwagers mit Hans Urs von Balthasar." In *Dramatische Erlösungslehre,* edited by Józef Niewiadomski and Wolfgang Palaver, 137–46. Innsbruck: Tyrolia, 1992.

Vonier, Anscar, O.S.B. *A Key to the Doctrine of the Eucharist.* Bethesda, Md.: Zacchaeus, 2003.

Waal, Franz B. *Primates and Philosophers: How Morality Evolved.* Princeton: Princeton University Press, 2006.

Wallace, William, O.P. *The Modeling of Nature: Philosophy of Science and Philosophy of Nature in Synthesis.* Washington, D.C.: The Catholic University of America Press, 1996.

Walsh, Liam G., O.P. "The Divine and the Human in St. Thomas's Theology of Sacraments." In *Ordo sapientiae et amoris: Image et message de Saint Thomas d'Aquin à travers les récentes études historiques, herméneutiques et doctrinales,* edited by Carlos-Josaphat Pinto de Oliveira and Jean-Pierre Torrell, 321–52. Fribourg: Editions Universitaires Fribourg, 1993.

———. "Sacraments." In *The Theology of Thomas Aquinas,* edited by Rik Van Nieuwenhove and Joseph Wawrykow, 326–64. Notre Dame, Ind.: University of Notre Dame Press, 2005.

Wawrykow, Joseph. *God's Grace and Human Action: 'Merit' in the Theology of Thomas Aquinas.* Notre Dame, Ind.: Notre Dame Press, 1995.

Weinandy, Thomas G., O.F.M. Cap. *The Father's Spirit of Sonship: Reconceiving the Trinity.* Edinburgh: T & T Clark, 1994.

———. "The Soul-Body Analogy and the Incarnation: Cyril of Alexandria." *Coptic Church Review* 17, no. 3 (1996): 59–66.

———. *Does God Suffer?* Notre Dame, Ind.: University of Notre Dame Press, 2000.

———. "Jesus' Filial Vision of the Father." *Pro Ecclesia* 13, no. 2 (2004): 189–201.

———. "The Beatific Vision and the Incarnate Son: Furthering the Discussion." *The Thomist* 70, no. 4 (2006): 605–15.

Weinberg, Stephen. *Dreams of a Final Theory: The Scientist's Search for the Ultimate Laws of Nature.* New York, Pantheon, 1993.

Weisheipl, James A., O.P. *Friar Thomas d'Aquino.* Garden City, N.Y.: Doubleday, 1974.

Weismann, Friedrich, Brian McGuinness, and Joachim Schulte. *Wittgenstein and the Vienna Circle.* Oxford: Basil Blackwell, 1979.

Westerman, Pauline C. *The Disintegration of Natural Law: From Aquinas to Finnis.* Leiden: Brill, 1998.

White, Thomas Joseph, O.P. "The Voluntary Action of the Earthly Christ and the Necessity of the Beatific Vision." *The Thomist* 69, no. 4 (2005): 497–534.

———. "Von Balthasar and Journet on the Universal Possibility of Salvation and the Twofold Will of God." *Nova et Vetera* (English) 4, no. 3 (2006): 633–66.

———. "Jesus' Cry on the Cross and His Beatific Vision." *Nova et Vetera* (English) 5, no. 3 (2007): 525–51.

———. "Ditheletism and the Instrumental Human Consciousness of Jesus." *Pro Ecclesia* 17, no. 4 (2008): 396–422.

Wiederkehr, Dietrich. "Mysterium paschale und die Leidensgeschichte der Menschheit." In *Mysterium Salutis,* edited by Magnus Löhrer, Christian Schütz, and Dietrich Wiederkehr, 243–46. Einsiedeln: Benziger, 1981.

Wippel, John F. *The Metaphysical Thought of Thomas Aquinas: From Finite Being to Uncreated Being.* Washington, D.C.: The Catholic University of America Press, 2000.

Wittgenstein, Ludwig. *The Blue and Brown Books.* Oxford: Blackwell, 1958.

———. *Schriften.* Frankfurt am Main: Suhrkamp, 1960.

Wright, N. T. *Jesus and the Victory of God.* Minneapolis: Fortress Press, 1996.

———. *The Resurrection of the Son of God.* Minneapolis: Fortress Press, 2003.

Yocum, John. "Sacraments in Aquinas." In *Aquinas on Doctrine: A Critical Introduction,* edited by Thomas G. Weinandy, Daniel A. Keating, and John Yocum, 159–81. London: T & T Clark, 2004.

ENCYCLICALS AND OTHER MAGISTERIAL DOCUMENTS

Pope Urban IV. *Transiturus.* 1264.

Pope Leo XIII. *Rerum Novarum.* 1891.

Pope Leo XIII. *Mirae Caritatis.* 1902.

Pope Pius X. *Pascendi Dominici Gregis.* 1907.

Pope Pius XI. *Quadragesimo Anno.* 1931.

———. *Casti Connubii.* 1932.

Pope Pius XII. *Mediator Dei.* 1947.

Pope John XXIII. *Mater et Magistra.* 1961

——. *Pacem in Terris.* 1963.

Pope Paul VI. *Mysterium Fidei.* 1965.

——. *Populorum Progressio.* 1967.

——. *Humanae Vitae.* 1968.

——. *Octogesima Adveniens.* 1971.

Pope John Paul II. *General Audiences: Theology of the Body.* 1979.

——. *Laborem exercens.* 1981.

——. *Sollicitudo rei socialis.* 1987.

——. *Centesimus annus.* 1991.

——. *Fides et Ratio.* 1998.

——. *Veritatis splendor.* 1993.

——. *Evangelium vitae.* 1995.

——. *Ecclesia de Eucharistia.* 2003.

Pope Benedict XVI. *Sacramentum Caritatis.* 2007.

Vatican Council II: The Conciliar and Post Conciliar Documents. Edited by Austin Flannery. Wilmington: Scholarly Resources, 1975.

Catholic Church. *Catechism of the Catholic Church: With modifications from the editio typica.* New York: Doubleday, 1997.

Congregation for the Doctrine of the Faith. *Dominus Iesus.* 2000.

Contributors

Guy Bedouelle, O.P., is rector of the Catholic University of the West in Angers, France. He previously was professor of church history at the University of Fribourg and president of the Center for Dominican Studies of Saulchoir in Paris. He is the author of many books, among them *In the Image of St. Dominic: Nine Portraits of Dominican Life, Saint Dominic: The Grace of the Word, The History of the Church,* and *The Reform of Catholicism, 1480–1620.*

Bernhard Blankenhorn, O.P., is a candidate for the S.T.D. at the University of Fribourg, where he is studying dogmatic theology under Gilles Emery, O.P. He has published articles in *Angelicum* and *Nova et Vetera.*

Stephen L. Brock is professor of medieval philosophy at the Pontifical University of the Holy Cross (Rome) and a member of the Pontifical Academy of St. Thomas. He is the author of *Action and Conduct: Thomas Aquinas and the Theory of Action,* which has been translated into Spanish and Italian. He is also the editor of *L'attualità di Aristotele* and of *Tommaso d'Aquino e l'oggetto della metafisica.* His essays have appeared in *The Thomist, Nova et Vetera,* and *The Review of Metaphysics,* and other journals.

Benoît-Dominique de La Soujeole, O.P., is professor of dogmatic theology at the University of Fribourg. He is one of the leading dogmatic theologians in France of his generation and an expert especially in ecclesiology, sacramentology, and Mariology. Many of his important essays have appeared in the *Revue thomiste.* He is the author of *Le sacrement de la communion, Introduction au mystère de l'Église, Éléments pour une spiritualité de l'Église,* and *Initiation à la théologie mariale.*

Lawrence Dewan, O.P., is professor of philosophy at Dominican University College (Ottawa). A member of the Pontifical Academy of St. Thomas Aquinas, he is widely recognized as one of the foremost Thomist metaphysicians of his generation and the author of a great number of important and probing essays on Thomist metaphysics and moral philosophy. He is the author of *Form and Being: Studies in Thomistic Metaphysics, St. Thomas and Form as Something Divine in Things,* and *Wisdom, Law, and Virtue: Essays in Thomistic Ethics.*

Archbishop *J. Augustine DiNoia, O.P.,* is secretary of the Congregation for Divine Worship and the Discipline of the Sacraments. He received his Ph.D. in theology from Yale University, served many years as professor of systematic theology at the Dominican House of Studies in Washington, as editor of *The Thomist,* and as director of the John Paul II Cultural Center in Washington, D.C. He is a member of the Pontifical Academy of St. Thomas. He is the author of *The Diversity of Religions.*

Mary Ann Glendon is Learned Hand Professor of Law at Harvard University, and served as U.S. ambassador to the Holy See from 2008 to 2009. She is the author of *Abortion and Divorce in Western Law, The Transformation of Family Law, Rights Talk: The Impoverishment of Political Discourse, A Nation Under Lawyers, A World Made New: Eleanor Roosevelt and the Universal Declaration of Human Rights,* and most recently of *Traditions in Turmoil.*

Reinhard Hütter is professor of theology at Duke University Divinity School, has recently been visiting professor at the University of Jena, Germany, and has served as the president of the Academy of Catholic Theology in 2010–2011. He is also a member of the Pontifical Academy of St. Thomas and distinguished fellow of the St. Paul Center for Biblical Theology. He is the author of *Suffering Divine Things: Theology as Church Practice* and *Bound to Be Free: Evangelical Catholic Engagements in Ecclesiology, Ethics, and Ecumenism.* He has co-edited four books, most recently *Reason and the Reasons of Faith.* He has been editor of the journal *Pro Ecclesia;* he is the co-editor of *Nova et Vetera* and serves on numerous editorial boards of journals and academic series, and he has published widely in theological and philosophical journals in the United States, England, Germany, and Italy.

Joseph W. Koterski, S.J., is associate professor of philosophy at Fordham University. He is editor-in-chief of *International Philosophical Quarterly* and the author most recently of *An Introduction to Medieval Philosophy: Basic Concepts.* He is also co-editor of *Prophecy and Diplomacy: The Moral Teaching of Pope John Paul II, Karl Jaspers on Philosophy of History and History of Philosophy, The Two Wings of Catholic Thought: Essays on Fides et Ratio,* and *Culture and Creed.* His essays have appeared in *The New Scholasticism, Augustinian Studies, The Heythrop Journal,* and *American Catholic Philosophical Quarterly.*

Matthew L. Lamb is professor of theology at Ave Maria University. He previously taught for many years at Boston College and Marquette University. He is the author of *Commentary on St. Paul's Epistle to the Ephesians by St. Thomas Aquinas; History, Method, and Theology: A Dialectical Comparison of Wilhelm Dilthey's Critique of Historical Reason and Bernard Lonergan's Meta-Methodology, Solidarity with Victims: Toward a Theology of Social Transformation,* and he is editor of *Creativity and Method: Essays in Honor of Bernard Lonergan.* He is the author most recently of *Eternity, Time, and the Life of Wisdom* and the co-editor of *Vatican II: Renewal within Tradition.* He is also the author of more than 135 theological articles.

Matthew Levering is professor of theology at the University of Dayton. He is the co-editor of *Nova et Vetera* and the founding chair of the Board of the Academy of Catholic Theology. He is the author of numerous books among which are *Christ's Fulfillment of Torah and Temple: Salvation According to St. Thomas Aquinas, Scripture and Metaphysics: Aquinas and the Renewal of Trinitarian Theology, Sacrifice and Community: Jewish Offering and Christian Eucharist, Biblical Natural Law: A Theocentric and Teleological Approach, Participatory Biblical Exegesis: A Theology of Biblical Interpretation, Christ and the Catholic Priesthood: Ecclesial Hierarchy and the Pattern of the Trinity,* and *Jewish-Christian Dialogue and the Life of Wisdom: Engagements with the Theology of David Novak.* Among his co-edited books are *Aquinas the Augustinian, Reading John with St. Thomas Aquinas, Rediscovering Aquinas and the Sacraments, Vatican II: Renewal within Tradition.*

Steven A. Long is professor of theology at Ave Maria University. He previously has taught at the University of St. Thomas (Minnesota) and at the Catholic University of America. He is the author of *The Teleological Grammar of the Moral Act,* and of *Natura Pura On the Recovery of Nature in the Doctrine of Grace.* (He is currently preparing his metaphysical work, *Analogia Entis,* for publication with University of Notre Dame Press.) With Christopher Thompson he is editor of *Reason and the Rule of Faith: Conversations in the Tradition with John Paul II,* drawn from the Lilly-funded seminars in the series Habits of Mind: The Vocation of the Catholic Intellectual. His essays have appeared in *Revue thomiste, The Thomist, Communio, Nova et Vetera,* and *The National Catholic Bioethics Quarterly.*

Alasdair MacIntyre is senior research professor of philosophy at the University of Notre Dame. He taught previously at Duke University, Vanderbilt University, Boston University, and Brandeis University. He is the author of *After Virtue, Whose Justice? Which Rationality?, Three Rival Versions of Moral Enquiry,*

Dependent Rational Animals, and most recently of *Edith Stein: A Philosophical Prologue 1913–1922, Ethics and Politics, The Tasks of Philosophy,* and *God, Philosophy, Universities.*

Graham J. McAleer is professor of philosophy at Loyola University in Maryland. He is the author most recently of *To Kill Another: Homicide and Natural Law.* His essays have appeared in *Nova et Vetera, The Journal of the History of Ideas, The Thomist,* and *Modern Theology.*

Richard Schenk, O.P., is professor of theology at the Dominican School of Philosophy and Theology (Berkeley) and the Graduate Theological Union. Previously, he served as concurrent director of the Hannover Institute of Philosophical Research and founded its department for philosophy and theology. He is a member of the European Academy of Science and Arts and also served as the founding president of the Academy of Catholic Theology. He is the author of *Die Gnade vollendeter Endlichkeit* and critical editor of Robert Kilwardby's *Quaestiones in librum IV Sententiarum.* His numerous essays have appeared in *Nova et Vetera, Dialog, Communio, Journal of Religion and Culture,* and *Forum Katholische Theologie.* He also contributed many entries to the major theological encyclopedias: *Lexikon für Theologie und Kirche, Theologische Realenzyklopädie,* and *The New Westminster Dictionary of Church History.*

Craig Steven Titus is research professor at the Institute for the Psychological Sciences and researcher and vice-director of the St. Thomas Aquinas Institute for Theology and Culture at the University of Fribourg, Switzerland. He is the author of *Resilience and the Virtue of Fortitude* and the editor or co-editor of eight books, among which are *The Pinckaers Reader, Sujet moral et communauté,* and *Renouveler toutes choses en Christ: vers un renouveau thomiste de la théologie morale.* He is editor of *The Psychology of Character and Virtue, Philosophical Psychology: Psychology, Emotions, and Freedom, Christianity and the West: Impact on Art and Culture,* and *On the Wings of Faith and Reason: The Christian Difference in Culture and the Sciences.* He has published several articles in learned journals, including in *The Thomist* and *Revue d'Ethique et de Théologie Morale, Journal of Psychology and Christianity, Edification,* and *New Blackfriars.*

Thomas Weinandy, O.F.M. Cap., is executive director for the Secretariat for Doctrine at the United States Conference of Catholic Bishops. He previously was for many years lecturer in history and doctrine at the University of Oxford, England. He is the author of numerous theological works, among which are *Does God Change? The Word's Becoming in the Incarnation, In the Likeness*

of *Sinful Flesh: An Essay on the Humanity of Christ, The Father's Spirit of Son-
ship: Reconceiving the Trinity,* and *Does God Suffer?* Most recently he published
Athanasius: A Theological Introduction. He is also co-editor of *The Theology of
St. Cyril of Alexandria: A Critical Appreciation, Aquinas on Doctrine: A Critical
Introduction,* and of *Aquinas on Scripture: An Introduction to His Biblical Com-
mentaries.*

Thomas Joseph White, O.P., is assistant professor of theology at the Dominican
House of Studies. He is the author of *Wisdom in the Face of Modernity.* He is the
co-editor of *Divine Impassibility and the Mystery of Human Suffering* and the editor of *The Analogy of Being: Invention of the Anti-Christ or Wisdom of God?* He
is also the author of several essays published in *Pro Ecclesia, Nova et Vetera,* and
The Thomist.

Index of Names

O'Neill, Coleman, viii, 17
Olivi, Peter John, 51n68

Pannenberg, Wolfhart, 115, 118
Paul VI, 36–37, 39, 58, 60, 257, 280
Peter of Poiters, 335 n15
Peterson, Erik, 33–35
Pieper, Josef, 331, 338 n27
Pierce, C. S., 354
Pinckaers, Servais, viii, 17, 120, 274–75, 312–29,
    331, 366
Pius X, 94
Pius XI, 280
Pius XII, 36–37, 72n123
Plato, 145, 149, 212, 263, 279, 320, 323, 344
Plotinus, 87
Porter, Jean, 330–52
Proust, Marcel, 119
Pseudo-Dionysius. *See* Dionysius

Rahner, Karl, vii–viii, 26 n6, 110, 117, 170, 176,
    177n14, 197–200
Ratzinger, Joseph. *See* Benedict XVI
Rawls, John, 356
Reid, Thomas, 359
Rhonheimer, Martin, 285–86, 308–11
Rist, John, 278
Roland of Cremona, 137n3
Romero, Oscar, 197
Rommen, Heinrich, 275–77
Rowland, Tracey, 353–54
Rufus, Richard, 179

Sabatier, August, 94n6
Sala, Giovanni, 319–20
Sartre, Jean-Paul, 259 n 9, 264–65
Scheeben, Matthias, 71–72
Scheler, Max, 354–55, 361, 363
Schillebeeckx, Edward, 77–78, 98–100, 147n25
Schleiermacher, Friedrich, 94n6
Schwager, Raymund, 201
Selvaggi, F., 67n104
Simon, Yves, 265 n16, 276–77
Simplicius, 344

Sirico, Robert, 353
Smith, Adam, 354 n4, 355–56, 359, 363
Smith, Janet E., 285, 308–11
Sölle, Dorothee, 201
Sombart, Werner, 354–55, 363
Sophocles, 268
Southern, Richard, 272
Speyr, Adrienne von, 201
Spicq, Ceslas, viii, 17
Stefanu, Stefanos, 320n31
Stein, Edith. *See* Teresa Benedicta of the Cross
Sylvester of Ferrara, 57–58

Tauler, Johannes, 121
Taylor, Charles, 119
Teilhard de Chardin, Pierre, 100
Teresa Benedicta of the Cross, 121
Thérèse of Lisieux, 121
Thrasymachus, 279
Torrell, Jean-Pierre, 17, 80n2, 140n9, 142 n13

Ulpian, 273
Undset, Sigrid, 119
Urban IV, 35

Vonier, Anscar, 61–63

Wallace, William, 114
Walton, Sam, 356
Weigel, George, 353
Wiederkehr, Dietrich, 202
William of Auvergne, 137n3, 177, 179 n21
William of Auxerre, 137n3, 178
William of Macclesfield, 18
William of Meliton(i)a, 137n3, 17n15
William of Ockham, 51
Wippel, John, 43
Wittgenstein, Ludwig, viii, 27n10, 33
Woolf, Virginia, 119
Wright, N. T., 115, 116 n56
Wycliffe, John, 63n93, 77–78

Zwingli, Ulrich, 78, 172n4

Ressourcement Thomism: Sacred Doctrine, the Sacraments, and the Moral Life was designed and typeset in Arno by Kachergis Book Design of Pittsboro, North Carolina. It was printed on 60-pound Natures Book Natural and bound by Thomson-Shore of Dexter, Michigan.